CALIFORNIA

Northern Mountains p489

North Coast & Redwoods p202

Gold Country p543

Lake Tahoe p564

Napa & Sonoma Wine Country p151

Yosemite & the Sierra Nevada p595

San Francisco p55

Marin County & Bay Area p108

Central Coast p245

Sacramento & the Central Valley p518

Palm Springs & the Deserts p444

Santa Barbara County p294

Los Angeles p335

Disneyland & Orange County p386

San Diego & Around p415

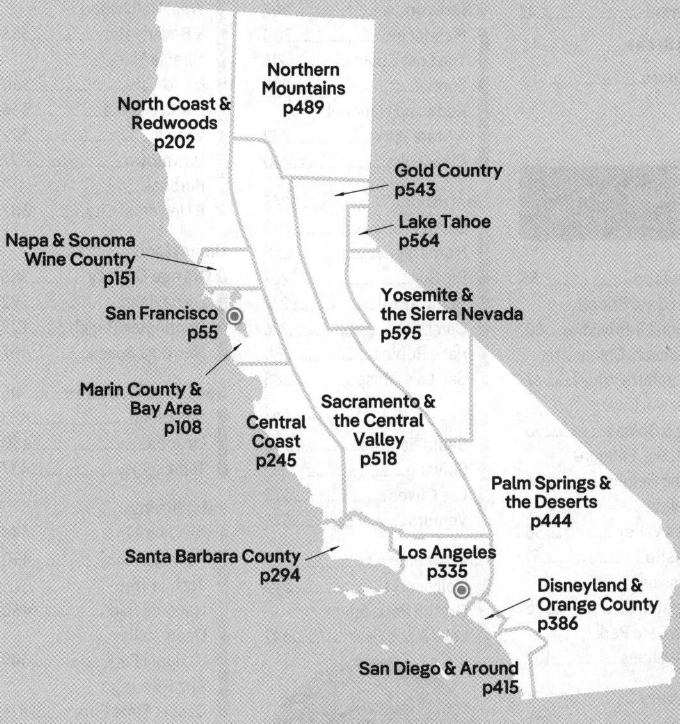

Alexis Averbuck, Alison Bing, Celeste Brash, Ashley Harrell, Anita Isalska, Megan Leon, Julie Tremaine, Ryan Ver Berkmoes, Wendy Yanagihara

CONTENTS

Plan Your Trip

The Journey Begins Here 4
Map 8
Our Picks 10
Regions & Cities 28
Itineraries 32
When to Go 40
Get Prepared 42
The Food Scene 44
The Outdoors 48

The Guide

San Francisco 55
Golden Gate Bridge, the Marina & Presidio 60
North Beach, Chinatown & Fisherman's Wharf 67
Downtown, Civic Center & SoMa 76
Japantown, Fillmore & Pacific Heights 83
The Haight & Hayes Valley 86
The Castro 91
The Mission & Dogpatch 95
Golden Gate Park & the Avenues 102

Marin County & Bay Area 108
Sausalito 114
Point Reyes 121
Oakland 125
Berkeley 132
Palo Alto 139
San Jose 143
Half Moon Bay 145

Napa & Sonoma Wine Country 151
Napa 156
St Helena 165
Sonoma 173
Petaluma 180
Santa Rosa 183
Sebastopol 186
Russian River Valley 193
Healdsburg 197

North Coast & Redwoods 202
Mendocino 208
The Lost Coast 216
Eureka 225
Redwood National & State Parks 232
Clear Lake 240

Central Coast 245
Santa Cruz 250
Monterey 258
Big Sur 267
Highway 101 272
Cambria 276
Paso Robles 280
San Luis Obispo 285

Santa Barbara County 294
Santa Barbara 300
Solvang 312
Los Olivos 320
Ventura 326

Los Angeles 335
Hollywood 340
Griffith Park, Silver Lake & Los Feliz 347

US Open of Surfing (p403), Huntington Beach

Pinot noir wine grapes, Sonoma Valley (p177)

West Hollywood & Beverly Hills 353
Miracle Mile & Mid-City 360
Santa Monica 366
Venice 372
Downtown 377
Burbank & Universal City 382

Disneyland & Orange County 386
Disneyland 392
Huntington Beach 402
Newport Beach 407

San Diego & Around 415
San Diego 420
La Jolla 430
Temecula 437

Palm Springs & the Deserts 444
Palm Springs 450
Joshua Tree National Park 460
Death Valley National Park 469
Anza-Borrego Desert State Park 476
Mojave National Preserve 482

Northern Mountains 489
Mt Shasta Region 494
Mt Lassen Region 502
Redding & Shasta Lake 511

Stand-up paddleboarding and kayaking in Sand Harbor (p588), Lake Tahoe

Sacramento & the Central Valley ... 518
- Sacramento ... 524
- Sacramento Valley ... 534
- San Joaquin Valley ... 536

Gold Country ... 543
- Auburn ... 548
- Nevada City ... 555
- Sonora ... 559

Lake Tahoe ... 564
- South Lake Tahoe & Stateline ... 570
- Tahoe City ... 579
- Northern Shore ... 584
- Truckee ... 589

Yosemite & the Sierra Nevada ... 595
- Yosemite National Park ... 600
- Sequoia & Kings Canyon National Parks ... 611
- Eastern Sierra ... 619

Toolkit

Arriving ... 630
Getting Around ... 631
Money ... 632
Accommodations ... 633
Family Travel ... 634
Health & Safe Travel ... 635
Outdoor Safety ... 636
Food, Drink & Nightlife ... 638
Responsible Travel ... 640
LGBTIQ+ Travelers ... 642
Accessible Travel ... 643
Driving Highway 1 ... 644
Nuts & Bolts ... 645

Storybook

A History of California in 15 Places ... 648
Meet the Californians ... 652
The Myth of California ... 654
Where Diversity Reigns Supreme ... 658
Climate Crisis ... 660
In-N-Out Burger ... 662

Tha Bay Bridge (p82), San Francisco

CALIFORNIA

THE JOURNEY BEGINS HERE

Growing up in Oakland (p125), I thought I would never move away from the Bay Area. It's downright perfect: weather, culture, beauty, people. What more could I want? Then life happened. And I became a painter and a travel writer, with time banked: years, in places from Greece to NYC, New Orleans and even Antarctica. Yet whenever I cruise any of the Bay's bridges, I remember what I've always loved: the sparkle of the water, the promise of the day. Anything can happen here, from seafront oyster lunch with a local wine and a good friend to a night out dancing to the world's best music. Every street is a mix of people, a mix of experiences; some local, some imported. No wonder the place remains magnetic – there really is something like a California Dream, and here we are all welcomed home.

Alexis Averbuck

Instagram: @alexisaverbuck

Alexis lives in Sonoma County and on Greece's Hydra Island where she paints and writes about her adventures.

My favorite experience is hiking the Sonoma County coast (p192) as the mist clears and the Pacific rolls in, crashing on the rock pinnacles and clean-cut cliffs.

WHO GOES WHERE

Our writers and experts choose the places that for them, define California.

SUNDRY PHOTOGRAPHY/SHUTTERSTOCK ©

Growing up in the **Bay Area** (p108) defined a head trip. It's a crazy, vibrant and dynamic place where you learn never to be surprised – by anything! This extends to my favorite drive in the world: Hwy 1 south from Pacifica to Santa Cruz, where I grew up. Each of the hundreds of times I've driven it, I've discovered something new: another hidden beach, a tide pool, a cafe run by a chef with a kooky, wonderful vision – the list goes on.

Ryan Ver Berkmoes

A longtime journalist and proudly native Californian, Ryan has written guidebooks that span the globe.

PAIGEFALK/GETTY IMAGES ©

In 2020 I traveled to Humboldt County to research a hiking guide, planning to stay a few months. On journeys through the **Lost Coast** (p216), I became enchanted with how rays of sunlight shine through redwood branches and become illuminated on fog, and the whoosh sound made by pebbles along the shoreline. Near the tiny town I used as a base, people were plunging into swimming holes all summer, and neighbors were gifting each other produce. I still haven't left.

Ashley Harrell

Instagram: @where_smashley_went

Ashley is a California-based freelance journalist who has co-authored more than 50 Lonely Planet books.

When driving, I cherish the moment when lofty **Mt Shasta** (p494) comes into view, either welcoming me to California or acting as a farewell to the state's intense, natural beauty. I get goosebumps from the energy that the great mountain radiates. But nothing beats the indescribable high from the cleansing air and something that feels beyond this world on the mountain itself!

Celeste Brash

Instagram: @cjbrash

Celeste is a travel nerd, outdoor enthusiast and pearl farmer based in French Polynesia and the USA.

PETER BOWMAN/SHUTTERSTOCK ©

To me, **Ojai** (p332) embodies a sort of hazily mythical, cinematic vision of California that draws spiritual seekers and creative souls. The valley isn't a secret, but those desiring retreat and refuge find it in Ojai's sunlit trails, mountain backdrop and rural pace. It's authentically country but sophisticated at the same time, and it's just a naturally beautiful place.

Wendy Yanagihara

Instagram: @wendyyanagihara

Wendy has contributed to over 50 guidebooks for Lonely Planet since 2003.

VENTU PHOTO/SHUTTERSTOCK ©

Everyone has an opinion on **Los Angeles** (p335), ranging from true love to frustration, as with any city. The one thing everyone can get on board with is that LA is about its people: it's about the kaleidoscope of diversity that is strewn in every corner, every restaurant and every small neighborhood, and it's what truly makes this city pulsate with life unlike any other.

Megan Leon

Instagram: @lagringabkk

Megan is a food and culture writer and In-N-Out Burger's biggest fan.

ROBERT MULLAN/SHUTTERSTOCK ©

MIMI DITCHIE PHOTOGRAPHY/GETTY IMAGES ©

Some cities dazzle you; others feel like a jacket that fits just right. For me, **San Luis Obispo** (p285) is one of those perfect fits. From the first time I walked through its tree-lined streets and shady plazas, I was home. This is 'SLO Cal': mellow, friendly and unhurried. But what keeps me coming back are the adventures close by: volcanic mountains, beautiful beaches and wine country.

Anita Isalska

Instagram: @lunarsynthesis

Anita is a British-born writer based in San Francisco. Read her stuff on anitaisalska.com.

CRISTI POPESCU/SHUTTERSTOCK ©

On a stopover in **San Francisco**, (p55) I wandered through Chinatown into City Lights Books. In the basement I noticed a sign painted by a 1930s cult: 'I am the door.' It's true. San Francisco is the threshold between fact and fiction, past and future, body and soul. That was 20 years ago. I'm still here. You've been warned.

Alison Bing

Twitter: @AlisonBing

Alison has survived SoCal sandstorms, NorCal cult potlucks and Bay Area robot wars to tell only-in-California stories.

TIME STOOD STILL PHOTO/SHUTTERSTOCK ©

California is vast and varied, but if there's one place to get the purest 'California experience,' it's **San Diego** (p420). Around this city, you can visit the mountains, wine country and the beach in the same day, eat some of the state's very best food, taste the thriving brewery scene, explore Gold Rush history and experience the incredible blend of cultures.

Julie Tremaine

Instagram: @julietremaine

Julie is a travel and food writer exploring the world one bite at a time.

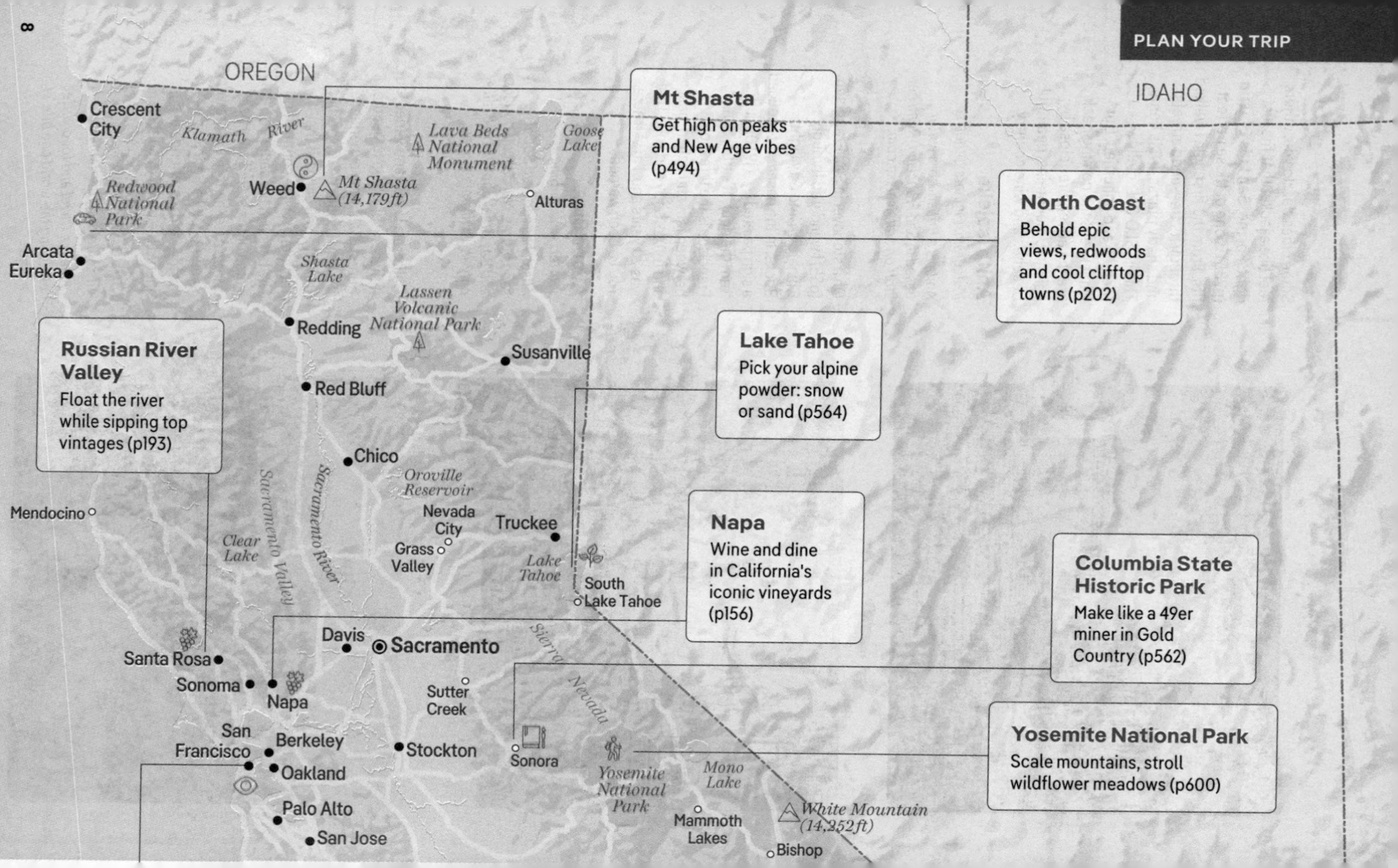
OREGON
IDAHO
Crescent City
Klamath River
Lava Beds National Monument
Goose Lake
Weed
Mt Shasta (14,179ft)
Alturas
Redwood National Park
Arcata
Eureka
Shasta Lake
Lassen Volcanic National Park
Redding
Susanville
Red Bluff
Chico
Oroville Reservoir
Nevada City
Grass Valley
Truckee
Lake Tahoe
South Lake Tahoe
Mendocino
Clear Lake
Sacramento Valley
Sacramento River
Santa Rosa
Sonoma
Napa
Davis
Sacramento
Sutter Creek
Sierra Nevada
San Francisco
Berkeley
Oakland
Stockton
Sonora
Yosemite National Park
Mono Lake
Palo Alto
San Jose
Mammoth Lakes
White Mountain (14,252ft)
Bishop
Mt Shasta
Get high on peaks and New Age vibes (p494)
North Coast
Behold epic views, redwoods and cool clifftop towns (p202)
Russian River Valley
Float the river while sipping top vintages (p193)
Lake Tahoe
Pick your alpine powder: snow or sand (p564)
Napa
Wine and dine in California's iconic vineyards (p156)
Columbia State Historic Park
Make like a 49er miner in Gold Country (p562)
Yosemite National Park
Scale mountains, stroll wildflower meadows (p600)

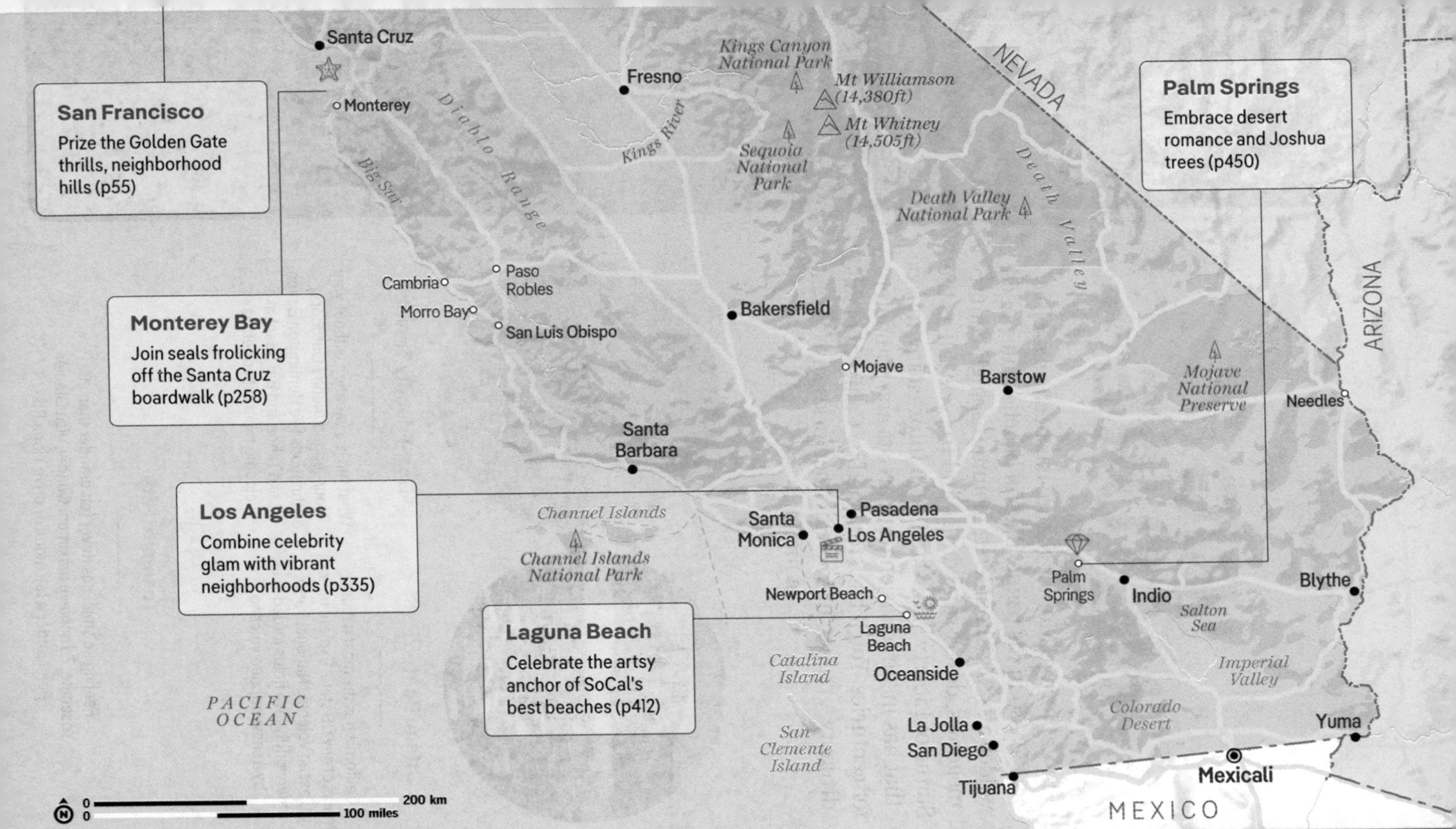
San Francisco
Prize the Golden Gate thrills, neighborhood hills (p55)
Monterey Bay
Join seals frolicking off the Santa Cruz boardwalk (p258)
Los Angeles
Combine celebrity glam with vibrant neighborhoods (p335)
Laguna Beach
Celebrate the artsy anchor of SoCal's best beaches (p412)
Palm Springs
Embrace desert romance and Joshua trees (p450)
Santa Cruz
Monterey
Big Sur
Diablo Range
Fresno
Kings River
Kings Canyon National Park
Mt Williamson (14,380ft)
Mt Whitney (14,505ft)
Sequoia National Park
Death Valley National Park
Death Valley
NEVADA
ARIZONA
Cambria
Paso Robles
Morro Bay
San Luis Obispo
Bakersfield
Mojave
Barstow
Mojave National Preserve
Needles
Santa Barbara
Channel Islands
Channel Islands National Park
Santa Monica
Pasadena
Los Angeles
Newport Beach
Laguna Beach
Catalina Island
San Clemente Island
Oceanside
La Jolla
San Diego
Tijuana
Palm Springs
Indio
Salton Sea
Blythe
Imperial Valley
Colorado Desert
Yuma
Mexicali
MEXICO
PACIFIC OCEAN
0
200 km
0
100 miles

BIG NATURE

In California, Mother Nature has been as prolific as Picasso in his prime. Blissful beaches, unspoiled wilderness, big-shouldered mountains, high-country meadows, desert sand dunes and trees as tall as the Statue of Liberty – this land is an intoxicating mosaic that has inspired visionaries, artists and wanderers for centuries. You'll be astonished by California's wild diversity – plunge in to create memories sure to last a lifetime.

Off the Beaten Path

California has the most national parks of any US state. Explore remote Lassen Volcanic National Park's otherworldly lava fields lorded over by a snow-capped volcano.

Dog-Friendly Travel

What fun is a vacation without your four-legged friend? Outdoorsy destinations like Huntington Beach, Lake Tahoe and Big Bear Lake welcome them with open paws.

Yosemite Hits

Feeling so small has never felt grander than in Yosemite. To achieve maximum wonder, visit Glacier Point under a full moon or drive Tioga Rd.

Death Valley National Park (p469)

BEST NATURE EXPERIENCES

Get lost ambling among ancient groves at **Redwood National & State Parks ❶**, home to the world's tallest trees. (p232)

Twist your way through canyons, zoom across salt flats and stop at North America's lowest point in larger-than-life **Death Valley National Park ❷**. (p469)

Hit the **Lost Coast Trail ❸**, where hardy backpackers tackle 24.6 miles of rugged, unspoiled coastline. (p217)

Embrace epic **Lake Tahoe ❹**, from downhill ski runs and mountain-bike trails to lakeside ambles, all wrapped in the Sierras. (p564)

Explore the underwater wilderness at **Crystal Cove State Marine Conservation Area ❺**, then hike its mountain trails. (p410)

EPIC EPICUREAN

California is the epicenter of good eating in the USA. Where else is the natural bounty fresher or more varied, the kitchen creativity more boundary-pushing or the flavors and textures more international? New cravings have been invented at California's cultural crossroads for over 200 years, so don't hold back! Get adventurous with anything from roadside food trucks to Cal-Japanese tasting menus, and Michelin-starred gastronomic temples to foraged-food cooking – there's something for everyone.

Taco Mania

Tacos are a staple of the SoCal food scene, especially in LA and San Diego where the humble Baja-style fish taco is a local obsession.

Farmers Markets

Farmers markets abound (check cafarmersmkts.com and cdfa.ca.gov), celebrating bounties of local veg, seafood, mushrooms, inventive baked goods and more.

America's Cornucopia

California is the top US producer of vegetables and organic foods – expect everything from pistachios to radicchio, and olive oil to hillside honey.

FROM LEFT: MELINA MARA/THE WASHINGTON POST VIA GETTY IMAGES ©, JULIA E HEATH/SHUTTERSTOCK ©, MARIAH TAUGER/LOS ANGELES TIMES VIA GETTY IMAGES ©

Dubu kimchi in Koreatown (p364), Los Angeles

BEST FOODIE EXPERIENCES

Duck inside SF's **Ferry Building** ❶, a landmark for good taste that features local, sustainable food producers and a legendary farmers market. (p82)

Go on a culinary adventure in Napa and Sonoma wine country. Start in downtown **Napa** ❷ and roam out to smaller spots like Healdsburg. (p158)

Explore LA's **Koreatown** ❸, just one of the state's many ethnically Asian neighborhoods. (p364)

Mingle with hipsters, office jockeys and visitors at **Grand Central Market** ❹, a gourmet food hall in Downtown LA going strong since 1917. (p380)

Delight in truly local cuisine at East Bay's **Cafe Ohlone** ❺, which showcases the foods of California's native Ohlone people. (p134)

ADVENTURES OUTDOORS

An irresistible combo of forests, mountains, ocean and desert, California's outdoors is nothing short of extraordinary and the menu of active options seemingly inexhaustible. So get out of the car and get your blood pumping. Make memories while hiking in a fairy-tale forest, plunging into a gem-colored mountain lake, clambering around massive dunes or schussing down epic slopes. Adventure, after all, is about embracing the season and terrain as well as the unique experiences.

CA is for Camping

Bed down under a blanket of stars at California's myriad national, state and regional parks. Joshua Tree is surrounded by evocatively eroded boulders and fan-palm oases.

Hot Springs

Volcanic mud baths, like those in Calistoga, may be exactly what the doctor ordered after a day of wine-tasting, or dip into natural hot-spring pools found across the state.

Rafting the American River

California's premier white-water destination is ready-made for families and thrill-seekers alike. Embark on a short expedition or a full-on multiday adventure.

Yosemite Falls (p606), Yosemite National Park

BEST OUTDOOR EXPERIENCES

Rock-climb or hike your way through **Pinnacles National Park** ❶, exploring boulders, spires and mountains. (p275)

Summit thrilling **Mt Shasta** ❷, before wilding out at Lassen Volcanic National Park with its azure crater lakes. (p496)

Paddle a redwood outrigger canoe through the estuary near **Mendocino** ❸ in search of harbor seals and harmony. (p211)

Ascend into the Sierra Nevada at **Yosemite National Park** ❹, where waterfalls tumble into glacier-carved valleys and wildflower meadows bloom. (p600)

Cycle your way around Napa and Sonoma wine country, on mountain-biking trails or mellower cruises like **Dry Creek Valley** ❺ or Sonoma Valley. (p199)

COASTAL PLEASURES

Life's a beach in California, but there's so much more along the coast. When the coastal fog lifts, the state's 840 miles of shoreline truly does its 'golden' moniker justice. Summer weather reigns supreme year-round in the south; rock crags, mists and drama define the north. Find family fun in La Jolla, ogle world-class surfers in Huntington Beach, mingle with eccentrics in Venice Beach, cuddle at sunset in a Big Sur cove or find yourself on the stunning Lost Coast Trail.

FROM LEFT: CRISTI POPESCU/SHUTTERSTOCK ©, J.D.S/SHUTTERSTOCK ©, IV-OLGA/SHUTTERSTOCK ©

Beach Scenes

Endless summers are fueled by Ferris wheels and carnival games, coupled with soul-stirring sunsets in Santa Monica, Venice Beach and Santa Cruz.

Surf's Up!

Even if you never set foot on a board, you should totally check out Cali's epic surf breaks like those around Huntington Beach, La Jolla (Trestles) and Santa Cruz (Steamer Lane).

Iconic Big Sur

That coastline in all those car commercials? Definitely Big Sur: cradled by redwood forests, the coast is a place of hidden waterfalls and heart-hammering bridges.

Point Reyes National Seashore (p121)

BEST COASTAL EXPERIENCES

Escape civilization on SoCal's isolated islands at **Channel Islands National Park** ❶, nicknamed 'California's Galapagos.' (p331)

Hike the tawny **Marin Headlands** ❷ across SF's Golden Gate Bridge north to wild, wonderful Point Reyes National Seashore. (p117)

Summit the Pomo Canyon Red Hill Trail to behold the wild **Sonoma Coast** ❸ unfurling at your feet with bluff trails leading onwards. (p192)

Hit the beach in the OC to tan among celebutantes and play among toddlers at **Laguna Beach** ❹ and Newport Beach. (p412)

Make your mark in **Malibu** ❺, where tide-pooling, surfing and sunseeking vie for your attention. (p371)

CLASSIC ROAD TRIPS

Road-tripping is the ultimate way to experience California, so fill the gas tank and buckle up for unforgettable drives through scenery that tugs at your heart and soul. Wheel through sensuous wine country, humbling redwood forests, epic desert expanses, endless miles of coastal highway and sky-touching Sierra Nevada peaks. Just make sure that rental car has unlimited miles – you'll need 'em all.

FROM LEFT: DXKFOTO/SHUTTERSTOCK ©, MAKS ERSHOV/SHUTTERSTOCK ©, THOMAS DE WEVER/GETTY IMAGES ©

Route 66

Get your kicks on America's 'Mother Road,' which brought Dust Bowl refugees, Hollywood starlets and hippies to California the end of the rainbow.

Pacific Coast Highway

Whether you follow the entire 656 miles or just a short stretch of coast-hugging Hwy 1, you'll hit the Insta jackpot – dramatic sea cliffs, playful seals and the Golden Gate Bridge.

Avenue of the Giants

This incredible 32-mile road is canopied by the world's tallest trees – redwoods all, some of which were seedlings during the Roman Empire.

Joshua Tree National Park (p460)

BEST ROAD-TRIPPIN' EXPERIENCES

Pick your portion of Hwy 1: Golden Gate Bridge and Marin Headlands, Big Sur, 17-Mile Drive or the **North Coast** ❶. You can't lose. (p214)

Zip between historic towns in the rolling Gold Country of the Sierra Nevada foothills on aptly named **Hwy 49** ❷. (p543)

Trace the rugged side of the Sierra Nevada on the **Eastern Sierra Scenic Byway** ❸ (Hwy 395), passing alpine lakes and hot springs. (p620)

Cruise springtime California deserts, like **Joshua Tree National Park** ❹, when wildflower blooms light up the sere sands. (p462)

Get a designated driver to roll from Carneros to St Helena and **Westside Rd** ❺, sampling the world-renowned wines of Napa and Sonoma. (p196)

E FEHRENBACHER/SHUTTERSTOCK ©

Fox Theater (p128), Oakland

SPARKLING CITIES

California's cities have more flavors than a jar of jelly beans. They will seduce you with a cultural kaleidoscope that ranges from art museums, architectural showpieces and vibrant theater to tantalizing food scenes and high-octane nightlife.

Quick! What's the Capital of California?

At the confluence of California's two most powerful waterways – the American and Sacramento Rivers – lies the tidy grid of streets of the state capital, Sacramento.

Dig Deeper

California cities run deeper than their beaches, hipsters and reality-TV entourages might have you believe. Ultimately, it's the cultural diversity that can make the biggest impression.

BEST CITY EXPERIENCES

Indulge in trendsetting food, social movements, art and technology in **San Francisco** ❶. (p55)

Hit the wonderland that is **Los Angeles** ❷, visiting everything from Hollywood dives to the Getty Museum. (p335)

Meet laid-back living and rove **Oakland's** ❸ myriad restaurants, breweries and shops. (p125)

Enjoy **San Diego's** ❹ breezy confidence and sunny countenance. (p420)

Hop between craft breweries, tasting rooms and restaurants in smaller cities like **Petaluma** ❺ or Santa Rosa. (p180)

Danish pastries, Solvang (p312)

QUIRKY CALI

California is full of bizarre roadside attractions and hidden surprises. SoCal's deserts and the North Coast, both traditional magnets for free spirits, deliver a disproportionate share of kooky gems. LA and SF are just as jam-packed with oddities, from outdoor sculpture gardens to dinosaurs by the freeway – it's all part of the DNA.

Real-Life Rosebud

Tour William Randolph Hearst's over-the-top Hearst Castle and see where the real-world Citizen Kane played, featuring zebras, a bejeweled swimming pool, lavish interiors and stunning views.

Slab City

Mingle with artists and misfits in this off-grid community that sprawls across the sun-scorched desert floor at the foot of Salvation Mountain, a colorful showpiece of American folk art.

BEST OFFBEAT EXPERIENCES

Get your chakras in order at the crystal shops and on a Vortex Tour on **Mt Shasta** ❶. (p496)

Explore another dimension at the **Integratron** ❷, a giant 'rejuvenation and time machine' near Joshua Tree. (p467)

Blend patchouli aromas at the **Sebastopol** ❸ farmers market, then tour the recycled sculptures of Patrick Amiot. (p186)

Sample Danish flavors and local wines at **Solvang** ❹ (p312)

Head to San Francisco's **Marina** ❺ for sound experiments and more. (p65)

Napa Valley (p156)

FROM GRAPE TO GLASS

Wherever you are in California, a vineyard is near. World-class vintages are grown and bottled here, just waiting to be tasted. Raise a toast to California's wine-producing regions that are pioneering sustainable practices and brimming with sensory wonders.

Organic vs Biodynamic

Organic means grapes aren't exposed to chemical fertilizers, pesticides or herbicides. Biodynamic means integrated farming intended to sustain healthy ecosystems.

Cider & Beer Too

California is tops for more than wine: it has the most craft breweries in the nation and a killer cider game, with heritage apple orchards throughout.

BEST WINE EXPERIENCES

Sample some of America's best wines in famous **Napa Valley ❶**. (p156)

Sip pinot noir on a tour of sylvan **Santa Ynez Valley ❷** hillsides quilted with oaks, olive trees and vineyards. (p325)

Cycle the Sonoma Valley to Glen Ellen and **Kenwood ❸** wineries. (p179)

Discover one of California's best-kept secrets, the **Russian River Valley ❹** – it boasts sparkling wines, pinot noirs and chardonnays. (p196)

Embrace the Central Coast's excellent wine-tasting around **Paso Robles ❺**. (p281)

MOVIE MAGIC

To Shakespeare all the world may have been a stage, but in California it's actually more a film set. And although movies were born in France, they certainly came of age in Hollywood. You can stand in celebrities' footprints, take in famous filming locations or hop on a bus to see where the stars live.

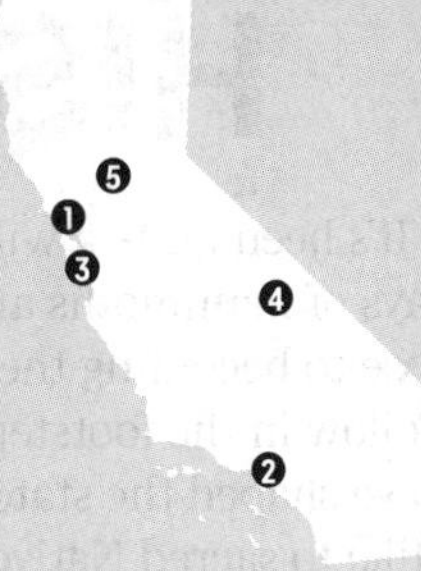

Get Into It

For a century California has made audiences laugh, cry and come back for more. To witness the magic, join a live studio audience or tour a movie studio in LA.

Hollywood Selfies

Snap a selfie outside Grauman's Chinese Theatre, then duck into Hollywood & Highland for a photo op with the iconic Hollywood sign and revel in your 15 minutes of social-media fame.

Theme Parks

Kids love action-packed days with beloved cartoon characters at Disneyland Resort, legendary Universal Studios Hollywood and more, with movie-themed rides, live shows and slick special effects.

BEST CINEMATIC EXPERIENCES

Relive film-noir classics like John Huston's *The Maltese Falcon* and Alfred Hitchcock's thriller *Vertigo* in **San Francisco** ❶. (p55)

Throw a director's megaphone around **Los Angeles** ❷ and you'll hit a celluloid sight, from Mulholland Dr and Hollywood Blvd to Malibu. (p335)

Play like a 'Lost Boy' on the Boardwalk at **Santa Cruz** ❸ horror-flick locations. (p252)

Get misty-eyed over old-fashioned Westerns filmed in **Lone Pine** ❹. (p620)

Look for Lady Bird in **Sacramento** ❺, birthplace of filmmaker Greta Gerwig and the movie's filming location. (p524)

HIGH ON HISTORY

It's been quite a wild ride for California from the days of mammoths and saber-toothed tigers to being close to becoming the world's fourth-largest economy. Follow in the footsteps of countless generations that have shaped the state in ways both dark and golden. Hike to sacred Native American waterfalls, confront the moral complexities of the mission system, reflect upon the frenzied rush for gold and finish up with a martini in Humphrey Bogart's favorite watering hole.

FROM LEFT: ZACK FRANK/SHUTTERSTOCK ©, BENNY MARTY/SHUTTERSTOCK ©, DAVID PAUL MORRIS/GETTY IMAGES ©

Cultural Crossroads

Native American tribes, Spanish Colonial *presidios* (forts) and Catholic missions, Mexican pueblos (towns) and mining ghost towns have all left traces here for you to find.

Alcatraz

Watch Clint Eastwood in *Escape from Alcatraz* before visiting 'The Rock' – America's first military prison – on a tiny history-rich island rising in the San Francisco Bay.

Land Back Movement

California is increasingly attempting to return some of the land stolen from Native Americans – from 500 acres on the Lost Coast to part of the Oakland hills.

HP Garage, Palo Alto (p139)

BEST HISTORICAL EXPERIENCES

Follow in the tracks of Western pioneers and hardscrabble miners in Gold Country's **Columbia State Historic Park** ❶. (p562)

Roam **Downtown Los Angeles** ❷ from Olvera St to Chinatown (two of them!) and Little Tokyo, soaking up some of California's founding cultures. (p377)

Visit the garage where Bill Hewlett and David Packard kicked off the Silicon Valley revolution in **Palo Alto** ❸. (p139)

Dive deep in **Sonoma** ❹ history as far back as the 1820s at an adobe mission and taste the wine that inspired the breakaway Bear Flag Republic. (p173)

Witness a painful chapter of the USA's past at **Manzanar National Historic Site** ❺, the WWII Japanese American internment camp. (p620)

LUX BLUE/SHUTTERSTOCK ©

Sunset in California

ROMANTIC GETAWAYS

Whether you're on your honeymoon or simply treating your sweetie, California is tailor-made for romance. Bed down in a Victorian B&B or in a tent under a canopy of stars. Clink glasses in a winery bistro or at a mountaintop picnic. Surrender to R&R in a chic spa or hike out to an isolated forest cabin.

San Francisco Charm

SF is aces for romance, from its majestic Golden Gate Bridge and dreamy Marin Headlands to flirty Poet's Corner.

Vineyard Love

Let wine country do the wooing at perfect inns like Napa's Auberge du Soleil or Hennessey House, or Beltane Ranch near Sonoma.

BEST ROMANTIC EXPERIENCES

Heed the call of romance in **Mendocino** ❶, the former whaling village with cottages and quiet country inns. (p208)

Surrender to the classy desert town of **Palm Springs** ❷; dine under the stars and lounge poolside. (p450)

Find bliss in **Big Sur** ❸, where waterfalls splash in rainbow mists and cliffs cradle purple-sand beaches. (p267)

Bask in good vibes in sparkling **Malibu** ❹, built for cozy cuddling and beach strolls. (p371)

Join the posh recluses in russet-walled **Santa Barbara** ❺. (p304)

Sea lions, Monterey Bay (p258)

NATURE ENCOUNTERS

Wildlife encounters are just a part of California. Sea otters and seals frolic around harbor piers, while whales cruise offshore. From black bears in the forests to monarch butterflies in eucalyptus groves, tortoises in the desert and skies filled with migrating birds, this state is a critter's paradise.

Wildflowers

Many local plants have adjusted to long periods of almost no rain, growing during wet winters, blooming in February, then drying out until the first rain falls.

Underwater Life

Commune with coral-reef creatures and giant colonies of pinnipeds while hiking, snorkeling or kayaking offshore at places like the uninhabited Channel Islands.

BEST WILDLIFE EXPERIENCES

See birds passing on the Pacific Flyway at **Klamath Basin National Wildlife Refuge ❶**. (p501)

Listen to the roar of elephant seals at **Año Nuevo State Natural Reserve ❷**. (p148)

Roam the peninsula of **Point Reyes National Seashore ❸** with migrating whales offshore. (p121)

Visit **Monterey Bay ❹** for its wonderful aquarium, wildlife-spotting by kayak and whale-watching. (p260)

Search for golden eagles, foxes and bighorn sheep at **Anza-Borrego Desert State Park ❺**. (p476)

REGIONS & CITIES

Find the places that tick all your boxes.

North Coast & Redwoods

TALL TREES AND WILD COASTLINE

Lumber barons wised up and conserved primeval redwood forests along the misty, rugged and wild North Coast. Let your offbeat flag fly in Humboldt County, and swap seafaring stories at spectacular coastal fishing villages, like Elk and Mendocino, as you explore some of California's most majestic landscapes.

p202

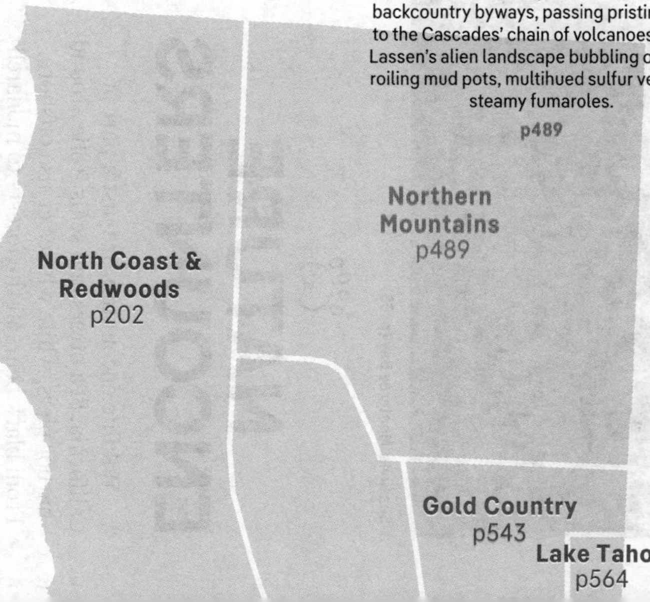

Northern Mountains

CALIFORNIA'S UNSUNG MOUNTAIN PARADISE

Mt Shasta is a magnet for shamans, New Age poets and ice-axe-wielding alpinists. There's more wilderness as you head north along backcountry byways, passing pristine lakes to the Cascades' chain of volcanoes and Mt Lassen's alien landscape bubbling over with roiling mud pots, multihued sulfur vents and steamy fumaroles.

p489

Gold Country

DELIGHTFUL TOWNS, BEAUTIFUL PARKS AND HISTORY

Head for the Sierra Nevada foothills like the tens of thousands of pioneers who arrived here during California's gold rush, and you'll find the Wild West alive and well in historic gold-mining country. Get thrills on river-rafting trips, chills on underground cave tours and swills at rustic winery tasting rooms.

p543

Lake Tahoe

BEACHES, SKIING, MOUNTAINS AND CASINOS

North America's largest alpine lake is a year-round playground. Come for Olympic-worthy skiing and boarding in winter, or cool off on the beaches in summer. Hiking and mountain biking the backcountry takes you to the wildest sides of the Sierras. Flashy casinos and cosy lakeside cabins are a bonus.

p564

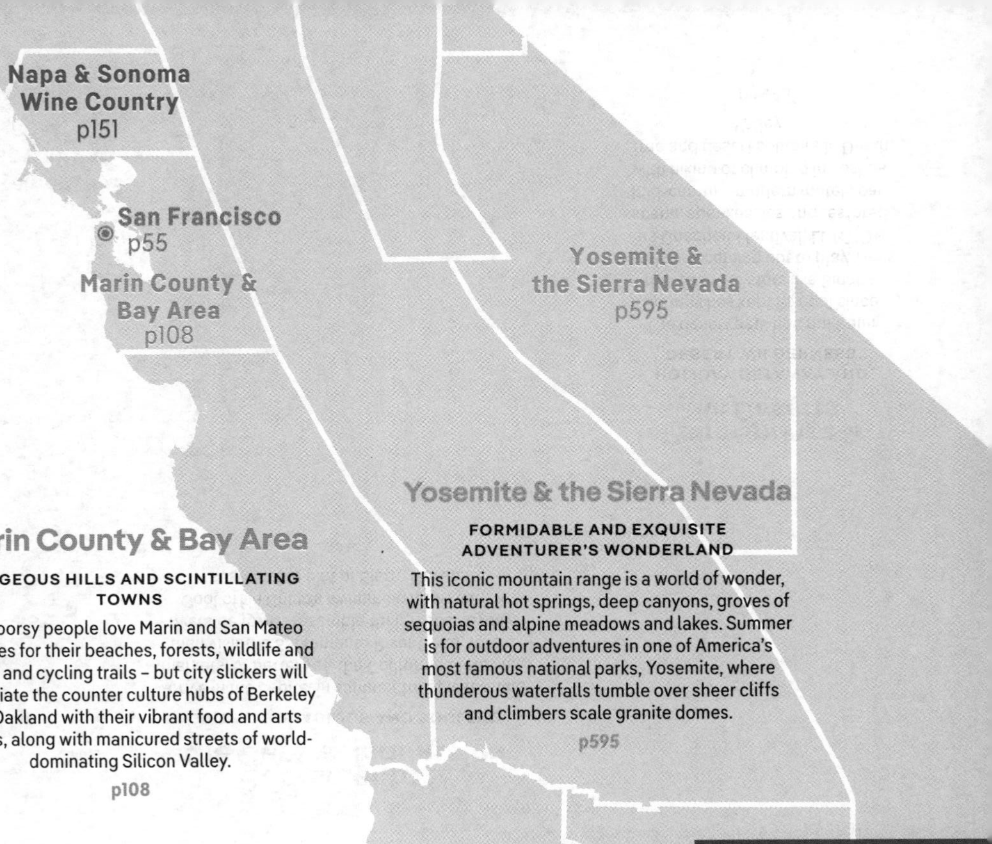

Napa & Sonoma
Wine Country
p151

San Francisco
p55

Marin County &
Bay Area
p108

Yosemite &
the Sierra Nevada
p595

Napa & Sonoma Wine Country

GLORIOUS VINEYARDS AND UNIQUE TOWNS

The sun-washed valleys and cool coastal fog make Napa and Sonoma Counties California's most iconic wine-growing regions. But local ranches and hippie free-thinking also thrive, yielding bountiful arm-to-table meals, unusual small towns and interesting blends of luxe and laid-back, with a killer coastline to boot.

p151

San Francisco

WHERE THE WEST GETS ITS WILD IDEAS

San Francisco, with its charming streets and cable cars, keeps pushing boundaries through trendsetting food, social movements, art and technology. This city is defined by bold moves and rich history, with multicultural influences spanning centuries – just like its iconic Golden Gate Bridge – and remaining fresh and inspiring all the way.

p55

Marin County & Bay Area

GORGEOUS HILLS AND SCINTILLATING TOWNS

Outdoorsy people love Marin and San Mateo Counties for their beaches, forests, wildlife and hiking and cycling trails – but city slickers will appreciate the counter culture hubs of Berkeley and Oakland with their vibrant food and arts scenes, along with manicured streets of world-dominating Silicon Valley.

p108

Yosemite & the Sierra Nevada

FORMIDABLE AND EXQUISITE ADVENTURER'S WONDERLAND

This iconic mountain range is a world of wonder, with natural hot springs, deep canyons, groves of sequoias and alpine meadows and lakes. Summer is for outdoor adventures in one of America's most famous national parks, Yosemite, where thunderous waterfalls tumble over sheer clifts and climbers scale granite domes.

p595

Central Coast

WILD COAST MADE FOR ESCAPES

Surf south from serene Santa Cruz with its old-timey beach boardwalk, stop to whale-watch at wildlife-rich Monterey Bay, then hike past Big Sur's coastal waterfalls and gawk at Hearst Castle en route to studious San Luis Obispo and its bountiful Paso Robles wine country.

p245

Sacramento & the Central Mountains

GRITTY, BODACIOUS AND SOULFUL

Arrive in the capital in summer for epic farmers markets, or better yet, the California State Fair, then visit the Sacramento River Delta, where riverside towns resemble their 1930s heyday. Cool off in Chico's swimming holes over a sustainable pint of Sierra Nevada.

p518

Palm Springs & the Deserts

HOLIDAY GETAWAY AND DESERT WILDERNESS

The desert gets hot, but Palm Springs has kept its cool since the '50s with stars like Sinatra and Elvis coming out to play. Now its Coachella festival, LGBTIQ+ scene, speakeasies and restored mid-century-modern motels pair with hiking or climbing in Joshua Tree and desert solitaire in Death Valley.

p444

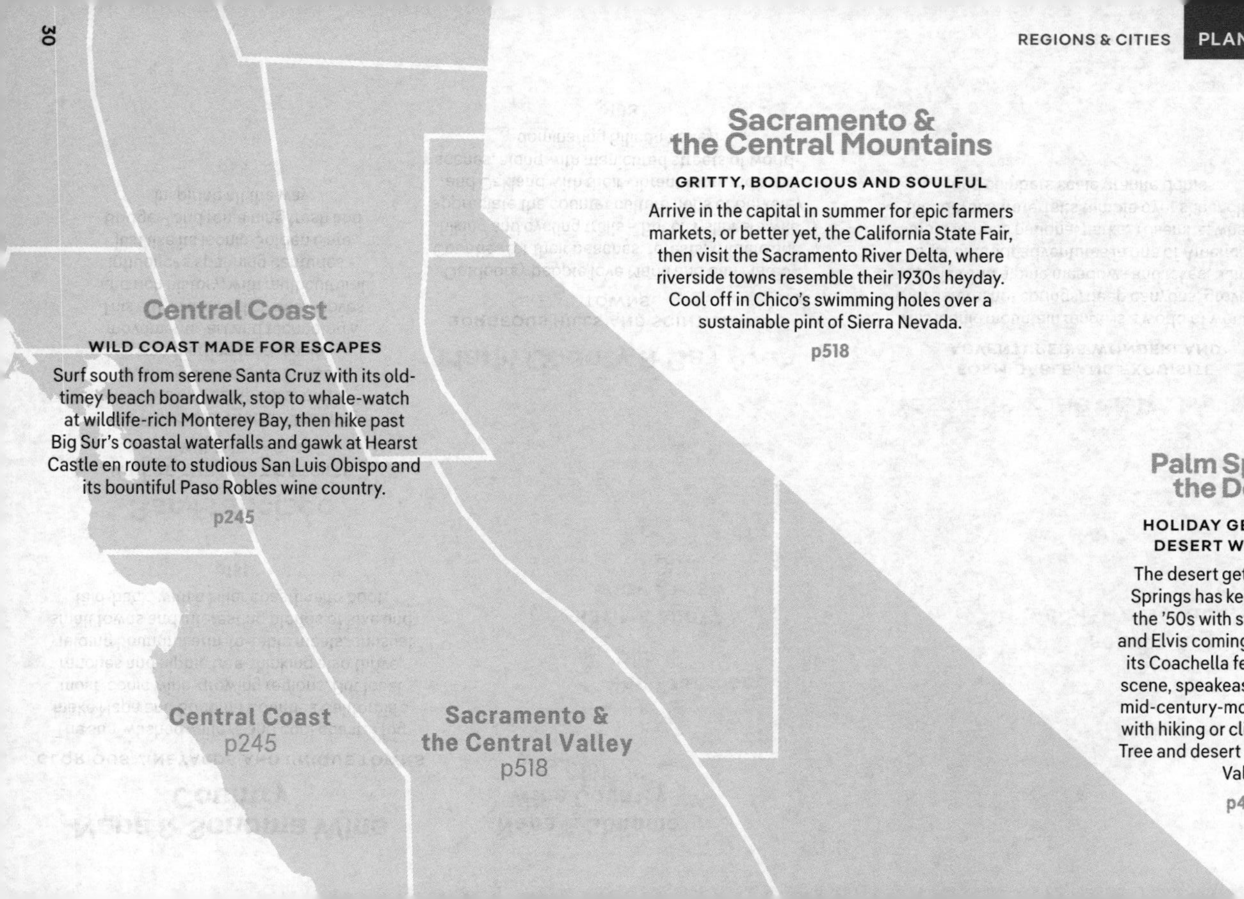

Central Coast
p245

Sacramento & the Central Valley
p518

Santa Barbara County

SPANISH COLONIAL COASTAL BEAUTY

Santa Barbara keeps a low, Spanish Colonial profile with pristine streets and high hedges along white-sand beaches, with world-class vineyards right next door in the oak-dotted Santa Ynez Valley. Sparkling waters invite snorkeling, diving or kayaking in nearby Channel Islands National Park.

p294

Los Angeles

THE VIBRANTLY DIVERSE HEART OF CALIFORNIA

There's more to life in La La Land than just sunny beaches and air-kissing celebrities. Explore its bounty of art and architecture, feast on eclectic cuisines and visit sharply contrasting and lively neighborhoods, each with rich histories dating from the earliest days of Spanish colonization.

p335

Santa Barbara County
p294
Los Angeles
p335
Palm Springs & the Deserts
p444
Disneyland & Orange County
p386
San Diego & Around
p415

Disneyland & Orange County

SUN, SAND & SURF

The OC's beaches are packed with strapping surfers, volleyball champions and retouched reality stars. If you think this scenery is surreal, check out the hyper-reality of the Disneyland Resort and the rest of the theme parks that keep the kids enthralled, meeting life-size characters from their favorite flicks.

p386

San Diego & Around

EXPLORE CALIFORNIA'S COOLEST CITY

California's southernmost city seems like it's on permanent vacation, with a near-perfect year-round climate on its beaches and a booming craft-brewery scene. Explore further with Balboa Park's quirky museums and the architecture along El Prado promenade, or wander laid-back beach towns seeking the ultimate fish taco.

p415

JAMES KIRKIKIS/SHUTTERSTOCK ©

Giant Dipper (p252), Santa Cruz

ITINERARIES

San Francisco to LA

Allow: 8 days **Distance:** 440 miles

You have a week to settle California's longest-running debate: which is the state's better half, north or south? Is it fog-mantled San Francisco with its magnificent bay, or sun-kissed Los Angeles and its beaches unfurling hither and yon. But wait, what about all that in the middle – raw coastline, wine country, cool college towns and celebrity idylls?

1

SAN FRANCISCO ⏱2 DAYS

Spend two days eating magnificently, riding cable cars and exploring **San Francisco** (p55), from the iconic Golden Gate Bridge (pictured) to Golden Gate Park. Look at street art in the Mission and stroll the historic North Beach neighborhood. Sail to Angel Island or Alcatraz, discover the weirdest tech in the west at the Exploratorium and find inspiration at SFMOMA.

1¾ hours

2

SANTA CRUZ ⏱1 DAY

Hwy 1 leads you south past lighthouses and strawberry farms, staggering bluffs and fishing harbors to the beach boardwalk at laid-back **Santa Cruz** (p250). While you're there, take a roller-coaster ride on the Giant Dipper, watch surfers at Steamer Lane (pictured), stroll the downtown or get wild at Natural Bridges State Beach and the Forest of Nisene Marks.

1¾ hours

3

BIG SUR ⏱1 DAY

Edge around the Monterey Bay, stopping to beachcomb and wildlife-watch before diving into California's best aquarium in maritime Monterey. Continue winding south along thrilling cliff edges to soul-stirring **Big Sur** (p267), where redwood forests rise and waterfalls crash onto the beach. Camp or post up in a romantic B&B to soak it all in.

2½ hours

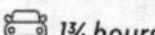

GRAPHICATO/SHUTTERSTOCK ©, DALTON JOHNSON/SHUTTERSTOCK ©, DOUG MEEK/SHUTTERSTOCK ©

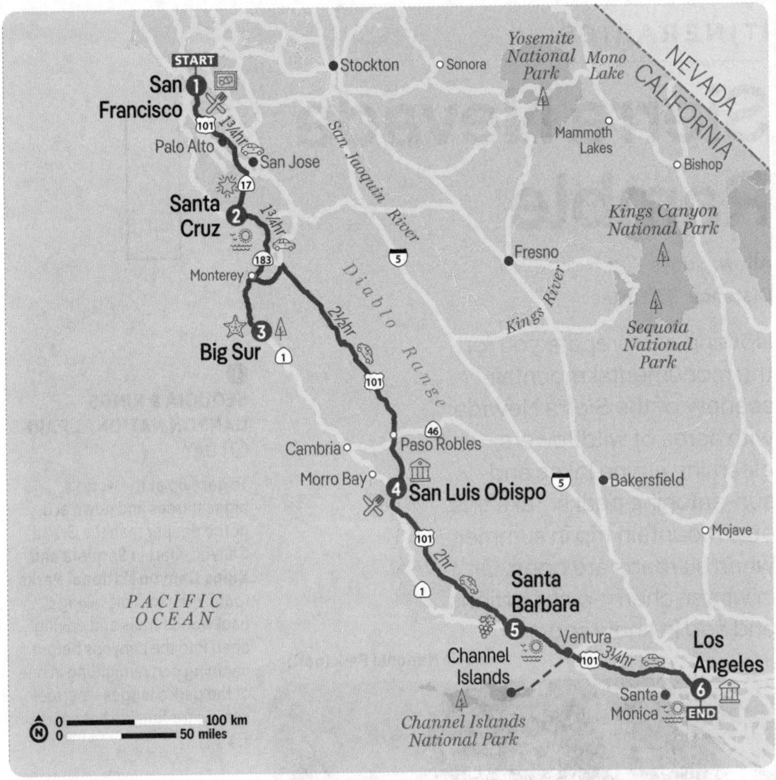

START
San Francisco 1
101
1¾hr
Palo Alto
San Jose
17
Santa Cruz 2
1¾hr
183
Monterey
Big Sur 3
1
2½hr
101
Cambria
46
Paso Robles
Morro Bay
4 San Luis Obispo
101
2hr
1
Santa Barbara
5
Ventura
101
3¼hr
Los Angeles
6
Santa Monica
END
Channel Islands
Channel Islands National Park
PACIFIC OCEAN
Stockton
Sonora
Yosemite National Park
Mono Lake
NEVADA
CALIFORNIA
Mammoth Lakes
Bishop
San Joaquin River
5
Diablo Range
Fresno
Kings River
Kings Canyon National Park
Sequoia National Park
5
Bakersfield
Mojave
0 100 km
0 50 miles

4

SAN LUIS OBISPO ⏱1 DAY

Book ahead to ensure a stop at the eccentric Hearst Castle, the Julia Morgan–designed estate of William Randolph Hearst. Then take coastal Hwy 1 onward past offbeat beach towns like Cambria, Cayucos and Morro Bay (which is crammed with wildlife). Arrive in **San Luis Obispo** (p285) hungry for local barbecue dinner and a walk around the downtown.

2 hours

5

SANTA BARBARA ⏱1 DAY

Follow the monarch-butterfly trail to retro-1950s Pismo Beach, the first of many beach stops on your way to happy hour in seaside **Santa Barbara** (p300), at the edge of Santa Ynez Valley wine country. Rub shoulders with Oprah, Harry and Meghan in Montecito.

Detour: *Hop on a boat from Ventura to explore Channel Islands National Park (p331) ⏱4 hours*

3¼ hours

6

LOS ANGELES ⏱2 DAYS

Cruise south to Malibu, where hiking trails compete with brilliant beaches, then end in **Los Angeles** (p335) for Hollywood star-spotting, world-class museums and live music on the Sunset Strip. Sample its rich neighborhoods, from Silver Lake and Los Feliz to Koreatown and Venice Beach, where you can join the nonstop parade of goth punks, bodybuilders and hippie drummers.

ITINERARIES

Sierra Nevada Ramble

Allow: 6 days

Distance: 330 miles

Nothing can prepare you for the monumental mountain scenery of the Sierra Nevada, with acres of wildflowers, gleaming alpine lakes and sun-catching peaks. Take this epic mountain trip in summer, when all roads are open. Or, in winter, cherry-pick portions and add in snow sports.

Sequoia National Park (p611)

1

SEQUOIA & KINGS CANYON NATIONAL PARKS

1 DAY

To gaze up at the world's biggest trees and down at a gorge deeper than the Grand Canyon, start in **Sequoia and Kings Canyon National Parks** (p611). Plan for time hiking backwoods trails and driving deep into the canyons before camping or overnighting in one of the park's lodges – perfect venues for fireside hot cocoa.

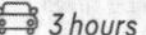

3 hours

2

YOSEMITE NATIONAL PARK

2 DAYS

Go west, then north to **Yosemite National Park** (pictured above; p600), where thunderous waterfalls and granite monoliths overhang a verdant valley. Soar over the Sierra Nevada's snowy rooftop on high-elevation Tioga Rd to reach Mono Lake.

Detour: *Take Hwy 395 south to Mammoth Lakes (p624), an all-seasons adventure base camp. It's another 100 miles to Lone Pine (p620) in the shadow of Mt Whitney.* *2–6 hours*

2 hours

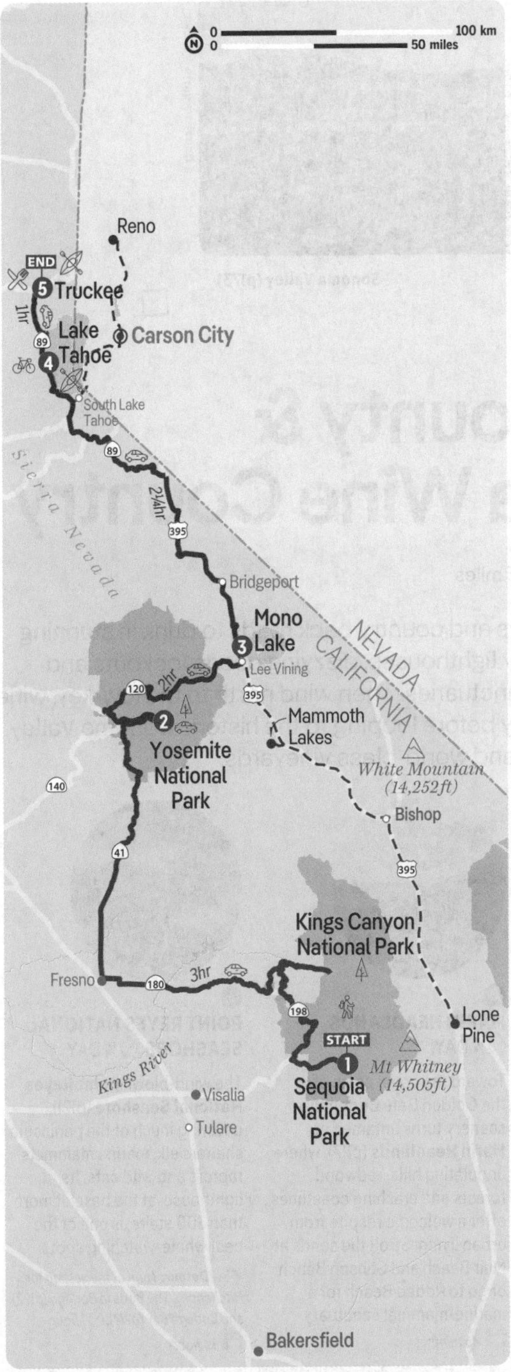

3

MONO LAKE ⏱1 DAY

Gaze out over **Mono Lake** (p626) and spot its odd-looking tufa formations reflecting in the mirror-like surface. Then rent a kayak so you can paddle up close and check them out. Afterward, visit Bodie State Historic Park, the Eastern Sierra's haunting gold-rush ghost town and listen for the whistle of *High Noon.*

🚗 *2¼ hours*

4

LAKE TAHOE ⏱1 DAY

Head to **Lake Tahoe** (p564), a deep-blue jewel framed by jutting peaks. The startlingly clear blue waters invite splashing, kayaking and even scuba diving. Meanwhile, mountain bikers careen down epic single-track runs and hikers follow trails through thick forests to staggering views.

***Detour:** Roll to Nevada for casino nightlife in Reno (p588).* ⏱*6 hours*

🚗 *1 hour*

5

TRUCKEE ⏱1 DAY

Amble back into the Old West as you hop between craft breweries and a surprising array of restaurants. **Truckee** (p589) is the perfect base for rafting the Truckee River, windsurfing on nearby Donner Lake or giving yourself the willies at Donner Memorial State Park as you hike trails where the Donner Party perished.

TIMOTHY S. ALLEN/SHUTTERSTOCK ©

Sonoma Valley (p173)

ITINERARIES

Marin County & Sonoma Wine Country

Allow: 4 days **Distance:** 135 miles

Follow coastal highways and country back roads to drink in stunning vistas from 19th-century lighthouses, dizzying ocean lookouts and beaches with marine sanctuaries. Then wind north to the low-key, wine-rich Russian River Valley before looping to the historic Sonoma Valley with its charming town and world-class vineyards.

1 SAUSALITO ½ DAY

Just north of the Golden Gate Bridge, **Sausalito's** (p114) pretty houses descend neatly down a hillside into a downtown with stunning bay views – the perfect spot for brunch. Northwest of downtown, poke around Sausalito's picturesque houseboat docks.

***Detour:** Reserve ahead to visit the old-growth redwoods at Muir Woods National Monument (p118). 1 hour*

20 minutes

2 MARIN HEADLANDS ¼ DAY

Toward the coast north of the Golden Gate Bridge the scenery turns untamed at **Marin Headlands** (p117), where undulating hills, redwood forests and crashing coastlines offer a welcome respite from urban living. Stroll the sands at Muir Beach and Stinson Beach, or go to Rodeo Beach for a marine-mammal sanctuary.

45 minutes

3 POINT REYES NATIONAL SEASHORE ¼ DAY

The wind-blown **Point Reyes National Seashore** (p121), covering much of the peninsula, shelters elk, marine mammals, raptors and wild cats. Its lighthouse, at the base of more than 300 stairs, is one of the best whale-watching spots.

***Detour:** Thrill at the setting for Hitchcock's* The Birds *in Bodega (p192) and Bodega Bay (p214). 1 hour*

1¼ hours

JON CHICA/SHUTTERSTOCK ©, SAM EDWARDS/SHUTTERSTOCK ©, MATTHIEU GALLET/SHUTTERSTOCK ©

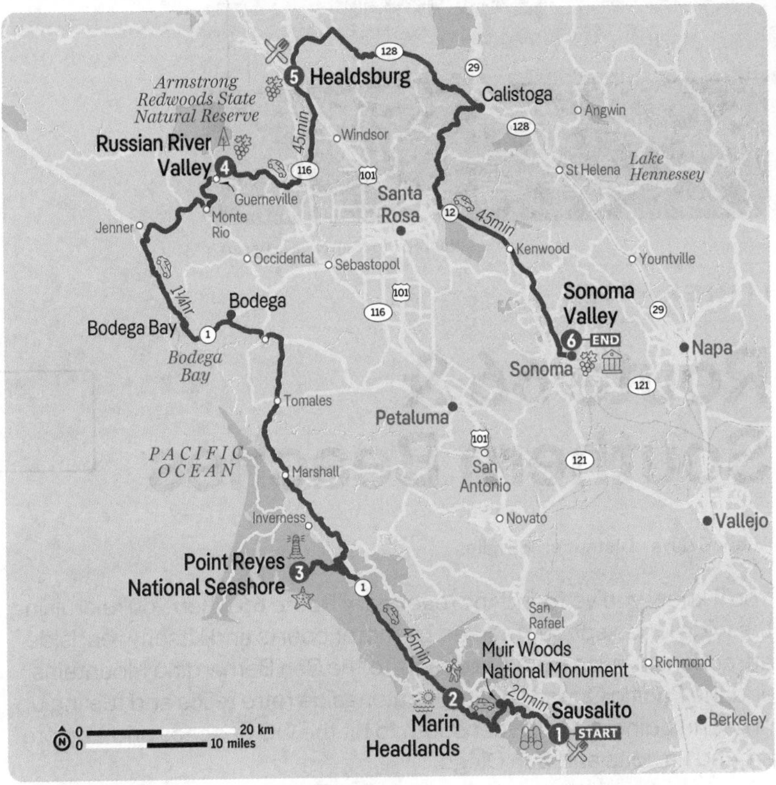
128
29
Healdsburg
Armstrong Redwoods State Natural Reserve
Calistoga
Angwin
128
Russian River Valley
45min
Windsor
Lake Hennessey
116
101
St Helena
Guerneville
Santa Rosa
12
45min
Monte Rio
Jenner
Kenwood
Occidental
Sebastopol
Yountville
1¼hr
101
Sonoma Valley
Bodega
29
Bodega Bay
116
1
END
Napa
Bodega Bay
Sonoma
121
Tomales
Petaluma
101
PACIFIC OCEAN
San Antonio
121
Marshall
Inverness
Novato
Vallejo
Point Reyes National Seashore
1
45min
San Rafael
Muir Woods National Monument
Richmond
20min
Sausalito
Marin Headlands
START
Berkeley
20 km
10 miles

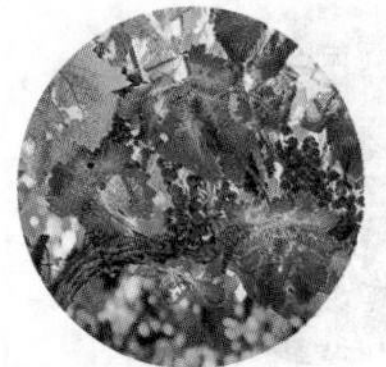

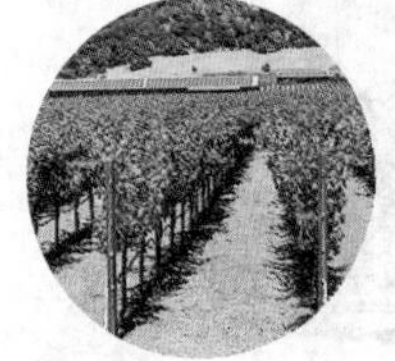

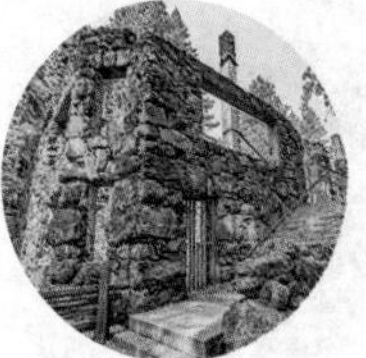

4

RUSSIAN RIVER VALLEY ⏱1 DAY

Cruise up **Russian River Valley** (p193) to gather good vibes in ancient redwood groves at Armstrong Redwoods State Natural Reserve. Float down the Russian River in an inner tube, and join Sonoma County's freethinkers for sunset toasts in organic vineyards – there are 50 wineries within a 20-minute drive of Guerneville.

🚗 *45 minutes*

5

HEALDSBURG ⏱1 DAY

Take beautiful Westside Rd north, stopping at wineries along the way. You're in the thick of wine country now. Plan for lunch in **Healdsburg** (p197), then unwind in Dry Creek Valley's farmstead wineries, or slightly north at Alexander Valley's many organic vineyards.

Detour: *Mellow out even further at hot springs in Calistoga (p170), Harbin or Orr.* ⏱ *3 hours*

🚗 *45 minutes*

6

SONOMA VALLEY ⏱1 DAY

A world apart but only an hour from San Francisco, **Sonoma Valley** (p173) is a 17-mile stretch of wild imagination, with pioneering sustainable vineyards and 13,000 acres of parkland heroically reclaimed from wildfires. Tour the wineries then stretch your legs at Jack London State Historic Park (pictured above), the famous author's former ranch. Finish in Glen Ellen or historic Sonoma.

FELIPE SANCHEZ/SHUTTERSTOCK ©

Route 66 (p486), Mojave Desert

ITINERARIES

Route 66 & Southern Beaches

Allow: 5 days **Distance:** 365 miles

You'll know you've found the legendary Route 66 when you're cruising the wide-open spaces marked by motor courts and kitschy roadside attractions. Cruise from the desert to the San Bernardino Mountains and the Pacific Ocean, pulling up alongside retro relics and fueling up in neon-lit diners. Then veer south to hit the OC beaches and explore around La Jolla and San Diego.

1 MOJAVE DESERT 1 DAY

The Golden State was the promised land at the end of a long road. Today, motoring across the **Mojave Desert** (p482) is a relative breeze compared to times of yore. Get a diner lunch in famous Western towns like Barstow and Daggett.

Detour: Feeling the desert mood? Head north to Death Valley National Park (p469), the state's austere epicenter. 5 hours

2 hours

2 PALM SPRINGS 1 DAY

Take a turn off Route 66 to reach the San Bernardino National Forest, where you can hike, camp and play at Big Bear and its lake before reaching retro-glam in **Palm Springs** (p450), where poolside cocktails meet desert oases and Joshua trees.

2 hours

3 LOS ANGELES 1 DAY

Route 66 emerges in Pasadena and **Los Angeles** (p335) before dead-ending into Hwy 1 in Santa Monica (pictured) with a grand coastal-view payoff. You can stop and explore LA for as long as time allows, or breeze through on your way out to the coast.

Detour: If you're in an outdoors mood, head to Santa Monica and Malibu (p371) for trails and beaches. 4 hours

1½ hours

TSUGULIEV/SHUTTERSTOCK ©, GG-FOTO/SHUTTERSTOCK ©, REISESCHATZI/SHUTTERSTOCK ©

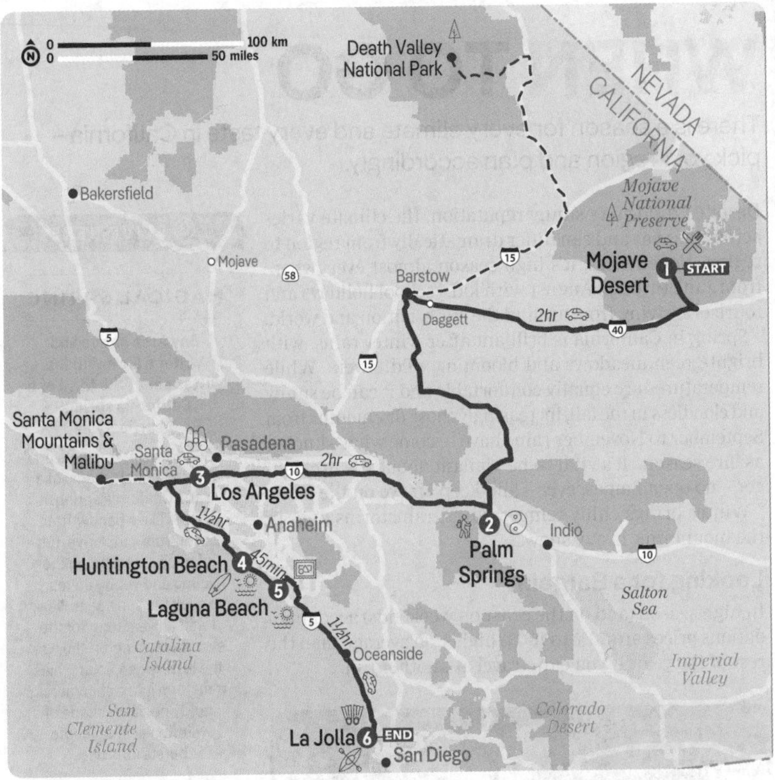

0 100 km
0 50 miles
Death Valley National Park
NEVADA
CALIFORNIA
Mojave National Preserve
Bakersfield
Mojave
58
15
Barstow
Mojave Desert
1 START
Daggett
2hr
40
5
15
Santa Monica Mountains & Malibu
Santa Monica
Pasadena
2hr
10
3 Los Angeles
1½hr
Anaheim
2 Palm Springs
Indio
10
Huntington Beach 4
45min
5 Laguna Beach
5
1½hr
Salton Sea
Catalina Island
Oceanside
Imperial Valley
San Clemente Island
Colorado Desert
La Jolla 6 END
San Diego

4

HUNTINGTON BEACH ½ DAY

In **Huntington Beach** (p402), aka 'Surf City USA,' SoCal's obsession with wave riding hits its peak. If you look down, you'll see names of legendary surfers in the sidewalk Surfers' Hall of Fame. On the pier, catch views of daredevils barreling through tubes. Otherwise, Huntington City Beach is a perfect place to snooze on the sand.

45 minutes

5

LAGUNA BEACH ½ DAY

On your way south, Crystal Cove State Park (pictured above) has more than 3 miles of open beach, an underwater scuba park and 2400 acres of woodland. Emerge at **Laguna Beach** (p412), an early-20th-century artist colony of coves, cliffs and bungalows. Laguna celebrates its bohemian roots with summer arts festivals and the acclaimed Laguna Art Museum.

1½ hours

6

LA JOLLA 1 DAY

La Jolla (p430) is a ritzy town of shimmering beaches, downtown boutiques and cliff-top mansions. Take advantage of the sunshine by kayaking and snorkeling at La Jolla Cove, or go scuba diving and snorkeling in San Diego-La Jolla Underwater Park, which harbors a variety of marine life and reefs. It's the perfect base for exploring the area and San Diego, too.

WHEN TO GO

There is a season for every climate and every taste in California – pick your region and plan accordingly.

Despite California's sunny reputation, the climate varies across the year and can differ dramatically from region to region. Nonetheless, it's high season almost everywhere from June through August with kids' school holidays and tourists arriving from around the state, nation and world.

Spring in California is brilliant after winter rains, with bright-green meadows and blooming wildflowers. While temperatures are equally comfortable and it can be sunny and cloudless in the fall, increasingly those dry months from September to November rains have become what's known as 'fire season.' It's vital to be vigilant about the fire danger – no open flames, ever – and keep an eye on the news.

Winter brings chilly temperatures, rainstorms and, in the mountains, heavy snow.

Looking for a Bargain?

In high season (and on the coast on weekends) accommodations prices are 50% to 100% higher on average than the rest of the year. If you can, travel at another time.

I LIVE HERE

MAGICAL SPRING

Bay Area native and writer Carrie Wilkins writes about the thrill of a California spring. @carrieelysia

'As I grew up, I recognized the undeniable magic of a warm California spring. It arrives like a handwritten letter from a lost love, full of hope – beckoning the young and young at heart to seek the sun again. Now, I wait all year long for the symphony of color: the way the lush, green, rolling hills transform into a shimmering gold and every shade of wildflower imaginable bursts into view.'

Flowers at Lake Tahoe (p564)

MOUNTAIN DRIVING

In California's mountains, winter storms can require the use of snow tires or chains for your vehicle. Keep an eye on the CalTrans website (dot.ca.gov) whenever snowy weather is forecast during your travels.

Weather Through the Year (San Francisco)

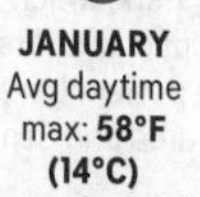

JANUARY	FEBRUARY	MARCH	APRIL	MAY	JUNE
Avg daytime max: **58°F (14°C)**	Avg daytime max: **61°F (16°C)**	Avg daytime max: **62°F (16°C)**	Avg daytime max: **63°F (17°C)**	Avg daytime max: **64°F (17°C)**	Avg daytime max: **67°F (19°C)**
Days of rainfall: 8	Days of rainfall: 8	Days of rainfall: 8	Days of rainfall: 4	Days of rainfall: 2	Days of rainfall: 0

DESERT SEASONS

Unlike in the rest of California, summer is low season in the deserts where temperatures exceed 100°F (38°C). It's blistering to even try to walk around, let alone hike its gorgeous trails. Go in spring instead, when wildflower blooms can be mind-blowing, or high-season winter.

I LIVE HERE

WINTER WEALTH

Oakland-born fashion designer Amy Brenneman travels between the SF Bay Area, France and Indonesia. @Hi_rol

'Every winter I come home to the Bay Area and I hit the Berkeley hills for a sunset hike. Saffron-tinted light filters through the redwoods and warms the soft spongy trail, the air perfectly crisp and cool. Upon reaching the top, I look out over the Golden Gate Bridge in the distance, calmly perched in winter clarity, promising a golden state of mind.'

The Big Festivals & Parades

Headliners, indie rockers, rappers and DJs converge outside Palm Springs at the **Coachella Valley Music & Arts Festival** (p448) for an annual musical extravaganza. **April**

California celebrates LGBTIQ+ pride for the entire month of June, with costume parades, film fests and streets parties. **SF Pride** (p93) sets the global parade standard, with over a million people, tons of glitter and ounces of bikinis. **Palm Springs** (p449) celebrates in November. **June & November**

A million people come to the **California State Fair** (p529) in Sacramento to ride the Ferris wheel, cheer on pie-eating contests, browse blue-ribbon agricultural and arts-and-crafts exhibits, taste Californian wines and beers, and hear bands. **July**

Outside Lands (p107) bring three days of play in Golden Gate Park with music and comedy plus gourmet food, beer and wine. **August**

Outside Lands (p107)

Local & Quirkier Festivals

Blanketed in snow, Lake Tahoe's **WinterWonderGrass** (p568) festival lights up the alpine lake with roots music and craft beers. **March**

Hot rods and hot action fete the classic film at **Salute to American Graffiti** in Petaluma (p182) and **Graffiti Summer** in Modesto (p538). **May & June**

Head to the hills (specifically Quincy) for the **High Sierra Music Festival** (p510), one of the best laid-back music fests in the state, played over one long weekend. **July**

Old-school jazz cats, cross-cultural sensations and fusion rebels all line up to play the West Coast's legendary **Monterey Jazz Festival** (p249), held on the Central Coast over a long weekend. **September**

COASTAL FOG

Especially in Northern California, summer is marked by coastal fog that doesn't always burn off. So San Francisco can be socked in and chilly when just inland in Oakland it's a sunny 75°F (24°C). September is the best month for the North Coast.

JULY	AUGUST	SEPTEMBER	OCTOBER	NOVEMBER	DECEMBER
Avg daytime max: **67°F (19°C)**	Avg daytime max: **68°F (20°C)**	Avg daytime max: **71°F (21°C)**	Avg daytime max: **70°F (21°C)**	Avg daytime max: **64°F (17°C)**	Avg daytime max: **58°F (14°C)**
Days of rainfall: 0	Days of rainfall: 0	Days of rainfall: 0	Days of rainfall: 2	Days of rainfall: 6	Days of rainfall: 8

LEFT: SUNDRY PHOTOGRAPHY/SHUTTERSTOCK ©; RIGHT: LMPC/GETTY IMAGES ©

Hiking in Fern Canyon (p234)

GET PREPARED FOR CALIFORNIA

Useful things to load in your bag, your ears and your brain

Clothes

Casual layers California is a laid-back, anything-goes kind of place, especially when it comes to fashion – but beware the changeable weather. Travelers who've only ever seen California on TV are in for a shock along the coast, where marine fog reprimands anyone in shorts all morning, rolls back in the afternoon to make you wish you'd worn sweat-proof sunscreen, and returns by evening to mock skimpy date-night outfits. The mountains can be cold and deserts blazing hot. Layer up with sweaters, wraps or light jackets. LA is more fashion-conscious and San Francisco more relaxed or iconoclastic; most other cities are quite informal.

Local Language?

In California, language goes way beyond 'dude.' Many Californians are multilingual – more than 200 different languages are spoken here. The top five are English, Spanish, Chinese, Tagalog and Vietnamese. Around 43% of state residents speak a language other than English at home. Dive in and go for it: you may find someone who speaks your native tongue.

Shoes Walking shoes are essential for cities and trails alike. Even on nights out, stilettos or gnatty oxfords are not necessary – just dress however you like.

READ

Where I Was From (Joan Didion; 2003) California-born essayist shatters palm-fringed fantasies.

If They Come in the Morning (Angela Davis; 1971) Chronicles of the Black Power movement collected by one of its leading figures.

Grapes of Wrath (John Steinbeck; 1939) Award-winning novel of Dust Bowl migration on Route 66 to California's Central Valley.

The Big Sleep (Raymond Chandler; 1939) Iconic Phillip Marlow mystery set in Los Angeles sets the bar for gumshoes.

Manners & Rules

Californians are casual by nature, but a few (unspoken) rules still apply.

Attitude Smiles go a long way here. Be friendly, even in a disagreement.

Greetings Shaking hands when meeting is a tad formal, but it's expected for business dealings and by some older adults.

Bargaining Haggling over the prices of goods usually isn't appropriate, except at outdoor markets and with sidewalk vendors.

Smoking Don't light up indoors (it's illegal) or anywhere else you don't see others doing it. Some restaurants have patios or sidewalk tables where smoking is tolerated (ask first, or look around for ashtrays), but don't expect your neighbors to be happy about secondhand smoke.

Cannabis While people aged 21 and older can buy cannabis, smoking or consuming marijuana in public or on federal land (national parks, Marin Headlands etc) is illegal.

Eating out Californian restaurant etiquette tends to be informal. Only a handful of restaurants require more than a dressy shirt, slacks and shoes that aren't flip-flops. At other places, T-shirts, shorts and sandals are fine.

Tipping (p632) At restaurants, 15% to 25% is expected anywhere you receive table service. Counter service can still rate 10%, though it's not obligatory.

Driving It is illegal to drive under the influence of anything (alcohol, marijuana) or to carry open containers. When wine tasting, have a designated driver and keep any open bottles in the trunk.

WATCH

Vertigo (Alfred Hitchcock; 1958; pictured above) The famous noir thriller set in San Francisco, starring James Stewart and Kim Novak.

LA Confidential (Curtis Hanson; 1997) Neo-noir tale of corruption and murder in 1950s LA.

Boyz n the Hood (John Singleton; 1991) Groundbreaking coming-of-age story set in LA's South Central neighborhood.

Laurel Canyon (Lisa Cholodenko; 2002) Gripping tale set in the iconic neighborhood of the '60s and '70s music scene.

Milk (Gus Van Sant; 2008) The biopic of Harvey Milk, the first openly gay man to hold a major US political office.

LISTEN

LA Woman (The Doors; 1971) Iconic band from the 1960s LA counterculture rock scene, along with the likes of Janis Joplin and Jimi Hendrix.

All Eyez on Me (2Pac; 1996) Tupac Shakur's last album features the song 'California Love' and West Coast stars like Dr Dre and Snoop Dogg.

I've Got a Tiger by the Tail (Buck Owens; 1965) The Bakersfield Sound put the 'western' in country and western, along with performers like Merle Haggard.

Dookie (Green Day; 1994) First major-label release by the Bay Area punk band includes monster hits 'When I Come Around' and 'Welcome to Paradise.'

California burrito

THE FOOD SCENE

California cuisine is a team effort that changes with every season – and it has changed the way the world eats.

As you graze the Golden State, you'll often want to compliment the chef – and they will pass it on to the staff, local farmers, fishers, winemakers and artisan food producers who make their menu possible. 'Let the ingredients speak for themselves!' is the rallying cry of California cuisine. Most types of America's fruit and vegetables are grown here, and you get the pick of the crop year-round. With fruit, vegetables, meats and seafood this fresh, heavy sauces and fussy garnishes aren't required to make meals memorable.

California cuisine also reflects the contributions of some of the world's top food cultures. The state's deep Mexican and Latin American heritage means burritos regularly outshine burgers. And California has some of the best Asian cuisine available outside Asia. The California stew is also peppered with Mediterranean traditions – where the climate and soil are similar to California's – and Afro-Caribbean and southern soul cooking.

Thus fusion is not a fad but second nature in California, where international takes blend beautifully with local ingredients.

Global Soul Food

California belonged to Mexico before it became a US state in 1850, and almost 40% of the population today is Latinx. It's no surprise, then, that Mexican classics remain go-to comfort foods, and upscale restaurants add novel twists to staple tamales and tacos. This blending of local produce and international cuisines defines California's great culinary advantage: an experimental attitude toward food. Even in its Wild West days

Best California Dishes

CALIFORNIA BURRITO
Mega-meal bursting out of a giant flour tortilla.

DUNGENESS CRAB
November-to-June favorite, eaten whole and in sandwiches.

SALMON
Appearing on menus statewide, fresh-caught and prepared in myriad ways.

ARTICHOKES
Giant and springtime delicious, from farms around Castroville.

when gold-rush miners and Chinese workers lived side by side, necessity and proximity meant everyone ate adventurously and cross-culturally, pairing whiskey and wine with tamales and Chinese noodles. Check out Tanya Holland's *California Soul: Recipes from a Culinary Journey West*.

Vegan & Vegetarian

To all those accustomed to making do with dressed-up side salads: relax, your needs are not an afterthought here. Decades before Alicia Silverstone championed a vegan diet, LA, SF and North Coast restaurants were already catering to vegans. You won't have to go out of your way to find vegetarian and vegan options: bakeries, bistros and even mom-and-pop joints in the remote Sierras are ready for meat-free, dairy-free, eggless requests. Locate vegetarian and vegan restaurants and health-food stores at happycow.net.

Wonderful Wines, Craft Brews

Powerful drink explains a lot about California. Mission vineyards first planted in the 18th century gave Californians a taste for wine, and the mid-19th-century gold rush brought a rush on the bar. By 1850, San Francisco had 500 saloons selling hooch to prospectors who'd struck it rich – or didn't. Today, California's traditions of wine, beer and snazzy cocktails are continually reinvented by creative winemakers, craft brewers and microdistillers – and, for the morning after, specialty coffee roasters come in mighty handy.

DIANE N. ENNIS/SHUTTERSTOCK ©

FOOD & WINE FESTIVALS

Wine & Food Affair (p155) Tour over 100 Sonoma County wineries in November; a specialty dish is paired with their vintages.

California Avocado Festival (p299) Guacamole for days in Santa Barbara County in early October.

Sonoma Harvest Fair (p155) In October, get your spittoon ready for the country's biggest wine-tasting festival.

Capitola Art & Wine Festival (p249) Sip a seaside chardonnay while browsing local art in this Central Coast hamlet in September.

Kelseyville Pear Festival (p243) Things get juicy in Lake County in September as they celebrate their local fruit.

San Joaquin Asparagus Festival (p533) In April, Stockton celebrates the slender green spears; there's live music and more.

Gravenstein Apple Fair (p189) Tuck into pies galore in Sonoma County in mid-August.

Gravenstein apples

MS S. ANN/SHUTTERSTOCK ©

Wine in Napa Valley (p156)

FORAGED FOOD
From wild chanterelles beneath California oaks to hillside miner's lettuce.

OYSTERS
From Hog Island Kumamoto in Tomales Bay to Grassy Bar in Morro Bay.

CIOPPINO
Iconic San Francisco fish stew in a rich tomato broth.

CALIFORNIA ROLL
Sushi roll invented in 1960s LA using crab, avocado and cucumber.

Specialties: Food Trucks

When sit-down meals fail to satisfy, make raids on local food trucks – fleets are standing by across the state. California's legendary food trucks serve up everything from tacos *al pastor* (marinated pork) or Indian curry-and-naan wraps to Chinese buns packed with roast duck and fresh mango.

Come prepared with cash and sunblock: most trucks don't accept plastic cards, and lines can be long at peak hours.

You'll often find batches of food trucks grouped together – sometimes in organized food parks – or single purveyors in habitual spots, like a supermarket parking lot. Ways to locate trucks coming soon to a curb near you include searching for 'food truck' and your location on Google maps, looking at food-critic picks on local news websites, and checking dedicated food websites such as eater.com. For mouthwatering reviews of legendary Cal-Mex street food, check out **LA Taco** (lataco.com).

Food Truck Hits

If you can think of a cuisine, somewhere in the state there's a food truck for it.

Dim sum Chinese small plates and dumplings
Kalbi Korean flavor-bursting marinated, grilled beef short ribs
Jollof rice Spicy West African rice
Cuitlacoche Corn smut, a sort of mold – a delicacy the world over
Korean tacos Grilled, marinated beef and spicy pickled kimchi
Pho Vietnamese noodle soup
Southern California fish tacos Grilled fish tacos, ideally fresh
Birria Meat stew from Jalisco, usually using goat

Taco truck

But expect every type of fusion or comfort food, too – think wood-fired pizza or grilled cheese and Tater Tots. Many food trucks also offer sweets like churros (sweet Mexican fried dough) or fresh-fruit hand pies.

MEALS OF A LIFETIME

Benu (p79) Splash out on brilliant wine-paired tasting menus that look like minimalist art in San Francisco.

SingleThread (p198) Be dazzled at this celebrated restaurant in Healdsburg where food masquerades as nature.

Rooh (p79) Indian creativity with farm-fresh ingredients – vibrant and delectable in SF and Palo Alto.

Chez Panisse (p134) Where it all started – worship at the temple of Alice Waters in Berkeley.

Mister Jiu's (p72) Wonderfully innovative Chinese cuisine and a charming banquet-hall ambience in SF.

Providence (p346) Seafood washes elegantly ashore with flavors from Asia and the Med on beautiful LA plates.

THE YEAR IN FOOD

SPRING

When the sun comes out, farmers markets fill city streets with salad makings, fish-taco trucks flock to California beaches, and lines bend around the block for organic artisanal ice cream studded with just-picked berries.

SUMMER

Beach barbecues are better with wild coho salmon, Brentwood corn on the cob, fresh salsa made with heirloom tomatoes, and grilled peaches topped with edible lavender flowers.

FALL

Experience your first crush at harvest in wine country, get lost in corn mazes and pumpkin patches, and give thanks for California's bounty of fresh-fruit pies.

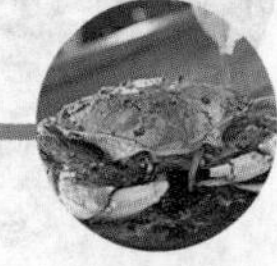

WINTER

Make the most of long winter nights with Dungeness crab, oysters and sand dabs. Celebrate Lunar New Year with lucky mandarins, and let citrus-spiked craft cocktails warm you.

Chez Panisse (p134)

DAVID A LITMAN/SHUTTERSTOCK ©

Sea lions at Moss Landing (p257)

THE OUTDOORS

Hike among desert wildflowers in spring, dive into the Pacific in summer, mountain-bike through fall foliage and ski down wintry mountain slopes.

California is an all-season magnet for outdoor fun, and people come from all over the world for the pleasure. Beach life and surf culture define California's freewheeling lifestyle, so consider permission granted to play hooky and hit the waves. Amble on smooth coastal bluff trails or hike multiday backpacking treks into the backcountry. If you want to get your adrenaline pumping, try scuba diving past coastal shipwrecks, scale sheer granite cliffs or go white-water rafting on the rapids.

Swimming & Surfing

If your California dream vacation means bronzing on the beach and paddling in the Pacific, head directly to Southern California. With miles of wide, sandy beaches between Santa Barbara and San Diego, you can be living the dream at least six months of the year. Ocean temperatures are tolerable by May or June, peaking in July and August. The rest of the year, use a wetsuit.

Northern California beaches are blustery and dramatic, with high swells crashing into rocky bluffs – not great for casual swimmers but perfect for the **Titans of Mavericks** (titansofmavericks.com), the world's most challenging big-wave pro surfing competition, held annually near Half Moon Bay. If you've never set foot on a board, California's your chance. Surfing is an obsession up and down the coast, particularly in Santa Cruz, Orange County and San Diego.

Adrenaline Sports

SNOW SPORTS
For sheer variety, the downhill skiing and snowboarding resorts ringing **Lake Tahoe** (p572) are unbeatable.

KAYAKING & CANOEING
Paddle Sonoma County's meandering **Russian River** (p195) as it flows by vineyards and redwoods out to the ocean.

KITEBOARDING & WINDSURFING
Let the wind lift you at **Crissy Field** (p63) in San Francisco or **Mission Bay** (p426) in San Diego.

FAMILY ADVENTURES

Go sand sledding on **LA's beaches** (p375).
Skywalk through the towering redwoods at **Sequoia Park Zoo** (p228).
Kayak with otters and seals in **Moss Landing** (p257).
Take surf lessons on the beaches around **Santa Barbara** (p304) or at **Huntington Beach** (p403).
Go snow-tubing in the Sierras at **Lake Tahoe** (p589).
Explore the nature-rich coast at **Point Reyes National Seashore** (p121).
Look for bison in **Golden Gate Park** (p107).
Go horseback riding in **Palm Springs** (p453) through an oasis bedecked with palms.
Loop-de-loop on rides at **Disneyland** (p392), **Knott's Berry Farm** (p401) and **Santa Cruz Beach Boardwalk** (p252).
Zip around skate parks, like the one in **Monte Rio** (p195).

Walking & Hiking

With epic scenery, California is the perfect place to explore the state's iconic highlights on foot. Stroll the beach at sunset or trek past Joshua trees in desert oases. Summit 14,000ft craggy peaks and admire alpine lakes. Walk under the world's tallest, largest and oldest trees. In spring and early summer, the Golden State is touched with a painter's palette as wildflowers bloom down coastal hillsides, across mountain meadows and along desert sands.

Legendary long-distance trails cut right through the state, too, including the 2650-mile **Pacific Crest National Scenic Trail** (PCT), which takes hikers from Mexico to Canada. Running mostly along the PCT, the 211-mile **John Muir Trail** (JMT) links Yosemite Valley and Mt Whitney via Sierra Nevada's high country. Trace the footsteps of pioneers and Native Americans along the 165-mile **Tahoe Rim Trail**, and you'll swear you've never seen a bluer lake or brighter sky. But there are still more trails to blaze here: the **California Coastal Trail Association** (coastwalk.org) is already more than halfway through building a 1200-mile trail along California's shoreline.

BEST SPOTS

For the best outdoor spots and routes, see the map on p50.

Hiker on the Pacific Crest Trail (p443)

Cycling & Mountain Biking

California has outstanding cycling terrain offering varying experiences: leisurely spins along the beach, adrenaline-fueled mountain rides or multiday coastal road-cycling tours. Even heavily trafficked urban areas may have good cycling routes, especially in SoCal. For example, choose the scenic route along LA's beachside **South Bay Bicycle Trail**.

The cycling season runs year-round in most coastal areas, although fog may rob you of views in winter and during 'May gray' and 'June gloom.' Avoid the North Coast and the mountains during winter (too much rain and snow at higher elevations) and SoCal's deserts in summer (too dang hot).

SCUBA DIVING & SNORKELING
Along the coast, rocky reefs and kelp beds teem with sea creatures like those at **Channel Islands National Park** (p331).

WHITE-WATER RAFTING
California has plenty of white water, like the **American River** (p552); hurtling down the rapids beats any roller coaster.

WHALE-WATCHING
Spot migrating gray, blue, humpback and sperm whales from viewpoints like the **Pigeon Point Light Station** (p149).

CLIMBING
Rock climbing abounds in the national parks (Half Dome!), the Sierras and other mountains, like **Mt Shasta** (p494).

ACTION AREAS

Where to find California's best outdoor activities.

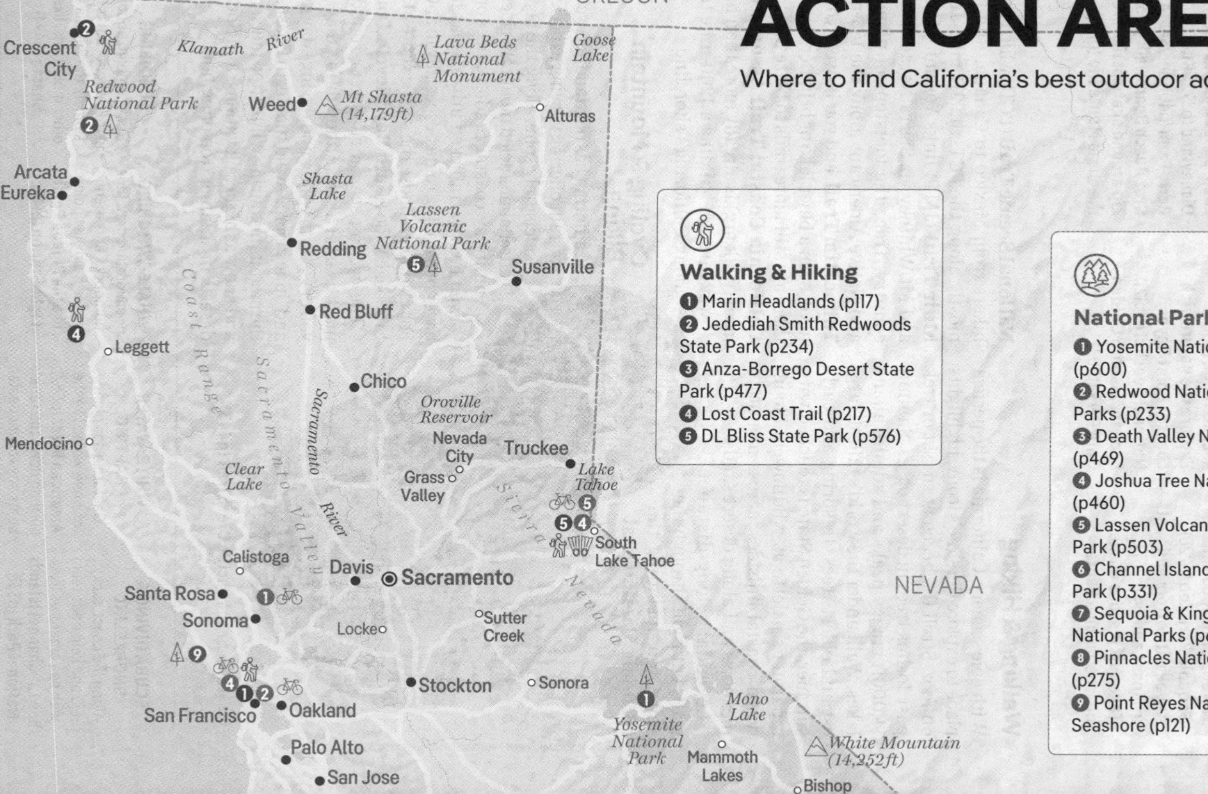

Walking & Hiking

1. Marin Headlands (p117)
2. Jedediah Smith Redwoods State Park (p234)
3. Anza-Borrego Desert State Park (p477)
4. Lost Coast Trail (p217)
5. DL Bliss State Park (p576)

National Parks

1. Yosemite National Park (p600)
2. Redwood National & State Parks (p233)
3. Death Valley National Park (p469)
4. Joshua Tree National Park (p460)
5. Lassen Volcanic National Park (p503)
6. Channel Islands National Park (p331)
7. Sequoia & Kings Canyon National Parks (p611)
8. Pinnacles National Park (p275)
9. Point Reyes National Seashore (p121)

Cycling & Mountain Biking
1 Napa Valley (p162)
2 Golden Gate Bridge (p62)
3 Santa Barbara (p306)
4 Mt Tamalpais State Park (p120)
5 Lake Tahoe (p573)
6 Joshua Tree National Park (p465)
Diving & Snorkeling
1 La Jolla (p430)
2 Crystal Cove State Marine Conservation Area (p410)
3 Monterey Bay (p261)
4 Emerald Bay Maritime Heritage Underwater Trail (p577)
5 Point Lobos State Natural Reserve (p266)
Surfing for Beginners
1 La Jolla (p430)
2 Santa Cruz (p252)
3 Malibu (p371)
4 Newport Beach (p407)
5 Carpinteria (p311)
PACIFIC OCEAN
Santa Cruz
Monterey
Big Sur
Diablo Range
Fresno
Kings River
Kings Canyon National Park
Mt Williamson (14,380ft)
Mt Whitney (14,505ft)
Sequoia National Park
Death Valley National Park
Cambria
Paso Robles
Morro Bay
San Luis Obispo
Bakersfield
Mojave
Barstow
Mojave National Preserve
Needles
ARIZONA
Santa Barbara
Channel Islands
Santa Monica
Los Angeles
Mojave Desert
Newport Beach
Laguna Beach
Palm Springs
Indio
Blythe
Salton Sea
San Nicolas Island
Catalina Island
Oceanside
Imperial Valley
Colorado Desert
La Jolla
San Diego
San Clemente Island
Tijuana
Mexicali
Yuma
MEXICO
0 200 km
0 100 miles

CALIFORNIA

THE GUIDE

Chapters in this section are organised by hubs and their surrounding areas. We see the hub as your base in the destination, where you'll find unique experiences, local insights, insider tips and expert recommendations. It's also your gateway to the surrounding area, where you'll see what and how much you can do from there.

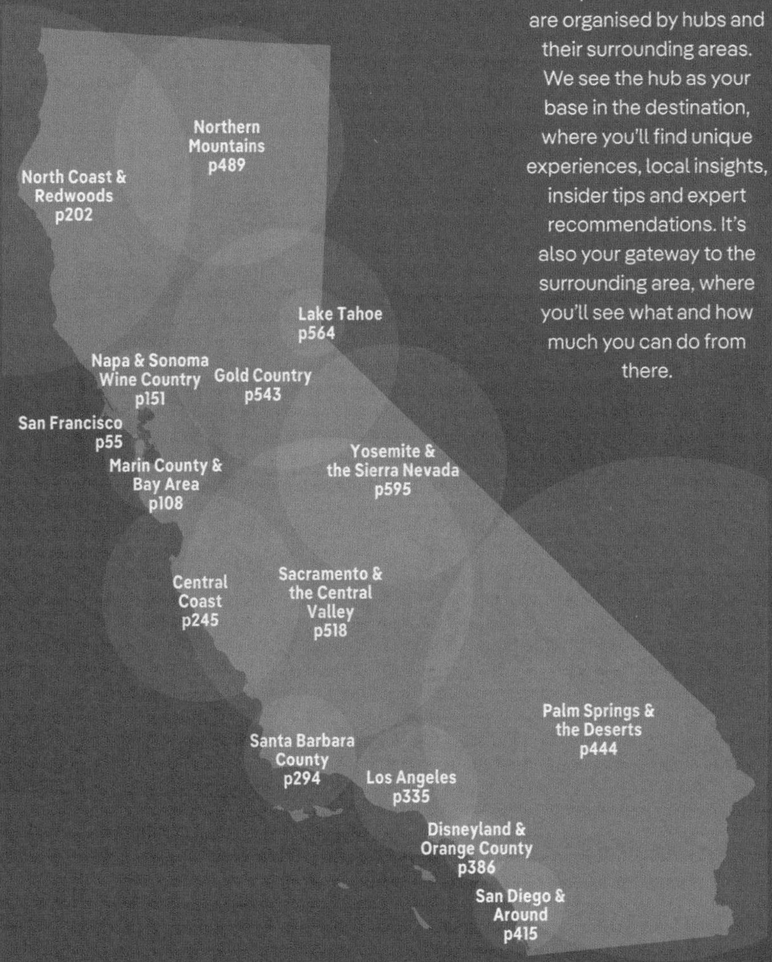
Northern Mountains p489
North Coast & Redwoods p202
Lake Tahoe p564
Napa & Sonoma Wine Country p151
Gold Country p543
San Francisco p55
Marin County & Bay Area p108
Yosemite & the Sierra Nevada p595
Central Coast p245
Sacramento & the Central Valley p518
Palm Springs & the Deserts p444
Santa Barbara County p294
Los Angeles p335
Disneyland & Orange County p386
San Diego & Around p415

Wildflowers on the beach at Point Reyes National Seashore (p122)

GARY C. TOGNONI/SHUTTERSTOCK ©

ARKANTO/SHUTTERSTOCK ©

Above: The Painted Ladies on Alamo Square (p84); Right: Cable car in Chinatown (p67)

THE MAIN AREAS

GOLDEN GATE BRIDGE, THE MARINA & PRESIDIO
Panoramic parks in ex-military posts. p60

NORTH BEACH, CHINATOWN & FISHERMAN'S WHARF
Iconic sights and legendary food and drink. p67

DOWNTOWN, CIVIC CENTER & SOMA
Startups, museums and parties galore. p76

JAPANTOWN, FILLMORE & PACIFIC HEIGHTS
Victorians, shopping and showtime. p83

SAN FRANCISCO

WHERE THE WEST GETS ITS WILD IDEAS

As fog swirls around California's creative hub, you'll never guess what's coming next – but you can say you tasted, heard and saw it first in San Francisco.

Adventurous food, wild entertainment, trippy tech: a weekend in San Francisco may seem like a quick trip into the future, except that it's been this way from the start. Oysters and acorn bread topped the menu in the Mexico-run Ohlone settlement of San Francisco c 1848 – but a year and some gold nuggets later, Champagne and chow mein were served by the bucket. Gold found in nearby Sierra Nevada foothills turned a sleepy 800-person village into a port city of 100,000 freewheeling prospectors, opera divas, con artists and hardworking laborers from across the globe.

Sound familiar? It will once you've spent a few days here. San Francisco's high-tech Gold Rush may be over – if you believe the headlines – but look around and you'll notice the city has already kicked off another creative comeback. Through boom and bust, the free spirits here have endured. During WWII, soldiers accused of insubordination and homosexuality were dismissed in San Francisco, as though that would teach them a lesson. Instead San Francisco's counterculture thrived, inspiring West Coast jazz and Beat poetry. When the Central Intelligence Agency tested LSD on author and willing volunteer author Ken Kesey, he slipped some into Kool-Aid at SF's Trips Festival. The psychedelic '60s took off, and the Summer of Love brought free food, love and music to the Haight. The Castro became a symbol of gay liberation, electing Harvey Milk as America's first out gay official in 1977. When SF witnessed devastating losses from HIV/AIDS in the 1980s, the community rallied, establishing global models for epidemic treatment and prevention.

San Francisco has continued to float outlandish new ideas – social media, mobile apps, biotech, green energy – even amid pandemics and economic downturns. As in San Francisco's early days, new ideas keep arriving here from around the world. So come on in: you're just in time for San Francisco's next act, and it's your turn on stage.

THE HAIGHT & HAYES VALLEY
Counterculture and concerts. p86

THE CASTRO
Out and proud, 24/7. p91

THE MISSION & DOGPATCH
Murals, fabulous meals and Latinx landmarks. p95

GOLDEN GATE PARK & THE AVENUES
Natural wonders and outlandish art. p102

Find Your Way

SF is only 7 x 7 miles, laid out on a slightly wonky but simple grid around the diagonal axis of Market Street. The entire Bay Area is well mapped by Google and Apple (both headquartered locally) – but look out for unmapped hills, one-way streets, pedestrian-friendly 'Slow Streets' and self-driving cars.

Golden Gate Bridge

Golden Gate Bridge, the Marina & Presidio
p60

Tunnel Tops

PACIFIC OCEAN

Legion of Honor

Golden Gate Park & the Avenues
p102

de Young Museum

Academy of Sciences

Golden Gate Park

San Francisco Botanical Garden

WALKING & BIKING

Ditch the car and spare yourself parking hassles–this city is best covered on foot. Only two of the city's 48 hills are staggeringly steep – to summit Nob Hill and Russian Hill, hop on a cable car or rent an electric bike from SF's Lyft bikeshare app.

CABLE CARS

SF's original steampunk transport is frequent, slow and scenic, running from 6am to 12:30am daily. To avoid queues for tickets and save money, get a day-use Muni Passport.

0 — 2 km
0 — 1 miles

Alcatraz

North Beach, Chinatown & Fisherman's Wharf
p67

Coit Tower
Exploratorium
City Lights Books

Yerba Buena Island

Japantown, Fillmore & Pacific Heights
p83

Asian Art Museum

SFMOMA

Downtown, Civic Center & Soma
p76

SFJAZZ

San Francisco Bay

The Haight & Hayes Valley
p86

The Castro
p91

Rainbow Honor Walk

Dolores Park

The Mission & Dogpatch
p95

San Francisco International (10.5mi)

FROM THE AIRPORT

The Bay Area's main airport is San Francisco Airport (SFO), a 30- to 45-minute drive south of SF. Rideshare services pick up curbside outside International Terminal Departures and on level 5 of the domestic parking garage. BART offers 20- to 30-minute train rides connecting downtown and SFO.

MUNI BUS & STREETCARS

Schedules vary by line, but service is infrequent after 9pm. Bring exact fare or get a reloadable Clipper card, also good for BART and cross-bay ferries. Anyone under the age of 19 rides free.

Plan Your Days

Make the most of California sunshine while it lasts, but don't be mad when the fog rolls in – San Francisco is at its most magical on misty days and mysterious nights.

SERGII FIGURNYI/SHUTTERSTOCK ©

Alcatraz (p71)

Day 1

Morning

- Hop off the cable car in **Chinatown** (p70) and wander historic alleyways to **City Lights** (p69) for a poetry pit stop. Parrots squawk encouragement on your hike up to **Coit Tower** (p69) for 360-degree panoramas. Follow your nose back downhill to North Beach or Chinatown.

Afternoon

- Head to the waterfront to discover scientific superpowers in the **Exploratorium** (p80), hang around historic ships with sea lions, or catch your pre-booked ferry to **Alcatraz** (p71), where D-Block solitary raises goose bumps.

Evening

- Make your island-prison break in time for **Abacá happy hour** (p72), seafood at dockside **Scoma's** (p72) or Cal-Chinese banquets at **Mister Jiu's** (p72).

You'll Also Want To...

Other cities may surprise you – but in San Francisco, you'll surprise yourself. Start by taking these only-in-SF dares.

REVEAL TOP SECRETS

In the **Presidio** (p64), uncovering military secrets is a walk in the park.

GET PSYCHEDELIC

Join mind-bending experiments in progress in the **Marina** (p65).

MEET FREE THINKERS

Get moved to poetry at **North Beach** (p69) literary landmarks.

LIZ HAFALIA/THE SAN FRANCISCO CHRONICLE VIA GETTY IMAGES ©, KARLIS DAMBRANS/SHUTTERSTOCK ©, M. VINUESA/SHUTTERSTOCK ©

Day 2

Morning

- Wander **Calle 24** (p99) past mural-covered bodegas to **Balmy Alley** (p98), where the Mission muralista movement began. Pick up **La Taqueria burritos** (p99) to enjoy in **Dolores Park** (p98), pausing for mural photo-ops at the **Women's Building** (p98).

Afternoon

- Roll downhill for **Bi-Rite Creamery ice cream** (p101) and **Creativity Explored** shows (p99), then head into the **Haight** (p86) to spot Victorian 'Painted Ladies' and colorful counterculture landmarks around the hippie-historic Haight/Ashbury intersection.

Evening

- Early walk-ins score sensational small plates at **Frances** (p93). Follow rainbow-lit **Honor Walk** (p92) to the Castro's history-making gay hot spots and iconic **Castro Theatre** (p92).

Day 3

Morning

- Follow the **Coastal Trail** (p106) from Ocean Beach around Land's End bluffs, and discover Golden Gate Bridge vistas and priceless art treasures at the Legion of Honor.

Afternoon

- After lunch at **Mamahuhu** (p106), head to **Golden Gate Park** (p103) to befriend butterflies in the **Academy of Sciences'** (p103) rainforest dome, sip tea by the **Japanese Tea Garden** (p103) koi pond, or cloud-watch inside the **de Young Museum's** (p103) *Skyspace* installation.

Evening

- Plan dinner around showtime at the rock-legendary **Fillmore** (p85), groovy **SFJAZZ** (p88) or dragtastic **Oasis** (p82) – and party on in SoMa clubs.

FIND YOUR SF SOUNDTRACK
Explore 100 years of music history in the **Fillmore** and **Japantown** (p85).

FLY YOUR RAINBOW FLAG
Bask in the rainbow glow of SF's world-changing LGBTIQ+ icons in **the Castro** (p91).

FREE YOUR INNER FLOWER CHILD
Relive the Summer of Love in the hippie **Haight** (p86).

SEE THE FUTURE FIRST
Glimpse where art and tech are headed next in **Dogpatch** (p99).

GOLDEN GATE BRIDGE, THE MARINA & PRESIDIO

PANORAMIC PARKS IN EX-MILITARY POSTS

Talk about a comeback: less than a decade after the Great Quake wrecked the city, San Francisco built a palatial fairground along swampy northern waterfront for the 1915 Panama-Pacific Expo. Afterward, fair buildings were dismantled, but the beloved Palace of Fine Arts remained, and the deco Marina took root around it.

This waterfront creatively reinvented itself following the 1989 quake, turning now-obsolete military bases into public playgrounds to enjoy art, nature and Golden Gate Bridge views. Chestnut St restaurants offer more selection than the Presidio, where a few park concessions and food trucks dot former military parade grounds. In Fort Mason's scenic shipyards, everyone's busy making art, not war – and Greens continues its revolution in vegetarian fine dining started in 1979. Meanwhile in the Fillmore bar zone between Union and Greenwich Streets, nicknamed the Bermuda Triangle, SF's straight singles disappear for weekends at a time – only to resurface Mondays as startup chief growth officers.

TOP TIP

Urban hikers flock to the Marina, SF's flattest neighborhood, for easy access to scenic Presidio hiking trails. The marine layer rolls in fast, so wear layers and consider renting an e-bike for hasty retreats. Street parking is tricky on weekends – try waterfront parking at Crissy Field or Marina Green parks.

Golden Gate Bridge (p62)

HIGHLIGHTS
1 Golden Gate Bridge
2 Tunnel Tops

SIGHTS
3 Arion Press
4 Baker Beach
5 Battery Bluff
6 Crissy Field
7 Fort Mason
8 Military Intelligence Service Historic Learning Center
9 Pet Cemetery
10 Spire
11 Wave Organ

EATING
12 Greens
13 Off the Grid

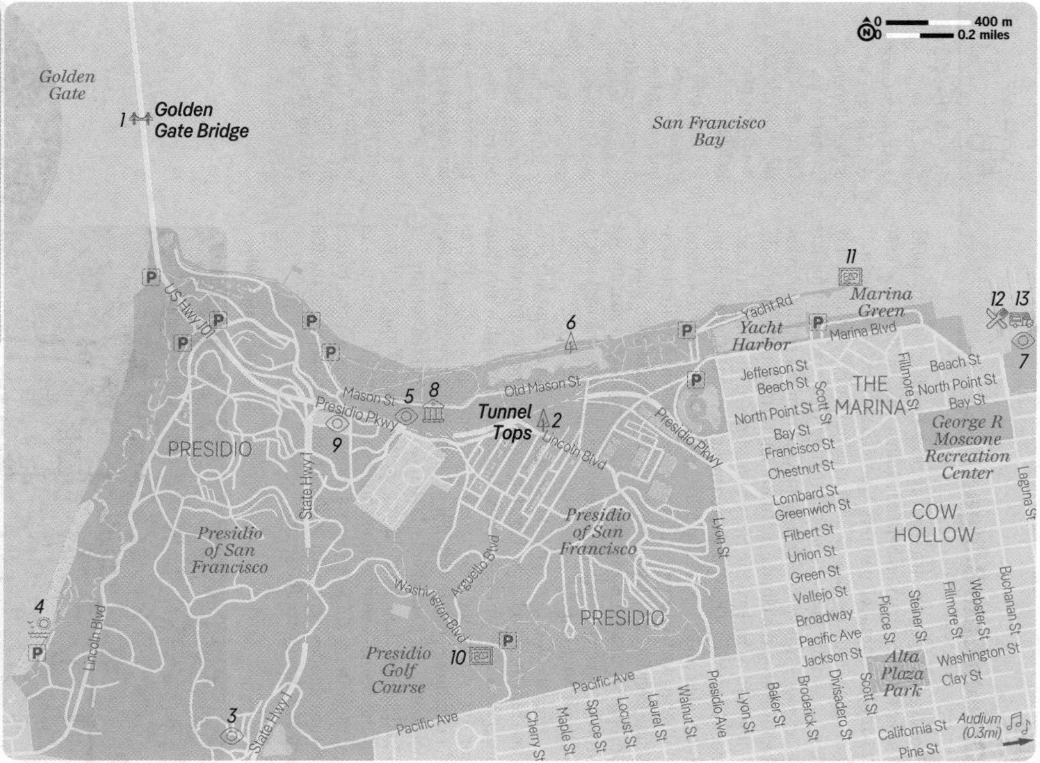

Golden Gate
Golden Gate Bridge
San Francisco Bay
Yacht Rd
Yacht Harbor
Marina Green
Marina Blvd
US Hwy 101
Mason St
Presidio Pkwy
Old Mason St
Tunnel Tops
Lincoln Blvd
PRESIDIO
Presidio of San Francisco
State Hwy 1
Washington Blvd
Arguello Blvd
Presidio Golf Course
Pacific Ave
Lyon St
THE MARINA
Jefferson St
Beach St
North Point St
Bay St
Francisco St
Chestnut St
Lombard St
Greenwich St
Filbert St
Union St
Green St
Vallejo St
Broadway
Jackson St
Scott St
Fillmore St
Beach St
North Point St
Bay St
George R Moscone Recreation Center
Laguna St
COW HOLLOW
Pierce St
Steiner St
Webster St
Buchanan St
Washington St
Clay St
Alta Plaza Park
California St
Pine St
Audium (0.3mi)
Cherry St
Maple St
Spruce St
Locust St
Laurel St
Walnut St
Presidio Ave
Baker St
Broderick St
Divisadero St
400 m
0.2 miles

Fort Mason (p65)

Golden Gate Bridge

MONUMENTAL MAGIC TRICKS

No other bridge puts on a show like this. On clear days, the Golden Gate Bridge glows ember-red against the blue sky – thanks to 25 diligent daredevil painters, who scale towers 80 stories high and apply 1000 gallons of International Orange paint weekly. But the bridge saves its most breathtaking magic act for late afternoons, when the fog rolls in. One minute, reddish towers balance atop the clouds; a minute later, they've disappeared.

It's hard to believe the Navy almost nixed SF's signature art deco landmark. The War Department owned the land flanking the bridge, and the Navy wanted it built of solid concrete, painted dull gray with caution-yellow stripes. Luckily, architects Gertrude Comfort and Irving Morrow joined forces with engineer Joseph Strauss on a winning counter-proposal: a soaring yet sturdy suspension bridge, painted a color that ensured safety without blighting the landscape.

Before the War Department could insist on an eyesore, laborers dove into the treacherous Bay riptides to sink bridge foundations in 1933. Workers braved powerful currents and high winds daily for four years, and despite standard-setting safety measures – including newly invented hard hats and a reinforced safety net that saved 19 workers who fell from bridge scaffolding – 11 builders lost their lives during construction. Today, a plaque on the bridge's southern entrance honors their courage and extraordinary achievement: a pioneering suspension bridge almost 2 miles long, with 746ft suspension towers. For the full effect, hike or bike the span.

TOP BRIDGE VIEWS

Over, under, east or west: which Golden Gate Bridge view is best? Depends on your timing. For sunny midday picnics overlooking the bridge, head to Tunnel Tops. During the morning commute, duck underneath the bridge at Fort Point to hear traffic hum overhead – and see where Alfred Hitchcock filmed Vertigo's thrilling ending. Sunny afternoons are prime time for hikers and cyclists crossing the bridge on eastern and western sidewalks, respectively. To beat fast-moving fog back to SF, rent an e-bike.

Golden Gate Bridge

TUNNEL TOPS BRIDGE PHOTO-OPS

These spectacular end-to-end bridge views were once only glimpsed by passing commuters – until nonprofit Presidio Trust turfed the tops of highway tunnels, cleverly creating a panoramic public park dubbed **Tunnel Tops**.

Battery Blaney

Battery Bluff

AWESOME ARMY ART

Between Tunnel Tops and Crissy Field, a sunny walkway wanders past three concrete monoliths hunkering into the hillside. What look like ultramodern sculptures are US Army bunkers (1899–1902) nicknamed Blaney, Baldwin, Sherwood and, a bit on the nose here, Slaughter. These **gun batteries** never saw any action, and were hidden from public view beginning in 1936. Now that the brutalist batteries are accessible, you might glimpse bands posing on them for moody publicity shots, or couples leaning into angular shadows for a semiprivate smooch.

Tunnel Tops

PANORAMIC PICNICS

San Francisco's most inspired **picnic spot** sits atop a traffic jam. Thanks to a $118 million effort to reclaim unsightly concrete traffic bottlenecks as public green space, you can enjoy spectacular Golden Gate Bridge views on a grassy lawn while commuters zoom underfoot. Picnic Place offers panoramic barbeque grills and wheelchair-accessible communal tables (reserve free online). Kids race downhill to the Outpost's concrete-chute slides and reclaimed-cypress playhouses. Weekends at 4pm, gather 'round the Campfire Circle to hear park rangers share stories about Buffalo Soldiers, indigenous healers and WWII spies. From Presidio Steps, catch sunsets over the Bay or watch fog swallow the bridge.

Crissy Field

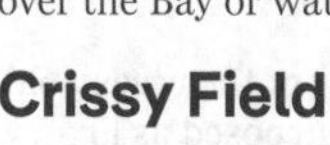

Crissy Field

AIRSTRIP TURNED COASTAL NATURE PRESERVE

War is for the birds at Crissy Field, a military airstrip turned waterfront nature preserve with glorious Golden Gate views. Where military aircraft once ran reconnaissance missions, kite-flyers share airspace with rare shorebirds above a reclaimed tidal marsh. You too can get airborne at **House of Air**, a repurposed airplane hangar lined with 42 trampolines. A freeform parade of joggers, hikers and strollers cover beachside trails, while sandpipers and wetsuited windsurfers brave chilly bay waters at Crissy Field's East Beach. Puppies have staked their claim on Crissy Field's grassy knoll, where they offer free lessons in the art of lolling. On foggy days, everyone flocks to the certified-green **Warming Hut** to warm up with fair-trade coffee while browsing wildlife books.

BEST PRESIDIO PICNIC PURVEYORS

Dynamo Donut Kiosk
SF's best doughnuts in sensational seasonal flavors, including chocolate horchata and carrot cake. $

Cafe Rx
Fresh soup/salad/ sandwich lunch combos dispensed weekdays at the Presidio's former pharmacy. $

Presidio Popup
Food trucks patrol the Presidio's Main Parade Lawn from 9am to 4pm. $

Presidio Bowl & Grill
Get grass-fed beef and veggie burgers to go, or stay to score strikes over hot wings and beer. $

Lucca Deli
Turbo-loaded Italian classics, from meat-stuffed muffuletta to spicy-salami Calabrian. $

MORE IN GOLDEN GATE BRIDGE, THE MARINA & PRESIDIO

Top-Secret Presidio

THE PARK'S BEST SECRETS

Spies, nudists, hidden masterpieces and pets called Blinky and Stinky – this former US army base reveals fascinating secrets along now-public hiking paths . Hiding in plain sight in the northeast corner of the Presidio is whitewashed Building 640, a WWII spycraft and language school that's now a museum. Step inside the **Military Intelligence Service Historic Learning Center** to see the drafty bunkhouse where Japanese American soldiers were trained by the US military, then deployed on high-risk intelligence missions to Pacific Rim battlegrounds.

Meanwhile, in accordance with US Executive Order 9066, their families and communities were rounded up and incarcerated as supposed 'enemy aliens' – including 70,000 Nisei (US-born citizens of Japanese heritage). To prove their loyalty, more than 30,000 Japanese Americans served in the US military, including the all-Nisei 442nd regiment, the most decorated unit in US history, whose extraordinary service is highlighted here. The Center's riveting displays also track the San Francisco–based Japanese American Citizens League's civil rights lawsuits over 40 years, establishing key civil rights precedents and an official 1988 US government apology to Japanese Americans incarcerated during WWII.

Follow Presidio trails leading west from the Golden Gate Bridge through windswept cypresses to **Baker Beach**, where you'll find beachgoers braving the elements to picnic, toss Frisbees and build sand castles until Pacific tides roll in. When rays poke through the marine layer, sun shines where it usually doesn't on the clothing-optional north end of Baker Beach. Access is beyond the boulders – adults only and no photography, please.

Behind the Presidio's Golf Clubhouse parking lot, another hiking trail leads to a contemporary art landmark: Andy Goldsworthy's towering wooden **Spire**. Built from fallen Presidio cypress trees in 2006, Goldsworthy's 100ft sculpture was intended to be eclipsed by new cypresses planted around it – but when the sculpture was damaged in a fire, San Franciscans rallied to rebuild it. Goldsworthy has repurposed fallen trees into three more art treasures hidden in the Presidio woods: **Wood Line**, **Tree Fall** and **Earth Wall**.

Literary masterpieces lurk in the shadow of the creepy old Presidio military hospital (improbably repurposed as luxury condos). **Arion Press** is 100 years old and still letter-pressing fresh poetry by Pulitzer Prize winners, painstakingly setting

WHERE TO STAY IN THE MARINA & PRESIDIO

HI Fisherman's Wharf
Major bargain: scenic waterfront hostel in ex-barracks with kitchen, games, free breakfast and parking. $

Lodge at the Presidio
At this officers' post turned eco-lodge, handsome guestrooms have commanding bridge views. $$$

Hotel del Sol
Live the California dream in this mod motel with courtyard pool, colorful rooms and sweet deals. $

Baker Beach and the Golden Gate Bridge (p62)

type by hand and cranking pages through antique Heidelberg presses. Casual visitors can catch gallery exhibits, but bibliophiles should, ahem, book ahead for Thursday 3pm tours of the basement foundry lined with drawers of fascinating, almost-extinct fonts – including the lead type used to print the original UN Charter.

Tucked behind Crissy Field under a highway overpass is the Presidio's **Pet Cemetery**, where soldiers and their families honored beloved dogs, cats, hamsters and bunnies. Weathered wooden headstones memorialize Blinky and Stinky ('Not really! Bye now love'), while carved granite tombstones praise Raspberry and Mr Twister ('P.S. He was like a beautiful flower that bloomed for 13 years – he was the end of my rainbow').

Mind-Bending Marina Experiments

HEAR, SEEAND TASTE SOMETHING NEW

There's more to the Marina than boats and bars. Follow the trail past yacht club docks along a jetty poking into the Bay, and you'll discover an aural oddity: the **Wave Organ**. Eerie sounds wheeze from repurposed SF cemetery statues and plumbing parts, ingeniously reconfigured into an acoustic sculpture by artists Peter Richards and George Gonzalez. If

SF'S FAVORITE PHOTO-OP

Like many a fine romance, the **Palace of Fine Arts** was never meant to last, and yet it did. California Arts and Crafts architect Bernard Maybeck originally built this Greco-Roman folly from wood, burlap and plaster as a temporary exhibit for the 1915 Panama-Pacific International Expo, but after the fair, San Francisco kept it as a souvenir. By the 1960s, the fake ruin was near-destroyed, and had to be recast in concrete. Generations of San Franciscans have posed for wedding photos under its rotunda, with its frieze showing 'Art under attack by materialists, with idealists leaping to her rescue' – a timeless sentiment.

Union St Inn
Plush Edwardian B&B with generous breakfasts in the parlor and six antique-filled guestrooms. **$$$**

Infinity Hotel
Sleek yet comfortable, with bonus bidets, steam showers and roof-deck views from here to infinity. **$$**

Marina Motel
Sitcom-set vintage motel with bougainvillea-covered archways and kitschy-cute rooms with kitchenettes. **$**

OLD-FASHIONEDS FOR FUTURISTS

Lose track of time over aged Tom Collins or freshly roasted coffee at the **Interval**, the bar-cafe that doubles as the headquarters for Stewart Brand's nonprofit **Long Now Foundation**, dedicated to long-term thinking – hence Brian Eno's fourth-dimensional digital artwork over the bar, the interdisciplinary library overhead and the sculptural prototype of a 10,000-year clock.

Over leisurely drinks, you can join fellow futurists and Long Now members imagining a world where art and technology aren't judged by sales or likes, but by their long-term impact on human history.

MICHAEL VI/SHUTTERSTOCK ©

The Wave Organ

trippy experimental music strikes a chord with you, don't miss the **Audium**. Since 1967, Stan Shaff and his son Dave have performed original compositions here on a unique instrument: an auditorium lined with 176 floor-to-ceiling speakers, blending found sounds from the city outside into meditative 'room compositions.'

The Marina's most eye-opening sights are at **Fort Mason**, a former WWII military base where San Franciscans now take subversive glee in making experimental art, not war. On Pier 2, **Herbst Pavilion** includes Fog Design+Art Fair and West Coast Craft Fair in its arsenal of artistic events, while dockside nonprofit **SF Camerawork** has showcased boundary-pushing photographers in jaw-dropping gallery shows since 1974. Stick around the shipyards for premieres of original commissioned works like *Halie! The Mahalia Jackson Musical* at historic **Magic Theatre** – or take center stage yourself at BATS Improv comedy workshops.

Attention: Fort Mason's mess hall is now commandeered by women star chefs at **Greens**, inventing flavor-bomb vegetarian dishes with organic ingredients from Buddhist Green Gulch Farm since 1979. Reserve ahead for bayfront tables with breathtaking Golden Gate Bridge views, or savor bar bites with Buddha-hand-infused cocktails at redwood-stump tables. Can't decide what to eat? Head to Fort Mason's parking lot, where **Off the Grid** food trucks throw down on Friday nights, and farmers markets overflow with organic possibilities on Sunday and Wednesday mornings.

WHERE TO EAT IN THE MARINA

Atelier Crenn
Chef Dominique Crenn's nightly menu is a poem, and her otherworldly inventions leave diners starry-eyed. **$$$**

Viva Goa
Melt hearts and SF fog with tangy, warming Goan xacutti coconut-seed curries and pillowy naan. **$$**

Kaiyō
SF surf-and-turf with Japanese Peruvian flair, from sushi and ceviche to Nikkei-style marinated grilled meats. **$$**

NORTH BEACH, CHINATOWN & FISHERMAN'S WHARF

ICONIC SIGHTS; LEGENDARY FOOD AND DRINK

Look past the souvenir shops, and you'll notice San Francisco's original Wild West neighborhoods have lost none of their character. In the 1800s, these were the stomping grounds of rebel rancher Juana Briones, San Francisco's *fundadora* (founder), main midwife and first woman entrepreneur. The Gold Rush brought new communities to her doorstep, including Chiletown, Sydneytown, Manilatown and Chinatown. Plump dumplings and rare teas are still served under pagoda roofs on Chinatown's Stockton and Grant Streets, while history-making Chinatown alleys are filled with temple incense, mah-jongg tile clatter and lion dancers practicing for Lunar New Year celebrations. Wild parrots circle over Italian cafes and bohemian bars in neighboring North Beach, where regulars find inspiration for the next great City Lights poetry book, sequel to *The Godfather* (written at Caffe Trieste) or outrageous stand-up comedy act. Fisherman's Wharf still has active fishing fleets, crab shacks and sea lions barking at passersby – plus a Maritime Museum featuring historic tall ships and a fabulous mural-lined bathhouse for stinky sailors.

TOP TIP

Since the 1880s, cable cars have remained the best way get to and from this area. Muni buses and T-line streetcars are often packed, and way less fun. Public parking is available underneath Portsmouth Square and at Good Luck Parking Garage, where spots are stenciled with fortune-cookie wisdom collected by artist Harrell Fletcher.

Caffe Trieste

NORTH BEACH, CHINATOWN & FISHERMAN'S WHARF

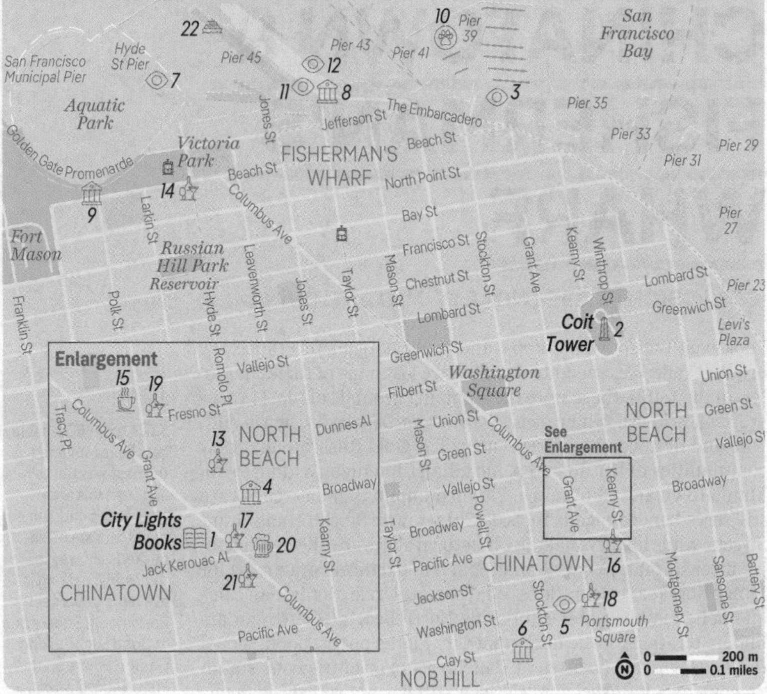

HIGHLIGHTS
1 City Lights Books
2 Coit Tower

SIGHTS
3 Aquarium of the Bay
4 Beat Museum
5 Chinatown
6 Chinese Historical Society of America
7 Hyde Street Pier
8 Musée Mécanique
9 National Maritime History Museum
10 Pier 39
11 Pier 45
12 USS Pampanito

DRINKING
13 15 Romolo
14 Buena Vista
15 Caffe Trieste
16 Comstock Saloon
17 Devil's Acre
18 Li Po
19 Saloon
20 Spec's Twelve Adler Museum Cafe
21 Vesuvio

TRANSPORT
22 Sea Forager Expeditions

Chinese Historical Society of America

Chinese Historical Society of America

EYE-OPENING INSIGHTS

Picture what it was like to be Chinese in America during the Gold Rush, Cold War and Civil Rights movement at this 1932 landmark, which Hearst Castle architect Julia Morgan built as Chinatown's YWCA. CHSA historians unearth fascinating artifacts: WWII Chinatown nightclub posters, Frank Wong's Chinatown miniatures, and Bruce Lee's martial arts costumes and philosophy library. Exhibits track Chinese American historical milestones, tracing recent anti-Asian discrimination back to the Chinese Exclusion Act, which officially excluded Chinese immigrants from US citizenship and civil rights from 1882 to 1943.

Coit Tower

Coit Tower

CENSOR-DEFYING ART

The exclamation mark on San Francisco's skyline is Coit Tower, featuring staggering views from the open-air roof platform and wraparound 1930s lobby murals celebrating SF workers. Federally funded Works Progress Administration (WPA) murals by 26 local artists capture Depression-era SF: speakeasies and soup kitchens, police confronting protestors, and intrepid reporters covering the scene for multilingual newspapers. Before Coit Tower opened in 1934, authorities denounced the murals as communist and tried to censor them – but San Franciscans voted to preserve them, and today they're a national landmark. Book docent-led mural tours online – tour all of them, or just the seven recently restored hidden stairwell murals.

City Lights Books

FREE SPEECH LANDMARK

Words were dangerous business in the 1950s, when library books were routinely banned, Hollywood screenwriters were blacklisted and comedians got arrested for swearing in SF nightclubs – but poet Lawrence Ferlinghetti founded City Lights Books anyway. City Lights' affordable paperbacks brought poetry to the people, sparking the Beat movement. Allen Ginsberg's *Howl and Other Poems* (1956) was an instant sensation – and Ferlinghetti and City Lights manager Shigeyoshi Murao were promptly arrested for 'willfully and lewdly' publishing poetry with homoerotic content. They fought the charges on artistic merits and won a landmark case that set global standards for free speech. Celebrate your freedom to read freely in the upstairs Poetry Room, browse the latest publications and peruse basement nonfiction sections covering Stolen Continents and Muckraking.

City Lights Books

Wander Chinatown Alleys

CELEBRATE RESILIENCE AND REINVENTION

The 41 alleyways packed into Chinatown's 22 blocks have seen it all: gold rushes and revolutions, incense and opium, fire and icy receptions. Look up and you'll notice pagoda-topped temples built over barbershops, restaurants and laundries. From 1870 to 1943, discriminatory laws restricted Chinese immigration, employment and housing – so there was nowhere to go but up.

Grant Ave is Chinatown's economic heart, but its soul is Waverly Place, lined with flag-festooned temple balconies. Follow wafting sandalwood incense up three flights of stairs to Tin How Temple, where services have been held since 1852 – even after San Francisco's 1906 earthquake and fire, while altars were still smoldering. Entry is free and donations customary for temple upkeep; no photography, please.

Turn into laundry-lined Spofford Alley, where Prohibition bootlegger battles were waged and Sun Yat-sen plotted the overthrow of China's Qing dynasty at No 36. Now Spofford stays mellow until dusk, when Chinese orchestras strike up tunes and the clatter of epic mah-jongg games begins.

Colorful murals grace SF's oldest alleyway, formerly known as Mexico, Spanish and Manila St, after the women who once staffed back-parlor brothels here. Today, **Ross Alley** is better known for stealing scenes in action movies *(The Karate Kid Part II, Big Trouble in Little China)* and for the Chinese Culture Center's cutting-edge art installations at No 41. Sample SF-invented desserts at **Golden Gate Fortune Cookie Factory**, and take away life lessons in reinvention and resilience from Ross Alley.

Chinatown

IV-OLGA/SHUTTERSTOCK ©

BEST FOR DIM SUM

Good Mong Kok
Join the lines for shrimp har gow and other classics, whisked from vast steamers into takeout containers. $

City View
Arrive before the midday rush for first dibs on passing carts, from garlicky gai lan to tangy spareribs. $$

Lai Hong Lounge
For 30 years, SF families have bonded over tantalizing waits here for fragrant barbecue-pork buns and soup dumplings. $

Palette Tea House
Modern waterfront bistro pairs Wagyu potstickers and Sichuan seafood dumplings with select teas and cocktails. $$$

Alcatraz

THE BAY'S DREADED PRISON ISLAND

Even from afar, this infamous prison island is more chilling than San Francisco fog. For over 175 years, 'the Rock' was the site of brutal prisons, FBI raids and death-defying escape attempts. Visitors arrive by ferry near Building 64, where riveting videos reveal the sunny island's dark history. The original military dungeon built on Alcatraz in 1859 housed Civil War deserters, court-martialed soldiers and Native 'unfriendlies' – including 19 Hopi who refused to send their children to government boarding schools, where Hopi language and religion were forbidden.

The Alcatraz cellblock that still dominates the island became a maximum-security penitentiary in 1934, showcasing federal efforts to imprison Prohibition gangsters, from Chicago's Al Capone to Harlem's Bumpy Johnson. First-person accounts of daily life are included on the audio tour, covering mealtime rules, censored library books and 36 escape attempts (one successful).

When the last federal prison on Alcatraz closed in the 1960s, Native Americans claimed sovereignty and occupied the island, standing their ground against the FBI from 1969 to 1971. Thousands of Native Americans participated in the protest over 19 months, until public support pressured then president Nixon to restore Native territory and strengthen self-rule for Native nations. As you walk uphill, notice the signs Alcatraz Red Power Movement activists left behind – including 'Home of the Free Indian Land' on the water tower. Every Thanksgiving, the International Indian Treaty Council celebrates Indigenous People's Day with a sunrise ceremony on Alcatraz.

Alcatraz

ANGEL ISLAND'S IMMIGRATION PRISON

Alcatraz isn't the only notorious island in the Bay. In 1970, the former **Angel Island Immigration Station** was ready for demolition until researchers found inscriptions detainees had carved into the walls – including 220 poems expressing sadness and anger about unfair treatment here. From 1910 to 1940, over 500,000 people from 80 countries were sent here for interrogation, detention (sometimes for years) and often deportation – Asian immigrants were routinely refused entry under discriminatory US laws until 1943.

Take Golden Gate Ferry to read their indelible words at the **Detention Barracks Museum**.

BEST SEAFOOD ON FISHERMAN'S WHARF

Scoma's
On fishing docks, savor pier-to-plate Cal-Italian classics – seafood-studded tomato cioppino, creamy scallop pasta, crisp crab cakes – with award-winning wine pairings. $$$

The Codmother
Follow seagulls to the corner of Beach and Jones to find food-truck mavericks batter-frying fresh cod for decadent Baja fish tacos and legit fish-and-chips. $

Pier 45
Crab stands open seasonally on the boardwalk, but around the back, savvy shoppers trawl Pier 45 docks for salmon, crab and other daily hauls sold from fishing boats. $

ROBERT ALEXANDER/GETTY IMAGES ©

City Lights Books

MORE IN NORTH BEACH, CHINATOWN & FISHERMAN'S WHARF

Find Poetry in the Streets

HOME OF THE BEATS

As you walk Grant Street from Chinatown to North Beach, listen: pots clang, cups clatter, greetings boom and echo. These improvised urban rhythms inspired generations of Beat poets to rush into **Caffe Trieste** and scribble free-form poems onto napkins and bathroom walls (some are still there). Today, the **Beat Museum** preserves 1000+ artifacts from their 1950s heyday, including Allen Ginsberg's typewriter and Diane di Prima's Revolutionary Letters – the closest you can get to the complete Beat experience without breaking a law.

The heart of San Francisco's poetry scene remains City Lights Books (p69), founded by poet Lawrence Ferlinghetti to sell affordable paperbacks. When Ferlinghetti was named San Francisco's first official Poet Laureate in 1998, he proposed poetic justice: renaming alleys to honor poets instead of politicians. **Kenneth Rexroth Place** honors the haiku poet and translator with a brief byway linking Chinatown speakeasies and North Beach delis. Black Beat poet and Buddhist Bob

WHERE TO EAT IN NORTH BEACH, CHINATOWN & FISHERMAN'S WHARF

Mister Jiu's
From sourdough scallion pancakes to marrow mapo tofu, chef Brandon Jew champions Cal-Chinese cuisine. **$$$**

ABACÁ
Diners become *pamilya* (family), sharing Cal-Filipino fried chicken and pandan-waffle brunches and bar bites. **$$$**

Molinari
Sing along to Sinatra while deli maestros slice prosciutto and house-cured salami for generous panini. **$**

Kaufman was frequently jailed for 'resisting arrest' in rhyme, and was never lost for words – until Kennedy's assassination, when he took a vow of silence that lasted until the Vietnam War ended. **Bob Kaufman Alley** is disarmingly captivating, and profoundly silent.

Jack Kerouac Alley connects Kerouac hangouts City Lights and **Vesuvio** bar, via pavement quoting *On the Road:* 'The air so soft, the stars so fine, the promise of every cobbled alley so great...' Also notice Li Po's sidewalk poem: 'Between best friends, there is never enough wine.' Consider this your invitation to follow the Beats to Chinatown's legendary **Li Po** bar, to debate the meaning of life and poetry on barstools by the golden Buddha.

THE POET'S CHAIR

In City Lights' upstairs **Poetry Room** (p69), everyone's invited to sit in the designated Poet's Chair and read (or write) a poem – founder Lawrence Ferlinghetti's hand-lettered sign recommends: 'Stash your sellphone and be here now.'

Ahoy, Sailor

AQUATIC ADVENTURES ON DRY LAND

The waterfront isn't just for looks – you can hop on a schooner, stare down sharks, suntan with sea lions and catch your own dinner here. The adventure begins at ship-shape **National Maritime History Museum**, built in 1939 as a public bathhouse for stinky sailors and now a treasure-box of aquarium-inspired art deco murals, mosaics and slate friezes by celebrated Black Californian sculptor Sargent Johnson. Major museum events include sea shanty sing-alongs aboard historic ships, occasional sailing excursions, and the Moby Dick Marathon, an epic 24-hour reading of the novel Melville wrote after his sea voyage to San Francisco.

Time travelers, your ride awaits at historic **Hyde St Pier**, where one ticket lets you board magnificent triple-masted 1895 schooner *CA Thayer,* adorable 1907 steam tugboat *Hercules,* elegant 1890 steam paddleboat *Eureka* and iron-clad 1886 square-rigger *Balclutha.* During WWII, San Francisco docks launched Navy fleets into the Pacific – including the 1943 submarine **USS Pampanito**, which survived six tours of duty. Explore below decks with the self-guided audio tour to hear submariners' heart-pounding stories of sudden dives, torpedo battles and tense stealth-mode silences. Ready for action? The Pampanito is docked alongside **Musée Mécanique**, a vintage arcade where you can battle Space Invaders, start a Wild West saloon brawl and get your fortune told for under a buck.

Walk underwater without getting wet at **Aquarium of the Bay**, where glass tubes lead you into bay waters past mesmerizing moon jellies, underneath shark tanks and

WHY I LOVE CITY LIGHTS BOOKS

Alison Bing, writer

On a stopover between Hong Kong and New York in San Francisco, I wandered through Chinatown fog fragrant with incense and roast duck into City Lights Books. In the basement near the Muckraking section, I noticed a sign painted by a 1930s cult: 'I am the door.' It's true. San Francisco is the threshold between fact and fiction, past and future, body and soul. That was 20 years ago. I'm still here. You've been warned.

Cafe Jacqueline
Sharing a fog-like seafood soufflé means it's love; sharing silky chocolate means it's forever. **$$$**

Go Duck Yourself
Fourth-generation crispy duck takeout cleverly rebranded and expanded, with signature sauces and bao kits. **$**

Z&Y
Spice up date nights with signature Sichuan dandan noodles, and leave your lips buzzing. **$$**

THE WHARF'S TRIPPY, HIPPIE LANDMARK

Beniamino Bufano's St Francis sculpture greets wharf visitors outside the **Longshoremen's Union Hall**, a hexagonal midcentury landmark where union dockworkers unwind after tough shifts – though it's best known for one epic party. Bill Graham launched the 1966 Trips Festival here, featuring headliners Janis Joplin, the Warlocks (now better known as the Grateful Dead) and novelist Ken Kesey, who spiked the punch with government-issue LSD intended to create the ultimate soldier.

During this 'acid test,' futurist Stewart Brand hallucinated military computers shrinking into his hand, bringing computing power to the people – 40 years later, Steve Jobs thanked him for the inspiration.

through manta-ray ballets. San Francisco's favorite 'sea-lebrities' are the **Pier 39** sea lions, who took over the yacht marina after the 1989 Loma Prieta earthquake. Thanks to California wildlife protections and abundant local herring, these lovable layabouts became wharf regulars – up to 1000 sea lions haul out here between January and July.

Wondering what's for dinner yet? Watch the fishing boats come in alongside **Pier 45**. If you arrive before local chefs, you can buy today's catch directly from the boats. On Saturday afternoons, peek inside **Fishermen's and Seamen's Memorial Chapel** at the stained glass captain's wheel and plaques honoring neighbors lost at sea. The antique altar banner honoring Madonna del Lume, Sicilian protector of fisherfolk, isn't just for show: she leads wharf parades at the annual Blessing of the Ships (first Saturday in October).

If you'd rather be fishing, join sustainable fishing expert Kirk Lombard on **Sea Forager Expeditions** along SF's waterfront to catch seasonal rock crab, herring, clams and prized monkey-faced eel – plus optional cooking classes to make proper SF seafood feasts. Kirk also leads eyebrow-raising Fisherman's Wharf tours, revealing 175 years of ship scandals, pirates' tales and juicy scuttlebutt (sailor's slang for gossip).

Now you have seafaring stories to swap over booze-spiked Irish coffee at the **Buena Vista**. At **Spec's Twelve Adler Museum Cafe**, the walls are plastered with merchant-marine memorabilia – and you'll be plastered too, if you try to keep up with the salty characters holding court in back. Surrounded by nautical mementos – including a massive walrus organ over the bar – your order seems obvious: pitcher of Anchor Steam, coming right up.

Dare to Enter the Devil's Acre

TOAST TO YOUR SURVIVAL

Tonight you're gonna party like it's 1899. Back then, San Francisco had some 3000 saloons plus 2000 'blind pigs' (speakeasies), competing for clients with signature cocktails. Through brawls and busts, Prohibition and pandemics, North Beach's swaggering Western saloons miraculously survived – and they're still slinging historically accurate whiskey cocktails and staggering gin concoctions.

Living large could turn lethal in the North Beach saloon district known as the Devil's Acre, where Gold Rush dandies in fancy waistcoats were literally shaken down for excess gold dust. San Franciscans still tend to dress down for drinks here – especially at **Saloon**, a hard-partying dive since 1861. Leg-

WHERE TO DRINK TEA IN CHINATOWN

Red Blossom
Sniff fragrant rare teas expertly curated by second-generation tea merchants Alice and Peter Luong.

China Live
Pull up stools by SF-landmark-tiled counters, and sip your way across oceans and mountains.

PlenTea
Bubble tea obsessions begin with fresh-brewed tea, organic milk and chewy *boba* (tapioca pearls).

IV-OLGA/SHUTTERSTOCK ©

Sea lions at Pier 39

end has it that when the city caught fire in 1906, loyal patrons saved Saloon by dousing it with hooch.

Over at **Comstock Saloon**, Victorian boozehounds relieved themselves in the trough under the bar between cocktails. Today, Comstock's cocktails are potent as ever, and live ragtime bands make bathroom lines downright entertaining. Comstock serves the city's definitive Martinez – the precursor to the modern martini, allegedly invented when a dedicated drinker demanded something to tide him over on the Bay ferry ride to Martinez.

A more contemporary Devil's Acre watering hole is called (wait for it) **Devil's Acre**, where even sworn enemies Call a 'Treuse – a signature cocktail with chartreuse, vermouth, egg white and mysterious 'Gold Rush bitters.' Wild Western nights continue at **15 Romolo**, the back-alley Basque saloon squeezed between Broadway burlesque joints. The strong survive the Suckerpunch (bourbon, sherry, hibiscus, lemon and Basque bitters), but the Basque Firing Squad (mezcal, Basque Patxaran liqueur, grenadine, lime and bitters) ends the night with a bang.

BEST PIZZA IN NORTH BEACH

Golden Boy
Join rock stars lining up for a late-night legend: Genovese focaccia-crust pizza at a bomb-shelter counter. $

Cotogna
Book ahead for James Beard Award-winning, wood-fired pizzas with perfectly blistered crusts. $$$

Liguria Bakery
Go before 11am to grab cinnamon-raisin focaccia or tomato focaccia with green onions, hot from the 100-year-old oven. $

Tony's Pizza Napoletana
Classic slices and original Up in Smoke combos: pizza plus a joint in a Jeremy Fish-designed box. $

WHERE TO STAY IN NORTH BEACH, CHINATOWN & FISHERMAN'S WHARF

Hotel Bohème
Poetry writes itself in North Beach's legendary bohemian retreat, with funky rooms named after Beat poets. $$

Argonaut
The wharf's cleverly converted historic cannery has snug guestrooms with exposed-brick walls and Bay views. $$$

Pacific Tradewinds Hostel
Chinatown's welcoming 4th-floor hostel has a friendly kitchen, free breakfasts and dorm bunks with lockers. $

DOWNTOWN, CIVIC CENTER & SOMA

STARTUPS, MUSEUMS AND PARTIES GALORE

Downtown San Francisco works hard for attention. Once the business day is done, San Franciscans promptly head home to vibrant neighborhoods – only a riveting show or happening club can lure them downtown. With many tech-enabled SF workers now fully remote, landmark Theater District entertainment venues are working even harder to attract crowds – and they're succeeding, with legendary drag shows, theater premieres, rock concerts and kinky leather street fairs.

Alongside the Theater District is Civic Center, the political center of the city, if not exactly its heart. The main draws here are San Francisco's spirited protests, SF Main library and treasure-box Asian Art Museum. Most downtown museums cluster around 4th and Mission Sts, including SFMOMA, the Museum of African Diaspora and Contemporary Jewish Museum. Downtown's unofficial playground is the sunny waterfront Embarcadero, where a promenade connects Fisherman's Wharf to Giants Stadium via the Exploratorium and foodie Ferry Building.

TOP TIP

Compared to other US cities, SF has lower-than-average rates of violent crime, but it faces many of the same challenges – including a housing crisis, opioid epidemics and overburdened healthcare systems. Visitors new to SF are advised to take share rides directly to/from Tenderloin destinations and SoMa nightclubs.

SFMOMA (p79)

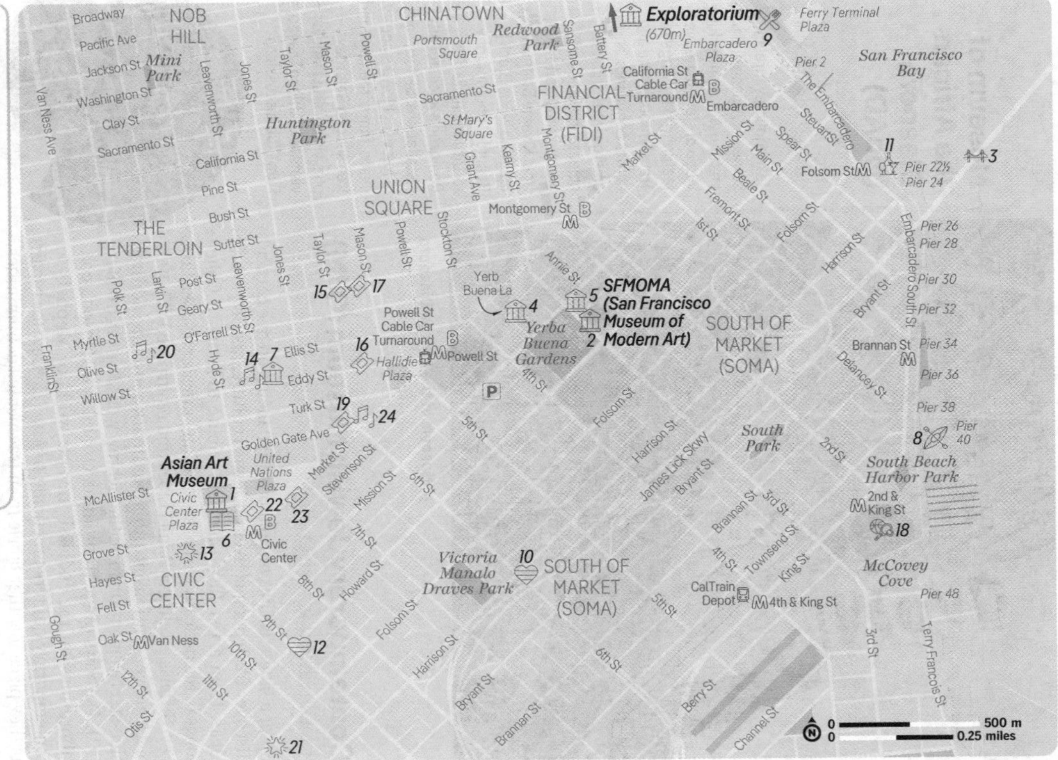

HIGHLIGHTS
1 Asian Art Museum
2 SFMOMA (San Francisco Museum of Modern Art)

SIGHTS
3 Bay Bridge
4 Contemporary Jewish Museum (CJM)
5 Museum of the African Diaspora (MoAD)
6 San Francisco Public Library
7 Tenderloin Museum

ACTIVITIES, COURSES & TOURS
8 City Kayak

EATING
9 Ferry Building

DRINKING
10 EndUp
11 Waterbar

ENTERTAINMENT
12 AsiaSF
13 Bill Graham Auditorium
14 Black Cat
15 Curran
16 EXIT Theater
17 Geary Theater
18 Giants Stadium
19 Golden Gate
20 Great American Music Hall
21 Oasis
22 Orpheum
23 Strand Theater
24 Warfield

Museum of the African Diaspora

TOP: ANNE CZICHOS/SHUTTERSTOCK ©; BOTTOM: XINHUA/LIU YILIN VIA GETTY IMAGES ©

Museum of the African Diaspora (MoAD)

GLOBAL BLACK CULTURE IN CONTEMPORARY ART

Take a journey through stories of African diaspora, starting with a powerful video of slave narratives featuring Maya Angelou. Travel through time and across continents, and emerge into exhibits celebrating Black art and cultures worldwide, from Kwame Brathwaite's uplifting 1960s Black Is Beautiful photography to Trina Michelle Roninson's ancestor altar installations. SF turns out in force for MoAD's poetry slams, film screenings and free second Saturdays – plus virtual artist studio visits and African Diaspora Film Club discussions.

Contemporary Jewish Museum (CJM)

MODERN JEWISH ART & CULTURE

Enter a blue-steel box miraculously balancing on one corner to discover fresh perspectives on Jewish culture, history, art and ideas, from artist Judy Chicago's tribute to Leonard Cohen's songs to the radically casual style of San Franciscan super-tailor Levi Strauss. Architect Daniel Libeskind repurposed SF's 1907 brick power station into this landmark museum, adding blue-steel elements to form the Hebrew word *l'chaim* (to life).

CJM's shows range from Frank Oz and Jim Henson's collaborations on the endlessly diverse world of Muppets to contemporary quilters practicing *tikkun* (Hebrew for repair) as they piece together fabric from fragmented communities.

Asian Art Museum

Asian Art Museum

TIME-TRAVELING ART ADVENTURES

Follow art and ideas across Asia all the way back to San Francisco. Three floors showcase highlights from this magnificent Asian art collection spanning 18,000 works and 6000 years. The museum's flow retraces Buddhism pilgrimage trails and trade routes from South Asia overland and across oceans to San Francisco, with contemporary Asian American artists offering fresh perspectives along the way.

Start on the 3rd floor with South Asian miniatures, detour through iridescent Iranian ceramics, and pass Javanese shadow puppets and Tibetan mandalas. Ahead are priceless Chinese jades and landscape paintings featuring poetry, frogs and farmers waiting for rain. Walk carefully past rare, translucent Korean celadon, and pause at the Japanese tea-ceremony room before returning to ground-level contemporary art galleries and events.

SFMOMA (San Francisco Museum of Modern Art)

IMMERSIVE ART EXPERIENCES

Take on SFMOMA's sprawling collection from the top, jumping into 7th-floor art installations, ducking into video projection rooms, meditating in the serene, minimalist Agnes Martin room and spotting familiar names and faces in the world-renowned photography collection.

From its start in 1935, SFMOMA was a visionary early investor in then-emerging art forms including photography, installations, video, performance art, digital art and industrial design. SFMOMA curators' bold early purchases of breakthrough works by muralist Diego Rivera and young Frida Kahlo remain highlights of the modern painting collection – the 1931 wedding portrait Frida Kahlo painted of herself with Diego is worth the admission alone – but the recent donation of pop art, abstract expressionist and contemporary masterpieces from the Fisher family (founders of the Gap) tripled the museum's collections.

Pace yourself with breathers at the outdoor terrace sculpture garden and cafe and cleverly curated museum stores, and don't miss the atrium murals and lobby masterpiece: Diego Rivera's **Pan-American Unity** mural. Commissioned for SF's 1940 Golden Gate International Expo, the mural shows California and Mexico linked by freedom struggles, shared roots and lofty dreams.

SFMOMA

ARTFUL DOWNTOWN DINNERS

Benu
Just behind SFMOMA, chef Corey Lee crafts exquisite dishes that look like minimalist masterpieces and pack monumental pan-Pacific flavor. $$$

Rooh
Gorgeous flavors dance across your tongue in perfectly composed progressive Indian dishes – tandoori artichokes, dahi puri with avocado-yogurt mousse, Madras curry shortribs. $$

Liholiho Yacht Club
Aloha is the secret ingredient in Liholiho's colorful, artfully casual dishes, meant for sharing with those friends you'd offer the last bite of shrimp-crusted Petrale sole or rendang curry NorCal lamb. $$

I LIVE HERE: MAKING HISTORY IN COMPTON'S TRANSGENDER CULTURAL DISTRICT

After starring on *Rupaul's Drag Race*, **Honey Mahogany** (@HoneyMahogany) co-founded SF's transgender cultural district and became the first Black transwoman elected Democratic Committee Chair – and she still slays in Oasis shows.

Street Cred
The highest concentration of transpeople in the world is here, but this isn't some trans Disneyland. America's first LGBTIQ+ uprising was the 1966 Compton's Cafeteria Riot, when transwomen fought police harassment at the corner of Turk and Taylor – now commemorated at our annual **Riot Party**.

District Highlights
You'll find drag burlesque at **Aunt Charlie's**, people doing incredible work for housing stability at **Glide**, live comedy at **Piano Fight**, and art-house theater at **CounterPulse**. Everywhere are unsung sheroes running public health initiatives, opening businesses and helping neighbors with groceries...as you do.

Exploratorium

STRANGER THAN SCIENCE FICTION

Can you stop time, sculpt fog or make sand sing? At San Francisco's hands-on, living laboratory of science and human perception, you'll discover superhuman abilities you never knew you had – and emerge with a renewed sense of wonder.

Designers of the Exploratorium's 600+ interactive exhibits have won MacArthur Genius grants for inventions that engage all the senses: try on static-electricity hairdos, star in animated motion-capture videos and send whispered messages to strangers across the room. Exploratorium exhibits are inspired by founder Frank Oppenheimer, a physicist who worked on the atom bomb (along with his older brother, J. Robert), but was then backlisted during the McCarthy era. He dedicated the rest of his life to promoting science in the public interest, teaching public school and founding the Exploratorium in 1969.

Today, the Exploratorium is truly immersive, covering a nine-acre glass-walled pier that juts straight into San Francisco Bay, and includes outdoor exhibits you can explore free of charge, 24 hours a day. For date nights where anything could happen (scientifically speaking), reserve tickets for After Dark Thursdays, when 18+ crowds bond over glow-in-the-dark mad scientist cocktails, technology-assisted sing-alongs and eye-opening special exhibits.

Exploratorium

GILBERTO MESQUITA/SHUTTERSTOCK ©

Be Thoroughly Entertained

IT'S SHOWTIME

Since the Gold Rush, San Francisco has earned its entertainment reputation nightly. All but one of the city's 20 landmark theaters were destroyed in the 1906 earthquake – yet while the city was smoldering, theater tents were pitched amid the rubble. Surviving entertainers began marathon free performances to raise spirits, and the city rebuilt at an astonishing rate of 15 buildings per day. In a show of popular priorities, SF's theater district was re-established before City Hall was rebuilt.

To see what's on in SF's Theater District, visit nonprofit Theatre Bay Area's website (theatrebayarea.org) and score discount tickets. At historic **Geary Theater**, American Conservatory Theater launched Tony Kushner's *Angels in America* and other Tony-winning shows by major playwrights, including Tom Stoppard, Dustin Lance Black, Eve Ensler and Robert Wilson. ACT's **Strand Theater** stages experimental works, and **EXIT Theater** hosts San Francisco Fringe Festival. Broadway shows and comedy specials are tested and filmed at the **Orpheum**, **Golden Gate** and **Curran** theaters.

For live music, you're in the right place. Marquee stars detour from stadiums to rock urban-legendary **Warfield** and **Bill Graham Auditorium**, where joints have been passed around in front of City Hall for decades. Indie rockers share the bill with global greats at the **Great American Music Hall**, the Tenderloin's opulent 1907 bordello turned all-ages venue – John Waters' annual Christmas show here is a delicious San Francisco treat. **Black Cat** features live music five nights a week, reviving the Tenderloin speakeasy where Miles Davis and other jazz greats recorded.

It's hard to believe SF nightlife almost didn't survive California's 1913 Red Light Abatement Act. Intended to curb prostitution and legitimize theater, it effectively enabled discrimination against women and LGBTIQ+ artists. After rebuilding SF postquake, women and LGBTIQ+ San Franciscans found themselves banned from their own theaters, bars, workplaces and apartments on grounds of 'lewdness' – except for the Tenderloin, where police were bribed to curb enforcement.

WWII veteran and original Black Cat drag hostess José Sarria became the first out gay American to run for public office in 1961, on a platform to stop anti-gay harassment. Sarria narrowly lost – and promptly declared herself Absolute Empress of San Francisco. Her Imperial Court became a fundraising and community health powerhouse during the AIDS pandemic,

SF'S LEATHER & LGBTQ CULTURAL DISTRICT

Whether your kink is cowboys, dungeons, disco or all of the above, SoMa's Leather & LGBTQ Cultural District will keep you thoroughly entertained. Public spankings and cheap beer are merely appetizers at **Folsom St Fair** and **Dore Up Your Alley Fair**. **SF Eagle** is a leather landmark for Sunday beer busts, barbecue and well-earned back-patio sunburns since 1981. Thirsty bikers hit **Hole in the Wall Saloon**, where original 1970s glow-in-the-dark gay erotica seems tame once you've been to the bathroom. Fashion statements are beside the point at **Powerhouse** underwear party nights, and so is cologne – testosterone and sweat are preferred scents here.

WHERE TO LUNCH AROUND CIVIC CENTER

Bodega SF
Soul-satisfying north Vietnamese specialties: tangy free-range chicken salad and decadent crab noodles. **$$**

La Cocina
Nepalese dumplings, Oaxacan tamales, Algerian couscous: all top-notch choices from enterprising women chefs. **$**

Swann Oyster Depot
Justifiably famous since 1912 for fresh oysters and crab salads – arrive before noon for counter stools. **$$**

establishing public health protocols that continue to save lives worldwide. Today the Tenderloin remains SF's most notorious district for criminalized activity, but also the home of essential community health services, LGBTIQ+ landmarks and historic entertainment venues. For exhibits exploring the Tenderloin's hidden histories, stop by the **Tenderloin Museum** and **San Francisco Public Library**'s James Hormel LGBTQIA Center.

The Tenderloin's trailblazing LGBTIQ+ entertainment scene never went away – it just moved to South of Market (SoMa) warehouses in the 1970s to accommodate crowds at late-night venues like the **EndUp** and Sunday 'tea dances' (the WWII euphemism for gay days at SF bars) in SF's landmark Leather & LGBTQ Cultural District (p81). Iconic SoMa spots include dedicated drag venue **Oasis** and **AsiaSF**, the city's original trans cabaret – stick around for afterparties DJed by divas, and rock out like an Absolute Empress.

TREAT YOURSELF AT THE FERRY BUILDING

While commuters rush to catch ferries, browse **Ferry Building food kiosks** and wait out rush hour over local beverages at **Red Bay Coffee, Fort Point Beer** or **Ferry Plaza Wine Merchant**. For sit-down meals, book **Boulibar** for Mediterranean flatbreads and pizzas straight from the wood-fired oven, or reserve ahead for sensational Cal-Vietnamese filet mignon shaking beef and signature Dungeness crab cellophane noodles at **Slanted Door,** chef Charles Phan's James Beard Award-winning bayfront bistro. Save room for dessert: ideally **Humphry Slocombe**'s Secret Breakfast (bourbon and corn flakes) ice cream or **Recchiuti Chocolates** and fleur de sel caramels.

Hit Your Stride on the Embarcadero

WORKOUTS ALONG THE WATERFRONT

There's no shame in hopping cable cars: San Francisco's 48 hills test even hard-core hikers and bikers. San Francisco's preferred workout is the Embarcadero, the sunny and mercifully flat Bayfront promenade. This is the starting point of SF's anarchic annual **Bay to Breakers** pseudo-marathon, when costumed racers run 12k to Ocean Beach – while jogging jokers dressed as salmon head upstream.

Year-round, San Franciscans stroll, skate, bike or jog the Embarcadero from Fisherman's Wharf past the Exploratorium (p80) to **Giants Stadium** (aka Oracle Park). Pause midway for **Ferry Building** treats supplied by NorCal food artisans, twice-weekly farmers markets and award-winning waterfront bistros.

But the defining landmark on the horizon is a work of mad genius. Joshua Norton lost his shirt and his mind in SF's Gold Rush before proclaiming himself 'Emperor of these United States and Protector of Mexico,' and ordering construction of a trans-bay bridge in 1872. Taxpayers took some convincing: the **Bay Bridge** wasn't completed until 1936. The eastern span collapsed in the 1989 Loma Prieta earthquake, taking 12 years and $6.4 billion to repair.

To grumbling taxpayers, Emperor Norton's idea didn't seem so bright anymore – until artist Leo Villareal installed 25,000 LED lights along the western span, mesmerizing commuters with a 1.8-mile-long light show that shimmers and pulses in never-repeating patterns. With crowdfunded support, **Bay Bridge Lights** runs from dusk until 2am. Watch the lights twinkle over oyster happy hours at Embarcadero's **Waterbar**, or get a closer look on twilight kayaking tours with **City Kayak**.

WHERE TO STAY DOWNTOWN

The Fairmount
Swagger into hilltop Fairmont to treat yourself to opulent suites and staggering tower views. **$$$**

White Swan Inn
Stage your own love-in at this shagadelic Nob Hill B&B, with cottage-core decor and groovy SF vibes. **$$**

Hotel Emblem
Start SF's next art movement in rooms equipped with poetry, inspiration boards and meditation bowls. **$$**

JAPANTOWN, FILLMORE & PACIFIC HEIGHTS

VICTORIANS, SHOPPING AND SHOWTIME

Don't let the quaint Victorian mansions fool you: this neighborhood rocks. You'll hear J-pop, taiko and TikTokkers in Japantown, and psychedelic soul, punk and Latin jazz at the Fillmore.

SF's most original soundtrack has deep roots. Starting in the 1880s, Japanese Americans settled Nihonmachi (Japantown) around Cottage Row. While Pacific Heights power-brokers built Victorian mansions, savvy builders copied their swagger in fabulous, affordable rowhouses downhill.

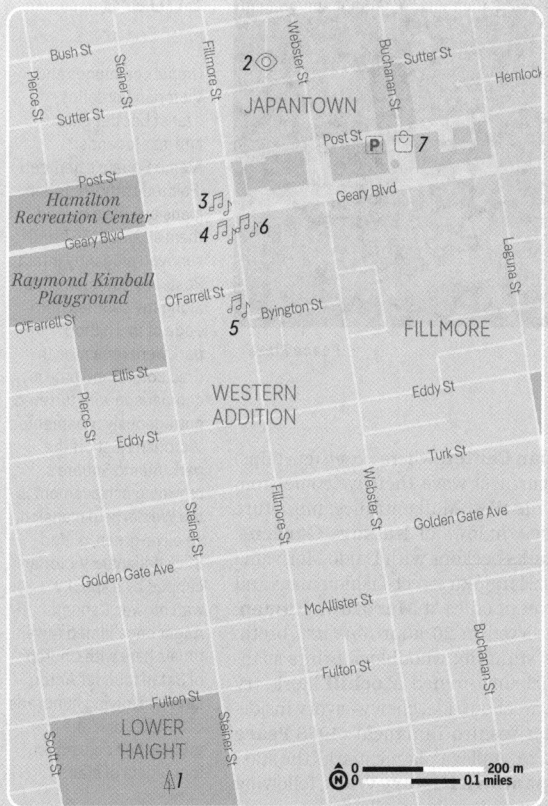

TOP TIP

Every San Franciscan has a favorite Victorian. To find yours, hit hot spots around Alamo Square and between Japantown's Sutter St and Washington St in Pac Heights. Many are whitewashed to suit minimalist modern tastes – the originally used vivid color schemes.

SIGHTS
1 Alamo Square
2 Cottage Row

ENTERTAINMENT
3 Boom Boom Room
4 Fillmore Auditorium
5 Sheba Piano Lounge
6 Social Study

SHOPPING
7 Japan Center

Cottage Row

JAPANTOWN'S HIDDEN, HISTORIC RETREAT

Take a quick detour from Sutter St into the 19th century, when this neighborhood was still a sleepy village. Serene clapboard cottages line the brick-paved promenade once known as Japan Street, after the Japanese Americans who called it home. They cultivated vegetables in cottage gardens to sell here, at Japantown's trailblazing farmer's market. Today, plum trees blossom and bonsai thrive in the central mini-park: an idyllic spot for sketching and sushi picnics.

Cottage Row

Peace Plaza

Japan Center

CULTURE IN A MALL

Time-travel to 1963 in **Japan Center,** where *noren* (curtains) and *maneki-neko* (cat figurines) wave their welcome from restaurant entryways. At the West Mall entrance, miniature maples greet you from the windows of **Katsura Gardens**. Upstairs, **Kinokuniya Books** beckons with Daido Moriyama photography monographs, Harajuku street-fashion mags and manga galore. Nerd out over noodles at **Marufuku Ramen**, hand-cut extra-thin and served in 20-hour *tonkotsu* broth. **Tokaido Arts** showcases stunning woodblock prints spanning four centuries. At kirizuma-roofed **Mochill** kiosk, try mochi doughnuts: crispy-sweet outside, chewy-savory inside. Outside, minimalist master Yoshiro Taniguchi's 1968 **Peace Pagoda** graces **Peace Plaza**. A plaza plaque marks the start of 10-block, self-guided **Japantown History Walk**, following the footsteps of Japantown's civil rights trailblazers.

Alamo Square

PAINTED LADIES

Hippie communes and Victorian bordellos, czarist bootleggers and jazz legends: Alamo Square's genteel 'Painted Lady' Victorian mansions have hosted them all since 1857, and survived elegantly intact. Postcard Row mansions along the southeastern edge of this hilltop park were repainted in drab colors, and pale in comparison with turreted, outrageously ornamented Victorians just off the park. Alamo Square's crowning achievement is the Westerfield mansion, an olive-green, gilded Stick Italianate Victorian capped by a spooky watchtower. Kenneth Anger once filmed tower rituals here with Church of Satan founder Anton LaVey, involving hundreds of candles and one grumpy lion coaxed up four flights of stairs.

MORE IN JAPANTOWN, FILLMORE & PACIFIC HEIGHTS

The SF Sound

A SOUFUL, PSYCHEDELIC SOUNDTRACK

Playlists can't get more eclectic than the historic soundtrack of this musically inclined neighborhood: '30s blues, '40s swing, '50s bop, '60s psychedelic rock, '70s punk, '90s hip-hop and timeless taiko drums. You might hear it all at Japantown's **Cherry Blossom Festival,** plus global pop hits.

Billie Holliday, Ella Fitzgerald, Dinah Washington and other top talent played tiny clubs that sprang up around Fillmore until the 1960s, when redevelopment squeezed out legendary venues from Jimbo's Bop City to Winterland, where the Sex Pistols played their last gig. But the Fillmore never lost its groove. Hepcats still play **Fillmore Jazz Fest**, reinventing standards that have echoed in these streets for decades. Down the block, sisters Israel and Net Alamayehu revive Fillmore jazz supperclub traditions at **Sheba Piano Lounge**, serving hot jazz combos and spicy Ethiopian vegetarian platters nightly. One landmark 1930s Fillmore blues venue remains: the **Boom Boom Room**, where top touring talents still bring crowds to the well-stomped checkered linoleum dance floor with blues, soul and funk. Around the corner at **Social Study**, weekend DJs remix vintage soul, funk and hip-hop on vinyl for laid-back, old-school Fillmore vibes.

When San Francisco's hippie scene exploded, psychedelic sounds spilled out of **Fillmore Auditorium** and into the streets: Jimi Hendrix, Janis Joplin, the Grateful Dead and Sly and the Family Stone blew minds and made careers here. SF silkscreen artists printed promotional posters in colors so trippy that they were nearly impossible to read. Today, the Fillmore's upstairs gallery is lined with these vintage posters, while bands that pack stadiums rock the 1250-capacity downstairs dance hall. For major shows, free Fillmore posters are still handed out.

DINNER BEFORE THE SHOW

Nari
Ingenious chef/owner Pim Techamuanvivit creates trippy Thai dishes as mindblowing as Fillmore shows, including oysters with water-beetle mignonette. $$$

State Bird Provisions
Savvy Boom Boom Room regulars know: 5pm walk-ins score first pick from carts loaded with California-inspired, dim-sum-sized 'provisions,' including the namesake: buttermilk-brined quail nested on sweet-and-sour onions. $$

On the Bridge
During SF Film Festival marathons at Kabuki Cinema, head to the Webster St footbridge for Japanese beer, curries and yoshoku-style fish-roe pasta – Patti Smith's favorite. $$

WHERE TO STAY IN JAPANTOWN

Hotel Kabuki
Beyond the sharp minimalist exterior are creature comforts like tie-dyed bedheads and wooden privacy screens. **$$**

Chateau Tivoli
Live like an opera diva in this opulent 1892 Victorian mansion near Alamo Square. **$$$**

Queen Anne
Star in your own costume drama at this rosy Victorian inn with massive mahogany beds. **$$**

THE HAIGHT & HAYES VALLEY

COUNTERCULTURE AND CONCERTS

To the rest of the world, hippies just seemed to happen – but at the corner of Haight and Ashbury Sts, you'll see exactly where '60s Flower Power took root like a dandelion in the sidewalk. More than a nostalgia trip, the Upper Haight is a standing invitation to let your freak flag fly – in an afternoon here, you can sing along, sniff flowers, skate gutters, sign petitions, encounter cults, spout poetry and feel totally alive.

Follow SF street skaters to the Lower Haight to see eye-popping concert posters at Haight Street Art Center, and discuss with regulars at legendary Lower Haight bars. Overcome powerful bar-stool inertia for world-class jazz, opera and classical shows in Hayes Valley, or join epic mosh pits at the Independent. Reserve ahead for dinner at one of Hayes Valley's gourmet bistros, or keep it casual at the hip mid-Haight hot spot known as NoPa (North of PanHandle) along Divisadero St.

TOP TIP

The park that runs parallel to Haight St is called the Panhandle – and panhandling has been part of the Upper Haight scene since the '60s, from busking street musicians to teens scrounging for bus fare. The Haight's neighborly, nonjudgmental nonprofits are here to help everyone, and the Haight Ashbury Food Program welcomes volunteers.

Haight St shops

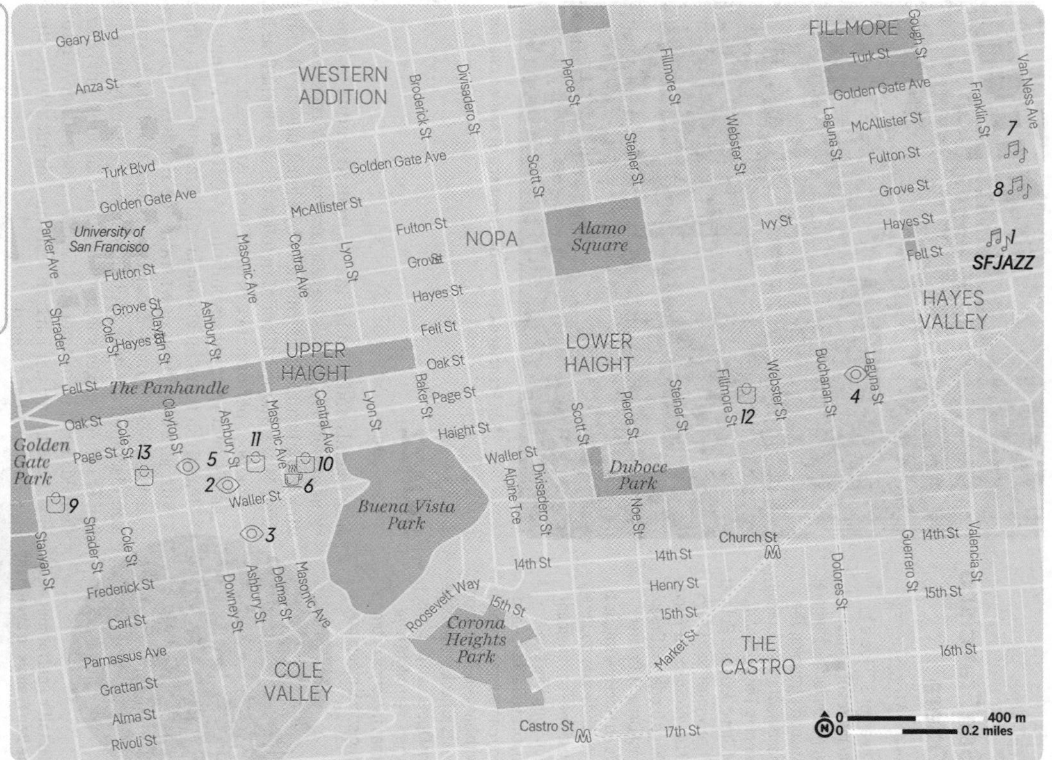

HIGHLIGHTS
1 SFJAZZ

SIGHTS
2 635 Ashbury St
3 Grateful Dead House
4 Haight Street Art Center
5 Haight-Ashbury Free Clinic

DRINKING
6 Coffee to the People

ENTERTAINMENT
7 San Francisco Opera
8 San Francisco Symphony

SHOPPING
9 Amoeba Music
10 Bound Together Anarchist Book Collective
11 Piedmont
12 Sparc
13 Wasteland

Mavis Staples performing at SFJAZZ (p88)

San Francisco Opera

ARIAS WITH A TWIST

Cheer for SF Opera premieres of original works, including Margaret Atwood's gripping *The Handmaid's Tale,* Grammy-winning *The (R)Evolution of Steve Jobs* and Pulitzer Prize-winner Nilo Cruz's *El Último Sueño de Frida y Diego* (Frida and Diego's Last Dream). Painter David Hockney's radical sets and haute-couture costumes complement Eun Sung Kim's bold musical direction – and you can appreciate both with bargain $26 balcony seats. Check the website for Opera Lab pop-ups, where you might hear divas freestyle or tenors sing social media posts.

San Francisco Opera's performance of *Andrea Chenier*

TOP: CARLOS AVILA GONZALEZ/THE SAN FRANCISCO CHRONICLE VIA GETTY IMAGES ©; BOTTOM: NOUNPUSHER PHOTOGRAPHY/SHUTTERSTOCK ©

SFJAZZ

WHERE GENIUS COMES TO PLAY

Jazz legends and singular talents from Argentina to Yemen shine at North America's biggest jazz center. Witness extraordinary mainstage performances by global talents like soul icon Mavis Staples, Ukrainian folk futurists DakhaBrakha, punk-poet performance artist Laurie Anderson and Oakland's own trumpet revolutionary Ambrose Akinmusire. Hear fresh takes on classic jazz albums and poets riffing with jazz combos in downstairs Joe Henderson Lab, featuring breakthrough local talents like Oakland harpist/soundsculptor Destiny Muhammad and achingly uplifting San Francisco singer/songwriter Diana Gameros. Enjoy jazz-themed cocktails in modern, LEED-certified Miner Auditorium – even upper-tier bargain seats have drink holders, stage views and brilliant sound.

Metallica performing with the San Francisco Symphony

San Francisco Symphony

CLASSICAL MUSIC BREAKTHROUGHS

When cutting-edge conductor and composer Esa-Pekka Salonen raises his baton, the whole audience holds its breath, anticipating another world-class performance by the Grammy-winning SF Symphony. Salonen opens the symphony to fresh inspiration with world premieres of original works, exciting rising-star guest conductors and screenings of *Star Wars* and *Black Panther* with a live orchestra. Spirited collaborations showcase major talent – including violinist Itzhak Perlman, pianist Yuja Wang and SF's own rock demigods, Metallica. Score $20 terrace seats and you can sit right behind the musicians.

Ready for an encore? Hidden behind Davies Symphony Hall is **SoundBox**, an intimate backstage space where symphony musicians and guest artists riff and experiment.

RUSLANKALN/GETTY IMAGES ©

San Francisco locals

MORE IN THE HAIGHT & HAYES VALLEY

Get Haight-Ashbury Flashbacks

LET YOUR FREAK FLAG FLY

Was it the fall of 1966 or the winter of '67? Dude, if you can remember the Summer of Love, you probably weren't here. The fog was laced with pot, incense and burning draft cards, and the corner of Haight and Ashbury Streets became the turning point for a generation of free spirits. The Haight's counterculture kids called themselves freaks and flower children; *San Francisco Chronicle* columnist Herb Caen derisively dubbed them hippies.

The hippie spirit endures here. On an average Upper Haight Saturday, you can sign Green Party petitions, commission a poem and hear Hare Krishna on keyboards and Jimi Hendrix on banjo. Tie-dyes and psychedelic art are always in style here – hence the prized tie-dyed concert tees on the wall at **Wasteland**, and original silkscreen prints at **Haight Street Art Center**.

The Haight still entertains crowds and radical ideas, too. Legendary glitter-bearded, psychedelic drag troupe The Cockettes were part of a '60s Haight commune dedicated to free food and

HAIGHT ST PUB CRAWL

Toronado
The city's best beer selection, including 40-plus beers on tap and seasonal microbrews.

Noc Noc
Who's there? Underground cartoonists, anarchist hackers and Burning Man founders, that's who.

Club Deluxe
Strong highballs guarantee you'll be swinging to jazz combos before the night is through.

Aub Zam Zam
Find boho bliss in this vintage Persian jazz bar, serving top-shelf cocktails at low-shelf prices since 1941.

The Alembic
The Victorian tin ceilings are hammered and you could be too, unless you sip the potent seasonal concoctions.

WHERE TO CURE THE MUNCHIES

Ragazza
Supreme NorCal pizza: wood-fired thin crust piled with farm-fresh ingredients and artisanal salumi. **$$**

Brenda's Meat & Three
Life-affirming California Creole revives marathoners and partiers – especially lip-smacking shrimp and grits. **$$**

Otra
Heirloom masa tacos and other NorCal Latin dishes come with a twist and a kick. **$$**

HIPPIE HILL

The ultimate hippie hangout is **Golden Gate Park** (p103), where the 1967 Human Be-In invited everyone to 'tune in, turn on, drop out.' You can still dig those groovy vibes at the free annual **4:20 Festival** and drop-in drum circles at **Hippie Hill**.

art, and you too can try on glitter drag at **Piedmont**, the Haight's original drag fashion house. Those '60s ideals never went away, either: there's free food at **Haight Ashbury Food Program**, free music shows at **Amoeba Music** and annual **Haight St Fair,** and free thinking at **Bound Together Anarchist Book Collective**. If you don't recognize Emma Goldman in the storefront *Anarchists of the Americas* mural, the all-volunteer staff will cheerfully supply you with biographical comics by way of introduction. The people, united, will never be decaffeinated at **Coffee to the People**, where the fair-trade coffee is strong enough to revive the Sandinista Movement and tables are covered with slogans from every social movement since the '60s.

Follow the music to Haight and Ashbury, where street musicians keep jamming at the intersection that changed rock history. Janis Joplin and her girlfriend Peggy Caserta lived at **635 Ashbury St** during the Summer of Love, while the Victorian at 710 Ashbury St miraculously survived earthquakes and the tenancy of Jerry Garcia, Bob Weir, Pigpen and sundry Deadheads. Still known as the **Grateful Dead House**, this was the site of the band's scandalous 1967 drug bust – and their landmark press conference demanding the decriminalization of marijuana.

Fifty years later, the state of California complied. You'll notice the clock at Haight and Ashbury is permanently set to 4:20 – recognized globally as 'international bong hit time,' a Bay Area term coined in 1971. With ID, adults can buy weed legally at trailblazing neighborhood marijuana dispensary **Sparc**, an early advocate of medical marijuana. Bad trips were mercifully treated gratis at **Haight-Ashbury Free Clinic**, pioneering non-judgmental, free 'rock medicine' still offered at SF festivals. The clinic's hand-carved 1967 sign still hangs at Haight and Cole Sts next to a mural of its motto: 'Healthcare is a right, not a privilege.'

Across Haight street, see how far humanity has come in Joana Zegri's 1967 **Evolution Rainbow mural**, showing life forms evolving from the Pleistocene era to the Age of Aquarius. A shop owner painted over it in the '80s – and faced community boycotts until it was restored. In the hippie heart of the Haight, the Age of Aquarius isn't over yet.

GO GOURMET

Rich Table
Mind-bending dishes like porcini doughnuts, sardine chips and burrata funnel cake blow up Instagram feeds nightly. $$$

Zuni
All style, no gimmicks – Zuni has been elevating menu staples into NorCal classics since 1979. $$$

Nojo Ramen Tavern
Discuss SFJazz shows between slurps of noodles and rich, housemade chicken paitan broth, topped by specialty slow-braised chicken. $$

Souvla
Upgrade from standard gyros to spit-fired lamb atop kale with Greek yogurt dressing, or tangy chicken salad with pickled onion and mizithra cheese. $

WHERE TO GET DOWN AND FUNKY

Independent
Funk with George Clinton, groove with reggae legends and watch this space for surprise shows.

Madrone Art Bar
Bust signature moves inside this art installation and bar at Motown Mondays and global disco nights.

Rickshaw Stop
Beats won't quit at this rainbow-spectrum black-box club, with all-ages '80s tribute nights.

THE CASTRO

OUT AND PROUD, 24/7

Ride up the rainbow-lit elevator at Castro Muni station, notice the giant rainbow flag forever unfurling over Harvey Milk Plaza and let it all sink in: honey, you've arrived. This is the best place on the planet to be out and proud, surrounded by people living their truth.

The Castro seems effortlessly free and fabulous – but this freedom was hard-won. When Castro businessman Harvey Milk was elected the nation's first openly gay official, he commissioned Gilbert Baker and Lynn Segerblom to create a symbol of community pride: the original rainbow flag, now at the Castro's GLBT History Museum. But ten months after taking office, Milk was assassinated. While the community was regrouping in 1981, a new threat emerged: AIDS. With zero federal support, the Castro wiped its tears and got to work, providing compassionate healthcare at STRUT and establishing pandemic protocols that still save lives worldwide. Your arrival is perfectly timed for the Castro's latest comeback, showing the world how to come out, play safe and make progress against any odds.

TOP TIP

SF wishes you well, offering community healthcare for all. The Castro's nonprofit STRUT center provides private, free and low-cost services, including PrEP HIV prophylaxis, STI testing, substance counseling and support groups. Founded in 1979, nonprofit Lyon-Martin Health Services provides dedicated primary care for women, trans and nonbinary folks regardless of ability to pay.

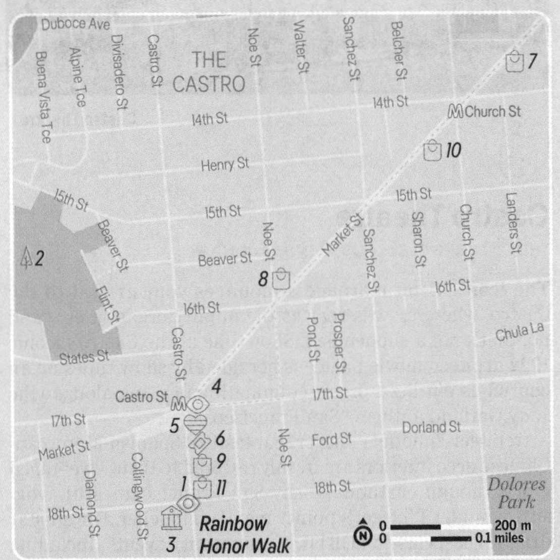

HIGHLIGHTS
1 Rainbow Honor Walk

SIGHTS
2 Corona Heights
3 GLBT History Museum
4 Jane Warner Plaza

DRINKING
5 Twin Peaks Tavern

ENTERTAINMENT
6 Castro Theatre

SHOPPING
7 Apothecarium
8 Castro Farmers Market
9 Cliff's Variety
10 Crossroads
11 Fabulosa Books

GLBT History Museum

GLBT History Museum

PROUD MOMENTS IN SF HISTORY

Time-travel through 50-plus history-making years in the Castro at America's first gay museum. Experience proud moments and historic challenges through moving personal stories and touchstone SF artifacts – including Harvey Milk's 1970s campaign literature, SF's original handsewn 1978 rainbow Pride flag and 1980s Keith Haring flyers urging SF to 'Act Up, Fight AIDS.' The shop features books researched at the museum, historic event posters – yes, SF's 1970 Gay-In was an actual event – and fridge magnets echoing Harvey Milk's words: 'You gotta give 'em hope.'

Rainbow Honor Walk

LIGHTING THE WAY FORWARD

See how far we've come with Castro sidewalk plaques honoring LGBTIQ+ luminaries. Along Market and Castro Sts, 68 global trailblazers point the way forward, from Nobel Laureates to San Francisco's own self-declared Absolute Empress José Sarria. Many of the portraits etched in bronze are familiar faces: civil rights leader James Baldwin, artist Keith Haring, author Virginia Woolf and SF disco diva Sylvester. Each also has a brief bio, so you can get better acquainted with the backstories of trans Zuni leader We'Wha, women's healthcare advocate Phyllis Lyon and Iranian singer Fereydoun Farrokhzad. Honorees are suitably bathed in rainbow-lit glory every night.

Castro Theatre

Castro Theatre

THE CASTRO'S FABULOUS LIVING LANDMARK

The iconic neon marquee announces your arrival to the Castro, where crowds roar as the mighty organ rises – and no, that's not a euphemism. Showtime at the Castro's iconic 1922 art deco movie palace is heralded by show tunes on an enormous Wurlitzer organ, culminating in a sing-along to the Judy Garland anthem, 'San Francisco.'

Architect Timothy Pflueger's fantastical Spanish-Moroccan-Chinese deco interiors are freshly restored to their jewel-toned glory, though earthquake-shy San Franciscans still avoid sitting under Pflueger's pointy metal chandelier. For all-star drag revues, classic LGBTIQ+ community events (including SF Gay Men's Chorus Holiday Spectacular) and film festival premieres – including the world's biggest LGBTIQ+ film fest, **Frameline Film Festival** – there's no finer palace on earth.

Rainbow crosswalk in the Castro

OUT FOR DINNER IN THE CASTRO

Frances
Cozy Castro bistro, serving market-inspired, well-priced set menus of 10 to 15 dishes to dazzle dates. $$$

Anchor Oyster Bar
Since 1977, Anchor has been Castro's port of call for sustainably sourced local oysters and SF cioppino (seafood stew). $$$

Beit Rima
Bond over meze inspired by chef Samir Mogannam's mom, including garlicky *ful* (fava spread) and smoky *shish taouk* (grilled chicken). $$

Mama Ji's
Extended happy hours call for chef Lily's homestyle Sichuan food, including Mother Chen's bean curd. $$

MORE IN THE CASTRO

Follow the Rainbow

GAY DAYS AND NIGHTS

The nightlife here is urban-legendary, but when the sun comes out, the Castro really shines – being out in broad daylight is a freedom this community fought for, and celebrates every day. Take the vintage F-line streetcar down Market to **Jane Warner Plaza**, recognizable by rainbow-themed art installations and regulars soaking in as much sun as legally possible – you might notice some strategically placed socks.

Look up: the **Castro Theatre** marquee is winking its neon welcome. Look down: the Rainbow Honor Walk invites you to walk in the footsteps of LGBTIQ+ trailblazers. To hear more of their stories, duck into **Fabulosa Books** for biographies by local authors – or step into GLBT Museum for a quick trip through Castro history. If you're here for Pride month in June, you

UP LATE...OR EARLY

When Castro bars close, late-night venues continue past sunup in SoMa. Stick around SoMa's **Leather and LGBTQ District** (p81) for Sundays and daytime street parties, when the sun shines where it usually doesn't.

WHERE TO STAY IN THE CASTRO

Hotel Castro
Wake up inspired amid stunning guestroom photomosaics of Harvey Milk and other LGBTIQ+ icons. **$$$**

Parker Guesthouse
Make your gay getaway in style at this Edwardian estate, covering two sunny yellow mansions. **$$$**

Beck's Motor Lodge
Spiffy and central, the Castro's original 1958 motel is recently renovated, with a roof deck and free parking. **$$**

DANCE PARTY SCENE

Drag dynamo **Juanita More** throws the most euphoric dance parties in town, including **BeatPig**, **Princess** and disco galas benefitting local LGBTIQ+ nonprofits. Lines along Market are probably for legendary lesbian nights at the **Café** or drag-star disco at **Beaux**. Crowds pack **440 Castro** for furry Sundays and weekend nights, when go-go boys twirl. At **The Lookout**, sports fans skip the big game for SF's other Sunday contact sports: drag disco brunch and Jock, where you'll see more jockstraps than in the 49ers locker room. Queer arts collective **Comfort and Joy** organizes Castro's mesmerizing, neon-lit **Glow street fair** and brings blissful Radical Faerie energy to **Sprung**.

can witness history in the making at Castro's Pink Party before SF's million-strong Pride parade.

Gay pride literally stops traffic at Castro and 18th Sts, where crosswalks are rainbow-striped. On the southeast corner, activists gather petition signatures, street altars honor community members and anything goes when someone hits play on a boom box – could be another Beyoncé flash mob, daredevil cheerleading formation or lip-sync battle. On the northwest corner, the outdoor bulletin board shows what's top of mind lately: circuit parties, parenting support groups, drag political fundraisers, lost cats, bands seeking guitarists and – the perennial favorite – missed connections.

Castro cafes offer excellent coffee, easy conversation and free copies of the *Bay Area Reporter,* the community's newspaper since 1971, with a handy BARtab supplement to help you make plans for tonight. To get you geared up for any occasion, **Crossroads** offers first-rate deals on secondhand clothes, **Cliff's Variety** has you covered for wigs and costume supplies, and **Apothecarium** cannabis dispensary sells edibles and smokes in a lounge featured in *Architecture Digest.*

Late afternoon, the scene picks up as neighbors ditch work for **Castro Farmers Market** (Wednesdays, March through November) or short, steep hikes up 520ft-high **Corona Heights** for romantic sunsets with panoramic views over the Castro. When goose bumps set in, follow the the vintage rainbow sign to Castro's best people-watching at **Twin Peaks Tavern**, the first gay bar in the USA with windows open to the street – this calls for a toast to freedom.

The night is yours: stick around for dinner and a Castro Theatre show, or hit concerts and clubs downtown. Or let the action find you at 18th St bars where everyone comes out to play: nonbinary club kids, gay sports fans, politicians in drag, lesbian playwrights and leather daddies. When the music's right, the rainbow glow of Castro dance floors is probably visible from space. But if there's not enough of a scene for you at any particular bar, this is the Castro: make one.

BEST HAPPY HOURS IN THE CASTRO

Midnight Sun
Midnight Sun lives up to its motto with good vibes, strong drinks, bear Fridays and Latinx-fabulous Media Noche.

Moby Dick
Since 1977, epic Castro nights start here with sailor's specials, pool, pinball and naughty-nautical vibes.

The Edge
Drag divas and leather daddies bond over show-tune sing-alongs, but it takes a PhD to win at pop music trivia nights.

THE MISSION & DOGPATCH

MURALS, FABULOUS MEALS AND LATINX LANDMARKS

Wander the Mission with a book in one hand and a burrito in the other, amid murals, sunshine and the usual crowd of filmmakers, grocers, techies, skaters and novelists. Here you can score fresh looks, old books and the ultimate Mission souvenir: a new talent, inspired by the vibrant local arts scene.

The Mission's namesake is whitewashed adobe Misión San Francisco de Asís, known as Mission Dolores (Mission of the Sorrows) – tragically apt for the indigenous conscripts forced to build it from 1776 to 1782. Subjected to harsh living conditions and introduced diseases, an estimated 5000 Ohlone and Miwok laborers were buried on Ohlone land appropriated by the Mission.

Today, multistory murals cover Calle 24 (24th St), SF's Latino Cultural District. Mission St was once SF's 'miracle mile' of deco cinemas and swanky shops, but now Valencia St is lined with trendy boutiques and bars. The cutting-edge arts scene is gravitating to waterfront Dogpatch, where dockside warehouses house galleries, startups and restaurants.

TOP TIP

The Mission is a magnet for weekend visitors with restaurants, boutiques, galleries, bars and lively street scenes. You'll notice income disparities between the minimum-wage workers and tech execs who live here, side by side. If you're walking around at night, be mindful east of Valencia and around deserted Dogpatch warehouses.

Mission Cultural Center for Latino Arts (p99)

THE MISSION & DOGPATCH

HIGHLIGHTS
1 Dolores Park

SIGHTS
2 826 Valencia
3 Aesthetic Union
4 Balmy Alley
5 Clarion Alley
6 Crane Cove Park
7 Creativity Explored
8 Institute for Contemporary Arts San Francisco (ICASF)
9 Letterform Archive
10 McEvoy Foundation for the Arts
11 Minnesota Street Project
12 Mission Cultural Center for Latino Arts
13 Museum of Craft & Design
14 Precita Eyes
15 SF Center for the Book
16 Women's Building

ACTIVITIES, COURSES & TOURS
17 18 Reasons
18 Chase Center
19 La Raza Skatepark

EATING
20 La Palma Mexicatessen
21 La Reyna
22 Mission Community Market

ENTERTAINMENT
23 Brava Theater

SHOPPING
24 Adobe Books
25 Higher Purpose Cannabis
26 Medicine for Nightmares
27 Mission Comics
28 Mission Skateboards
29 Needles & Pens
30 RH

Dolores Park

Dolores Park

SUNNY HANGOUT AND CULTURAL HOT SPOT

Welcome to the Mission's living room, where friends gab, puppies run and kids roll. Grassy slopes are dedicated to the fine art of lolling, while lowlands host soccer, Frisbee and political protests. Good weather brings picnics and cultural events, including Easter's Hunky Jesus drag contest, free summer movie nights and San Francisco Mime Troupe performances.

Climb to the southwestern corner for superb views of downtown, framed by palm trees. Hard to believe this park was once a Jewish cemetery, then a refugee camp for San Franciscans displaced by fire in 1906. Across 20th St, the fire hydrant that saved the neighborhood is still painted golden.

Women's Building

MISSION'S MONUMENT TO WOMEN

The nation's first women-run community center has served San Francisco since 1979, and it's graced with a magnificent mural painted by seven Mission muralistas with 100 volunteer assistants in 1994. Their five-story-high *MaestraPeace* mural shows global feminist icons and goddesses, weaving a glorious fabric to hold community together. On the Lapidge St side, you'll spot Nobel Peace Prize winner Rigoberta Menchú at the top, reproductive rights advocate and former US Surgeon General Dr Joycelyn Elders in the center, and artist Georgia O'Keeffe peeking out from the side.

Balmy Alley

Balmy Alley

FIFTY YERS OF EPIC ARTWORK

Inspired by Diego Rivera's 1930s San Francisco murals and provoked by US foreign policy in Latin America, Mission muralistas set out to transform the political landscape, one mural at a time. Working with their neighbors along Balmy Alley, Mujeres Muralistas ('Women Muralists') began painting garage doors here in 1973, turning a neglected backstreet into a safe passage and point of pride for the neighborhood.

Today, decades of epic murals maintained by mural arts nonprofit Precita Eyes cover Balmy Alley, from early Frida Kahlo homages to the 1985 Placa ('Mark-making') collective memorial for El Salvador activist Archbishop Óscar Romero. Muralists from Precita Eyes lead weekend walking tours covering Balmy Alley and dozens more neighborhood murals, with proceeds funding mural upkeep.

Discover New Talents

FIND YOUR CREATIVE MISSION

Tech tends to pull focus in SF, but there's a creative groundswell underway in the Mission – if you know where to look. Duck into **Clarion Alley** to discover spray-paint masterworks curated by a street artists' collective, including Tanya Wischerath's portraits of SF's transgender trailblazers as saints. Few murals survive tests of time and taggers in this open-air gallery, but with Clarion alums like Barry McGee, Alicia McCarthy and Chris Johansen, this alley has produced more stars than most art schools. To see breakthrough talents at work, head to nonprofit **Creativity Explored**, where developmentally disabled adults create artwork destined for museum retrospectives, international acclaim and Marc Jacobs handbags.

To make your own Mission art statement, take a graphic arts workshop at **Mission Cultural Center for Latino Arts**, putting pride and protest into posters since 1977. At **Aesthetic Union**, prints are pulled from a vintage Heidelberg press with a few choice words ('vote like a freak,' 'and now...hope') – and you can print your own slogan at letterpress workshops.

Wordsmiths can't miss **826 Valencia**, the nonprofit writing and publishing center fronted by a pirate store for all your pirate needs – eye patches, spyglasses, mermaid repellent – plus McSweeney's literary anthologies and books written by kids on the premises. To meet comic-book heroes in person, head to **Mission Comics** for signings, giveaways and gallery shows by major cartoonists, including *Poison Ivy* cover artist Jessica Fong and *Supergirl* writer Mariko Tamaki. Stock up on chapbooks and 'zines at **Needles and Pens**, and learn how to bind your own at **SF Center for the Book**.

If all this Mission creativity is making you hungry, make your own feast at nonprofit **18 Reasons**, where chef-led classes range from essentials (knife skills, cheese-making and cookies) to specialties (quesabirria, lasagna and Malaysian cakes). Create your own market menu with fresh produce from 30 local farmers at Thursday's **Mission Community Market** – for shortcuts, pick up Flour Chylde pastries and Chaac Mool's *cochinita pibil* (slow-roasted pork).

FOOD-SCENE STARS

Reem's Mission
Reem Assil serves sensational Palestinian Californian comfort food hot from the oven, including fresh-baked *mana'eesh* flatbread. $

Old Skool Café
This nonprofit, youth-run restaurant offers culinary training for at-risk youth, serving SF's most decadent brunch of Creole soul food. $$

Chicano Nuevo
Local street-food legend Abraham Nuñez reinvents Mission party food and updates Old Fashioneds with smoky mezcal. $

Osito
Gather around the fire to watch chef Seth Stowaway work his magic with multicourse meals that capture seasonal California inspirations. $$$

Follow Your Bliss down Calle 24

WALK AMONG LEYENDAS (LEGENDS)

From the moment you step onto Calle 24, SF's Latino Cultural District, your feet fall into an easy rhythm. Enticing aromas

WHERE TO EAT MISSION BURRITOS

La Taqueria
The James Beard Award winner satisfies purists: grilled meats, slow-cooked beans, mesquite salsa and flour tortillas. $

La Corneta
Upgrade to first class: get super prawn burritos with spicy onions and salsa verde. $

El Farolito
Late-night, value-priced, forearm-sized feasts, crammed with carnitas or smoky carne asada. $

I LIVE HERE: MISSION INSPIRATIONS

Alejandro Murguía is San Francisco's Poet Laureate, American Book Award winner, co-founder of Mission Cultural Center for Latino Arts and Professor of Latinx Studies at San Francisco State University.

Mission Festivals
Poetry is all around us. You'll hear Mayan blessings in Balmy Alley for **Flor y Canto Literary Festival**, Brazilian samba songs at **Carnaval** and multilingual poetry in *panaderías* and at Brava Theater during the Mission's **Paseo Poético**.

Literary Landmarks
At 24th and Folsom, a Precita Eyes mural honors Alfonso Texidor, who edited the poetry section of *El Tecalote*. Juana Alicia's new mural at the **Mission Branch Library** is a flowering *nopal* (cactus) – a symbol of resistance on a library built by capitalist Andrew Carnegie. How poetic.

beckon: flowering trees, fresh coffee, *pan dulce* at historic *panaderías* (bakeries). Monumental murals unfold around you, reaching around Victorian bay windows. Storefronts bedecked with *papel picado* (cut-paper streamers) invite you to stop and look, turning your walk into a dance step. Now you understand why 4000+ people stroll this street every day, and why it's known as el corazón de la Misión – the beating heart of the Mission.

Calle 24 murals always look fresh thanks to **Precita Eyes**, the mural arts nonprofit that restores historic murals, organizes new mural commissions and leads mural walking tours. You can't miss Precita Eyes' Calle 24 storefront, graced by a stunning new **mosaic** of flower goddess Xochiquetzal by muralist and founder Susan Cervantes. To see where the Mission mural movement took off, turn into Balmy Alley (p98). During Día de los Muertos, Balmy Alley is lined with *ofrendas* (altars) honoring ancestors and community icons, with offerings of orange-anise *pan de muerto* from **La Reyna** *panadería*.

Skaters roll through Balmy Alley between two skater hot spots: **La Raza Skatepark** and **Mission Skateboards**. Owner and street-skate legend Scot Thompson makes it his mission to equip newbies and pros alike with artist-designed decks, custom tees and stacks of San Francisco's own *Thrasher* magazine.

Books are another Calle 24 obsession. When neighborhood bookstores lost business to online megastores, readers rallied, turning **Adobe Books** and **Medicine for Nightmares** into member-supported collectives. Don't miss raucous Calle 24 bookstore events and premieres at **Brava Theater**, staging original works by women, BIPOC and LBGTQI+ talents in a fabulous 1926 deco theater.

Follow the sound of applause from Brava to La Palma Mexicatessen, where that clapping means *tortilleras* are busy making organic tortillas by hand. Load up on tacos and *huaraches* (stuffed masa) to enjoy at 24th and York Minipark, for picnics on the mosaic-encrusted back of Quetzalcoatl. The serpent-god first appeared in murals here in 1972, when neighbors rallied to turn a derelict lot into Calle 24's community hub. Quetzalcoatl's transformative powers remain undeniable, inspiring all who walk Calle 24.

Outlandish Art in Dogpatch

IMMERSIVE ART BY THE DOCKS

Ever since T-line streetcars made the waterfront Dogpatch district accessible from downtown, locals have started to realize there's life beyond Golden State Warriors games at **Chase Center**. Between monumental port machinery are stunning Bay views, best viewed on sunny strolls through

WHERE TO DRINK IN THE MISSION ATMOSPHERE

Trick Dog
Drink in SF inspiration with wildly original, award-collecting cocktails inspired by poetry and Mission muralists.

Wild Side West
Lesbian-owned since the '60s, when Janis Joplin started pool-table make-out sessions.

The Homestead
During Prohibition, this 120-year saloon served soda with shots in secret table compartments.

Chase Center

Crane Cove Park or the rooftop cafe of the new **RH** flagship home-decor store. Take a closer look between futuristic tech startups and the psychedelic **Portola Music Festival** at Pier 80, and you'll notice Dogpatch's old shipping warehouses are overflowing with art.

Art took root in Dogpatch five years ago, when venture-capitalist arts patrons Deborah and Andy Rappaport opened **Minnesota Street Project** to house subsidized artists' studios and galleries displaced by downtown rents. Minnesota Street Project shows are free and fearless, including Anglim/Trimble showcases of provocative Bay Area artists, Harwood Gallery's meticulously crafted dreamscapes and Rena Bransten's colorful, conceptual Californian sculpture.

Immersive art shows are cropping up across Dogpatch. New nonprofit **Institute for Contemporary Arts San Francisco (ICASF)** is covered inside and out with experimental art on urgent topics, from climate change to reparations. Entry is free here and at **McEvoy Foundation for the Arts**' themed shows of California artists. Otherworldly craft installations transform factory-floor galleries at **Museum of Craft & Design**, while nonprofit **Letterform Archive** highlights the Bay Area's impressive output of protest signs, book arts and punk 'zines. After Dogpatch gallery-hopping, head to **Ungrafted** for blind flights of California vintages with somms Rebecca Fineman and Chris Gaither. Or head to local Latina-owned weed startup **Higher Purpose Cannabis**, where high art takes on new meaning.

MISSION DESSERTS WORTH THE WAIT

Craftsman & Wolves
Artful pastries taste even better than they look on Instagram, including the jewel-like white chocolate 'jade stone.' $

Tartine
Celebrate birthdays late/early with cajeta-drizzled tres leches cake and pucker-up passion-fruit Bavarians. $

Bi-Rite Creamery
Sunshine in Dolores Park means lines down the block for salted caramel sundaes and seasonal balsamic strawberry ice cream. $

Stonemill Matcha
Teatime is really just an excuse for black sesame cream puffs and silken matcha cream pie. $

WHERE TO CATCH MISSION SHOWS

Bottom of the Hill
Top of the list for punk icons and indie rockers; worth checking out for their names alone.

The Chapel
Musical prayers are answered in a 1914 California arts-and-crafts landmark with heavenly acoustics.

ODC
Catch risky, raw performances by dance innovators, and learn new moves at ODC Dance Commons.

GOLDEN GATE PARK & THE AVENUES

NATURAL WONDERS AND OUTLANDISH ART

You've probably heard that SF has a wild streak a mile wide, but that streak also happens to be 4.5 miles long. Golden Gate Park lets locals do what comes naturally: roller-discoing, drum-circling, starfish-petting, orchid-sniffing and stampeding toward the Pacific with a herd of bison.

Hard to believe these lush 1017 acres were once scrubby sand dunes, and that San Franciscans have preserved this stretch of green since 1866, over the private interests of casinos and resorts. Thanks to SF's mystical microclimates and natural eccentricity, the park is home to rare flora from around the world and extraordinary sights at every turn: massive free concerts, miniature yacht regattas, underground art treasures, chatty penguins and hushed redwood groves. Join San Franciscans and come out to play in the park at the California Academy of Sciences, de Young Museum and Gardens of Golden Gate Park.

TOP TIP

Even when downtown basks in California sunshine, fog hangs around Golden Gate Park all the way to the ocean. Bring a windbreaker to block coastal gusts, and warm layers to handle temperatures that can range from 50°F to 70°F (10°C to 21°C) on the same day – July and 'Fogust' can get downright frigid.

Japanese Tea Garden in Golden Gate Park

Osher Rainforest Dome, Academy of Sciences

Academy of Sciences

WHERE SF GOES WILD FOR SCIENCE

Just when you thought San Francisco couldn't get any wilder, blue butterflies alight on your shoulders in the Osher Rainforest Dome and penguins waddle your way in the African Hall. The Academy's tradition of weird science dates from 1853, and acclaimed architect Renzo Piano's 2008 remodel brought thousands of live animals under a 2.5-acre wildflower-covered roof. Night owls party on at 21+ NightLife Thursdays, featuring cocktails and time-traveling Planetarium shows. Kids may not technically sleep during Academy Sleepovers, but they could jump-start promising careers as scientists.

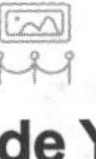

de Young Museum

GROUNDBREAKING GLOBAL ART

Follow sculptor Andy Goldsworthy's artificial earthquake fault line through the courtyard to discover groundbreaking immersive shows, from Faith Ringgold's storytelling quilts to Ansel Adams' sweeping, silvery Yosemite photographs. The de Young boldly pursues ideas across centuries, continents and art forms, so you never know what awaits in the next gallery – you could be face to face with Oceanic ceremonial masks or Ramses the Great's golden sarcophagus. Take the elevator up to the 144ft sci-fi observation tower for park panoramas, or cloudwatch in James Turrell's sublime *Skyspace* installation, hidden under the sculpture garden. Keep your ticket for free same-day entry to the Legion of Honor (p107).

de Young Museum

Gardens of Golden Gate Park

NATURAL WONDERS

Urban life is overrated, with traffic jams and office blocks – but at Golden Gate Park, that's all behind you. Thanks to San Francisco's microclimates and dedicated gardeners, flora from around the world bloom here year-round in the **San Francisco Botanical Garden**, while century-old bonsai weather the storms in the **Japanese Tea Garden**. Inside the **Conservatory of Flowers**' grand greenhouses, rare orchids blush alongside carnivorous plants.

This urban-garden dreamscape seems far-fetched now, but it was considered impossible when backed by San Franciscan voters in 1866. Plans fell to civil engineer William Hammond Hall, who insisted that instead of planned casinos and racetracks, Golden Gate Park should showcase nature. Today a day pass grants you same-day entry to both gardens and the conservatory.

GOLDEN GATE PARK & THE AVENUES

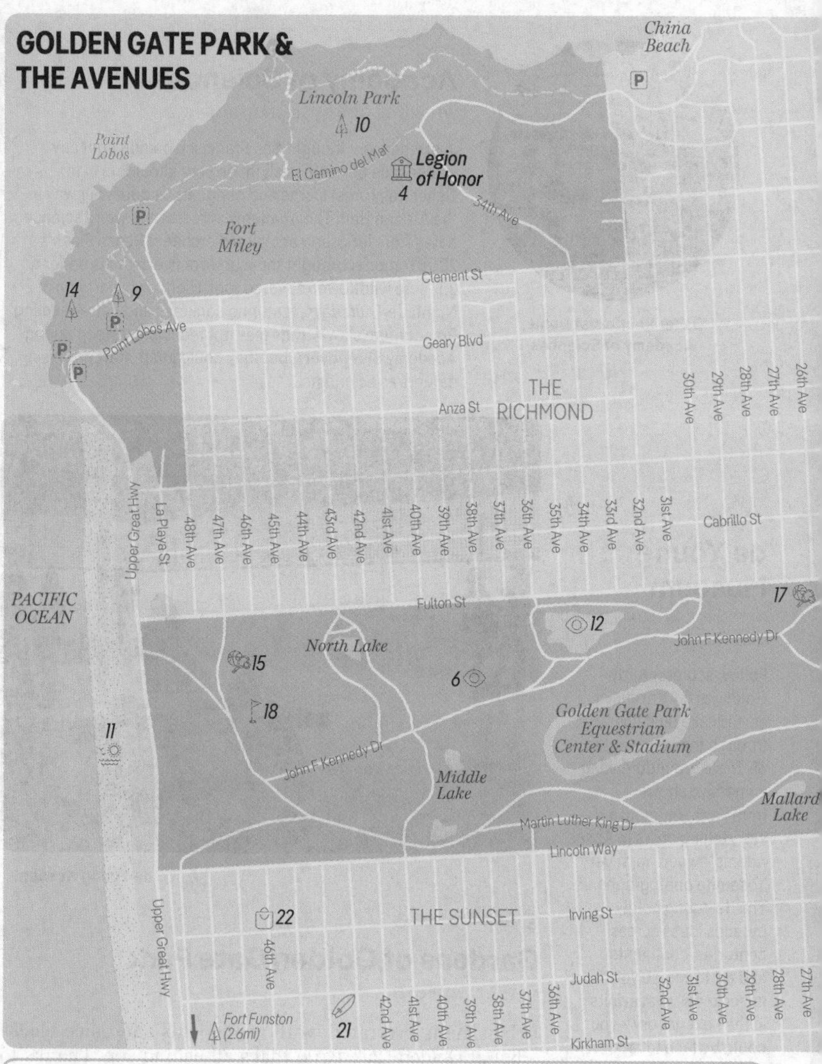

HIGHLIGHTS
1 Academy of Sciences
2 de Young Museum
3 Golden Gate Park
4 Legion of Honor
5 San Francisco Botanical Garden

SIGHTS
6 Bison Paddock
7 Conservatory of Flowers
8 Japanese Tea Garden
9 Lands End
10 Lincoln Park
11 Ocean Beach
12 Spreckles Lake
13 Stow Lake
14 Sutro Baths

ACTIVITES, COURSES & TOURS
15 Archery Range
16 Children's Playground
17 Disc-Golf Course
18 Golden Gate Municipal Golf Course
19 Horseshoe Pits
20 San Francisco Lawn Bowling Club

SHOPPING
21 Aqua Surf Shop
22 Mollusk

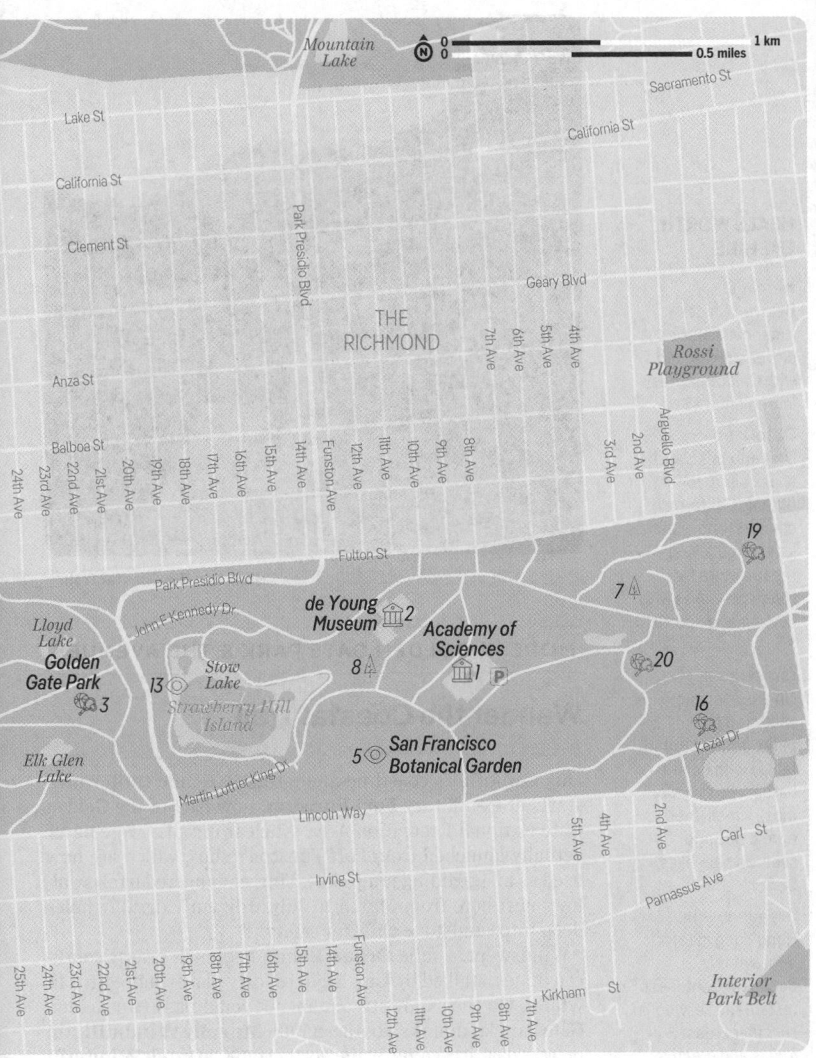
Mountain Lake
0 1 km
0 0.5 miles
Sacramento St
Lake St
California St
California St
Clement St
Park Presidio Blvd
Geary Blvd
THE RICHMOND
7th Ave
6th Ave
5th Ave
4th Ave
Rossi Playground
Anza St
Arguello Blvd
Balboa St
24th Ave
23rd Ave
22nd Ave
21st Ave
20th Ave
19th Ave
18th Ave
17th Ave
16th Ave
15th Ave
14th Ave
Funston Ave
12th Ave
11th Ave
10th Ave
9th Ave
8th Ave
3rd Ave
2nd Ave
19
Fulton St
Park Presidio Blvd
7
de Young Museum
2
John F Kennedy Dr
Lloyd Lake
Academy of Sciences
Golden Gate Park
Stow Lake
8
1
20
13
3
Strawberry Hill Island
16
Kezar Dr
5
San Francisco Botanical Garden
Elk Glen Lake
Martin Luther King Dr
Lincoln Way
5th Ave
4th Ave
2nd Ave
Carl St
Irving St
Parnassus Ave
25th Ave
24th Ave
23rd Ave
22nd Ave
21st Ave
20th Ave
19th Ave
18th Ave
17th Ave
16th Ave
15th Ave
14th Ave
Funston Ave
12th Ave
11th Ave
10th Ave
9th Ave
8th Ave
7th Ave
Kirkham St
Interior Park Belt

WIRESTOCK CREATORS/SHUTTERSTOCK ©

Hikers on the Coastal Train

MEALS WORTH THE HIKE

Mamahuhu
Beloved Chinese American classics cleverly revamped with California-fresh ingredients. $$

Outerlands
Drift into this beach-shack bistro for organic Californian comfort food with just-baked levain bread; return for Dutch pancakes with housemade ricotta. $$

Um.ma
On this sociable, sheltered back patio, gather around tables with built-in barbecues for *kalbi* (ribs), kimchi fried purple rice and seafood pancakes. $$$

Dragon Beaux
Hong Kong meets Vegas at this decadent Cantonese restaurant, serving succulent roast meats and creative dumplings, including brandy-laced XO dumplings. $$

MORE IN GOLDEN GATE PARK & THE AVENUES

Wander the Coastal Trail

THE CITY'S BEST NATURE HIKE

Hug California's coastline along this 10.5-mile trail, which starts at ex-military **Fort Funston**, now part of the Golden Gate National Recreation Area. Nuclear missiles were never actually launched from Fort Funston's silos, which are now used as hang-gliding jump sites. Tiny, endangered bank swallows nest here from March to July, diligently drilling holes deep into sandstone cliffs for safety.

Windswept, 4-mile **Ocean Beach** begins in grassy southern dunes, stalked by long-legged snowy plover shorebirds in winter. On the sandy stretch ahead, you'll pass two Golden Gate Park landmarks: southern 1908 **Murphy Windmill** still powers park irrigation, while northern 1902 **Dutch Windmill** is surrounded by tulips each spring. You'll also meet hardy beachcombers and hard-core surfers braving Pacific riptides (casual swimmers, beware). If you're up for a gnarly challenge, hit **Mollusk** for specialty boards and **Aqua Surf Shop** for rental gear and instructor recommendations. The original

WHERE TO SIP HOT DRINKS IN GOLDEN GATE PARK & THE AVENUES

Beach Chalet
Enter past 1930s frescoes and head upstairs to watch Ocean Beach surfers do their thing.

Plough & the Stars
Come for Irish coffee and properly pulled pints of Guinness, stay for a Celtic jam session.

Java Beach Café
Warm up after Ocean Beach with cascara, a tangy, refreshing tisane brewed with hibiscus flowers.

site of Burning Man, Ocean Beach allows bonfires only in 16 artist-designed fire pits until 9:30pm, March through October.

Casual strollers pick up the freshly restored Coastal Trail near **Sutro Baths** ruins, where seals bark encouragement to hike through the sea cave for end-of-the-world views. Head around **Lands End** bluffs for pine-framed Pacific views, with glimpses of shipwrecks at low tide and Golden Gate Bridge (p62) panoramas.

Pass wedding-party photo-ops and golf players at **Lincoln Park**, and duck into the **Legion of Honor** to find unexpected art treasures, from Monet water lilies to John Cage soundscapes. The Legion is a tribute to California's WWI veterans gifted to the city by 'Big Alma' de Bretteville Spreckels, San Francisco's sculptor's model turned billionaire philanthropist. Upstairs, contemporary artworks interact with Big Alma's collections of Rodin sculptures and Impressionist paintings. Downstairs, blockbuster shows range from Guo Pei's fantasy couture to Picasso's sketchbooks. Afterward, descend gloriously tiled Lincoln Park Steps (near 32nd Ave) for destination dining in the avenues.

Offbeat Outdoor Adventures

BECOME AN ALTERNA-ATHLETE

Design your own try-anything triathlon in Golden Gate Park (p103), where park features include fly-casting pools, competition-standard **horseshoe pits**, an 18-hole competitive **disc-golf course** plus an affordable nine-hole public golf course. **San Francisco Lawn Bowling Club** has kept the ball rolling since 1901 at America's first public lawn-bowling green. At the park's **archery range**, coaches from Golden Gate Junior Olympic Archery Division offer traditional archery classes (ages 8+).

Kids rule the park's historic southeastern **children's playground**, which features a new climbing wall, daredevil concrete slides and a vintage 1912 Loof carousel. For tiny yet fierce competitions, check out weekend miniature yacht regattas on **Spreckles Lake**, where the boat you're rooting for may be beaten by a turtle. Think you could best a turtle in a boat race? Try it: pedal boats, rowboats and electric boats are available for rent on **Stow Lake**.

John F Kennedy Dr is closed to motor vehicles east of Crossover Dr on weekends to accommodate runners, cyclists, skateboarders and meandering dreamers. On weekends here, join epic roller disco sessions and get free swing dance lessons at Lindy Hop in the Park.

For more action, the park offers four soccer fields, 21 tennis courts, 12 miles of equestrian trails, 7.5 miles of bicycle trails and running paths galore. Hit your stride and stampede to the **Bison Paddock**, home to SF's mellow resident herd since 1899.

SHOWS IN THE PARK

Hardly Strictly Bluegrass
The West goes wild over three days of free concerts in the Park.

Flower Piano
More than 50 San Francisco pianists serenade the Botanical Garden.

Outside Lands
One of America's best festivals for marquee acts, plus gleeful debauchery at Wine Lands.

Night Bloom
Flower power lives on at the Conservatory of Flowers, with a psychedelic light show set to music.

4:20
Hippie Hill is more funky and fragrant than usual on April 20, when bands perform free shows.

WHERE TO SCORE BAKED GOODS IN GOLDEN GATE PARK & THE AVENUES

Pineapple King
Fluffy pineapple-sweetened buns that'll haunt your dreams, with flavor-bomb fillings. **$**

Cinderella Bakery
Royal Russian pastries – cherry strudel, *blinchiki* (crepes) with caviar – at neighborly prices. **$**

Ariscault
Buttery croissants that melt in your mouth, plus flakey, caramelized-sugar-crusted koign amann. **$**

MARIN COUNTY & BAY AREA

GORGEOUS HILLS AND SCINTILLATING TOWNS

From wild walks by the Pacific to ferries on the bay, and from redwood splendor to bounteous tables, Marin County and the Bay Area endlessly beguiles.

The San Francisco Bay Area encompasses a bonanza of natural vistas and wildlife. Cross the Golden Gate Bridge into Marin County and visit wizened ancient redwoods body-blocking the sun, and herds of elephant seals chilling on the sands of Point Reyes. Gray whales blow spray off the filigreed coast, while hawks prowl the skies over the wild sands and shaggy hills of the Marin Headlands.

In the East Bay, Oakland is the diverse, radically proud place San Francisco once was. Berkeley sparked the state's locavore food movement and, together with its long-standing university, continues to be at the forefront of environmental and left-leaning political causes. North, you'll find gritty bayside towns and national-park sites recalling nearly forgotten chapters of history.

Academic, urbane and beguiling, Stanford University is the soul of Palo Alto, which in turn is the heart of Silicon Valley, the land of startup legends and louche billionaires. Travel the world without leaving San Jose, the low-key powerhouse anchor to the valley's fortunes.

Meandering along endlessly beautiful coast south of San Francisco, Hwy 1 traces 70 miles of undeveloped coastline south to Santa Cruz. Spot whales offshore, and seals and sea otters close in. Lose count of the sandy cove beaches and ribbons of dunes amid wetlands and redwoods. Pause for an hour or a day in Half Moon Bay, Pescadero or another tiny town.

SUNDRY PHOTOGRAPHY/SHUTTERSTOCK ©

THE MAIN AREAS

SAUSALITO
Gateway to Marin County's wonders. p114

POINT REYES
Pure, wild nature. p121

OAKLAND
Edgy and dynamic. p125

BERKELEY
Lively yet genteel. p132

MANISHA26/SHUTTERSTOCK ©

Left: View of San Francisco Bay from Sausalito (p114); Above: Point Reyes (p121)

PALO ALTO
Silicon Valley's well-heeled center. p139

SAN JOSE
Vibrant and multicultural. p143

HALF MOON BAY
Top stop on Hwy 1. p145

Find Your Way

The Bay Area surrounds the San Francisco Bay, which breaks up this large region into very individualistic areas – there's no mistaking San Jose for Berkeley, and so on. The coasts are more unified in their raw beauty and intrigue.

Sausalito, p114
Reachable by ferry, this town right on the bay has bohemian roots, and is the gateway to the Marin Headlands, Muir Woods, Hwy 1 and Point Reyes.

Berkeley, p132
The famous university town is a delight to explore on foot, from the campus to the surrounding neighborhoods. Head north for surprising national-park sites.

Oakland, p125
The big city across the bay from San Francisco offers intriguing, walkable and contrasting neighborhoods, with some of the best eating in the region.

Point Reyes, p121
This beautiful national seashore has miles of wave-tossed beaches, some teeming with enormous elephant seals. Stop for an afternoon or longer before continuing on Hwy 1.

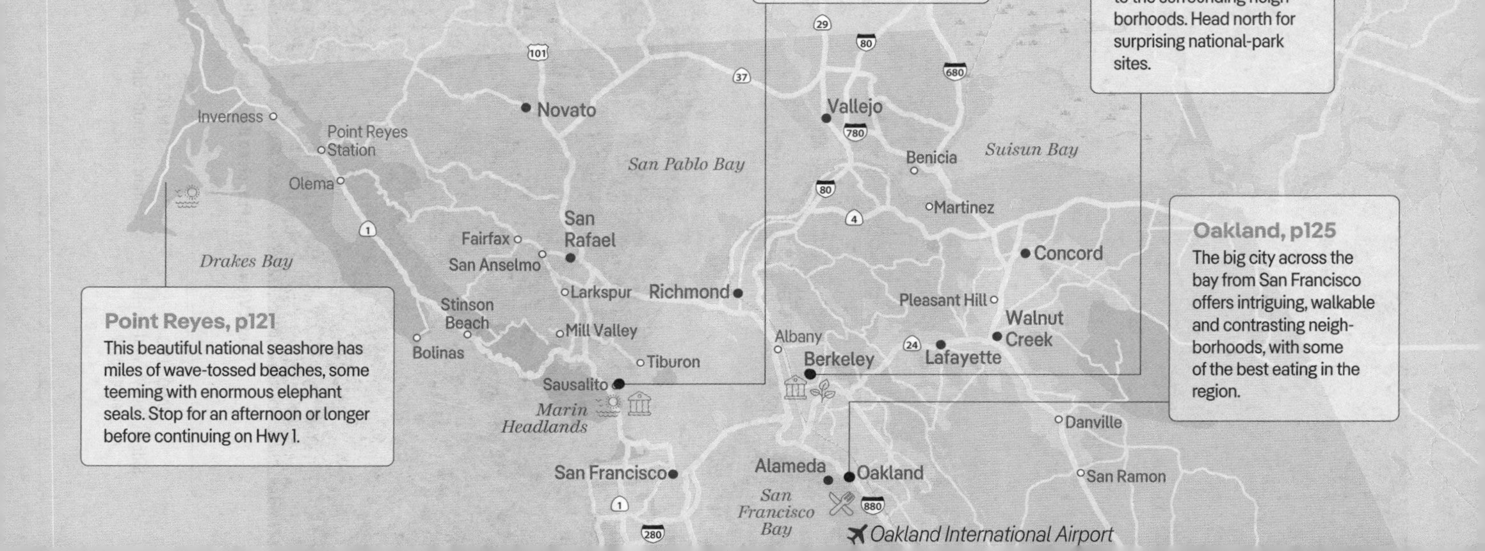

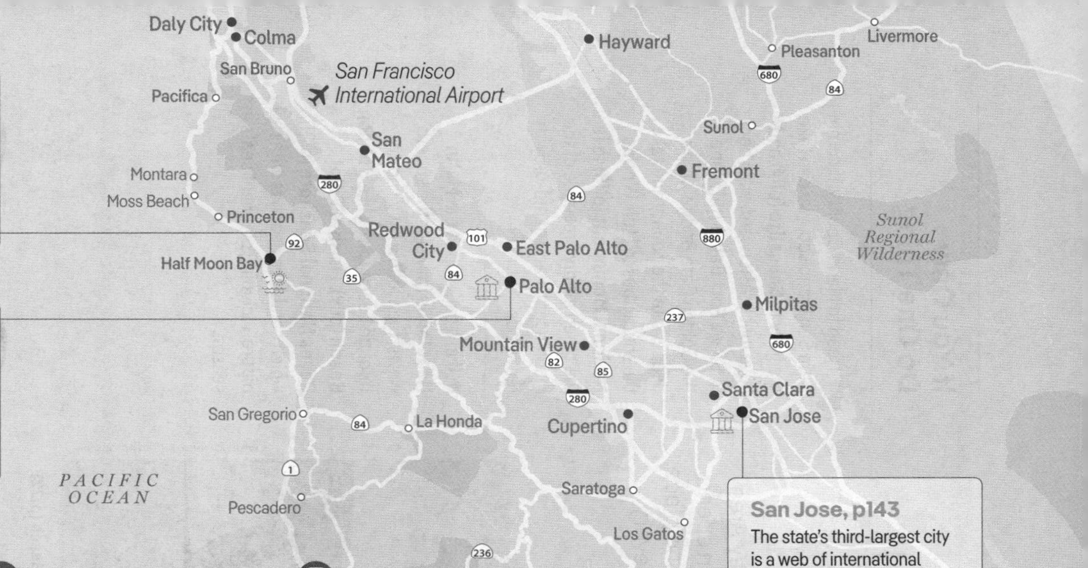

Daly City
Colma
San Bruno
Pacifica
San Francisco International Airport
Hayward
Pleasanton
Livermore
Sunol
San Mateo
Fremont
Montara
Moss Beach
Princeton
Redwood City
East Palo Alto
Half Moon Bay
Palo Alto
Milpitas
Sunol Regional Wilderness
Mountain View
Santa Clara
San Jose
San Gregorio
La Honda
Cupertino
PACIFIC OCEAN
Saratoga
Pescadero
Los Gatos
680
84
280
92
101
35
880
237
82
85
1
236
0 — 50 km
0 — 25 miles

Half Moon Bay, p145

This is the anchor of the sensational segment of Hwy 1 between San Francisco and Santa Cruz. Be overawed by myriad beaches and parks north and south.

Palo Alto, p139

The heart of Silicon Valley has an enticing downtown and the genteel charms of Stanford University. Further afield are beautiful open spaces and top tech titans.

San Jose, p143

The state's third-largest city is a web of international neighborhoods where you can enjoy Mexican, Vietnamese, Japanese and other cultures. It's near top Silicon Valley sights.

FERRY

An ever-expanding network of ferries connects the cities around the bay in fast and wonderfully scenic style. It's the way to visit Sausalito and a fine way to reach Larkspur and the Smart train north. Oakland and Alameda are also easily reached.

CAR

The ideal way to explore the Bay Area. Hwy 1 north and south of the Golden Gate is best experienced with the freedom of your own wheels. There's no need for a car in the main cities of the East Bay and Peninsula.

TRAIN

The Bay Area is well-connected by train. BART has fast services from San Mateo via San Francisco to all the major points in the East Bay. Caltrain is another winner, knitting together the Peninsula from SF to San Jose, via Palo Alto.

Plan Your Time

Marin County and the Bay Area is a region where you can spend your time savoring just one place, or you can indulge your every peripatetic urge.

XAVIER HOENNER/SHUTTERSTOCK ©

Elephant seal at Drakes Beach (p122)

If You Only Do One Thing

- Head to Marin County. If coming from San Francisco, you can take the ferry to **Sausalito** (p114) and have lunch. Afterward, walk back to SF via **Fort Baker** (p115) and the Golden Gate Bridge. Or go deeper into the county and take the shuttle bus to **Muir Woods National Monument** (p118) to feel the otherworldly presence of the magnificent stand of old-growth redwoods.

- If in a car, stop at the **Marin Headlands** (p117) for the superb views, then follow Hwy 1 north through beach towns like **Stinson Beach** (p119). Finish at **Point Reyes National Seashore** (p121), which combines beaches with raw nature, including elephant seals in season.

Seasonal Highlights

Winter may bring rain, but Bay Area temperatures inspire envy elsewhere in the USA. Spring and fall are beautiful, while summer weather ranges from chilly to blazing.

JANUARY

Winter storms (in non-drought years) mean driftwood on the beaches, pounding **surf** and **salmon running** in some redwood-forest streams.

MARCH

With spring, **hillsides** trade burlap brown for impossibly vibrant green speckled with orange California poppies.

MAY

Alameda puts on black for the **World Goth Day Festival**; Berkeley honors authors at the **Bay Area Book Festival**.

LUCY AUTREY WILSON/SHUTTERSTOCK ©; CATAHOULAGIRL/SHUTTERSTOCK ©; IMAGES@ARTIST-AT-LARGE/STOCKIMO/ALAMY ©

Three Days to Travel Around

- After don't-miss Marin County, add in the essential East Bay. **Oakland** (p125) and **Berkeley** (p132) abut, and with their utterly different personalities will give you days and days of diverse activities and eating.

- In Oakland, stop by the **Oakland Museum of California** (p127) for an enlightened look at the state. Walk around **Lake Merritt** (p129), and stop by **Jack London Sq** (p127) for a drink where the man himself drank.

- In Berkeley, walk the **Cal campus** (p134) and enjoy some superb meals. Then pop north to Richmond for the **Rosie the Riveter WWII Home Front National Historic Park** (p137).

If You Have More Time

- Get your vehicle and cruise Hwy 1, south from **Pacifica** (p148). In fact, you may wish to do this if you only have one day. The **70 miles to Santa Cruz** (p147) make this stretch of the fabled road one of the world's most beautiful drives. Stop off at any beach that catches your eye, but know that to see them all would require a month or more. There are coves like **Gray Whale Cove State Beach** (p149) and wide-open expanses like **Gazos Creek State Beach** (p149).

- Stop for lunch at **Half Moon Bay** (p145) or **Pescadero** (p149) and circle back to SF, or continue to Santa Cruz and beyond.

JUNE
The region's bodacious foods star at the **Marin County Fair**, as do rides, barnyard animals and fireworks.

AUGUST
Silicon Valley celebrates art, agriculture, science, engineering and all things tech at the **Santa Clara County Fair**.

OCTOBER
Mill Valley Film Festival screens independent films; the **Half Moon Bay Art & Pumpkin Festival** (p146) celebrates the Halloween icon.

DECEMBER
Children's Fairyland in Oakland hosts one of the Bay Area's most interesting and culturally diverse winter festivals: **Fairy Winterland**.

SAUSALITO

Sausalito

Los Angeles

Perfectly arranged on a secure little harbor on the bay, Sausalito is undeniably lovely. Named for the tiny willows that once populated the banks of its creeks, it's famous for its colorful houseboats bobbing in the bay. Much of the well-heeled downtown has uninterrupted views of San Francisco and Angel Island.

Sausalito is a major tourist hub, jam-packed with souvenir shops and fair-to-middling boutiques. It's the first town you'll encounter after crossing the Golden Gate Bridge from San Francisco (the car-accessible viewpoint at the north end of the bridge is justifiably popular for its sweeping views).

Sausalito began as a busy lumber port with a racy waterfront. Dramatic changes came in WWII when Sausalito became the site of Marinship, a huge shipbuilding yard. After the war a new bohemian period began. Today, the town defines genteel.

TOP TIP

Day-trippers turn up in droves and parking can be a pain. If you're just visiting town and/or hiking locally, take the ferry from San Francisco. If you're combining a visit to Sausalito with the nearby Marin Headlands and Point Reyes, then a car is essential – but prepare for parking challenges.

SIGHTS
1 Bay Area Discovery Museum
2 Bay Model Visitor Center
3 Fort Baker
4 Horseshoe Bay

SLEEPING
5 Cavallo Point

EATING
6 Scoma's
7 Venice Gourmet Delicatessen & Pizzeria

Sausalito

Interactive Bay Exhibit & Delish Dining

WANDER CENTRAL SAUSALITO

One of the coolest things in this beautiful town, fascinating to both kids and adults, is the **Army Corps of Engineers' Bay Model Visitor Center**. Housed in one of the old Marinship warehouses, it's a 1.5-acre hydraulic model of San Francisco Bay and the delta region that shows how the whole bay works.

For a sit-down meal with a view, try the very popular **Scoma's**. Their old-school classics such as cioppino (a piquant seafood stew) and Crab Louie salads are excellent. Or you can assemble a fab picnic at **Venice Gourmet Delicatessen & Pizzeria**.

Epic Fort, Seafront & Museum

EXPLORE FORT BAKER

Below the north tower of the Golden Gate Bridge, **Fort Baker** hides in plain sight. This 1905 army base with one of the world's best views helped guard the entrance to the bay along with the better-known Fort Point on the south side. It's surprisingly uncrowded. Stroll **Horseshoe Bay**, watch the wintertime crab fishers, and get a snack or a meal from one of several good outlets. You can even spend the night in former officers' quarters at the luxe Cavallo Point Lodge.

A highlight is the Bay Area Discovery Museum, an excellent hands-on delight designed for children that includes a large playground area with a shipwreck.

WALKING SAUSALITO & THE GOLDEN GATE BRIDGE

One of the Bay Area's best walks begins and ends in San Francisco (p55) and features some of the region's best scenery.
Catch a mid-morning ferry to Sausalito, enjoying the views of Alcatraz and Angel Islands. Stroll the town and get refreshments and even a picnic. Follow East Rd south along the natural shoreline until you reach Fort Baker. Walk under the Golden Gate Bridge, and curve up the access road until you reach the popular viewpoint.

Cross the bridge on the eastern sidewalk (the west side is for cyclists). Dress warmly! It's 1.7 miles across the walkway – take your time for the stellar views. It's 5 miles from Sausalito to the San Francisco side of the bridge.

GETTING AROUND

Golden Gate Ferry links regularly with San Francisco's Ferry Building. Blue & Gold Fleet ferries sail from the Fisherman's Wharf area. These 30-minute rides afford fabulous bay views.

Golden Gate Transit buses cross the Golden Gate Bridge to/from San Francisco.

Beyond Sausalito

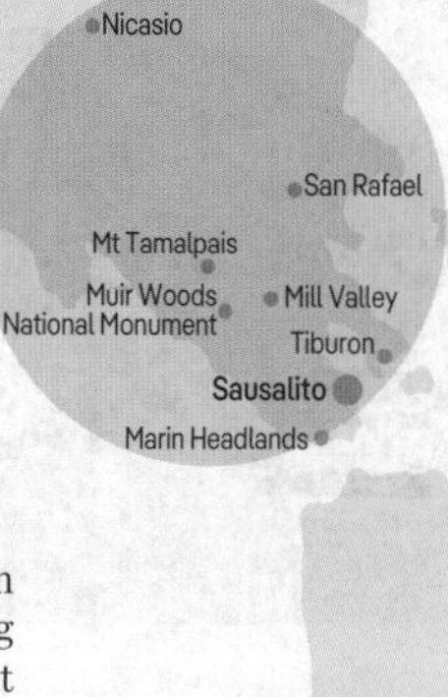

Spend a day or a week exploring the natural wonderland of Marin County. It's like a concentrate of outdoor goodness.

Just across the Golden Gate Bridge from San Francisco, Marin County is a collection of wealthy, wooded hamlets that cling tenuously to their haute hippie roots as an ever-more-affluent tech-era population moves in. It's a place of superb natural beauty and myriad adventures, which unfold west and north of Sausalito.

Geographically, Marin County is a near mirror image of San Francisco, although Marin is much wilder and more mountainous. Redwoods grow on the coast-side hills, surf crashes against remote cliffs and beaches, and hiking and cycling trails crisscross scenic Marin Headlands, Muir Woods and Mt Tamalpais. These glorious natural surrounds make Marin County an excellent day trip or weekend escape from San Francisco, or the perfect pause on a longer coastal California journey.

TOP TIP

Hwy 1 cuts over to the Marin coast after Sausalito. But explore other sinuous roads linking the Hwy 101 corridor with the wild west.

The Marin Headlands and the view of the Golden Gate Bridge (p62) and San Francisco (p55)

Rodeo Beach

Awesome Views, Hikes & Animal Sanctuary

MAGNIFICENT NATURAL DIVERSITY

The cliffs and hillsides of the **Marin Headlands**, a mere 15 minutes by car from Sausalito, rise majestically at the north end of the Golden Gate Bridge, their rugged beauty all the more striking given the fact that they're only a few miles from San Francisco's urban core. A few forts and bunkers are left over from a century of US military occupation. It's no mystery why this is one of the Bay Area's most popular hiking and cycling destinations: as the trails wind through the near-pristine headlands, they afford stunning views of the sea, the bridge and San Francisco, and lead to isolated beaches and secluded picnic spots.

The historical **Point Bonita Lighthouse** is a breathtaking half-mile walk from Field Rd parking area. Harbor seals haul out seasonally on nearby rocks.

At the western end of Bunker Rd sits spectacular **Rodeo Beach**, partly protected from wind by high cliffs. All along

OASIS IN THE BAY

In the middle of San Francisco Bay, **Angel Island** was a hunting and fishing ground for the Miwok people, and served as a military base, an immigration station with an awful past, a WWII Japanese internment camp and an anti-aircraft missile site. There are thought-provoking forts and bunkers amid natural beauty.

You can hike the 5-mile perimeter trail or to the summit of 788ft **Mt Livermore**, or picnic in a protected cove looking out at the seemingly close yet distant urban grid. On most days crowds are small, even though access is easy by ferry from San Francisco, Sausalito and Tiburon. Bikes can be rented.

Camping on Angel Island mixes serene isolation with an evening lightshow around the bay.

WHERE TO EAT BEYOND SAUSALITO

Angel Island Café
Casual snack bar near the ferry dock, packing fine picnics. Hours vary; on summer weekends there's live music. **$**

Sam's Anchor Cafe
Decades-old waterfront cafe known for vintage cocktails and excellent seafood dishes and burgers. **$$**

Kitchen Sunnyside
New-age socialists mix with tech billionaires at this high-end comfort-food cafe in Mill Valley. **$$**

GOOD EATING IN MARIN COUNTY

Traveling beyond Sausalito in Marin County, you can eat well, from the coast to the valleys and on to the sunny bay. People drive long distances for the world-class Japanese food at **Village Sake** in Fairfax; the *izakaya* (Japanese pub-style fare) are paired with craft beers and sake. It's worth heading west of San Rafael to San Anselmo for **Madcap**, an iconic farm-to-table bistro with an Asian accent. Sublime barbecue from the US South is served at **Pig in a Pickle** in Corte Madera. Famous for its hearty meals, **Parkside Cafe** is next to the sand in Stinson Beach; outside, the snack bar serves burgers, sandwiches, baked goods and ice cream – expect a queue.

ZACK FRANK/SHUTTERSTOCK ©

Muir Woods National Monument

the coastline you'll find cool old battery sites – abandoned concrete bunkers dug into the ground with fabulous views. Start at **Battery Townsley**, a half-mile walk or bike ride up from the Fort Cronkhite parking lot. The **Coastal Trail** leads to Muir Beach.

Above Rodeo Beach, the **Marine Mammal Center** rehabilitates injured, sick and orphaned sea mammals before returning them to the wild. Reserve a slot in advance and you can see adult seals and pups being cared for from an observation deck.

Small Hikes to Big Trees

MUIR WOODS' GRAND REDWOOD GROVES

Wander among an ancient stand of the world's tallest trees in 550-plus-acre **Muir Woods National Monument**, a 30-minute drive from Sausalito. The shortest option, the 1-mile **Main Trail Loop**, is a gentle walk alongside Redwood Creek to the 1000-year-old trees at **Cathedral Grove**; it returns via **Bohemian Grove**, where the tallest tree in the park stands more than 258ft high. It's a good 2-mile hike up

WHERE TO SHOP BEYOND SAUSALITO

Bolinas People's Store
Small co-op grocery store near the beach, with picnic tables. Serves fair-trade coffee and sells organic lunch items.

Nicasio Valley Cheese Company
Sample soft cheeses at one of Marin County's most renowned cheesemaking shops.

Book Passage
One of the Bay Area's best bookstores, just off Hwy 101 in Corte Madera. Hosts big-name author appearances.

to the top of the aptly named Cardiac Hill to reach the **Dipsea Trail**, which climbs over the coastal range and down to Stinson Beach.

You can also walk down into Muir Woods by taking trails from the Panoramic Hwy, such as the **Bootjack Trail** from the Bootjack picnic area, or from Mt Tamalpais' Pantoll Station campground, along the **Ben Johnson Trail**.

Note that visitors to Muir Woods are required to reserve and pay in advance either for parking at the park itself or shuttle transportation from Sausalito parking lots and the ferry dock. Check online for details and current conditions.

Try to come midweek, early in the morning or late in the afternoon, when tour buses are less common. Even at busy times, a short hike will get you out of the densest crowds and onto trails with huge trees and stunning vistas. A lovely cafe serves local and organic goodies and hot drinks.

Quaint Views

WONDERFUL WATERFRONT TIBURON

At the end of a small peninsula jutting out into the bay 15 minutes' drive from Sausalito, **Tiburon** is blessed with gorgeous views and a small and appealing village center. **Upper Main St**, also known as Ark Row, is where old houseboats have taken root on dry land and metamorphosed into classy shops and boutiques. Rent a bike and follow the shoreline.

Wealth, Bohemian Style

CHARMING MILL VALLEY

It's still hanging on to its bohemian roots, but beautiful **Mill Valley**, nestled under the redwoods at the base of Mt Tamalpais only 15 minutes by car from Sausalito, is nowadays home to pricey houses, luxury cars and expensive boutiques. It's one of the Bay Area's most picturesque hamlets. Once served by a logging railroad, the old train station is now home to the excellent **Depot Bookstore & Cafe**.

Hike Marin's Peak

MAKE YOUR MARK ON MT TAM

Looming over Marin County and just a 15-minute drive from Sausalito, majestic **Mt Tamalpais** (Mt Tam; 2572ft) holds more than 60 miles of hiking and biking trails, lakes, streams, waterfalls and an impressive array of wildlife – from plentiful newts and hawks to rare foxes and mountain lions. Wind your way through meadows, oaks and madrone trees to breathtaking

DON'T-MISS BEACH TOWNS

Between the Marin Headlands and Point Reyes are three coastal towns (on or near Hwy 1) where the character in line next to you at the coffee bar might be a Hollywood celebrity, an aging rocker or a lifelong hippie.

Muir Beach is a quiet hamlet with a pretty gray-sand beach. Hike here from the headlands or Muir Woods. Wide, blond **Stinson Beach** is positively buzzing on warm, sunny weekends. The town has a handful of eateries and lots of vacation rentals. **Bolinas** got on the map, as it were, for the residents' habit of tearing down signs on the highway so non-locals wouldn't know how to get here. It mixes old-world charm with a big surf scene.

WHERE TO STAY BEYOND SAUSALITO

Waters Edge Hotel
A large deck extends over the bay in Tiburon; tasteful rooms have an elegant minimalism, with romantic water views. **$$$**

HI Marin Headlands Hostel
Wake up to grazing deer at this spartan 1907 military compound snuggled in the woods. Comfortable beds. **$**

Pelican Inn
Twee English cottage in Muir Beach with cozy rooms and pub food such as locally sourced fish-and-chips. **$$**

TOP STATE PARKS IN MARIN

About 6 miles northeast of San Rafael, **China Camp State Park** preserves a Chinese shrimp-fishing village that was here for decades beginning in the 19th century. Hidden behind a vast outcrop, fishers and their families were able to live here away from the rampant racism found across California.

Today's Marin County was once home to the Coastal Miwok people. **Olompali State Historic Park** is on the site of a village that was inhabited from about 6000 BCE until 1850. It's just off Hwy 101 in Novato. In the coastal hills along Sir Francis Drake Blvd, **Samuel P Taylor State Park** has groves of redwoods and streams that fill with spawning salmon in winter.

vistas over the San Francisco Bay and the Pacific Ocean, with towns, cities and forested hills rolling into the distance.

Mt Tamalpais State Park encompasses about 10 sq miles of parklands and more than 60 miles of trails. Don't miss the summit of **East Peak**. Panoramic Hwy climbs from Hwy 1 through the park, then winds downhill to Stinson Beach.

Must-See Architecture

SAN RAFAEL AND A MASTERPIECE

The oldest and largest town in Marin, a quick 15-minute drive north of Sausalito, **San Rafael** is slightly less upscale than most of its neighbors but doesn't lack atmosphere. Its strollable downtown has plenty of good places to eat.

Just north, the region's premier architectural sight is the eye-catching **Marin County Civic Center**, the wild masterpiece by Frank Lloyd Wright (1867–1959), who didn't live to see its 1962 completion. Wright designed the horizontal hillside buildings to flow with the natural beauty of the county's landscape, with sky-blue roofs, sand-colored walls and a gold tower pointing to the heavens. Self-guided tours are fascinating, but check for the regular free guided tours. The **Sunday Marin Farmers Market** here is one of the Bay Area's best.

To the south, **San Quentin State Prison** is the notorious hulking mass best viewed from the Larkspur ferry.

A Gorgeous Detour

STUNNING MARIN INTERIOR

Tiny **Nicasio** is in the midst of horse ranches and beautiful, grassy open hillsides in Marin County's geographic center, a 40-minute drive from Sausalito. **Lucas Valley Rd** is a more scenic and less crowded alternative to Sir Francis Drake Blvd, and allows various loop drives to and from Point Reyes.

GETTING AROUND

Ferries from San Francisco serve Tiburon and Larkspur. The latter connects with the Smart train, which runs north to San Rafael and on to Santa Rosa via Petaluma.

On weekends, San Francisco's Muni bus serves the Marin Headlands, Rodeo Beach and several other stops. Golden Gate Transit and Marin Transit operate local bus services along the Hwy 101 corridor. Other destinations include Mt Tamalpais State Park, Stinson Beach, Bolinas and Point Reyes.

POINT REYES

Point Reyes
San Francisco
Los Angeles

Windswept Point Reyes peninsula is a rough-hewn beauty that has always lured marine mammals and migratory birds; it's also home to scores of shipwrecks. In 1579, Sir Francis Drake landed here to repair his ship, the *Golden Hind*. During his five-week stay he mounted a brass plaque near the shore claiming this land for England. In 1595, the first of many ships lost in these waters went down. To this day bits of cargo still wash up on shore. Despite modern navigation, the dangerous waters here continue to claim the occasional boat.

Point Reyes National Seashore protects 100 sq miles of pristine ocean beaches and coastal wilderness and has phenomenal outdoor opportunities. Hikes take you to remote corners where you can spot huge animals and walk wave-tossed beaches where your footprints will be the only human evidence amid driftwood, seashells and shorebird scratchings.

TOP TIP

A mile west of Olema, the Bear Valley Visitor Center has maps, information and worthwhile exhibits. It's a vital first stop to find out about wildlife-spotting conditions, including beach closures and mandatory shuttle buses to busy areas. The Earthquake Trail details the San Andreas Fault, which runs right through here.

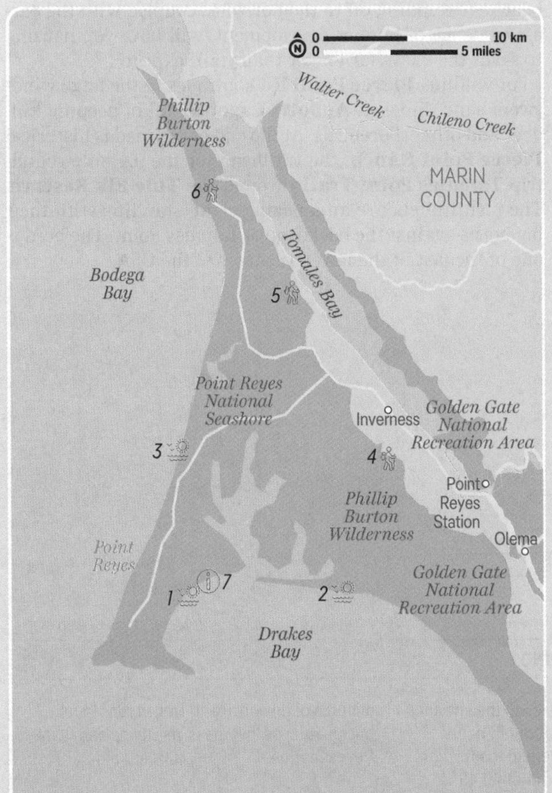

SIGHTS
1 Drakes Beach
2 Limantour Beach
3 Point Reyes Beach

ACTIVITIES, COURSES & TOURS
4 Inverness Ridge Trail
5 Pierce Point Rd
6 Tomales Point Trail

INFORMATION
7 Kenneth Patrick Center

POINT REYES WILDLIFE

Point Reyes has an extraordinary range of wildlife, including 80 species of mammals and nearly 30 species of reptiles and amphibians. The largest animals here are the **elephant seals**, which number upwards of 2000 on shore during late winter and early spring. As they rest after months of feeding non-stop at sea, you can walk close to the adult males snoozing on the sand. Each weighs from 4400lb to 6000lb. Look for pups from January to March; August is the only month when you're unlikely to find any elephant seals at Point Reyes.

Offshore, late December through mid-April is migration season for **gray whales**. You can often spot these behemoths from shore.

Hit the Beaches

POINT REYES' WORLD-CLASS COAST

Virtually every strip of sand is a long drive from anywhere at Point Reyes, but every one is worth the effort.

Limantour Beach is a great all-around beach with an array of wilderness hikes and stunning sunsets. **Drakes Beach** is backed by white sandstone cliffs and is arguably the most gorgeous of the main beaches. There's also the seasonal **Kenneth Patrick Center**, which offers information, especially in elephant-seal mating season. West-facing **Point Reyes Beach** offers 11 miles of solitude. On many days – especially from late fall to spring – the sky turns an iridescent vermilion at sunset. Bring a blanket, lean against a dune and enjoy the show.

Trails, Seabirds & Elk Reserve

HIKING THE POINT REYES WILDERNESS

Trails crisscross Point Reyes over hillsides and along the shoreline.

For views, the **Inverness Ridge Trail** heads for around 3 miles up to **Mt Vision** (1282ft), affording spectacular vistas of the entire national seashore. Seeing the raw beauty of the beaches extending off to the horizons, coupled with the barest evidence of human development, will have you pausing to savor the views for longer than you'd expect.

For wildlife, **Pierce Point Rd** continues to the huge windswept sand dunes at **Abbotts Lagoon**, full of peeping killdeer and other shorebirds. At the end of the road is historical **Pierce Point Ranch**, the trailhead for the 9.4-mile round-trip **Tomales Point Trail** through the **Tule Elk Reserve**. The plentiful elk are an amazing sight, standing with their big horns against the backdrop of Tomales Point. The herd is one of the last in the lower 48 states of the USA.

GETTING AROUND

Barring bad traffic, you can reach the entrance to the national seashore in about 1½ hours from San Francisco. From here to the furthest reaches of the park can take another 45 minutes of driving. Marin Transit runs local buses as far as Inverness via Olema and Point Reyes Station.

Beyond Point Reyes

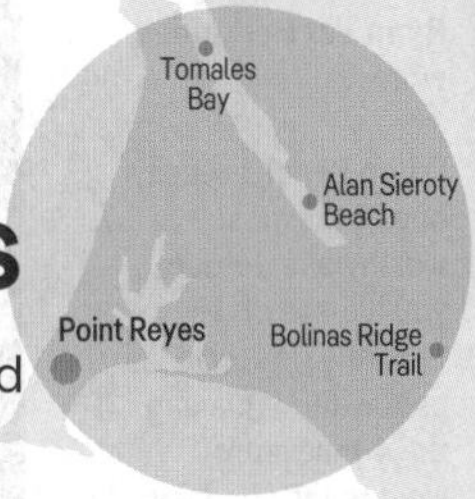

The beauty and bounty of nature extends beyond Point Reyes to the little towns situated on the beautiful byways wending along the coast.

If you have a timetable for your journey along Hwy 1 in the Point Reyes area, toss it out the window. There are many alluring little villages where you can sample the products of the dairies and ranches that thrive in the rolling green hills. Plan on stopping often.

Point Reyes Station is the hub of western Marin County. Since the 1960s the region has been populated by artists. Today, Main St is a diverting blend of art galleries, tourist shops, restaurants and cafes. The town has a lively saloon, local cheese vendors and the superb little store Point Reyes Books, where the staff curate a fine selection of titles relating to the region, many written by local authors.

TOP TIP

Olema, at the entrance to Point Reyes National Seashore, is good mostly for coffee. Inverness, the one town inside the park, has very limited dining options.

Cycling the Bolinas Ridge Trail (p124)

WHY I LOVE DILLON BEACH

Ryan Ver Berkmoes, writer

Dillon Beach is easily one of the most worthwhile detours you'll make off Hwy 1 – rarely do I drive past without making the 4-mile jaunt west to the sand. But first, I stop at the 19th-century village of **Tomales**, where the Dillon Beach road begins, for its good cafes, including Route One Bakery & Kitchen (the pizza is superb).

The road to Dillon Beach passes outcrops of weirdly sinuous boulders. Down at the sand, there's plenty of parking and a welcoming relaxed attitude. Firewood is sold at the park entrance and you can have a bonfire on the wide, flat beach. The views of Tomales Point at Point Reyes National Seashore across the water are a treat.

JESSICA RUSCELLO/SHUTTERSTOCK ©

Barbecue Tomales Bay oysters

Oysters Galore

OH SHUCKS!

Fresh oysters from **Tomales Bay** are a much-loved local specialty. From south to north, there are three waterfront restaurants on Hwy 1, 15 to 20 minutes' drive north of Point Reyes Station.

The relaxed **Marshall Store** is perfect for slurping down barbecue or raw Tomales Bay oysters, sourced from the restaurant's own farm. Smoked-seafood plates are also good.

Hog Island Oyster Company farms oysters and sells them at this roadside outlet. There's not much to see: just some picnic tables, an outdoor cafe and a window selling the famously silky oysters and a few other provisions.

At vintage 1930s **Nick's Cove** perched over Tomales Bay, trophy heads are mounted on knotty-pine walls and there's a roaring fireplace. The seafood dishes – including the local oysters – are impeccable.

Hiking, Beaches & Kayaking

EMBRACE OUTDOOR FUN

The **Bolinas Ridge Trail**, a 10.5-mile series of ups and downs for hikers or cyclists, has great views, and starts about 1 mile east of Olema (the main entry point for **Point Reyes National Seashore**), off Sir Francis Drake Blvd.

Just 5 miles north of Point Reyes Station, **Alan Sieroty Beach** is a tiny peninsula on glassy Tomales Bay that's good for families and swimming.

Long-running **Blue Waters Kayaking** offers guided tours of Tomales Bay; otherwise, you can get a kayak delivered to your lodgings and paddle to secluded beaches on your own. Book ahead for full-moon and bioluminescence excursions.

GETTING AROUND

You'll need your own wheels to get around the region beyond Point Reyes.

OAKLAND

Oakland is where the Bay Area's diverse, artsy and radical folks have enshrined a free-thinking way of life. Oaklanders are fiercely proud that their home retains the mixed ethnic tableau and unapologetic left-wing politics San Francisco once enshrined, and they know this backdrop is threatened by million-dollar residential homes, already present even in formerly middle-class neighborhoods.

Oakland is full of historical buildings and colorful businesses. With such easy access from San Francisco via BART or ferry, it's worth spending part of a day exploring here on foot or by bicycle.

Oakland's eateries are among the best and most innovative in the Bay Area, due to its cultural diversity and the fact that up-and-coming chefs can more readily afford to start a business here. The city abounds with budget-friendly favorites. Uptown, Temescal and Rockridge attract culinary trendspotters. Oakland's busiest and hippest bars are in the Uptown district, often just a short stumble from BART.

Oakland

Los Angeles

TOP TIP

Broadway is the backbone of downtown Oakland, running north from touristy Jack London Sq at the waterfront. The genteel Rockridge neighborhood lies west of Broadway along College Ave, near the Berkeley border. Downtown, Telegraph Ave branches off Broadway and heads north to Berkeley via the vibrant Temescal neighborhood (between 40th and 51st Sts).

Oakland City Hall (p126)

CARY KALSCHEUER/SHUTTERSTOCK ©

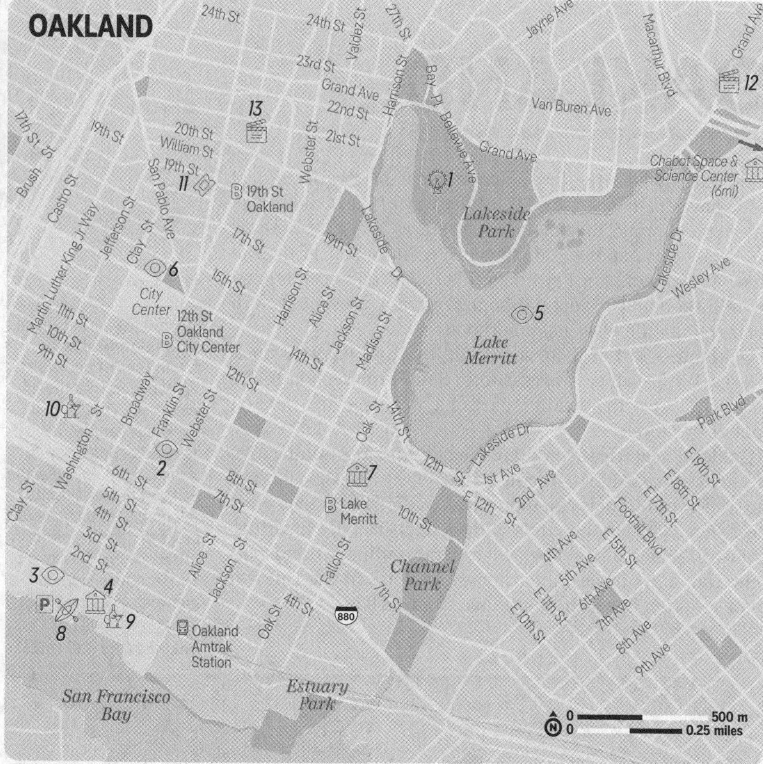

SIGHTS
1 Children's Fairyland
2 Chinatown
3 Jack London Square
4 Jack London's Cabin
5 Lake Merritt
6 Oakland City Hall
7 Oakland Museum of California

ACTIVITIES, COURSES & TOURS
8 California Canoe & Kayak

DRINKING
9 Heinold's First & Last Chance Saloon
10 Oeste

ENTERTAINMENT
11 Fox Theater
12 Grand Lake Theatre
13 Paramount Theatre

The City's Heart

DOWNTOWN OAKLAND AND CHINATOWN

Pedestrianized **City Center**, between Broadway and Clay St, 12th and 14th Sts, forms the heart of downtown Oakland. There's also a car-free corridor along 13th St between Broadway and Franklin. Nearby Oakland City Hall is a beautifully refurbished 1914 beaux-arts building.

Old Oakland west of Broadway between 8th and 10th Sts, is lined with restored historical buildings dating from the late 19th century. The area has a lively restaurant and after-work scene. Stop in at happening **Oeste** for a great music-and-drinks scene coupled with a delicious wide-ranging menu, plus a hopping rooftop bar.

East of Broadway and bustling with commerce, Oakland's no-nonsense **Chinatown** centers on Franklin and Webster

Leeks and fennel at the farmers market

Sts, as it has since the 1850s. Come and partake of wholesale drama like Napa cabbage price wars.

The top draw is the **Oakland Museum of California**. Dedicated to California, it has rotating exhibitions on artistic and scientific themes, and permanent galleries covering the state's diverse ecology and history, as well as California art, from traditional landscapes to reimagined cartography. It's the museum celebrating the state – for better and worse – that should be in the capital, Sacramento, but isn't.

A Square with a Past & a View

WATERSIDE JACK LONDON SQ

The waterfront where writer and adventurer Jack London once caroused now bears his name. Jack London Sq offers grand opportunities for kayaking around the harbor or strolling the docks, especially when the **Sunday farmers market** takes over. Contemporary redevelopment has added generic urban condos, plus popular restaurants and bars. **California Canoe & Kayak** rents kayaks and stand-up paddleboarding (SUP) sets. Book ahead for moonlight paddles along the waterfront.

BEST RESTAURANTS IN OAKLAND

Millennium
Beloved in Rockridge for vegan surprises like pumpkin tamales and parsnip *okonomiyaki* (Japanese savory pancakes). $$

Horn Barbecue
West Oakland's own celebrity chef, Matt Horn, serves the salivating masses his renowned brisket and pulled pork. $$

Commis
Chef James Syhabout's paean to innovative dining, on Piedmont Ave. Reserve a counter seat for the kitchen show. $$$

FOB Kitchen
Filipino restaurant in Temescal. Order anything with pork plus the garlic rice. There's a popular weekend brunch. $$

WHERE TO DRINK IN OAKLAND

Wood Tavern
An array of top California wines on offer in Rockridge, plus locally sourced, casual food.

Alem's Coffee
At this East African cafe on Temescal's edge, the outdoor patio is a popular community gathering place in the morning.

Snail Bar
In Temescal, natural and organic wines are just some of the uncommon treats; small-plate pairings change weekly.

INTERNATIONAL BLVD TACOS

Running southwest from Oakland's center, International Blvd lives up to its name. It's the crucible for a world of Bay Area cultures. One of the most famous is its extraordinary Mexican fare, which you can enjoy at restaurants, hole-in-the-walls and busy taco trucks.

When Michelin discovered the sublime little **Taqueria El Paisa**, International Blvd had reached a new level of recognition. The tacos are good beyond all superlatives: simple, fresh and garnished with nopals (cactus).

Tortas Ahogadas Mi Barrio celebrates Jalisco-style food, which includes *tacos dorados*. Savor the fiery salsa.

Just north, at a parking lot on Fruitvale Ave, the **El Novillo** taco truck gives you too many choices: taco or burrito? Which of the many meats?

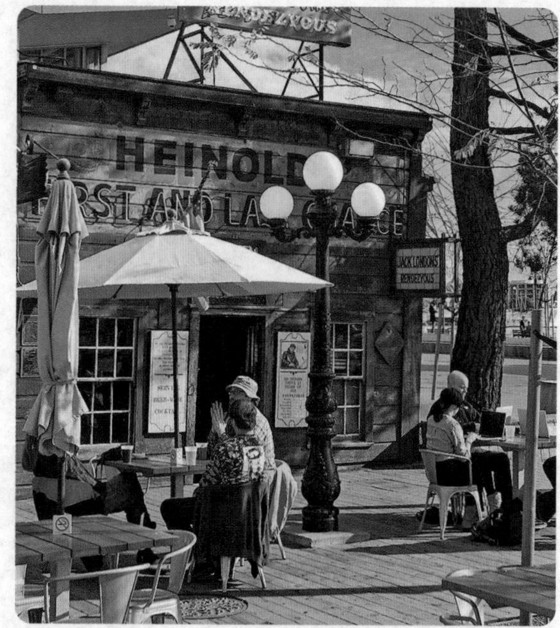

JAMES KIRKIKIS/SHUTTERSTOCK ©

Heinhold's First & Last Chance Saloon

On the edge of the square, **Jack London's Cabin** is reconstructed in part using the logs from his original 1898 cabin in the Yukon territory of Canada, and the historical wooden hovel allows visitors a peek inside life during the gold-rush era. Seemingly more popular is a **statue of a wolf** (or maybe a sled dog, or is it *The Call of the Wild's* Buck?), which kids love to pose with.

Stop by nearby **Heinold's First & Last Chance Saloon**, an 1883 bar constructed from wood scavenged from an old whaling ship and, yes, a favorite of London's. Keeled to a severe slant during the 1906 earthquake, the building has a tilt that might make you feel self-conscious about stumbling before you even order (avoid the tilt by drinking at the pretty outdoor tables).

Art-Deco Arts District & Grand Lake

BUSY UPTOWN AND LAKE MERRITT

North of downtown Oakland, the **Uptown** district contains many of the city's art-deco beauties, such as the **Fox Theater** and **Paramount Theatre**, and a lively arts, restaurant

WHERE TO DRINK IN OAKLAND

North Light
Temescal cocktail bar with a bookstore; albums provide tunes amid the book-lined walls. Creative booze mix.

Kingfish Pub
Century-old beloved dive bar in Temescal that was once a bait shop. Play shuffleboard on the back patio.

Ghost Town Brewing
Under-the-radar brewery in West Oakland with 15 beers usually on tap. Locrain is a superb pale ale.

and nightlife scene. The area stretches roughly between Telegraph and Broadway, bounded by Grand Ave to the north.

Follow Grand Ave east of Broadway and you'll run into the shores of **Lake Merritt**. Grand Ave (north of the lake) and Lakeshore Ave (east of the lake) are pedestrian-friendly streets with interesting shops, restaurants, cafes and bars.

An urban respite, Lake Merritt is a popular place to stroll or go running (a 3.2-mile paved path circles the lake), with bonsai and botanical gardens, a bird sanctuary, green spaces, a boathouse and gondola rides. Look for another landmark theater, the 1926 **Grand Lake Theatre** on the lake's northern edge. It's the home of the wildly popular **Noir City film festival**, hosted by TCM's Eddie Muller, celebrating film noir movies.

Kids of all ages love the lakeside **Children's Fairyland**, a 10-acre attraction that dates from 1950, and hasn't changed a whole lot since – we mean that as a compliment! With its little Aesop theater and Peter Rabbit's garden, it ticks all the nostalgia boxes for a sweeter, simpler time that actually probably didn't exist. The park's oldest ride – an *Alice in Wonderland*–themed carousel dubbed the **Wonder-Go-Round** – was beautifully restored in 2019.

Interactive Space Center & Planetarium

TO INFINITY AND BEYOND

Stargazers will go gaga over the **Chabot Space & Science Center**, a kid-oriented science and technology center in the Oakland Hills with loads of exhibits on subjects such as space travel and eclipses, as well as cool planetarium shows. It's the official visitor center for the South Bay's NASA Ames Research Center. Check out the gear that will be used on future space missions.

WALKING WEST OAKLAND

Battered by the 1989 earthquake, bedeviled by homeless encampments, surrounded by freeways jammed with suburbanites and a busy container port, **West Oakland** embodies every non-gentrified aspect of the city's history.

It's here that the Black Panther Party began its uncompromising campaign for African American rights and independence. Its free lunch programs for school kids are still revered today. A few decades earlier, CL Dellums led the railway porters union as it fought not just for better wages but also the civil rights of people across the USA.

Throughout West Oakland vibrant murals celebrate the area's heritage and culture. Experience the past and present on the excellent **Black Liberation Walking Tour** (blwt.org), which draws on personal stories to bring the neighborhood alive.

GETTING AROUND

Oakland is well connected. Amtrak serves Sacramento, the Central Valley and San Jose. BART serves the East Bay, Oakland's airport and San Francisco through the Transbay Tube. AC Transit runs a dense network of bus routes, and ferries link Jack London Sq to San Francisco's Ferry Building.

Beyond Oakland

The East Bay is not all Oakland and Berkeley. Natural and cultural attractions range from the bay to the peaks.

Excellent restaurants and bars, a creative arts scene, offbeat shopping, woodsy parks and better weather are just some of the attractions that lure people to the East Bay.

Alameda is an actual island, thanks to a narrow channel separating it from Oakland. Its surrounding waterfront has sensational bay views and attractions to fill an afternoon. Elsewhere, the string of towns heading south to Fremont and its vast Tesla factory (where Chevy Novas were once made) define no-nonsense.

Squeezed into a plot at the base of the soaring white Bay Bridge, Emeryville was once the home of thriving Ohlone villages, which featured towering shell mounds built from bay oyster and clam shells. Today, it is mostly known for Pixar Animation Studios (not open for visitors).

TOP TIP

It's best to have your own wheels for exploring the East Bay beyond Oakland, especially for reaching the region's highest point.

Alameda

SNAPASKYLINE/SHUTTERSTOCK ©

USS Hornet

A Base for Drinking

BAR-HOPPING IN ALAMEDA

The west end of **Alameda**, only 10 minutes by car from Oakland, was once a major naval air station. Long closed, the former base is slowly being transformed into a new neighborhood. Most significantly, several vast old hangars near the USS *Hornet* have been repurposed as Spirits Alley, which features artisanal distilleries, wine-tasting rooms and breweries.

Top draws include **St George Spirits**, the alley's anchor, and **Building 43 Winery**. Be sure to check out the striking panoramic views of the San Francisco skyline across the bay, and ward off those hangovers with food-truck goodness.

For even more colorful imbibing, **Forbidden Island Tiki Lounge** is in the heart of the island and is one of the Bay Area's most infamous tiki bars.

Historic Warship

USS HORNET, HOME FROM THE MOON

When they splashed down after their lunar landing, the Apollo 11 astronauts were lifted aboard the **USS Hornet**, a Cold War–era aircraft carrier that began life in WWII. It's now docked amid the old naval base near Spirits Alley, a 10-minute drive from Oakland, and is open for tours. There's an array of historic aircraft on display in the hangar deck and up top on the wind-blown flight deck. The *Hornet's* role in the Apollo missions is fully covered.

THE EAST BAY'S TALLEST POINT

At 3849ft, **Mt Diablo** is more than 1200ft higher than Mt Tamalpais in Marin County. On a clear day (early on a fog-free morning is best) the views from Diablo's summit are vast and sweeping, from the bay and the Pacific in the west to the Sierras in the east. Additional draws include 170 miles of hiking trails, rock climbing, stargazing, wildflowers in springtime and the tarantula-mating season in the fall.

Looming over the open lands and suburbs of Contra Costa County 14 miles east of Oakland, Mt Diablo is most easily accessed off I-680 at Danville or Walnut Creek. You can also drive to the summit, where there's a visitor center.

GETTING AROUND

Alameda is reached by buses from Oakland and two ferry lines from San Francisco. BART heads south down the East Bay, as do Amtrak and AC Transit buses. Emeryville is the end point for Amtrak's long-distance *California Zephyr* train.

BERKELEY

Berkeley is synonymous with protest, activism and left-wing politics. Here, 'woke' is an essential attribute, not an aspersion.

But beyond those tropes is a busy, attractive city, a blend of yuppie, hippie and student, all existing side by side with great Asia-Pacific regional restaurants, twee toy stores, Latin American grocers, high-end organic food halls and the misty green campus of the University of California, Berkeley (aka 'Cal'). It's easy to stereotype 'Bezerkeley' for some of its recycle-or-else PC crankiness and occasional overbearing self-righteousness. But some of that attitude is justified: at the end of the day Berkeley has, more often than not, been on the right side of environmental and political issues that have defined the rest of the nation.

Green spaces in the hills and on the flats of the bay, plus enticing neighborhoods, make Berkeley a good day trip or stop from anywhere in the Bay Area.

TOP TIP

Telegraph and Shattuck Aves are packed with cafes, cheap restaurants and bookstores. Berkeley's Little India runs along the University Ave corridor. College Ave in Elmwood near Rockridge is lined with shops and bakeries. The popular Gourmet Ghetto stretches along Shattuck Ave north of University Ave.

The Campanile (Sather Tower) at the University of California, Berkeley

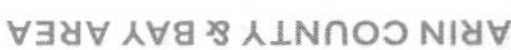

SIGHTS
1 BAMPFA
2 Bancroft Library
3 Campanile
4 Phoebe A Hearst Museum of Anthropology
5 Sather Gate
6 Sproul Plaza
7 Telegraph Avenue
8 University of California, Berkeley

ENTERTAINMENT
9 Aurora Theatre Company
10 Berkeley Repertory Theatre
11 Freight & Salvage Coffeehouse

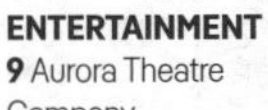

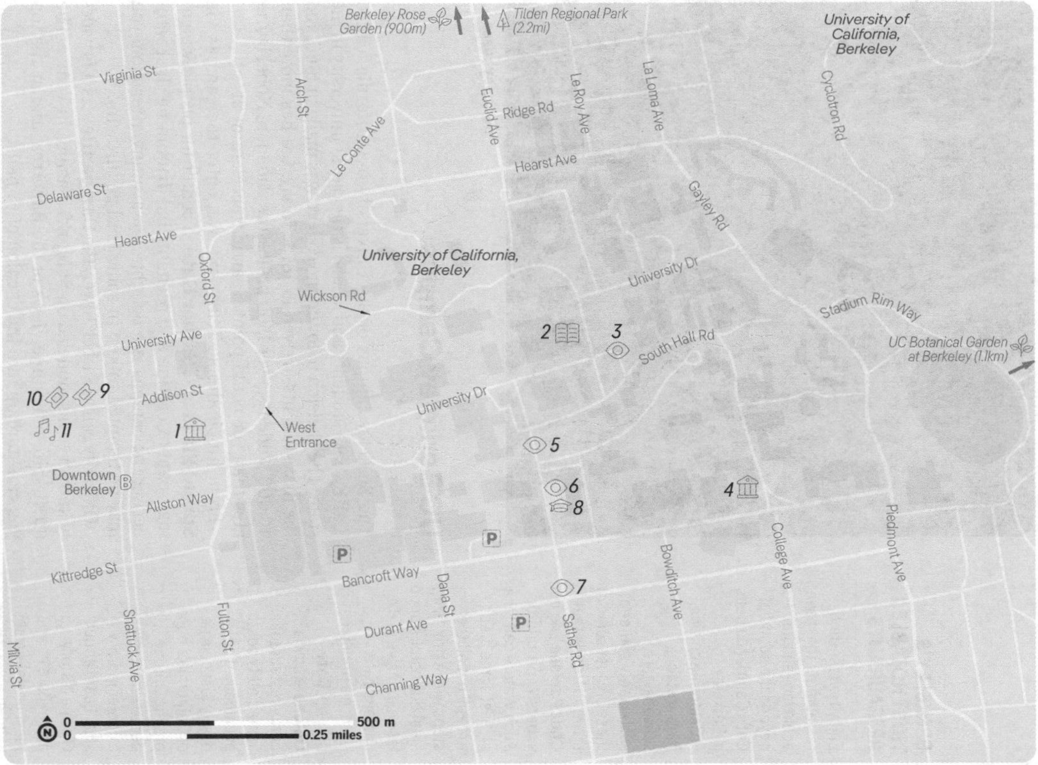

Berkeley Rose Garden (900m)
Tilden Regional Park (2.2mi)
University of California, Berkeley
Virginia St
Arch St
Euclid Ave
Le Roy Ave
La Loma Ave
Cyclotron Rd
Ridge Rd
Le Conte Ave
Hearst Ave
Delaware St
Hearst Ave
Gayley Rd
University of California, Berkeley
Oxford St
Wickson Rd
University Dr
Stadium Rim Way
University Ave
South Hall Rd
UC Botanical Garden at Berkeley (1.1km)
Addison St
University Dr
West Entrance
Downtown Berkeley
Allston Way
Kittredge St
Bancroft Way
Dana St
Bowditch Ave
College Ave
Piedmont Ave
Durant Ave
Sather Rd
Shattuck Ave
Fulton St
Milvia St
Channing Way
0
500 m
0
0.25 miles

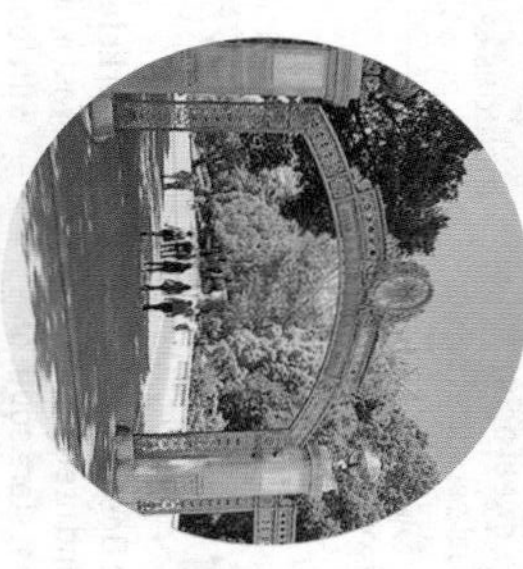

Sather Gate (p134)

BERKELEY'S MOST NOTABLE RESTAURANTS

Enjoy trendsetting restaurants that have achieved fame far beyond the sound of Cal's Campanile bells in Berkeley.

California cuisine, farm-to-table, seasonal fare, sustainably sourced: these are just some of the food trends that **Chez Panisse** and its superstar proprietor Alice Waters can take at least some credit for. Pull out all the stops with a prix-fixe meal downstairs or go less expensive in the upstairs cafe.

Once a popular pop-up, **Cafe Ohlone** is now a buzzy restaurant immediately south of campus. The nearly lost cuisine of California's once prolific Ohlone people is given a contemporary spin. Learn about Ohlone history and culture as you feast on delicacies including dandelion soup, sweet acorn pancakes, sorrel salad and wood-smoked venison.

ALFRED GEORG SONSALLA/GETTY IMAGES ©

Berkeley roses

UC Berkeley Campus

IT'S ALL ABOUT CAL

The Berkeley campus of the University of California (called 'Cal' by both students and locals) is the oldest university in the state. The decision to found the college was made in 1866, and the first students arrived in 1873. Today, Cal has more than 40,000 students, over 1500 professors and more Nobel laureates than you could point a particle accelerator at.

From hippie-dippie Telegraph Ave, enter the campus via **Sproul Plaza** and **Sather Gate**, a center for people-watching, soapbox oration and pseudotribal drumming. Just wandering the campus is a delight – on a sunny afternoon, you may be tempted to join in some Frisbee throwing.

Officially called Sather Tower, the **Campanile** – as it is widely known – was modeled on St Mark's Basilica in Venice. The 307ft spire offers fine views of the Bay Area, and at the top you can stare up into the carillon of 61 bells.

The small **Phoebe A Hearst Museum of Anthropology** includes exhibits from indigenous cultures around the world, including a large collection highlighting Native Californian

WHERE TO SHOP IN BERKELEY

Moe's Books
New and used books in a vast store south of campus. Renowned for its knowledgeable staff.

Berkeley Bowl Marketplace
Vast indie supermarket filled with foods from around the Bay Area and the world; huge produce department.

Acme Bread
One of the region's best bakeries, beloved for its take on classic sourdough bread.

cultures. Inside a stainless-steel exterior, **BAMPFA** (Berkeley Art Museum and Pacific Film Archive) holds multiple galleries showcasing a limited number of artworks, from ancient Chinese to cutting-edge contemporary. Its film series is top-notch.

The **Bancroft Library** houses, among other gems, the papers of Mark Twain, a copy of Shakespeare's folios and a diary from the Donner Party. Its public exhibits include the surprisingly small gold nugget that sparked the 1849 gold rush.

An array of memorial plaques on the wall outside of Room 3407 in **Gilman Hall** tells you you've found the chemistry lab where plutonium was discovered in 1941. It became the core element of the first atom bombs.

Cruising Downtown

HEAD OUT ON THE TOWN

Berkeley's downtown, centered on Shattuck Ave between University Ave and Dwight Way, has few traces of the city's tie-dyed reputation. It abounds with shops, restaurants and restored public buildings.

The nearby arts district revolves around the acclaimed thespian stomping grounds of the **Berkeley Repertory Theatre** and **Aurora Theatre Company**, and live folk music from around the globe at the historic **Freight & Salvage Coffeehouse**, all on Addison St.

Down by the bay, **waterfront trails** afford sweeping views to the Golden Gate.

Verdant Gardens & Hikes

EXPLORING THE BERKELEY HILLS

Nature begins in the hills right at the east end of campus. With 34 acres and more than 10,000 types of plants, the **UC Botanical Garden** at Berkeley has one of the most varied collections in the country. Flora from every continent except Antarctica is lovingly tended here, with special emphasis on Mediterranean species that grow in California. The **Berkeley Rose Garden** is 2 miles northwest.

Further up in the hills, 2079-acre **Tilden Regional Park** is Berkeley's best. It has nearly 40 miles of hiking and multiuse trails of varying difficulty, from paved paths to hilly scrambles, including part of the magnificent **Bay Area Ridge Trail**. The wonderfully wild-looking **Botanical Garden** celebrates native California plants.

BERKELEY'S LANDMARK ARCHITECT

Julia Morgan's ties with Cal began when she became the first woman to graduate from the civil engineering program. She is best known as William Randolph Hearst's favorite architect and the designer of Hearst Castle (p279), but over her prolific career she designed more than 700 buildings, including some noteworthy Berkeley creations.

Julia Morgan Hall (1911) is in the UC Botanical Garden and exemplifies her low-slung designs clad in redwood. At the southwest corner of campus, the **Berkeley City Club** (1929) picks up many of Hearst Castle's Moorish and Romanesque design elements.

The **Berkeley Playhouse** (1910) on College Ave is beautifully understated. A bit east, **St John's Presbyterian Church** (1910) is on the National Register of Historic Places.

GETTING AROUND

Berkeley is well served with three BART stations. AC Transit buses cover the main roads and provide links across the East Bay. There's limited ferry service to San Francisco.

Beyond Berkeley

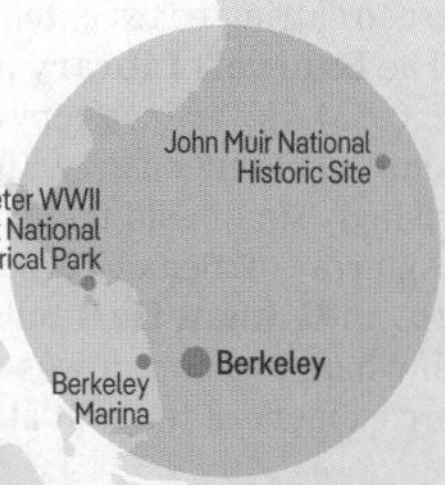

Follow the bay to visit sights that, while far from the tourist glitz of San Francisco, Marin and Napa, are nonetheless uniquely compelling.

As you head north and east around the bay toward the Sacramento Delta, many of the most interesting sights and activities beyond Berkeley are close to the water. This includes three national parks, including one that is one of the nation's least visited.

Historic old cities dot the shore. Vallejo, on the north side of San Pablo Bay, was once the state's capital (1851–1853). Across the narrow Carquinez Strait, compact little Crockett is a tiny dash of vintage charm in the shadow of its huge C&H sugar factory and the I-80 bridge.

Barely 3 miles east, 19th-century Port Costa has popular weekend roadhouses next to busy train tracks built right along the water.

TOP TIP

When driving East Bay freeways such as the I-80, be aware that they become heavily congested during morning and evening rush hours.

Berkeley Marina (p138)

THOMAS WINZ/GETTY IMAGES ©

Rosie the Riveter WWII Home Front National Historic Park

Rosie the Riveter's Home

HISTORIC MEMORIAL TO HUMAN RIGHTS

The struggle for civil rights and women's equality is the focus of one of the East Bay's most significant historical sites, the **Rosie the Riveter WWII Home Front National Historic Park**. Located on the bay in Richmond, 15 minutes by car from Berkeley, this impressive National Parks Service facility has a fine museum. It's inside the historic Ford Building complex near the location of four adjoining Kaiser shipyards that achieved the almost unbelievable feat of building 747 freighters and warships during WWII.

Thousands of workers toiled in shifts around the clock, seven days a week. To meet the insatiable need for labor, scores of women were brought into the workforce, along with a huge number of African Americans, who had faced severe discrimination in California.

Displays cover the huge societal changes spawned by the shipyards and the challenges the workers faced in finding housing and a basic life balance. Tragically, there were few jobs in Richmond after the postwar closure of the shipyards other than the pollution-belching refineries near the bay – these remain operational to this day. The city is still stunted

LITTLE-KNOWN & MOVING MEMORIAL

On July 17, 1944, 320 sailors and civilians were killed when ammunition being loaded onto a freighter exploded at the Port Chicago military base, near Concord.

The disaster was heard and felt in Oakland 30 miles away and beyond. The ship being loaded vanished. Despite the disaster's scope, it's little known today. Most of those killed were African American sailors, working under horrific conditions. During WWII the US military was still segregated and African Americans were given the worst jobs.

Today the **Port Chicago Naval Magazine National Memorial** is a simple and poignant monument at the blast site. It receives few visitors as the location is an active military base, and visits require advance reservations.

WHERE TO EAT BEYOND BERKELEY

Brezo
Next to the Rosie the Riveter park, Brezo serves local and Mexican fare and has a large patio. **$**

Bull Valley Roadhouse
Port Costa roadhouse dating from 1897, with classic American fare and potent cocktails. **$$**

States Coffee
House-roasted coffee served in the heart of Martinez; good snacks and baked goods. **$**

decades later. Look for the large freighter, the SS *Red Oak Victory*, docked near the visitor center. It's one of the last surviving ships to be built here.

CYCLING THE RICHMOND-SAN RAFAEL BRIDGE

Cruising on two wheels across the Golden Gate Bridge is one of the Bay Area's iconic cycling experiences. But there's another, longer, bridge that you can now ride across. No, it's not the Bay Bridge, but rather the unheralded, unloved **Richmond-San Rafael Bridge** in the North Bay. One entire lane of the two-deck span has been walled off for bikes, which has been a real boon for exploring the region. Using the San Francisco-Larkspur Golden Gate ferry as well as BART in Richmond, you can create a huge circle ride from the city. The 5.5-mile bridge affords grand views of Marin, Alameda and Contra Costa Counties and the bay while you ride.

Kayaking & Stand-Up Paddleboarding

ACTION ON THE WATER

As well as making for a lovely postcard or iconic snapshot, San Francisco Bay offers plenty of options for getting out on the water. Once you've rented gear, you'll find myriad locations from which to launch all around the bay.

Cal Adventures is run by the UC Aquatic Center at the **Berkeley Marina**, just 10 minutes by car from Berkeley. It organizes sailing, windsurfing, SUP and sea-kayaking classes and gear rental.

John Muir's Home

VIBE OUT WITH THE FAMOUS NATURALIST

Naturalist John Muir's former residence is part of the **John Muir National Historic Site**. It sits in a pastoral patch of farmland in bustling, modern Martinez, far up the bay, a 30-minute drive from Berkeley. Though Muir wrote of sauntering through the Sierra Nevada with a sack of tea and bread, it may be a shock for those familiar with the iconic Sierra Club founder's ascetic, weather-beaten appearance that this house (built by his father-in-law in 1883) is a model of Victorian Italianate refinement, with a tower cupola and a daintily upholstered parlor.

Muir's 'scribble den' has been left as it was during his life, with crumbled papers overflowing from wire wastebaskets and dried-bread balls – his preferred snack – resting on the mantelpiece.

Acres of the family's fruit orchards still stand, and visitors can enjoy seasonal samples. The grounds include the 1849 **Martinez Adobe**, part of the ranch on which the house was built, and oak-speckled hiking trails on nearby **Mt Wanda**, named for one of Muir's daughters.

GETTING AROUND

Richmond is well served by BART and Amtrak. AC Transit buses provide local coverage in Alameda County. Further east, services become more sparse and having your own wheels is the one practical way to tour around.

PALO ALTO

Palo Alto is Silicon Valley's ritziest city. Even a modest bungalow here may cost over $2 million, while upscale boutiques, restaurants, bars and beauty spas crowd downtown streets.

It's also the mythical heart of Silicon Valley. Bill Hewlett and David Packard got their start here in their legendary garage (you can see it at 367 Addison Ave). Steve Jobs lived and died here. Larry Page and Sergey Brin were students at Stanford University here when they started Google. The list goes on. But it's not all lightness and joy. Palo Alto was the home of Elizabeth Holmes and Theranos, and the ethics of the billionaire venture capitalists of Sand Hill Rd and tech oligarchs are regularly questioned.

Sprawled across nearly 13 sq miles just west of downtown, Stanford University lays claim to being the city's soul. Built by Leland Stanford, one of the Central Pacific Railroad's founders and a former governor of California, it has grown to become a prestigious, wealthy and conservative institution.

TOP TIP

Stanford University maintains a self-consciously rural appearance and adjoins a namesake luxury shopping center. Both are west of the busy Caltrain tracks. Downtown is a walkable delight. Past pricey neighborhoods and Hwy 101, East Palo Alto is a separate city, which enjoys little affluence. Further on, parks and trails line the bay shore.

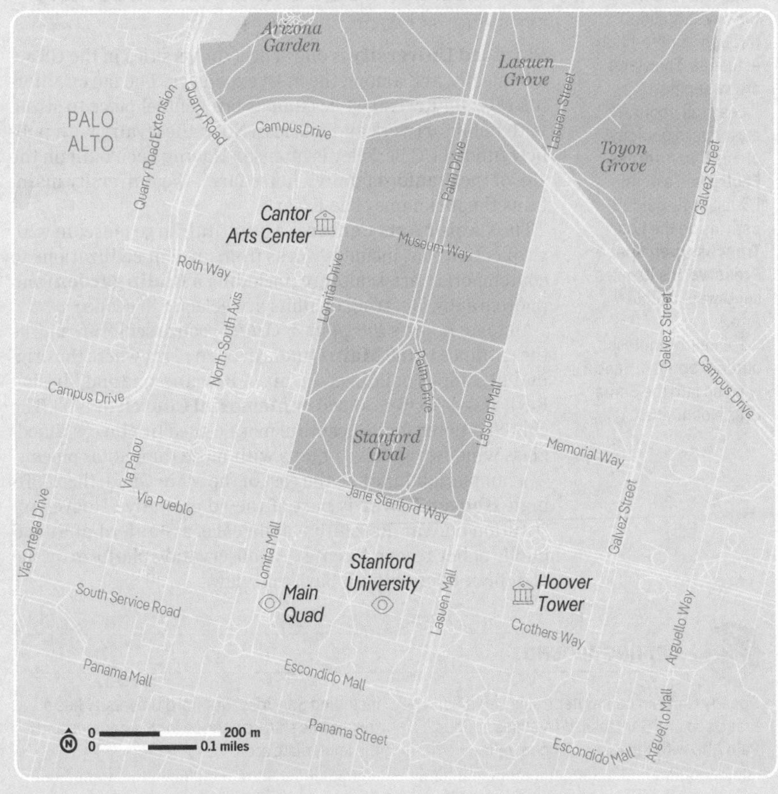

PALO ALTO OUTDOORS

West of the campus, the 3.7-mile paved **Stanford Dish Loop** is a favorite with runners, walkers and science nerds who want to get an up-close look at the 150ft-diameter radio telescope (nicknamed 'the Dish') that once broadcast signals to NASA's Voyager spacecraft. It's a steep up-and-down route and offers spectacular views.

The **Baylands Observation Deck and Boardwalk** is the hub for hiking trails that follow the bay shoreline through wildlife-filled estuaries. The views are sweeping.

Learn all about earthquake geology on the **San Andreas Fault Trail**, a gentle 1.5-mile self-guided path inside the **Los Trancos Open Space Preserve**. It's 10 miles southwest of Palo Alto.

For nearly endless outdoor options, head west up into the Santa Cruz Mountains.

INGUS KRUKLITIS/SHUTTERSTOCK ©

Stanford University

Get Academic at Stanford University

ENRICHING ARCHITECTURE AND MUSEUMS

Stanford University is one of best universities in the US academically, and among the most expensive. The faux California Mission Revival–style campus is a genteel place to stroll, with public artwork and murals. (Note: the rivalry with publicly funded UC Berkeley is intense.) Having been built on the site of the Stanford family's horse farm, the university maintains the nickname 'The Farm.'

The **Cantor Arts Center** is a beautiful, large museum with a collection that includes works from ancient civilizations to contemporary art, sculpture (including a **Rodin garden**) and photography. Rotating exhibits are eclectic in scope.

Auguste Rodin's *Burghers of Calais* bronze sculpture marks the entrance to the **Main Quad**, an open plaza where the original 12 campus buildings – a mix of Romanesque and Mission Revival styles – were joined by **Memorial Church** in 1903. The church is noted for its beautiful mosaic-tiled frontage, stained-glass windows and five organs with more than 8000 pipes.

A campus landmark to the east of the Main Quad, the 285ft-high **Hoover Tower** is part of the conservative Hoover Institution on War, Revolution and Peace, a Stanford-affiliated public policy research center. An observation platform on the 14th floor offers superb Bay Area views.

GETTING AROUND

Speedy Caltrain commuter trains serve San Francisco and San Jose. VTA buses connect Palo Alto with the rest of Silicon Valley, including San Jose. Stanford University has a free public shuttle service for the campus and the immediate area.

Beyond Palo Alto

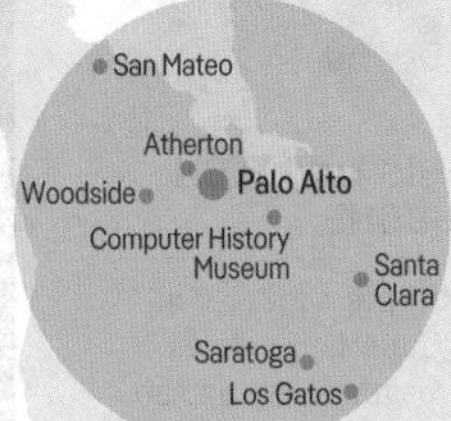

Roam the land where billionaires are spawned and enjoy your own tech fantasy. Divert to bay and mountain pleasures.

South of San Francisco, squeezed tightly between the bay and the coastal foothills, a vast swath of cities, towns and suburbia continues toward San Jose. Dotted inside this area are famous names such as Silicon Valley, Menlo Park and Mountain View.

You won't find Silicon Valley on any map: it's a nickname coined in the 1970s. As silicon chips form the basis of modern microcomputers, and the Santa Clara Valley – stretching from Palo Alto through Sunnyvale and Cupertino to San Jose – is thought of as the birthplace of the tech revolutions, the region is dubbed 'Silicon Valley.' It's hard to imagine that through the 1960s it was still a region of apricot, Bing cherry and walnut orchards.

TOP TIP

Choose your freeway: Hwy 101 is the spine of Silicon Valley, while the I-280 is the less congested, prettier alternative.

Apple Park Visitor Center (p142), Cupertino

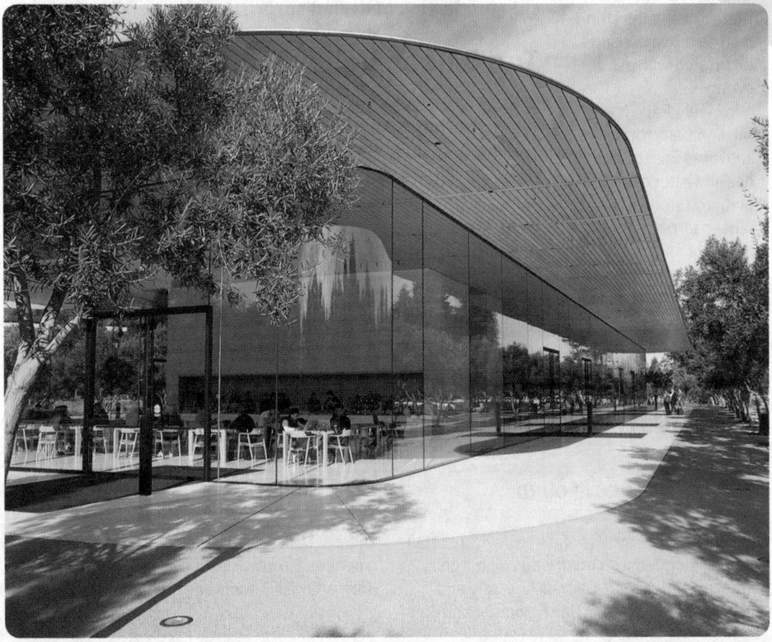

VISITING TECH ICONS

Apple is located in Cupertino, with a visitor center and an Apple Store, a sleek cafe and a rooftop deck that allows a glimpse of the company's infamous 'flying saucer' headquarters. The basement bathroom corridors look eerily reminiscent of the sets for the Apple TV+ series *Severance*, about an evil corporation dedicated to mind control.

Google, in Mountain View, has no visitor center but there's a Google Merchandise Store in a shabby strip mall next to a parking lot littered with used syringes.

In Menlo Park, **Meta**, the company formerly known as Facebook, has no visitor center or merch store. Cheap plastic tarps bearing the Meta name cover the Facebook 'thumbs up' signs once popular for selfies.

TADA IMAGES/SHUTTERSTOCK ©

Intel Museum

Museums of Tech

PAEANS TO FAMOUS INNOVATIONS

The vast and fascinating **Computer History Museum** in Mountain View has themed exhibits drawn from its 100,000-item collection and is only a 10-minute drive from Palo Alto. Artifacts range from the abacus to iPod prototypes (remember those?). Docents are often industry luminaries who've got time to kill now that their IPOs have vested.

The storied chipmaker Intel – one of the reasons Silicon Valley got its name – runs the engaging **Intel Museum** in Santa Clara, which covers the use of silicon in producing microchips, several decades of nearly unbelievable innovation in chip production and – not surprisingly – Intel's involvement.

Top Silicon Valley Towns

EXPLORING BEYOND PALO ALTO

There are several noteworthy towns and cities in the region, which mostly flow seamlessly from one to the next. **San Mateo**, a 10-minute drive from Palo Alto, has good bayshore parks, such as the Coyote Point Recreation Area. **Atherton** is the wealthiest zip code in the USA, with old-money families that predate Silicon Valley. **Woodside** has good casual-chic roadside cafes on Hwy 84 and is the gateway to the magnificent open lands of the Santa Cruz Mountains along Skyline Blvd. **Santa Clara** has tech companies surrounding its namesake university, which is home to the 1777 Mission Santa Clara de Asís. Well-heeled **Saratoga** and **Los Gatos** have atmospheric town centers that are enjoyable for strolling – a local rarity.

GETTING AROUND

Silicon Valley's streets and freeways are often traffic-clogged with frustrated Lamborghini drivers (and others). Caltrain links city and town centers between San Francisco and San Jose. VTA provides fill-in bus and light-rail services. However, your own wheels are best for visiting this sprawling area.

SAN JOSE

Though culturally diverse and historical, San Jose – carpeted with Silicon Valley's suburbia – has always been in San Francisco's shadow. Founded in 1777 as El Pueblo de San José de Guadalupe, San Jose is California's oldest Spanish civilian settlement. Its downtown is fairly modest for a city that's California's third-most populated – though it does bustle with twenty-something clubgoers on weekends, in part thanks to its large namesake state university. And a huge new development by Google near the stadium and train station will transform the center.

Industrial parks, high-tech computer firms, surprisingly leafy neighborhoods and strip malls are sprawled across the city's landscape. Underneath all this is fertile land where some of the world's most bounteous orchards once grew.

This West Coast multiethnic melting pot has excellent restaurants scattered throughout. While sights are few, the city is a good pit stop on the way south to Santa Cruz and Monterey or north to San Francisco.

TOP TIP

Drive 9 miles northwest of downtown San Jose to the tiny old village of Alviso, which is in the wetlands at the south end of the bay. This is big-sky country and there are hikes galore across the trails of the Don Edwards San Francisco Bay National Wildlife Refuge.

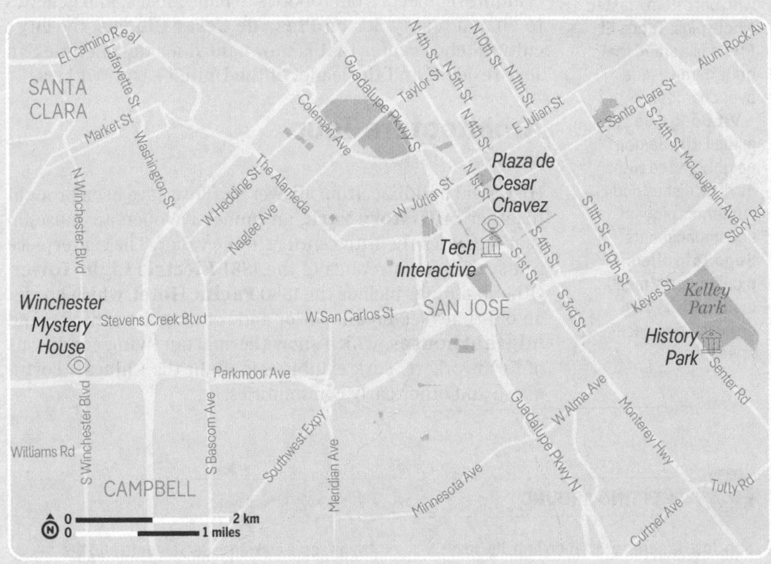

SAN JOSE'S DIVERSE FOOD SCENE

Fab places to eat include **Original Joe's**, a downtown institution with an Italian accent serving casual meals including sublime burgers. In Japantown, **Gombei** serves Japanese comfort food. Close by, **Shuei-Do Manju Shop** is beloved for its house-made *mochi* (rice-based pastries).

Luna Mexican Kitchen, along The Alameda, brings a farm-to-table ethos to sophisticated Mexican fare. At the other end of the budget, the **Tacos El Lider** food truck serves renowned tacos made with pork from roasted whole pigs. **Tacos El Plebe** is a stand that grills carne asada over charcoal.

Vịt Đồng Quê stars in the Little Saigon neighborhood with its duck dishes and authentic, piquant accompaniments. **Sogo Tofu** offers picnic-worthy meals made with its own organic Taiwanese-style tofu.

Winchester Mystery House

Mysteries & Histories

SAN JOSE'S TOP SIGHTS

The prime San Jose attraction is also the strangest: **Winchester Mystery House** is a ridiculous yet fascinating and elaborate Victorian mansion filled with 160 mostly non-utilitarian rooms with dead-end hallways and a staircase that runs up to a ceiling. It was the obsession of Sarah Winchester, who seemingly couldn't live without constant hammering. Guided tours cover the basics and previously little-seen corners.

Tech Interactive is an excellent technology museum that examines subjects from robotics to biofeedback, and genetics to virtual reality. It's on **Plaza de Cesar Chavez**, the city's cultural civic center that is now named for the onetime San Jose resident and the leader of the United Farm Workers.

Architecture Tour

WALK INTO THE PAST

Historical buildings from all over San Jose have been brought together in **History Park**, an immersive open-air museum that recreates the 19th century in the valley. The centerpiece is a scaled-down replica of the 1881 **Electric Light Tower**. Other buildings include the 1880 **Pacific Hotel**, which houses an old-timey ice-cream parlor and rotating art exhibits, and **migrant houses**, which show the spartan living conditions of farmworkers. Park exhibits highlight the Chinese, Portuguese and other early communities.

GETTING AROUND

San Jose is a transportation hub. Its busy airport has international and domestic flights and is a good alternative to San Francisco's. Caltrain offers excellent service up the Peninsula to San Francisco. Amtrak regional trains serve Oakland, Sacramento and the Central Valley. Amtrak's wonderful long-distance *Coast Starlight* runs north to Seattle and south to LA.

HALF MOON BAY

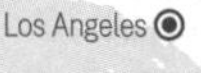

Home to a long coastline, mild weather and Mavericks, one of the biggest and scariest surf breaks on the planet, Half Moon Bay and neighboring Miramar and El Granada are prime real estate.

The Ohlone people lived here for thousands of years before Spanish missionaries set up shop in the late 1700s; it was developed as a beach resort in the early 1900s. Today, it's the main coastal town between San Francisco (29 miles north) and Santa Cruz (49 miles south).

Although the shallowness of the bay means it should really be called Quarter Moon Bay, the long stretches of sandy beach and coastal bluffs attract surfers, hikers and active-minded weekenders. The small downtown is architecturally historic and has enough interesting shops and cafes to make it worth a stroll.

Much development is strung out along Hwy 1. Note that this is one of the foggiest places in Northern California – bring layers.

TOP TIP

Mavericks is an intense surf break that became world famous thanks to arresting videos beginning from the 1990s – waves here can top 60ft after storms. A surf competition was held here sporadically until 2016. To see the action, take binoculars and hike around Pillar Point west of the namesake harbor.

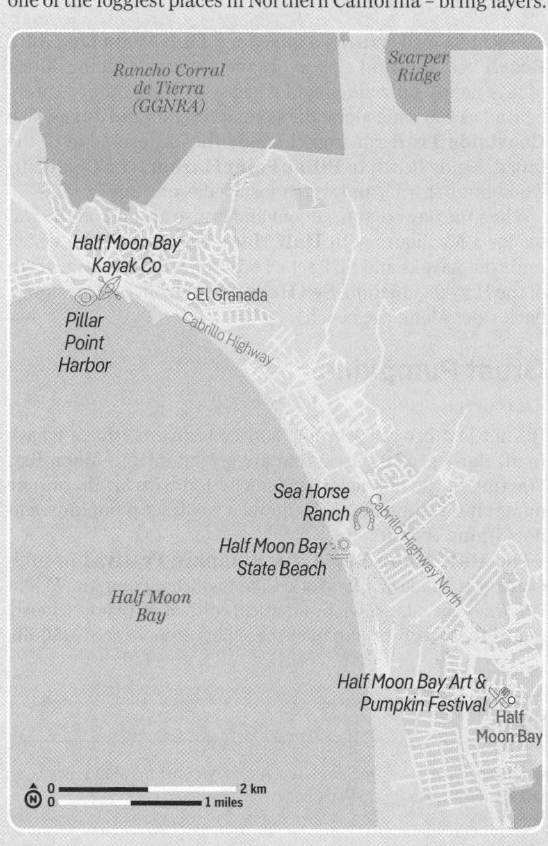

GREAT EATING & DRINKING IN HALF MOON BAY

Seafood stars at several Half Moon Bay waterfront restaurants, each serving clam chowder and Bay Area standards like Louie salads and Dungeness crab sandwiches. **Barbara's Fishtrap** is an old-school joint at Pillar Point Harbor. Nearby, **Sam's Chowder House** causes Hwy 1 traffic backups and serves a fine lobster roll.

Also at the harbor, **Hop Dogma Brewing Co** serves tasty brews. It's one of several fab drinking spots here serving great food, including **Jettywave Distillery** and **Old Princeton Landing Public House and Grill**.

In town, **Moonside Bakery & Cafe** knows how to make a croissant and is a top-end diner for breakfast and lunch. **Dad's Luncheonette** on Hwy 1 serves remarkably creative hamburgers and specials.

BTEIMAGES/SHUTTERSTOCK ©

Half Moon Bay pumpkins

Swim, Hike, Kayak & Ride Along the Coast

HIT THE BEACH

Crescent-shaped and over 4 miles long, **Half Moon Bay State Beach** is a beautiful ribbon of sand along the Pacific. Much of it is nearly untrodden and it's easy to leave other visitors behind as you walk along the sandstone cliffs and dunes. The **Coastside Trail** runs north along the eastern edge of the broad, sandy beach to **Pillar Point Harbor**. Look for driftwood after storms and watch for whales offshore.

When the bay is calm, get out and cruise around on the water for a few hours with **Half Moon Bay Kayak Co**, which rents out kayaks and SUP sets. Located just over a mile north of the Hwy 92 junction, **Sea Horse Ranch** offers daily horseback rides along the beach.

Great Pumpkins

HALLOWEEN HIJINKS

It's not just brussels sprouts and houseplants (that's what's in all those greenhouses) that are grown in Half Moon Bay. Starting in the fall, fields become dotted with bright orange pumpkins. Leading up to Halloween you'll see pumpkins vendors lining Hwy 1.

The **Half Moon Bay Art & Pumpkin Festival** in mid-October is famous for its World Championship Pumpkin Weigh-Off, where beasts grown by fanatical cultivators (who zealously guard their secrets) can bust the scales at more than 2500lb.

GETTING AROUND

SamTrans provides useful local bus services, including to the Caltrain Hillsdale train station in San Mateo. Another route runs along Hwy 1 to Pacifica.

Beyond Half Moon Bay

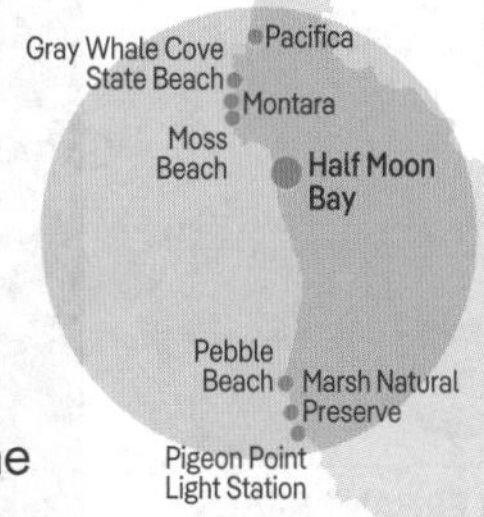

Gray Whale Cove State Beach
Pacifica
Montara
Moss Beach
Half Moon Bay
Pebble Beach
Marsh Natural Preserve
Pigeon Point Light Station

One of the California's highlights, the famous drive on Hwy 1 south from San Francisco is one of the state's unmissable pleasures.

The 70-mile stretch of coastal Hwy 1 from San Francisco to Santa Cruz is one of California's most bewitching oceanside jaunts. Outside of Half Moon Bay, it's a sinuous ribbon of road, passing beach after beach. From Pacifica to the end of San Mateo County is 41 miles; just enjoying this stretch can easily fill an entire day, even before you reach Davenport and the splendors of Santa Cruz County.

Besides the easily accessed beaches alongside Hwy 1, there are countless others hidden from view. If you see a string of vehicles with surfboard racks parked roadside, you'll find a trail across the fields leading to some impossibly lovely cove reached by an often perilous cliffside trail.

TOP TIP

Hwy 1 is dotted with seasonal produce stands and full-time vendors of locally produced goods such as wine and fruit pies.

Fitzgerald Marine Reserve (p149)

ELEPHANT SEALS ON THE BEACH

Near the Santa Cruz County line, **Año Nuevo State Natural Reserve** is home base for one of the world's largest breeding colonies of northern elephant seals. Up to 10,000 boisterous beasts breed, give birth, duke it out and snooze year-round along this shore.

Protected after nearly being hunted to extinction, elephant seals returned to Año Nuevo Beach in 1955. During the birthing time from mid-December to the end of March (peak season), visitors are only permitted access to the reserve on heavily booked guided tours. For the rest of the year the 3- to 4-mile round-trip sandy hike to the beach is self-guided.

BERKAN SARIDILEK/SHUTTERSTOCK ©

Pigeon Point Light Station

Laid-Back Beach Town & Cliff Trail

SURFING, HIKING AND CYCLING

The lazy beach town of **Pacifica**, just 15 miles south of downtown San Francisco and 20 minutes by car north of Half Moon Bay, signals the end of the city's urban sprawl and the start of the wild Pacific coastline. Pacifica is not particularly interesting; its real claim to fame is as the gateway to the spectacular run south of Hwy 1.

Pacifica State Beach is long, scenic and gets pounded by surfable waves (gear rental is available nearby at **Nor-Cal Surf Shop**).

Immediately south of Pacifica is the **Devil's Slide**, a gorgeous coastal cliff area now bypassed by a tunnel. Hikers and cyclists cruise along the **Devil's Slide Coastal Trail**, a paved 1.3-mile section of the old highway. Parking areas perch above the sheer, filigreed cliffs, with waves crashing below and pelicans flying overhead.

WHAT TO SEE INLAND FROM HWY 1

Skyline Blvd
Follows the ridge of the Santa Cruz Mountains for vistas from the ocean to the San Francisco Bay.

Hwy 84
Runs for 28 curvaceous miles between Hwy 1 and Palo Alto, passing parks, redwoods and open lands.

Butano State Park
Witness nature's recovery from the 2020 wildfires in a park webbed with hiking trails.

Coastal Villages on Wildlife-Rich Beaches

RUMRUNNERS AND STARFISH

Montara and **Moss Beach**, both only 10 minutes by car from Half Moon Bay, are tiny hamlets punctuating a stretch of coast dotted by cliffs and sand. Just north, **Gray Whale Cove State Beach** is one of the coast's many popular clothing-optional beaches.

At Moss Beach, **Fitzgerald Marine Reserve** protects tide pools teeming with sea life such as colorful starfish, crabs and urchins. A small visitor center provides an introduction to the wealth of life along the coast.

Overlooking the cove where bootleggers used to unload Prohibition-era liquor, the heated ocean-view deck of the **Moss Beach Distillery** is perfectly positioned to catch sunset.

Nature Preserve & Jade-Pebble Beach

LUSH WETLANDS AND GEM-LIKE ROCKS

Located about 20 minutes's drive south of Half Moon Bay, **Marsh Natural Preserve** is on the inland side of Hwy 1, at the turn for Pescadero. A tangle of trails winds through these verdant wetlands. Adjacent **Pescadero State Beach** features a long strand (keep an eye out for seals) that's backed by dunes and interrupted by rocky tide pools.

Pebble Beach is part of **Bean Hollow State Beach**. The shore is awash with bite-sized eye candy of agate, jade and carnelian. The eroded sandstone cliffs have shapes that Antoni Gaudí would've been envious of.

Lovely Lighthouse & Best Hostel Ever

BEAUTIFUL BEACON, WHALES OFFSHORE

Occupying a small outcrop, the 115ft-high **Pigeon Point Light Station** (1872) is one of the West Coast's tallest lighthouses. It's 30 minutes by car from Half Moon Bay. The bluff is a prime spot for spotting gray whales in winter. One of this coast's rare places to stay is also the most coveted: the **HI Pigeon Point Lighthouse** hostel. Book well ahead and don't miss the hot tub.

South of the lighthouse, **Gazos Creek State Beach** has a long series of sandy expanses, where untrodden sand plus blustery wind and ceaseless waves are the norm. Note how the devastating 2020 fires in the Santa Cruz Mountains came right down to Hwy 1 and crossed over to the ocean's edge.

SEA BREEZES & ARTICHOKES IN PESCADERO

A foggy speck of coastal crossroads between Half Moon Bay and Santa Cruz, 19th-century Pescadero is 2 miles inland from Hwy 1. Start at **Harley Farms Goat Dairy**, where you can get close to the cloven-hoofed sources of the delicious soft cheese that's for sale along with other deli items. In town, **Duarte's Tavern** is always thronged by happy masses feasting on crab cioppino, cream of artichoke soup and olallieberry pie; reserve a table in advance. Across the street, **Arcangeli Grocery Company** is a prime purveyor of picnics for the beach, famed for its hot-from-the-oven stuffed artichoke-herb bread, a doughy loaf made with white flour that some enjoy more than others.

GETTING AROUND

SamTrans buses link Pacifica to the Daly City BART station. They also cover Hwy 1 south to Half Moon Bay. Further south, you'll need your own vehicle to follow the coast. Experienced cyclists brave the narrow shoulders of Hwy 1 from Pacifica to Santa Cruz.

Above: Napa Valley Wine Train (p158); Right: Chardonnay in Carneros (p162)

THE MAIN AREAS

NAPA
Wine epicenter. **p156**

ST HELENA
Quaint northern Napa Valley hub. **p165**

SONOMA
History-rich town. **p173**

PETALUMA
Historic downtown with gastronomic flair. **p180**

NAPA & SONOMA WINE COUNTRY

GLORIOUS VINEYARDS AND UNIQUE TOWNS

California's premier wine valleys sparkle with a constellation of cool communities. Iconic landscapes blend fantastic food and wine plus a hefty dash of local flair.

In a single day in Napa Valley, you can wallow in volcanic mud in Calistoga, learn how to make roux in St Helena and spend a wild night among giraffes on a Wine Country safari. That's after tasting some of the world's best vintages. Here, organic family wineries dare to make wines besides classic cabernets, while bicyclists commuting between former stagecoach stops wave hello to sous-chefs weeding organic kitchen gardens to seed farm-to-table menus.

Head west to Sonoma County to wander thousand-year-old redwoods, pop open a bottle of bubbly with a saber in Healdsburg and meet the budding talent behind farm-to-spliff dispensaries in Sebastopol. The region remains a magnet for free spirits. Adventure author Jack London attracted like-minded bohemians to Sonoma Valley while romantics and rebels roamed the Russian River Valley, frolicking in the redwoods and establishing Guerneville as a pioneering LGBTIQ+ resort.

Good living seems to come naturally here, but people work hard to make that possible. Napa and Sonoma Counties have faced firestorms, earthquakes, droughts and floods. But after each disaster, America's fanciest stretch of farmland rebounds. Today, these verdant valleys are rich with preserved parklands, pioneering regenerative agriculture and close-knit networks of first responders, small business owners and hospitality workers. So raise a toast to Napa and Sonoma: living proof that with exceptional dedication and a splash of liquid courage, California dreams really do come true.

SANTA ROSA
Interesting Sonoma County capital. **p183**

SEBASTOPOL
Artsy bohemian hangout. **p186**

RUSSIAN RIVER VALLEY
Wine and river playground. **p193**

HEALDSBURG
Laid-back chic, wine, art and food. **p197**

Find Your Way

Napa and Sonoma Counties and their myriad smaller valleys are surprisingly vast. We've picked the places that capture their history, culture and natural landscape, and each of them offers a chance to taste your own Wine Country.

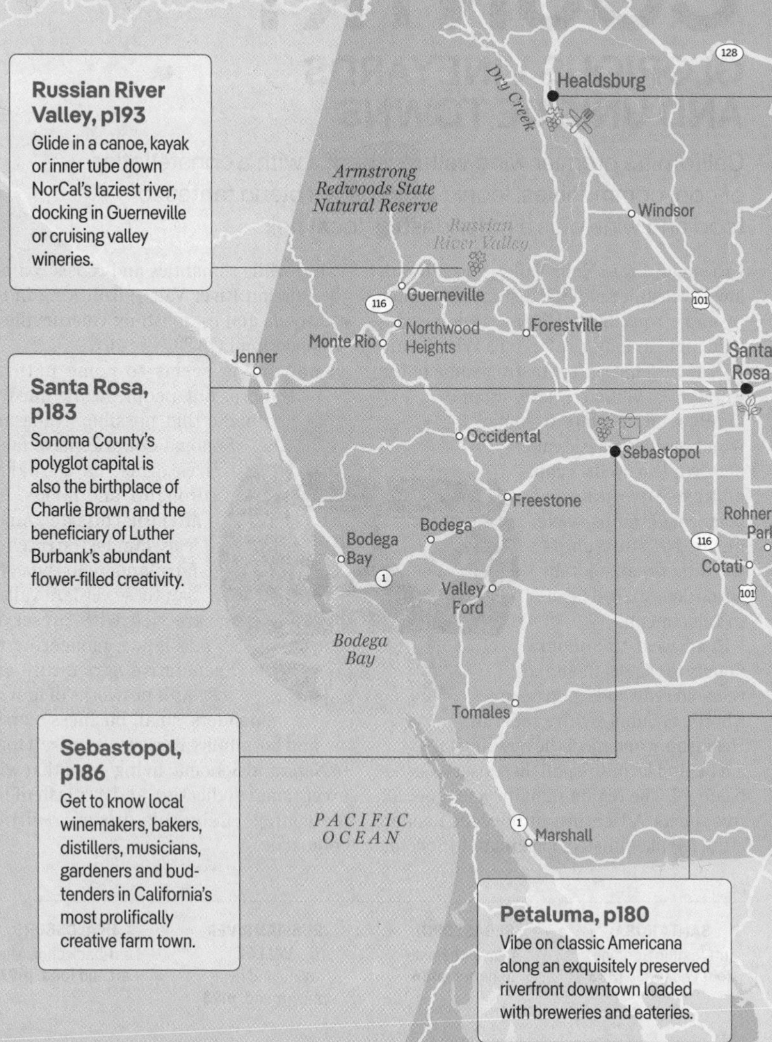

Russian River Valley, p193
Glide in a canoe, kayak or inner tube down NorCal's laziest river, docking in Guerneville or cruising valley wineries.

Santa Rosa, p183
Sonoma County's polyglot capital is also the birthplace of Charlie Brown and the beneficiary of Luther Burbank's abundant flower-filled creativity.

Sebastopol, p186
Get to know local winemakers, bakers, distillers, musicians, gardeners and bud-tenders in California's most prolifically creative farm town.

Petaluma, p180
Vibe on classic Americana along an exquisitely preserved riverfront downtown loaded with breweries and eateries.

Healdsburg, p197

Wine-taste and boutique-browse your way around the plaza before cycling to nearby vineyards or debating the merits of all the dinner restaurants.

St Helena, p165

This charming town is a treat in its own right, with a historic center, but it's also a hub for northern Napa Valley vineyards.

Napa River

29

Napa

Sonoma

Petaluma

116

12

121

101

San Antonio

121

Napa, p156

Wine and dine like a rock star, with California's most prized reds, world-acclaimed chefs' tasting menus, and restorative brunches at five-star resorts.

Sonoma, p173

Stroll beneath palm trees along the adobe-lined plaza into California's past. Then seek sustenance at myriad restaurants and tasting rooms.

CAR

Hitting the road is the best way to explore Wine Country. This way you can discover its secluded valleys and cool-cat towns, and tour the wineries scattered across the countryside. Don't drive buzzed, though – book a tour or a rideshare instead.

TRAIN

Sonoma-Marin Area Rail Transit (SMART) offers rail services in Sonoma and Marin Counties from the Sonoma County Airport to downtown San Rafael. The Napa Valley Wine Train takes you from downtown Napa to St Helena and back in tourist coaches.

BICYCLE

Wine Country is a dream for cyclists. For many, the highlight of a California trip is the sun-dappled, winery-lined roads and trails linking valley wineries. They're scenic, mostly flat, and easy enough for beginners.

N 0 — 20 km
0 — 10 miles

Plan Your Time

Go with the flow in Wine Country: stroll small towns or cycle to sun-drenched vineyards before having a siesta and a meal that defines 'farm-to-table.' Or venture to the coast for riverfront redwoods and rugged oceanscapes.

JAMIE PHAM/ALAMY ©

Cuvaison Winery (p162)

Short on Time

● If you're an oenophile new to the region, then Napa's where you have to head. Start at town tasting rooms like **Gamling & McDuck** (p158) before roaming out to vineyards in **Carneros** (p162), where vines meet marshland and the Bay beyond. Pick your poison: high-end art at **Donum Estate** (p163) or **Hess Pearsson Estates** (p162), or relaxed family vineyards at **Robledo** (p162) and killer views at **Cuvaison Winery** (p162).

● North up the valley, the tastings continue, and if you've reserved well in advance, dine in **Yountville** (p164); otherwise, play it casually in **St Helena** (p165) or **Calistoga** (p170) – then wash all your cares away with a **hot-springs soak** (p171).

Seasonal Highlights

Make reservations in restaurants and hotels in summer. Hotel rates jump during September and October's grape-crushing season. Many operations are diminished on winter weekdays.

MARCH

Cinephiles will delight in the five-day **Sonoma Valley Film Festival**, which has been running for over 20 years.

MAY

Napa's three-day **BottleRock** (p160) festival of music, food and wine attracts marquee names with intergenerational appeal.

JULY

Peak season for floating the Russian River brings the **Monte Rio Variety Show**, with unannounced celebrity guests like Conan O'Brien.

ARAYA DIAZ/GETTY IMAGES FOR BILLI PRODUCTIONS LTD. ©; STERLING MUNKSGARD/SHUTTERSTOCK ©;VIVL/SHUTTERSTOCK ©

Three Days to Explore

- Continue your Wine Country adventure with coffee and a look inside the adobe mission on **Sonoma's plaza** (p174). Then meander along the valley's vine-lined roads, stopping frequently for tastings at spots like **Gundlach-Bundschu** (p176). Explore **Bartholomew Estate** (p176), an oak-dotted winery and preserve, then channel *The Call of the Wild* at **Jack London State Historic Park** (p179).

- Get a teeny taste of western Sonoma County, which makes Napa and Sonoma look uptight by comparison. Grab lunch in Santa Rosa at **Mitote Food Park** (p185) before making a beeline for **Sebastopol** (p186). Tour organic farms before oysters and chilled wine at **Rocker Oysterfeller's** (p191) in Valley Ford.

If You Have More Time

- Settle in for a while in the Russian River area where you can combine **a float on the river** (p195) with mescal cocktails at **El Barrio** (p195) in Guerneville or seafood on the coast at **River's End** (p195) in Jenner or at Bodega Bay. Time your trip for Occidental's **Friday Farmers Market** (p191) and dance outside at dusk.

- Wine-taste your way up **Westside Rd** (p196) to **Healdsburg** (p197). If it's a Tuesday or Saturday morning, Healdsburg's abundant **farmers market** (p199) is a must for wares well beyond food, or on a mid-year's Tuesday afternoon, plan to picnic at a **free summer concert** (p199) on the plaza.

AUGUST

High summer sees Guerneville's **Lazy Bear Week** (p195) and Sebastopol's **Gravenstein Apple Fair** (p189) lighting up Sonoma County.

SEPTEMBER

The grape crush begins along with **Women's Weekend** (p195), when queer women and trans folx bring the party to Guerneville.

OCTOBER

America's biggest wine competition, **Sonoma Harvest Fair**, pairs well with the **Sonoma County Art Trails** open studio tours.

NOVEMBER

During **Wine & Food Affair** (p197) let your taste buds be your guide to 100 Sonoma County wineries offering a featured dish and wine pairing.

NAPA

Your first stop in Napa may be the only one you need for a dream Wine Country getaway. With laid-back downtown tasting rooms, historic music halls featuring major musicians, and Oxbow Public Market offering affordable gourmet fare, downtown Napa is where Napans come to relax.

Napa's riverbank parks are part of the town's sustainable 'living river' design to manage seasonal floods. And its lush hillsides kick off the steady carpet of wineries running straight up the valley.

It's hard to believe that in 2014 this was the epicenter of a magnitude 6.0 earthquake, causing $1 billion in damage. While Napa was rebuilding, the 2017, 2019 and 2020 fires hit – and when winter rains finally came, so did Napa River floods. Yet through it all Napa kept rebuilding, steadily and thoughtfully, and Napa remains the sweet spot where wine flows and conversation meanders, just like the Napa River.

TOP TIP

Skyline Wilderness Park blooms with springtime wildflowers and California perennials in its Martha Walker Native Plant Habitat. There's also over 25 miles of hiking and mountain-biking trails, an archery range and disc-golf course. Picnicking with wine is allowed, as is camping with both tents and RVs.

Napa

4KODIAK/GETTY IMAGES ©

SIGHTS
1 1st St

ACTIVITIES, COURSES & TOURS
2 Culinary Institute of America at Copia
3 Napa Valley Gondola
4 Napa Valley Wine Train

EATING
5 Oxbow Public Market
6 The Dutch Door
7 Winston's

DRINKING & NIGHTLIFE
8 Brown Downtown
9 Contimo Provisions
10 Gamling & McDuck
11 Krupp Brothers Downtown Tasting Room
12 Outland
13 Rebel Vinters
14 Trade Brewing
15 Vintners' Collective

ENTERTAINMENT
16 Napa Valley Opera House

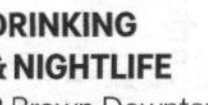

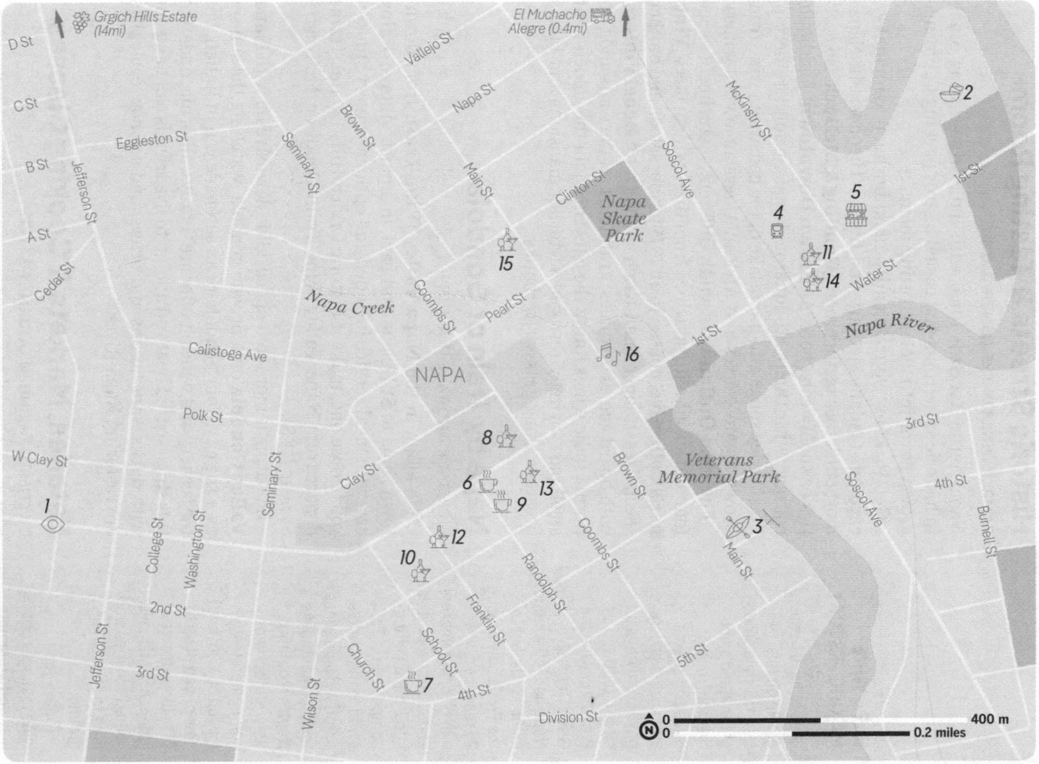

FOR GASTRONOMES

You really can't beat California for food and wine. To learn more about the state's **food scene**, see p44.

Historic Streets & Tasting Rooms

SAMPLE WINES IN THE CENTRAL CITY

Napa's buzzy **1st St** is lined with indie wine-tasting rooms in historic storefronts and casual bistros packing California-grown flavor into globe-trotting menus.

Get to know your friendly neighborhood winemaker/cartoonist Adam McClary and his cat Theodosia in Napa's most punk-rock tasting room, **Gamling & McDuck**. No neckties or snooty cabs here. At **Brown Downtown**, find liquid courage with Duppy Conqueror, Jamaican folklore hero of Bob Marley songs and namesake of the epic white wine from Brown Estate, Napa's first African American–owned winery.

Flights at **Outland** are wildly different, featuring between four and six all-natural wines from three winemakers. **Vintner's Collective**, housed in an 1875 former saloon and brothel, specializes in super small-batch wines. Or hit **Rebel Vinters**, with board games on tables, graffiti art on the walls and California indie wines lining the bar. Then join the golden-hour stroll past lovingly restored Victorian mansions and take a breather along grassy riverbanks.

NAPA WINE-MAKING HISTORY

Grapes have been grown on this 5-by-35-mile strip of farmland since the gold rush. But earthquakes and juice-sucking phylloxera bugs struck, followed by Prohibition and the Great Depression. Napa had 140 wineries in the 1890s, but by the 1960s only around 25 remained.

In 1976, winemakers entered a few bottles into a blind tasting competition in Paris – and to the world's surprise, Napa wines took top honors. As Napa's reputation grew, global wine conglomerates moved in. With land now priced at up to $1 million an acre, independent, family-owned wineries work hard to stand their ground.

Today, Napa wine tasting is not just world famous but it also allows you to get ahold of many vintages only available on-site.

Napa by Train or Gondola

KICK BACK AND TAKE IT ALL IN

Chug along in the **Napa Valley Wine Train** from downtown Napa to St Helena and back in a plush vintage dining car, with meal service included and optional winery stops (if you choose one, make it historic Grgich Hills Estate). Trains depart from Napa Valley Wine Train Depot on McKinstry St near 1st St.

If floating is more your speed, glide downstream with **Napa Valley Gondola** on a private gondola, watching the sun set over the city. Your gondolier can serenade you in Italian, but the scenery and wine on offer are totally California, dude. On this single-oared boat you and up to five friends can hang out with ducks, spot herons and otters, and see how ecologists are restoring Napa River.

Eateries, Markets & Cooking Classes

DAYTIME GRAZING IN GOURMET STYLE

Deliciousness abounds in Napa. Start the day at **Winston's** for amazing baked goods and stick-to-your-ribs breakfast sandwiches with a happy brunching crowd. Midday is prime for bodacious sandwiches at **Contimo Provisions** (they also make killer biscuit sandwiches) or all-organic casual food at **The Dutch Door**. If tacos are your jam, head for out-of-the-

WHERE TO FINE-DINE IN NAPA

Compline
Cozy, unpretentious bistro/wine bar offering a short, seasonal menu of hearty dishes. **$$$**

Kenzo Napa
Michelin-starred Japanese magic paired with top wine and sake in chic minimalist harmony. **$$$**

Bistro Don Giovanni
With copper pans, garden fountains and black-vested waiters, the Don ladles on Italian charm. **$$$**

Wine tasting in Napa

way taco truck **El Muchacho Alegre**, parked at 751 Jackson St in a residential neighborhood north of the center.

But why commit to just one dining establishment when you could graze at a dozen of Napa's finest? At the **Oxbow Public Market**, assemble the meal of your California dreams with all-star dishes – perhaps Hog Island Oyster Co oysters mignonette, C Casa duck-confit tacos and Eiko's *hamachi* sushi bonbons with Fieldwork Brewing Company farmhouse ale, followed by Ritual Coffee espresso. Or if it's breakfast time, don't miss Model Bakery's treats.

Also in the Oxbow area, downtown Napa's **Culinary Institute of America at Copia** offers drop-in cooking classes, demos, documentaries and star-chef panels too spicy for TV. Hit the free **Chuck Williams Culinary Arts Museum** upstairs, buy Marketplace gadgets and signed cookbooks downstairs, or have meal at the **Grove**.

If you'd like to throw in a little wine and beer tasting while you're in the Oxbow area, **Krupp Brothers Downtown Tasting Room** and **Trade Brewing** are just across the street from each other.

WINE-TASTING TIPS

Swirl, sniff and swish. Swirl your wine in the glass to release aromas, then have a good sniff to excite your salivary glands. Take a small sip and swish it around your mouth so all your taste buds get in on the action.

Sip and spit. If you love what you're tasting, you'll want to try plenty – and that means pacing yourself. It's fair game to spit out your last sip, or even pour leftovers into the spittoon (aka 'chuck bucket').

Remember to eat. Some wineries serve bites; otherwise snack in between.

Consider joining wine clubs carefully. Your pourer may suggest joining their wine club (to buy discounted bottles annually). Don't feel pressured, especially if you're tipsy and fuzzy on the details.

WINERIES NEAR CENTRAL NAPA

Palmaz
Julio and Amalia Palmaz produce Napa's most buzzworthy wines on their 600-acre hillside estate.

Matthiasson Winery
Get back to nature at this sustainable winery, a short drive away on Napa's western low slopes.

Hendry
Joyful, knowledgeable wine aficionados make this low-key winery a perennial favorite.

BEST PLACES TO STAY IN NAPA

Blackbird Inn
Relax in a ruggedly handsome 1902 California Craftsman cottage with eight plush rooms. $$$

Hennessey House
Star in your own romantic costume drama at this lovely lavender Victorian mansion packed with modern comforts. $$

Archer
Live like a vintner who's just won Double Gold at downtown Napa's most happening hotel. $$$

Milliken Creek Inn
Enjoy understatedly elegant small-inn charm with boutique-hotel service and Napa indulgence. $$$

AGWILSON/SHUTTERSTOCK ©

BottleRock

Local Live Music & Festivals

GROOVING AND MOVIES

Hitting high notes since 1880, the opulent **Napa Valley Opera House** has survived earthquakes and fires to find its second wind, and is making a late-breaking career shift into jazz. The **BlueNote Napa** calendar features weekend global jazz talent and midweek locals' nights – and the drink menu here puts other clubs to shame, with cult wines and house-brewed craft beer.

Plan to be in Napa in May for breakout-hit three-day music, food and wine festival **BottleRock**, where huge lineups have included marquee names such as Pink, Janelle Monáe, Red Hot Chili Peppers and Blondie. Or celebrate the silver screen at November's star-studded, food-focused **Napa Valley Film Festival**, where movies about food and wine are obvious crowd-pleasers, but the roster includes documentaries and narrative films as well.

GETTING AROUND

Downtown Napa is centrally located in Napa Valley, between scenic Silverado Trail to the east and busy St Helena Hwy/Hwy 29 to the west. The multiuse Napa Valley Vine Trail connects downtown Napa to Yountville.

Napa Valley Vine bus C gets you around downtown Napa; bus 10 gets you from downtown Napa to St Helena and Calistoga. Napa Valley Vine bus 11 links downtown Napa to the Vallejo Ferry Terminal, where ferries run to San Francisco. Alternatively, you can get a rideshare from the Vallejo Ferry Terminal. Express bus 29 connects El Cerrito del Norte BART station to downtown Napa and Calistoga.

Beyond Napa

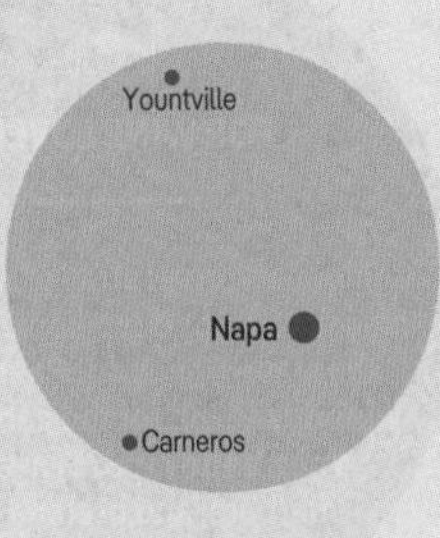

The southern Napa Valley, from Carneros to Yountville, kicks off the region's exquisite wine, art and culinary game in style.

Radiating out from Napa town, the southern stretches of the Napa Valley range from the moist pinot noir coastal vineyards, rimmed by marshes, in Carneros, to fancy-pants Yountville further inland. Wineries abound, more than we can list here. Whether you're in for the day, or have a week to roam, you'll find the best the region has to offer – from excellent vintages, eye-blowing vistas and world-class meals to lonesome country lanes and old-school roadside diners.

It also happens to be an area rich in art collections and installations, so plan ahead a bit to reserve entry at these wineries and make the most of your time.

TOP TIP

Carneros is an AVA (American Viticultural Area) spanning Napa and Sonoma Counties. Though online addresses indicate one county or another, the sights are all in the same vicinity.

Vineyards in Carneros (p162)

Moody Wetlands, Vaunted Vineyards

CARNEROS' EASYGOING DELIGHTS

FOR WINE LOVERS

California's broad array of wine regions means you'll find top tipples all across the state. Check out **Paso Robles' wineries** (p281) for top cabs or **Santa Ynez Valley** (p325) near Santa Barbara, and pretend you're in the movie *Sideways*.

This stretch of bayfront lowlands spanning both Napa and Sonoma Counties is 15 minutes' drive south of Napa. Historically it was shared by Patwin people to the east and Coastal Miwok to the west. Mexican shepherds named it Los Carneros ('The Rams') back in the 1830s – and until recently, sheep had the run of the place. In the 1960s, savvy farmers reckoned that thin-skinned pinot noir grapes might actually prefer the foggy, damp microclimates that made woolly sheep feel right at home. Now preserved wetlands stand alongside the rolling vineyards, making a drive or cycle through this zone an otherworldly jaunt off the Napa beaten path. The **Napa River Bay Trail** loops south of Carneros along the shore.

Take an exquisite break with some of the region's most majestic views at **Cuvaison Winery**, where undulating vineyards join ponds in the distance. Low-key **McKenzie-Mueller Winery** is tucked into the heart of Carneros' vineyards, while **Hudson Napa Valley**, surrounded by vast succulent gardens, beckons with more great views.

Closer to Sonoma, **Robledo** winery was built from the ground up by Reynoldo Robledo, who started in the industry as a farm worker in 1968 and became Sonoma's go-to vineyard expert. His kids run the winery now, and welcome you to estate tastings at the hand-carved bar.

Peckish? Look for the cow on the roof of roadside **Angelo's Wine Country Deli**, south of Carneros. Angelo Ibleto makes fat sandwiches here with smoked meats and *un pizzico d'amore* (a pinch of love). Wrap up with live local music at easygoing **Kivelstadt Cellars & WineGarten**.

CYCLING NAPA VALLEY

What better way to cruise the vineyards than by bike? The **Napa Valley Wine Trail** connects vineyards, wineries, downtown Napa and Yountville via 12.5 miles of walking and cycling paths. The trail is just a piece of an ambitious 47-mile stretch that will eventually connect the Vallejo Ferry Terminal to Calistoga. For now, to bike onward to Calistoga, take tree-lined **Silverado Trail** instead of hot, traffic-heavy Hwy 29. You can rent a bike or book a tour at **Napa Valley Bike Tours** or **Calistoga Bike Shop**.

Art Collections Paired with Wine

FINE ART, SCULPTURE AND WINE TASTING

Climb a winding country road 20 minutes' drive west of Napa up beyond vineyards through oak forests to an ivy-covered hilltop stone winery at **Hess Pearsson Estates**. Here, wine tastings can be paired with California's finest private contemporary-art collection. Thought-provoking installation art starts with Leopoldo Maler's 1974 burning typewriter – a homage to his uncle, a newspaper editor killed by Argentina's

WHERE TO EAT AROUND NAPA

Folktable
Top Chef's Casey Thompson's downhome cosmopolitan food includes truffle hand pies. **$$**

Boon Fly Café
Leisurely weekend brunches with killer eggs Benedict, handmade doughnuts and excellent burgers. **$$**

Lou's Luncheonette
Two words: fried chicken. Oh, and po'boys and burgers too. **$**

di Rosa Center for Contemporary Art

junta. Other highlights include Anselm Kiefer's sculpture of lead shingles from Cologne Cathedral, and Andy Goldsworthy's giant ball of manzanita branches.

Scrap-metal sheep dotting the hillside hint that something unusual is afoot on 217 acres of Carneros countryside at **di Rosa Center for Contemporary Art**. This groundbreaking collection was the personal passion of free-spirited reporter-turned-grape-farmer Rene di Rosa, who hung hyperrealist Robert Bechtle paintings on the ceiling and installed spooky Tony Oursler videos in his cellar. Today, the gatehouse gallery showcases Viola Frey's monumental 1970s ceramic sculpture, David Best's art cars, and works by visiting California artists, while inspiration overflows into the **Sculpture Meadow**.

Craving some Ai Weiwei with your chardonnay? The jaw-dropping contemporary-art collection at nearby **Donum Estate** is surrounded by lavender fields, vineyards and an organic farm. Take the tour, glass of chardonnay in hand, roaming Yayoi Kusama's polka-dotted pumpkin, Gao Weigang's brass-tube maze and Keith Haring's embracing figures.

If you're an architecture buff, head north to **Quixote Winery** – that gold-leafed onion dome sprouting from the grassy knoll is the work of Austrian eco-architect Friedensreich Hundertwasser, whose signature crayon-colored ceramic pillars frame broken-tile mosaic walls.

WINERY BOOKING TIPS

Almost all of the wineries in Napa and Sonoma are reservation-based, so book ahead. They do accept walk-ins, though, when they have an open spot, and the best way to figure that out is as follows.

Napa Valley Welcome Center
Contact them to find last-minute openings. They sometimes have wine-tasting passes (ask for passes at your hotel, too).

Tock
Check this online service, which lists many wineries and shows availability.

Telephoning
The old-fashioned method still works and is worth trying – you might get lucky!

If you don't feel like driving, book a ride with **Designated Drivers Napa Sonoma**, or a wine tour with **Active Wine Adventures**, **Platypus Wine Tours**, **Laces and Limos** or **Beau Wine Tours**.

WHERE TO STAY AROUND NAPA

Windhaven Cottage
Live the Wine Country life in a wooden cottage surrounded by edible gardens and vineyard views. **$$**

Poetry Inn
Contemporary inn with staggering views over Stag's Leap vineyards. Recite sonnets on your balcony. **$$$**

Petit Logis
Wake to the aroma of croissants from next-door Bouchon Bakery in Yountville. **$$**

LOVELY PICNIC SPOTS

Strict zoning laws make it tricky to find places to picnic legally in Napa. If you're heading to a winery, call ahead to see if picnicking is allowed (it's customary to buy a bottle of your host's wine if it is). If you don't finish your wine, stash it in the trunk – California law forbids driving with an uncorked bottle in the car.

Here's a short list of prime picnic spots, in south-north order: **Skyline Wilderness Park**, **French Laundry Gardens**, **Pride Mountain** and **Old Faithful Geyser**.

ARNIEBY/SHUTTERSTOCK ©

Bouchon Bakery, Yountville

Culinary All-Stars

TWEE YOUNTVILLE'S GASTRONOMIC EXPLOSION

Planets and Michelin stars are mysteriously aligned over **Yountville**, a tiny Western stagecoach stop 20 minutes' drive north of Napa that's been transformed into a global dining destination. It sounds like an urban legend – until you take a stroll down Yountville's quiet, tree-lined Washington St.

Say hey to interns weeding French Laundry's herb gardens and trainee sommeliers grabbing lunch at **Tacos Garcia**. You've just met the talents behind a thousand meals of a lifetime each week – and you can probably buy them a beer later. **French Laundry** itself dazzles through nine opulent courses (if you can get a reservation), but you can also grab to go at **Bouchon Bakery** (just wait in the hefty line), or both sup and stay over at trendy **North Block** in the village center.

For a bit of wine tasting, head across the valley floor to a batch of excellent wineries: **Robert Sinskey Vineyards**, **Antica Napa Valley**, **Shafer Vineyards** and **Regusci Winery**.

GETTING AROUND

Summer and fall weekend traffic crawls, especially on Hwy 29 between downtown Napa and St Helena at around 5pm, when wineries close. If you're driving, Carneros is about 15 minutes from downtown Napa, 10 minutes from downtown Sonoma and an hour from San Francisco. For scenic drives from Yountville, follow Silverado Trail north, or take Mt Veeder Rd through pristine countryside west of Yountville. The Napa Valley Vine bus doesn't stop in Yountville proper but across Hwy 29 at the Veteran's Home.

ST HELENA

St Helena
San Francisco
Los Angeles

Even people with places to go and wine to drink can't resist a closer look at St Helena (pronounced ha-LEE-na). One or two blocks down Main St, cars suddenly swerve to the curb so that passengers can photograph this road that looks exactly like a Western movie set. But this scene is the real deal: three blocks of Main St are a designated National Historic District, covering 160 years of California history – including the 1913 Cameo Cinema, one of the oldest movie theaters still in operation in America.

Today, Main St is lined with restaurants, gourmet shops and tasting rooms. Further up the street, the 1889 Greystone Cellars château is home to the Culinary Institute of America. If you're thirsty, you're in luck: there's more than an acre of wine grapes per resident in St Helena.

TOP TIP

St Helena is packed with fabulous restaurants and loaded with nearby wineries where you'll need reservations. If you haven't booked, you can self-cater at the local Sunshine Foods market or Napa Valley Olive Oil Company. St Helena Welcome Center has information and lodging assistance and can help with winery bookings.

St Helena

CHARLES O'REAR/GETTY IMAGES ©

ST HELENA

ACTIVITIES, COURSES & TOURS
1 Culinary Institute of America

SLEEPING
2 Wydown Hotel

EATING
3 Charter Oak
4 Gott's Roadside
5 Model Bakery
6 WF Giugni & Son

SHOPPING
7 Napa Valley Olive Oil Company

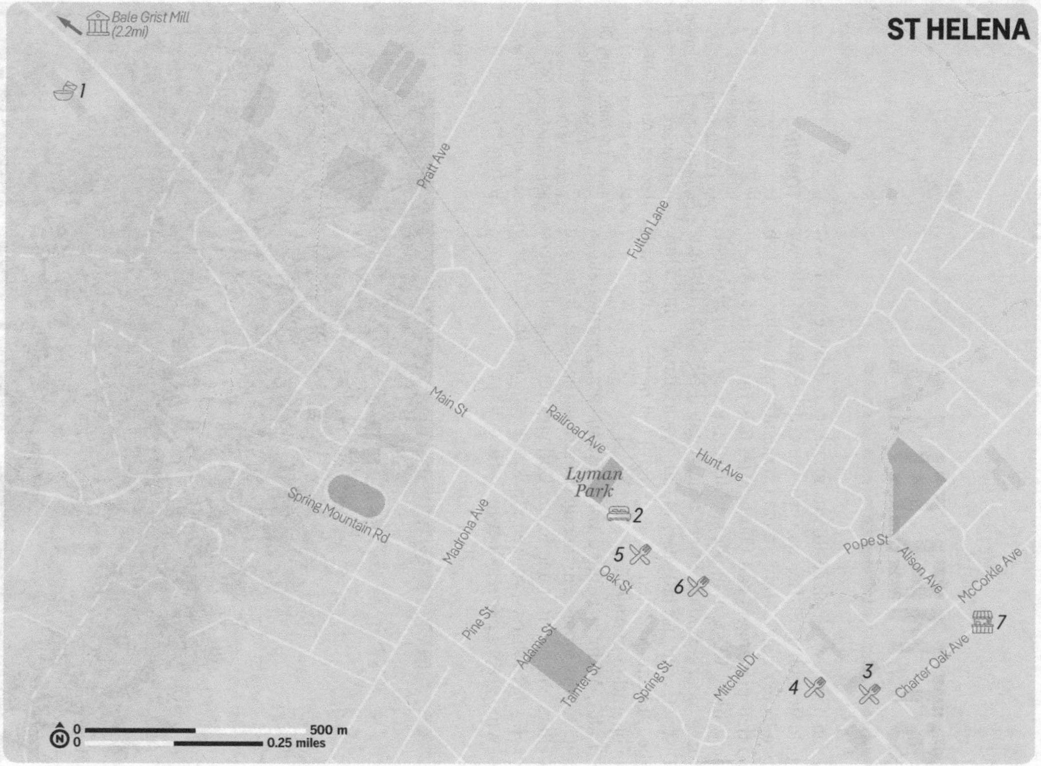

Bale Grist Mill (2.2mi)
Pratt Ave
Fulton Lane
Main St
Railroad Ave
Hunt Ave
Lyman Park
Spring Mountain Rd
Madrona Ave
Oak St
Pope St
Alison Ave
McCorkle Ave
Pine St
Adams St
Tainter St
Spring St
Mitchell Dr
Charter Oak Ave
0 500 m
0 0.25 miles

Culinary Institute of America (p168)

Ballooning over Napa Valley

Stroll Through History with Creature Comforts

ST HELENA'S CHARMING DOWNTOWN

How did one little town get so lucky? From the start, St Helena had two things going for it: true romance and a family of savvy businesswomen. This area was native Wappo land until it was claimed by Spain, and became a territory of Mexico – more specifically, the property of Dona Maria Ygnacia Soberanes, the niece of Mexican commander General Vallejo.

When Maria fell for English Protestant Dr Edward Turner Bale, it caused an uproar. But the couple worked out a deal: Dr Bale became a Mexican citizen and converted to Catholicism, winning over the Vallejo family – and co-ownership of Maria's 28 sq miles of land.

The couple had six children together by 1849, when the news arrived via stagecoach: gold had been discovered in California. Dr Bale headed for the hills during the gold rush, but this time he was out of luck. He died within months, leaving Dona Maria with kids, mining debts and a legal fight to own her own land as a woman – back then this wasn't allowed under US law.

BALLOONING & FLYING IN WINE COUNTRY

If you think Wine Country scenery is breathtaking, wait until you see it from 3000ft up in the air. The biplane and balloon rides here have limited capacity, so book ahead and prepare yourself for a once-in-a-lifetime, adrenaline-rush experience.

Napa Valley's signature hot-air-balloon flights leave early, at around 6am or 7am, when the air is coolest and mists are rising from the vineyards. Many offer a champagne toast or brunch on landing. Call **Balloons Above the Valley**, **Napa Valley Balloons**, or **Aloft**, Napa's most established ballooning outfit.

The **Vintage Aircraft Company** flies over Sonoma in old-school biplanes with an expert pilot who'll do loop the loops on request.

WHERE TO SHOP IN ST HELENA

Woodhouse Chocolates
Graze delectable chocolates handmade by CIA-trained mother-and-daughter team Tracy and Christina Anderson.

New West KnifeWorks
Gleaming, high-performance knives, hand-carved cutting boards and colorful blown-glass olive-oil decanters.

Lolo's Consignment
Forgot a sweater for wine-cellar tastings, or are stilettos slowing your roll through vineyards? Hit Lolo's.

FOR BURGER LOVERS

If you enjoyed Gott's Roadside, check out another quintessential California burger purveyor, **In-N-Out Burger** (p664).

Dona Maria sold off parcels of land that had potential as vineyards, but saved the best for her daughters, giving the **Bale Grist Mill** – still grinding flour today – to Isadora and prime vineyards to Caroline. Romance and business converged again when Caroline married German winemaker Charles Krug. Together they planted vineyards and founded Napa's first commercial winery in 1858. The vineyards are still producing, and now belong to Mondavi.

Whether it's wine or romance that leads you to St Helena, you're in the right place. You can stop by century-old businesses still open today, including jam-packed **Napa Valley Olive Oil Company**, brimming with picnic possibilities, and the excellent **WF Giugni & Son** deli. Get renowned baked goods at Model Bakery, or hit retro burger joint **Gott's Roadside** to sprawl on the lawn and feast on grass-fed beef burgers oozing with Point Reyes blue cheese.

Stay in a historic boutique hotel like **Wydown Hotel**, and enjoy a romantic dinner at **Charter Oak**, a sensational restaurant in an 1878 sherry distillery. When you drink wine here, raise a toast to Dona Maria and Caroline: two women who put that wine in your glass and their hearts into building this irresistibly charming town.

BEST WINERIES NEAR ST HELENA

Tres Sabores
Soulful zin that's the toast of Napa Valley, sauvignon blanc named a *New York Times* top 10 pick and a collectors' favorite rare rosé.

Joseph Phelps
Here's the secret to Phelps' iconic red blend Insignia, made with each season's best grapes since 1974: there are no rules.

Sinegal Estate
Dating from 1879, with lush gardens and a pond, featuring cabernet sauvignon and franc, pinot noir and sauvignon blanc.

Cooking & Wine-Tasting Classes

CELEBRATE FOOD AND WINE

Final exams never tasted as good as the ones served at the renowned **Culinary Institute of America (CIA)** inside an 1889 stone château. Taste A-students' work at the **Gatehouse Restaurant** and bakery-cafe, and educate your palate at weekend wine-tasting classes and cooking demonstrations. Get in on the action with hands-on one-day classes and load up on gourmet school supplies in the gadget- and cookbook-filled shop. For more classes and demos, visit the CIA at Copia in downtown Napa (p159).

GETTING AROUND

Parking in downtown St Helena is next to impossible on summer weekends. Tip: look behind the visitor center. Napa Valley Vine connects St Helena to downtown Napa and Calistoga on bus 10, and provides transit around town on the St Helena Shuttle. To schedule a pickup, call 707-963-3007 or access their website or app during operating hours.

Beyond St Helena

Vaunted vineyards and spritzing hot springs carpet the northern end of the Napa Valley radiating out from St Helena.

Today, when wine aficionados look at this green valley around Oakville and Rutherford, they see red – thanks in no small part to Robert Mondavi, the visionary vintner who knew back in the 1960s that Napa was capable of more than jug wine. His marketing savvy launched Napa's premium reds to cult status. Meanwhile up the road, trailblazing winemaker Mike Grgich made history in 1976 with the first Napa chardonnay to win over French judges in international wine competitions. Further north, Calistoga bubbles with mineral hot springs, and the hills around this part of Napa Valley are studded with excellent wineries – more than you can explore on one trip.

TOP TIP

The best hiking is at Bothe-Napa (with yurts and campsites) and Robert Louis Stevenson State Parks. Find biking information and rentals at Calistoga Bike Shop.

Frog's Leap, Rutherford (p170)

A WINERY FOR EVERY MOOD

Vineyard walks Sutro Wine, Hanzell Vineyards, Donum Estate

Natural and sustainable wines Preston, Porter Creek, Pax Wines

Drinking for a cause Equality Vines

Inspiring views Iron Horse, Bella, Soda Rock Winery

Rebels and trailblazers Merry Edwards, Gundlach-Bundschu, Ceja

Hidden gems Porter-Bass, Carpenter Wine, Emmitt-Scorsone Wines

Food and wine pairings Flowers, Idlewild, Mayo Family Winery

Collector favorites Bohème Wines, Talisman Wines

Wonderful Wineries

ROAM VINEYARDS ACROSS THE VALLEY

Cruise 10 minutes from St Helena to the eastern hills for a spectacular drive along Sage Canyon Rd by **Lake Hennessey** (where you can stop and fish for a bit) to reach oak-topped Pritchard Hill and the thrilling **Chappellet Winery**. Magnificent views vie for your attention as you taste in the barrel-filled vaulted redwood winery itself. Pair it with the much humbler **Nichelini Family Winery**, perched on a dramatic ravine. It was founded in 1890 and has been in the same family ever since. You can continue along to **Lake Berryessa** for more water sports and picnic spots.

On the other side of Lake Hennessy, and also family-owned, **Amizetta Vineyards** has sweeping views back toward the lake and books up – plan ahead to survey the panorama during a personalized wine-tasting experience.

On the valley floor, pop into organically farmed **Ghost Block Estates** or nearby **Frog's Leap**, where you can follow vineyard cats through enchanted gardens, and drink in the views from the loft of an 1884 barn.

Go west, high atop Spring Mountain and smack on the county boundary, to reach family-owned **Pride Mountain Vineyards**. Winemaker Matt Ward and David Orozco's sustainable-farming vineyard team shares credit for their cult-status cabernet and merlot.

Laid-Back Life in the Valley

FROM TACOS TO MICHELIN STARS

Sprawling winery complexes along Hwy 29 dominate the landscape with gilded signs and gated entrances – including **Mondavi** and **Grgich Hills**. You'll recognize the hamlets of **Oakville** and **Rutherford** when you hit the historic 1881 Oakville Grocery, 10 minutes' drive south of St Helena. Turn off Hwy 29 onto cross-valley roads, and you'll find the excellent **La Luna Taqueria & Market**, where the wine-fridge sign says 'Tacos y vinos' – accept the invitation. Offbeat organic wineries abut low-key high-end ho tels hidden in the heart of Napa Valley, such as **Rancho Caymus**, built by pioneering vintner Mary Tilden Morton, and **Auberge du Soleil** with its vaunted restaurant, a prime spot for champagne-soaked proposals.

Hot Springs, Safaris & Champagne

GET WILD IN CALISTOGA

With soothing natural hot springs, bubbling volcanic mud pools and a dramatically spurting geyser, Nilektsonoma (Cal-

WHERE TO STAY IN CALISTOGA

Brannan Cottage Inn
Stay in the 1862 gingerbread cottage of Samuel Brannan, the hustler/entrepreneur who founded Calistoga. **$$$**

Cottage Grove Inn
Get cozy in sweet whitewashed cottages with wood-burning fireplaces, hot tubs and rocking-chair porches. **$$$**

Francis House
Splash out for a full-blown gracious country mansion experience, complete with pool and tennis court. **$$$**

Oakville Grocery

istoga), 15 minutes' drive north of St Helena, was renowned across Talahalusi (Napa Valley) by the indigenous Wappo (Brave) people for some 8000 years. Then in 1859 a braggart named Samuel Brennan came along and claimed to have discovered the place. The town's odd name comes from Brannan, believing it would develop like the New York spa town, Saratoga. Apparently Sam liked his drink and at the founding ceremony tripped on his tongue, proclaiming it the 'Ca-li-stoga' of 'Sara-fornia.' The name stuck.

By 1873 Brannan had lost a fortune promoting Calistoga as California's signature spa resort. But look around Calistoga today and you might think he'd pulled it off.

At **Indian Hot Springs** guests can glide from mud baths to an Olympic-sized outdoor spring-fed pool then move on to

ROBERT LOUIS STEVENSON IN NAPA

Honeymoons in Napa Valley are often epic – but the 1880 honeymoon of Robert Louis Stevenson and Fanny Osbourne was epically awful. Robert was sick and they were broke, so they wound up squatting in an abandoned bunkhouse at extinct volcanic cone Mt St Helena's Silverado Mine, now part of **Robert Louis Stevenson State Park**, which is criscrossed with trails. At St Helena's **Robert Louis Stevenson Museum** you can peruse artifacts of the author's life and learn how the honeymoon trip inspired Stevenson's travel memoir *The Silverado Squatters*, making his reputation for harrowing adventure stories that eventually included *Treasure Island* and *Strange Case of Dr Jekyll and Mr Hyde*.

WHERE TO EAT IN CALISTOGA

Bella Bakery
Your friendly neighborhood top-notch bakery and coffee bar, with perfect quiche and chocolate-layer cake. **$**

Lovina
Garden lunches here are a dream – and inspiration for chef Leticia Martinez. **$$**

Buster's Southern BBQ
Napa Valley's favorite back-to-basics barbecue stop, with sunny outdoor tables. **$**

THE DIRTY LOWDOWN

Calistoga mud isn't just wet dirt: it's a blend of volcanic ash, peat and hot mineral spring water. If you're wondering why some baths cost more, it might be the silkier mud with higher volcanic ash content... or maybe it's the marketing.

Mud-bath packages take one to 1½ hours, combining semi-submergence in warm mud, hot mineral water soaking and a steam bath or blanket-wrap. Variations include thin, painted-on clay-mud wraps (called 'fango' baths, good for those uncomfortable sitting in mud), herbal wraps and seaweed baths. Check for midweek deals from lodging sites and the **Calistoga Visitors Center**. Reservations are essential so book ahead, especially for summer weekends.

Old Faithful Geyser

Sam's Social Club for bubbly bathrobed happy hours. Across the street, the 1952 spa-motel **Dr Wilkinson's** offers de-stress sessions in mineral-water pools, extra-squishy mud baths and 'beer brew' (hops-infused mineral baths).

Most spa treatments are adults-only, but **Old Faithful Geyser** keeps tykes entertained, as do mineral hot-springs pools at 1947 **Calistoga Motor Lodge and Spa** and best-value **Roman Spa Hot Springs**. Or really spice it up over the hill at **Safari West** with a jeep trip among giraffes, zebras and flamingos, plus overnight glamping. En route check out the **Petrified Forest**, where three million years ago a volcanic eruption at Mt St Helena blew down the stand of redwoods, now petrified.

For more adult bubbly, explore the historic sparkling-wine caves at Green Certified **Schramsberg** and glimpse the traditional French champagne riddling and racking methods before sampling the *tête de cuvées* (best of the vintage). Don't-miss wineries include **Vincent Arroyo** and **Olabisi** for exclusive small-batch wines.

GETTING AROUND

Downtown Calistoga is flat, easy and charming to walk or bike around. Napa Valley Vine bus 10 gets you from Calistoga to St Helena and downtown Napa. Vine operates a Calistoga Shuttle, providing door-to-door service within city limits. To schedule a pickup, call 707-963-4229 or access their app or website during operating hours.

SONOMA

Enchanting downtown Sonoma seems a world apart from mundane everyday life. Stroll streets lined with long-standing trees and Victorians and you'll find heritage inns, indie boutiques and some 30 tasting rooms. A bicycle ride away are more parks, historic sites, sensational family-owned restaurants and (how did you guess?) wineries.

Native Americans originally converged here at the village of Huichi to trade goods and songs. Many died in outbreaks of measles and smallpox that arrived with the friars of Mission Solano. When Mexico secularized California's missions and the lands were officially returned to Native Americans, those land deeds were not honored. Instead, Sonoma's mission vineyards were claimed by settlers.

On one particularly drunken night in 1846, a band of settlers took over the Sonoma barracks and proclaimed a breakaway Bear Flag Republic. Not a shot was fired, and after a confusing month US forces claimed Sonoma as US territory.

TOP TIP

There are lots of historic inns and romantic cottages suitable for a midrange budget, but those counting pennies will have better luck in Santa Rosa or Petaluma. Off-season rates plummet. Reserve ahead, and ask about parking, as some inns don't have parking lots. Sonoma Valley Visitors Bureau offers loads of local information.

Mission San Francisco Solano (p175)

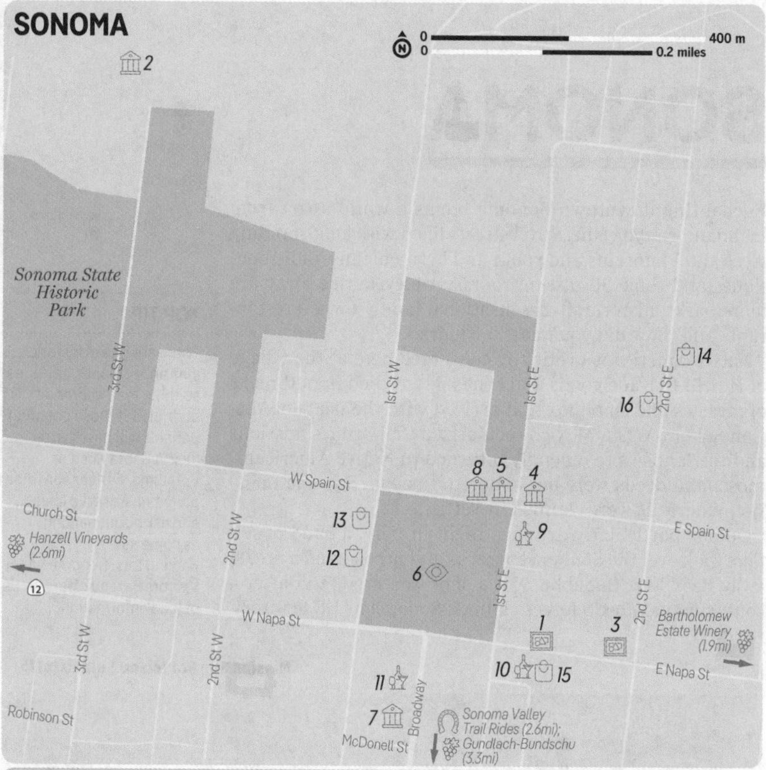

SONOMA

SIGHTS
1 Arts Guild of Sonoma
2 General Vallejo's Home
3 La Haye Art Center
4 Mission San Francisco Solano
5 Sonoma Barracks
6 Sonoma Plaza
7 Sonoma Valley Museum of Art
8 Toscano Hotel

DRINKING & NIGHTLIFE
9 Bedrock Wine
10 Enoteca Della Santina
11 Pomme Cider

SHOPPING
12 Chateau Sonoma
13 Global Heart Fair Trade
14 Patch
15 Tiddle E Winks
16 Vella Cheese Co

Plaza Ringed by Monuments

AMBLE THROUGH CALIFORNIA HISTORY

The city of Sonoma's pride and joy is the plaza – the largest town square in all of California, it's surrounded by local history, a venerable old theater, food and oh, yes, drinking options. There are free jazz concerts in its lush gardens, too (6pm

WHERE TO EAT IN SONOMA TOWN

Sausage Emporium
Bang-on brunches include namesake sausages and rich sandwiches alongside wine and craft beers. **$**

Delicious Dish
Succulent burgers, fresh-catch fish sandwiches and salads with fries at a field-side diner with patio. **$**

Tasca Tasca
Sea, garden, land: choose your next culinary adventure and this inspired tapas bar will take you there. **$$**

to 8:30pm every second Tuesday of the month from June to September). Arrive early and bring a picnic.

Anchored by adobe **Mission San Francisco Solano**, the plaza's sights allow you to time travel across 200 years of California history – one ticket for the **Sonoma State Historic Park** covers them all. The 21st and final California mission was built in 1823 by Native American conscripts and lasted just 11 years. Mexico's Comandante of Northern California, General Vallejo, commissioned the other big adobe, **Sonoma Barracks**, to house his troops in 1834. Displays capture 19th-century life and describe how Sonoma's Bear Flag Republic started. The lobby of the 1886 **Toscano Hotel** is beautifully preserved – have a peek inside.

The stately 1852 home of General Vallejo is a half-mile northwest. When Mexico lost California to the USA, Vallejo lost his official position, but the master strategist quickly became a US citizen, a California senator and spring-water supplier to the city of Sonoma.

Pair Local Art & Libations

CREATIVITY FOR ALL THE SENSES

Sonoma remains staunchly independent-minded and proud of its creativity, which is on display at **Sonoma Valley Museum of Art** and the **Arts Guild of Sonoma**. Collective **La Haye Art Center** fills a converted foundry where you can tour its gallery and meet the artists – sculptor, potter and painters – in their studios. Next door, cozy **Cafe La Haye** champions produce sourced within 60 miles.

At **Bedrock Wine Co** pair your art with wines in a historic saltbox cottage hung with tintype portraits and antique Sonoma maps. Maverick winemaker Morgan Twain-Petersen is reviving California's old vine-field blends with grapes sourced from tiny NorCal blocks, including classic zinfandels and obscure varietals like Alicante Bouschet.

Or, compare quaffs at **Pomme Cider**, with its convivial cascades of cider on tap, or at the burnished barroom of **Enoteca Della Santina**, where they also serve Italian dishes from their neighboring restaurant.

Shopping in Sonoma Town

SOMETHING FOR EVERYONE

Right in downtown Sonoma, **Patch** is California's oldest community-run urban farm, beloved by neighbors and protected from developers for at least 150 years. Across the street, **Vella Cheese Co** has been making spaghetti Western for almost

BEST SONOMA TOWN RESTAURANTS

Sonoma Food Tour
ably takes you to the highlights of the area for a taste.

El Molino Central
Unforgettable Wine Country meals combine sustainably homegrown ingredients and Sonoma's Mexican culinary traditions at this 1930s roadside mainstay. $

Valley
Smack on Sonoma Plaza, this welcoming wine bar dishes up creative, seasonal offerings such as California comfort food. $$

Animo
Sensational Basque-meets-Korean home-cooking. Now that's a mouthful! $$$

Girl & the Fig
Celebrated bistro with hearty feasts of rustic French fare. $$$

WHERE TO STAY IN SONOMA TOWN

Cottage Inn & Spa
Private patios for morning pastries, with a tinkling fountain and on-site spa. What's not to love? **$$**

An Inn 2 Remember
Steps from Sonoma Plaza, this vintage 1910 charmer offers warm welcomes and private, comfortable lodgings. **$$**

Fairmont Sonoma Mission Inn & Spa
Historic resort on the grounds of one of Sonoma's original missions. **$$$**

100 years – their two-year-aged dry jack is meant for shaving atop rustic dishes.

Step back in time at **Tiddle E Winks**, a retro 1950s variety store packed with nostalgic fun for all ages: wind-up toys, classic board games and penny candy.

French whimsy meets California quirk at **Chateau Sonoma**, Sarah Anderson's curiosity cabinet of a shop. **Global Heart Fair Trade** has unique handmade gifts, festive clothing and jewelry, recyclable decorations and artisanal chocolates in support of a worthwhile cause: all sales ensure living wages for makers.

GETTING ACTIVE

Walkers will love the trails winding through **Montini Open Space Reserve** above Sonoma, with their rolling grassland and oak woodlands. Trailheads at 1st St W and 4th St W in Sonoma lead to two overlooks, and the trail from 4th St is ADA-accessible. Montini's **Valley of the Moon trail** connects to the beautiful, volunteer-maintained **Sonoma Overlook Trail**, which also starts at 1st St W. It's 3 miles of spectacular hiking through oaks, bay trees and native wildflowers.

Downtown Sonoma is small, flat and perfect for biking. **Wine Country Cyclery** rents bikes, e-bikes and tandem bikes (aka 'divorce-makers'). Rentals include helmets and – crucially – a winery map. Book ahead.

Vineyards Near Sonoma Town

FAMILY-FRIENDLY WINERIES

Several Sonoma wineries were damaged by fires in 2017 and 2019, yet most have regrouped and replanted with more climate-resilient grape varietals and new fire-preventing measures. The inspired vintages they're producing are proudly featured on Sonoma menus.

California's oldest family-run winery, **Gundlach-Bundschu**, looks like a castle, and everyone gets a royal welcome at the bar. Six generations of Bundschus have kept the delightful dry gewürztraminer flowing since 1858. Bike down a country lane past farmstead donkeys for a tour of the 1800-barrel cave and a picnic by the pond. Concerts regularly rock Gun-Bun's redwood barn and outdoor ampitheater.

Sonoma's most idyllic winery, **Hanzell Vineyards**, has views to die for over Sonoma all the way to San Francisco Bay. Take your seat in the historic stone barn for exceptional organically produced chardonnays and pinot noirs.

Sprawling **Bartholomew Estate Winery** was established in 1857 at the birth of California's wine industry under Hungarian count Agoston Haraszthy, and now its certified-organic vineyards produce sauvignon blanc, cabernet sauvignon and zinfandel. Picnics are allowed in the estate's sun-dappled private park (free and open to visitors); there's a 3-mile trail through vineyards, oaks, madrones and redwoods. Pass the pond to reach an overlook with sweeping vistas. You can also go riding on horseback with **Sonoma Valley Trail Rides**.

For wineries, restaurants and lodging in Carneros further south, see p162.

GETTING AROUND

Sonoma Hwy (Hwy 12) is lined with wineries and runs from Sonoma, past Glen Ellen, through Kenwood to Santa Rosa, then on to western Sonoma County. You can get a rideshare to downtown Sonoma, where many sights, wine-tasting rooms and restaurants are within walking or cycling distance. Have your own wheels to explore the valley and its wineries. Public transportation is not convenient; check transit.511.org.

Beyond Sonoma Town

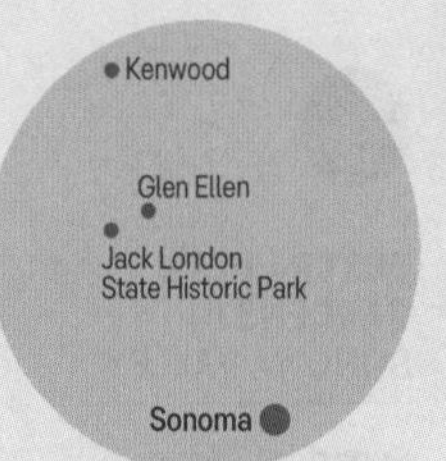

Century-old vines and charming settlements that are both fun-loving and down-to-earth fill the Sonoma Valley.

The rhythm of Sonoma Valley is an easy groove to fall into, following tracks worn over thousands of years. Here you're tracing the steps of Miwok, Pomo and Wintun people who converged in this lush valley to feast, relax and swap stories. They called this place the Valley of the Moon, and the mystical name has stuck locally.

Heading up the valley from Sonoma, the tiny, quaint 19th-century resort town of Glen Ellen is full of surprises: acclaimed restaurants, recycled art masterpieces, rare Japanese maples, wilderness horseback rides, stiff martinis and luxury cottage hideaways. Further north, the batch of vineyards known as Kenwood lures you with wine-pairing feasts and hikes up Sugarloaf to appreciate where you've been.

TOP TIP

Campers can hike into sites at Hood Mountain Regional Park or drive in at Sugarloaf Ridge State Park.

Jack London State Historic Park (p179)

BEST PARKS & GARDENS IN SONOMA VALLEY

Sugarloaf Ridge State Park
Around 25 miles of fantastic hiking and biking: on clear days, Bald Mountain views stretch to the Pacific.

Sonoma Valley Regional Park
Oak woodlands with trails, including the ADA-accessible 1.2-mile **Valley of the Moon** trail, picnic areas and dog park.

Sonoma Botanical Garden
World-renowned 25-acre botanical garden specializing in the flora of Asia.

Hood Mountain Regional Park
Wilderness trails for hiking, biking and horseback riding.

RICHARD CUMMINS/ALAMY ©

Kunde winery

Creative Haunts & Delicious Treats

THE CHARMS OF GLEN ELLEN

A 20-minute drive north of the town of Sonoma, tiny **Glen Ellen** (population 1200) is a jumble of little cottages behind white picket fences along a poplar-lined creek. Back in 1905 it was a swinging resort town with natural hot springs that lured California's rich and renowned, including the world's most famous author at the time, Jack London.

The town has remained a magnet for trailblazing writers and artists, including gonzo journalist Hunter S Thompson and food writer MFK Fisher – you can tour her **Last House** on the wildflower-laden **Bouverie Perserve** (egret.org) by appointment.

Pixar animator John Lasseter's **Lasseter Family Winery** contains the **Justi Creek railway**. And over decades at **13623 Arnold Dr**, junk-art maestro Chuck Gillet has reassembled rusted farm tools and auto parts into post-apocalyptic gargoyles. 'Private but peek freely,' says the sign.

You're in the heart of Sonoma, one of the world's most prestigious pinot noir regions, and **Talisman Wines** has award-

WHERE TO STAY IN SONOMA VALLEY

Beltane Ranch
African American millionaire and civil-rights pioneer Mary Ellen Pleasant built this beautiful ranch in 1892. **$$**

Olea Hotel
Relax in impeccable luxury in the oak-blanketed hills of Glen Ellen. **$$$**

Glen Ellen Inn & Martini Bar
Have a stiff martini then hit the sheets at these welcoming cottages and inn. **$$**

winning vintages to prove it. Founder/winemaker team Scott and Marta Rich collaborate with legendary pinot growers from Carneros to the Sonoma coast.

Don't miss the chance to swing into **Les Pascals Patisserie** for flaky, butter-glossed croissants, impeccable baguettes, savory quiches and decadent tarts. For a full, sit-down meal go south of town to beloved **Mill at Glen Ellen**, where casual fare can be adapted to vegans and vegetarians.

FOR HIKERS & MOUNTAIN BIKERS

California's combination of regional, state and national parks mean gorgeous walks, hikes and rides are always within easy reach. Find out more on p48.

Jack London's Ranch

GET THE CALL OF THE WILD

Even a novelist can farm land as fertile as Sonoma's, as you'll see 25 minutes' drive north of Sonoma town at **Jack London State Historic Park**, where the adventure author of *The Call of the Wild* and his wife, editor and fellow writer Charmian Kittredge London, built Beauty Ranch as their writing retreat and pioneering organic farm. At the **museum,** insightful displays cover Jack's death-defying travels and his controversial ideas, including socialism and Darwinism. Don't miss Jack's rejection letters in the downstairs bookstore. From the museum, it's a hilly half-mile walk to the ruins of their Wolf House, passing **Jack's gravesite** along the way.

Sonoma Valley Wineries

THE VINEYARDS OF KENWOOD

Rolling grass- and vine-covered hills rise from Sonoma Valley. Its 40-odd wineries get less attention than Napa's, but many are equally good. If you love zinfandel, syrah and pinot noir, you're in for a treat. A few **Kenwood area** landmarks (there is no town per se; rather a collection of vineyards 25 minutes' drive north of Sonoma town) have stood the test of time – including the little 1860s red schoolhouse, now **Muscardini Cellars**, tasting room.

Friendly **Kunde winery**, on a historic ranch of vast vineyards, offers mountaintop tastings with impressive valley views and guided hikes (reserve in advance). Or just stop by for a tasting (a rarity, in reservation-required Wine Country).

At **VJB Cellars** taste triumph in prized Italian wines grown in Sonoma that aren't otherwise often imported to the USA, including robust white friulano and summer-stormy aleatico rosé. They've got a delish restaurant too. Another beauty is **Hamel Family Wines**.

BEST PLACES TO EAT IN SONOMA VALLEY

Glen Ellen Star
Food & Wine star chef Ari Weiswasser keeps the mood relaxed in Glen Ellen. $$$

Mayo Family Winery & Reserve Room
Wining and dining are better together with an inspired seven courses of seasonal small plates with reserve wines. $$$

TIPS Roadhouse
Casual New Orleans-style road food is the order of the day in Kenwood. $$

Wine Truffle Boutique
When chocolate, wine and ice cream are all you need in Glen Ellen. $

GETTING AROUND

Sonoma Valley has around 40 wineries. If you want to go vineyard hopping, you'll realistically want a car or bicycle. Glen Ellen is a nice bike ride from Sonoma – just 7 miles on quiet country roads. Kenwood is another 5 miles north. Or you can book a service like Designated Drivers Napa Sonoma.

PETALUMA

The historic town of Petaluma, just a short drive south of Santa Rosa and west of downtown Sonoma, is Sonoma County's sleeper hit. One of California's oldest cities, built around a river and served by rail, it used to be a conduit for the northern counties' abundance on its way south to the burgeoning Bay Area, and the region was renowned for its chicken farms and dairies.

Now Petaluma grabs attention for its walkable, quaint downtown, packed with eateries, taprooms and wine bars, and its foggy and wind-whipped wine appellation, dubbed 'the Petaluma Gap.' The region's chardonnays, pinot noirs and syrahs have earned a reputation for their elegance and complexity. It's also home to two of the Bay Area's premier breweries.

Petaluma is a fine place to while away the day, exploring the food-and-drink havens of the city's old brick-building downtown center, then party into the night.

TOP TIP

Sample local dairy goodies at Angela's Ice Cream and check with Petaluma Visitors Center to find out which rural dairies and creameries are open to the public. The word Sonoma describes a town, a valley and a much bigger county, so always check *where,* when someone says 'we're in Sonoma.'

Petaluma

KWANCHANOG NOIINWONG/SHUTTERSTOCK ©

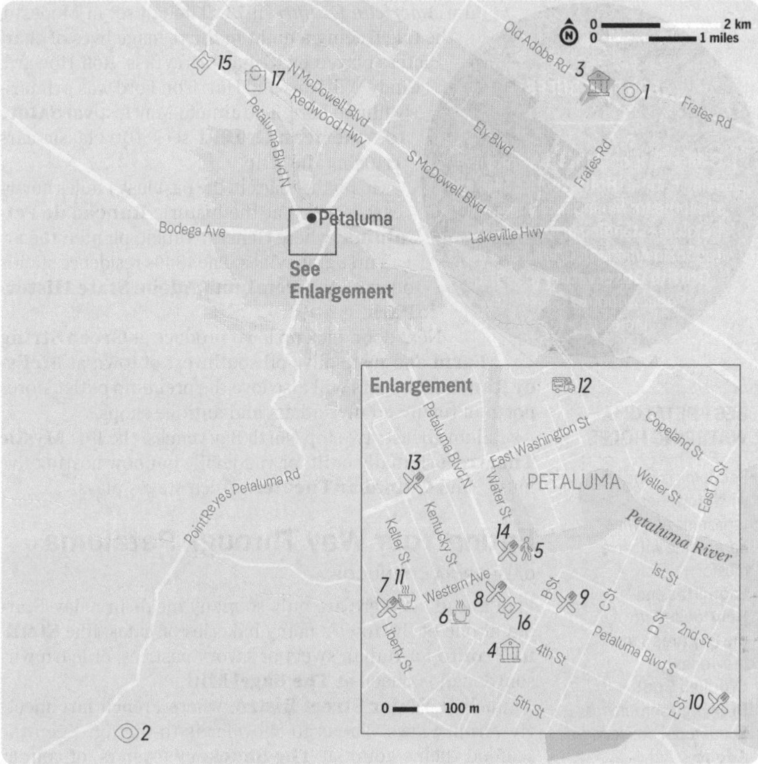

SIGHTS
1 Green String Farm
2 McEvoy Ranch
3 Petaluma Adobe State Historic Park
4 Petaluma Historical Library & Museum

ACTIVITIES, COURSES & TOURS
5 Riverfront Walk

EATING
6 Stellina Pronto
7 Stockhome
8 Street Social
9 Sugo Trattoria
10 Table Culture Provisions
11 The Bagel Mill
12 The Block
13 The Shuckery
14 Water Street Bistro

ENTERTAINMENT
15 Cinnabar Theater
16 Mystic Theatre

SHOPPING
17 Premium Outlet Stores

Bay Area Boomtown

CRUISING THE PETALUMA STRIP

Petaluma was established in 1858 and its charming downtown area (packed with unique iron-front architecture that survived the 1906 earthquake) and lovingly preserved Victorians are on the National Register of Historic Places. Learn more at the free **Petaluma Historical Library & Museum**, housed in a spectacular neoclassical building and providing a bounty of local information and weekly walking tours between May and October.

Strolling the **riverfront walk** is a treat, though kayaks have replaced the paddleboats and steamers of yore. If things around town start to look a bit familiar, perhaps you're flashing back to George Lucas' seminal, Academy Award–nominated

WELCOME TO FLATBACK

The word Petaluma comes from the Miwok words *pe'ta* (flat) and *lu'ma* (back), referring to the gentle openness of the valley behind the hill. Mexico's Comandante of Northern California, General Vallejo, then used it for his giant Rancho Petaluma, granted to him in 1834.

film *American Graffiti* (1973). Though set in Modesto, the tale tracing a night in the teenage lives of characters played by Richard Dreyfuss, Ron Howard, Cindy Williams and Harrison Ford was primarily filmed here. The annual May festival **Salute to American Graffiti** sees 400 classic cars cruising the strip.

Go further back in the past just 4 miles northeast of town at the historic **Rancho de Petaluma**, where General Vallejo planted the area's first grapevines. The 1830s residence stands today as the **Petaluma Adobe State Historic Park**.

Next door, pick up local produce at **Green String Farm** and taste olive oil southwest of town at **McEvoy Ranch**. Shoppers will also love the premium outlet stores north of town and myriad art and antique shops.

Petaluma boasts two top North Bay venues: the 1911 **Mystic Theatre**, originally built for vaudeville but now hosting live music, and **Cinnabar Theater**, which stages plays.

FOR FILM BUFFS

California is both the USA's movie-making capital (**Hollywood**; p340) and a favorite for filming locations, with Petaluma standing in for **Modesto** (p538) in *American Graffiti* and the **Griffith Observatory** (p348) in *Rebel without a Cause*, to name just a few.

BEST PETALUMA WATERING HOLES

Petaluma is loaded with breweries, taprooms and wine bars, some with live music.

Lagunitas and **HenHouse** Two of the Bay Area's top breweries.

Crooked Goat Brewing Taproom for Sebastopol brewery.

Adobe CreekTaproom Outpost of Novato brewery.

Brewsters Beer Garden Live music lights it up.

La Dolce Vita Wine Lounge Myriad wines with small plates.

Vine and Barrel Talkative owner serving wines and tapas.

Griffo Distillery & Tasting Bar Stock up on spirits and quaff cocktails.

Eating Your Way Through Petaluma

CALIFORNIA CORNUCOPIA

Plan ahead, as there are only so many meals in a day. Start out at one of the town's many bakeries or cafes, like **Stellina Pronto** for Italian sweet or savory pastries, or learn why sourdough is queen at **The Bagel Mill**.

Lunch at **Water Street Bistro**, where French fare meets riverfront views. The crab chowder is to die for. Keep the seafood theme going at **The Shuckery** (oysters, of course, paired with wine or sangria) or mix it up at **Stockhome** for Swedish-Mediterranean delights (say what!?).

In the evening, go classic at **Sugo Trattoria**, or enjoy the always-inventive tasting menus at **Table Culture Provisions**. Nip into the 100-year-old Lan Mart Building to discover fabulous new kid on the block **Street Social**, where you never know what you'll get, with wildly creative dishes changing constantly.

For a more casual night, slide into **The Block**, home base for a rotating lineup of food trucks, including a permanent pizzeria that'll satisfy any wood-fired cravings. Gather around one of the firepits and grab a local microbrew, too.

GETTING AROUND

Reach Petaluma from San Francisco via the Golden Gate Transit bus or SMART rail, which continues north to Santa Rosa and its airport.

Getting around by car is easiest and parking spots abound outside of the walkable town center.

SANTA ROSA

Sonoma County's capital is a city of flowering neighborhoods and bold initiatives, beginning with its 1841 founding by *ranchera* María Ygnacia López de Carrillo. Her son Julio Carrillo became a forward-thinking urban planner, laying out Santa Rosa's neat city grid with a public square at the center. Cheerful retro storefronts still beckon visitors into local shops, and historic Railroad Sq greets commuters arriving on tracks first laid by local Chinese laborers in the 1870s, the location immortalized in area museums and Alfred Hitchcock's *Shadow of a Doubt* (1943).

The city makes international news each year when Russian River Brewing Co releases its brilliantly bitter double IPA Pliny the Elder. which prompts campouts at the door, and remains a place of pilgrimage for craft-beer lovers year-round.

It's hard to believe Santa Rosa has been hit with so many earthquakes and wildfires, but the city named for the patron saint of police and nurses was always destined to be a survivor.

TOP TIP

Make a fun trip by taking the SMART train from the Sonoma County Airport station (1 mile from the airport via Sonoma County Transit bus 55) or Santa Rosa's Railroad Sq to Marin's Larkspur ferry terminal (via Petaluma), where you can catch the Bay Ferry to San Francisco.

Railroad Sq (p185)

SANTA ROSA

SIGHTS
1 4th St
2 Luther Burbank Home & Gardens
3 Museum of Sonoma County
4 Railroad Sq
5 South of A St Art District

EATING
6 Abyssinia
7 Betty's Fish & Chips
8 Bird & the Bottle
9 Goguette
10 Hang Ah
11 Mitote Food Park
12 Red Bird Bakery

DRINKING & NIGHTLIFE
13 Dierk's Midtown Cafe

SHOPPING
14 Lola's

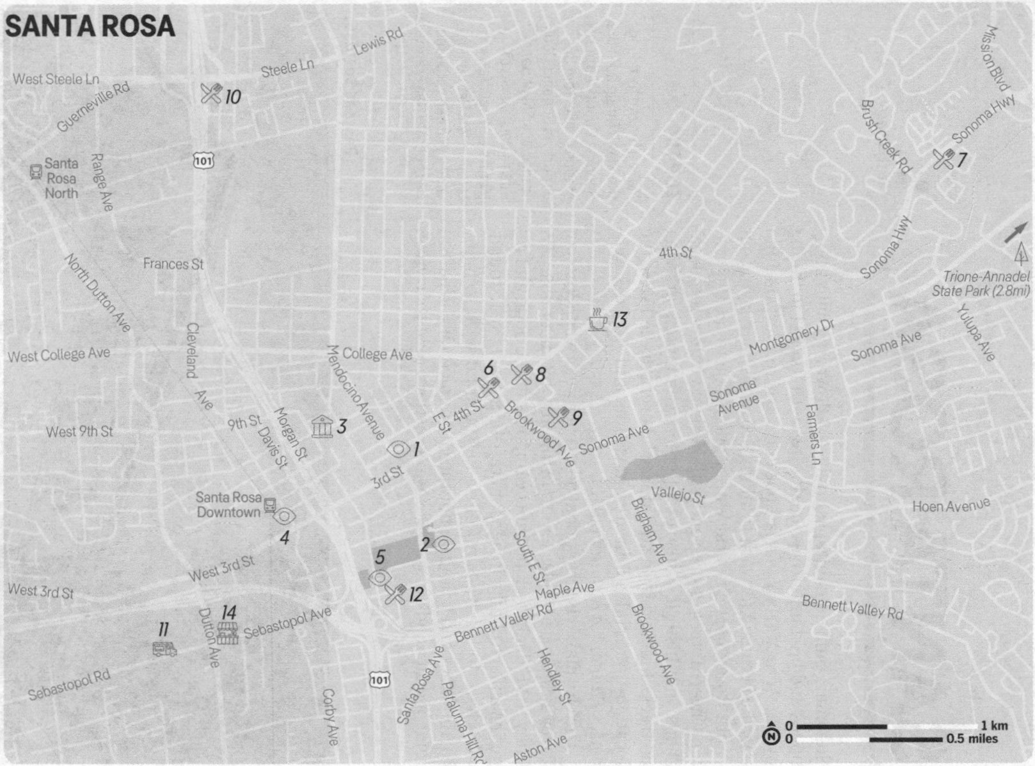

FOR ART LOVERS

In addition to reveling in the *Peanuts* museum or local winery Paradise Ridge, where outdoor sculptures thrill on a gorgeous hillside, experience more art at **San Francisco's downtown museums** (p78).

Walking Streets, Trails & Museums

NEIGHBORHOOD CHARMS

Wine Country's biggest city channels modern-day Americana, with cottage rose gardens, bicyclists peddling rails-to-trails greenway **Joe Rodota Trail**, hikers trekking **Trione-Annadel State Park** and life booming in the culturally Latinx **Roseland** neighborhood.

The main heart and shopping stretch is **4th St** along central Old Courthouse Sq. It re-emerges across the freeway at historic **Railroad Sq**. Walk the tree-shaded, mural-lined streets of the **South of A St Art District**, and stop and smell the flowers – many are fragrant varietals like the Santa Rosa plum developed for delight, utility and sustainability just up the street at **Luther Burbank Home & Gardens**. This is where pioneering horticulturist Luther Burbank (1849–1926) cultivated 800 hybrid plant species over 50 years.

Take a trip through Sonoma County's past, present and future in the **Museum of Sonoma County** in side-by-side history and art museums.

International Food Tour

TASTES FOR EVERY PALATE

Santa Rosa is a world tour in excellent eats, from dim sum at **Hang Ah** to Ethiopian at **Abyssinia**, and French patisserie and bread at **Goguette** to down-home cooking at **Dierk's Midtown Cafe**, **Red Bird Bakery** and **Betty's Fish & Chips**.

The Roseland area on Sebastopol Rd is ruinous to any diet, with **Mitote Food Park** full of 'taco trucks' actually making specialties from all over Mexico alongside a bar, and countless taquerias and markets like **Lola's**.

When you're not sure what you're craving, try a little bit of everything at **Bird & the Bottle**, from grilled lamb meatballs to duck confit tacos.

'GOOD GRIEF, CHARLIE BROWN!'

Beloved worldwide, the *Peanuts* comic strip was drawn in Santa Rosa by cartoonist Charles M Schulz. The wonderful-for-all-ages **Charles M Schulz Museum** follows the journey of Snoopy, Charlie Brown, Lucy and the gang from their 1950 introduction to last laughs in 2000. Downstairs are original Schulz drawings. Upstairs are artists' tributes to *Peanuts,* plus an exacting recreation of Schulz' art studio: markers on a reclaimed-wood desk and a video of Schulz drawing – a fluid poem in ink.

If you fly into Charles M Schulz Sonoma County Airport, you can take your pic with Snoopy in the terminal. Keep an eye out for giant fiberglass statues all over the city, part of the **Peanuts on Parade** celebration of the characters.

GETTING AROUND

Sonoma County Airport Express shuttles between Sonoma County Airport and San Francisco and Oakland airports. SMART train, Golden Gate Transit and Greyhound buses run between San Francisco and Santa Rosa.

Central Santa Rosa is flat and walkable, but it sprawls, so take local CityBus (using a Bay Area–wide Clipper Card) if you don't have your own wheels. Downtown parking garages are cheaper than street parking.

SEBASTOPOL

No amount of fermented fruit can explain free-spirited Sebastopol. In the 19th century, independent Pomo villagers and immigrant apple farmers formed a US township in the Pomo homeland of Bitakomtara. According to legend, an epic 1850s bar brawl here was jokingly compared to the famous Crimean War battlefront, underway at the time, and the nickname Sebastopol stuck.

While the rest of Wine Country started growing grapes, Sebastopol kept growing heirloom apples, vegetables and wildflowers developed by local horticulture hero Luther Burbank. Back-to-the-land hippies brought fresh ideas to western Sonoma County, including organic farming, home beekeeping and marijuana cultivation. Now even the traffic medians are pesticide free, and the entire town is a nuclear-free zone.

Anywhere you go, you can't miss the local characters, some more famous than others. Tom Waits lives on the outskirts, and Grateful Dead drummer Mickey Hart occasionally jams. Sebastopol just keeps bringing legends to life.

TOP TIP

Sebastopol Area Chamber of Commerce & Visitors Center offers maps and information. Buy *Sebastopol Walks* by Richard Nichols for town walks plus country rides and rambles on the Joe Rodota Trail, through bird-watchers' paradise wetland Laguna de Santa Rosa (whose foundation hosts exhibits and activities) and beyond.

Wineyard in Sebastopol

TIMOTHY S. ALLEN/SHUTTERSTOCK ©

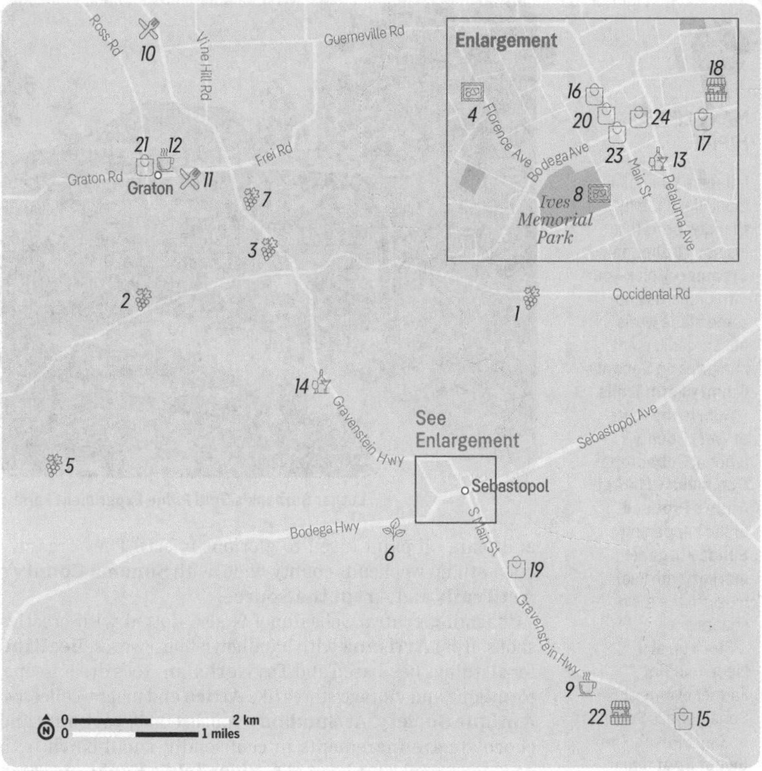

SIGHTS
1 Balletto
2 Char Vale
3 Emeritus
4 Florence Ave
5 Freeman
6 Luther Burbank's Gold Ridge Experiment Farm
7 Merry Edwards
8 Sebastopol Center for the Arts

EATING
9 Hardcore Espresso
10 Mom's Apple Pie
11 Underwood Bar & Bistro
12 Willow Wood Market Cafe

DRINKING & NIGHTLIFE
13 Hopmonk Tavern
14 Horse & Plow

SHOPPING
15 Antique Society
16 Artisana
17 Attico
18 Barlow Market
19 Beekind
20 Copperfield's Books
21 Graton Gallery
22 Midgley's Country Flea Market
23 Sumbody
24 Toyworks

Fantastical Sculptures, Local Creativity & Vintage Wares

ART FOR ART'S SAKE

A cow rides a tractor, a rocket blasts off the lawn and a dinosaur grabs a red convertible for lunch: it's all happening on **Florence Ave**, in dozens of sculptures Patrick Amiot made for neighbors' yards from recycled junk. You'll spot plenty more throughout the county.

Around the corner at **Sebastopol Center for the Arts**, see the world from the perspective of Sonoma County's boundary-pushing artists, working in media from fiber arts to glass

MAKE LIKE A HIPPIE

Immerse yourself in local life at family-friendly farms (like luscious **Bohemian Creamery**), pick-your-own orchards and some of the world's best organic plant nurseries on **Sonoma County Farm Trails**.

Admire the fruits of West County's labor at **Sebastopol Community Market**, **Andy's Produce** or the happening **Sunday organic market**, with live music in the town square.

Stock up at Meet Your Pot Farmer events at Sebastopol's **Solful** or Santa Rosa's **The Sweet Spot** farm-to-spliff cannabis dispensaries.

Visit Santa Rosa's family-owned **Birkenstock Village** to complete your look with a pair of Birks.

WAYNE HSIEH78/SHUTTERSTOCK ©

Luther Burbank's Gold Ridge Experiment Farm

and plain ol' paint (used to glorious effect). They organize open-studio weekends county-wide, with **Sonoma County's Art Trails** and **Art at the Source**.

Charming central Sebastopol is also dotted with creative shops, from **Artisana** with handhewn housewares, **BeeKind** for all things bee-based and **Toyworks**, any tot's dreamscape, to antique and vintage stores like **Attico** and macro-collective **Antique Society**. At **Sumbody**, mushrooms, goat milk and chocolate are ingredients in ecofriendly, small-batch bath products. Feed your head at **Copperfield's Books** or search for treasures on Sunday at **Midgley's Country Flea Market**.

Seek bodily sustenance at **Hardcore Espresso** or in nearby **Graton's Willow Wood Market Cafe** with California comfort food plus champagne cocktails, or **Underwood Bar & Bistro**, both near Graton Gallery.

Apples, Wines, Daisies & Good Times

HEARTY HORTICULTURE AND HARD CIDER

Sebastopol had a reputation for boozy shenanigans long before Sonoma County's wine industry took off, because the heirloom-apple orchards that thrived here weren't originally intended for roadside bakery Mom's Apple Pie. They were used to make hard cider – a tradition upheld today at **Hopmonk Tavern** and **Horse & Plow** tasting room, and cele-

WHERE TO SATISFY YOUR SWEET TOOTH IN SEBASTOPOL

Screamin' Mimi's
Delectable homemade ice cream served by the ounce. Choose from a seasonal lineup of flavors. **$**

Pascaline
French patisserie-cafe and favorite local hangout for delicate pastries and bistro-style brunch. **$**

Sebastopol Cookie Co
Aromas entice at this indie bakery making restorative triple-chocolate cookies, snickerdoodles and more. **$**

JUDEAND/SHUTTERSTOCK ©

Barlow Market

brated twice annually at **Gravenstein Apple Fair** and **Apple Blossom Festival**.

The old apple cannery on the edge of Sebastopol was repurposed into the **Barlow Market**, home to Sebastopol's upstart makers, including celebrated Crooked Goat Brewery, Region tasting room, Pax Wines, Kosta Browne Wines and Spirit Works Distillery.

About 150 years ago horticulturalist Luther Burbank cultivated fruit trees and daisies (like popular Shasta daisies, the 1901 hybrid of flowers from three continents) at **Luther Burbank's Gold Ridge Experiment Farm** (wschs.org/farm), which is open to the public. You can also reserve ahead to taste namesake Gold Ridge Farms' organic apple and olive-oil products.

In the 1970s, while chef Alice Waters established California cuisine, **Merry Edwards** was championing California wine from her vineyard – becoming the first woman in Napa's Winemakers' Hall of Fame while putting California pinots on the map.

Redwoods encircle the **Freeman vineyards**, trapping mists that winemaker/founder Akiko Freeman captures in cool-climate pinots and chardonnays. Vineyards are actually a minority crop on **Littorai**, a 30-acre biodynamic estate where bees, birds and beneficial insects create an integrated ecosystem.

Sebastopol is ringed by vineyards, so you can just keep going, with **Emeritus**, **Balletto** and **Char Vale**...

BEST EATS IN SEBASTOPOL

Ramen Gaijin
Upbeat mood fueled by (so spicy!) pork-belly ramen and (so tasty!) short ribs. $$

Incas Peruvian Cuisine
Savory heaping dishes from chicken stew to braised lamb shank. $

The Barlow
Two-acre village of indie food producers, artists, winemakers, coffee roasters and distillers. $$

Fern Bar
Come for '70s atmosphere, stay for Sonoma-proud shared plates. $$

La Bodega Kitchen
Inspired vegan food paired with wine from the adjoining wine store. $$

GETTING AROUND

Central Sebastopol is best walked or biked, and trails radiate through the countryside. Cyclists can take the paved Joe Rodota Trail to Santa Rosa and then the SMART train south (Petaluma or Larkspur Landing's Bay Ferry to San Francisco). Sonoma County Transit buses include a free local shuttle (Route 24).

Beyond Sebastopol

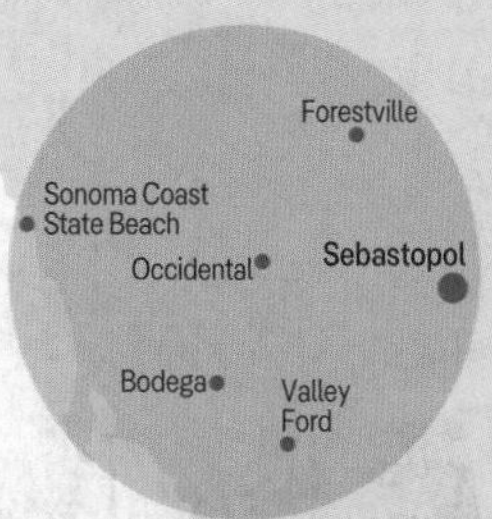

Trace the valleys cleaving forested mountains out to the Pacific Coast, reveling in homegrown fare and easygoing settlements along the way.

Hills undulate from Sebastopol and Graton to the Pacific in the west and up to the Russian River in the north. The valleys golden in summer, while in winter and spring, rain-greened pastures rise to the redwood- and oak-topped hills. Vineyards carve up the acreage as do historic communes and quintessential Northern California hamlets.

World-class wineries, a nationally famous day spa and excellent creameries, bakeries and restaurants spice up the mix. So too do heartfelt gatherings like Occidental's farmers market, where live music fills the night sky as folks from the hills around come down and say hi.

This is a region in which to kick back, drop out and see what happens.

TOP TIP

A vehicle is essential for traversing these resplendent hills – bus services are scant and only hard-core cyclists should brave the narrow roads.

Union Hotel, Occidental

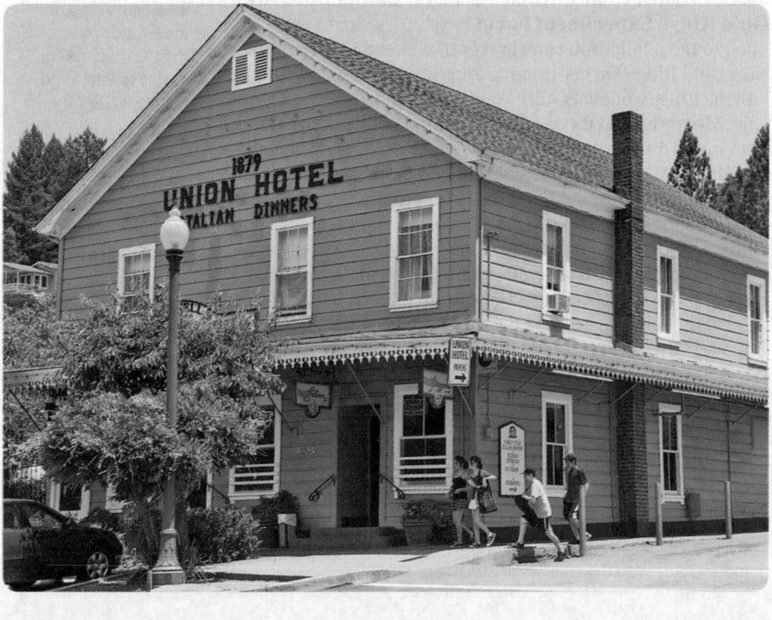

Vineyard Valleys

QUAFFING WINES AND NIBBLING FRESH LOAVES

Raise a toast 20 minutes' drive northwest of Sebastopol at **Iron Horse Vineyards** with sparkling wines that have been served at White House inaugurations. Over at **Furthermore Wines**, start with pinot, break for bocce, then return to the urgent matter of pinot, or better yet, their mysterious rosé of pinot noir.

Roll along pastoral Green Valley, surrounded by rolling farmland, apple orchards and vineyards, plus the occasional Shetland pony, to the small town of **Forestville**. The main drag is lined with old-timey storefronts, and everyone knows when Jessie Frost is baking – the aroma of her organic breads at **Nightingale Breads** changes traffic patterns. Stop for a bite, then visit the beloved **RYME tasting room** before continuing on to River Rd and the quaint red barn where the family-owned **Martinelli winery** has been bucking convention since 1887. That's when a young Tuscan winemaker eloped to California to grow grapes on notoriously steep, rocky Jackass Hill, yielding award-winning zinfandels, pinots and muscats.

Farmers Market Party & Offbeat Treats

OCCIDENTAL'S HIGH LIFE

Located 20 minutes' drive west of Sebastopol, **Occidental** (population 876) is the surprising mountain-top lumber town that time forgot and trees reconquered – with help from visionary ecologists and back-to-the-land hippies.

The power of countercultural thinking is celebrated when partying breaks out May to October at the **Friday Farmers Market**. Crafts, flowers, cheese, organic produce, mushrooms and giant pans of Pacific seafood paella fill the street and musicians light up the evening as friends and family mingle. Grab great draft brews at **Altamont General Store** and sit curbside and watch the world go by, or combine family-style epic ravioli with local vintages at the **Union Hotel**.

Drop by **Bohème Cellar Door** for wine tasting. At **Hinterland and Neon Raspberry** everything is recycled, organic and/or women-made with punk attitude.

North of town, you might pause to zipline through the redwoods at **Sonoma Canopy Tours** before winding down the hill to reach the Russian River at Monte Rio.

BEST EATS AROUND OCCIDENTAL

Hazel
Join a fabulous dinner party – wine flows and *oohs!* erupt as dishes arrive bubbling from wood-fired ovens. $$$

Rocker Oysterfeller's
Valley Ford's oyster and New Orleans–style cooking delight. $$

Farmhouse Inn
The region's Michelin-starred River Rd gourmet landmark, with refined locally raised organics. $$$

Howard Station
Open since the 1870s and serving generous brunches. $

Fork Roadhouse
Get cozy by the fireplace at this rural ranch house, or take out farm-to-table fare with a wild streak. $$

FOR THE REBELS

Occidental is a West County epicenter of free thinking. To read more about California's unique ways of thinking, see **The Myth of California** (p654).

WHERE TO STAY AROUND OCCIDENTAL

Inn at Occidental
Escape the ordinary at this 16-room Victorian inn with heirloom quilts for getting cozy in the redwoods. **$$**

Raford Inn
Countryside B&B surrounded by palm trees and vineyards, featuring wine receptions and generous breakfasts. **$$**

Occidental Lodge
Request the newer rooms with boho flair at this budget option that still resonates with its original 1973 motel vibes. **$**

FANTASTIC FREESTONE

From the instant you turn onto **Bohemian Hwy** at Freestone, you're in for a wild ride. Freestone is a former stagecoach stop with a current population of 32, yet the road is lined with cars. People arrive from far and wide to nibble on planet-sized sticky buns at **Wild Flour**, taste water-buffalo gelato at **Freestone Cheese**, and get buried up to their necks in cedar chips – a Japanese tradition – at **Osmosis Day Spa**. The spa ritual here begins with organic tea in the bonsai garden, then proceeds to a redwood tub full of soft, fermenting cedar and rice bran – the woodsy aroma and dry-enzyme action will warm you to the bone. It's one-of-a-kind in North America, and attracts celebs and hippies alike.

GEORGE ROSE/GETTY IMAGES ©

Martinelli Winery (p191)

Sonoma County's Best Drive

FROM REDWOOD MOUNTAINS TO WIDE-OPEN OCEAN

Sonoma County's most memorable drive may not be through the grapes (though Westside Rd is a contender; see p196), but along these 10 miles of winding byway from Occidental to the ocean. It's best in the late morning, when fog lifts and sun filters through the trees.

Reach the ridgeline on **Coleman Valley Rd**, head left onto Joy Rd and right onto Fitzpatrick Lane to find a hidden glory: the **Grove of the Old Trees** (landpaths.org). Picnic or stroll the easy 1-mile loop trail.

Back on Coleman Valley Rd, pass gnarled oaks and craggy rocks to ascend 1000ft, until the vast blue Pacific unfurls at your feet. The road ends at coastal Hwy 1, where you can explore **Sonoma Coast State Beach**, then navigate southeast to reach the tiny town of **Bodega** (not Bodega Bay) to see the iconic church and schoolhouse where Hitchcock shot his 1963 classic, *The Birds,* and eat oysters in serene **Valley Ford**.

GETTING AROUND

There's no good way to get around here via public transportation – buses, while they do run, are infrequent. Seasoned cyclists ply country lanes – be alert whether you're on two wheels or four.

RUSSIAN RIVER VALLEY

The Russian River has long been a good-time summer-weekend destination for Northern Californians who come to canoe, hike redwood forests, barbecue, taste wine and live life at a lazy pace.

Though the source of the Russian River is north in Ukiah, and the valley begins outside of Healdsburg, when locals talk about hitting 'The River,' they mean the wide stretch starting around lively Guerneville, winding past mellow Monte Rio and Duncans Mills, and flowing into the Pacific at Jenner. For thousands of years, indigenous Pomo people called this river on the east side of their homelands the Ashokawna ('eastern water'). But once Russians established Fort Ross as a trading post for bear pelts, it became known as the Russian River.

Lately, Russian River Valley vineyards have taken their place among California's important wine appellations, especially for cold-weather grapes like pinot noir. Easy days floating on the river call for toasts, ably supplied by local wineries and Sonoma County microbreweries.

TOP TIP

Get top-tier year-round guided birding tours throughout the region with Teresa and Miles Tuffli, whose website (imbirdingrightnow.com) is a font of info on the abundant birds of the river. For fishing info and supplies, visit King's Sport & Tackle. The Russian River Visitor Center provides additional insights in Guerneville (russianriver.com).

Canoeing on the Russian River (p195)

RUSSIAN RIVER VALLEY

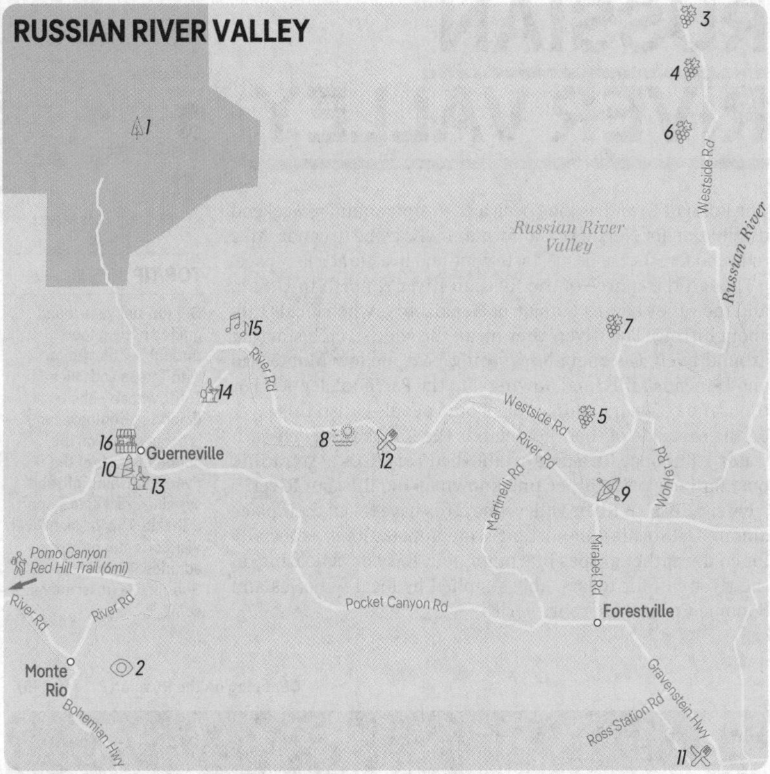

Russian River Valley
Russian River
Westside Rd
River Rd
Martinelli Rd
Wohler Rd
Mirabel Rd
Pocket Canyon Rd
Gravenstein Hwy
Ross Station Rd
Bohemian Hwy
Guerneville
Forestville
Monte Rio
Pomo Canyon Red Hill Trail (6mi)

SIGHTS
1 Armstrong Redwoods State Natural Reserve
2 Bohemian Grove
3 De La Montanya
4 Flowers
5 Gary Farrell
6 MacRostie
7 Porter Creek
8 Sunset Beach

ACTIVITIES, COURSES & TOURS
9 Burke's Canoe Trips
10 Johnson's Beach

EATING
see 16 Boon Eat + Drink
see 16 Main Street Bistro
11 Mom's Apple Pie
12 Russian River Pub

DRINKING & NIGHTLIFE
see 16 El Barrio
13 Equality Vines
see 16 Rainbow Cattle Company
14 Stumptown Brewery

ENTERTAINMENT
15 Rio Nido Roadhouse

SHOPPING
16 Big Bottom Market
see 16 Farmers Market
see 16 Guerneville Bank Club

WHERE TO STAY NEAR GUERNEVILLE

Mine + Farm
Modern B&B in a 1906 farmhouse next to Korbel Vineyards and near Sunset Beach. **$$$**

Highlands Resort
Mellow out in the redwoods at Guerneville's most relaxed LGBTIQ+ and straight-friendly resort. **$$**

Fern Grove Cottages
Star in your own retro rom-com at these vintage garden cottages, right on the edge of Guerneville. **$$$**

Beaches, Restaurants & Bars with LGBTIQ+ Flair

PLAYING IN GUERNEVILLE AND ALONG THE RIVER

The Russian River's biggest vacation spot, Guerneville (pronounced *GURN*-vill) only has about 4700 residents but almost doubles in size on hot summer weekends, when folks come from all over to hike redwoods, float the river and hammer cocktails poolside. This town has flaunted a 'good time had by all' vibe since the 1870s, and it hasn't lost its honky-tonk reputation yet. Just ask burly gay partiers in town for **Lazy Bear Week**, sun-worshiping lesbians on **Women's Weekend** and assorted San Francisco hipsters along for the ride.

Downtown Guerneville is a year-round destination, with cafes, indie-maker boutiques, straight-friendly gay bars, wine tasting for a cause at **Equality Vines**, and fun casual dining at places like **Boon Eat + Drink**.

If you actually came to Russian River for the river, Guerneville's **Johnson's Beach** is the epicenter of inner tubes, paddleboat rentals and beach concessions. There's good river access east of Guerneville at **Sunset Beach**, plus sandy beaches and swimming holes downstream toward Monte Rio.

For picnic supplies, Guerneville Bank Club and Big Bottom Market make everything from sandwiches to ice cream. The small **farmers market** meets on Wednesday afternoons.

Main Street Bistro and **Rainbow Cattle Company** have been Guerneville go-tos for decades and newcomer **El Barrio** slings creative mescal- and tequila-heavy cocktails.

Just east, **Stumptown Brewery** gets packed, **Rio Nido Roadhouse** rollicks around a tree-shaded pool, and the **Russian River Pub** is where Santa Rosa restaurateur Guy Fieri made his start.

Floating or Paddling the River

GOOF OFF WITH RIVER OTTERS

During summer and fall the absolute best thing to do on the Russian River is to float down it, on a tube or whatever inflatable thing you can find, with some friends and a flask in hand, passing posing herons. It'll cost you nothing (other than the price of your floaty), and **Regional Parks River Shuttle** can drop you at Steelhead Beach and pick you up at Sunset Beach on summer weekends. Or rent a canoe or kayak from **Burke's Canoe Trips** at Johnson's Beach or Monte Rio Beach.

Plan for at least four to five hours – the river is slow-moving so you'll have to do more paddling than you expect – and pack supplies (like drinking water).

NORTHWOOD & MONTE RIO

Golfers, bucket-list **Northwood Golf Course** is a gorgeous vintage 1920s Alister MacKenzie-designed nine-hole course in the redwoods. It used to be the course for the Bohemian Grove, which was connected by a walking bridge across the river. Now it's open to all. Just beside the course, the **Northwood Restaurant** serves sin-worthy breakfasts and Bloody Marys, plus there's a patio beneath the redwoods and occasional karaoke. Yes, karaoke! Neighboring **Bia Cafe** rustles up delish breakfast sandwiches and espresso drinks. Or bounce over to **Monte Rio**, where Paul at **Rio Cafe** serves fresh salads, burgers, mac 'n' cheese, pizzas and more with a wry smile, and the kids can hit the **Skate Park** next to **Lightwave Coffee and Kitchen**.

WHERE TO EAT DOWNRIVER FROM MONTE RIO

Gold Coast Coffee & Bakery
Stop in Duncans Mills for a gooey butterhorn or thin-crust pizza, plus occasional live local music. **$**

Cafe Aquatica
Jenner's waterfront cafe makes for lazy days sitting at the river-ocean confluence, coffee or crab roll in hand. **$**

River's End
Spectacular ocean views, an old-school fully stocked bar and seasonal menus of local fare. **$$**

FOR OCEAN LOVERS

River Rd/Hwy 116 ends at epic coastal Hwy 1. To continue north through kooky villages, artsy towns and mile upon mile of open coastal ranges alongside the vast Pacific, check out the **Cruising Hwy 1** road trip (p214).

Around Monte Rio, you'll pass the notorious **Bohemian Grove**, where since 1872, prominent male leaders – including several US presidents, famous actors and industry moguls – have gathered to frolic nude in 4 sq miles of private redwoods.

In winter, the river can flood during heavy rains, and beach vendors close. But it's a fine time for watching osprey and blue heron ply the moody river mists from the shore.

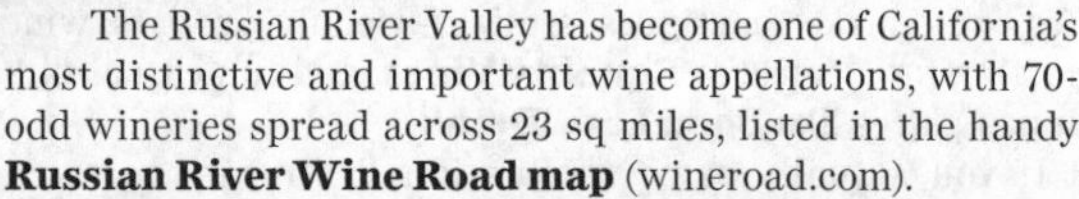

Wine Tasting in the Russian River Valley

IDYLLIC WINE ROAD

The Russian River Valley has become one of California's most distinctive and important wine appellations, with 70-odd wineries spread across 23 sq miles, listed in the handy **Russian River Wine Road map** (wineroad.com).

The highest concentration is along **Westside Rd**, between Guerneville and Healdsburg, a world-class country drive through redwood hills, sun-drenched vineyards and mossy oaks, even if you aren't a wine taster.

MacRostie is tops for gorgeous views and pinots that regularly rack up high points from critics. At **Flowers**, foodie bites and wine pair perfectly, like chardonnay and fennel-pollen-sprinkled *gougères,* and ridge-top pinot noir with black nori.

Step inside the 1930s tool shed at **Porter Creek** for sensational, sustainable pinot noir, syrah, viognier and chardonnay – casual wine tasting at its best.

Room for more? Hit the **Gary Farrell** and **De La Montanya** vineyards.

RUSSIAN RIVER VALLEY WINES

Nighttime coastal fog drifts up the Russian River Valley, then usually clears by midday. Pinot noir does beautifully here, as does chardonnay, which also grows in hotter regions but prefers the longer 'hang time' of cooler climes. Visit wineries lining wonderful Westside Rd, or one of the region's best hidden wineries: **Porter-Bass**, where mists swirl around redwoods and biodynamic vines yield outstanding vino, poured for you at a wood-plank bar.

Old-Growth Redwoods & Ocean Trails

ANCIENT GROVES AND HILLTOP VIEWS

The oldest tree in Guerneville's magnificent 805-acre **Armstrong Redwoods State Natural Reserve** is a true survivor: 309ft high, 1400 years old and named after a lumber baron. Colonel James Armstrong bought these woodlands in 1874 to log, but changed his mind when he saw the old-growth redwoods. Follow the well-maintained loop trail.

Hikers should not miss one of the Greater Bay Area's premier trails, the **Pomo Canyon Red Hill Trail**, from Pomo Canyon up and over coastal hills to Shell Beach. It's 6.5 miles if you walk it as a loop.

GETTING AROUND

West County's winding roads get confusing and there's limited cell-phone service – carry a proper map or download your maps for offline use. The couple of Sonoma County Transit buses that serve the area (lines 20 and 28) are very infrequent. Take the Regional Parks River Shuttle on summer weekends to avoid parking nightmares.

HEALDSBURG

Healdsburg

San Francisco

Los Angeles

Today, Healdsburg seems to have it all – looks, style, taste and plenty of money – but its history is a real-life telenovela. It began with forbidden romance, when rebellious SoCal teenager Joséfa Carrillo fell for wisecracking Massachusetts-born sea captain Henry Fitch. Joséfa and Henry planned to homestead a 75-sq-mile ranch on leased Wappo land in Sonoma, but Henry died of pneumonia in 1849, leaving Joséfa widowed at age 39, with 11 kids and a not-yet-working ranch. An uninvited guest named Harmon Heald squatted on the property until the US government auctioned it off to bidders, including Heald.

When the dust finally settled in 'Heald's-burg' in the 1860s, a Victorian village flourished around the town's sun-dappled square and ranchlands were planted with farms and vineyards.

Nowadays Healdsburg is a gourmet magnet, with farm-inspired bistros and wine-tasting rooms. You can bicycle along vineyard-lined West Dry Creek Rd and Westside Rd, where California sunshine and valley mists produce wonderfully nuanced wines.

TOP TIP

Events take place across Sonoma County's Alexander, Dry Creek and Russian River Valleys (check wineroad.com). At the Wine & Food Affair, about 100 wineries pair a featured dish with their wines. The neoclassical Carnegie Library in downtown Healdsburg contains a museum covering Sonoma County life.

Preston Farm & Winery

BEYOND WINING & DINING

Healdsburg's center is dotted with crafty shops packed with creative wares and contemporary art galleries, such as **Erickson Fine Art**, **Jam Jar** and **Gallery Lulo**, or **Upstairs Gallery** above the **Levin** bookstore.

Explore Dry Creek Valley's natural side, with **Getaway Adventures**, who offer active tours from all-ages bike and wine tours to Russian River kayak/bike rides, as well as excursions to the coast or Napa.

Hop in a canoe or kayak from **River's Edge Kayak & Canoe Trips** and paddle down Healdsburg's lazy stretch of Russian River, or try stand-up paddleboarding.

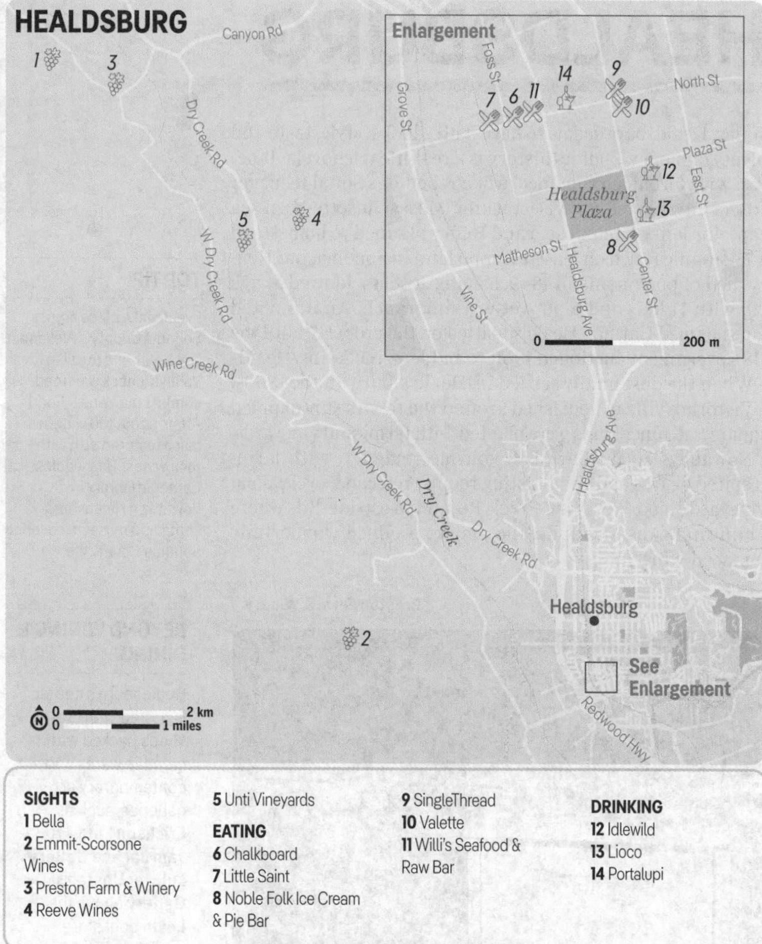

SIGHTS
1 Bella
2 Emmit-Scorsone Wines
3 Preston Farm & Winery
4 Reeve Wines
5 Unti Vineyards

EATING
6 Chalkboard
7 Little Saint
8 Noble Folk Ice Cream & Pie Bar
9 SingleThread
10 Valette
11 Willi's Seafood & Raw Bar

DRINKING
12 Idlewild
13 Lioco
14 Portalupi

Sparkling Plaza, Tasting Rooms & Gastronomy

PARADE OF SENSATIONS

Stroll Healdsburg's verdant central plaza, lined with cool boutiques, bookstores and tasting rooms. Drink all along Northern California's coast from the comfort of your lounge seat at Lioco, specialist in coastal chardonnays and pinot noirs. At **Idlewild** especially fascinating Piedmontese wines are quietly made by 4th-generation winemaker Sam Bilbro. Also of Italian origin, the wines at **Portalupi** include unexpected sparking barbera.

The most difficult problem with eating in Healdsburg is choosing where to go. You can splash out a gastronomic temple like **SingleThread**, where edible Sonoma landscape is the first of 11 sensational seasonal courses, which range from vineyard 'cover crop' grains to forest-floor-foraged morel dashi – a tour de force of nature. SingleThread farmer Katina Connaughton and chef-husband Kyle helped found **Little Saint**, where chef de cuisine Bryan Oliver now masterminds the plant-based menu.

'Healdsburg-inspired' aptly describes Dustin and Aaron, the locally born brothers behind **Valette**, and the meals they share with friends and strangers alike. You might spot Dustin at Healdsburg Farmers Market, hauling a wagonful of produce destined for his menus.

That small, seasonal, ingredient-driven bistro every chef dreams of opening comes to life at **Chalkboard**, a snug wine grotto with a sunny back patio.

Next door, slurp ocean-fresh oysters with crisp white wines at **Willi's Seafood & Raw Bar**.

And what's not to love about **Noble Folk Ice Cream & Pie Bar**? It's a dessert dream beyond ice cream – lemon-lavender cupcakes, brownie cubes and raspberry brown-butter macarons are tastier than they'll look on your Insta feed.

Crushing on Rural Wineries

DRY CREEK VALLEY ESCAPE

Hemmed in by 2000ft-high mountains, **Dry Creek Valley** is relatively warm, ideal for sauvignon blanc and zinfandel, and in some places cabernet sauvignon. Roll down the valley's undulating country lane – one of Sonoma County's great back roads, ideal for cycling.

The caves at **Bella** are as pretty as the name suggests and are impressively hardworking, turning grapes from 105-year-old estate vines into prize zinfandels and syrah. From the tasting-room window at **Unti Vineyards**, rolling vineyards look like sun-drenched Tuscan hills – and that's exactly what you'll taste in your wineglass: organically farmed Mediterranean noble grapes that thrive in these conditions. Dry Creek's best find is **Emmitt-Scorsone Wines**, hidden on a back road, where upstart cult wine labels **Judge Palmer** and **Domenica Amato** are made, and where the winemaker pours sneak previews between tasks.

Patio tastings at **Reeve Wines** let you admire the vineyards and sheep pastures as you sip poetry-inducing rosé of pinot noir and alluring single-vineyard sangiovese. **Preston Farm & Winery** grows heirloom produce and raises livestock to support an integrated ecosystem – sheep handle weeding, and artichokes and radishes help with pest control. The farm store sells produce and olive oil, while the bar pours citrusy sauvignon blancs.

PLAZA LIFE

Healdsburg's inviting plaza is always a chill place to people-watch and picnic. In summer, join **free concerts** each Tuesday afternoon – local food vendors set up by 5pm and tunes start at 6pm.

On sunny Tuesdays and Saturdays the **farmers market** (healdsburgfarmersmarket.org) begins with warm hellos from Sonoma County farmers, inspiring cooking demos and live music. Graze regional delicacies, such as Dry Creek peaches, Lata's samosas, Volo chocolate's bean-to-bar treats, Valley Ford Creamery's award-winning Estero Gold cheeses and organic Preston olive oil. Find unique handmade gifts, including Lissa Herschleb's stamped ceramic earrings and Michael Rosen's stoneware mugs. Since 1978 the market has also hosted seasonal events, from zucchini races to pumpkin-carving contests.

GETTING AROUND

Sonoma County Transit buses travel around Healdsburg and connect it to neighboring cities. Parking is easier once you get out of the plaza zone. Since 1976, Spoke Folk Cyclery have been getting visitors to vineyards on rental bikes.

Beyond Healdsburg

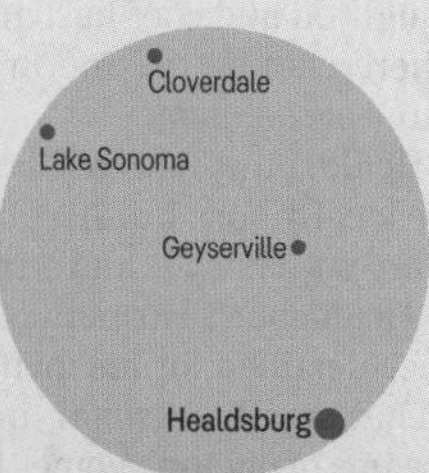

The vast Alexander Valley and small-town Geyserville and Cloverdale, where country living thrives, embrace you in a sense of quiet escape.

As Hwy 101 begins its long journey north from Healdsburg, the valley widens, with pastures and vineyards carpeting the way. Folks start to become fewer and farther between, and Geyserville and Cloverdale are way off the tourism radar. They offer down-to-earth gateways to the Alexander Valley, one of the most completely planted wine regions in Sonoma, with its inviting wineries and equally inviting winemakers. It's a kind of rural living that doesn't really feel like the Bay Area at all.

Just 6 miles south of Healdsburg, the city of Windsor is a sleepy place that makes for a more budget-friendly base than Healdsburg. Famous Russian River Brewing Co has a tasting room and brewery here that's less thronged than their Santa Rosa pub.

TOP TIP

Stay in the area at the Old Crocker Inn, the historic Cloverdale ranch of Victorian railroad baron Charles Crocker.

Grape vines in Alexander Valley

NATURE'S CHARM/SHUTTERSTOCK ©

Wild West Vibes, Pools & Unexpectedly Fine Dining

GEYSERVILLE'S CREATURE COMFORTS

Welcome to **Geyserville**, population 671. It's 12 minutes' drive north of Healdsburg…but where are the geysers? Wander the town's old wooden boardwalk, and you'll find Wild West character and a **sculpture trail**, but no sign of the geothermal wonders that initially attracted visitors in 1847. The hot springs are located underground, and produce 20% of California's renewable energy. To get into hot water, reserve a spot at the vast hilltop swimming pools at the **Francis Ford Coppola Winery**. Newly reopened **Cyrus** has already earned a Michelin star, and ably delights with exquisite Sonoma County fusion in a modern glass dining room.

Grapes, Grapes & More Grapes

ALEXANDER VALLEY WINERIES

As you explore the serene historic **Alexander Valley** (alexander valley.org) vineyards around Geyserville and Cloverdale, follow Hwy 128 to the tasting room of **Soda Rock Winery** for excellent California zinfandel. Down the road you'll find Chalk Hill AVA vineyards flourishing at indie, women-run wineries. Try velvety pinots at **Carpenter** under a sheltering oak and hike the vineyard at **Sutro** with brilliant 5th-generation winemaker Alice Sutro. At **Hanna** taste the sunny, rustic, estate-grown chardonnay, zinfandel and cabernet.

Lake Boating, Fishing, Hiking & Biking

THE PLEASURES OF LAKE SONOMA

A teal lake and wilderness preserve amid golden Sonoma foothills 20 minutes' drive north of Healdsburg, scenic **Lake Sonoma** was made by the US Army. In 1983, the US Army Corps of Engineers built Warm Springs Dam for practical purposes, including flood control and irrigation – and the result was this sporting jackpot, with a lake for boating and fishing, miles of trails for hiking and biking, a hillside archery range and a fish hatchery that's helped restore Sonoma's once-endangered steelhead.

FOR LAKE LOVERS

California is home to the brilliant, alpine **Lake Tahoe** (p564), best for beaches and boating in summer and skiing in winter.

BEST CASUAL EATS BEYOND HEALDSBURG

Diavola Pizza
A contender for California's most perfectly crispy thin-crust, wood-fired pizza, with house-cured *salumi* and sausage. $$

Russian River Brewing Co
At this renowned brewery you'll need to balance the flight of beers or brewery tour with pub grub. $

Tomi Thai
Windsor's stellar Thai restaurant makes it worth the trip for the huge array of traditionally prepared dishes. $

Plank Coffee & Tea
House-roasted espresso drinks and an impressive 50 loose-leaf teas, plus homemade quiche and baked treats. $

GETTING AROUND

You'll need a car or private transportation to get around beyond Healdsburg.

NORTH COAST & REDWOODS

TALL TREES AND WILD COASTLINE

Rugged and scenic, California's North Coast is imbued with spectral fog and an outsider spirit.

Locals on California's northern coast like to say they live 'behind the redwood curtain.' The sky-high trees create not only a physical barrier but also a palpable psychological divide: much about this wild, remote and even slightly foreboding region has long been a mystery. In the past, most travelers never made it this far – unless, of course, they were trimming weed. And it's telling that a stretch of this shoreline became 'lost' after the state's highway system deemed the region impassable in the 1930s.

Little by little, though, the curtain is starting to slip. During the summer, when large pockets of California are on fire, smoky or generally sweltering, people head for the fog-shrouded north. They're escaping into the tranquil, fern-filled redwood groves and hiring a forest-bathing guide to help them reconnect. They're backpacking over secluded coastal bluffs, spying on elk and scanning the horizon for migrating whales. They're dropping by the lesser-explored wine appellations, venturing into hidden coves with a blanket and a local bottle, then retreating to cozy, fire-warmed Victorian mansions.

AHTURNER/SHUTTERSTOCK ©

The big question, though, is whether tourism (or anything else) can replace the region's former cash crop. Nobody in the Green Triangle can make a living growing the legal stuff anymore, but they'll certainly take you on a tour of a pot farm, massage you in a cannabis spa and certify you a 'gangier.' Yes, a sommelier of ganja.

THE MAIN AREAS

MENDOCINO
Dreamy coastal village. **p208**

THE LOST COAST
Rugged wilderness beach. **p216**

EUREKA
Passes for urban. **p225**

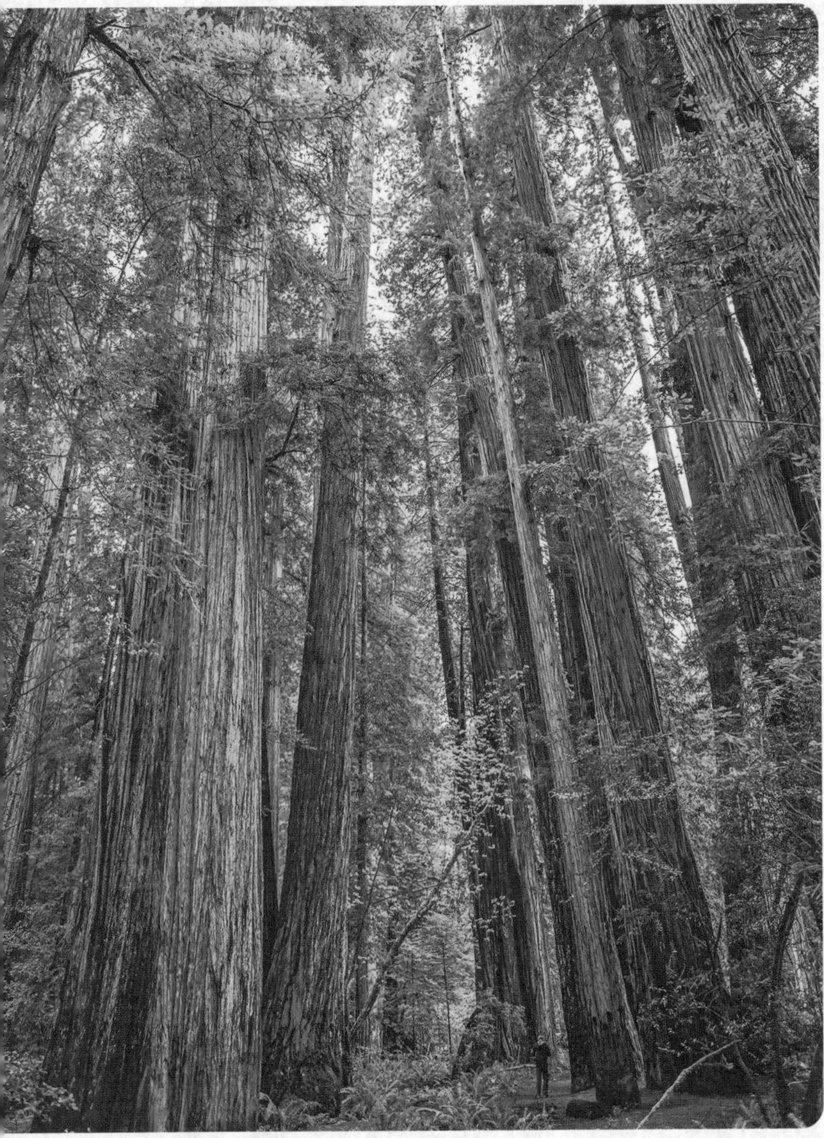

ANDREAS C. FISCHER/SHUTTERSTOCK ©

Left: Punta Gorda Lighthouse (p219); Above: Jedediah Smith Redwoods State Park (p234)

REDWOOD NATIONAL & STATE PARKS
Neck-craning, mind-blowing forests. **p232**

CLEAR LAKE
Big lake, lesser-known wine. **p240**

Find Your Way

Stretching over more than 300 miles of coastline, nearly 200,000 acres of redwood parkland and vast swaths of little-known wine country, the North Coast has a place for you.

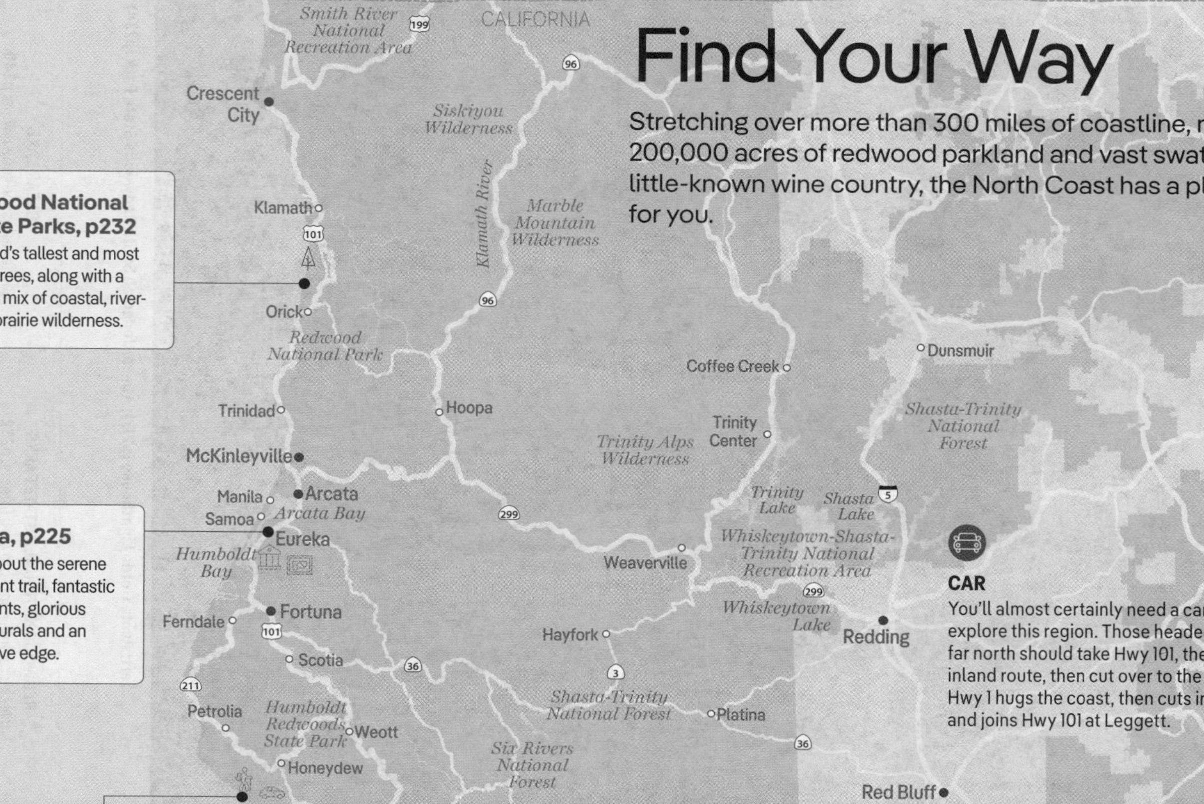

Redwood National & State Parks, p232
The world's tallest and most ancient trees, along with a luxuriant mix of coastal, riverine and prairie wilderness.

Eureka, p225
It's all about the serene waterfront trail, fantastic restaurants, glorious street murals and an alternative edge.

CAR
You'll almost certainly need a car to explore this region. Those headed to the far north should take Hwy 101, the faster, inland route, then cut over to the coast. Hwy 1 hugs the coast, then cuts inland and joins Hwy 101 at Leggett.

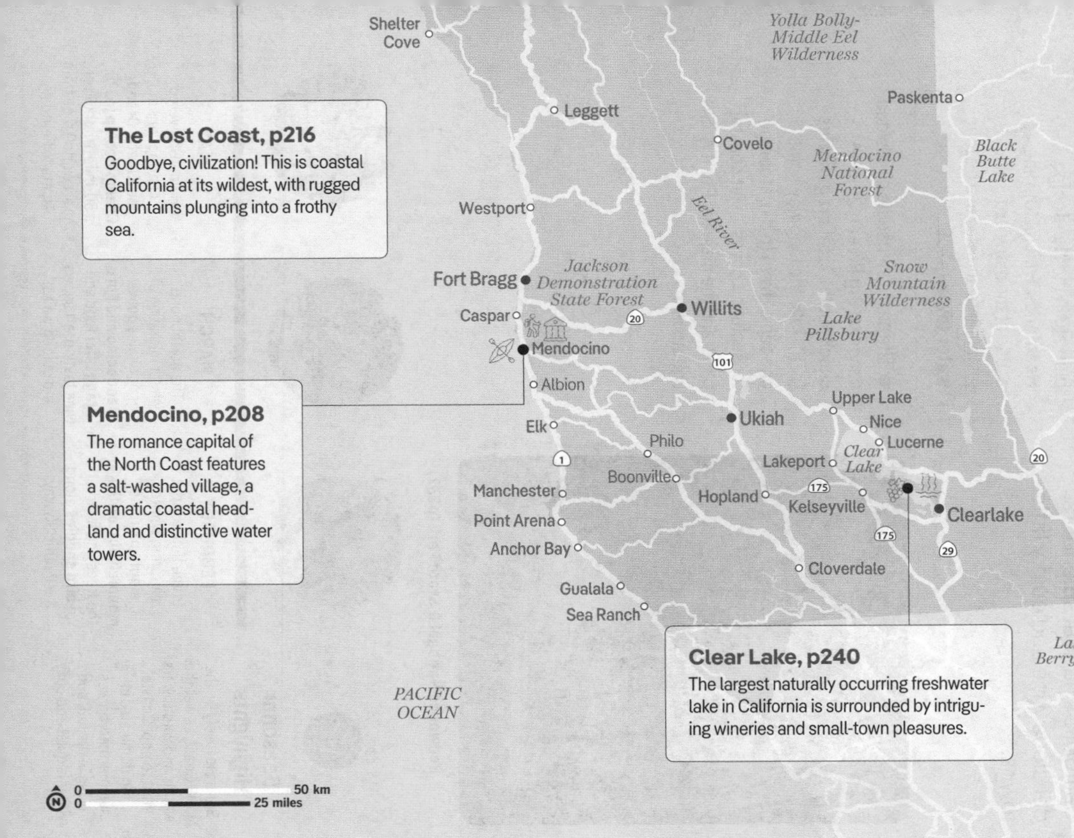

The Lost Coast, p216

Goodbye, civilization! This is coastal California at its wildest, with rugged mountains plunging into a frothy sea.

Mendocino, p208

The romance capital of the North Coast features a salt-washed village, a dramatic coastal headland and distinctive water towers.

Clear Lake, p240

The largest naturally occurring freshwater lake in California is surrounded by intriguing wineries and small-town pleasures.

BUS

Those willing to piece together bus travel through the region will face a time-consuming headache, but connections are possible to most towns. Companies include Greyhound, the Mendocino Transit Authority, the Redwood Transit System and Redwood Coast Transit.

AIR

California Redwood Coast Humboldt County Airport is located north of McKinleyville. It has regular services to San Francisco and Los Angeles. In the far north, Crescent City is home to the tiny Del Norte County Regional Airport, which has a daily service to Oakland.

Plan Your Time

The North Coast is a place to slow down and appreciate California's natural splendors, delicious wine and quirky little towns.

JACKSWAN TURNER/SHUTTERSTOCK ©

Redwoods National & State Park (p232)

Pressed for Time

- If you only have a weekend, **Mendocino** (p208) is relatively easy to reach and puts the region's best foot forward. Drive up Hwy 101 and cut through **Anderson Valley** (p213), where travelers can sip excellent wine. Stroll the gorgeous bluff along the **Mendocino Headlands Trail** (p210), dine at one of the many exquisite restaurants and stay in a historic **water tower** (p209).

- The next day, paddle a redwood canoe up **Big River** (p211) and check out the local **art galleries** (p211). Take the long way home on scenic **Hwy 1** (p214), stopping for secluded coves, quiet coastal parks and the majestic Point Arena lighthouse.

Seasonal Highlights

Spring is lovely on the North Coast, as weather warms and wildflowers start to pop. Coastal fog dominates in summertime, harvest is big in the fall, and winter is quiet and cozy.

FEBRUARY

Prime time to spot migrating **whales**, **elephant seals**, **monarch butterflies** in the trees and hundreds of **bird species** along the Pacific Flyway.

MARCH

The northbound winter migration of gray whales peaks; **Mendocino and Fort Bragg** offer food and wine tasting, art shows and guided walks.

MAY

Human-powered contraptions in the **Kinetic Grand Championship** (p228; a 50-mile 'triathlon of the art world') race from Arcata to Ferndale.

OCIMADFOTO/SHUTTERSTOCK ©, RWV/SHUTTERSTOCK ©, BRIAN CAHN/ZUMA WIRE/ALAMY ©

A Few Days to Travel Around

● After a couple of days in Mendocino, continue north to the mighty **Avenue of the Giants** (p222), perhaps stopping for a guided **forest bathing** (p223) experience. Be sure to hit up some kitschy **roadside stops** (p222) and take the **scenic route** (p218) over to the Lost Coast, where you can stay by the sea.

● In the morning, tackle a portion of the renowned **Lost Coast Trail** (p217) to Punta Gorda Lighthouse and its famous elephant seals. Then drive north to **Ferndale** (p222), California's quaintest town, to admire the 'butterfat mansions' and stay the night in a lovely **Victorian** (p222) filled with period furnishings.

If You Have More Time

● Head to **Redwood National & State Parks** (p232) to hang out with the world's tallest trees. Start in Jedediah Smith Redwoods with the new **Grove of the Titans** (p235) hike, then make the **scenic drive** (p238) down the coast, going **canoeing** (p238) with a Yurok tribesman and learning why *The Lost World: Jurassic Park* was filmed at **Fern Canyon** (p234). Sleep in a **Sue-meg State Park** (p238) cabin or a B&B in **Trinidad** (p238), then hike the dramatic headlands spotting sea lions and whales. Finally, explore **Eureka** (p225) and **Arcata** (p231), getting to know the artists, pot farmers and others who call it home.

JUNE

Fire season starts. From Bodega Bay all the way to Crescent City, **hiking**, going to the **beach**, river **swimming**, camping and **farmers markets** are in full swing.

JULY

The **Northern Lights Music Festival**, the **Mendocino Music Festival** and other events pop up all over the region. Fog tourists arrive.

OCTOBER

The **wine regions** celebrate their harvest with food-and-wine shindigs, grape-stomping and barrel tastings; some events start in September.

NOVEMBER

Rain and fog envelop the coast, and having a **wood-burning stove** becomes super cozy. Prices drop and crowds thin out.

MENDOCINO

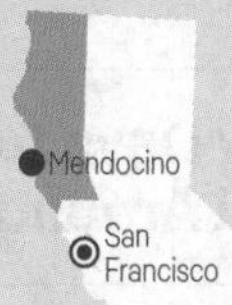

Built on a headland by transplanted New Englanders in the 1850s, the salt-washed settlement of Mendocino thrived late into the 19th century thanks to ships transporting redwood timber from here to San Francisco. The mills shut down in the 1930s, and the town was infiltrated in the 1950s by artists and bohemians. Today, fewer than 1000 residents remain, but the romantic seaside village receives some 1.8 million visitors each year, and water shortages have become a chronic problem.

With rose gardens and white-picket fences, quaint B&Bs and New England–style redwood water towers, Mendocino becomes all the more desirable during fire season, when 'fog tourists' descend. They come to saunter along the headland trail and soothe their muscles in saunas and hot tubs, to dine at exquisite restaurants and to shop for luxury goods at boutique galleries and cute shops. Their willingness to drop large amounts of cash has resulted in this destination's fitting nickname: 'Spendocino.'

TOP TIP

To avoid crowds, come midweek or in the low season, when the vibe is mellower and prices more reasonable. Regardless of when you will visit, book hotels, restaurants and activities as far in advance as possible.

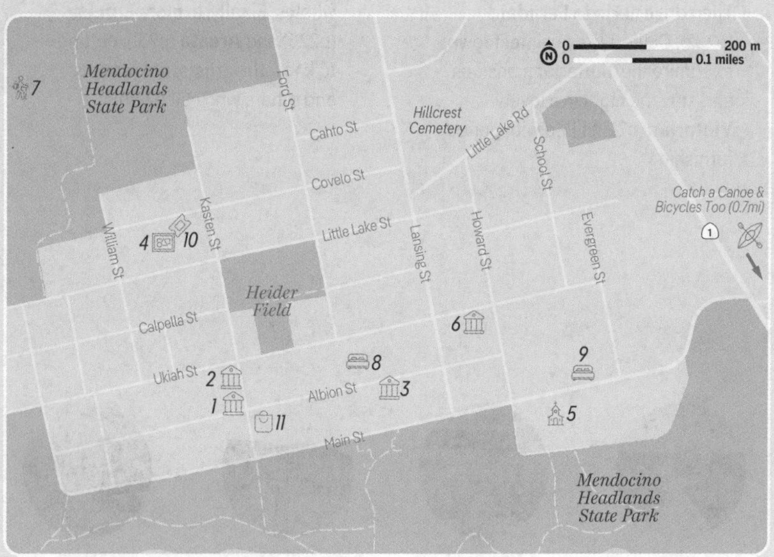

SIGHTS
1 Artists' Co-op of Mendocino
2 Highlight Gallery
3 Kelley House Museum
4 Mendocino Art Center
5 Mendocino Presbyterian Church
6 Water Gallery

ACTIVITIES, COURSES & TOURS
7 Mendocino Headlands State Park

SLEEPING
8 MacCallum House Inn
9 Sweetwater Inn and Spa

ENTERTAINMENT
10 Helen Schoeni Theatre

SHOPPING
11 Loot & Lore

Mendocino's water towers

Why All the Water Towers?

A QUIRKY HISTORY

Mendocino isn't called 'The Town of Water Towers' for nothing. Back in the late 19th century, more than 100 redwood water towers and accompanying windmills (which powered pumps that pulled water from underground wells) loomed above the Main St storefronts, churches and Victorian homes. Today, only a couple dozen remain, and many of those can be visited on a water-tower history tour given by Anne Semans, the director of the excellent **Kelley House Museum** (which features changing exhibits on early California and Mendocino). The water-tower system, Semans tells her guests, was created to tap Mendocino's shallow water table with the help of the frequent high winds atop the bluff. Some tanks supplied one home, while others provided for entire blocks, and still more were used by hotels and for fire suppression.

Some of the old water towers have even been converted into accommodations. At the **MacCallum House Inn**, a restored tower has become a two-story suite with a top-floor sauna and views of Mendocino Bay. **Sweetwater Inn and Spa** rents out three towers that all date from the 1800s and

WRECK OF THE FROLIC

In 1850, a ship retired from the opium trade – the *Frolic* – struck a reef near **Point Cabrillo**, about 3 miles north of Mendocino, and ran aground. Jerome Ford, who came from San Francisco to salvage the cargo, was too late as the Pomo Indians (who had inhabited the region for some 10,000 years) had already recovered the Chinese luxury goods onboard. But Ford took notice of the coast's real treasure: the enormous redwoods. He teamed up with entrepreneur Henry Meiggs, who bought a sawmill and had it transported to Big River. During the mill's 50-year run, it yielded a billion board feet of timber, used to build San Francisco and then rebuild it after the 1906 earthquake.

BEST SHOPPING IN MENDOCINO

Gallery Bookshop & Bullwinkle's Children's Books
Stocks a great selection of books on local topics and specialized outdoor guides.

Out of This World
Birders, astronomy buffs and science geeks head directly to this binocular, telescope and science-toy shop.

Highlight Gallery
Displays handcrafted wood furniture, fine art, ceramics, sculptures, jewelry and textiles, all created by NorCal artisans.

BEST STAYS IN MENDOCINO

Stanford Inn & Resort
Superlative resort with a solarium-enclosed pool, organic gardens and a delish vegan restaurant. $$$

Alegria
Romantic hideaway – decks have views over the coast and rooms have fireplaces. $$

Mendocino Hotel
The town's first hotel, this place is a relic of the Old West. $

Mendocino Grove
Glamping gem by the sea with safari-style tents and elegant bathhouses. $$

Brewery Gulch Inn
An arts-and-crafts-style resort built with salvaged redwood, in verdant gardens south of Mendocino. $$$

ALESSANDRARC/SHUTTERSTOCK ©

MacCallum House Inn (p209)

come with access to clothing-optional hot tubs. Peek around town, and you'll notice others that have been converted into vacation rentals, artists' studios, stairwells and even an occult shop – **Loot & Lore** – which hawks witchy jewelry and ritual supplies.

MORE WHALES

For some of the state's best marine-mammal watching, head south to **Channel Islands National Park** (p331), where a whopping 27 species of cetacean have been spotted, including gray, blue, humpback, minke, sperm and pilot whales.

Hiking the Mendocino Headlands Trail

DIZZYING CLIFFS BY THE SEA

A short walk from the town, this convenient but spectacular trail follows the dramatic edge of the headland and is flanked with berry bramble, wildflowers and cypress trees perched over steep bluffs. The trail runs the length of **Mendocino Headlands State Park**, and is best hiked from east to west, starting at **Mendocino Presbyterian Church** on Church St, a fine example of Carpenter Gothic architecture and a California Historical Landmark. You can also hike from west to east, and there are several parking areas near different stretches of the trail, meaning you can drop in on those sections without hiking the whole thing.

As you stroll along the edge of the rocky headland, the ocean views will include rock formations and dramatic arches, and you'll encounter several short spur trails

BEST PLACES TO EAT AND DRINK IN MENDOCINO

Luna Trattoria
Atmospheric restaurant serving Northern Italian favorites: wood-fired pizza, house-made pasta and stellar lasagna. **$$**

Goodlife Cafe & Bakery
Locals and tourists mingle in this unpretentious, noisy and cozy cafe over baked goods and comfort food. **$**

Cafe Beaujolais
Iconic California-French fusion restaurant in an 1893 farmhouse restyled into an urban-chic dining room. **$$$**

to hidden viewpoints that are especially lovely around sunset, and often deserted. You might even spot a passing whale! Seize the opportunity to descend the stairs to the wide, picturesque coves and relax in the sand, where people often construct elaborate driftwood structures. When you're back up on the bluff, listen to the foamy sea lapping against the hollowed-out caves below.

Paddling a Redwood Canoe

BIG ADVENTURE ON BIG RIVER

'Everyone must believe in something. I believe I'll go canoeing,' Henry David Thoreau once said. Mendocino offers a unique opportunity to do so in redwood outriggers built from reclaimed barn wood by a local craftsperson. The adventure begins beneath the Big River bridge at **Catch a Canoe & Bicycles Too**, owned and operated by the adjacent and fabulous Stanford Inn & Resort (p212). Knowledgeable staff members help your family (including the dog) into a canoe and send you up the river equipped with maps and insight into the region.

The redwood-flanked banks of this tidal estuary (the second longest in California at 8.3 miles) remain undeveloped for the duration, having been purchased in 2002 through a massive fundraising effort and becoming part of Mendocino Headlands State Park. Back in the 1800s, though, logging companies built dams and stacked logs along the water, then in wintertime dynamited the dams to float the logs to the mill. Remnants of this process, including 'sinker logs,' can still be found today.

As you glide through the estuary, you'll notice it is otherwise pristine and frequented by friendly harbor seals, hunting river otters, nesting ospreys and double-crested cormorants, who keep a rookery high in the trees. Paddling through their world is all the more enjoyable in the narrow, efficient canoes, which offer a foot-operated rudder system and twin hulls that provide remarkable stability. To fully enjoy this classic Mendocino experience, bring a picnic and a camera.

Partaking in Art

A HUB FOR CREATIVE PURSUITS

In Mendocino, you can't throw a paintbrush without hitting an artist. It's been that way since the late '50s, when Bill Zacha bought a large property in the middle of town and turned it into the **Mendocino Art Center**. Today, the sprawling compound remains a haven for artists as well as an educational institution and creative retreat, hosting exhibitions,

BEST WHALE-WATCHING SPOTS

Mendocino Headlands State Park
In wintertime, the Ford House Museum & Visitor Center offers guided whale-watching walks.

Point Arena Lighthouse
One of the two tallest lighthouses on the West Coast (tied with nearby Pigeon Point) at 115ft.

Point Cabrillo Light Station
Stout 1909 lighthouse in a 300-acre wildlife preserve north of Mendocino.

Sue-meg State Park
Coastal bluffs jut out to sea and sandy beaches abut rocky headlands.

Klamath River Overlook
On a clear day, this is one of the best whale-watching spots in California.

Ravens
A vegan revelation, serving produce from the organic gardens of the Stanford Inn. Great cooking classes, too. **$$**

Dick's Place
A dive bar with a great jukebox. The perfect spot to check the other Mendocino and do shots with rowdy locals. **$**

Trillium Cafe
Inspired, seasonal California cuisine served in a cozy dining room, alfresco with ocean views or to go in a picnic box. **$$**

I LIVE HERE: BEST PLACES TO BE INSPIRED

Joan and Jeff Stanford have owned the Stanford Inn & Resort (@stanford_inn) since 1980. Joan conducts creative playshops, while Jeff teaches meditation. They wrote a vegan cookbook together and recommend these Mendocino experiences.

Hiking to Russian Gulch Waterfall
Walk the soft trails alongside streams and breathtaking redwoods, allowing thoughts to turn to wonder and fresh ideas to flow.

Attending Open Paint Out
The Mendocino Art Center's plein air festival attracts artists from all over the country. Meet the artists and revel in their joyous competition.

Canoeing Big River
Narrow beaches along this undeveloped estuary provide wonderful picnic sites and opportunities to soak in the sounds and sights of the forest.

SAWBEAR/SHUTTERSTOCK ©

A canoe on Big River (p211)

renowned art classes and the 81-seat **Helen Schoeni Theatre**, which is home to the **Mendocino Theatre Company** (mendocinotheatre.org).

Whether you have a passion for ceramics, fine arts, fiber arts, jewelry or sculpture, taking a class at the art center is a surefire way to meet local artists and tap into the essence of Mendocino. Another way to get your art fix is to browse some of the local galleries. The **Highlight Gallery** on Kasten St features the finest work of Northern California painters, woodworkers, sculptors and artisans, while the **Water Gallery** is a working artist's studio housed in a water tower on Ukiah St. Just down the road, the **Artists' Co-op of Mendocino** has been showing the work of traditional and contemporary fine artists since 1988. For further inspiration, simply walk around this incredibly scenic town and the remarkable natural places in its surroundings.

Mendocino's galleries hold openings on the second Saturday (and sometimes the first Friday) of each month, usually from 5pm to 7pm. Check mendocinobeacon.com for exact times and details.

GETTING AROUND

You're definitely going to want a car. But the Mendocino Transit Authority does run buses along The Coaster Rte 60 between the Navarro River Junction and Albion, Little River, Mendocino and Fort Bragg.

Beyond Mendocino

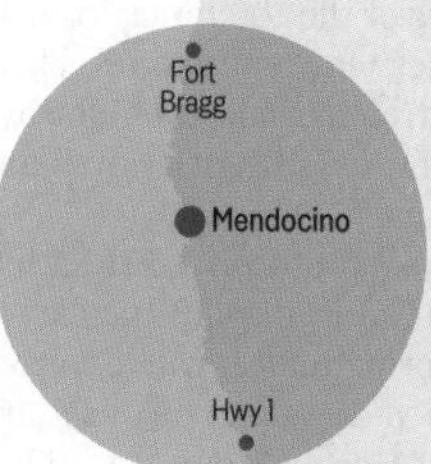

Experience a beach of sea glass, a brilliant coastal drive, a tranquil wine valley and an unpretentious neighbor to the north.

Whatever direction you've headed in for a day trip from Mendocino, congratulations – you've made an excellent choice. To the south lies one of California's classically beautiful drives, the coastal Hwy 1, which cuts a winding course on isolated cliffs high above the crashing surf. Off Hwy 1 to the east you'll climb into Anderson Valley, an agricultural gem most famous for its apple orchards, idyllic vineyards and friendly folks. And just to the north there's workaday Fort Bragg, a one-time lumber and fishing town being reinvented as a tourism destination, with a legendary beach covered in sea glass, an eye-catching botanical garden and a vintage-train company that also offers a rail-bike experience.

TOP TIP

Don't rush it. If you see an inviting, deserted cove, a patch of unusual wildflowers or an intriguing winery, pull over and explore.

Glass Beach (p215), Fort Bragg

CRUISING HIGHWAY 1

Over the 100 miles from Mendocino to Bodega Bay, you can revel in an uninterrupted stretch of coastal highway that skirts rocky shores, secluded coves and wind-sculpted beaches.

First stop is **1 Elk**, a hamlet famous for its stunning cliff-top views of towering rock formations. If you're celebrating something, bed down in one of the 10 adorable rooms at Harbor House Inn. The ocean views are eye-popping and the hyper-local restaurant just earned its second Michelin star. Continuing south, you'll find the **2 Point Arena Lighthouse**, which has guarded the unbelievably windy point since 1908. It's the tallest climbable lighthouse in California. Check in at the museum, then ascend the 115ft tower to inspect the Fresnel lens, panoramas of the sea and the jagged San Andreas Fault below. Another half-hour down the coast is a series of villages. **3 Gualala** is a hub for weekend getaways and sunny weather. Sea Ranch is a weather-beaten but ritzy subdivision with a lot of exclusive-looking vacation homes, empty beaches and ocean bluffs open to the public. One of the best reasons to spend the night around these parts is **4 Salt Point State Park**, a 6000-acre stunner with sandstone cliffs dropping into a kelp-strewn sea and hiking trails crisscrossing windswept prairies and wooded hills. It's especially popular with mushroom foragers. From there, the road twists and turns past rhododendron groves, a reconstruction of a 19th-century Russian fur-trading fort, a seal colony at Jenner's harbor and the fishing fleets of **5 Bodega Bay** (yes, from Hitchcock's classic flick *The Birds*) before sending you into the San Francisco Bay Area.

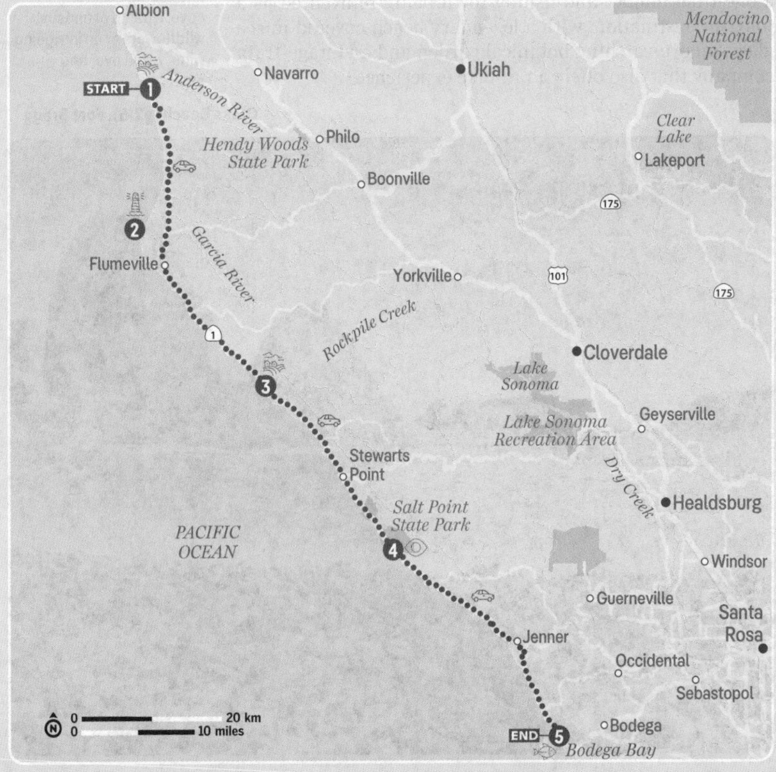

KATE FIEDLER/SHUTTERSTOCK ©

Mendocino Coast Botanical Gardens

Hangin' in Fort Bragg

MENDOCINO'S UNPRETENTIOUS COUSIN

Fort Bragg has the same banner North Coast activities as Mendocino – beachcombing, surfing, hiking and kayaking – but an outing here is definitely cheaper and considerably less precious. South of downtown at **Noyo Harbor**, roll up to a fish shack (there are many to choose from, but we like **Sea Pal Cove**) and chow down on fried seafood as you watch the fishing boats haul in the day's catch. Then head to town and take a ride on the historic **Skunk Train**, which got its nickname in 1925 for its stinky gas-powered steam engines (today it runs on diesel). One- or two-hour trips pass through the **Pudding Creek Estuary**, offering views of blue herons, ospreys, otters and redwood forests. You can also hire two-person rail bikes for a 7- or 25-mile round-trip guided tour along the same route as the train, with new moonlight rides in summertime. Book in advance as it's popular.

Don't leave Fort Bragg without a visit to the **Mendocino Coast Botanical Gardens** and its serpentine paths and wheelchair-accessible trails wandering along 47 seafront acres south of town. This Northern California wonder displays native flora, rhododendrons and heritage roses, and the succulents section alone makes it worthwhile. The organic garden is harvested by volunteers to feed area residents in need.

LEGENDARY GLASS BEACH

Starting in the early 1900s, Fort Bragg residents tossed untold amounts of detritus off a bluff and into the surf, expecting it would simply disappear. Instead, the refuse was returned to them as sea glass, as rock formations created unique wave patterns that tumbled the trash and pushed it back to the beach.

Not only did the sea transform Fort Bragg's trash, but it also put the otherwise unremarkable town on the map. In the '90s, people began traveling here to admire the shining booty, and in 2006 a local sea captain opened the **Sea Glass Museum**, one of the planet's most extensive collections. It's a must-see, and although much of the beach has been picked over, it remains a famous destination.

GETTING AROUND

Wheels are ideal to navigate the areas surrounding Mendocino. But Mendocino Transit Authority operates buses along major roads in the area, with Rte 60 connecting Fort Bragg to the Navarro River Junction, where Rte 75 goes east to Boonville and south to Point Arena and Gualala. Rte 95 connects Point Arena, Gualala and Bodega Bay.

THE LOST COAST

Los Angeles

In these increasingly crowded times, travelers who aim to get as far from civilization as possible will adore the Lost Coast. The longest stretch of undeveloped coastline in the state is a superlative backpacking destination and a glimpse into California's past, with foggy, windswept coves and rugged, 4000ft peaks that plunge into a frothy sea. Up and down this secluded shoreline, playful seals peek above the surf and majestic Roosevelt elk graze on grassy bluffs and within sky-high forests.

The coast became 'lost' when the state's highway system deemed the region unruly in the mid-20th century, and bypassed it. There is one sizable and difficult-to-reach community, however: Shelter Cove, perched on a south-facing bluff surrounded by the King Range National Conservation Area. Some folks arrive via the airstrip, while others brave the narrow, curvy road. While tourism may be a mainstay of the economy, locals are oftentimes leery of outsiders. Don't expect a sunny California welcome.

TOP TIP

Wildflowers bloom from April through May and gray whales migrate from December through April. The warmest, driest months are June to September, but days are foggy and the weather can change quickly. In fall, the weather is clear and cool.

Hiker on the Lost Coast

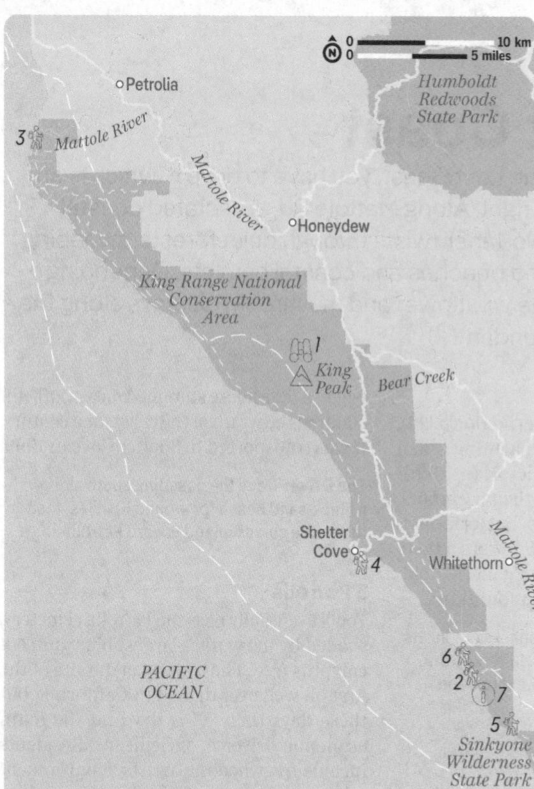

SIGHTS
1 King Peak

ACTIVITIES, COURSES & TOURS
2 Jones Beach
3 Mattole Beach
4 Shelter Cove
5 Sinkyone Wilderness State Park
6 Whale Gulch

INFORMATION
7 Needle Rock Visitor Center

Hiking the Lost Coast

GET INTO THE WILD

The best way to see the Lost Coast is to hike, and the most popular journey is the 24.6-mile **Lost Coast Trail** between **Shelter Cove** and **Mattole Beach**. The trail is mostly level, passing untouched beaches and crossing over rocky outcrops and streams. The long hike isn't for everyone, as it requires three days, a permit, bear canisters, a tide chart and an expensive shuttle back to your car (unless you hike it twice).

If you're hard-core but only have a day or two, take any of the King Range's strenuous upland trails off the beach toward

BEST PLACES TO EAT AND DRINK ON THE LOST COAST

Mi Mochima
From out of nowhere comes delicious and authentic Venezuelan cuisine: empanadas, arepas, *patacón* sandwiches. $$

Gyppo Ale Mill
Brews a dozen of its own ales and knocks burgers, brats and salads out of the park. Also lawn games and firepits. $$

Mario's Marina Bar
The local hangout in Shelter Cove has killer ocean views from its patio and frequent live music. $

ROAD TRIP

The Lost Coast

Before you can hike the Lost Coast, you have to drive it, which is an experience in its own right. Along Mattole Rd, an isolated coastal stretch, the narrow two-laner twists through quiet forests, sweeping grasslands, black-sand beaches and coastal hamlets. Depending on the time of year, the wildflower and mushroom displays along the drive can be quite abundant.

1 Ferndale

Your road trip starts in Ferndale (p222), one of California's most charming small towns for its distinctive Victorians. Built in the early 19th century with dairy profits, these are known locally as 'butterfat palaces.' A stroll down Main St offers a taste of small-town America, with galleries, old-world emporiums and soda fountains.

The Drive: After grabbing any snacks or trinkets you desire, hop on little-driven Matthole Rd and drive for 40 minutes southwest to Cape Mendocino.

2 Cape Mendocino

You'll roll through a high alpine forest and past Capetown, a former stagecoach stop, before meeting the sea at Cape Mendocino, where a lighthouse stationed on a 400ft cliff endured the wrath of the coast for a century. It was transported to Shelter Cove in 1998.

The Drive: Trace the coastline south along a black-sand beach for around 10 miles, then follow the curves inland toward Petrolia.

3 Petrolia

You'll eventually pass the Petrolia cemetery, shaded by the world's largest blue gum eucalyptus tree. The town was the site of the first oil well ever drilled in California, but these days the well is dry and the main economic driver is agriculture. Residents include freewheeling artists, environmentalists, pot-growers and other eccentrics.

The Drive: From Petrolia, it's a 15-minute drive west to Mattole Beach.

Punta Gorda Lighthouse

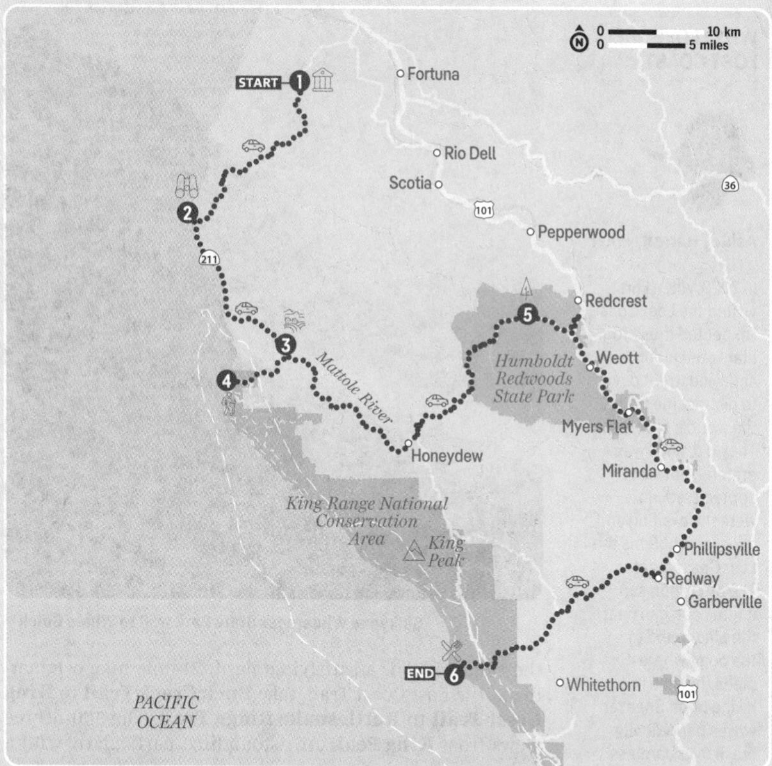

4 Mattole Beach

The sandy mouth of the Mattole River meets the sea at the north end of the King Range Conservation Area. There are campsites and picnic areas, along with the trailhead for the Lost Coast Trail (p217), which stretches 24.6 miles south to Shelter Cove. For a taste of the journey, hike the first 3.5 miles to Punta Gorda Lighthouse, which has remnants of shipwrecks, curious tide pools and enormous elephant seals.

The Drive: Double back the way you came and continue on Mattole Rd to Humboldt Redwoods State Park, or take the turnoff at Honeydew for back roads leading to Shelter Cove.

5 Humboldt Redwoods State Park

If you went with option two, you've exited the Lost Coast but entered perhaps the most scenic drivable stretch of redwood forest in the world. There's a reason people make car commercials along this snaking corridor, which stretches from Honeydew all the way to Hwy 101. The redwoods are large, abundant and close to the road, making it a tight squeeze to get through.

The Drive: If you took the redwoods route, it's still possible to end in Shelter Cove by taking Hwy 101 south. Once you're on the highway, it's about an hour's drive.

6 Shelter Cove

A last outpost of civilization, Shelter Cove came into existence 50 years ago after Southern California swindlers subdivided the land, built an airstrip and flew in potential investors, fast-talking them into buying seaside properties for retirement. What they didn't mention was that a steep, winding, one-lane dirt road provided the only access. Oh, and the seaside plots were eroding into the sea. There's still only one route, but now it's paved, and the town features several good restaurants and a fantastic brewery.

WHY I LOVE THE LOST COAST

Ashley Harrell, writer

In 2020, when I first visited the Lost Coast, I expected those fog-blanketed mountains and windswept coves to distract me from the world's problems. They did, and I was grateful, but what I appreciated more were the exciting and unusual problems the Lost Coast created. The afternoon sun, it turns out, can heat the black sand to the point where it melts the glue in a hiking boot. Sneaker waves periodically crash over careless backpackers. Sometimes, you share a campsite with a rattlesnake. You get through it, somehow. You come out stronger. You vow to return as soon as possible.

RICHARD SHEAK/SHUTTERSTOCK ©

Sinkyone Wilderness State Park trail to Whale Gulch

the ridgeline. For a satisfying, hard, 21-mile hike originating at the Lost Coast Trail, take **Buck Creek Trail** to **King Crest Trail** to **Rattlesnake Ridge Trail**. The 360-degree views from **King Peak** are astounding, particularly with a full moon or during a meteor shower.

For those interested in shorter and less challenging hikes, there's **Sinkyone Wilderness State Park** about an hour's drive south of Shelter Cove. From the **Needle Rock Visitor Center** you can hike in both directions along the coast, but the northern trail to **Whale Gulch** is the prettier route. The 4.5-mile out-and-back features golden bluffs and majestic wild elk, along with a spur trail down to **Jones Beach**, where the foaming sea drags bullwhip kelp to the bases of startling rock formations.

GETTING AROUND

There's no public transport on the Lost Coast, and the only reliable shuttle with permits to transport backpackers through the area is Lost Coast Adventure Tours. It operates daily shuttles from Shelter Cove to Mattole Beach.

Beyond the Lost Coast

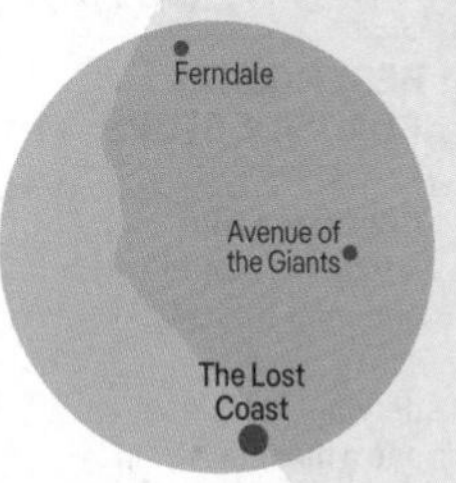

California's quaintest town and tallest trees are just outside the state's most beguiling coastal wilderness.

The Lost Coast is extremely remote, but it does not exist in a vacuum. On your way in or out, there are some very enticing stays, restaurants and roadside attractions to get into.

If you're coming in from the south on Hwy 101, Leggett and Standish-Hickey State Recreation Area are good for a delicious meal, a hike and a dip in one of the region's best swimming holes. Further up Hwy 101, you can also combine a drive through the famous Avenue of the Giants with your approach to the coast. Or, if driving down Hwy 101 from the north, the adorable town of Ferndale makes for a delightful gateway into the wild.

TOP TIP

Don't rush through or try to do everything, particularly along the Avenue of the Giants. Pick one or two groves or hikes to thoroughly enjoy.

Humboldt Redwoods National Park (p222)

YAYA ERNST/SHUTTERSTOCK ©

BEST NORCAL ROADSIDE STOPS

Confusion Hill
A tourist trap and enduring curiosity with a 'gravity-defying' fun house and a mountain train ride.

Drive-Thru Tree Park
Home of Leggett's chandelier tree, a redwood that keeps growing despite a gaping hole beneath it.

Legend of Bigfoot
A bigfoot-themed gift shop with a large wooden statue of Patti herself and more carved-out folklore.

Peg House
A general store, live-music venue and garden restaurant with the famous slogan: 'Never don't stop.'

Exploring Ferndale

SOAK UP THE BUTTERFAT

Many travelers use Ferndale as a base for exploring the Lost Coast or Avenue of the Giants, but there are attractions right at its doorstep, too. Half a mile from downtown via Bluff St, you can enjoy short tramps through fields of wildflowers, beside ponds and past a mature Sitka spruce forest (rarer even than redwood) at 110-acre **Russ Park**. The **cemetery**, also on Bluff St, is surprisingly cool, with graves dating from the 1800s and expansive views to the ocean.

If the town's history interests you, spend a night in one of its old-timey hotels. **Gingerbread Mansion** is the crème de la crème, an 1894 Queen Anne–Eastlake and Ferndale's most photographed building. The inside is no less extravagant, with each room uniquely adorned in floral wallpaper, patterned carpeting, grand antique furniture and perhaps a fireplace, wall fresco or stained-glass window. Two blocks away you'll find the **Shaw House**, an emblematic 'butterfat palace' that also happens to be California's oldest B&B and the first permanent structure in Ferndale (completed by founding father Seth Shaw in 1854). The lodgings are set back on extensive grounds and original details remain, including painted wooden ceilings.

Mega-famous restaurateur Guy Fieri is from Ferndale, so as you might guess, there's some really good grub. Pie shops, ice-cream stores, a butcher/deli and chocolate shop line Main St, and a **farmers market** has locally grown veggies and locally produced dairy – including the freshest cheese you'll find anywhere. For some small-town flair at breakfast, head to **Poppa Joe's** diner, a former pharmacy dating back to 1870. Trophy heads hang from the walls, the floors slant and old men come to play poker. Ferndale does not have much nightlife, but there are a couple of good **cafes** in the center of town and the **theater** has year-round productions ranging from *The Rocky Horror Show* to stand-up comedy nights and contemporary plays.

Hiking the Avenue of the Giants

TRUE TALES OF TALL TREES

Tree huggers, take note: the sprawling redwood groves within **Humboldt Redwoods State Park** rival (and some say surpass) those in Redwood National Park, which is a long drive further north. Admittedly, the landscapes here are less diverse and the individual trees are slightly shorter, but we're talking 380ft versus 370ft. The quickest, easiest way to enjoy

BEST PLACES TO STAY

Benbow Historic Inn
A monument to 1920s elegance and a National Historic Landmark, this Garberville spot could easily be a museum. **$$$**

Victorian Inn
A venerable hotel in an old bank building in Ferndale, with period-style wallpaper and funky antiques. **$$**

Standish-Hickey State Recreation Area
Great campground with river swimming and 9 miles of hiking trails in redwoods. **$**

Gingerbread Mansion

the park is simply to exit Hwy 101 when you see the **Avenue of the Giants** sign, and take the smaller, two-lane alternative to the interstate; it's an incredible 32-mile stretch and there are plenty of great stops along the way.

Assuming you are coming from the south, **Stephens Grove** is the first to offer truly impressive redwoods, which have stretched up tall thanks to the nutritious alluvial flat, or flood plain, on which they stand. Parking is easy and there's a short, 0.7-mile hike – the **Governor William D Stephens Loop Trail** – that's a perfect introduction to the park. If you're interested in a longer hike within lesser-explored territory, drive another 6 miles north to the **Children's Forest**. This is another alluvial flat, and there's rarely anyone here, particularly if the seasonal bridge isn't up over the South Fork of the Eel River. The hike begins at the **Williams Grove Day Use Area**, from which it's a half-mile to the river. After the crossing, the mile-long loop trail brings hikers into a grove that endured a large wildfire in 2003. After about a decade, the resilient forest had regained its beauty, and the only evidence of the fire was a burned-up park sign.

Another 10 miles north you'll find **Founders Grove**, the most visited area of the park thanks to its convenient location

FOREST BATHING

No, this has nothing to do with swimming. Forest bathing – or *shinrin-yoku,* as its Japanese inventors call it – is about sitting and walking near trees, taking in the forest through all the senses. The practice started in the 1980s as a way to combat high rates of suicide among Japan's working class, but its therapeutic benefits have popularized it worldwide. And what better trees to bathe in than California's mighty redwoods?

You can attempt this on your own, but it's more effective and interesting to have a guide. The region's only certified guide is **Justin Legge** (redwoodguide.org), a naturalist and outdoor recreation specialist. His sessions in and around Humboldt Redwoods State Park have been known to blow away even the most dogged of skeptics.

BEST PLACES TO EAT

Chimney Tree
Local grass-fed beef burgers, fresh-baked pies and soft-serve ice cream on the Avenue of the Giants. **$**

Benbow Inn Restaurant
Fancy meals served in the elegant dining room or alfresco. Get a cocktail at the bar, then a delicious steak. **$$$**

Peg House
The burgers, oysters and brownies are standouts, but everything's amazing at this roadside gem. **$**

WHERE TO STAY ON THE LOST COAST

Tides Inn
Perched above Shelter Cove's tide pools, the squeaky-clean rooms offer excellent views. $$

Usal Beach Campground
A somewhat lawless Lost Coast campground, accessed from the south via Hwy 1. $

Needle Rock Campground
Next to the visitor center in Sinkyone Wilderness State Park, with 10 basic sites and a cozy barn. $

Inn on the Lost Coast
Family-friendly oceanfront hotel; some suites boast private hot tubs, saunas and fireplaces. $$$

Founders Grove (p223)

beside the Hwy 101 off-ramp. Unless you are dead set on doing the easiest and most popular thing, skip it and instead hit the nearby but lesser-explored **Rockefeller Grove**. Here you can contemplate nature in peace, or jump on the **Bull Creek Flats Trail**, a 10-mile hike around what's been called 'the world's tallest forest.' For another story about resilience, drive about 10 miles north to the **Grieg-French-Bell Grove**, a lovely setting thick with ferns and sorrel and more tall trees. One in particular, the **Girdled Tree**, is missing a large section of its bark. Humans peeled it away in 1901 for reassembly at a convention in San Francisco, but miraculously, the tree did not die.

GETTING AROUND

There's no public transport around Ferndale, and you also need your own wheels to explore Humboldt Redwoods State Park. Bring a bicycle and you can ride the entire length of the Avenue of the Giants.

EUREKA

On the edge of the largest bay north of San Francisco, Eureka is an artsy sort of place with a charming historic district behind the strip-mall sprawl of Hwy 101, which cuts through the heart of the city. Main draws include Victorian architecture, a serene waterfront trail, fantastic restaurants and glorious street murals. But Eureka's been struggling to find its economic footing.

After the Wiyot tribe was violently expelled from the region in the 19th century, the city was established as a major logging hub. When that went out of style, Humboldt County's seat rode high on the marijuana black market. Legalization has crashed the local cannabis industry, leaving the city's residents thinking about what's next. Tourism is on the rise, and large investments have recently come from Cal Poly Humboldt, the state's new polytechnic, as well as the offshore wind industry and even Big Tech.

TOP TIP

Look around. Art is everywhere: on the walls, on the utility boxes, on the sidewalk and tucked into the shrubbery. Seriously. Visit during the region's famous Kinetic Grand Championship, a sculpture race that sees human-powered art vehicles take to the streets.

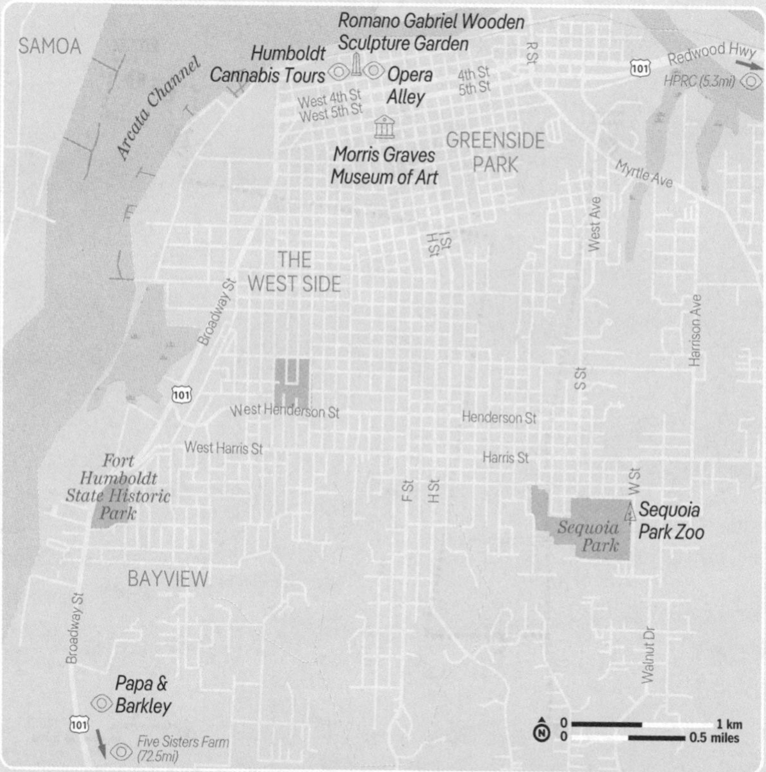

SAMOA
Arcata Channel
Humboldt Cannabis Tours
Romano Gabriel Wooden Sculpture Garden
Opera Alley
West 4th St
West 5th St
4th St
5th St
R St
101
Redwood Hwy
HPRC (5.3mi)
Morris Graves Museum of Art
GREENSIDE PARK
Myrtle Ave
West Ave
I St
H St
THE WEST SIDE
Broadway St
Harrison Ave
S St
101
West Henderson St
Henderson St
West Harris St
Harris St
Fort Humboldt State Historic Park
F St
H St
W St
Sequoia Park
Sequoia Park Zoo
BAYVIEW
Broadway St
Walnut Dr
Papa & Barkley
101
Five Sisters Farm (72.5mi)
0 1 km
0 0.5 miles

CYCLE EUREKA'S VICTORIANS

Victorian lumber-baron mansions dot Eureka, and some of the best can be appreciated on a self-guided cycling tour.

Start at the **1 Carson Mansion** at M and 2nd Sts, perhaps the most famous Queen Anne in the country. The hilltop 1880s home of lumber baron William Carson features stained-glass windows and wood from around the world. Sadly, there's no going in, as it's now a private men's club. On the opposite corner at 202 M St, the **2 Pink Lady Mansion** is a bubblegum Queen Anne bearing a domed turret and other dainty features. Built in 1884 as a wedding gift for Carson's son, today it serves as a vacation rental.

One block west and two south, you'll find another Victorian-style accommodation, **3 Carter House Inn**. The ornate orange-and-brown hotel is an ode to the Murphy House, an 1885 Victorian in San Francisco destroyed by the 1906 earthquake. Inn owner Mark Carter discovered the original blueprints in a Eureka antique shop in 1978, and his crew created a near-exact replica.

Next, pedal a mile southwest to **4 Hillsdale St**, and behold an entire block of breathtaking Victorians, each featuring different colors, patterns and adornments. Three blocks south on C St, **5 Abigail's Elegant Victorian Mansion** is yet another sumptuous Queen Anne, whose interior can only be described as a Victorian explosion.

Conclude the tour in Old Town at the **6 Inn at 2nd & C**, a historic hotel set within an 1888 Victorian built by Finnish immigrants. Once called the Eagle House, the mansion features four floors adorned in reclaimed wood and antiques plus the whimsical Phatsy Kline's Parlor Lounge, an ideal spot for a celebratory drink.

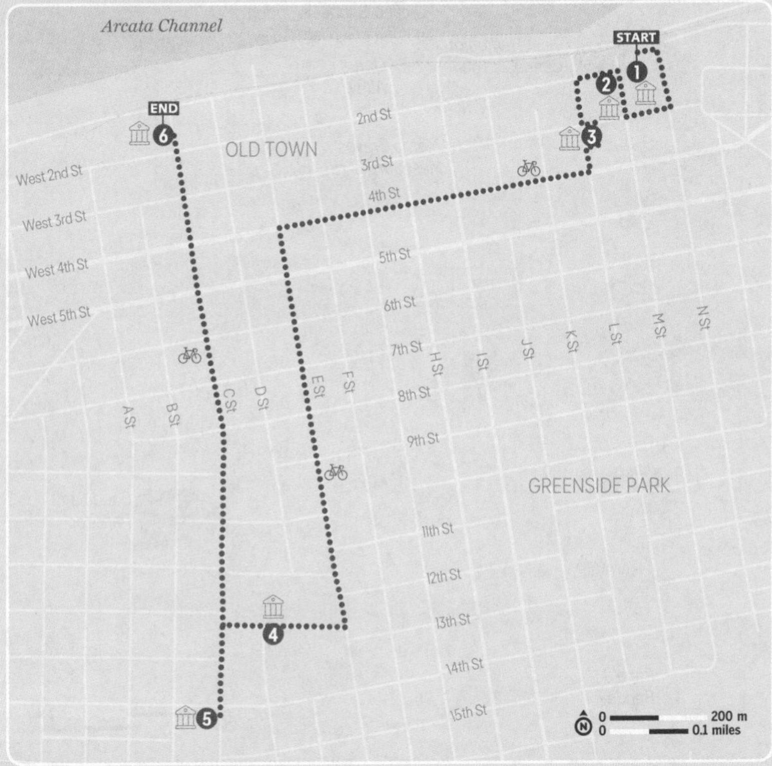

JAIRO RENE LEIVA/SHUTTERSTOCK ©

Carson Mansion

Appreciating Eureka's Art

MURAL TOURS, MUSEUMS AND MORE

Walk a block in Eureka and you'll experience art in one form or another. The walls are covered in murals (many created by the legendary Duane Flatmo), utility boxes feature paintings, and sidewalks are scrawled over with poems. The city crackles with creativity and teems with people who love to harness it.

One of the most joyous introductions to the scene is a few hours spent with exuberant local Robert 'Robot' Adams, who offers art, culture and mural tours in a pedicab. A popular one involves cruising **Opera Alley**, where Eureka's first Street Art Festival took place, to introduce visitors to the city's murals and striking architecture. Later, wander over to the **Romano Gabriel Wooden Sculpture Garden** in Old Town for whimsical outsider art enclosed by aging glass. For 30 years, wooden characters in Gabriel's front yard delighted locals. After he died in 1977, the city moved the collection here. For those seeking a more traditional setting, the **Morris Graves Museum of Art** is a rotating showcase of Pacific Northwest art within the 1904 Carnegie library, displayed across seven galleries and classrooms, a courtyard sculpture garden and a rotunda where artists perform on weekends.

If you visit during one of the city's many arts-inspired events, definitely attend. **North Coast Open Studios** takes place in

HISTORY IN THE HARBOR

At one time, seven ferries transported mill workers and their families across Humboldt Bay. After the Samoa Bridge opened in 1971, six of those went out of service, but the *Madaket* survived. Built in 1910 and refurbished in 1989, it's the oldest continuously operating passenger vessel in the USA.

Today, the boat is docked at the foot of **C St** and hosts history and wildlife tours around the bay, along with sunset cocktail cruises. Circling the bay, it glides past **Tuluwat Island**, the site of a 1860 massacre in which white settlers murdered women, children and elders of the Wiyot tribe. In 2019, Eureka returned the island to its ancestral caretakers, a first for a US city government.

BEST PLACES TO STAY IN EUREKA

Best Western Plus Humboldt Bay Inn
A city oasis with a pool and waterfall, plus a free stretch limo to take you to dinner. **$$**

Inn at 2nd & C
Glorious historic hotel tastefully restored to combine Victorian-era decor with every possible modern amenity. **$$**

Abigail's Elegant Victorian Mansion
A living-history museum in which innkeepers lavish guests with warm hospitality. **$$**

Redwood Skywalk

BEST DRINK SPOTS IN EUREKA

The Shanty
Coolest bar in town, popular with young hipsters for its pinball, pool and sweet back patio.

Lost Coast Brewery & Cafe
Award-winning brewery in a historic building, with free tours, tasty craft beer and outrageous spinach dip.

The Speakeasy
Squeeze in with the locals at this New Orleans–inspired bar with live blues and a convivial atmosphere.

Savage Henry Comedy Club
Intimate, lively comedy club that draws big names and hosts open-mics for budding amateurs.

June, when artists from across the county open their studios to the public. **Arts Alive** is a crafty downtown block party on the first Saturday of every month. At **Eureka's Friday Night Market**, musicians perform in Old Town as local farmers and artisans hawk their wares. The most famous event, of course, is the **Kinetic Grand Championship**. Founded by artist Hobart Brown in 1969, the human-powered art race takes place each Memorial Day weekend, over 50 miles of land, sand, water and mud. Attending this event is the best way to tap into the spirit of the eccentric Northern California artist community.

A Walk in the Redwood Canopy

A HIKE THAT'S 100FT HIGH

At the **Redwood Skywalk** attraction that opened in 2021 at Eureka's **Sequoia Park Zoo**, you can stroll up into a redwood grove and explore the ancient giants from 100ft above the forest floor. The elevated trail is the longest of its kind in the western USA, and the construction of its ascent ramp, launch deck, accessible main loop, seven viewing platforms and optional hanging bridge were all designed by 'en-tree-preneurs.'

BEST PLACES TO EAT

Brick & Fire
Delicious thin-crust pizzas, salads and mains highlighting local produce and wild mushrooms. **$$$**

Gill's by the Bay
A bit south of Eureka, this family-owned, waterfront seafood diner is festooned with whaling industry artifacts. **$$**

Samoa Cookhouse
In Samoa, this is the last operational logger-style cafeteria in the west. Friendly service; lip-smackin' food. **$**

Upon entering the zoo, wander past the flamingos on your left and the predator exhibit on your right, and soon you'll reach the ascent ramp that zigzags at a gentle incline up to the launch deck. From there, the fully accessible main walkways and platforms offer a rare glimpse into a mesmerizing ecosystem: curious barred owls perch in the canopy; gnarled, oversized burls protrude from massive trunks; and from above, you can peer over swirling patches of ferns and sorrel.

For the most intrepid visitors, there's the 'adventure leg': a series of Costa Rica–style hanging bridges that complete the **Sky Walk Loop**. Take your time, watch your footing, and relax as you become part of the life in the redwood canopy.

Marijuana Tourism

WHEN IN HUMBOLDT...

At one time, an estimated one-fifth of Humboldt County's population was farming its world-famous weed, and for decades, a good chunk of the economy was cash-only and tax-evading. In recent years, local incentives drew some black-market farmers out of hiding now that recreational marijuana is – in California and some other US states – legal. While the transition has been rough due to high regulatory fees and plummeting prices, there are several safe, informative ways for visitors to Eureka to learn about the local industry.

For newbies, purchasing legal weed can be like walking into a fancy wine store and not knowing your sauvignon blanc from your cabernet sauvignon. Enter the folks at **Humboldt Cannabis Tours**, who can take you on educational visits to the best local dispensaries – including **HPRC** in Arcata, which has been selling pesticide-free cannabis products since 1999 – or out to 'white market' farms, where you'll learn about the growing cycle from the Emerald Triangle's longtime cannabis farmers. At **Five Sisters Farm** you can also glamp in a deluxe tent and take an outdoor bath with a CBD bath bomb.

Several other businesses around Eureka are out to defy stoner stereotypes by offering a tourist-friendly look at cannabis culture (must be 21 and older). California's first cannabis spa, housed within the dispensary **Papa & Barkley**, offers massage to customers who have purchased THC-, CBD- and cannabis-infused topicals next door. For travelers with more than a casual interest, **Ganjier** (ganjier.com) is a certification program akin to sommelier training. Online courses prepare students to become trusted guides for consumers, then a two-day in-person training session and final exam take place on a 250-acre wilderness campus outside Eureka.

I LIVE HERE: BEST PLACES FOR A STROLL

Jennifer Fumiko Cahill, the arts and features editor of the *North Coast Journal* (@northcoastjournal) in Eureka, recommends these three strolls.

Sequoia Park Zoo's Redwood Skywalk Scale the ADA-accessible ramp into the redwood canopy and walk suspension bridges and platforms with interpretive signs about the flora and fauna unique to the treetops.

Hillsdale Street Just a couple blocks between C and E Sts are a museum's worth of Victorian and post-era homes, beautifully preserved and often playfully painted.

Old Town Mural Walk Visit eurekastreetartfestival.com and use its map of wild and dreamy murals created for the annual event to wind through the historic buildings.

GETTING AROUND

The Redwood Transit System operates buses between Eureka and cities to the north and south, making stops up and down Hwy 101. Greyhound also runs a bus service that stops here en route from San Francisco to Ukiah, and Eureka Transit Service operates local buses Monday to Saturday.

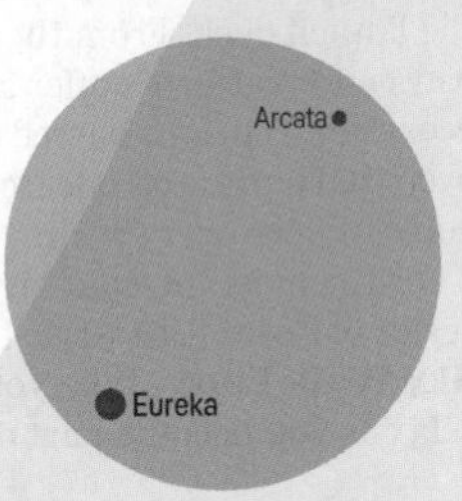

Beyond Eureka

Just outside the city, a hippie college town, a wildlife refuge and plenty of redwood adventures await.

Because of its central location and full array of services, Eureka is a convenient base for much of the redwood coast. But before you venture too far afield, it's worth exploring the neighboring attractions.

Just south of Eureka, you can enjoy some wetland solitude and watch geese migrate through Humboldt Bay National Wildlife Refuge. And mere minutes to the north is the region's most progressive town, Arcata, which surrounds a grassy central square that regularly swells with college students, campers, wanderers and tourists. Sure, it occasionally reeks of patchouli and its politics lean far left, but its earnest embrace of sustainability means organic products and produce are the norm, art-and-craft markets are rampant and vegans are well served.

TOP TIP

Don't miss the farmers market in Arcata Plaza every Saturday. Going on since 1978, it's a full-on display of hippie culture behind the redwood curtain.

Long-billed dowitchers in the Arcata Marsh & Wildlife Sanctuary

R. ALAN MEYER/SHUTTERSTOCK ©

Arcata Community Forest

Bliss Out in Arcata

EMBRACE YOUR INNER HIPPIE

When in Arcata, do as the locals do, and your body, mind, spirit and inner child will all appreciate it. That means rising early and getting into nature, whether you take a drive to spy on birds at **Humboldt Bay National Wildlife Refuge**, walk the redwood trails in **Arcata Community Forest** or go cycling through the **Arcata Marsh & Wildlife Sanctuary**, where trails meander over 225 acres of wetlands and wastewater is filtered clean.

Get brunch at **Cafe Phoenix**, an adorable little restaurant with nurturing hot and cold beverages, a healthy salad of the day, amazing burritos and house-made everything. Then it's time for an education. Head over to **Cal Poly Humboldt**, the state's newest polytechnic, for your appointment to tour the demonstration house at **Campus Center for Appropriate Technology (CCAT)**, a world leader in developing sustainable technologies. The converted residence uses less than 5% of the energy consumed by an average American home.

Pick up vegetarian curry at **Wildflower Cafe & Bakery** for dinner, then relax into the evening with an appointment at the **Finnish Country Sauna and Tubs,** essentially a Euro-crunchy bohemian dream, with private, open-air redwood hot tubs and a sauna situated around a small frog pond. Don't leave without hot chocolate and a homemade cookie from **Cafe Mokka**.

BEST PLACES TO STAY & EAT IN ARCATA

Front Porch Inn
Boutique oasis highlighting local history, art and recycled materials, with a dreamy bathhouse and elaborate theme rooms. $$$

Hotel Arcata
Anchoring the plaza, this renovated 1915 brick landmark has friendly staff and comfortable, old-world rooms. $

SALT Fish House
Low-lit, nautical-themed restaurant on the plaza with sustainable seafood, local produce and crafty cocktails. $$

Slice of Humboldt Pie
Everything from chicken pot pie to Mexican-chocolate pecan pie, and the savory empanadas also shine. $

GETTING AROUND

Arcata city buses stop at the Arcata & Mad River Transit Center. An even better way to get around town is to rent a bike from Revolution Bicycles or test out the Humboldt Bike Share program, which allows you to reserve bikes through the free Movatic app. There is a sizable network of cycle lanes in Arcata.

REDWOOD NATIONAL & STATE PARKS

Hidden away in the upper reaches of California's northwestern Pacific coast, Redwood National Park encompasses some of the world's tallest and most ancient trees, along with a luxuriantly verdant mix of coastal, riverine and prairie wildlands. The massive stands of old-growth California coastal redwoods *(Sequoia sempervirens)* here, draped in moss and ferns and towering up to 379ft tall, are managed in conjunction with three neighboring state parks – Prairie Creek Redwoods, Del Norte Coast Redwoods and Jedediah Smith Redwoods (the latter famed as a backdrop in the original *Star Wars* movie).

Collectively, the parks constitute an International Biosphere Reserve and World Heritage Site, yet they remain little visited when compared to their southern brethren, like the Sequoia National Park. It is worth contemplating that some of these trees have been standing here since time immemorial, predating the Roman Empire by 500 years. Prepare to be impressed.

TOP TIP

Take advantage of the region's many scenic drives to aimlessly explore. But with a particular destination in mind, don't rely on GPS, as digital navigation systems are notorious for misdirecting visitors in Redwood National & State Parks. Instead, consult park maps and use road signs to navigate the parks reliably.

Redwoods National Park

FERNANDO TATAY/SHUTTERSTOCK ©

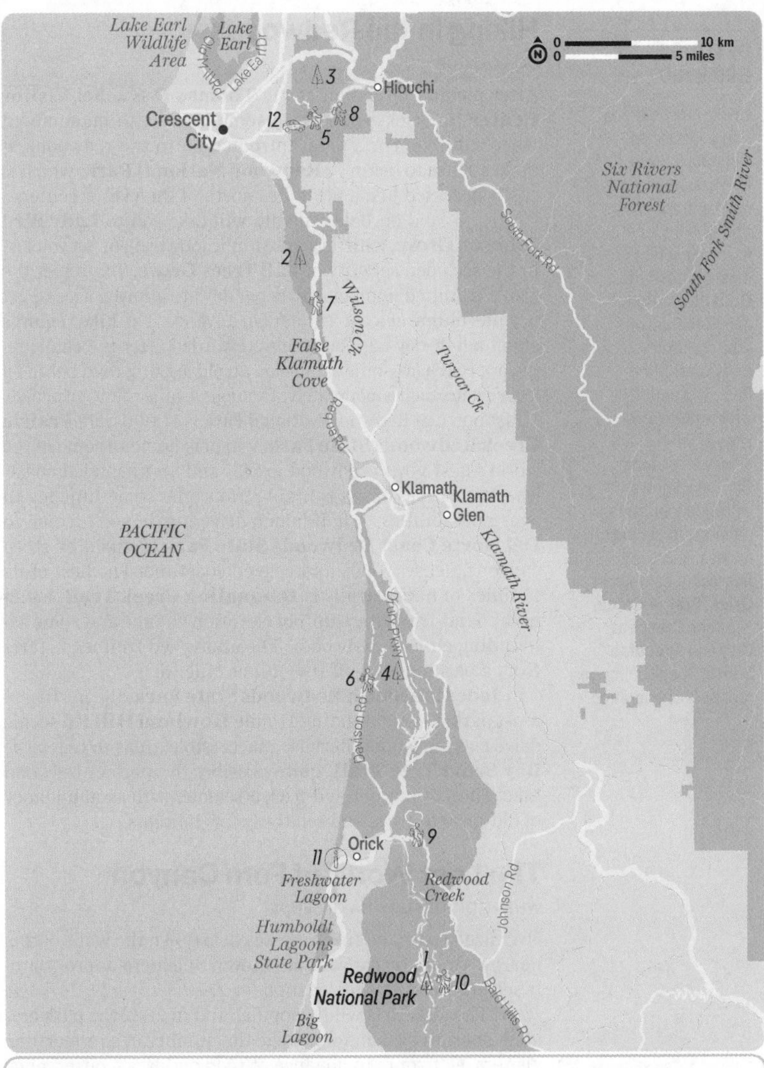

HIGHLIGHTS
1 Redwood National Park

SIGHTS
2 Del Norte Coast Redwoods State Park
3 Jedediah Smith Redwoods State Park
4 Prairie Creek Redwoods State Park

ACTIVITIES, COURSES & TOURS
5 Boy Scout Tree Trail
6 Coastal Trail
7 Damnation Creek Trail
see 6 Fern Canyon
8 Grove of the Titans Trail
9 Lady Bird Johnson Grove Trail
see 8 Mill Creek Trailhead
10 Tall Trees Grove Trail

INFORMATION
11 Thomas H Kuchel Visitor Center

TRANSPORT
12 Howland Hill Rd

GETTING ORIENTED

Unlike most national parks, Redwood National & State Parks do not have a main entrance and only charge fees in some sections, most notably the **Gold Bluffs Beach** and Fern Canyon area of Prairie Creek Redwoods State Park. The parks' widely dispersed sites of interest are signposted along the main highway, with side roads and parking lots providing access. There are five visitor centers: in **Orick**, **Prairie Creek**, **Hiouchi**, **Crescent City** and **Jedediah Smith**. Check online for hours of operation.

Hiking in the Redwoods

DO LOOK UP

After picking up a map at the **Thomas H Kuchel Visitor Center** in Orick, you'll have some choices to make about where to hike. For a great introduction to the redwoods, it makes sense to begin in **Redwood National Park**, which is easily accessed just a few miles north of the visitor center.

A trip inland on Bald Hills Rd will take you to **Lady Bird Johnson Grove**, with its gentle 1-mile loop trail, or get you lost in the secluded serenity of **Tall Trees Grove**. To protect the grove, a limited number of cars per day are allowed access; get permits online at least 24 hours in advance. The hike requires about a half-day trip, but you're rewarded after the challenging approach (a 6-mile ramble on an old logging road behind a locked gate, then a moderately strenuous 4-mile round-trip hike).

Just north of Redwood National Park is 14,000-acre **Prairie Creek Redwoods State Park**, which is home to some of the world's best virgin redwood groves and an unspoiled coastline. Its 75 miles of shady hiking trails offer something for all ages and abilities. A half-hour's drive north, you'll come to **Del Norte Coast Redwoods State Park**, defined by steep canyons, dense woods and rugged coastline. The best of its 15 miles of hiking trails is **Damnation Creek Trail**, a 4.2-mile round-trip with 1100ft of elevation change and some astounding cliffside redwoods. The unmarked trailhead starts from a parking area off Hwy 101 at Mile 16.

In **Jedediah Smith Redwoods State Park**, the northernmost park, the outstanding 11-mile **Howland Hill Rd** scenic drive cuts through otherwise inaccessible areas to reach the **Boy Scout Tree Trail**, quite possibly the perfect redwood hike. The 5.6-mile out-and-back is remote, with an abundance of old-growth trees and relatively few humans.

The Lost World of Fern Canyon

WHERE DINOSAURS MAKE SENSE

Oversized ferns and fuzzy mosses drip down the walls of this narrow, dramatic canyon that Steven Spielberg appropriately selected as a filming location for *The Lost World: Jurassic Park*. The feature is wildly popular and in 2022 the park created a permit system to manage the number of summertime visitors. Get yours in advance at redwoodparksconservancy.org/permits/fern-canyon-permits.

To reach Fern Canyon, take Hwy 101 to Davidson Rd and drive west through Elk Meadow and onto the dirt road, continuing 6 miles to Gold Bluffs Kiosk. Pay the entry fee ($8),

BEST PLACES TO STAY AND EAT

Elk Meadow Cabins
Sandwiched between two redwood parks, bright cabins have equipped kitchens and elk on the lawn. **$$**

Lost Whale Inn
High above crashing waves north of Trinidad, this spacious, modern, light-filled B&B has stunning views. **$$$**

Larrupin Cafe
Everyone loves this upscale, one-of-a-kind restaurant with eclectic decor and amazing mesquite-grilled food. **$$$**

Fern Canyon

then drive 3 bumpy miles to the parking lot. From there, walk north on the **Coastal Trail** in appropriate footwear: the trail intersects on many occasions with a winding, pebble-filled creek and it's likely that your lower extremities will get wet.

You'll traverse coastal meadows and along the base of a bluff before reaching a lush forest. When you see the yawning entryway into Fern Canyon, you've arrived, and almost immediately you'll notice the 30ft walls festooned in living wallpaper including five different kinds of ferns. Above the canyon walls you'll spot Sitka spruce and other conifers soaring high, and if you look closely at the walls, you may spy a salamander or a frog.

Continuing through the canyon, you'll notice tiny, Instagram-perfect waterfalls tricking down from above, and eventually you'll reach a natural flight of stairs. Ascend them and take in the views of the canyon from above as you complete the 1-mile loop. To enhance and prolong the experience, continue your hike along one of the area's other magnificent trails.

Explore the Grove of the Titans

SECRET TREES REVEALED

Welcome to the Grove of the Titans, one of the world's most impressive and gargantuan thickets of coast redwoods. The grove had thrived for more than 1000 years before scientists discovered it in 1998 and gave the superlative trees names

MAGNIFICENT ROOSEVELT ELK

Roosevelt elk roam the coast and forestland up against Fern Canyon, and encountering these majestic creatures is as cool as it is worrisome, particularly during their August to October mating season. Bulls can weigh up to 1000lb and do damage with their antlers and legs, while cows with calves can also become aggressive.

Human–elk conflict has been on the rise in Northern California, and scientists are making a concerted effort to study elk in hopes of identifying solutions. Protect yourself and the elk by staying at least 75ft away while admiring them.

You may notice elk burgers advertised at **Snack Shack**, the only meal option in Orick. Note that the meat is from farmed elk, not the park's wild creatures.

BEST SCENIC DRIVES

Newton B Drury Scenic Parkway
An 8-mile parkway running parallel to Hwy 101 through ancient redwood forests.

Bald Hills Rd
A winding jaunt through the hills and prairies of Redwood National Park with an occasional lupine super-bloom.

Howland Hill Rd
A 10-mile, unpaved stunner through the towering ancient redwoods of Jedediah Smith State Park.

NATE HOVEE/SHUTTERSTOCK ©

Jedediah Smith Redwoods State Park (p234)

DON'T VISIT HYPERION

The Grove of the Titans isn't the only redwood attraction that's been damaged by visitors. The world's tallest tree, **Hyperion** (380ft), has also been over-loved. Ever since the tree's remote location within Redwood National Park got shared on the internet, people have been making the challenging (and frankly, unrewarding) trek to visit it. Because Hyperion is surrounded by other enormous trees, it's not even possible to tell that it's the tallest.

In 2022, park officials took action and closed the area around Hyperion to visitors. They placed warning signs in the park and on the website that visiting Hyperion would result in a $5000 fine and potential jail time. Definitely not worth it!

like Screaming Titan, Lost Monarch and El Viejo del Norte. Then, about a decade ago, Instagram photos and geotags began revealing their secret locations within Jedediah Smith Redwoods State Park, and interested tourists started showing up, disturbing the habitat, carving new paths and trampling the fragile root systems.

Flash-forward to 2022, and not only were visitors welcomed to the Grove of the Titans, but a new 3-mile rerouted trail with 1300ft of elevated boardwalk had been installed to keep them from destroying the place. The trail, along with new signage and bathrooms, was a collaboration between state and national parks agencies, Tolowa Dee-Ni' Nation, Save the Redwoods League and Redwood Parks Conservancy. It's now one of the top draws to the redwoods parks.

Visitors access the grove through the **Mill Creek Trailhead** off Howland Hill Rd. The new route threads around and between the giants and even underneath some fallen trunks. In addition to awe-inspiring redwoods, the trail meanders past big-leaf maple, Sitka spruce, sword ferns, azaleas and orchids, and observant hikers may spot banana slugs or newts.

GETTING AROUND

Redwood National & State Parks are most easily reached with your own vehicle. The parks' attractions are scattered along a 60-mile stretch of Hwy 101 and Hwy 199 between Orick and Gasquet.

Public transport is limited; Monday through Saturday, Redwood Coast Transit bus 20 passes through the park three times daily on its run from Crescent City to Arcata. There are scheduled stops at Prairie Creek Redwoods State Park and the national park office in Orick; upon request, drivers may drop passengers at other park locations.

Humboldt County Airport in McKinleyville (28 miles south of Orick) is the closest commercial airport.

Beyond Redwood National & State Parks

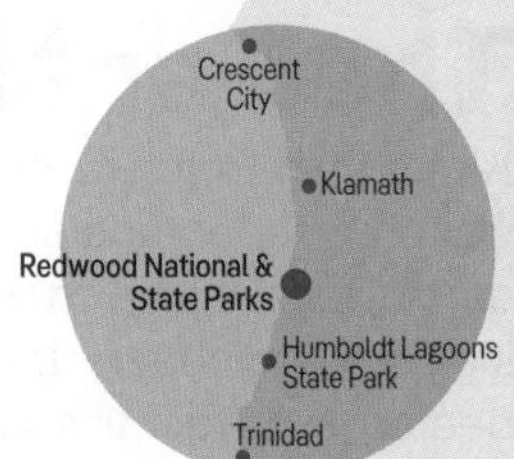

The coastal cities and state parks surrounding Redwood National & State Parks are tranquil escapes with eye-popping scenery.

Along California's northernmost coastline and in between its redwood parks, the beauty is relentless and at times hard to believe. Just south of Redwood National Park, Trinidad is a postcard-perfect seaside village perched before a jaw-dropping headland and dramatic offshore rock islands. Straddling the redwood parks you'll find Humboldt Lagoons State Park, a kayaking and bird-watching paradise that also happens to be the largest lagoon system in North America. North of Prairie Creek Redwoods sits Klamath – the heart of Yurok country – where the eponymous river meets the ocean. And west of Jedediah Smith Redwoods is Crescent City, a commercial fishing hub with a windswept, New England–style lighthouse.

TOP TIP

Leave time to bask in the haunting natural grandeur of it all. While there are scores of mid-century motels, sleep outdoors if possible.

View of the Trinidad State Beach from the Trinidad Head Trail (p237)

ROAD TRIP

The Far North Coast

Along this stretch of Hwy 101, curving roads and misty trails bring visitors to spectacular natural wonders like nothing else found on earth. Begin with a cruise along coastal Scenic Drive (the name says it all) toward cheery Trinidad, which somehow manages an off-the-beaten-path feel despite a constant flow of visitors.

1 Trinidad

Pop into the cute shops, do a seafood-with-views brunch at Seascape, and walk it off on the Trinidad Head Trail, which offers superb coastal scenery and excellent whale-watching (December to April). If the weather is nice, stroll the gorgeous cove at Trinidad State Beach; if not, make for the Cal Poly Humboldt's Telonicher Marine Laboratory. It has a touch tank, aquariums and an enormous whale jaw.

The Drive: Head 13 minutes north to the 640-acre Sue-meg State Park (formerly Patrick's Point, renamed to honor the Yurok tribe's wishes).

2 Sue-meg State Park

Coastal bluffs jut out to sea and sandy beaches and teeming tide pools abut rocky headlands. Sumêg is an authentic reproduction of an indigenous Yurok village, with hand-hewn redwood buildings. The 2-mile Rim Trail, a former Yurok trail around the bluffs, circles the point with access to huge rocky outcrops. Don't miss Wedding Rock, one of the park's most romantic spots, and Agate Beach, where lucky visitors spot bits of jade and sea-polished agate.

The Drive: Make your way back out to Hwy 101 through thick stands of redwoods on the approach to Humboldt Lagoons State Park.

3 Humboldt Lagoons State Park

The park has long, sandy beaches and a string of coastal lagoons. Big Lagoon and prettier Stone Lagoon are both excellent for kayaking and bird-watching. Sunsets are

ALESSANDRARC/SHUTTERSTOCK ©

Battery Point Lighthouse in Crescent City

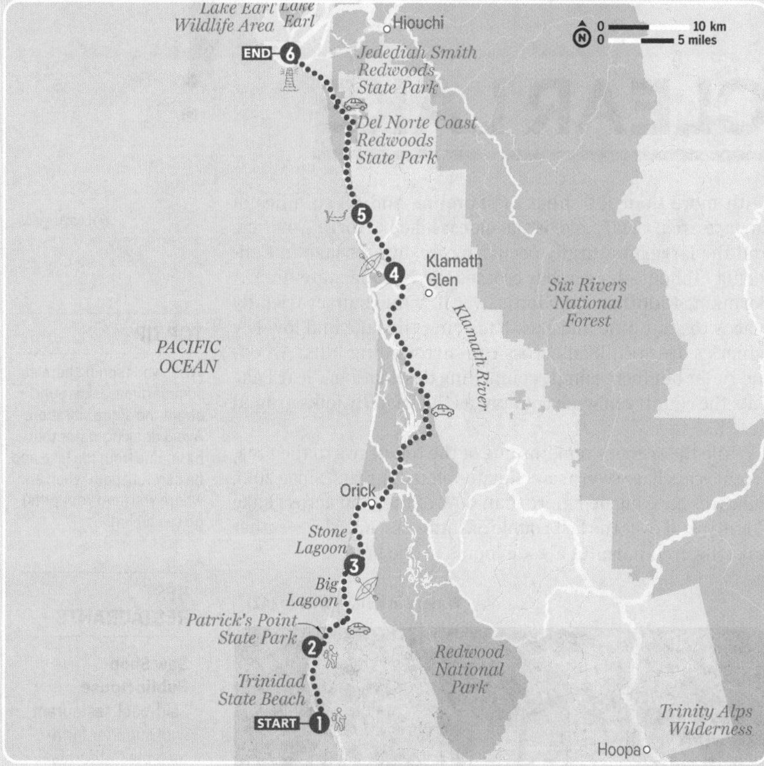

spectacular, with no structures in sight. At the Stone Lagoon Visitor Center, now run by the Yurok tribe, there are exhibits on indigenous history and culture, along with information about endangered California condors recently released in the region.

The Drive: Continue north for about 30 miles on Hwy 101 to Klamath.

4 Klamath

The tiny town's heart is the striking Yurok Country Visitor Center, which features cultural displays, crafts and activities, including guided canoe and jet-boat tours along the Klamath River. Klamath and much of the surrounding area is ancestral land, and in a long-awaited victory for the tribe, the river's dam was recently removed.

The Drive: Ten minutes up Hwy 101, giant statues of Paul Bunyan and Babe the Blue Ox tower over the parking lot at Trees of Mystery.

5 Trees of Mystery

This shameless tourist trap has a gondola running through the redwood canopy and a fun 'Tall Tales Forest' where chainsaw sculptures tell the tale of Paul Bunyan. The End of the Trail Museum, located behind the gift shop, has a large collection of Native American arts and artifacts, which indigenous leaders are attempting to repatriate.

The Drive: Another half-hour's drive north and you'll reach Crescent City.

6 Crescent City

Highlights include the Smith River (a gloriously undammed waterway), Tolowa Dunes State Park (a quiet haven for migrating birds and resident porcupines) and an 1856 lighthouse on a tiny rock island that you can visit at low tide.

CLEAR LAKE

With more than 100 miles of shoreline and 68 sq miles of surface area, Clear Lake is the oldest lake in North America, and the largest naturally occurring freshwater lake in California (Tahoe is bigger, but crosses the Nevada state line). A dormant, 4300ft volcano lords over it, while budget-friendly places to stay, dine and kick back ring the lake and low-key wineries are sprinkled across the surrounding hills. An off-the-radar but increasingly compelling destination, Clear Lake puts the country in wine country, as the friendly folks around here like to say.

While the scenery remains one of the top draws to the area, recent years have seen a few climate-related threats. Since 2015, wildfires have burned more than 60% of the land across Lake County, and over the last couple of summers, hot, dry weather has triggered harmful algae blooms in the lake.

Winery in Kelseyville (p242)

SHAY BAKSTAD/SHUTTERSTOCK ©

TOP TIP

When vacationing here in summertime, ask around about the algae situation. Avoid drinking water that has come from the lake and be careful about when and where you (and your pets) go swimming.

BEST RESTAURANTS

Saw Shop Public House
Laid-back restaurant with superior farm-to-table California cuisine and delicious cocktails. $$

Park Place
Lakeport's premier dining venue offers classic Italian and American dishes and killer views from the roof deck and patio. $$

RED's @ the Skyroom
A local favorite at the airport serving seasonal cocktails and salads and from-scratch California comfort food. $$

Blue Wing Saloon
Cozy up on the heated veranda with casual American fare and live music at the historic Tallman Hotel restaurant. $$

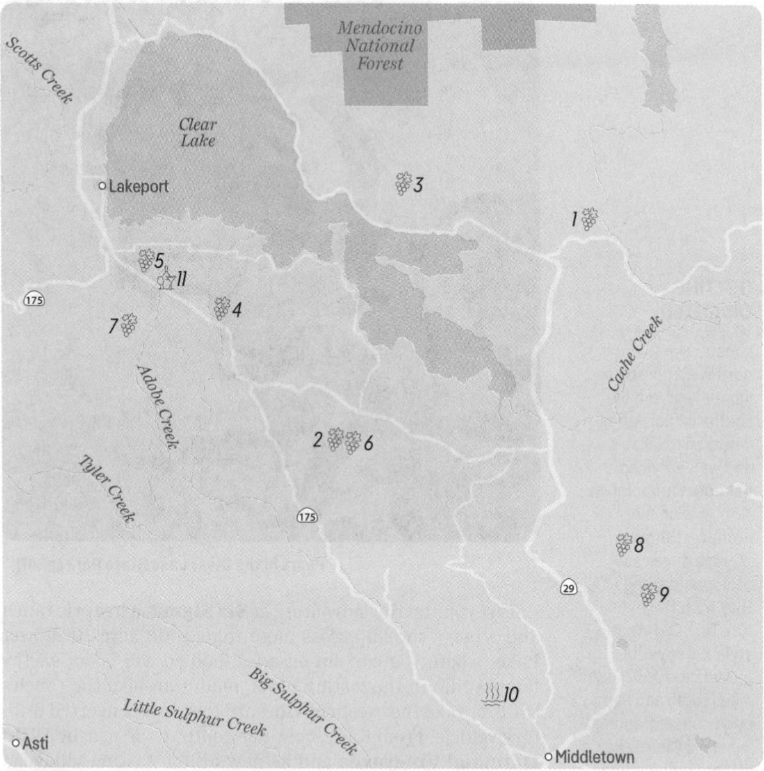

SIGHTS
1 Bed & Barrel at Stonehouse Cellars
2 Boatique Winery
3 Brassfield Estate Winery
4 Chacewater Winery & Olive Mill
5 Kaz Winery
6 Laujor Estate Winery
7 Olof Cellars
8 Six Sigma
9 Wild Diamond Vineyards

ACTIVITIES, COURSES & TOURS
10 Harbin Hot Springs

DRINKING
11 Shannon Mercantile

A Wine Country Less Traveled

YOU'RE NOT IN NAPA ANYMORE

There are some 30 wineries around Clear Lake. Most lie in volcanic soils more than 1300ft above sea level, and many provide grapes for neighboring Napa wineries. All are incredibly welcoming, and typically waive tasting fees if you purchase a bottle.

BEST ACTIVITIES AROUND CLEAR LAKE

Lakeport Auto Movies
One of America's few surviving and wonderfully nostalgic drive-in movie theaters. Showings Friday and Saturday nights.

Mt Konocti
A 2-mile round-trip hike rewards with views for miles and some interesting historical sites along the way.

Clear Lake State Park
A lakeside park and launching point for swimming, boating, kayaking and fishing. Also has trails and a visitor center.

Pears in the Clear Lake State Park (p241)

GETTING ORIENTED

Locals refer to the northwest portion as 'upper lake' and the southeast portion as 'lower lake.' Likable and well-serviced **Lakeport** (population 4947) sits on the northwest shore, a 20-mile drive east of Hopland along Hwy 175 (off Hwy 101). Tiny, Old West-style **Kelseyville** (population 3657) is 7 miles south and has a large concentration of wineries. **Clearlake**, off the southeastern shore, is the biggest town.

The old-timey village of **Upper Lake** is the most attractive destination up north. Down south, a former stagecoach stop called **Middletown** lies 18 miles south of Clearlake and just 4 miles from Harbin Hot Springs, one of California's premier nude-bathing experiences.

Start your tasting adventure at **Six Sigma**, a historic ranch and winery spread across more than 4000 acres in Lower Lake, where you can sip on a full-bodied cab or an earthy tempranillo in the tasting room, mountain-bike the ranch's trails or take the excellent vineyard tour in a converted military vehicle. From there, continue south to the nearby **Wild Diamond Vineyards** and its new hilltop tasting village, a collection of tables under shade canopies and surrounding what resembles a Las Vegas poolside cabana. The best part: you can sip astoundingly good reds while looking down on Napa (literally).

Hop onto Hwy 29 and start driving toward Kelseyville, where many of the ries are concentrated. At **Olof Cellars**, attend the informative winemaker-led tastings and sample some of the excellent reds, which are aged a minimum of three years. Olof produces just 500 cases annually; the bottles of nebbiolo, barbera and petit verdot are a steal. Six minutes south at cult favorite **Kaz Winery**, they're all about blends. Whatever is in the organic vineyards goes into the wine – and they're blended at crush, not during fermentation.

At **Laujor Estate Winery**, do the classic tasting and ask about what makes the relatively new grape-growing region, Red Hills AVA (American Viticultural Area), so special. (Hint:

BEST NON-WINERY PLACES TO STAY

Tallman Hotel
An elegant Upper Lake hotel featuring a shady garden, walled-in pool, brick patios and classy porches. **$$**

Suites on Main
Two-story collection of bright, contemporary suites with full kitchens, a backyard garden and views of Kelseyville. **$$**

Reese Ranch Retreat
A 17-acre ranch in Upper Lake offering glamping and animal encounters, including goat yoga and a zebra experience. **$**

it's the mountain climate, volcanic soil and lack of pesticides.) Then head over to **Boatique Winery** for more Red Hills AVA sampling, as well as an outstanding view of Mt Konocti and a prized collection of antique wooden boats (the west's largest, apparently). Continue on to Kelseyville proper, where **Chacewater Winery & Olive Mill** offers tastings of organic wine and olive oil, much of which is award-winning. Bring your favorite bottle to the picnic area out back where you can play horseshoes or bocce in front of the olive groves. If you have even more time, head over to the **Shannon Mercantile**, a buzzy new tasting room with 12 wines on tap, plus picnic areas and cornhole. Or make a trip across the lake to **Brassfield Estate Winery**, a stunning Tuscan-style village in the High Valley appellation, surrounded by magnificent gardens.

If an entire day of wine tasting isn't enough, why not just sleep at a winery? Boatique and Chacewater have short-term rentals on their property, and Laujor has one just above its tasting room. For an even more special experience, check out **Bed & Barrel at Stonehouse Cellars**. Set on 145 acres of secluded countryside, this winery rents a room and a suite within a luxury home, as well as a stylish and cozy three-bedroom ranch. All guests have access to vineyard hiking trails, a pool, a hot tub and a large patio with a barbecue grill. The resident innkeeper and chef prepares a bomb breakfast.

KELSEYVILLE PEAR FESTIVAL

Held on the last Saturday in September, Lake County's largest one-day event is a real hoot and a showcase of the region's agricultural heritage, including the almighty pear. Think parades, live music and dancing on three stages, a giant decorative pear, a pie-eating contest, a scarecrow contest and plenty of street vendors. There are special exhibits all over town, which could included a tractor and engine show, or a display on the history of Kelseyville farming within the Pear Pavilion. The event has grown from just 1500 attendees in 1993 to more than 10,000 in 2022. It's highly appropriate slogan? 'Catch the small-town magic.'

Hippie Hot-Springing

STRIP DOWN AND HEAT UP

Harbin Hot Springs is the oldest hot springs in California, and visiting these clothing-optional baths is practically a rite of passage. There's a youthful, no-frills vibe, and it's also decidedly hippie-dippie (don't be surprised when the bare-chested woman soaking next to you starts groaning and humming mantras). If you're comfortable in the buff, it can be a revelatory experience.

The heart and soul of the 1700-acre retreat center is the spring-fed pool area, with eight baths of varying temperatures, plus a sauna and sundeck offering sweeping valley views. Lodging is in creekside caravans, domes or hilltop cottages. Budget travelers can also pitch a tent or sleep in the car and pay for 24-hour access. Overnight visits feel a bit like going to adult summer camp, with yoga classes, drum circles, full-moon gatherings and the like. Reserve well in advance.

Day use gives you up to six hours to explore the facilities and dine at the organic (and mostly vegetarian) **Dancing Bear Cafe**. At least one person in your party will have to become a member; membership starts at $10 for a month.

GETTING AROUND

Having your own vehicle is definitely the way to go, although Lake Transit operates weekday routes between Clearlake and Calistoga. Buses serve Ukiah from Lakeport. Since piecing together routes and times can be difficult, it's best to phone ahead.

Above: Surfers in Santa Cruz (p252); Right: Big Basin Redwoods State Park (p256)

THE MAIN AREAS

SANTA CRUZ
Surfing, beaches and hikes. p250

MONTEREY
Marine life and seaside pleasures. p258

BIG SUR
Road trips and wilderness. p267

HIGHWAY 101
Offbeat small-town history. p272

CENTRAL COAST

WILD COAST MADE FOR ESCAPES

Ruggedly beautiful and oftentimes wild, the Central Coast unites good-time surf towns with fearsome sea cliffs and misty redwood forests.

The Central Coast exudes freedom, and its wave-smashed beaches, dense forests and close-knit communities have long inspired great art. Big Sur and Monterey bewitched legendary writers such as John Steinbeck, Henry Miller, Jack Kerouac and Robert Louis Stevenson. Meanwhile San Simeon and Carmel were canvases for visionary architects like Julia Morgan and Hugh W Comstock. And that's just the towns by the shore; the agricultural inland has its own stories to tell. Hwy 101 courses through fields of grain, grapes and garlic, following the same route that Spanish colonists took in the late 18th century. They rolled through, founding mission settlements to convert Native Americans and establish a claim on the land. What remains of that time are churches, adobes and cemeteries, which bear witness to the history of Native American cultural erasure and death from European-introduced diseases.

Befitting its turbulent past, the Central Coast is literally tempestuous, too. This is a realm of sea fog and foaming surf. Its cultural attractions are intriguing as well, with sumptuous estates like Hearst Castle and Paso Robles' modern art scene.

For idle days by a sunny beach, you're better off further south. But for a more compelling collage of experiences – bustling boardwalks, sea kayaking, clifftop hikes, volcanic landscapes – come explore the Central Coast. It's not postcard-perfect California, and that's precisely what makes the Central Coast so thrilling.

CAMBRIA
Idyllic gateway to beaches. p276

PASO ROBLES
Laid-back wine country. p280

SAN LUIS OBISPO
Portal to coast and backcountry. p285

Find Your Way

There are beaches, wildlife and excellent hikes up and down the Central Coast, so don't try to do it all. Pick a couple of hubs and day-trip from these, or embrace total freedom by road-tripping.

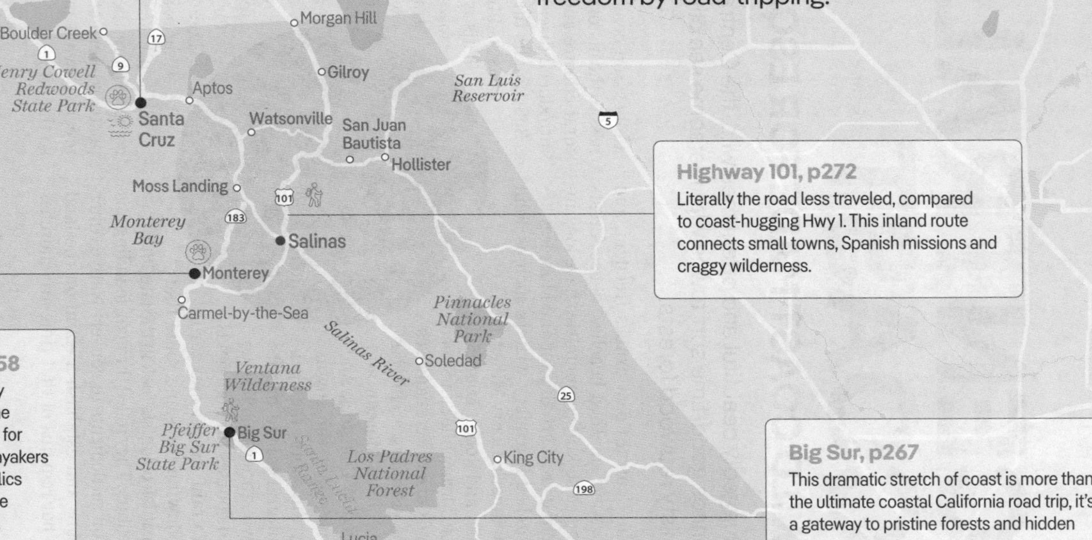

Santa Cruz, p250
Great vibes and even better surf breaks at this focal point for beach culture, with dreamy hikes through the rugged state parks nearby.

Monterey, p258
With a big, blue bay teeming with marine life, this is paradise for whale-watchers, kayakers and for seaside frolics – and don't miss the colossal aquarium.

Highway 101, p272
Literally the road less traveled, compared to coast-hugging Hwy 1. This inland route connects small towns, Spanish missions and craggy wilderness.

Big Sur, p267
This dramatic stretch of coast is more than the ultimate coastal California road trip, it's a gateway to pristine forests and hidden coves.

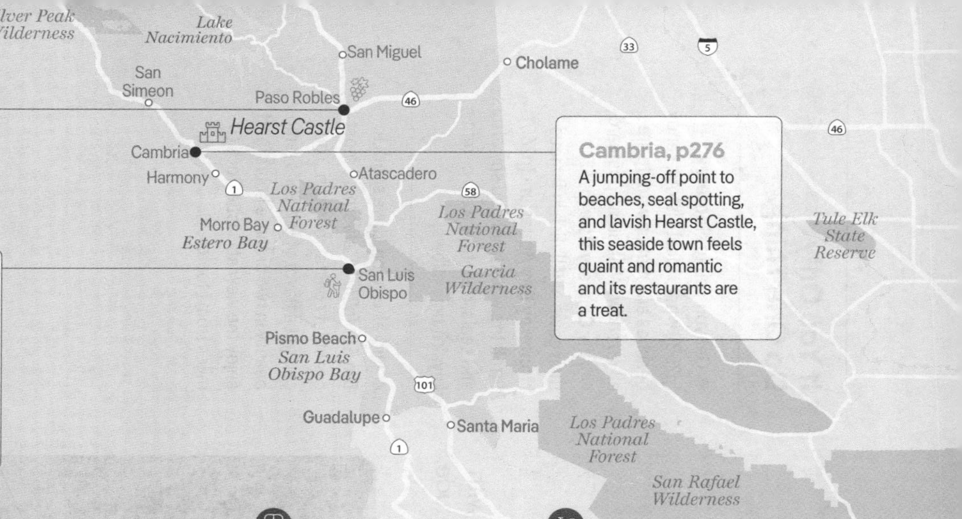

Paso Robles, p280

Lovers of wine (particularly reds) shouldn't miss this charmingly walkable city, with tasting rooms in town and vineyards all around.

Cambria, p276

A jumping-off point to beaches, seal spotting, and lavish Hearst Castle, this seaside town feels quaint and romantic and its restaurants are a treat.

San Luis Obispo, p285

The Central Coast's sweet spot: a mellow university town with a hodgepodge of historic buildings, plus beaches, vineyards and mountains all in easy reach.

CAR

The flexibility of having your own wheels pays off richly on the Central Coast. You'll experience road trips with epic scenery, detour to far-flung state parks and historic curiosities, and be able to stop at scenic lookouts on a whim.

TRAIN

You can reach major towns by taking the Coast Starlight train, which connects the San Francisco Bay Area with Monterey (via Salinas), Paso Robles and San Luis Obispo. To venture to smaller towns you'll need private transportation (or a lot of patience, given the patchy local buses and the occasional rideshares).

BICYCLE

Cycling is an excellent way to day-trip from major towns, especially bike-friendly Santa Cruz, Monterey and San Luis Obispo. Some road trips can be done by bike, too, such as 17-Mile Drive.

Plan Your Time

The Central Coast is a road-tripper's dream. Drive right beside the Pacific Coast, stopping at surf beaches, redwood forests and towns with free-and-easy California attitude.

Hwy 1 (p268), Big Sur

If You Only Do One Thing

- Get yourself to **Monterey** (p258), where local history, sandy beaches and marine wildlife are all on show. Walk along postcard-worthy **Cannery Row** (p262), then gawp at jellyfish in famous **Monterey Bay Aquarium** (p260). Stroll the waterfront and spy otters and seals, then take a dip or rent a kayak if time allows.

- Mid-afternoon, drive south to **Big Sur** (p267), California's most beautiful coastal road trip. You can get a flavor of Big Sur's remote beauty in two or three hours, and enjoy the view at Castle Rock (17 miles from Monterey).

Seasonal Highlights

The weather stays mild from spring through fall; summer gets uncomfortably hot inland. Nature is always putting on a show, thanks to migrations of marine mammals, birds and butterflies.

MARCH

Watch **otters** cuddling their pups along the coast, and coo over chubby baby **elephant seals** in Piedras Blancas.

APRIL

Time to **hike** among spring flowers! Montaña de Oro State Park blazes with color, and calla lilies bloom in Garrapata.

JUNE

It's warming up but not yet scorching inland, and conditions are perfect for beginner **surfers** (pro surfers, come back in fall).

Three Days to Travel Around

- Devote your first day to the greatest hits of **Monterey** (p258): Cannery Row, the aquarium and experiencing the bay in your chosen style (kayaking, diving or on a whale-watching cruise).

- Spend day two road-tripping **Big Sur** (p267), allowing time to admire Bixby Bridge, Pfeiffer Beach and the raw cliffside beauty of Ragged Point.

- On the third day, drive on to **San Simeon** (p278), meeting the elephant seals before heading up to William Randolph Hearst's 'enchanted hill,' aka **Hearst Castle** (p279). Join a tour of the media mogul's architecturally extravagant estate and finish the day in beachy sweet spot **Cambria** (p276).

If You Have More Time

- Begin a leisurely road trip in **Santa Cruz** (p250), spending a couple of days surfing, hiking among **redwoods** (p256) and kayaking with **sea otters** (p253). Next, hit **Monterey** (p258) and pretty **17-Mile Drive** (p265) before driving on to **Big Sur** (p267), allowing time to hike in **Julia Pfeiffer Burns State Park** (p268).

- Continue to **San Simeon** (p278) and tour ostentatious **Hearst Castle** (p279) before cutting inland to the exceptional **wineries of Paso Robles** (p281). Finish up in laid-back **San Luis Obispo** (p285), taking day trips to beauty spots like **Morro Bay** (p290).

JULY

The best time to see **humpback whales** in Monterey Bay. And vampires beware, **Gilroy's garlic festival** is in late July.

SEPTEMBER

Mild weather for **camping** in Big Sur and state parks, plus merriment at **Capitola Art & Wine** and **Monterey Jazz Festivals**.

OCTOBER

Paso Robles toasts **Harvest Wine Month** and vineyards across the region glow as their leaves turn red and gold.

NOVEMBER

Prime your camera: multitudes of **monarch butterflies** descend on Pacific Grove, Pismo Beach, Santa Cruz and other overwintering spots.

SANTA CRUZ

San Francisco
Santa Cruz
Los Angeles

Santa Cruz is where students, dropouts and tech royalty all compete for the best surf breaks. Located between Silicon Valley and Monterey, the city is famous for its beach boardwalk and surf culture. The Beat Generation of the 1950s and '60s established Santa Cruz as a refuge for artists, free thinkers and society opt-outs. The counterculture undercurrents never went away, but a lot of today's surfers and hippies have made big bucks in tech.

This is a choose-your-own-adventure coastal town, where you can test your physical limits surfing or hiking, raise microbrews with bros or scream your head off on the Giant Dipper. The combination of big waves, free-and-easy attitude and ever-so-slightly seedy nightlife is peak California.

Marine mist can hang low in the sky, diffusing the light to mystical effect. It also helps sustain the area's vineyards and state parks, with fern-floored redwood forests beckoning hikers to explore the nearby Santa Cruz Mountains.

Santa Cruz Beach Boardwalk (p252)

TOP TIP

Check Santa Cruz' calendar of festivals before you book. Standout events are the pre-1950s car festival Woodies on the Wharf (late June) and Capitola Art & Wine Festival (September), which brings a weekend of wine tasting, music and merriment just east of Santa Cruz.

VOLUNTEER AT DIG DAYS

For a deeper appreciation of the land and a chance to connect with eco-minded locals, join one of the **Dig Days** hosted by the Santa Cruz Mountains Trail Stewardship. These free events support local volunteers to dig and maintain trails at parks and preserves like San Vicente Redwoods and Cotoni-Coast Dairies. Check events and sign up at santacruztrails.org.

SIGHTS
1 Capitola State Beach
2 Capitola Wharf
3 Cowell's Beach
4 Natural Bridges State Beach
5 Santa Cruz Beach Boardwalk
6 Santa Cruz Wharf
7 Seymour Marine Discovery Center
8 UCSC Arboretum & Botanic Garden
see 1 Venetian Court

ACTIVITIES, COURSES & TOURS
see 2 Capitola Boat & Bait
9 Kayak Connection
10 Monarch Trail
11 Richard Schmidt Surf School
12 Santa Cruz Whale Watching

EATING
13 Gayle's Bakery
see 1 Margaritaville
14 Seabreeze Cafe
15 Shadowbrook
16 Verve Coffee Roasters

DRINKING
see 1 Capitola Wine Bar
17 Equinox Sparkling Wine
see 17 Santa Cruz Mountain Brewing

SHOPPING
18 Cowell's Surf Shop

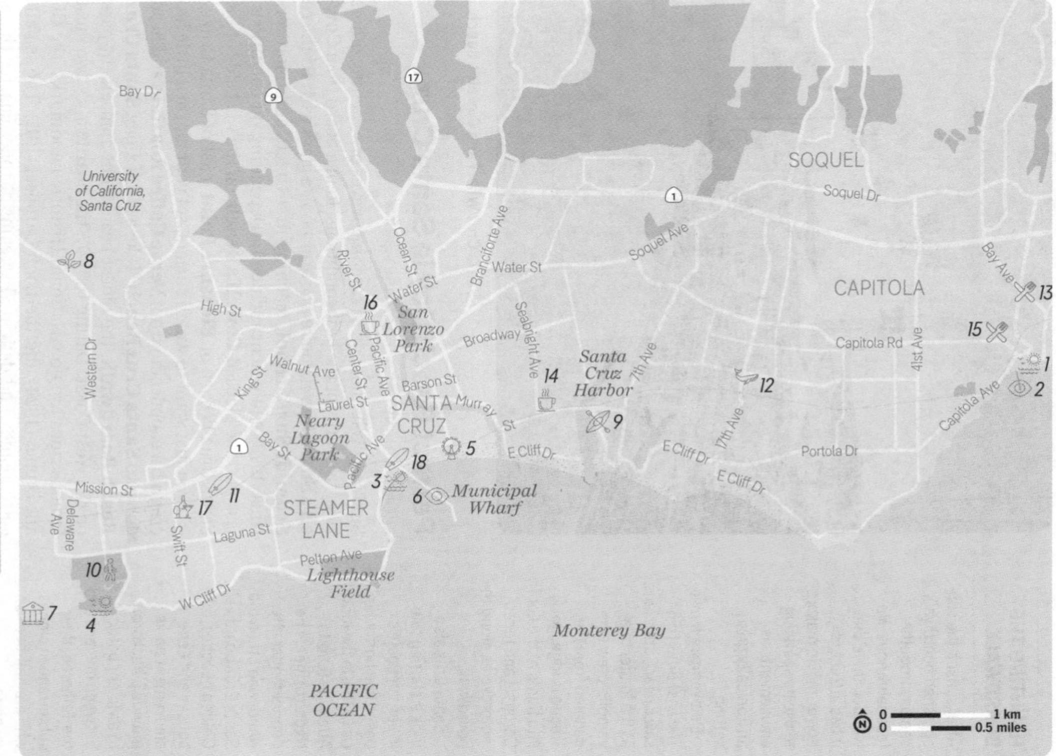

HAUNTING THE BOARDWALK

After sunset, the sun-splashed boardwalk seems altogether less salubrious. No wonder, then, that it has attracted horror-movie makers to use its sparkling amusements as an ironically grisly setting.

Cult vampire movie *The Lost Boys* (1987) saw Kiefer Sutherland as the leader of a vampire crew who dangled from the Trestle Bridge, got into fights at the Looff Carousel and raced motorcycles along the boardwalk.

Santa Cruz also took a starring role in Jordan Peele's unsettling horror film *Us* (2019). In the movie, Adelaide (Lupita Nyong'o) meets her doppelgänger after wandering off on the Santa Cruz boardwalk. Golden beaches, lake houses and eerie amusement parks provide a backdrop to a violent battle between humans and the Tethered, their subterranean clones who are hell-bent on revenge.

ARKANTO/SHUTTERSTOCK ©

Santa Cruz Wharf and Cowell's Beach

Perfect Beach Day in Santa Cruz

FROM MORNING SURF TO SUNSET DRINKS

Surf's up! Whether you're catching waves or watching others ride, rise early for the best conditions. Rent a board from **Cowell's Surf Shop** if you're a pro, or book a class with **Richard Schmidt Surf School**, teaching first-timers and improvers since 1978 (equipment included). Depending on conditions, lessons take place at **Cowell's Beach**, on the west side of the Santa Cruz Wharf, or **Pleasure Point** (east of Santa Cruz).

If you just want to watch surfers, set your alarm a little later: grab a cappuccino from **Verve Coffee Roasters** and head down to **Santa Cruz Beach**. Take a stroll along **Santa Cruz Beach Boardwalk**, the oldest beachfront amusement park on the West Coast. Dating to 1907, the boardwalk's two most famous rides are now National Historic Landmarks: the Giant Dipper (1924) and the Looff Carousel (1911). The sea air, cotton candy and delighted screams of roller-coaster riders might just transport you back to your childhood.

Next, grab brunch to fuel yourself up for a beach-bound hike. **Seabreeze Cafe** has an all-day breakfast menu with comforting classics like waffles, omelets and cinnamon rolls. Fully sated, head west to **Natural Bridges State Beach**, 2.5

WHERE TO EAT AND DRINK IN SANTA CRUZ

Oswald
European comfort food served at a long-running bistro: think cassoulet, lasagna, and rabbit three ways. **$$**

Penny Ice Creamery
Scoops of uncommon ice cream, made from homegrown ingredients and topped with toasted marshmallow fluff. **$**

Venus Spirits
A warehouse-chic craft distillery shaking cocktails made with whiskey, gin and aquavit. Snacks too.

miles from downtown. If it's sunny, enjoy a 3-mile walk from Santa Cruz Beach along Cliff Dr, drinking in views of the coast. You'll pass Lighthouse Field State Beach and boulder-studded Mitchell's Cove along the way.

Named for its arc-shaped sea stacks, Natural Bridges State Beach attracts multitudes of roosting seabirds. Watch them amass on the rocks while you paddle in the surf and walk along the tide pools to spot crabs and sea anemones.

Just north of the beach by the visitor center begins the short **Monarch Trail**, leading to a eucalyptus grove that hosts thousands of overwintering butterflies (p292), usually from October to January. The butterflies roost en masse, drinking milkweed nectar that sustains them through the winter (as well as giving them immunity to some predators).

Weather not suitable for rambling by the beach? One mile west is the **Seymour Marine Discovery Center**, part of UCSC's Long Marine Laboratory. Even if you don't go inside to check out the aquariums and touch pools, it's worth stopping by to marvel at the gargantuan blue whale skeleton outside.

As evening approaches, make your way north to the Ingalls St area, where **Equinox Sparkling Wine** pops bubbly made using the traditional methods of French champagne producers *(ooh la la)*. Finish up at **Santa Cruz Mountain Brewing**, which pours organic ales in a fun indoor-outdoor setting girded by food trucks.

Wildlife-Spotting Around Santa Cruz

SEA LIONS, OTTERS, PELICANS AND MORE

Surfers don't own these foamy waters: they're merely guests among thriving populations of marine mammals and seabirds.

Santa Cruz' coast is part of the **Monterey Bay National Marine Reserve**, and you barely have to go further than **Santa Cruz Wharf** to spot sea lions. There are portholes toward the far end of the landmark 1914 wharf where you can take a look at sea lions that can grow up to 8ft long and 800lb in weight.

But it's much more rewarding to get out on the water. In the morning, take a cruise out into the bay with **Santa Cruz Whale Watching** to seek out gray whales (December through April) and humpbacks (summer), not to mention sea lions and seals (the whole year round). Not sure of the difference? Sea lions are bigger and have large front flippers and ear flaps, whereas harbor seals have ear holes, shorter snouts and smaller front flippers. Next, get even closer by picking up gear from **Kayak Connection** and paddling the otter-filled waters around **Walton Lighthouse** or Moss Landing (p257).

I LIVE HERE: HIKING & CYCLING IN SANTA CRUZ COUNTY

Drew Perkins, Trails Planning Director, shares his favorite outdoor experiences in Santa Cruz County.

Some of my favorite trails are ones I've designed and built with the team at Santa Cruz Mountains Trail Stewardship. We built **West Engelsmans Reroute** in partnership with California State Parks in Wilder Ranch. I love the oceans views you get between the trees. Another great hiking trail is **Emma McCrary Trail** in Pogonip Open Space Preserve.

I am an avid mountain biker, and always recommend cyclists visit the **Flow Trail** we built in CAL FIRE's Soquel Demonstration State Forest. It's one of the projects I'm most proud to have been a part of.

BEST BREWERIES IN SANTA CRUZ

Humble Sea
Foggy IPAs are washed down with food-truck snacks at this indoor-outdoor tasting room with 10 taps.

Sante Adairius
Two taprooms off Hwy 1 near Santa Cruz and Capitola are worth a detour for their porters and West Coast IPAs.

Shanty Shack
Bohemian clientele, live music and 14 flavors on tap, from fruity sours to porters and pale ales.

BEST BEACHES AROUND CAPITOLA

New Brighton State Beach
Sandy shores hemmed with tree-capped bluffs, with walking trails and a campground. East of town.

Seacliff State Beach
Popular for swimming, strolling and sunsets. The sunken freighter, the SS *Palo Alto*, is off-limits. Three miles east.

Rio del Mar State Beach
Stretching south from Seacliff is this wide and sandy beach, far from the Capitola crowds. Four miles east.

Pleasure Point Beach
For skilled surfers and their admirers: a barely-there beach to launch your board into reliable breaks.

In the afternoon switch gears and admire feathered friends instead. Though dedicated birders will be up at dawn, you can marvel at huge pelicans, cormorants and snowy egrets all day long at state parks like Natural Bridges (p252). The **UCSC Arboretum & Botanic Garden** north of town is a great place to see hummingbirds (bring your best camera lens). Look out for curve-beaked thrashers and comical California quails too, as well as hawks and harriers wheeling overhead.

Revel in Capitola's Seaside Nostalgia

BEACHES, DINING AND GOOD VIBES

Rainbow-colored houses, easygoing locals and excellent surf beaches characterize Capitola, and many travelers prefer this quaint seaside town to its bigger, busier neighbor, Santa Cruz.

Start by picking up croissants, cheese twists or bear claws at local stalwart **Gayle's Bakery** before making your way south to Capitola Village. The colorful main drag, Capitola Ave, is lined with palm trees, swimwear stores and out-there arts-and-crafts boutiques. Get a palm reading and some salt-water taffy – you're on vacation!

After the bridge across Soquel Creek you'll find **Venetian Court**, the candy-colored beach condos that light up the social media feeds of countless visitors. Stay awhile on **Capitola State Beach** and take a stroll on **Capitola Wharf**. You can rent a stand-up paddleboard (SUP) or kayak from **Capitola Boat & Bait**, and launch it from the wharf stairs (just finish before the mid-afternoon winds pick up). Need a snack? Stay close to the beach by getting taco takeout from **Margaritaville** and picnicking right on the sand.

Come sundown, take the cable car up to romantic **Shadowbrook**, where elegant diners have tucked into Angus beef and shrimp scampi since 1947. Dress to impress. Finish up in friendly **Capitola Wine Bar** for local pinot noir and live music.

CLOSE WHALE ENCOUNTERS

Whale watching is possible up and down the California coast, but travelers report the closest encounters and best sightings in **Monterey Bay** (p260) and around **Channel Islands National Park** (p331).

GETTING AROUND

Exploring Santa Cruz is easiest by car, especially if you want to reach state parks and neighboring towns like Capitola. In town, easily available rideshare services will spare you the traffic and occasional parking pain. Cycling is a good option: rent wheels from Santa Cruz Bike Repair or Current eBikes.

Big Basin Redwoods State Park
Castle Rock State Park
Henry Cowell Redwoods State Park
Santa Cruz
Forest of Nisene Marks
Moss Landing

Beyond Santa Cruz

Roam redwood forests and kayak into a wildlife reserve in the natural beauty surrounding surfy Santa Cruz.

Yes, Santa Cruz is most famous for blond beaches, surf culture and an easygoing attitude. But those aren't the area's only drawcards: north of Santa Cruz is redwood country, where state parks like Big Basin and Henry Cowell bristle with ancient trees. Further east is Forest of Nisene Marks, a patchwork of more recently regrown forests. And just south of the Santa Cruz County border is Moss Landing, arguably the Central Coast's best place to observe seals and sea otters. Renting a kayak or SUP in Moss Landing and paddling into Elkhorn Slough, the state's second-largest estuary, puts you in a waterbound wonderland where marine mammals are so numerous it's a struggle to keep your distance.

TOP TIP

Break up your road trip: see redwoods between Silicon Valley and Santa Cruz, and visit Moss Landing between Santa Cruz and Monterey.

Sea otter, Moss Landing (p257)

BIGFOOT LEGENDS

What's big, hairy, and hides in California's redwood forests? According to some, the answer is Bigfoot, aka the Santa Cruz Sasquatch. Local legends about this shy, apelike creature stalking through remote North American forests persist, and some locals have devoted their entire lives to assembling evidence.

Get up to speed on the latest Bigfoot sightings and learn more about this persistent myth at the **Bigfoot Discovery Center**. The kindly curator Michael Rugg, a long-time enthusiast, will be happy to show you photos and clips – including the controversial 1967 Roger Patterson and Bob Gimlin footage of a hirsute figure sauntering through the wilderness. This small museum is opposite the entrance to Henry Cowell Redwoods State Park, south of Felton. Donations recommended.

TRACY IMMORDINO/SHUTTERSTOCK ©

Big Basin Redwoods State Park

Hike Among Stately Redwood Forests

BEAUTY SPOTS ALONG HWY 9

The scenic route between Silicon Valley and Santa Cruz is Hwy 9, which meanders to Santa Cruz County's loveliest state parks. Just 40 minutes' drive from Santa Cruz is **Castle Rock State Park**, where walking trails wind past sculpted sandstone, overlooking views of oaks, pine trees and coastal redwoods that carpet the valleys. A tree-lined detour along Rte 236 takes you to **Big Basin Redwoods State Park**, the oldest in California. A short loop trail (0.6 miles) leads you among redwoods up to 1800 years old, some of them blackened by the 2020 wildfires.

BEST FOREST TRAILS AROUND SANTA CRUZ

Redwood Grove Loop Trail
Short but mighty, this 0.8-mile walk in Henry Cowell ...dwoods takes you to giants ...ring 270ft.

Loma Prieta Epicenter
A 4.6-mile round trip in Forest of Nisene Marks, reaching the epicenter of the 1989 earthquake.

Saratoga Gap Trail
Until fire-scarred Skyline to the Sea Trail reopens, Castle Rock's best views are from this 5.6-mile loop.

Continue south along Hwy 9 to reach **Henry Cowell Redwoods State Park**, where old-growth redwoods are a habitat for bobcats and deer. Routes range from 1-mile loops to the taxing 7.5-mile Big Ben trail; grab a map at the entrance (it's easy to lose your bearings). Don't miss the colossal **Fremont Tree**, where you can step inside a 17ft-diameter trunk.

Further east is the **Forest of Nisene Marks**, named after a farming family matriarch who adored nature, and whose descendants donated the land to the state parks system in her memory. It's a dense patch of redwoods, chaparral and cottonwood trees, regrown after logging devastated the old-growth forests in the late 19th and early 20th centuries. Today it's an inspiring place to embrace the pin-drop silence of the forest.

IMMORTAL TREES

Santa Cruz' redwoods are mere youngsters compared to other trees in California. Case in point: the **Ancient Bristlecone Pine Forest** (p623) near Mammoth Lakes, where witchy-looking trees are an incredible 4000 or more years old.

Kayaking at Moss Landing

SPOT SEALS AND PLAYFUL OTTERS

Rent a kayak or SUP from the office of **Monterey Bay Kayaks** in Moss Landing, less than 30 minutes' drive from Santa Cruz. At first glance, the roaring highway and concrete stacks of a natural-gas power plant seem an unlikely setting for a marine preserve. But a short paddle under the highway bridge sends you into **Elkhorn Slough**, a 7-mile estuary. These sheltered waters brim with marine mammals and are aflutter with as many as 116 kinds of birds, including migratory species like peregrine falcons.

The banks of this serene waterway are lined by snoozing seals. You can see pelicans swoop down from the air, herons stalking the shallows, migrating birds like snowy plovers soaring overhead and huge moon jellies and Pacific sea nettle jellyfish pulsating in the water. But the stars of the slough are sea otters. No inhabitant of the California coasts garners coos of delight quite like these playful creatures, and more than 125 sea otters have been counted in Elkhorn Slough. Wildlife in Moss Landing is so abundant that you don't have to seek it out...and sometimes it comes directly to you. But getting too close to seals, seabirds and otters can disturb their feeding and breeding habits, so the onus is on you to keep your distance (ideally five kayak lengths away).

SLOUGH TIPS

Check wind speeds, or call the kayak rental before you head out. Blustery weather means sore arms or even upturned kayaks.

Sea fog burns off fast, so wear sunblock even if it's gray outside.

Time your trip for spring if you want to see cute otter pups cuddling their mothers. Fall and winter are prime time for migrating birds.

Don't land on banks and if an animal looks straight at you, you're too close. If an otter pops up nearby, gently paddle backward to increase the distance.

Be warned, the Federal Marine Mammal Protection Act means you can be slapped with a fine of $3000 for approaching otters.

GETTING AROUND

Touring state parks is best achieved with private transportation. It's possible to get between Santa Cruz and Moss Landing by bus (number 78), but services are infrequent.

MONTEREY

Midway between Santa Cruz and Big Sur, the Monterey Peninsula juts into the ocean from the southern edge of Monterey Bay. Sandy coves and rugged cliffs line the peninsula, though its focal point – for history, culture and wildlife – is the busy seaside town of Monterey.

Literary titan John Steinbeck immortalized Monterey in his 1945 novel *Cannery Row*, but you'll need to squint to picture the stinking fish canneries and steamy brothels described in the novel. Though Monterey has rough edges, downtown is polished to a shine, with hotels, restaurants and souvenir stores. It's one of Hwy 1's most celebrated stops, and there's no shortage of tourist traps, but even weary travelers are won over by Monterey's sparkling waterfront and spruced-up factory buildings.

Slightly north of Monterey is the genteel Pacific Grove neighborhood, while on the other side of the peninsula, connected by scenic 17-Mile Drive, is sun-splashed Carmel-by-the-Sea. Carmel wraps California's greatest hits into a gem-sized package: beaches, wine country and good fashion sense.

TOP TIP

Monterey's famous aquarium is justifiably a major drawcard, and online bookings are essential (tickets aren't sold at the door). Lines go right around the block in the mornings, so arrive in the early afternoon for minimal waiting time and plenty of time to admire the shoals of marine wonders.

Monterey Bay Aquarium (p260)

WIRESTOCK CREATORS/SHUTTERSTOCK ©

SIGHTS
1 Casa del Oro
2 Casa Serrano
3 Cooper-Molera Adobe
4 Custom House
5 House of the Four Winds
6 Hovden Cannery
7 Larkin House
8 Monterey Bay Aquarium
9 Old Fisherman's Wharf
10 Old Monterey Jail
11 Pacific House Museum
12 Point Cabrillo
13 Robert Louis Stevenson House
14 Stone Monument
15 Wing Chong Company Grocery

ACTIVITIES, COURSES & TOURS
16 Adventures by the Sea
17 Monterey Bay Kayaks
18 Monterey Bay Whale Watch

EATING
19 Happy Girl Kitchen
20 The Sardine Factory

SHOPPING
21 American Tin Cannery

WHY I LOVE MONTEREY

Anita Isalska, writer

What's better than a sun-splashed beach town with palm trees, white sand and otters somersaulting in the bay? When that town also has a glint in its eye. That's Monterey: it's a focal point for innocent seaside pleasures, like ice creams and bike rides and feeding time at the aquarium. It's also an erstwhile fishing town, whose seamy side was immortalized in John Steinbeck's *Cannery Row*. Historic downtown buildings once housed penniless artists, lovelorn writers and gold-rush villains. Their lives add to the enigma: Monterey is a blond beauty with an incredible backstory.

Meet Monterey Bay's Wildlife

SEALIFE SPOTTING INDOORS AND OUT

Monterey is a true menagerie of marine life, even before you set foot inside the famous aquarium. Begin on Ocean Blvd, north of Monterey's downtown. Look closely at the dazzling white sands off **Point Cabrillo** and you'll notice pudgy harbor seals basking on one of the best beaches in Monterey. A fence protects them from human disturbance, while docents wander around to explain seal breeding habits.

Head to the pretty cove at **Lovers Point** to spy on seabirds; it's a 30-minute walk, or you can rent a bike from Big Sur Adventures for a quick joyride. Either way, finish your morning with brunch at **Happy Girl Kitchen**, an eco-conscious cafe just two blocks from Ocean View Blvd.

By early afternoon, the crowds at **Monterey Bay Aquarium** will have thinned out, allowing you to enjoy this epic palace of undersea life without the hubbub. Stroll south to the aquarium and grab a pamphlet on your way in – it has essential info on feeding times for the rays, penguins and sea otters. The Jellyfish Galleries and colossal Open Sea tank garner the most photographs, but the most impressive exhibit is the three-story kelp forest. Some 2000 gallons of seawater are pumped in, fresh from the ocean, to replicate the Pacific's tidal swells.

By closing time, you're ready for an early dinner. **The Sardine Factory** is just nearby; illustrious past guests include Clint Eastwood and Prince Albert II of Monaco.

Walk it off along the coastline, heading south along Cannery Row and then Lighthouse Ave. Soon enough you will hear a cacophony of Monterey's famous sea lions bellowing and honking from the bay. The mixed-use trail continues past **Old Fisherman's Wharf**. After Monterey overfished its sardine supplies and the fish-canning boom went bust, the wharf turned to tourism; it's now thoroughly commercialized with seafood restaurants, candy stores and coffee places. Grab a snack and watch sea lions belly-flopping off the rocks before heading back downtown.

SEA-OTTER SIGHTINGS

Sea otters are a frequent sight along the Central Coast, but one of the best places to see them is from a kayak in **Moss Landing** (p257). Elkhorn Slough is an estuary teeming with marine mammals.

Plunge into Monterey Bay

SNORKEL, KAYAK AND SPOT WHALES AND SEA OTTERS

The town of Monterey sits at the heart of Monterey Bay National Marine Sanctuary, which extends 276 miles from the San Francisco Bay Area down to Cambria. You can spot sealife right from the shore, but it's more rewarding to get out on the water.

Not keen to get wet? **Monterey Bay Whale Watch** is one of the oldest local tour operators, and it's owned by marine

BEST SEAFOOD IN MONTEREY

Monterey's Fish House
At this family-owned stalwart, seafood is served with Italian flair; think crab ravioli and shellfish cioppino. $$

Crystal Fish
Light tempura and mouthwateringly fresh sushi fill the menu at this refined Japanese spot. $$

Schooners
An international smorgasbord of seafood, from oysters and local ceviche to cod with ramen noodles. $$$

A humpback whale in Monterey Bay

biologists. With any whale-watching expedition, you're rolling the dice: you could see anything from a distant plume of whale spray to the shiny bulk of a humpback mere feet from your boat. But whatever Mother Nature reveals, you'll experience an ecofriendly boat tour and gain an understanding of belugas, common dolphins and other denizens of the deep.

To get a little closer, rent a kayak or SUP. **Monterey Bay Kayaks** offers guided tours to vantage points where you can safely spot seals, sea lions and otters without disturbing their natural habitats and behaviors. If you prefer to go without a guide, **Adventures By The Sea** rents vessels – but stay five kayak lengths away from all mammals.

Finally, plunge beneath the waterline. Rent diving gear from **Aquarius Dive Shop**, who lead guided tours of marine wonderlands around Monterey and Carmel (reservations recommended). The sight of kelp forests fluttering in the ocean currents is eerily beautiful, and you can see pulsating moon jellyfish, buffalo cod and even sunfish. For an easier alternative, rent snorkel gear instead. Point Lobos (p266) is the best location, but locally in Monterey good areas are San Carlos, Del Monte and Lovers Point.

WHALE-WATCHING SEASON

Great news: much like humans, whales visit Monterey all year round. Their migration seasons overlap, meaning you have a chance of seeing colossal marine mammals whenever you travel. You can see humpbacks from March through November, but your best shot to see these mighty creatures raising a fin is in July and August.

The ocean's biggest behemoths, blue whales, have a shorter season: your optimum chance of sighting the world's biggest mammals is from May to October. Winter has action, too: from December to around mid-May, gray whales glide through Monterey Bay, and you can see killer whales too.

SOLO TRAVEL HIGHLIGHTS IN MONTEREY

Whaling Station Steakhouse
Sit at the bar in this lively restaurant for prime rib, classic cocktails and conversation. **$$**

Monterey Bay Kayaks
Guided tours, from 1½ to four hours long, lead you safely to the best wildlife spots.

Spindrift Inn
Free happy hours encourage guests to mingle. Afterwards retire to a baroque-style room with fireplace. **$$**

I LIVE HERE: LOCAL SEASIDE ACTIVITIES

Yerlany Mendez, Interpretive Programs Specialist at Monterey Bay Aquarium, shares her favorite seaside spots.

I enjoy going to Carmel Beach with my dogs, biking on the recreational trail from Seaside to Pacific Grove, and snorkeling in the shallow kelp of San Carlos Beach. You can visit these places at any time of the year. In spring you see baby deer on the recreational trail, and in summer you will see humpback whales off the coast. Winter may be chilly, but you can see the true power of the ocean waves.

San Carlos is the most special place. It's a calm beach with a shallow kelp forest. I did my first night dive there, when we saw octopuses and bioluminescent life!

Uncover Centuries of Monterey History

CANNERY ROW AND HISTORIC LANDMARKS

In his masterpiece *Cannery Row* (1945), John Steinbeck describes the neighborhood as 'a poem, a stink, a grating noise, a quality of light, a tone, a habit, a nostalgia, a dream.' The modern-day town has cleaned up its seedy streets (and no longer reeks of sardine canneries) but a walking tour uncovers interesting glimpses of Monterey's past.

Start at the **American Tin Cannery**, now a shopping mall. In the 1850s Chinese fishers established themselves at Point Ohlones and developed the fishing industry right here. Further south is the Norwegian-founded former **Hovden Cannery**, which sealed its final tin in 1973. Nearby, on the west side of Cannery Row between David Ave and Ariss Way, is the former **Wing Chong Company Grocery**, testament to the Chinese presence here. It was also the inspiration for a similarly named grocery in Steinbeck's *Cannery Row*.

To go deeper into history, continue on to the Pacific House Museum, opposite Old Fisherman's Wharf on Monterey's Recreational Trail. To the east is the old Custom House, the oldest government building in California, and just west, on the corner of Scott and Oliver Sts, is the town's first general store, **Casa del Oro** (1845). The 'House of Gold' is so named because it was a makeshift bank for those who struck it lucky during the gold rush.

A block north at Artillery and Pacific Sts, **stone monuments** mark the landing place of Sebastian Vizcaíno. The earliest European explorers sailed straight past Monterey, until Vizcaíno landed his galleons here in 1602. On this same spot, missionary Junípero Serra landed here in 1770, founding a chain of Spanish missions in the region.

Walk south along Pacific St for a string of grand old Spanish Colonial-style buildings. **Casa Serrano** (1843), the town's first school; **House of the Four Winds** (1835), named for its weather vane; and across the plaza, Old Monterey Jail (1854), a sturdy granite construction that became the temporary home for numerous gangsters and vigilantes.

Going east along Pearl St you'll see the town's first two-story house, the **Larkin House**, and the Cooper-Molera Adobe (1827), open weekends for walks around its sumptuously furnished interior and rose and herb gardens. A block southeast on Houston St is the **Robert Louis Stevenson House**, formerly a hotel where the author of *Treasure Island* (1883) hung out, writing articles for the local newspaper.

GETTING AROUND

Monterey does an excellent job of helping folks get around car-free. Not only is the center of town walkable (25 minutes from Cannery Row to downtown), it's also bike friendly, with numerous e-bike and bike-rental places. Even better, there's a free trolley from late June to Labor Day, serving downtown, Fisherman's Wharf, Cannery Row and the aquarium. There are (paid) parking lots and garages on Cannery Row.

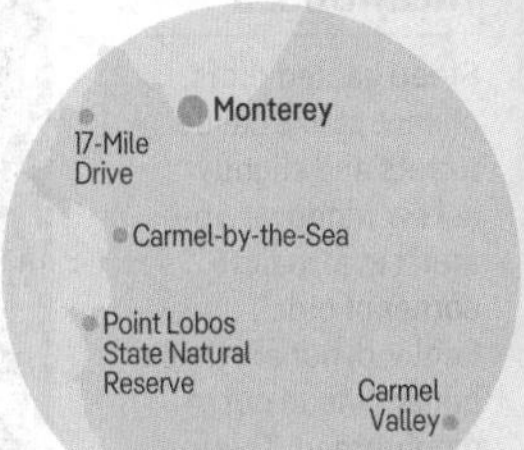

Beyond Monterey

Monterey's outskirts are pinch-me pretty: sashay through dreamy neighborhoods, take a photogenic road trip and see a kaleidoscope of butterflies.

Monterey
17-Mile Drive
Carmel-by-the-Sea
Point Lobos State Natural Reserve
Carmel Valley

Beyond downtown Monterey extend vineyards, hilly nature reserves and neighborhoods more manicured than movie sets. Monterey Peninsula's northern tip is home to Pacific Grove, a coastal city with a pious past. This was California's last 'dry' town, and it widely restricted liquor sales until 1969. Today it's the gateway to the enormously popular 17-Mile Drive, which winds around the peninsula.

Further south is Carmel-by-the-Sea, flanked by white-sand beaches to its west and wine country to the east. Once the stomping ground of literary trailblazers like Jack London and Sinclair Lewis, these days it feels like one large country club, where immaculately coiffed locals stroll by the beaches and clink mimosas over brunch.

TOP TIP

Every year around mid-October until mid-March, butterflies descend on Pacific Grove. The city's Museum of Natural History offers tips on where to see them.

Pacific Grove (p265)

COMSTOCK FAIRY-TALE HOUSES

Steep gabled roofs, chimneys like castle turrets and slightly askew windows: you aren't in a quaint corner of olde England, nor are these houses made out of gingerbread. This is **Comstock Historical Hill District**, where almost two dozen houses were designed by self-taught visionary architect Hugh W Comstock (1893–1950). He began by building the whimsical Hansel and Gretel Cottages (at Torres St, between 5th and 6th Avs) as a suitably magical workshop for his wife, Mayotta, who had a successful business selling handmade dolls, before building several other buildings with shingled roofs and timber beams. The houses are privately owned, so admire them at a distance. Get a map at Carmel's visitor center (on Ocean Av, between Junipero and Mission).

CRAIG LOVELL/EAGLE VISIONS PHOTOGRAPHY/ALAMY ©

Sauvignon blanc grapes at Joullian Vineyards

A Tasting Tour of Carmel Valley's Wine

SIP CABERNET SAUVIGNON AND MERLOT

The wineries in **Carmel Valley**, less than 30 minutes' drive from Monterey, are protected from Monterey's maritime fog, allowing warmer-climate grapes to thrive.

Begin your wine safari at **Blue Fox Cellars**. This boutique winery pours arneis, rosé of grenache and fruity merlot in a bewitching garden with views of cypress trees and the Santa Lucia Highlands. Nearby is **Boekenoogen Winery**, owned by a cattle-ranching and wine-growing family; it bottles wines on-site and offers daily tastings of cabernets, petite syrahs and more. Take a stroll around the village in between tastings, ideally pausing at **Corkscrew Cafe** for wood-fired pizzas (from mushroom and thyme to Italian sausage).

One more tasting before you leave? **Joullian Vineyards**, founded by Oklahoma transplants the Joullian and Sias families in the early 1980s, have established a flourishing home for cabernet sauvignon, merlot and sauvignon blanc, which you can sip in their rustic-chic tasting room.

BEST BOUTIQUE HOTELS IN CARMEL

Pine Inn
Built in 1889, this elegant hotel has a romantic and slightly eclectic design aesthetic. **$$$**

Svendsgaard's Inn
Bright and pleasant, with a fireplace lounge area and personalized service. Upscale and dog friendly. **$$$**

Hidden Valley Inn
Tucked away in the Carmel Highlands, this hotel is an ideal springboard into wine country. **$$**

After driving back to **Carmel-by-the-Sea**, keep the party going at tasting rooms around town. **Dawn's Dream Winery** is a casual spot with a focus on chardonnay and pinot noir; perch next to a barrel table in its exposed-wood tasting room and settle in. Finish up at **Barmel**, Carmel's life of the party, with live music and DJs on the weekend, as well as burgers and other bar food to sop up the damage.

FLIGHTS OF FLUTTERERS

You can see masses of butterflies at Pacific Grove Monarch Sanctuary every year between mid-October and mid-March, but **Pismo State Beach** (p292) is another hot spot for this mesmerizing migration.

Take a Joyride Along 17-Mile Drive

PACIFIC GROVE'S PICTURESQUE TOURIST BYWAY

Travelers flock to 17-Mile Drive, a scenic stretch of road that begins only 15 minutes' drive from Monterey, meandering through a private resort, **Pebble Beach**. Though you might scoff at the toll price, this gated road passes wave-smashed cliffs, champagne-colored beaches and all the splendor of the California coast. Also, you can claim back the toll if you spend $35 or more at Pebble Beach Resorts restaurants – ain't capitalism the greatest? Allow at least three hours.

Of the four access gates, the one from Hwy 1 is the most popular – but Sunset Dr in Pacific Grove is our favorite. Enter here and drive west to the coast, where the road snakes south past cypress groves, rugged cliffs and beaches the color of buttery shortbread.

Practically everyone stops at **Spanish Bay Beach**, so if it's crowded, press on to photo ops like **Restless Sea**, where turbulent Pacific sea swells cast foam across the rocks, and **Point Joe**, the site of past shipwrecks. At **China Rock**, you can see where Chinese fishers built their village in the 1880s. Further south, wildlife-watchers will want to point their binoculars at **Bird Rock**, home to pelicans and sea lions. Next up is the uniquely photogenic **Cypress Point Lookout**, followed by the **Lone Cypress**. It's far from the only tree of its kind, given the knotted cypress groves that cling to cliffs around Monterey, but this 250-year-old tree is perched on a crag, as if posing for a picture. At **Pescadero Point**, the southernmost tip of the route, you can see 'ghost trees,' where bone-like cypress trunks endure though the tree is long dead. After the road curls inland, you can rejoin Carmel Way south to Carmel-by-the-Sea.

CYCLING 17-MILE DRIVE

Want to dodge the toll, avoid the stress of parking in peak season or just experience the wind in your helmet-squashed hair? Then cycle 17-Mile Drive! You can rent wheels at **Big Sur Adventures**, which also offers guided e-bike tours (recommended for less confident cyclists; there are sections of road without bike lanes). Note that motorcycles aren't allowed on 17-Mile Drive.

SUSTAINABLE EATS IN CARMEL AND PACIFIC GROVE

Passionfish
Sustainably sourced fish and an emphasis on local ingredients like squid, sea scallops and Dungeness crab. **$$**

Julia's Vegetarian
Meat-free interpretations of curries, pasta and even lobster (mushroom) roll. Vegan options available. **$$**

Basil Seasonal Dining
Sourcing ingredients from local organic farms, Basil dishes up Italian-style home cooking like gnocchi and meatballs. **$$**

I LIVE HERE: GOURMET MONTEREY COUNTY

Greg Freeman, Chalone Vineyard winemaker, shares his favorite Monterey County food and drink experiences.

Monterey County is a mix of microclimates and micro-communities – try to see as much variety as possible, focusing on the people, cultures, food and scenery. See, swirl, smell, sip and savor the local chardonnays and pinot noir! Notice the bright acidity and the unique, deep flavors of fruit and minerality. Exceptional food abounds but I suggest **Sierra Mar Restaurant** in Big Sur, as it overlooks the Pacific Ocean, right at the very edge of the cliffs. **Dametra Cafe** has the best Middle Eastern food around and there is a guitarist/singer that gets the dining room up and dancing as you enjoy the best lamb, sauces and wines.

RANDY ANDY/SHUTTERSTOCK ©

Bluefish Cove, Point Lobos State Natural Reserve

Explore Pristine Nature in Point Lobos

CLIFFSIDE TRAILS AND UNDERWATER ENCOUNTERS

Point Lobos State Natural Reserve, 20 minutes' drive from Monterey, is a dramatic collision of steep cliffs, teeming tide pools, pine groves and coastal scrub. For walking trails less than a mile long, follow signs from the northwest parking lot to Cypress Grove or Sea Lion Point. Notable intrigues include the **Whalers Cabin Museum**, which has the still-standing remnants of huts built by the first wave of Chinese migrants to California in the early 1850s. Inside are whalebones, old photographs and antique Chinese ceramics. Weston Beach, 15 minutes' walk from the northwest parking lot, has tide pools where you can spot black abalone, sea stars and purple crabs.

Want to go deeper? Certified divers can explore 70ft-high kelp forests at one of two permitted plunge spots, **Whalers** and **Bluefish Cove**, and meet seals, otters and buffalo cod. Whether you dive in your own group or join a guided tour (recommended), you need to reserve well in advance. Book diving tours with Monterey-based **Aquarius Dive Shop** and **Bamboo Reef**.

GETTING AROUND

You'll need your own wheels (car or bicycle) for scenic journeys like 17-Mile Drive, but Carmel-by-the-Sea is small enough to explore on foot. Infrequent buses connect Carmel-by-the-Sea with Monterey and Point Lobos.

BIG SUR

When you imagine the great California road trip, wind in your hair as you soar along sinuous coastal roads, you're picturing Big Sur. Between the Pacific Ocean and the Santa Lucia Mountains, this inspiring section of coast extends south of Monterey, roughly between Carmel and San Simeon.

Spanish settlers nicknamed Big Sur 'the big country to the south' *(el país grande del sur)*, a moniker that promises wild, bracing landscapes – and these unspoiled coves, sheer cliffs and forested realms don't fail to enchant. Big Sur magnetized writers like Henry Miller, Jack Kerouac and Hunter S Thompson, but these days it's tourists and burned-out city slickers who arrive in droves.

Big Sur's landscapes are mighty, and its presence in California culture is colossal; but it's also fragile, isolated and thinly populated. Worried locals look on as streams of tourists bring traffic, litter, soil erosion and mudslides: tread lightly on your trip.

TOP TIP

Poetically enough, Big Sur has no official boundaries, nor a downtown, but the area just north of Pfeiffer Big Sur State Park has the most services. If you must visit highly trafficked photo ops like Bixby Bridge, it'll be more relaxing in the less touristed season from October through April.

Garrapata State Park (p268)

ROAD TRIP

Big Sur Road Trip

The coast-hugging road between Carmel-by-the-Sea and San Simeon is the most beautiful section of California's Hwy 1, connecting dazzling beaches, clifftop lookout points and forested state parks. Go with a full tank of gas (filling up is pricey), bring cash for state park entry, and download maps as cell service is spotty. You could rush this drive in a day, but take two days to enjoy some time in nature.

1 Garrapata State Park

Stretch your legs at Garrapata's under-explored state park on a short hike (or the tougher 4-mile loop trail). Further south, you'll find attractively rock-studded Garrapata Beach, reachable by a trail that is especially lovely between mid-February and early April. Note that 'garrapata' literally means 'tick' – cover your arms and legs.

The Drive: The next 4 miles to Bixby Bridge are dotted with pullover points, but views from the road are almost as good: craggy shorelines and flashes of the Pacific between stands of pine.

2 Bixby Bridge

The elegant, 260ft Bixby Bridge connects sheer sea cliffs that drop down to a golden beach. Castle Rock Lookout has good views, but only park for a photo op if it's safe to do so (tailgating and inattentive driving are common).

The Drive: Ocean views are on show for almost the entirety of this meandering, 8-mile stretch to Andrew Molera State Park, and brilliant beaches wink out after every bend.

3 Andrew Molera State Park

This undeveloped state park has 20 miles of trails weaving through redwood stands and wildflower meadows. For big views and historic artifacts, take the 2-mile Headlands Trail Loop past the 1860s Cooper Cabin to the Big Sur River.

Bixby Bridge

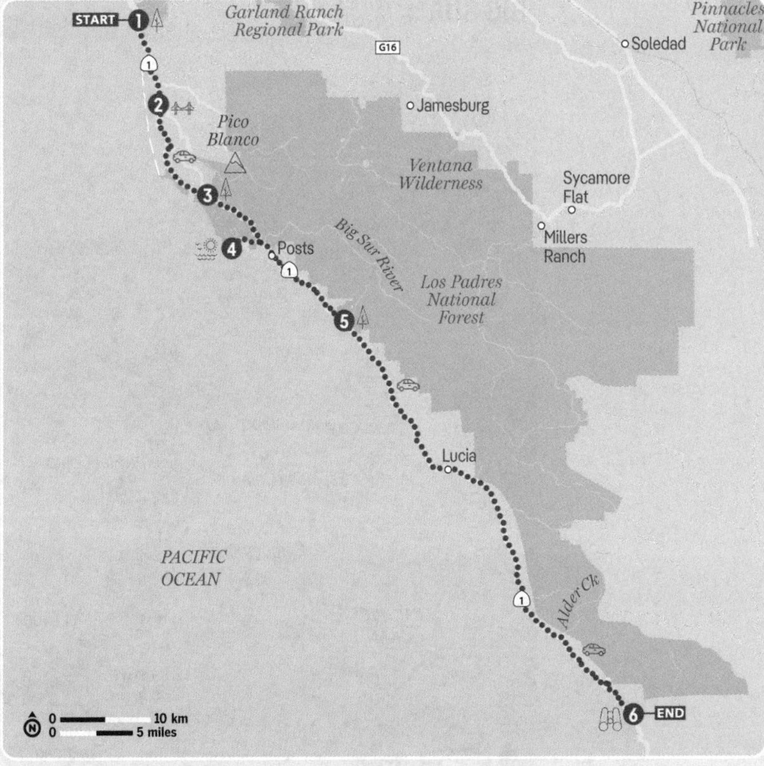

The Drive: The road nudges inland and the next 8 miles are lined with redwoods, before you turn off down the narrow road to Pfeiffer Beach.

4 Pfeiffer Beach

This beach is renowned for sand that appears purplish when the light hits just right, the gift of manganese garnet from crumbling hills nearby. In winter you can catch sunset lining up with Keyhole Arch, which makes this hulking rock formation look like a portal to another realm.

The Drive: After rejoining Hwy 1, the road twists and turns for 8 miles, first through forest and then along a serpentine stretch with Pacific Ocean views.

5 Julia Pfeiffer Burns State Park

Yet another beauty spot named after the early-20th-century Pfeiffer family, this park is a beloved stop for 80ft McWay Falls, which cascades onto the beach. When we last passed through, the half-mile overlook trail was partly closed due to erosion. For a shorter alternative, the popular Partington Trail reaches a rocky surf beach (45 minutes).

The Drive: Some 36 ocean-view miles extend to Ragged Point, sometimes shaded by redwoods. Sand Dollar Beach is an attractive midway stopoff.

6 Ragged Point

This headland marks journey's end. Ragged Point has stirring ocean views, and a short but steep walk goes down to an ashen-colored beach and the variable trickle of Black Swift Waterfalls.

The Drive: Finish up at Ragged Point's inn and restaurants, or continue another 15 miles south to San Simeon for elephant-seal spotting and the astonishingly opulent Hearst Castle.

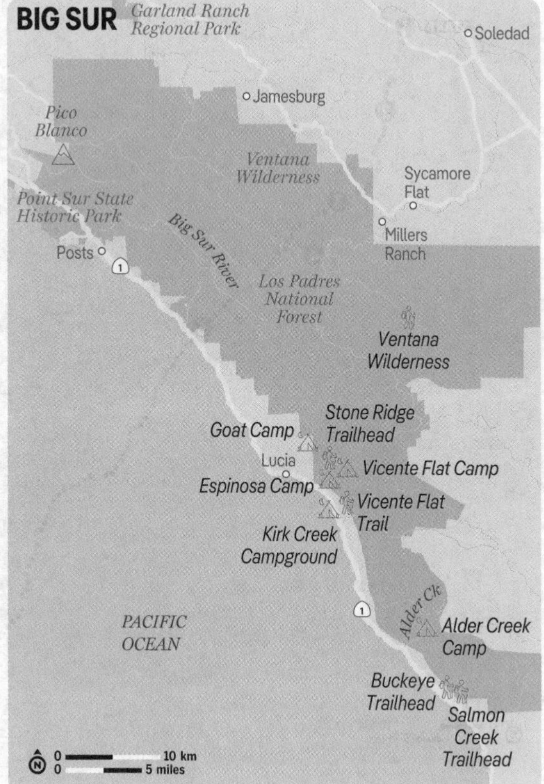

Go Back to Nature in the Ventana Wilderness

GET READY TO ROUGH IT

Tourists cling to the coast, but the Ventana Wilderness is Big Sur's back of beyond: more than 375 mountainous sq miles with a spiderweb of hiking trails. With a tent, broken-in hiking boots and a good level of fitness, a long weekend of wild treks awaits.

On day one, tackle the **Stone Ridge Trail**, a moderately tough hike that combines old-growth redwoods and moss-draped oaks with arguably the best coastal views in the Santa Lucia Mountains. The trailhead is by **Kirk Creek Campground** off Hwy 1; you'll follow the Vicente Flat Trail (sometimes spelled 'Vincente') and then the Stone Ridge Trail, which crisscrosses Limekiln Creek on its way to **Goat Camp**. Getting there and back (18 miles) is a tiring 12 hours; it's better to break it up at **Espinosa Camp** (3 miles' walk from

NB/TRAN/ALAMY ©

Kirk Creek Campground

Kirk) or **Vicente Flat Camp** (5 miles' walk) before finishing the final miles back to Kirk Creek Campground on day two.

Got a couple more days? Experienced backcountry hikers should drive to **Salmon Creek Trailhead** (16 miles south on Hwy 1) for the **Buckeye Trail**; it's 9 miles each way, and the return journey is easily broken up at bare-bones campgrounds. Follow the northwesterly trail toward Buckeye Campground, then Upper Cruickshank. Your calf muscles will grow even stiffer up to **Alder Creek Camp**, where you can camp overnight before making the return journey. Alternatively, arrange a friend or taxi to pick you up; Alder Creek has (rough) road access.

SAFE & SENSITIVE TRAVEL

Big Sur's coast road is intensely popular, while its wild hinterland is pristine. This fragile landscape demands that you travel with a light footprint.

Along Hwy 1, resist the urge to park roadside when there isn't much room. This contributes to soil erosion and can cause accidents. Be cautious of other drivers doing so, especially around Bixby Bridge.

Obey posted speed limits and drive steadily: it improves your fuel economy and reduces sudden braking, which makes you unpredictable to other drivers.

In the Ventana Wilderness, bring water and food, and pack out all trash. Use bearproof containers for food.

You need a license (free from readyforwildfire.org) to use portable stoves or light campfires. Don't light fires anywhere other than designated camping areas.

GETTING AROUND

You will need private transportation to reach the Ventana Wilderness, and a 4WD if you're planning to access campgrounds via bumpy Will Creek Rd. Road closures are common during extreme weather (like 2023's winter storms) so check ventanawild.org if you're unsure about driving conditions.

HIGHWAY 101

The Pacific Coast Highway (Hwy 1) is California's most iconic road trip, but the road less traveled is inland. The fastest route south from San Jose to San Luis Obispo, Hwy 101 accesses under-the-radar wine country, rough-around-the-edges small towns and rocky wilderness. South of San Jose is Gilroy, famous for its garlic festival, with an impressive Spanish mission in nearby San Juan Bautista. Next you'll reach Salinas, whose prolific lettuce-growing earned it the nickname 'Salad Bowl of the World.' More interestingly to travelers, it's the former home of legendary American author John Steinbeck. Further south is Soledad, a gateway town to Pinnacles National Park, a hangout for rock climbers and birds of prey.

Hwy 101's offbeat attractions aren't standout stars of California's Central Coast, but they sure are memorable – and they're a great way to break up a drive from the Bay Area to Paso Robles or San Luis Obispo.

TOP TIP

You can hit the main sights of Gilroy, San Juan Bautista and Salinas all in a day. If you're picking just one, San Juan Bautista has the most historic sights to explore. Devote at least half a day to do justice to Pinnacles National Park.

Gilroy Garlic Festival

SHEILA FITZGERALD/SHUTTERSTOCK ©

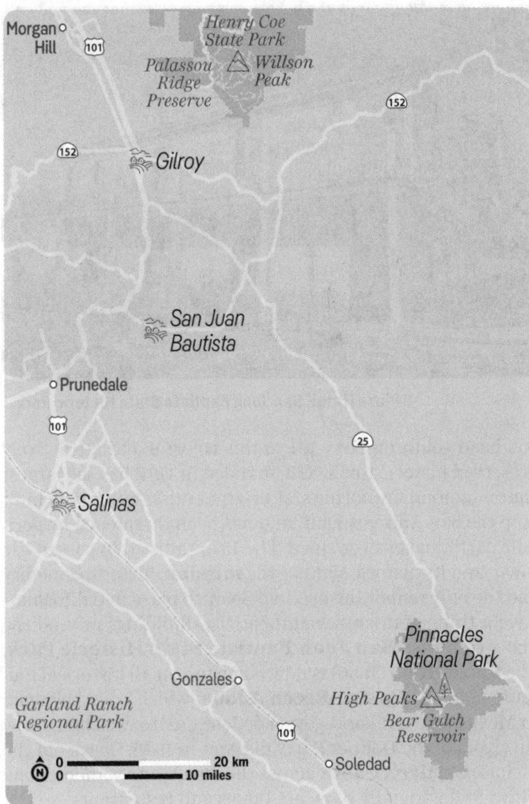

RIVER ROAD WINE TRAIL

Parallel to Hwy 101, a string of wineries follows the Salinas River. Foggy nights encourage cool-climate vines to thrive, resulting in outstanding chardonnay and pinot noir. Sip and swish the best of Monterey County in tasting rooms with views of the Santa Lucia Mountains, such as family-run **Hahn Estate** and boutique **Manzoni Estate**. Further flung (off Hwy 146 to Pinnacles National Park) is **Chalone Vineyard**, the oldest producing vineyard in all of Monterey County, with gloriously lofty views of the Salinas Valley. Chalone's pinots and chardonnays have a minerality resulting from the area's volcanic soil. You can learn more, or book a designated driver, at riverroadwinetrail.com.

Unsung Historic Towns off Hwy 101

'GARLIC CITY' AND SPANISH HISTORY

Just 12 miles apart, Gilroy and San Juan Bautista each offer a glimpse of California history. Start in **Gilroy**, famous for its annual **garlic festival** (on the last weekend in July). For most Californians heading south from San Jose on Hwy 101, Gilroy is only ever a pungent whiff as they drive past fields of garlic. Pull over to stroll through Gilroy's **Historic Downtown**, along Monterey St between 4th and 7th Sts: you'll see vintage brick storefronts dating to the early 20th century.

Don't stick around too long: the day's main attraction is **San Juan Bautista**. You'll pass cherry stalls and garlic vendors as

WHERE TO EAT AND DRINK IN GILROY AND SAN JUAN BAUTISTA

Papas and Eggs
Enjoy chilaquiles and Benedicts at this Mexican-accented brunch restaurant, north of downtown Gilroy. **$**

Jardines de San Juan
Bulging burritos, good margs and other satisfying Mexican fare on the edge of SJB's downtown. **$**

18th Barrel Tasting Room
Family-owned 18th Barrel is a convivial indoor-outdoor hangout for lovers of craft beer and wine.

DARK SIDE OF MISSION HISTORY

The beautiful churches and museums of 18th-century life at California's missions are popular with visitors, but they have complex and often disturbing histories. A common narrative is that kindly Franciscan priests coexisted happily with Native American people in missions.

Less often discussed is the linguistic and cultural erasure by missionaries, a deliberate strategy by the Spanish crown. There are written accounts documenting forcible displacement and enslavement of Native American people by the mission system, and there were countless deaths from diseases introduced by European colonists. Elias Castillo's book *A Cross of Thorns: The Enslavement of California's Indians by the Spanish Missions* (2015) presents evidence of violence and forced labor from Spanish government archives and letters.

ZACK FRANK/SHUTTERSTOCK ©

Plaza Hotel, San Juan Bautista State Historic Park

you head south on Hwy 101 to this colorful and attractively preserved historic town. SJB, founded in 1797, has the largest church among California's 21 original missions; it was built atop the San Andreas Fault and has been threatened by periodic earthquakes ever since. The 1876 railroad bypassed the town, and its historic sights – the **mission**, historic cemetery and the only remaining original Spanish plaza in California – have a trapped-in-amber authenticity. Buildings around the plaza comprise **San Juan Bautista State Historic Park**. The **Plaza Hotel** (1856) is now home to a small historical museum, and the **Castro-Breen Adobe**, which once belonged to Mexican general and governor José Castro, was bought by survivors of the Donner Party disaster in 1848. Check out the historic **Settler's Cabin** across the street, and wander along Third St for friendly bars, boutiques and restaurants.

Salinas for Literature Lovers

FOLLOW IN JOHN STEINBECK'S FOOTSTEPS

After well-heeled stops like Monterey and surfy Santa Cruz, the workaday town of Salinas can come as a shock to California road-trippers. More than rough around the edges, Salinas is the town where John Steinbeck (1902–68) was born and raised, before he forever changed America's literary canon with works like Pulitzer-winning *The Grapes of Wrath* (1939), *Of Mice and Men* (1937), and his love letter to working-class Monterey, *Cannery Row* (1945).

Start at the **National Steinbeck Center**, where Steinbeck's upbringing and creative works are presented through interactive exhibits and videos. This is one of America's biggest

WHERE TO EAT AND DRINK IN SALINAS

Villa Azteca
Oaxacan food, from cheese-stuffed squash blossoms to twists on mole, south of the Steinbeck Center. **$$**

Farmers Union Pour House
Wines, craft beers, boozy kombucha and a cozy brick-lined setting in downtown Salinas...cheers!

Alvarado Street Taproom
The Salinas outpost of Monterey's expanding craft brewery, pouring hoppy IPAs. Three miles southeast.

museums dedicated to an author and you can see old photographs, listen to Steinbeck's speeches and even see the camper in which Steinbeck traveled around the US.

Continue the theme at the **Steinbeck House**. Four blocks west of the Steinbeck Center, the restaurant inside the writer's erstwhile home prepares salads, sandwiches and pan-American classics – but whether or not you eat, it's worth seeing the beautifully renovated Victorian mansion.

True Steinbeck fans can head to the **Garden of Memories Cemetery**, 1.5 miles southeast of downtown, to see the Nobel Prize–winning author's final resting place. A simple plaque marks his grave (part of the Hamilton family tomb).

Round off the literary experience in Salinas' best bookstore, **Downtown Book & Sound**, a nostalgic warren of new and used books, vinyl and even VHS.

Traverse Craggy Pinnacles National Park

HIKE OR CLIMB ROCKY HEIGHTS

A half-hour (30-mile) detour east off Hwy 101, between Salinas and Paso Robles, underexplored **Pinnacles National Park** raises cathedrals of rock into the sky. Around 23 million years ago, massive volcanoes blew their tops, leaving behind pinnacles that gave this 40-sq-mile expanse its name. It's a rolling landscape of boulders, spires and mountains that reach 3304ft high at North Chalone Peak. Visitors come to hike, scale cliffs and gaze at California condors.

For an unchallenging loop trail with views of talus caves and craggy rock formations, embark on the **Moses Spring to Rim Trail** (2.2 miles round trip). It generally takes 1½ hours (maximum 500ft elevation) and is a good pick for families. For a short but stiff uphill hike with inspiring views of the High Peaks, hit the **Condor Gulch Trail** (1.7 miles one way).

Bring a flashlight for the **Visitor Center to Balconies Cavehike** (9.4 miles round trip, allow up to six hours). Returning from the cave, take the Balconies Cliffs route for superlative views of the park's massive rock formations.

Want more thrills? Routes suitable for intermediate rock climbers include **Rat Race** and the **Regular Route**; get climbing advice from the Friends of Pinnacles (pinnacles.org). Better yet, book a six-hour tour with **Adventure Out** (adventureout.com); instruction, gear and insurance are included.

FROGS, BATS & BIRDS OF PREY

Condors are visible in the park year round and they're quite a sight: bald-headed with 9ft wingspans, these carrion-eaters may have black or pink heads depending on their age, and adults have a distinctive white panel under their wings. If a bird holds its wings flat to soar, it's likely to be a condor. Turkey vultures are more common, and much smaller.

Bear Gulch Cave is home to Townsend's big-eared bats (but closed mid-May to mid-July for mating season), while Bear Gulch Reservoir is the habitat of multitudes of red-legged frogs; admire them from a distance, as they're endangered.

BACKCOUNTRY CAMPING

If the wild is calling and you're OK with roughing it, make the **Ventana Wilderness** (p270) your next stop. There are remote hiking trails and blissfully isolated campgrounds in the midst of mossy oak and redwood forests.

GETTING AROUND

Train travel is slow and services are infrequent; this strip of inland sights is best visited by car. Patient travelers can get to Salinas by train (it's a stop on the Coast Starlight) and Gilroy is reachable by Caltrain commuter services from San Jose. But if you aren't road-tripping, you'd best plan thoroughly: if we had to get stuck someplace in California, this isn't where we'd pick.

CAMBRIA

Between the southern end of Big Sur and Morro Bay, the seaside town of Cambria anchors an attractively windswept stretch of coast. Lively Cambria was built in the 1860s from leftover slabs of wood, giving it the nickname 'Slabtown.' When the timber industry came to a halt, tourism quickly took over as Cambria's moneymaker. Today Cambria has carefully cultivated a quaint ambience: it's rife with arty shops and farm-to-table restaurants, and vintage sights like Hearst Castle and a historic lighthouse heighten its attractiveness to weekenders and day-trippers from San Luis Obispo.

To Cambria's north is sparsely populated San Simeon, best known for its elephant-seal rookery, nearby Piedras Blancas lighthouse and access to hilltop Hearst Castle. To the south is Cayucos, a smaller, somewhat faded surf town with a Wild West feel, thanks to vintage signs and wooden saloons. A weekend is enough time to experience the best walks and sights.

TOP TIP

Staying in Cambria allows you to be close to dining, shopping and a pleasantly walkable downtown, but family travelers may prefer Cayucos for its pier and kid-friendly swimming beach. San Simeon has budget and midrange hotels but it's less compact and feels more remote.

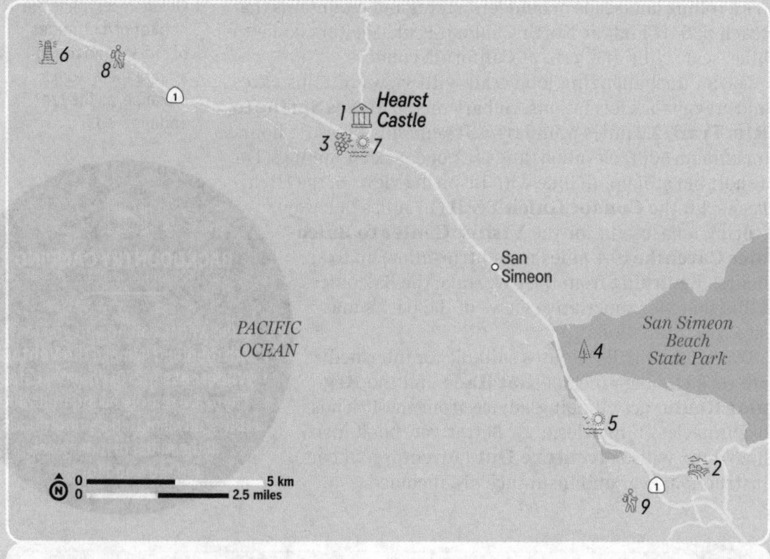

HIGHLIGHTS
1 Hearst Castle

SIGHTS
2 Cambria
3 Hearst Ranch Winery
4 Hearst San Simeon State Park
5 Moonstone Beach
6 Piedras Blancas Light Station
7 William Randolph Hearst Memorial State Beach

ACTIVITIES, COURSES & TOURS
8 Boucher Trail
9 Fiscalini Ranch Preserve

RANDY ANDY/SHUTTERSTOCK ©

Hikers in the Fiscalini Ranch Preserve

Quaint Cambria, from Seaside to Shopping

BRACING WALKS AND SMALL-TOWN QUIRK

In the morning, head to **Fiscalini Ranch Preserve**, where 17 short hiking trails offer picturesque routes between Monterey pine forests, wetlands and driftwood-strewn shores. Most popular are the Forest Loop Trail and the Bluff Trail; both are easy and roughly 1 mile long.

Grab lunch in **Cambria** (perhaps something spicy at **Robin's**), then take a walk along Main St to admire historic storefronts, antiques shops, arty cafes and, if it's a Friday, the **farmers market** that fills Main St from 2:30pm. Don't skip **Linn's Easy As Pie Cafe** for a slice of olallieberry (raspberry-blackberry hybrid) pie. While digesting this generous wedge of pie, take a turn around the **Cambria Historical Museum**, inside one of Cambria's oldest homes.

Next, head north to **Moonstone Beach**. If you're driving, take a quick detour past **Nitt Witt Ridge**, where a local artist and trash collector spent 50 years building a palatial home out of upcycled materials. At Moonstone, take a stroll along the beach boardwalk, roughly 1.5 miles through coastal prairies.

HISTORIC HARMONY

Embracing its novel, offbeat status, Harmony (population 18) is a worthwhile pullover between Cambria and Cayucos. Most people come to sip riesling, zinfandel and syrah at **Harmony Cellars**, a boutique winery that stays close to local winemaking traditions that began in the 19th century, but there's also an art studio and glassworks in this pocket-sized town. Kids in tow? Check Harmony Valley Creamery's website for when its scoop truck is around, doling up classic ice-cream flavors like mint chip, butter pecan and strawberry.

BEST EATS IN CAMBRIA

French Corner Bakery
Croissants, eclairs and lemon tarts are prepared with Parisian flair at this likable cafe. **$**

The Hidden Kitchen
A slow-food, nutrition-conscious approach to brunch and lunch, with a sister restaurant in Cayucos. **$**

The Sow's Ear
Creative California cuisine shares the menu with comfort food like chicken-fried steak and pot roast. **$$**

Piedras Blancas Light Station

BEST WALKING & CYCLING

Boucher Trail
A 4-mile there-and-back walk between Piedras Blancas Light Station and the elephant-seal lookout, taking in seasonal wetlands and coastal bluffs.

San Simeon Point Trail
This 2.5-mile round-trip hike (under two hours) from Hearst Castle State Beach has views of eucalyptus trees and foaming sea.

Ragged Point Route
This famous and challenging 37-mile return bike route runs along Hwy 1 between San Simeon and Ragged Point.

The beach is named for the precious stones washing up on the shore; take a close look at the rainbow of colored pebbles (but resist the urge to take any home).

Just off the beach is nautical-themed **Sea Chest Oyster Bar**, where you can grab an early dinner of calamari or clams. Moonstone Beach Boardwalk is just outside: a romantic spot to watch the sun set.

Wander the Shipwrecked Shores of San Simeon

WILDLIFE-SPOTTING AND MARITIME HISTORY

Start with a 4-mile round-trip hike, taking in the two main shoreside draws of the San Simeon area: the lighthouse and the elephant seals. Begin at **Piedras Blancas Light Station**, one of California's tallest lighthouses; it first blinked on in 1875, built after two ships from San Francisco sank after striking sunken rocks in 1869. Take a walk around the headland, gazing out at the rugged white sea stacks for which the lighthouse is named. Two-hour tours require reservations.

Follow the **Boucher Trail** east to reach the **elephant-seal vista point**. This observation deck peers out over a 4-mile-long beach. During breeding season (November to March),

SEASIDE SLEEPS

Fireside Inn
With a color palette reminiscent of surf and sea fog, this Moonstone Beach place captures the coastal aesthetic. **$$**

Shoreline Inn
Steps from Cayucos Beach, this well-renovated inn has family-friendly rooms with views of the pier. **$$**

Fogcatcher Inn
Cottages with mock-Tudor facades capture an English countryside ambience, complete with fireplaces. **$$**

elephant seals arrive en masse. Huge males (up to 5000lb) vie for female attention in growling, huffing standoffs, and from January you can see pups.

It's 2 miles back to Piedras Blancas, where you can pick up your car and continue east. Stop for a photo op of the skeletal pier at **William Randolph Hearst Memorial State Beach** before settling in at **Hearst Ranch Winery**. Picnickers are welcome to bring supplies to accompany tastings of syrah, malbec and petit verdot wines, but there's often a food truck (and always deli supplies like cheese and salami).

Finally, walk it off at the seasonal wetlands and coastal bluffs of **Hearst San Simeon State Park**, looking out for black-tailed deer and ground squirrels as you hike.

Tour Luxurious Hearst Castle

MEDIA MOGUL'S PRIVATE PALACE

Rivalling Graceland for its sheer opulence, Hearst Castle is a temple to extravagant wealth. Built by media mogul William Randolph Hearst (1863–1951), this 165-room hilltop estate is a place where no expense has been spared, and no two rooms are the same.

Tours are the only way inside; book ahead, it's deservedly popular. Allow half a day to get here, take a tour and stretch your legs on nearby beaches. The **Grand Rooms Tour** is a classic for first-time visitors. while the **Upstairs Suites tour**, if you can manage 367 steps, leads you through vaulted libraries and resplendent private suites.

After checking in at the visitor center, board the minibus for a 15-minute ride through groves of spruce and knotty manzanita. Up on the hill, guides lead groups along an architectural tour de force through ancient Egypt, Rome and Moorish Spain, tiptoeing past gold-tile floors and painstakingly reconstructed mosaics. Highlights are the column-framed **Roman pool** overlooking the hills (it takes 345,000 gallons of water to fill) and **Casa Grande**, styled like a Renaissance Spanish plaza. Though it looks hand-carved, it's poured concrete to withstand California's earthquakes.

The newspaper magnate Hearst inspired *Citizen Kane* (1941), Orson Welles' Hollywood cinematic epic, but the man himself was no recluse, entertaining Hollywood stars and royals. You'll learn more about his life during the (optional) 40-minute movie screening at the end.

PIONEERING ARCHITECT

Hearst Castle was a labor of love for the visionary architect Julia Morgan (1872–1957), who supervised its construction for 28 years. Morgan was the first woman admitted to Paris' prestigious École Nationale Supérieure des Beaux-Arts to study architecture, and California's first licensed female architect. Aside from Hearst Castle, Morgan also remodeled San Francisco's ornate Hearst Building, and designed the Craftsman-style Berkeley Playhouse (formerly a church). Though Morgan's works were ostentatious, she was known for being frugal, independent and devoted to her work.

GETTING AROUND

Most travelers drive, but the fairly flat, straight coast road (Hwy 1) makes it relatively easy to cycle from Cambria to Piedras Blancas or Hearst Castle. Infrequent RTA buses connect Morro Bay, Cayucos, Cambria and San Simeon, as long as you time your travels with care.

PASO ROBLES

San Francisco
Paso Robles
Los Angeles

A mellow, arty city in the midst of underrated wine country, Paso Robles is midway between San Francisco and Los Angeles. Some 25 miles inland, it's far enough from the tourist trail to escape international attention, but adored by in-the-know Californians for its 200-plus wineries, some scattered along Hwy 46 and many with tasting rooms in town (especially around Park and 13th Sts).

Paso Robles is much more laid-back than big-hitting California wine destinations like Napa Valley. There's a larger variety of wines, too, all of them benefiting from limestone-rich soil and cooling marine winds that blow in from the coast. Syrah, cabernet sauvignon and sauvignon blanc reign supreme, while typical buttery California chardonnay is persona non grata. Paso Robles originally grew to prominence as a spa destination and it remains an indulgent, revitalizing place to soak in hot springs, idle around looking at art and swirl a glass or three of wine.

TOP TIP

Wine tasting without a designated driver? Either tour tasting rooms in Paso Robles' walkable downtown, or secure local transportation. Book locally owned **SLO Safe Ride** (slosaferide.com) or **Fetch Transportation** (slofetch.com) for winery pickups and drop-offs, or create your own tour with **Wine Wrangler** (thewinewrangler.com).

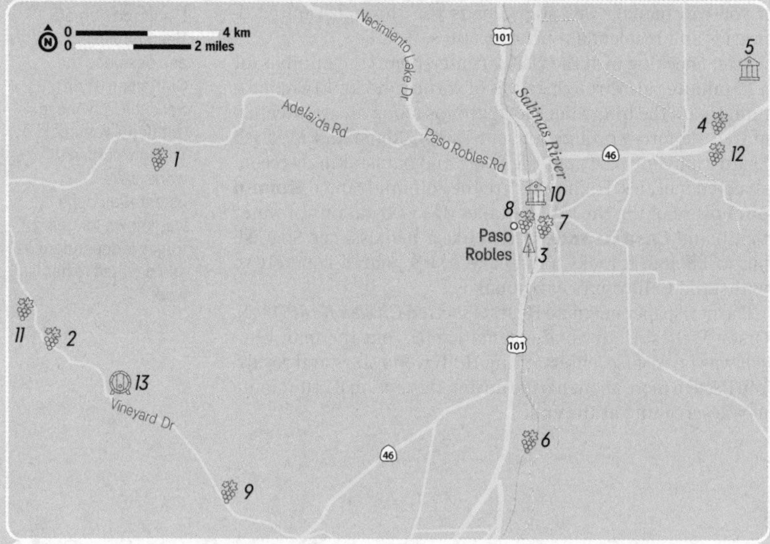

SIGHTS
1 Adelaida Vineyards
2 Dilecta
3 Downtown City Park
4 Eberle Winery
5 Estrella Warbird Museum
6 Field Recordings
7 Herman Story Wines
8 Indigené Cellars
9 Paix Sur Terre
10 Pioneer Museum
see 3 Studios on the Park
11 Thacher Winery
12 Vina Robles
13 Willow Creek Distillery

Spend a Wine-Tasting Weekend in Paso Robles

TASTINGS IN RELAXED WINERIES

On day one, take Hwy 46 east to **Eberle Winery**: unusually, this highly awarded winery offers tastings for free (that's how convinced they are that you'll buy a bottle or two). There's usually plenty of room for walk-ins at the bar, but book ahead and you can get a private tour of its 16,800 sq ft underground caves.

Just across Hwy 46 is **Vina Robles**. Founded by Swiss expats and operating for more than two decades, Vina Robles has six certified sustainable wine estates. Grab a formidable cheese plate or Alpine-style mac 'n' cheese while sampling the crisp albariño or cab sav. Keep an eye on the website for special events at the amphitheater.

Head back to Paso Robles' pretty town center, where you can experience wine country without feeling bad for your designated driver. Less than 10 minutes by rideshare along Hwy 101 to 'Tin City' is urban winery **Field Recordings**, which prides itself on finding unique wines from around the Central Coast; it's a rewarding spot to taste wildly different drops, from bracing nebbiolos to ramato-style pinot grigio (that is, Italian-style blush). Back in town, step inside eclectic **Herman Story Wines** – its tasting room is deliberately bare, forcing you to focus on the wine. Finally, **Indigené Cellars** is one of very few African American–owned wineries and its reservation-only tasting room is mere steps from the city park. Founder Raymond Smith's multi-award-winning wines include spicy cabernet sauvignon and chardonnay with tropical pineapple notes.

On day two, drive a loop west along Adelaida Rd to access the most attractively located wineries, set in gentle hills. **Adelaida Vineyards** (reservations required), the highest point in Paso Robles at 2320ft, has a tasting room fringed by walnut trees. Sustainable winemaking is at the heart of this lofty winery, which uses solar energy and water-preservation techniques in the production of its zesty rosé blends and plummy zinfandels.

Head south along Vineyard Dr, stopping at a couple more (**Thacher Winery** and **Dilecta** are excellent bets), then switch things up at **Willow Creek Distillery**. Have a tasting, and pick up a bottle of damson brandy or walnut liqueur,

WINE COUNTRY BY BICYCLE

Want a car-free wine-tasting experience in equally lovely surroundings? Make the **Edna Valley** (p287), 35 miles south on Hwy 101, your next stop. You can cycle between wineries, and it's just south of laid-back San Luis Obispo.

AFTER-DARK ARTWORK

An emerging hub for outdoor art, **Sensorio** is host to Bruce Munro's **Field of Light**, in which multitudes of light installations set the hills twinkling after sundown. As you walk through the outdoor installation, you'll see multicolored lighthouses made from wine bottles and the meadows sparkling with 58,800 glass spheres. The exhibit is in residence indefinitely, and Sensorio has plans to expand (check sensoriopaso.com for the latest). Book tickets ahead; it's roughly 5 miles northeast of Paso Robles (on Hwy 46).

FINE DINING IN PASO ROBLES

Les Petites Canailles
Its menu roves across France, with steak tartare, *moules frites* and Gruyère *tartelettes*. **$$$**

In Bloom
Settle in for an inventive six-course tasting menu, from Spanish-style octopus to gourmet s'mores. **$$$**

The Hatch
Comfort food from ribeye to rotisserie chicken receives sophisticated treatment at The Hatch. **$$**

HOT SPRINGS IN PASO ROBLES

Franklin Hot Springs
Slide into waters that simmer at a constant 97.3°F (36.3°C) at this no-frills spring, 4 miles southeast of downtown.

River Oaks Hot Springs
An upmarket spa experience with private mineral-water sessions as well as deep-tissue and hot-stone massages. Located 2 miles north.

Paso Robles Inn
Book a spa room at this downtown hotel to enjoy a private tub on your balcony.

CALEB LANDON/SHUTTERSTOCK ©

Wine tasting in Paso Robles

all inspired by Northern Italian recipes. Finish in style at **Paix Sur Terre**, a family-run winery offering tastings overlooking views of the vineyard.

Art & History in Paso Robles

VINTAGE SIGHTS AND MODERN ART

What do you do in Paso Robles before wine o'clock? Tap into the arts scene and local history. After grabbing espresso at Spearhead Coffee, wander across **Downtown City Park** (there's a farmers market on Tuesday mornings). On Pine St you'll find **Studios on the Park**, where you can peruse a gallery/fine-arts boutique and even meet local artists in residence. Check studiosonthepark.org for occasional events and art workshops for kids.

For a flavor of 19th-century Paso Robles, the **Pioneer Museum** is less than 1 mile north and has an old schoolroom and jail cell. If you have wheels, continue to the **Estrella Warbird Museum**, a 10-minute drive northeast of downtown, which showcases vintage military aircraft. Bonus: it's conveniently close to Hwy 46's best wineries, so you can segue into wine tasting in the afternoon.

GETTING AROUND

Downtown Paso Robles is safe and walkable. There's plenty of parking and the Amtrak station, en route from Oakland to LA, is in walking distance. Out-of-town wineries and sights like Sensorio need private transportation, but there are plenty of local taxi and pickup services to help.

Beyond Paso Robles

Paso Robles is enjoyably slow-paced but its surroundings are even sleepier, with relaxing wineries and atmospheric old buildings, including a Spanish mission.

If you want to clap eyes on centuries-old religious art, swirl syrah in a wood-lined tasting room or find a homestay in a converted ranch, San Miguel is the place. The main reason to visit this lonesome, frontier-feel town is its trio of impressive historic buildings. The town was founded in 1797 by the Spanish, who left behind the stately Mission San Miguel Arcángel parish church that is still in use today. Otherwise, downtown doesn't have much going on, and that's part of the appeal: there are vineyards on either side of Hwy 101, olive-oil groves pressing golden nectar, and outdoorsy locals taking to surrounding lakes and plains to cycle and hike.

TOP TIP

San Miguel is best experienced as a half-day trip; sticking around is truly for those with an appetite for slow living.

Mission San Miguel Arcángel (p284)

JAMES DEAN MEMORIAL

A lonely memorial to James Dean (1931–55), star of *Rebel Without a Cause* (1955), adorns an oak tree opposite the Jack Ranch Cafe in Cholame, 23 miles east of Paso Robles off Hwy 46. Dean's raw charisma propelled him to icon status and decades after his death in a car accident he remains associated with devil-may-care teen rebellion.

NAGEL PHOTOGRAPHY/SHUTTERSTOCK ©

Mission San Miguel Arcángel's interior

Travel Backwards in Time in San Miguel

HISTORIC CURIOS AND MISSION HISTORY

Begin at the **Mission San Miguel Arcángel**, just 15 minutes' drive from Paso Robles. This beautiful 1797 adobe complex is framed by a spiky garden of cactus and aloe plants. Walk through the vaulted arcade toward the church. Its beautiful frescoes of flowers, angels and the *ojo de Dios* (eye of God) were completed by Spanish-born trader and artist Esteban Carlos Munràs in the 1820s. The San Simeon Earthquake in 2003 caused critical damage to the mission, and restoration of the inner quadrangle continues to this day, but the incredibly well-preserved artwork on display still rivals some of California's better-known sites. Outside is a historic cemetery; note the guardian statue of patron saint Miguel taking a stab at Lucifer.

Just south is San Miguel's most striking photo op, the **Wieland Bell Tower**. This three-tiered brick tower memorializes WWII US Navy Chaplain Fidelis Wieland, and it has become an emblem at the gateway to the town. Further along is the **Rios-Caledonia Adobe** (1835), a treasured historic site with an original inn (now converted into a museum of mission life). Inside are artifacts from the daily lives of T'epot'aha'l people (or 'People of the Oaks'), the original stewards of the land around the Salinas River, as well as rooms furnished with 19th-century photographs illustrating mission life. Stay awhile to stroll in the gardens, which have century-old cacti and eucalyptus trees, a 1900s wishing well and a section of the old stage road (used up until 1938).

SPANISH MISSIONS

To see more relics of California's Spanish missions, **San Juan Bautista** (p273) is a must-see if you're heading north. Midway between Monterey and San Jose, SJB has an atmospheric state park conserving numerous historic buildings.

GETTING AROUND

You'll need private transportation to explore San Miguel and its lonesome surroundings. It's best visited as part of a road trip between the San Francisco Bay Area and San Luis Obispo, or as a half-day trip from Paso Robles.

SAN LUIS OBISPO

San Francisco
San Luis Obispo
Los Angeles

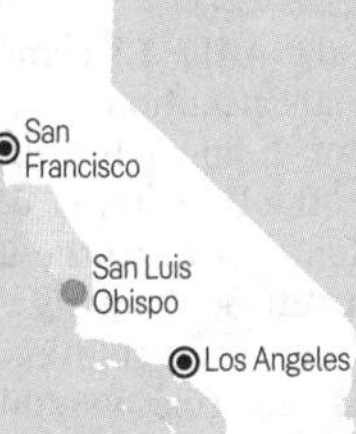

Outdoors-loving locals and students at California Polytechnic State University make their home in San Luis Obispo, while the rest of California looks on in envy. This compact city is roughly midway between San Francisco and Los Angeles, and lies snuggled among the volcanic Nine Sisters peaks. It's friendly, unpretentious and enjoys easy access to the rugged interior and some of the Central Coast's best beaches. For travelers, it's an ace base for half- and full-day trips south to Avila and Pismo Beach, east to Edna Valley wine country, or further north to wild Big Sur. Must-see sights are few; SLO is all about ambience, whether that's the outdoor cafe scene or the extraordinary hikes mere steps from downtown.

Like many of California's towns, SLO grew from a mission founded by Junípero Serra, in 1772. The town still has a strong Spanish accent, and the vintage architecture and tree-shaded streets give downtown an almost European feel.

TOP TIP

Several good, midrange hotels are clustered northeast of downtown (off Monterey St), within walking distance of the historic district. Expect to drive or take a rideshare to the Madonna Inn (unless you're staying there). Other excursions, like Edna Valley, are doable by bicycle.

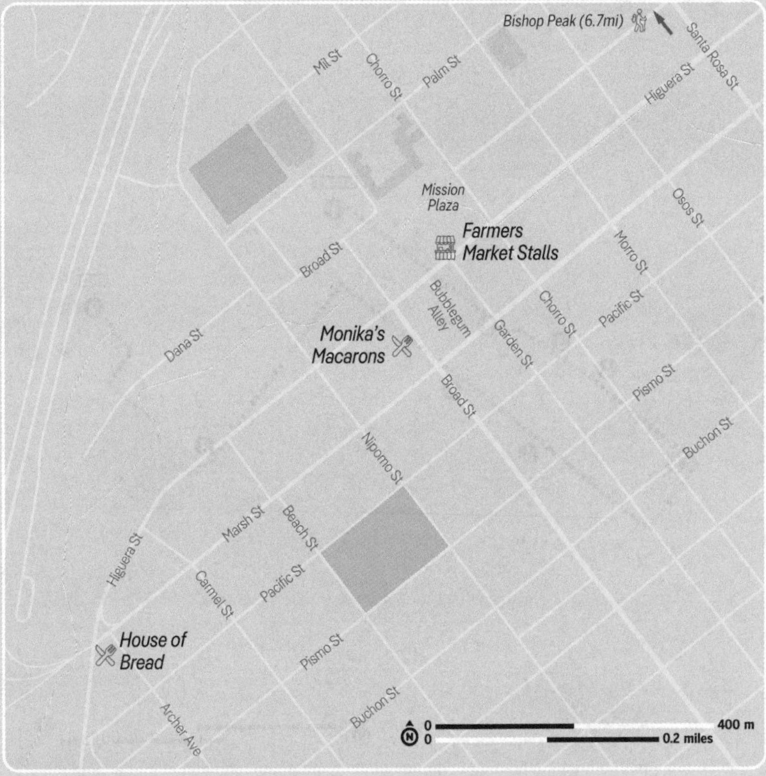
Bishop Peak (6.7mi)
Santa Rosa St
Mill St
Chorro St
Palm St
Higuera St
Mission Plaza
Osos St
Farmers Market Stalls
Morro St
Broad St
Bubblegum Alley
Garden St
Chorro St
Pacific St
Monika's Macarons
Dana St
Broad St
Pismo St
Buchon St
Nipomo St
Marsh St
Beach St
Higuera St
Carmel St
Pacific St
House of Bread
Pismo St
Buchon St
Archer Ave
0
400 m
0
0.2 miles

DOWNTOWN SLO WALKING TOUR

Start at the **1 Fremont Theater**, which steals attention with its shark-fin-shaped sign. It opened in 1942, mere months after the US entered WWII. Go west along Monterey St to the **2 Sinsheimer Bros Building**. Formerly a general store owned by two brothers, this 1884 landmark has cast-iron columns and elegant neoclassical features. Continue to Mission Plaza where you'll see the **3 Mission San Luis Obispo de Tolosa**, founded in 1772. Step inside the church, walk through cactus- and vine-wreathed gardens and tour the museum.

For more local history, head to the corner of Broad and Monterey Sts: you can browse antiques and old photographs inside the red-brick **4 San Luis Obispo County Historical Museum**. Further west along tree-lined Monterey St, you'll see the **5 San Luis Obispo Children's Museum** on the corner with Nipomo St. If you have little ones in tow, shepherd them inside for interactive displays and retro toys galore. Otherwise, head east on Higuera St, SLO's main shopping drag since the late 19th century, named after a Spanish founding family.

Just before the end of the second block, you'll see **6 Bubblegum Alley** on the right, where wads of chewed-up gum have been tacked onto the walls since the '60s. Continue along Higuera St, pausing to look at the imposing 1930s **7 Wineman Building** before heading south along Osos St.

After three blocks you'll see the **8 Grace Church**, a 1930s Colonial-style building. Meander across Mitchell Park onto Pismo St toward your final stop: the **9 Dallidet Adobe**. This 1850s building was home to SLO's first commercial wine and brandy maker Pierre Hypolite Dallidet and his family.

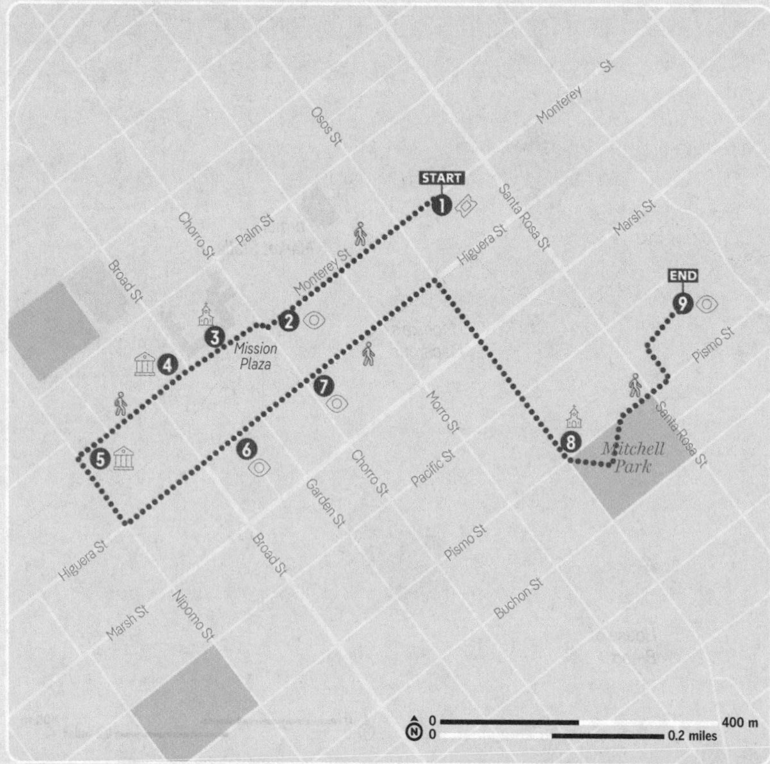

EDNA VALLEY CYCLING TOUR

A bicycle is the best way to experience the cool-climate wine country southeast of San Luis Obispo. The fog-kissed terroir allows winemakers to cultivate world-class chardonnays and pinot noirs, all with views of the Santa Lucia Mountains.

Start your ride from **1 San Luis Obispo** after renting wheels from downtown outfits like Foothill Cyclery, heading south along Johnson Rd, then Orcutt Rd. Here begins the Tiffany Ranch Loop, a 20-mile circuit linking the Edna Valley's wineries. At **2 Baileyana** mineral-note chardonnays and peachy pinot noir rosés are poured in a historic tasting room, formerly the 1909 Independence Schoolhouse. Further southeast along Orcutt Rd is **3 Chamisal Vineyards**, which prides itself on champagne-inspired sparkling wines and fruit-forward pinot noirs.

Turn right along Tiffany Ranch Rd, then right again to reach **4 Kynsi Winery**, tended to for more than 30 years by winemaking innovators Don and Gwen Othman. Reservations are recommended for tasting the spicy pinots and espresso-dark syrahs. Dry-white fans should save themselves for the **5 Claiborne & Churchill Winery**, which specializes in gewürztraminer and riesling. Get a tasting paddle and cheese plate to enjoy at a tree-shaded table.

Room for more? **6 Tolosa Winery** has a premium feel (reflected in its prices). Elegant architecture and manicured gardens create a plush setting where you can taste vibrant chardonnays and its flagship, full-bodied pinot noirs, before pedaling back into San Luis Obispo.

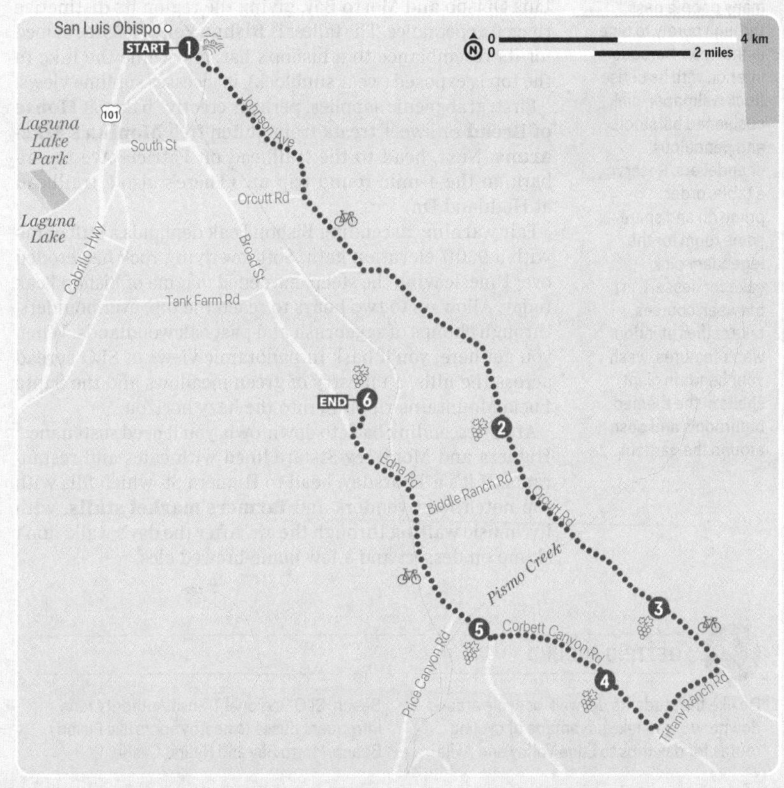

MADONNA INN

To some, it's a kitschy pink fantasia whose turrets, monster sign and twinkly glass windows beckon from Hwy 101. To others, it's an eyesore with wedding-cake decor. But what travelers can all agree on is the Madonna Inn shouldn't be missed. Its 110 themed hotel rooms give you the choice of chariot-shaped beds, animal-print decor, Austrian chalet chic and much more. But many people pass through purely to dine in the neon-baroque interior, with its cerise flock wallpaper, pink cushioned barstools and pendulous chandeliers. Reserve a table, order prime rib and spare some room for the legendary pink cake for dessert. In between courses, take selfies at indoor water features, wash your hands in giant shells in the themed bathrooms and pose around the gardens.

LOGAN BUSH/SHUTTERSTOCK ©

Wineman Building (p286)

Climb SLO's Tallest Peak

HIKE TO 360-DEGREE VIEWS

The Nine Sisters chain of volcanic plugs stretches between San Luis Obispo and Morro Bay, giving the region its distinctive rugged appearance. The tallest is **Bishop Peak** (1559ft), named for its resemblance to a bishop's hat, and while the hike to the top is exposed (wear sunblock), it accesses sublime views.

First, grab picnic supplies: perhaps creative bakes at **House of Bread** or sweet treats from gluten-free **Monika's Macarons**. Next, head to the trailhead off Patricia Ave to embark on the 4-mile round trip up. (There's also a trailhead at Highland Dr.)

Fair warning: ascending Bishop Peak demands a stiff climb with a 950ft elevation gain. Soft, overlying rock has eroded over time, leaving the steep, hardened magma of Bishop Peak today. Allow up to two hours to reach the top, over boulders, through clumps of sagebrush and past oak woodlands. When you get here, you'll bask in panoramic views of SLO spread across the hills, a tapestry of green meadows and the Santa Lucia Mountains rippling into the hazy horizon.

After descending back to downtown, you'll need sustenance: Higuera and Monterey Sts are lined with cafes and restaurants. If it's a Thursday, head to Higuera St, which fills with top-notch food vendors and **farmers market stalls**, with live music wafting through the air. After the day's walk, don't skimp on dessert and a few home-brewed ales.

GETTING AROUND

Do like the students do: walk or cycle around downtown, and take advantage of cycling routes for day trips to Edna Valley and Avila Beach. SLO Regional Transit Authority runs infrequent buses to nearby spots like Pismo Beach, Morro Bay and Hearst Castle.

Beyond San Luis Obispo

Beaches, hot springs and quaint seafront towns: day trips are part of the joy of staying in San Luis Obispo.

San Luis Obispo's enviable location gives it the best of California, from Pacific-lashed beaches to ancient peaks. These remarkable surroundings make SLO much greater than the sum of its parts: the variety of day trips is truly a delight.

From SLO, it's 15 minutes' drive to the coast. Don't expect Malibu: this stretch of coast has more eucalyptus trees than sun-kissed palms, and has as many creaky, vintage seafronts as polished promenades. Northwest is Morro Bay, a popular fishing village with a rustic feel, while directly west rises Montaña de Oro State Park. Heading south, you can visit chic Avila Beach or Pismo Beach. Wherever you are, scurry indoors to nurse a sour ale when the fog descends.

TOP TIP

Weather patterns can be unpredictable on this stretch of coast. Expect morning fog, scattered sunshine, and unusually sunny Novembers and Decembers.

Montaña de Oro State Park (p292)

GIOVANNI'S FISH MARKET & GALLEY

Purveyor of crisp, deep-fried fish, and multiyear winner of Morro Bay's chowder cook-off, casual Giovanni's is the place to go for seafood any which way. Shrimp tacos, fried oysters or poke bowls – it's all good, it's all fresh and the outdoor dining area overlooks the bay.

MANUELA DURSON/SHUTTERSTOCK ©

Morro Bay's rock

Sightsee in the Shadow of Morro Bay's Big Rock

VOLCANIC FEATURES AND SEASIDE CHARM

Fishing village **Morro Bay**, 15 minutes' drive northwest of San Luis Obispo, has been spruced up over the years, bringing visitors to its kayak-friendly waters, seafront amusements and trusty restaurants.

Locals dub the town 'Three Stacks and a Rock' for its concrete smokestacks (part of Morro Bay Power Plant) and standout geological feature: a volcanic plug that rises out of the bay. Part of the 21-million-year-old Nine Sisters volcanic chain, the rock is a 576ft hunk of dacite lassoed to the shore by a causeway. It's an impressive sight, and much tourist activity revolves around getting views of the rock. Take the short **Morro Strand Trail** from Cloisters Park along the state beach for a head-on view.

Continue along the Embarcadero, where you can spot sea otters frolicking in the bay and listen to barking sea lions. Detour east along Main St for Morro's best coffee at **Top Dog**, and to rummage the bookshelves at **Coalesce**.

Come evening, put your name down at **The Galley**, a

GEOLOGICAL MARVELS

If Morro Bay's big rock has you itching to discover more of the Central Coast's geological features, strike out for **Montaña de Oro State Park** (p292). You can get views of the Nine Sisters volcanic chain and hike fearsome cliffs and golden beaches.

WHERE TO SLEEP IN MORRO BAY

Morro Bay State Park Campground
South of town, awake beneath eucalyptus trees just steps from the park's walking trails. $

Anderson Inn
Boutique waterfront hotel with nautical trimmings. Some rooms have fireplaces and walk-in showers. $$

456 Embarcadero Inn & Suites
Classic, neutral-toned rooms and tasteful suites with bay-facing balconies just south of downtown. $$

reservation-free seafood restaurant specializing in 'naked fish' that also has a top-secret clam chowder recipe. While you wait for a table, grab a beer from a pub nearby or walk along the waterfront, watching lights twinkle on the water.

SCALE A VOLCANIC MOUNTAIN

The tallest of the Nine Sisters volcanic mountain chain is **Bishop Peak** (p288), and reaching the top of this 1559ft plug is a popular day hike from San Luis Obispo.

Walk in Los Osos' Fairy-Tale Forests

EASY HIKES AMONG OAKS

A satellite just 15 minutes' drive west of San Luis Obispo, **Los Osos** (literally 'the bears') was named after grizzly sightings when Spanish military officer Gaspar de Portolá's expedition came through in 1769. It's the gateway to Montaña de Oro State Park but has its own natural beauty, too.

Start exploring at **Los Osos Elfin Forest**, which has 90 acres of pygmy oak woodlands. A short boardwalk loop trail makes it easy to meander through the marsh and scrubland, admiring pixie-size trees (some as short as 4ft tall). It's ideal for birdwatching and kids will love toad- and lizard-spotting here.

Around 2 miles southeast, off Los Osos Valley Rd, is another gem-sized forest: **Los Osos Oaks State Reserve**. Like the Elfin Forest, its oaks have gnarled branches that evoke a fairytale atmosphere, but here the trees tower 25ft high. Along the relatively flat 1.5 miles of trails you might see wood rats and quail scurrying through the brush.

Pedaling & Paddling in Avila Beach

CYCLING, SEA STACKS AND CHARDONNAY

Less than 15 minutes by car from San Luis Obispo, chic Avila Beach feels enjoyably secluded. Thanks to a sheltered beach and good cycling trails it's a relaxing place to enjoy the outdoors before retreating to an upscale spot to wine and dine.

First, rent a bike or e-bike: there are multiple spots off Front St. Follow the **Bob Jones Trail**, which begins at the northwest end of the main beach, and cycle northeast across the creek. The mostly flat trail follows the water's edge under the shade of sycamore trees; look out for signs to the 'Secret Garden,' where a food truck and minibar might be selling wines, beers and pastries to break up your journey. When you pedal back, go beyond the beach and continue west along Avila Beach Dr, where you'll see boat-speckled waters on the way to **Fisherman's Beach**.

Rent a kayak or SUP from **Avila Beach Paddlesports**; from here, you can paddle in waters well protected by a breakwater, and get views of Port San Luis Lighthouse right from the water.

BEST BAY ACTIVITIES

Central Coast Outdoors
Kayak by day or at sunset on guided excursions with this knowledgeable outfit. Landlubber tours such as cycling, too.

Kayak Shack
Canoes, kayaks and SUPs are rentable by the hour from this no-frills spot south of downtown Morro Bay.

Pacific Charters Sport Fishing
Private fishing charters where you'll land rockfish and spot dolphins under the tutelage of Captain Shawn.

Morro Bay Whale Watching
See gray whales and humpbacks from the *Dos Osos*, a small open-deck boat with uninterrupted views.

NAUTICAL BOOZERS IN MORRO BAY

The Siren
The mermaid logo points the way to sea-themed cocktails, moreish bar snacks and regular live music.

Three Stacks and a Rock
Grab a wooden paddle (tasting paddle, that is) of IPAs and stouts overlooking views of the bay.

The Libertine Pub
Choose from 60 beer taps while you enjoy ocean views from the wooden deck.

You'll spot sea stacks covered in pelicans (and pelican poop), and meet otters and playful seals as you bob in the gentle waves.

After hanging up your paddles and returning your bike, pick your choice of sea-view restaurants back in Avila Beach, such as French-inflected **Blue Moon Over Avila** or venerable steak-and-pasta spot **Custom House**.

MONARCH-BUTTERFLY MIGRATION

Several Central Coast locations host seasonal gatherings of these scarlet-and-black winged beauties, but **Pismo State Beach Monarch Butterfly Grove** is one of the best. Between late October and February, monarch butterflies travel thousands of miles to roost in eucalyptus trees over the winter, picking sheltered groves like Pismo's (close to the North Beach Campground). Their numbers have been tragically trending downward: in July 2022, the International Union for Conservation of Nature (IUCN) sounded the alarm for this declining species by red-listing monarchs as endangered species. Observe with care, and at a distance.

Beach Hopping Around Pismo

DUNES, TIDE POOLS AND SECLUDED COVES

The sweeping shores and wind-sculpted dunes of **Pismo Beach** are less than 15 minutes' drive from San Luis Obispo, and they're perfect for a beach-bum weekend. On day one, start at **Pismo City Beach** to paddle, people-watch and stroll the pier; get away from the crowds by descending to the beach at Wilmar Stairs.

Picnic at Pismo Preserve (across the highway) before continuing west to **Spyglass Beach** and **South Palisades Park** (take the south stairs); in both spots you can peer at tide pools and see waves smash against sea stacks. Head north to **Pirates Cove** (near Avila Beach; note that the trail downhill is steep). There isn't an eye patch in sight – in fact, the beach is clothing-optional! – but Pirates Cove was a rum-running hideout during the Prohibition era. There's also a short trail to a sea 'cave,' actually a tunnel that forms a natural rocky picture frame.

On day two, it's best to have a car. Go south to **Pismo State Beach**, where walking trails thread through sand dunes and along a freshwater lagoon. The tightly packed sand of **Grover Beach** is the only section of state beach in the US that you can drive on. You'll need a 4WD; trundle with care (15mph maximum).

Drive on **Rancho Guadalupe Dunes Preserve**, a lost-in-time landscape of rolling dunes. Pioneering film director Cecil B DeMille built the colossal movie set for his biblical epic *The Ten Commandments* (1923) right here. Some say the film set is still buried in the dunes... Learn more at the **Dunes Center** in Guadalupe (Santa Barbara County).

Explore Craggy Coastal Realms in Montaña de Oro State Park

CLIFFSIDE TRAILS AND SANDY COVES

Sculpted by volcanoes, Montaña de Oro State Park (30 minutes' drive from San Luis Obispo) has turned out quite the masterpiece. Waves crash against alabaster cliffs and natural rock bridges, and trails for walkers, cyclists and horse-

WHERE TO DINE AND DRINK IN AVILA BEACH

Kraken Coffee Company
Hands down the best beans in town, plus breakfast burritos, pastries and ice cream. **$**

Gardens of Avila
Californian ingredients with Mediterranean flair in a garden setting at Sycamore Mineral Springs Resort. **$$$**

Libertine Brewing Company
The Avila location of a Central Coast chain pours sour ales and Belgian-style beers.

Pismo Beach

back riders thread their way across coastal plains. During spring the hills glow with wildflowers, hence the park's name 'Mountain of Gold.'

The **Bluff Trail** (3.5 miles) is a spectacular introduction to the park, leading from the main parking lot along the cliffs. Views are dramatic, especially of the foaming arc of waves washing into Spooner's Cove (named after early 1890s landowner Alden B Spooner II, who established a ranch and dairy here). Along the way you'll notice Miguelito shale, made from layers of organic matter compressed over six million years, now forming distinctively textured cliffs and sea stacks. Linger a while on grainy **Spooner's Beach** and check out the tide pools on the north side of the cove.

Presiding over these 12.5 sq miles is 1347ft Valencia Peak. To explore the park's tallest peak, the **Valencia Peak Trail** (4.5 miles) zigzags from Spooner's Cove parking lot up the flank of the mountain, with panoramic views rewarding the effort. Almost as tall is **Oats Peak**, and its eponymous trail is a longer, but much less steep ascent from Islay Creek Campground (11 miles).

BEST OF MONTAÑA DE ORO'S NATURAL SIGHTS

Hazard Canyon Reef
Best for tide pooling. Visit at low tide to see sea anemones and hermit crabs. Access from the Dune Trail.

Oats Peak Trail
Best for springtime. Bluebell and primrose flowers carpet the park interior, and the trail has great views.

Spooner's Cove
Best for beach picnics. Backed by cliffs, this picturesque beach is a favorite among families.

Coon Creek Beach
Best for solitude. Accessed by the Point Buchon Trail (just south of park bounds).

RUGGED HIKING TERRAIN

If your feet are itchy for more rugged hikes, **Pinnacles National Park** (p275), less than two hours north of San Luis Obispo, is paradise for ramblers and climbers.

GETTING AROUND

Cycling is an excellent way to get between San Luis Obispo and Avila Beach or Edna Valley, and infrequent buses connect SLO with Morro Bay and Pismo Beach. Between May and early September, a free trolley connects Avila and Pismo Beach on Friday afternoons and weekends. But, as in most places on the Central Coast, road-tripping is easiest if you want to cover multiple stops.

SANTA BARBARA COUNTY

SPANISH COLONIAL COASTAL BEAUTY

Hike, bike and surf year-round in a Mediterranean climate where pinot noir, Ojai Pixie tangerines and avocados thrive on the southern end of Calfornia's Central Coast.

The Santa Barbara coastline was originally inhabited by the Chumash people, who harvested and hunted from the oak-studded hills and the rich waters of the Santa Barbara Channel. Using tar from natural beach seeps, they built seafaring canoes that allowed them to settle on the northernmost of the Channel Islands.

In 1786, Spanish Franciscan missionaries dedicated the tenth California mission on the feast day of Santa Barbara, thereby blessing the city with its name and one of its most famous landmarks. With its beautiful beaches, front-country foothills and mild year-round climate, SB has long attracted visitors and new residents.

Over the last two decades, Santa Barbara County has developed into a wine country destination (it was named 2021 Wine Region of the Year by *Wine Enthusiast* magazine). With its transverse mountain range and unique patterns of fog and diurnal shift, a wealth of high-quality, small-production wines are yet another pleasure to savor.

JOSEPH SOHM/SHUTTERSTOCK ©

In addition to wine, its bountiful produce is celebrated with local festivals centered on the lemon and avocado. Appreciation for farmers, and what they literally bring to the table, continues to be an undercurrent of life here. That, and a commitment to the land and ocean in which the residents love to play.

Join the locals in enjoying a slower pace of life, dolphins surfacing near shore and the green flash at sunset, with blobs of tar.

THE MAIN AREAS

SANTA BARBARA
Coastal beauty. p300

SOLVANG
Danish kitsch. p312

LOS OLIVOS
Wine-tasting central. p320

VENTURA
Harbor charm. p326

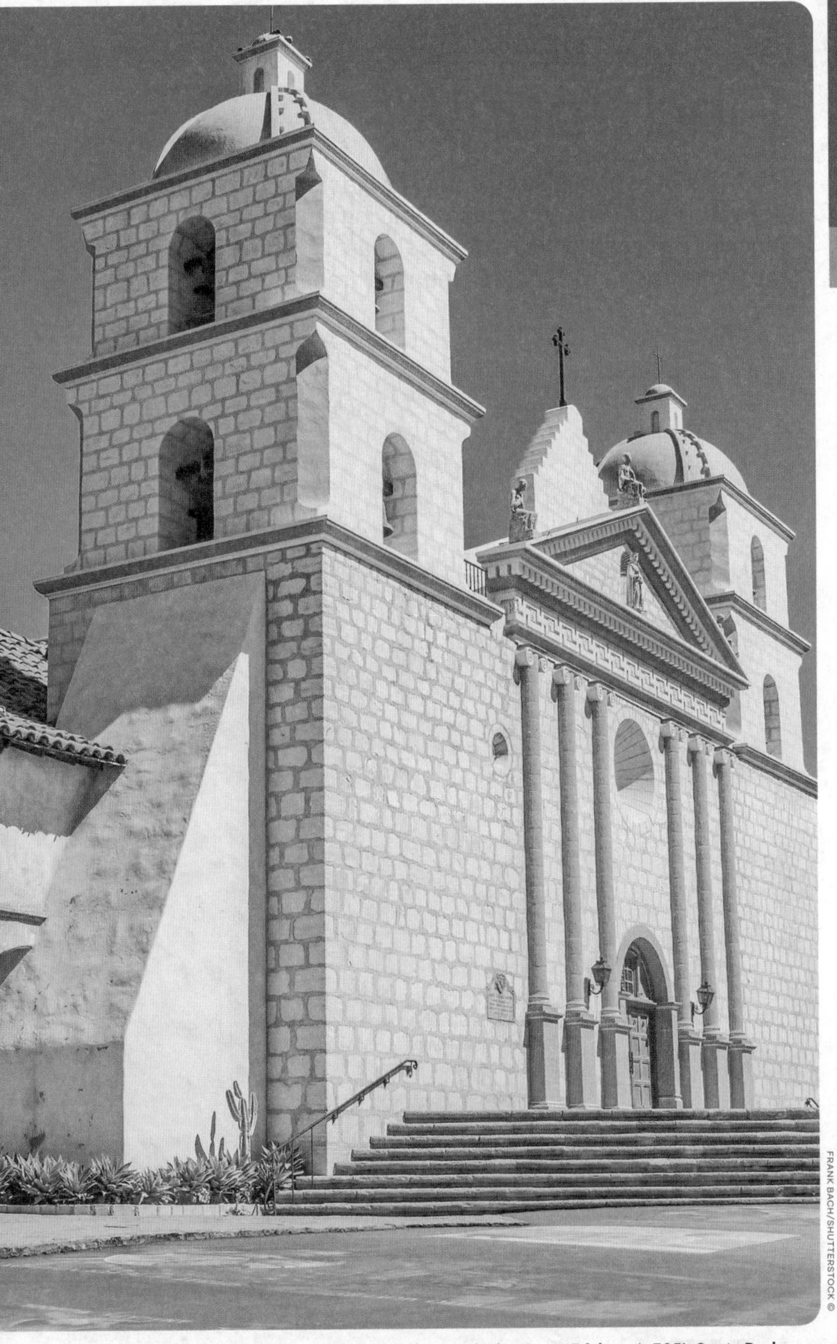

Left: Cyclists in Ojai (p332); Above: Mission Santa Bárbara (p305), Santa Barbara

Find Your Way

Santa Barbara occupies an easily navigable slice of coastal plain between mountains and ocean. Outlying areas of interest are reached by scenic drives along the coast or through the foothills of the Santa Ynez and Topatopa mountain ranges.

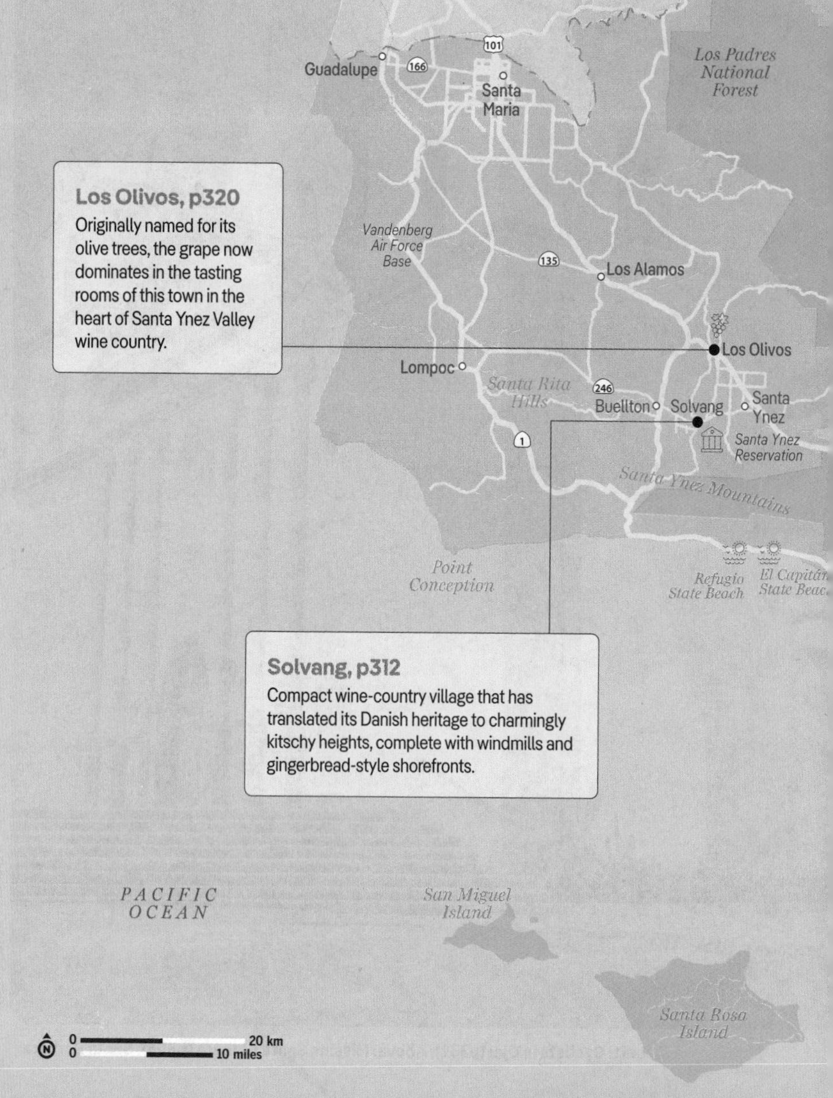

Los Olivos, p320
Originally named for its olive trees, the grape now dominates in the tasting rooms of this town in the heart of Santa Ynez Valley wine country.

Solvang, p312
Compact wine-country village that has translated its Danish heritage to charmingly kitschy heights, complete with windmills and gingerbread-style shorefronts.

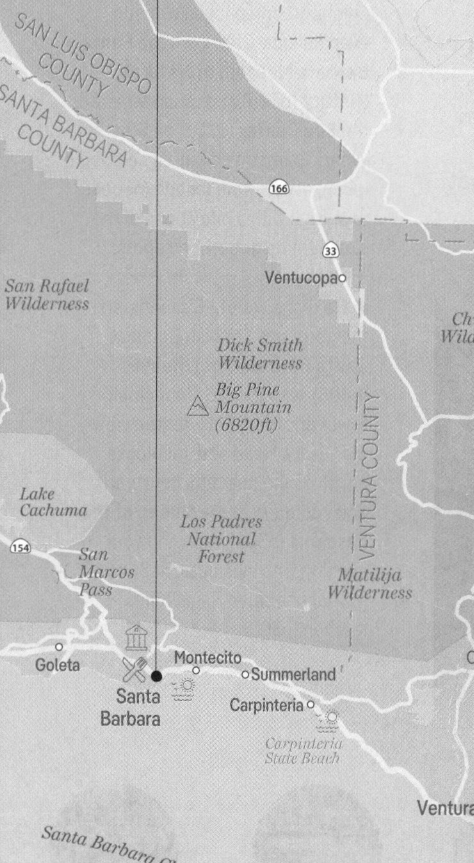

Santa Barbara, p300

Streets of Spanish Colonial architecture stretch from the foothills to Pacific beaches, offering outdoor fun on trail and ocean, complemented by epicurean pleasures.

Ventura, p326

Alluringly retro beach town with an under-the-radar appeal in its beaches, harbor and downtown; plus it's the departure point for Channel Islands National Park.

CAR

To visit outlying destinations from Santa Barbara, it's most convenient to drive, although most towns are small enough to explore on foot once you've arrived. Street parking is free or inexpensive throughout the region.

BICYCLE

The city of Santa Barbara has bike-friendly crosstown routes with painted bike lanes on some of its major streets, but for the most part its bike lanes are narrow or shared with vehicle traffic. Santa Ynez Valley is more spread out and suitable for bike touring.

BUS

Santa Barbara MTD buses cover the city proper, with service as far as Goleta and Carpinteria. Santa Ynez Valley Transit runs buses between Buellton and the town of Santa Ynez, while Gold Coast Transit has a route between Ventura and Ojai.

Plan Your Time

Santa Barbara makes the most logical base for easy access to beach, foothills and city. Stay in Solvang or Los Olivos if wine-tasting is your mission, or retreat in low-profile style to Ojai.

KEVIN YUAN/SHUTTERSTOCK ©

Funk Zone (p301), Santa Barbara

If You Only Have One Day

- Start in Santa Barbara's **Funk Zone** (p301), a compact neighborhood packed with fun, even for kids. Check out the **Santa Barbara Museum of Natural History** (p305) and touch tanks at the **Sea Center** (p305) on Stearns Wharf. Savor an ocean-air seafood lunch, or pair wine tasting (or beer, or spirits) with a bite at one of the excellent neighborhood spots.

- Next check out SB's landmarks: the gorgeous Spanish Colonial **Santa Barbara Courthouse** (p305), with the 3rd-floor clock tower affording 360-degree views of the city. Head several blocks up, stroll the peaceful courtyard and cemetery at the **Queen of the Missions** (p305), then end your evening with live music at Soho (p306) or a sip at Sama Sama Kitchen (p301).

Seasonal Highlights

California poppies start bursting in mid-February or March, followed in April or May by the blossoms of jacaranda trees. Year-round, different whale species travel through the Santa Barbara Channel.

FEBRUARY

Santa Barbara International Film Festival lights up the Arlington Theatre with screenings and talks with filmmakers and celebrities.

MAY

Artists create a patchwork of amazing chalk art at the Santa Barbara Mission for the **I Madonnari** street painting festival.

JUNE

Since 1974, the only-in-SB **Solstice celebration** revolves around a whimsically artsy parade continuing into a weekend festival in the park.

SIDE SHOW STOCK/GETTY IMAGES ©; KNUMINA STUDIOS/SHUTTERSTOCK ©; RANDY SPRAGUE/SHUTTERSTOCK ©

A Long Weekend to Play

- After exploring **Santa Barbara** (p300) on the first day, head further afield the next.

- Take a country drive to an estate winery or two in the **Santa Ynez Valley** (p325), or to the small towns of **Los Alamos** (p324) or **Los Olivos** (p320) for sipping and exploring on foot; don't forget to pick up a tin of Danish cookies in **Solvang** (p312).

- Next, while away a day in **Ojai** (p332) to soak up sunshiny, new-agey vibes and diverse, healthy cuisine. Make time to venture outdoors to hike Santa Barbara's **front country** (p310), or paddle a kayak or stand-up paddleboard (SUP) around the **harbor** (p304) for close encounters with seals, pelicans and bat rays.

Five Days or More

- Spend a day or two exploring **Santa Barbara** (p300) and get on the water, whether it's a surf lesson, a paddle around the harbor or a whale-watching cruise. Try catching an SB farmers market on Tuesday afternoon or Saturday morning to pick up snacks and see locals at their most relaxed.

- Take advantage of a longer stay with forays to **Ojai** (p332) for hiking, horseback riding or a spa day. Consider hiring a local guide for a wine-tasting tour in the **Santa Ynez Valley** (p325), and stop longer in **Solvang** (p312) to feed ostriches, find the taproom speakeasy and feast like a California-style Viking.

AUGUST

Santa Barbara's biggest annual celebration, **Old Spanish Days** (simply 'Fiesta' locally) celebrates the city's Spanish, Mexican and Chumash heritage.

SEPTEMBER

Kick up your dancing clogs at **Danish Days** in Solvang with music, parades, food and celebration of all things Danish.

OCTOBER

Little Carpinteria swells with visitors in early October for **Avocado Festival**, featuring live music, food and drink, and bountiful guacamole.

DECEMBER

Boats at Santa Barbara and Ventura harbors get their holiday sparkle on at each of their **Parade of Lights**.

SANTA BARBARA

Santa Barbara has long been a weekend getaway for Angelenos, for obvious reasons – about an hour-and-a-half drive up the coast, it's cozily nested between the Santa Ynez Mountains and the Pacific Ocean, graced with Spanish Colonial architecture and chill, beach-town vibes. The self-branded American Riviera inarguably hits a sweet spot of beautiful natural setting, plentiful outdoor and cultural activities and great dining and drinking options. In one day it's easy to get a good hike in, jump in the ocean and top it off with world-class wine tasting. SB retains a small-town feel while still being a university city with diverse cultural events, a gorgeous outdoor music venue and thriving arts scene. The city's background is rooted in agriculture and a vibrant Mexican heritage, both of which remain integral to its identity today.

TOP TIP

Downtown Santa Barbara is crisscrossed with one-way streets parallel and perpendicular to State St. Look out for wrong-way drivers, whizzing e-bikes and crossing pedestrians. Parking at city lots is free for the first 75 minutes, after which it's $2.50 an hour.

Santa Barbara

GEORGE ROSE/GETTY IMAGES ©

Municipal Winemakers' tasting room

Tasting in the Funk Zone

SANTA BARBARA'S URBAN WINE TRAIL

While the Funk Zone is ground zero for SB wine tasting, consider it a starting point (maybe also an ending point – your mileage may vary). That said, the high concentration of tasting rooms, eateries, breweries and galleries could entrap you for an entire day.

There's limited street parking, but large prepaid lots on Garden St and Cabrillo Blvd usually have space. Pick up divine pastries and coffee at **Helena Ave Bakery** and pop into vintage shops and galleries like **Blue Door**, Shopkeepers (p308) and **Helena Mason Art Gallery** as they open for the day.

If you don't have specific wineries in mind, start at the **Valley Project** on Yanonali St, where the chalkboard art gives a quick primer on the lay of the wine-country land. Nearby, **Margerum Wine Company** has an elegant feel while **Municipal Winemakers** offers a fun, unpretentious vibe. Muni pours a couple of complex, botanically infused non-alcoholic wines alongside its traditional lineup. Ask your server to recommend destinations based on what you like.

Not into wine? **Lama Dog Tap Room** pours a rotating selection of craft beers, with a bottle shop and convivial little

OUTSIDE THE ZONE

The Funk Zone may contain the densest concentration of tasting rooms in town, but clusters of others are located around SB's downtown. Pick up a **Santa Barbara Urban Wine Trail map** (urbanwinetrailsb.com) to find worthwhile gems along the **Haley St** corridor, along State St and around the whitewashed, bouganvillea-laced **El Paseo arcade** on Anacapa St.

The purchase of an **Urban Wine Trail tasting card** ($200) entitles you to one-time free tastings at participating wineries as well as day-of-tasting discounts. You could also simply use the map as an orientation tool, as many worthwhile wineries aren't part of the Urban Wine Trail program but are located in the highlighted neighborhoods.

WHERE TO EAT IN DOWNTOWN SANTA BARBARA

Bibi ji
Santa Barbara–style Indian food: with a slab of local *uni* (sea urchin) and an extensive wine list. **$$**

Corazón Cocina
Worth the long line at SB Public Market for bright, fresh ceviches and regional-specialty tacos. **$**

Sama Sama Kitchen
Southeast Asian cuisine with a California angle, paired with spicy cocktails and refined wine list. **$$**

SIGHTS
1 Helena Mason Art Gallery
2 Leadbetter Beach
3 Santa Barbara Courthouse
4 Santa Barbara Maritime Museum
5 Santa Barbara Museum of Art
6 Sea Center
7 Shoreline Park
8 Sullivan Goss Art Gallery

ACTIVITIES, COURSES & TOURS
9 Cal Coast Adventures
10 Paddle Sports Center
11 Santa Barbara Bicycles
see 19 Santa Barbara Surf School
12 Wheel Fun Rentals

EATING
13 Helena Ave Bakery
14 Loquita
15 Santo Mezcal
16 Shoreline Café
17 The Lark

DRINKING & NIGHTLIFE
18 Biergarten
29 Cutler's Artisan Spirits
20 Lama Dog Tap Room
21 Municipal Winemakers
22 Test Pilot
23 Valley Project

ENTERTAINMENT
24 Arlington Theatre
25 Granada Theatre

SANTA BARBARA

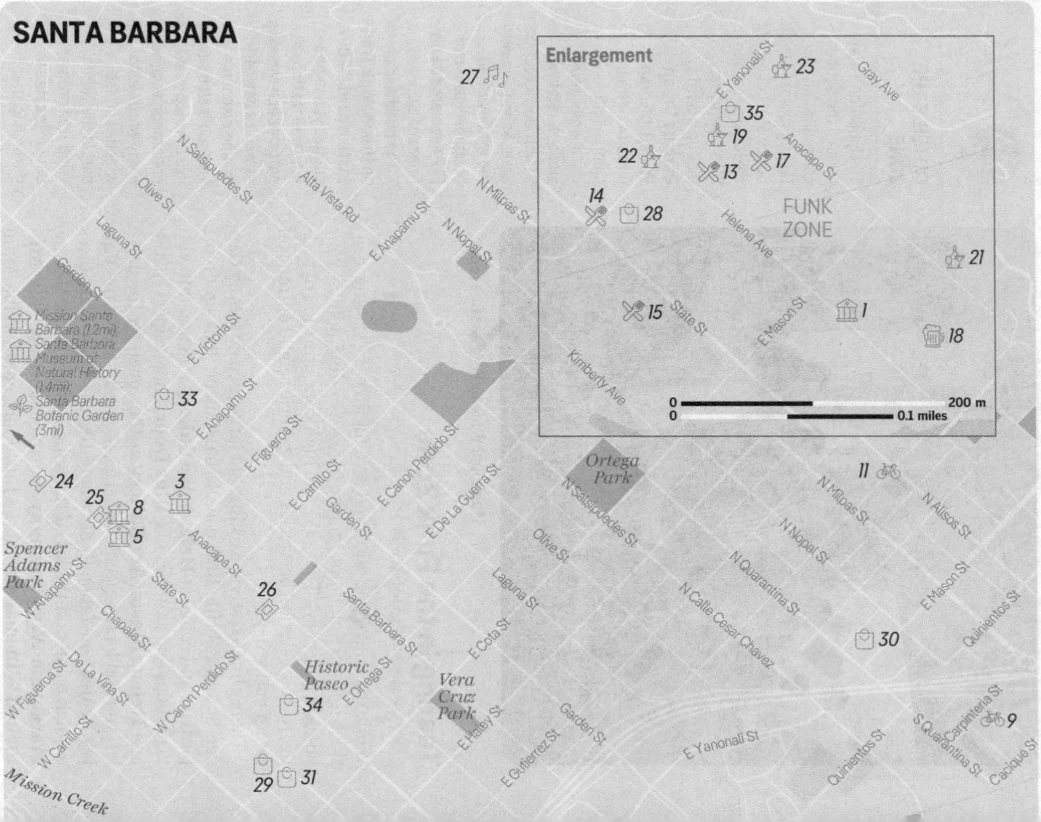

Enlargement
FUNK ZONE
E Yanonali St
Gray Ave
Anacapa St
Helena Ave
State St
E Mason St
Kimberly Ave
0 200 m
0 0.1 miles
23 35 19 22 13 17 14 28 21 15 1 18
27
N Salsipuedes St
Olive St
Laguna St
Garden St
Alta Vista Rd
E Anapamu St
N Milpas St
N Nopal St
Mission Santa Barbara (1.2mi)
Santa Barbara Museum of Natural History (1.4mi)
Santa Barbara Botanic Garden (3mi)
E Victoria St
E Anapamu St
E Figueroa St
E Carrillo St
E Canon Perdido St
E De La Guerra St
Garden St
33 24 25 8 3 5 26 34 29 31 30 11 9
Spencer Adams Park
W Anapamu St
Anacapa St
State St
Chapala St
De La Vina St
W Figueroa St
W Carrillo St
W Canon Perdido St
Mission Creek
Santa Barbara St
Historic Paseo
E Ortega St
E Cota St
Vera Cruz Park
E Haley St
E Gutierrez St
Garden St
Laguna St
Olive St
Ortega Park
N Salsipuedes St
N Quarantina St
N Calle Cesar Chavez
N Nopal St
N Milpas St
N Alisos St
E Mason St
Quinientos St
E Yanonali St
S Quarantina St
Carpinteria St
Cacique St

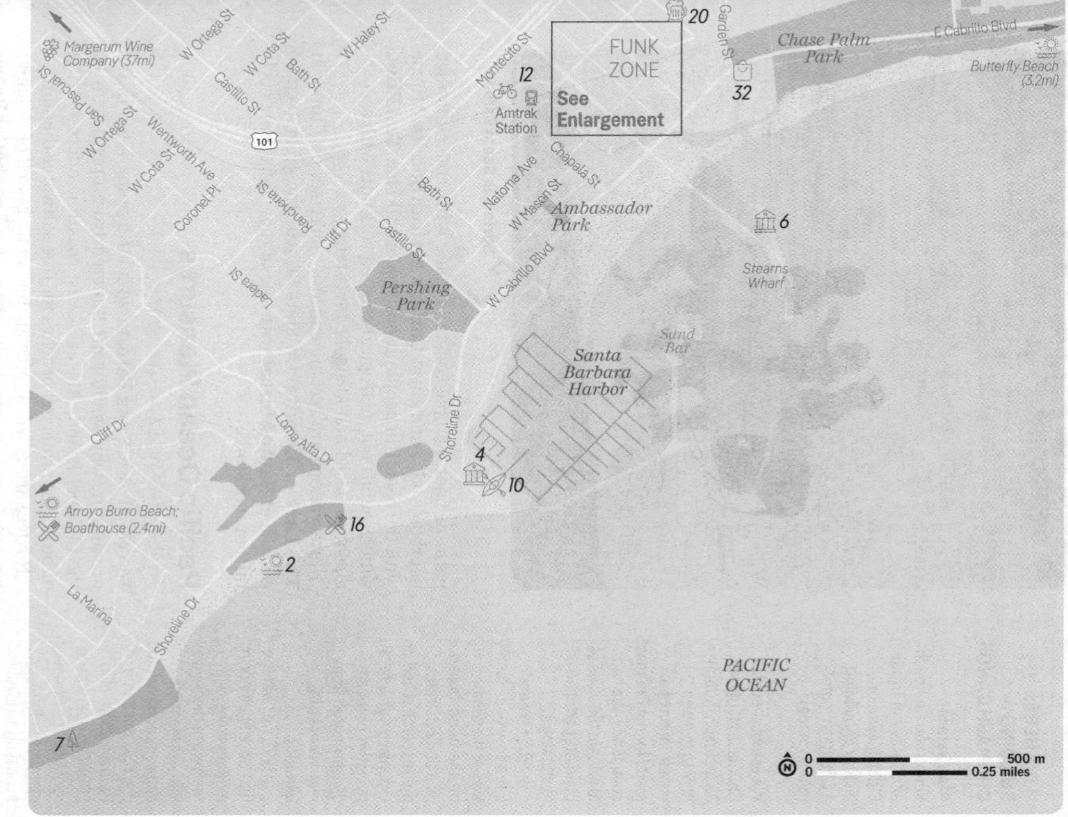

26 Lobero Theatre
27 Santa Barbara Bowl

SHOPPING
28 Blue Door
29 Idyll Mercantile
30 Pacific Pickle Works
31 Pura Luna Apothecary
32 Santa Barbara Arts & Crafts Show
33 Santa Barbara Company
34 Seaside Makers
35 Shopkeepers

I LIVE HERE: BUILDING A CHUMASH CANOE

Alan Salazar, Ventureño Chumash and Tataviam Tribal Elder, gives a brief history of building a Chumash *tomol* (plank canoe).

We established the Chumash Maritime Association in January 1997 to oversee construction of a *tomol* for the Chumash community. We had to relearn the skills of building, paddling and navigating it.

In 1912, Fernando Librado, whose family was of the *tomol* brotherhood, built one as a demonstration; our research relied on extensive notes taken by anthropologist JP Harrington from interviews with Librado.

In 1997, we built the first working *tomol* in modern times, with the help of the Santa Barbara Maritime Museum, and paddled it across the Santa Barbara Channel in 2001. Our goal was to revitalize the Chumash maritime culture, especially to involve our young people. Conditions permitting, we now do the channel crossing annually.

L PAUL MANN/SHUTTERSTOCK ©

Surfers in Santa Barbara

patio to boot. Sample cocktails made with house-distilled bourbon, vodka and gin at **Cutler's Artisan Spirits.** Mingle with the beautiful people at postmodern tiki bar **Test Pilot**, which rounds out its tropical-themed cocktails with seasonal, shrub-based non-alcoholic mocktails.

Reservations are recommended if you're set on dining at **The Lark** or **Loquita**. On State St, pair the green (vegan) ceviche at **Santo Mezcal** with one of their refreshing cocktails or mocktails.

Pacific Ocean Pleasures

SWIM, SURF, PADDLE, WHALE-WATCH

You could visit Santa Barbara without dipping a toe in the ocean, but...why would you? Buffered from open ocean by the Channel Islands, the east–west coastline offers a string of beautiful protected beaches for free saltwater therapy.

Novice surfers will appreciate the smaller swell of summer; most surf spots are best during the winter. **Leadbetter Beach** has a slow-rolling wave that makes it popular for lessons and beginners. Book surf lessons with **Santa Barbara Surf School** or **Surf Happens** to feel the stoke. **Arroyo Burro Beach** –

SPLURGY STAYS IN SANTA BARBARA

Hotel Californian
On the edge of the Funk Zone, this stylish spot puts waterfront and nightlife within strolling distance. **$$$**

El Encanto
This enchanting classic in the Riviera neighborhood looks out over the city from its foothill perch. **$$$**

Bacara
Modern elegance north of town, and with its own section of beach and luxurious space to stretch out. **$$$**

also known as Hendry's – is a nice surf spot with the added bonus of being SB's dog beach, and the **Boathouse** providing the perfect setting for post-beach lunch or happy hour.

At the harbor, rent a stand-up paddleboard (SUP) or kayak at **Paddle Sports Center**. Even within the breakwater, you'll encounter harbor seals, pelicans and rays on your paddle. Explore further, steering between the pilings of Stearns Wharf, or upwind toward Leadbetter Beach. Wildlife-watchers can book a **whale-watching tour** on the Santa Barbara Channel to see over 30 species of cetaceans, including migrating humpbacks, blue or gray whales (dependent on season).

Back on land, learn about SB's marine history, going back to its Chumash heritage, at the **Santa Barbara Maritime Museum**. On Stearns Wharf, get to know the local marine life in the touch tanks and exhibits at the Santa Barbara Museum of Natural History's **Sea Center**.

Classic Santa Barbara Landmarks

ARCHITECTURE, GARDENS AND NATURAL HISTORY

It may sound odd that the **Santa Barbara Courthouse** is a must-visit, but once you arrive, you'll see why couples have their weddings here. Taking up an entire city block, the Spanish Colonial Revival stunner is surrounded by lawn and sunken garden – great for midday naps and picnics. Even if you can't make it to a daily docent-led tour for a look at the intricately painted Mural Room (where VP Kamala Harris got hitched) and Moorish-style tile work, you should at least ride up to the 3rd-story clock tower to take in 360-degree views of the surrounding city, ocean and foothills. Take a virtual tour at sbcourthouse.org.

Next stop: the Queen of the Missions. Founded in 1786, **Mission Santa Bárbara** is only one of two California missions that have continuously operated since their establishment. Self-guided and docent-led tours explore the church, courtyard garden and cemetery where white settlers and unnamed Chumash lie. The Mission lawn and rose garden below are a local favorite for picnics.

Head a little further toward the foothills to the **Santa Barbara Museum of Natural History** in its creekside nook amid oak habitat. Find natural context in exhibits ranging from Chumash culture to indigenous wildlife and geology, then complement it with forest bathing at the nearby **Santa Barbara Botanic Garden**. The Channel Islands sector offers spectacular views and native island flora if you can't get to the islands themselves.

ARCHITECTURE WALKS

For an exceptionally insightful look at Santa Barbara's architectural highlights, take a $10 walking tour with a docent from the **Architectural Foundation of Santa Barbara**. Show up any Saturday and Sunday for a two-hour walk and talk.

The DIY **Red Tile Walking Tour** (santabarbaracarfree.org) stops at the most significant historical sites downtown, including **El Presidio de Santa Bárbara** with remnants of its original adobe structure.

Lest you think the American Riviera takes its red tile too seriously, check out a few of architect **Jeff Shelton's** playful, Seussian takes on the local vernacular. A downloadable walking tour map can be found online.

SPECIAL-OCCASION DINING IN SANTA BARBARA

Barbareño
Lunch is more casual at this Central Coast gem showcasing fresh, local produce, seafood and meats. **$$$**

Bouchon
Wine country cuisine – the standout experience here is shopping the farmers market with the chef before dinner. **$$$**

Yoichi's
Beautifully presented Japanese *omakase* (chef's choice) prix-fixe in a discreet little neighborhood spot. **$$$**

BEST LIVE-MUSIC VENUES

Santa Barbara Bowl
Even the nosebleeds are a sweet place to be at the Bowl, since you get a spectacular view of the city and ocean from the bar area. Shows end at promptly at 10pm as it's in a residential neighborhood.

SoHo
Going strong since 1994, this intimate venue hosts live local and touring bands. You can make dinner reservations to cozy up at a table for the show if you don't plan on dancing.

Red Piano
It does have a red piano, and 'Church on Monday' blues. In fact, it has live music every night of the week, enhanced by a friendly atmosphere and outdoor space.

Arts & Culture

THEATRE, LIVE MUSIC, VISUAL ART

Local landmarks themselves, many of SB's arts venues enhance their events with their own architectural beauty.

Entering the historic **Arlington Theatre** under its archways and sitting within a trompe l'oeil courtyard almost makes it feel like you're watching performances under a Spanish sky (complete with twinkling ceiling stars).

On the next block, the ornate **Granada Theatre** occupies the ground floor of the city's tallest building and is home to local institutions like the **State Street Ballet** and **Santa Barbara Symphony**.

A little further down State St, the elegant neoclassical **Santa Barbara Museum of Art** offers visual inspiration, occasionally holding workshops and events. Nearby, **Sullivan Goss Art Gallery** focuses on American artists of varying genres.

The **Lobero Theatre**, a few blocks down, is the oldest continuously operating theater in California. Founded in 1873 and renovated in Spanish Colonial Revival style in 1924, its acoustics make it perfect for chamber, folk and jazz performances.

From spring to fall, take in a show at the **Santa Barbara Bowl**, the city's beloved outdoor music venue tucked into a residential hillside. A shuttle runs from the entrance to the amphitheater, but part of the magic is walking up the woodsy path in shared anticipation with your fellow concertgoers.

Check the **UCSB Arts & Lectures** (artsandlectures.ucsb.edu) website for current listings, or keep it casual and discover the lively local music scene at the many breweries and cafes around town.

Cycle Santa Barbara

SEE SB ON TWO WHEELS

Santa Barbara is a great place to pedal around, whether meandering along the Cabrillo Blvd beachfront or taking a serious road tour into the foothills. Downtown SB is generally flat with some gentle climbs, and you can rent a bike to stitch together sightseeing stops. **Cal Coast Adventures** rents out bikes and also runs guided bike tours around the city.

The **Santa Barbara Bike Coalition** (movesbcounty.org) has an excellent map illustrating bike-friendly and alternative routes to help you plan a ride, and also links to **Cycle Cal Coast** (cyclecalcoast.com) with mapped-out loops for longer rides. For short, low-commitment jaunts, **Santa Barbara**

WHALE-WATCHING CRUISES

Double Dolphin
Offers a variety of sailing trips on a 50-foot catamaran with friendly crew, including whale-watching and sunset tours.

Condor Express
Whale-watching cruises on this 75-foot catamaran are narrated by trained naturalists and run by experienced crew.

Celebration Cruises
Has first-class, adults-only decks; opt to cruise on the electric Whisper yacht for a quiet ride.

CORY WOODRUFF/SHUTTERSTOCK ©

Granada Theatre

BCycles rents out e-bikes for $7 per 30 minutes, with docks located in multiple locations around town.

Rent a beach cruiser (half-day for $34) at **Wheel Fun Rentals** in the Funk Zone and ride along the palm-lined **Cabrillo bike path** southward about 2.5 miles to local favorite **Butterfly Beach**, or north past the harbor about a mile to Leadbetter Beach (p304) and on to **Shoreline Park** on the Mesa. Stop for a bite at the **Shoreline Cafe** for lunch with your toes in the sand, or head back to the Funk Zone and refresh with a beer flight and brats at **Biergarten**. If inspired, continue on to check out some of Santa Barbara's architectural landmarks, such as the Presidio (p305) and the Mission (p305).

Mountain bikers will find plenty of technical singletrack to negotiate after the thigh-burning climbs. Top tip: pick up and drop off a bike bell at the trailhead, as trails in the front country are multiuse and very popular with hikers.

I LIVE HERE: TOP MOUNTAIN-BIKING TRAILS

Chris Orr, recreation ecologist, suggests mountain biking trails for novice riders.

Romero Trail
Ride the fire road up and down – there's incredible views and it narrows down to feel like singletrack about a quarter of the way up. Of our front-country trails, it has the lowest grades to manage and least amount of technicality.

Elings Park
The trails are much less steep and much less technical than SB's mountain trails. It's right across from Douglas Family Preserve and above Hendry's Beach, offering the nice experience of a ride with great views followed by a beachside eat and drink afterward.

Ellwood
It offers another pretty extensive trail system with very mellow riding. It has awesome views of the beach and the islands, and is very novice-, family- and kid-friendly.

WHERE TO REFUEL DOWNTOWN

Handlebar Coffee Roasters
Popular local spot with beans roasted by former pro cyclists equally obsessed with the perfect cuppa. **$**

Juice Ranch
Fresh, cold-pressed juices, smoothies and wholesome cafe items with lots of vegan options. **$**

The Cruisery
Gastropub on State St with craft cocktails, generous portions, and a 'doggie flight' of water bowls outside. **$$**

BEST SB CHOCOLATIERS

Chocolate Maya
Using fresh farmers market ingredients and sustainably-sourced chocolate for their small-batch confections, they also sell artisanal bars from other makers.

Chocolats du CaliBressan
Divine salted-caramel Buddhas, coconut milk and curry truffles and single-origin chocolate by a French chocolatier.

Jessica Foster Confections
Small-batch chocolatier using local herbs, fruit and ingredients for handmade truffles, caramelized almonds and salted caramels.

Twenty-four Blackbirds
Specializing in single-origin chocolate, flavored caramels and beautifully marbled truffles.

Menchaca Chocolates
Micro-batch chocolates using direct trade cacao; also offers build-your-own chocolate bar experiences.

Shop Local

LOCAL MAKERS AND MARKETS

Santa Barbara is saturated with artists, indie boutiques and specialty shops, a fortunate and amazing thing considering the cost of real estate. It's tough to make a living in this town, which is why many residents like to support small makers and business owners by shopping local.

Since 1965, the **Santa Barbara Arts & Crafts Show** has set up every Sunday (and Saturdays of holiday weekends) along beachfront Cabrillo Blvd, with over half a mile of artists and craftspeople selling their work between Stearns Wharf and Calle Cesar Chavez. This tradition is now complemented by regularly scheduled, beautifully curated pop-ups like the women-of-color-run **Mujeres Makers Market** (mujeresmakersmarket.com) and **The Farmer and the Flea** (farmerandtheflea.co), both of which set up at El Presidio de Santa Bárbara (p305).

Downtown brick-and-mortar retail shops stocking locally made skincare, jewelry, clothing and homewares include **Seaside Makers** on State St, **Pura Luna Apothecary** and **Idyll Mercantile** on Chapala St and the **Santa Barbara Company** in a cute little cottage on E Victoria St. At **Shopkeepers** in the Funk Zone, find handmade, heirloom-quality goods from the 3rd-generation leather worker of Make Smith Leather Company.

Pickled veggies and shrub mixers by **Pacific Pickle Works** will round out your charcuterie board and cocktail cart, and the Tuesday afternoon and Saturday morning **farmers markets** (sbfarmersmarket.org) yield delicious local giftable victuals like lemon-spiked pistachios, toffee-studded almond butter and wildflower honey.

GETTING AROUND

Downtown Santa Barbara is based on a grid whose throughline is State St. State St's southeast end terminates at the shoreline and Cabrillo Blvd, and it's at this end where the Funk Zone lies and where the Amtrak station sits. Most visitors get around on foot, bike, rideshare or with their own vehicles; driving yourself is the way to go when traveling beyond city limits.

Beyond Santa Barbara

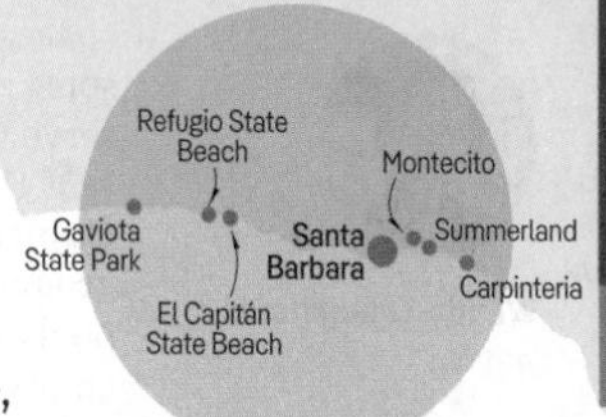

North on Hwy 101 opens up to wild coastline, while to the south you'll find some of the south county's most appealing small towns.

Northbound 101 moves through Goleta – 'The Good Land' – and branches off to the Santa Barbara Municipal Airport, the University of California, Santa Barbara and the university community of Isla Vista. After that, the scenery opens up to the wild Gaviota coastline and ranchlands (about 30 minutes by car) before turning inland to Buellton and Santa Ynez Valley wine country.

Southbound, the highway cuts through the rarefied enclave of Montecito (5 to 10 minutes by car), a land of lavish gated estates but accessible foothill trails and village restaurants. Just south is tiny Summerland (also 10 minutes from SB), with a crescent of gorgeous beach and strip of cute boutiques, followed by the low-key little beach town of Carpinteria (another 5 to 10 minutes along the coast). Easy to bypass on your way elsewhere, these small towns have unique allures awaiting those who make the time.

TOP TIP

The Santa Barbara coastline runs east-west, but locals give directions in reference to Hwy 101 – putting Summerland south and Goleta north of SB.

El Capitán State Beach (p310)

WHY I LOVE SANTA BARBARA

Wendy Yanagihara, writer

Running around my family's plant nursery and boogie-boarding all summer as a kid in Santa Barbara's sleepy south county, I had no idea how blessed I was to be rooted here. Now a grown-up who gets to live in this multicultural, agricultural community again, I'm continually grateful for the simple but profound joys like hiking a front-country trail whose creek is running, before paddling with an unexpected dolphin companion, and then sipping a local small-production wine, beer or kombucha with friends in our laid-back hometown paradise.

Explore the Wild Gaviota Coast

WILD COASTLINE NORTH OF SANTA BARBARA

The wild coast north of Goleta is a wealth of coastal open space, much of it privately owned, working ranchland with some parcels purchased by conservation organizations to preserve these rare oceanfront lands from future development.

Of three state beach parks along Hwy 101, the first is **El Capitán State Beach**, with a spacious and attractive campground of over 100 sites right above the beach. Explore tide pools, the nature trail along El Capitán Creek and miles of empty beach, stretching east and west from a south-facing point. A paved trail from the west leads all the way to **Refugio State Beach**, about 3 miles further northbound on Hwy 101. This crescent of beach is lined with stately palm trees and has over 60 campsites.

Furthest north, at the coastline where Hwy 101 veers inland, find **Gaviota State Park**, with interesting tilted shale beds embedded in the beach. Offshore, the park's waters form part of the **Kashtayit State Marine Conservation Area**. The trestle bridge above the beach is still used by Amtrak and freight trains, and camping is also available here.

Day hikers can access the **Gaviota Wind Caves** trail without paying a day-use fee, and hike just over a mile to the caves for beautiful windswept views of the coast below.

Touring South County Enclaves

MONTECITO, SUMMERLAND AND CARPINTERIA

Begin in Montecito with coffee and real French croissant at **Bree'osh** or **Renaud's** and stroll **Coast Village Rd** boutiques, keeping an eye out for mononymous luminaries like Oprah, Harry and Meghan roaming under the radar. Cross over the freeway at Olive Mill Rd and walk to **Butterfly Beach** to while away your morning before a wood-fired pizza at **Bettina** or Mexican favorite **Los Arroyos**.

To get a real sweat on, head into the foothills for a hike through front-country ceanothus and chaparral to reach views of the coastline as far south as Malibu. Find trail information at the **Montecito Trails Foundation** (montecitotrailsfoundation.info) website. Pursue more meditative walks through the wondrous landscape of **Lotusland** – by appointment only – an eccentric botanical garden on the former estate of opera singer Ganna Walska. End with a cocktail at **Honor Bar**.

A few miles further south lies the hillside beach town of Summerland, where Lillie Ave merchants boutiques like **Porch**

WHERE TO STAY ON THE GAVIOTA COAST

El Capitán State Beach Campground
Coveted beachside campground with miles of beach solitude if you're willing to walk. **$**

El Capitán Canyon
Glamp in El Capitán Canyon cabins and canvas yurts, where you can barbecue in style under the stars. **$**

Refugio State Park Campground
Lovely beachside campground with palms fringing the beach. **$**

MADELEINE CLEMENTS/GETTY IMAGES ©

Gaviota Wind Caves

and **Botanik** are stuffed with chic coastal decor and succulent art. On the ocean side of the freeway underpass, the bluff-top **Lookout Park** has a great playground, bocce court, picnic tables and path down to the beautiful slice of **Summerland Beach**.

Beyond Summerland, the agricultural town of Carpinteria still grows avocados, orchids and cherimoyas, but more recently has become a hotbed of marijuana cultivation. Stroll **Linden Ave** down to **Carpinteria State Beach**, browsing the indie shops and homegrown restaurants before seeking out the industrial park where locals chill at happy hour.

CARPINTERIA FERMENTATION OPERATIONS

Bordering the **Carpinteria Salt Marsh**, the generic-looking industrial park at the west end of Carpinteria Ave doesn't look like much. But walk around the back alley and you'll find a bubbly social zone with miniscule tasting rooms, empanadas, Turkish coffee, a specialty wine store and boutique chocolate. The dreamy **Apiary** brews beautiful and complex mead, cider and kombucha incorporating local honey, herbs and fruit.

Next door, nanobrewery **BrewLAB** always has a creative selection of top-notch small-batch beers on tap, from sours to stouts brewed with locally grown flora. At the end of the line, **Rincon Mountain Winery** pours tastings of their Carpinteria-farmed and -produced wine.

GETTING AROUND

It's easiest to drive, whether heading north to the Gaviota Coast or to Montecito and Summerland, but once there you can explore on foot. Santa Barbara MTD runs regular express buses to Carpinteria. Less frequently, you can catch local train service on Amtrak, with a platform blocks from Carpinteria State Beach.

SOLVANG

After red-tiled Spanish Colonial Santa Barbara, arriving in Solvang ('sunny fields' in Danish) is like experiencing a mildly kooky bout of culture shock. Founded in 1911 by three Danish-American educators, the Danish influence is authentic even if the decorative motif is over the top. Before the Danes, the Spanish established Mission Santa Inés here in 1804, and before that it was the ancestral land of the Native Chumash people.

Nowadays the Chumash tribe not only runs the nearby casino resort, but also tends vineyards and makes wine, as is the contemporary tradition of the Santa Ynez Valley. Long a destination for its butter cookies and Disneyfied Scandinavian window-dressing, Solvang does make a convenient central base for exploring Santa Ynez Valley wine country. And don't worry: there's plenty of good food besides *aebleskiver* and *pandekager* (Danish fritters and pancakes).

San Francisco

Solvang

Los Angeles

TOP TIP

Walk off some of your Solvang overindulgence or just take a break from touristy energy with an easy stroll along the oak-shaded creekside trail through Hans Christian Andersen Park. Take Atterdag Rd north from Mission Dr, veering left onto Chalk Hill Rd. The castle gate marks the entrance in true Solvang style.

Solvang

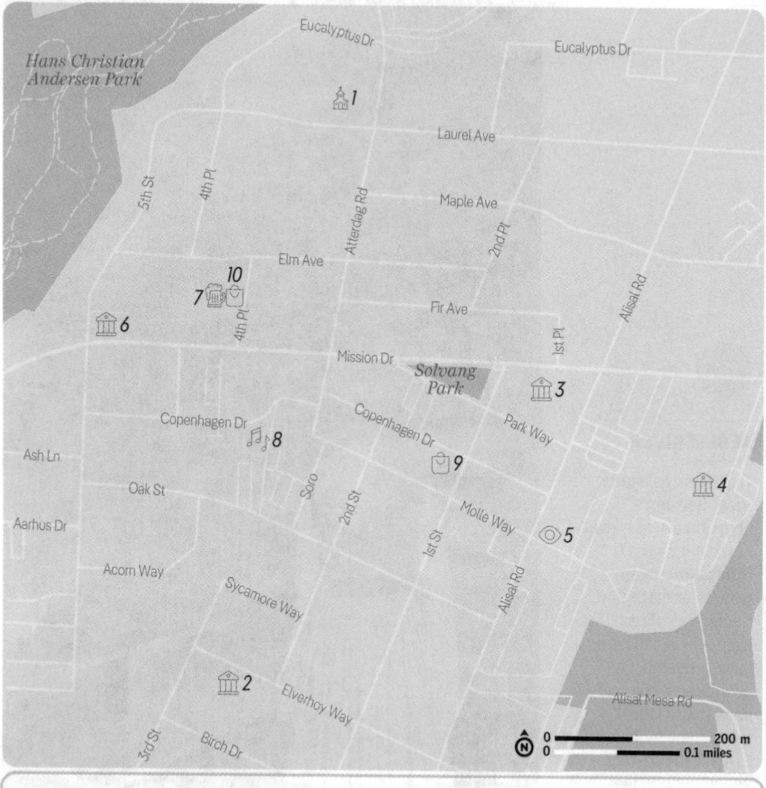

SIGHTS
1 Bethania Lutheran Church
2 Elverhøj Museum of History and Art
3 Hans Christian Andersen Museum
4 Mission Santa Inés
5 Rundetaarn
6 Wildling Museum of Art & Nature

DRINKING & NIGHTLIFE
7 Backroom

ENTERTAINMENT
8 Lost Chord Guitars

SHOPPING
9 Copenhagen House
10 Valley Brewers

Solvang's Danish Heritage

LEAN IN TO THE DANISH THEME

Solvang's Danishness goes deeper than the scent of sugary confections and ersatz windmills – details like stork statues on rooftops and the gabled rooftops themselves are nods to the town's actual Danish roots. Learn more at the charming **Elverhøj Museum of History and Art**, the former residence of an artist couple who modeled the beautiful tongue-and-groove home on 18th-century Danish design.

Back on main drag Mission Dr (Rte 246), the **Hans Christian Andersen Museum** houses a small collection of the author's handwritten letters, first-edition copies of his illustrated books and a model of his childhood home. A scaled-down replica of Copenhagen's **Little Mermaid** statue adorns a fountain across the road.

KIT LEONG/GETTY IMAGES ©

Elverhøj Museum of History and Art (p313)

AEBLESKIVER

Translated as 'apple slice,' Solvang's ubiquitous *aebleskiver* is a round, sweet fritter with a crispy exterior and a tender, doughy bite. Fresh from the pan, they're usually dusted with powdered sugar and served with jam. It takes some technique to make the perfect *aebleskiver*, as they need to be turned evenly on their special stovetop pan to get uniform doneness on all sides. You can buy cast-iron *aebleskiver* pans in town to make these festive balls of carby happiness at home.

On narrow Copenhagen Dr, **Copenhagen House** imports Danish furniture and jewelry as well as high-end kitchenware and designy trinkets. The shop's comings and goings are supervised by the stern-faced wooden figures of Solvang's founders, Reverend Benedict Nordentoft, Reverend JM Gregersen and Professor PP Hornsyld.

Several notable buildings around town were also inspired by monuments in Denmark, including **Bethania Lutheran**

WHERE TO EAT IN SOLVANG

Ramen Kotori
Authentic ramen, gyoza and Japanese-style small plates with fresh local seafood and farmers market produce. **$**

peasants FEAST
Seasonal, local American classics with an emphasis on freshness; superb takeout for winery picnics. **$**

First & Oak
Sample the tasting menu at this elegant restaurant with thoughtful wine pairings and outdoor seating. **$$$**

Church, whose stucco design echoes the more elaborate Gruntvig's Church in Copenhagen but also incorporates a Spanish-style red-tiled roof. Also taking inspiration from Copenhagen is Solvang's one-third-scale replica of the **Rundetaarn**. The stately brick round tower has no astronomical observatory but does house a pizzeria.

Slow Solvang

LOW-SPEED SIGHTS AND DELIGHTS

As tourist-saturated as Solvang can get, it has quiet corners worth finding. East of downtown along Mission Dr, the driveway to Solvang's **Mission Santa Inés** is an immediate escape. Fringed with olive trees, the mission garden is a peaceful spot to retreat for a moment. Pause in the cemetery to remember the Chumash people who were conscripted to build the mission here.

At the other end of town, the nonprofit **Wildling Museum of Art & Nature** explores how art can foster a closer relationship with nature. Take a few minutes to peek at the exhibits – local artists are often featured, with work ranging from traditional painting to multimedia installations.

One block over, turn off Mission Dr at 4th Pl and leave the tourist traffic behind you. You'll come across the home-brewing supply shop **Valley Brewers**, where the carboys and bags of hops may not hold any interest for you. Instead, pass the cashier to the dark hallway painted with bookshelves and push on the back wall – speakeasy-style – to enter the **Backroom**. This friendly taproom always has interesting beers on tap, many of them local, and a petite back patio to enjoy them in the sunshine.

End your evening with quality live music of the singer-songwriter variety at **Lost Chord Guitars**, a hole in the wall on Copenhagen Dr.

I LIVE HERE: SOLVANG DIVERSIONS

Alicia Valenzuela, tasting room host at Vega Vineyards, talks wine-adjacent activities in Solvang.

Ostrichland
It's cliché but an amazing experience if you've never done it. The ostriches are like dinosaurs, really majestic, and they come to you.

Vega Vineyards
We're family-friendly; kids can feed the animals here. We've got a mini highland bull named Tai, a mini pony named Cupid, sheep, two llamas, a potbellied pig and chickens.

Mad & Vin
One thing few people know about is the incredible brunch at the Landsby Hotel. There's never a line, the portions are great for the price, and the experience starts with the best pour-over coffee of your life.

GETTING AROUND

Solvang has an eminently walkable downtown – park in one of the free public lots south of Mission Dr and roam on foot. Copenhagen Dr is the main shopping and restaurant strip, with the surrounding streets fanning out to tasting rooms, hotels, and the residential area to the south.

Beyond Solvang

All roads lead to wine from gingerbread-house Solvang. Westward, the landscape opens into the rolling hills of Santa Ynez Valley vineyards.

Key scenes from the 2004 film *Sideways* took place in Buellton, and these days you can follow in the fictional footsteps of wayward main characters Miles and Jack with a *Sideways*-based tour. You may not be fanatical enough about the film to hit all the stops – in which case, write your own script. A drive along Santa Rosa Rd or Rte 246 is the simplest way to visit some of the region's best wineries while also enjoying a slow day trip through the valley's picturesque rolling hills cultivated in rows of vines.

TOP TIP

Buellton is the Santa Ynez Valley's main hub on Hwy 101. Get practical errands done here at the gateway to SB wine country.

Ampelos winery (p319), Lompoc

PHIL KLEIN/REUTERS/ALAMY ©

JOSEPH SOHM/GETTY IMAGES ©

Flying Flags RV Resort

Buellton Base Camp

EASY ACCESS AND CHEAP SLEEPS

Best as a local base camp, Buellton sits right off Hwy 101 and is a 5-minute drive to Solvang. While it doesn't have the kitschy charm of its more photogenic neighbor, it does offer relatively economical places to stay and some excellent, unpretentious spots to dine and taste wine.

Opt for luxury canvas tents, Airstreams or cabins at **Flying Flags RV Resort**, all of which come with pool access and are conveniently located for adventures further afield. It's glamping in suburbia in modestly hip style, where firepits and bocce courts foster a convivial mood. From here, you can walk to **Ellen's Danish Pancake House** for breakfast with the locals.

As advertised on multiple billboards along Hwy 101, **Pea Soup Andersen's** slings its famous split-pea soup in its comfortingly old-school restaurant. The recipe hails from France, brought to Buellton by Juliette Andersen, wife and business partner of Anton Andersen in the cafe they founded in 1924. The restaurant also sells bags of split peas with the soup recipe if you want to bring home a taste of historic Buellton.

SAN MARCOS PASS DETOURS

The drive over San Marcos Pass (Hwy 154) from Santa Barbara to the Santa Ynez Valley is a gorgeous one with a few detours worth making. The stunning **Chumash Painted Cave** sits right above the road, its interior viewable through a protective gate. Note that the 2-mile drive up to the cave is up a very narrow, twisting road.

About 3.5 miles further northwest along Hwy 154, take the Stagecoach Dr turnoff to **Cold Spring Tavern**, a former stagecoach stop established in 1868. This historic little forest haven serves Central Coast tri-tip sirloin and beer, and on weekend afternoons there's live music and the tavern at its best.

BUDGET SLEEPS IN BUELLTON

Flying Flags RV Resort & Campground
Drive up in your RV or book a glamping tent, vintage trailer or cabin. $

Sideways Inn
Look for the windmill and enjoy a pool, firepit and lounge after a day exploring. $

Pea Soup Andersen's Inn
Great choice for families; conveniently located and has a pool. $

SANTA RITA HILLS EXPLORATION

Savor the beauty of this drive through the green hills and curves of the Santa Rita Hills AVA (American Viticultural Area). The vines planted here are mostly pinot noir and chardonnay, though other varietals like grenache, syrah and viognier are cultivated here.

Start the loop in **1 Buellton** with your picnic fixings packed, taking Santa Rosa Rd to the west. About 6 miles down the bucolic, winding road, stop to taste at **2 Peake Ranch**, in its contemporary, airy tasting room with an outdoor patio looking out to the vineyard. On the same road, try the beautiful wines of **3 Alma Rosa Vineyard**, which organically farms its grapes in a commitment to sustainability. Alma Rosa was founded by Richard Sanford, the first vintner to plant pinot noir in Santa Barbara county in 1971. Just before Santa Rosa Rd intersects with Hwy 1, **4 The Hilt Estate** offers tastings by appointment only.

Turn right on Hwy 1 to drive the 2 miles to Lompoc's industrial **5 Wine Ghetto**, where you can sample multiple wineries' offerings, which is an efficient strategy if you're pressed for time.

Return to Buellton on Rte 246. Several wineries along the road are worth a stop, including the friendly family-owned and operated **6 Kessler-Haak** up Gypsy Canyon Rd with more pretty pinot noir, chardonnay and syrah. Moving east on Rte 246, you'll find the tasting experience to be relaxed and playful at the multi-generational, family-run **7 Babcock Winery**, which often has live music and other fun events. Next door , the stalwart **8 Melville Winery** offers a more elegant setting, either in the civilized tasting room or in the front vineyard.

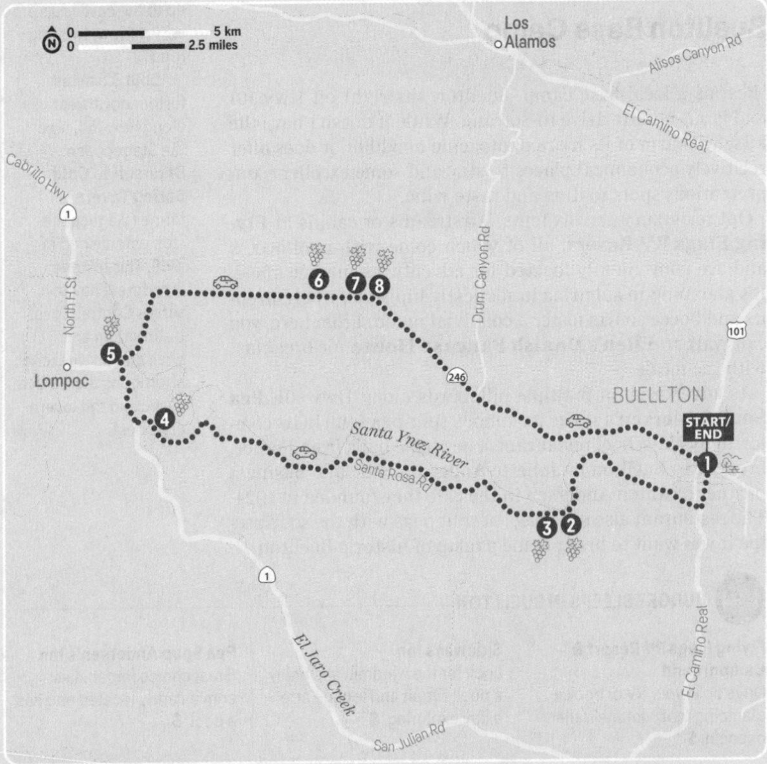

Chill out afterward with a beer at Firestone Walker Brewing Company's **Barrelworks Taproom**, pouring a variety of wild-ferment sours and Belgian strong ales. If wine is more your tipple, you'll find the excellent **Ken Brown Wines** and **Roark Wine Co** tasting rooms on the west side of Hwy 101.

Whatever you do, save room for **Industrial Eats**, where wood-fired pizzas and the sophisticated but simple small plates are best shared. In the evenings, hang out at the **Sideways Inn Lounge** for a local beer and Belgian frites.

Lompoc Wine Ghetto

INDUSTRIAL TASTING-ROOM COMPLEX

There's nothing hidden about Lompoc's Wine Ghetto, but it feels like you've discovered a local secret when you park among the nondescript industrial buildings in this warehouse complex. Just off the intersection of Hwy 1 and 12th St in the city of Lompoc, you could easily spend a day here tasting a representative spectrum of Santa Rita Hills terroir.

Each tasting room has its own creative feel reflective of its resident winemaker: from the self-effacing cartoon goats of **Flying Goat Cellars** labels (belying the artistry inside the bottle) to the bright and friendly **Fiddlehead Cellars**, pouring estate-grown wines made by pioneering woman winemaker Kathy Joseph.

Family-run **Ampelos** uses grapes from organically and biodynamically farmed vineyards to make their pinot noir and Rhône varietals. Taste through a solid breadth of Rhône and Burgundian varietals at **Zotovich** in the Santa Rita Hills Wine Center, adjacent to the Wine Ghetto.

Find a map of the Wine Ghetto at explorelompoc.com, and let your tasting room hosts suggest neighboring wineries to discover something new to you, just steps away.

JALAMA BEACH

Pronounced 'ha-LA-ma,' this out-of-the-way beach is a 45-minute drive from Lompoc. It's popular with kiteboarders and windsurfers, so be warned that it's often windy – enough for your unoccupied tent to catch air (don't ask us how we know). But because this isolated beach lies at the end of a narrow country road and its existence is far from obvious, it retains a wild feel despite having a comfortable little county campground and the rustic **Jalama Beach Store** serving burgers and breakfast. Reservations for the campsites and a handful of cabins can be made six months in advance.

GETTING AROUND

From Solvang, you'll need your own vehicle to explore the Santa Rita Hills and onward to Lompoc. Regular buses travel between Buellton and the town of Santa Ynez if you just want to get from A to B.

LOS OLIVOS

There's no denying the appeal of Los Olivos, with its clapboard ranch-chic aesthetic and relaxed wine country charm. Its petite size makes it the perfect choice if you've only got an afternoon to taste in the Santa Ynez Valley – within a grid of several blocks, you can walk to two dozen tasting rooms.

A stagecoach stop and then rail station on the Pacific Coast Railway in the 1880s, Los Olivos developed out of the rail boom; nowadays it thrives on booming wine industry tourism. Drive in from Hwy 154 onto Alamo Pintado or Grand Aves; they intersect momentarily at the flagpole, which marks the center of town and the beginning of your lovely day in Los Olivos.

TOP TIP

Adorable as Los Olivos is, anyone who tastes wine here inevitably finds that its public restrooms are bafflingly akin to unicorns. A few tasting rooms offer facilities to customers only – scout them out, but otherwise be prepared to brave the not-terrible porta-potties.

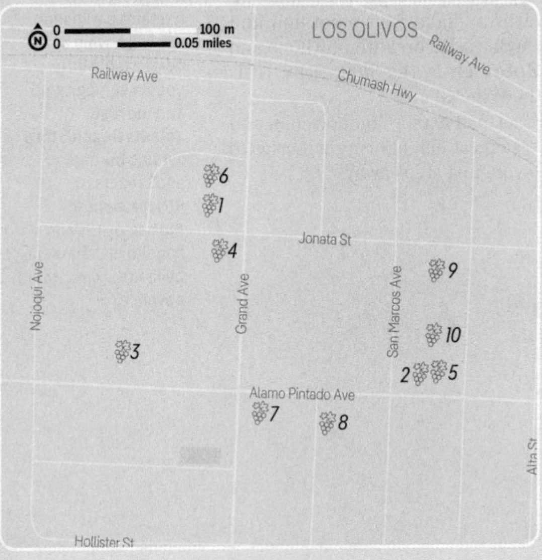

SIGHTS
1 Bien Nacido & Solomon Hills Estates
2 Blair Fox
3 Brewer-Clifton
4 Carhartt Family Wines
5 Holus Bolus
6 Saarloos and Sons
7 Solminer
8 Stolpman
9 Storm
10 Story of Soil

Carhartt Family Wines

Tasting in Los Olivos

WALKING AND WINE-TASTING

Wine-tasting in Los Olivos is a delicious reminder that life is good. It's a simple pleasure getting to taste through multiple wineries' offerings in the span of an afternoon without having to drive. (That said, do plan ahead for getting safely to your onward destination.) If you're cruising around with others, a good strategy for hitting several wineries is splitting your tastings with someone so you're not consuming the entirety of each pour. When tasting solo, sip and spit.

If you have no clue where to start, you'll find a super-approachable vibe at **Carhartt Family Wines**, which often has live music on their spacious patio, or at family-run **Saarloos and Sons**, which also does cupcake tastings.

Try the region's cool-climate Burgundian and Rhône varietals like chardonnay, pinot noir and syrah at the amazing small producers here like **Blair Fox**, **Storm**, **Holus Bolus** and **Story of Soil**. Sample less common varietals like interesting Austrian skin-contact grüner veltliner at **Solminer**, and be sure to taste at heavy-hitters like **Brewer-Clifton**, **Stolpman** and **Bien Nacido & Solomon Hills Estates**.

This town is mostly (okay, all) about the wine, but Los Olivos has boutiques and galleries to browse between tastings. Weekends often feel like a block party, with live bands and a festive atmosphere. Arrive early to find parking.

PUTTING THE OLIVES BACK IN LOS OLIVOS

Los Olivos comes by its name honestly. In the 1880s, a young rancher planted 5000 olive trees near Ballard. When the Pacific Coast Railway built its rail line from Los Alamos down to its new station, it eventually bequeathed the stop with the name Los Olivos in homage to the trees. Unfortunately, a harsh winter in 1889 killed most of the young olive trees.

In the mid-1990s, observing that the latitude and climate are similar to olive-growing regions in Spain and Italy, a few intrepid souls began planting olive trees in the Santa Ynez Valley expressly to produce olive oil. The happy, full-circle result is that you can now taste olive oil in Los Olivos.

GETTING AROUND

It might take you five minutes to walk from one end of downtown Los Olivos to the other – if you weren't here to taste wine. And since you likely are here for that, rest assured that overnight parking is allowed, in case you've tasted more enthusiastically than planned.

Beyond Los Olivos

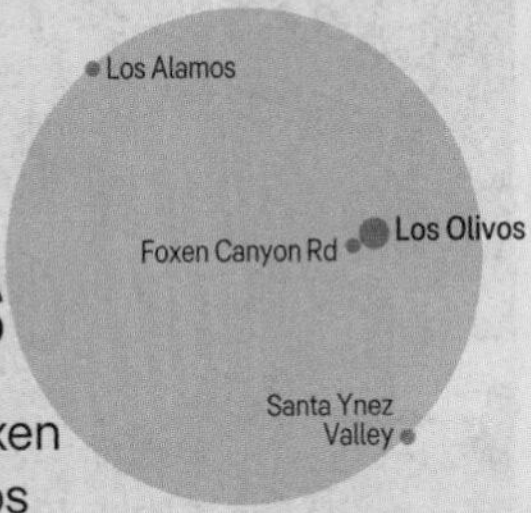

Dive deep into wine country, ranging along Foxen Canyon Rd to the surprising little outpost of Los Alamos.

Traveling the country roads around Los Olivos, it's easy to imagine this place before viticulture dominated the region. Road cyclists roll along Alamo Pintado Ave where homesteads follow agrarian cycles and horses graze slowly in blissful obliviousness to their good fortune.

Veer onto Zaca Station Rd to Foxen Canyon, the region's oldest AVA and home to some of Santa Barbara County's most venerable vineyards. The hilly topography and micro-climates mean that different varietals thrive in their specifically ideal conditions, so you'll travel from Rhône-heavy territory to a Burgundian clime as you head closer to the coast.

The winding road invites you to slow down and simply enjoy the scenery full of bucolic ranches, a tiny church and a sea of vineyard rows.

TOP TIP

The well-stocked Los Olivos Grocery is your go-to picnic provisioner – it's just south of Los Olivos proper, along Hwy 154.

Foxen Canyon Wine Trail

GARY CRABBE/ENLIGHTENED IMAGES/ALAMY ©

Rancho Sisquoc Winery

Foxen Canyon Wine Trail

TASTING ALONG RURAL FOXEN CANYON RD

From Hwy 154, Foxen Canyon Rd forks northward out of Los Olivos into beautiful oak-studded canyon country. Find a more exhaustive list of wineries and map at foxencanyonwinetrail.net.

Tastings at **Demetria** are by appointment only, but getting the keys to this estate is scoring the cheapest ticket to 'Tuscany' you'll ever find. Grapes here are organically and biodynamically grown, which is just an added bonus to this gorgeous estate tasting experience.

Next on the road northward, one of the oldest wineries in the Santa Maria AVA, **Foxen Winery** runs a sustainable operation and ranch-style, solar-powered tasting room serving spectacular pinot noir, syrah and chardonnay. Half a mile up the road, their **Shack** pours Bordeaux and Italian varietals.

Continue up to the sharp left, and stop for a walk around the blessedly isolated **San Ramon Chapel** for a look down at the valley and contemplation of names etched on the gravestones. Just down the hill is **Rancho Sisquoc Winery** –

I LIVE HERE: PICNICKING AT ESTATE WINERIES

Amy Christine, co-owner and winemaker at Holus Bolus & The Joy Fantastic, shares her picks for winery picnics.

Peake Ranch
The tasting room is in the vineyard, which is not the case everywhere. So you're sitting in the vines, away from the highway – it's quiet, modern, very comfortable and stunningly beautiful.

Demetria
Demetria is remote, up a really rugged private road. Once you're back there you're nestled into this cozy Santa Ynez environment, looking out at the vines with trees hanging over you, right in the midst of nature.

Melville
It's polished and a little more aristocratic, like you're sitting outside a European villa. You're tasting amid some of the vines, with a more elegant feel.

WHERE TO EAT IN LOS OLIVOS

Panino
Take a break from tasting with a takeout sandwich and a cool non-alcoholic beverage. **$**

Los Olivos Wine Merchant & Cafe
For a more formal sit-down lunch with organic ingredients grown on their own farm. **$**

Felix Feed & Coffee
A thoughtful refresh at Mattei's Tavern brings another daytime spot for a pre-tasting breakfast or lunch. **$$**

DAVID LITSCHEL/ALAMY ©

San Ramon Chapel (p323)

BEST WINE TOUR GUIDES

Sustainable Wine Tours
Founded by sommeliers, this small company brings guests to private tastings at wineries that are not open to the public.

Destination Vine
A small, concierge-style outfit with personable guides and customizable tours; run by a local duo.

Santa Barbara Wine Country Cycling Tours
Take in the fresh air and bike to your tastings with knowledgeable guides; tours on e-bikes are also available.

reserve picnic boxes ahead of your tasting and soak in the historic atmosphere.

End by pairing a picnic with delicate pinot noir and/or pinot bubbles in the peaceful valley environs of woman-run **Riverbench**. Both the cozy ranch house and outdoor tables are a lovely setting for tasting. Or opt for a livelier finish to your day with live music, bites and wine at **Presqu'ile**, whose scene-stealing tasting room and amphitheatre complement their beautiful wines.

High-Caliber Eats in Los Alamos

HWY 101 GOURMET HAMLET

Los Alamos might surprise you. What looks like a nowhere kind of highway stop with a gas station and roadside motel actually possesses four blocks of rustic sophistication. Appropriately nicknamed Lost Almost is not the most practical gateway to wine country, but it's an easy stop along Hwy 101 if you're passing through, and a destination itself.

Your first stop should be **Bob's Well Bread** for a transcendent *kouign amann* (Breton butter cake) or sit-down breakfast. For the gluten-free, the hearty brick of seeded GF bread

WHERE TO STAY IN LITTLE LA (LOS ALAMOS)

Alamo Motel
A stylish and popular choice, centrally located on Bell St, with an inviting lawn, firepit and bar shack. **$$**

Skyview Motel
Another remodeled retro number, this hip hilltop motel has a pool, restaurant and bar – it's a bit removed from town. **$$**

Victorian Mansion B&B
This attractive Victorian has an ornate interior with themed rooms. **$$**

is worth a detour to Los Alamos. From here, roam along Bell St to poke around antique shops and make hard decisions like where to eat next.

Mull it over with a glass of wine at **Lo-Fi** or **Lumen Wines** tasting rooms, pouring their noteworthy, small-production juice. Or browse **Casa Dumetz** and **Babi's Beer Emporium** to choose from wine, beers on tap, or selections from the bottle shop.

For casual wood-fired goodness, **Full of Life Flatbread** turns out beautiful flatbreads, organic salads and burnt ends from locally sourced beef. There's kid-friendly fine dining at **Pico**, also on the farm-to-table train, as is **Plenty on Bell** with well-executed comfort food. Or go for the Michelin-star experience at **Bell's**, serving California-style French food showcasing the region's fresh ingredients.

BALLARD

The tiny residential nook of Ballard was founded in 1880, making it the oldest community in the valley. It has a church and a school, and not much else except for the tucked-away **Ballard Inn**, an upscale B&B in modern farmhouse style. The inn is best for guests seeking a quiet escape, which is enhanced by **Bob's Well Bread Bakery at the Ballard Store** across the rural road. This satellite of the Los Alamos fixture brings its artisanal baked goods, breakfast and coffee to wake up sleepy Ballard's residents and guests alike.

Un-Wine in the Santa Ynez Valley

OLIVE-OIL TASTING AND LAVENDER FIELDS

Wine is queen around here, but there are other pleasures to be enjoyed in the Santa Ynez Valley. These rolling hills have traditionally supported agriculture and ranching, having nothing to do with the relatively new fermented-grape industry.

You might not realize, for example, that there is a miniature-donkey-sized hole in your existence. You'll need to make an appointment to visit **Seein' Spots Farm** – a small price to pay for the chance to snuggle the painfully cute creature that is the mini donkey. This farm breeds them responsibly and also rescues all kinds of other animals in need.

Also on the equine theme, you can take a horseback ride with **Vino Vaqueros** (which does end with a wine tasting). But the main event is riding through ranch and vineyard with experienced guides and horses; kids eight and up can ride, too.

Local tasting isn't limited to wine: try lavender honey and pick up lavender baking mixes and teas at **Clairmont Farm Lavender Co**. Its small shop also sells house-made skincare and mists, and visitors are free to enjoy the shade and walk amid the lavender; blooming season is in June and July.

Local olive farmers offer estate-grown tastings of their grassy, fruity and peppery olive oils in beautiful ranch settings, as at **Rancho Olivos** just outside of downtown Los Olivos.

GETTING AROUND

Your own vehicle or a driver are necessary to get around the Santa Ynez Valley's wine-country roads. From Los Olivos, Hwy 154 heads southeast to the town of Santa Ynez and onward to Santa Barbara via the San Marcos Pass. In the other direction, the 154 connects with Hwy 101.

VENTURA

Often overlooked by visitors in favor of Santa Barbara, Ventura is SB's more salt-of-the-earth sister, underrated only because she lacks the movie-star sheen. This coastal city (officially known as San Buenaventura) has an attractive old town anchored by the Mission San Buenaventura, plus a beachfront promenade and slightly retro little harbor village.

Ventura and its surrounding area were originally occupied by the Ventureño Chumash people, who built seafaring canoes and were skilled at spearfishing. During the era of Spanish colonialization, Junípero Serra established Mission San Buenaventura in 1782, the last of the California missions. In the early 1900s, oil drilling boomed, and some of E Main St's architecture has survived from that period.

Ventura harbor is the jumping-off point for Channel Islands National Park, about an hour-long boat ride across the Santa Barbara Channel. It's also the coastal gateway to Ojai, nestled in the Topatopa mountain range.

San Francisco
Ventura
Los Angeles

TOP TIP

Adjacent to Ventura, the agricultural city of Oxnard is California's biggest strawberry producer. During peak season, roughly April through June, you can often smell ripening strawberries even from Hwy 101. Pick up super-fresh, juicy berries from local farmstands, such as the ones at the T-junction of Telephone Rd and Olivas Park Dr.

Ventura's City Hall (p328)

SIGHTS
1 City Hall
2 Museum of Ventura County
3 San Buenaventura Mission
4 San Buenaventura State Beach
5 Ventura Botanical Garden
6 Ventura Pier
7 Ventura River Estuary

ACTIVITIES, COURSES & TOURS
8 Surfers Point
9 Ventura Promenade

EATING
10 Beach House Fish
11 Jolly Oyster

DRINKING
12 MadeWest

SHOPPING
13 Coalition Thrift Store
14 Findings Market
15 Patagonia

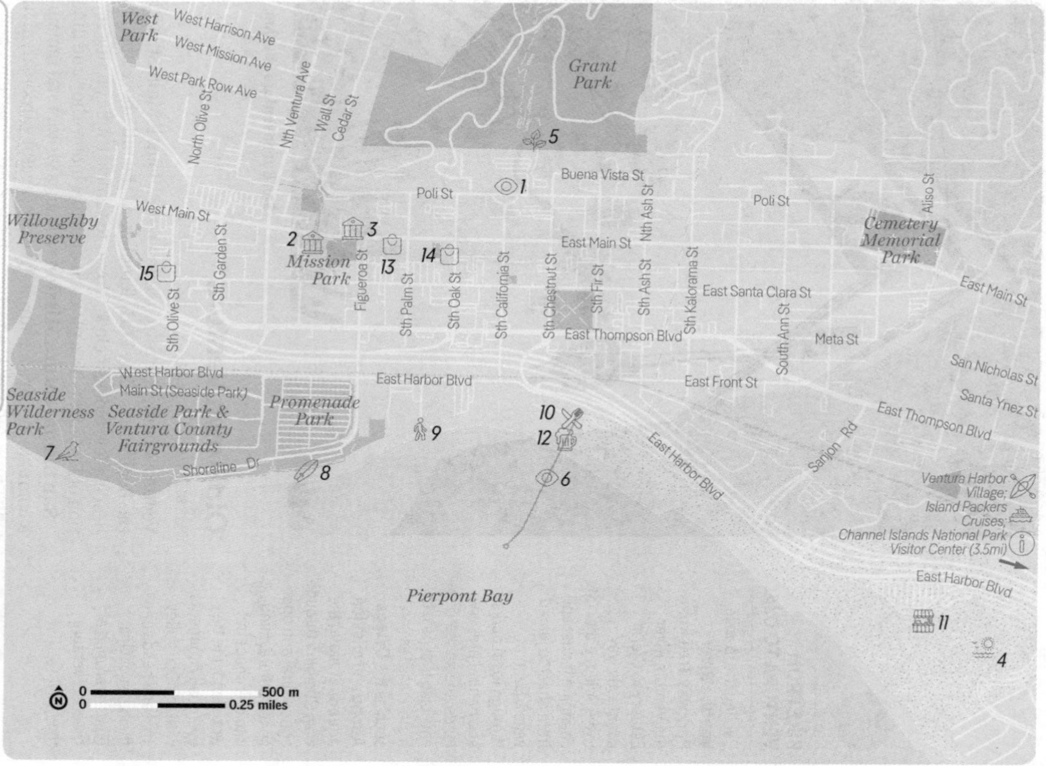

Ventura Keys homes (p329)

BIKE FROM VENTURA TO OJAI

Cycling the 16-mile **Ventura River Parkway Trail** from the Ventura River Estuary to Ojai is a fantastic way to experience the changing landscape from coast to inland valley. Running through local parks and natural preserve lands, the pedestrian-and-bike trail passes historical sites such as the **Ortega Adobe** and **mission aqueduct** along the way. Climbing through agricultural and open space before climbing into oak chaparral woodland, the trail eventually connects with the Ojai Valley Trail and heads into the heart of Ojai. Find a trail map at friendsofventura river.org.

BILL PERRY/SHUTTERSTOCK ©

San Buenaventura Mission

Old-Town Ventura

MISSION, OLD TOWN, BOTANICAL GARDEN

Ventura's naturally retro old town lies along E Main St, with the Beaux Arts **City Hall** looming on the hill above and the beach a few blocks below. Closed to vehicle traffic on this section of E Main St, it's a pleasant area to window-shop and dine.

San Buenaventura Mission welcomes visitors and remains a community parish church. In the peaceful garden area, its olive mill and brick filtering tank from the mission's aqueduct still stand. Across E Main St to the west, the **Museum of Ventura County** includes Chumash artifacts and historical displays as well as rotating exhibits that may be worth a look.

DRINKING AND NIGHTLIFE

Majestic Ventura Theater
Ventura's big music venue for touring bands, housed in a lovely 1920 Mission-style building.

Bank of Italy Cocktail Trust
Named for the historic building it occupies and the cocktails it mixes; also serves Italian-style bites.

Bombay Bar & Grill
Local live music, food, cocktails and a good beer selection in a lively party atmosphere.

Indie shops like **Findings Market** has beautifully curated, locally made wares. You'll also discover gobs of vintage and thrift shops like **Coalition Thrift Store**, benefiting local charities. Refuel at one of the slew of dining options, from tacos to Thai, and wine bars to craft brewhouses.

Walk it off at the **Ventura Botanical Garden** – free on Fridays – with its 2-mile trail zigzagging up a ridge. It's still bouncing back from the 2017 Thomas Fire, but the graded trail shows off expansive views of the city as you climb through South American and South African garden areas. And if the SoCal weather is colder than you expected, pick up a warm layer at **Patagonia's** flagship store (and global HQ) on W Santa Clara St.

CHANNEL ISLANDS

Day trips to **Channel Islands National Park** (p331) are a highlight of this region; book passage with park concessionaire Island Packers or take a spectacular guided kayaking tour with Santa Barbara Adventure Company to explore sea caves and view marine wildlife.

Ventura Oceanfront

OCEAN ACTIVITIES AND WATERFRONT ATTRACTIONS

Start with a beachfront walk on **Ventura Promenade** to soak up salt air with the bikers, skaters joggers and dog-walkers enjoying the paved pathway. Park at the end of California St and walk the pathway 1 mile west, watching surfers at **Surfers Point** on the way, to do a little birding at **Ventura River Estuary**. Strolling east along the shoreline will bring you to **San Buenaventura State Beach**, with 2 miles of beach and tree-shaded park.

Stop at the **Ventura Pier** for tacos at **Beach House Fish** and an oceanview pale ale at **MadeWest**. If you're there Fridays through Sundays, shuck your own oysters or have them grilled for you at the **Jolly Oyster**, a stand located in the state beach park.

To get on the water, rent a SUP, kayak or paddleboat at **Ventura Harbor Village** and paddle around the slips and cute harborside homes in the Ventura Keys neighborhood. Keep an eye out for sunning harbor seals, pelicans and egrets. The harbor village path is also a pleasant place for a stroll and a stop at the **Channel Islands National Park visitor center** if you can't make it out to the islands themselves.

Ventura Harbor is the launch point for trips to the Channel Islands with **Island Packers Cruises**, or dedicated **whale-watching** trips in the biodiverse Santa Barbara Channel.

BEST LOCAL SEAFOOD SPOTS

Brophy Brothers
An upstairs institution with harbor views and a busy, boisterous atmosphere with huge platters of steamed shellfish, fish specials and strong drinks; no reservations. $$

Rumfish y Vino
Lovely patio dining for excellent seafood with a Latin twist in old-town Ventura. $$

Spencer Mackenzie's
This casual counter-service joint slings ceviche, fish tacos, ahi pockets and poke a little east of old town. $

GETTING AROUND

Downtown Ventura is walkable with plenty of free or cheap parking. Because so many people who work in Santa Barbara live in Ventura County, the $8 (one-way) Commuter Express bus runs several trips daily during commute hours from Ventura to Santa Barbara. It's also possible to take the local Amtrak service between Ventura and Santa Barbara County towns on a more limited schedule.

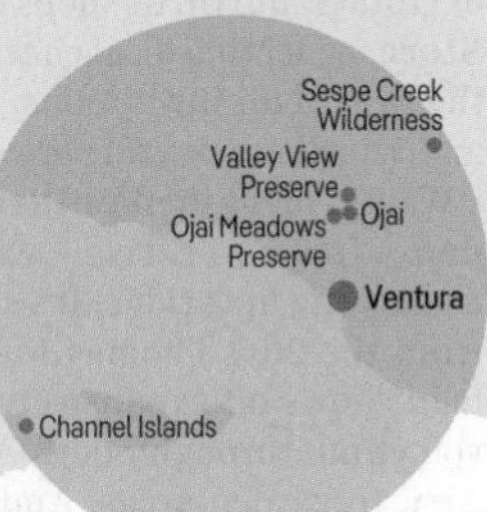

Beyond Ventura

From Ventura, journey inland to Ojai for slow living and sunshine, or cross the channel to windswept Channel Islands National Park.

When the coast is cool and tinged with fog, the chances are good that the sun is shining in Ojai. About a 20-minute drive into the oaky inland valley transports you to a different world altogether, where citrus groves and horse country meet spiritual seekers and Hollywood refugees. The lovely nest of a valley exudes good energy for rejuvenating and recreating.

Offshore, the Channel Islands topography defines the horizon line. Traveling across the channel is a 1½-hour journey over marine wilderness, where dolphin and whale encounters are the norm. Hiking on the wild, windswept islands is witnessing what the coastal mainland might have looked like a thousand years ago.

TOP TIP

Thousands of Ventura County residents commute to Santa Barbara for work. With Hwy 101 under construction, weekday mornings northbound and late afternoons southbound can get jammed – plan accordingly.

Lake Piru and the Topatopa Mountains, Los Padres National Forest (p333)

KELLY VANDELLEN/SHUTTERSTOCK ©

Dolphins in the Channel Islands

Channel Islands Day Trip

THE GALÁPAGOS OF NORTH AMERICA

Harbor seals bark you on your way as your boat departs Ventura Harbor into the **Santa Barbara Channel**. From there, it's all eyes on the ocean's surface as you scan for whale spouts or dolphins racing your vessel. It's not that unusual to find your boat in the middle of a superpod of dolphins numbering in the hundreds, or to have a curious whale approach as the boat idles.

Once you dock at the island, whichever it may be, it's yours to explore on foot. **Santa Cruz Island** is the most accessible of the five-island chain, with the most frequent boats making daily trips in the high season. At **Scorpion Anchorage**, displays explain the island's human history, with antique ranching equipment rusting in the sun. The 2-mile **Cavern Point Loop** heads through the campground and up to a bluff trail to a lovely overlook. A longer 5-miler goes to a viewpoint on **Potato Harbor** and the islands beyond.

Alternatively, meet up with your guide and suit up for **kayaking** into sea caves and isolated coves, exploring the ecosystem on the island's fringe. As you paddle, you'll marvel at

ISLAND CAMPING

Stay overnight to fully immerse yourself in the raw wilderness of the islands. Camping gifts you with the luxury of exploring after day-trippers have set sail for the mainland. You can reserve campsites up to six months ahead at recreation.gov.

Scorpion Canyon Campground on Santa Cruz Island has the most sites, only a half-mile from the boat dock with potable water and vault toilets. If you're backcountry camping, you'll have to bring your own water and haul it to the designated campgrounds.

Regardless of location, the super-intelligent ravens and island foxes know how to unzip zippers, so it's key to lock your food in the fox boxes for wildlife health.

CHANNEL ISLANDS TOUR OPERATORS

Channel Islands Adventure Company
National park concessionaire running kayak and snorkel tours at Santa Cruz Island.

Channel Islands Expeditions
Day trips to kayak and snorkel Anacapa or Santa Cruz Island, or overnight dive trips.

Island Packers
The company running boat transport to the islands also offers whale-watching trips from Ventura Harbor.

BEST DAY SPAS

Spa Ojai
Offers the full resort experience at Ojai Valley Inn, with private outdoor terraces, desert clay mud treatment with guided meditation, and light-flooded common areas.

Day Spa of Ojai
Owner Kim Wachter's Chumash heritage influences her treatments at this cozy downtown spa offering massages and skincare.

Body Essentials Ojai
With a customized approach to skincare, Ojai's oldest day spa has an infrared sauna, facials and massage.

Ojai Garden Spa
Gazebo massages outdoors in the garden of the Lavender Inn downtown; also offers skincare treatments.

CRAICPOT/SHUTTERSTOCK ©

Bart's Books, Ojai

the coppery blades of kelp swaying in contrast with the clear blue water, with fish darting within the kelp bed and bristling reef beneath.

Roaming Downtown Ojai

OUTDOOR BOOKSTORE, ART AND EATS

Holiday with Hollywood escapees in the magical place that is Ojai. Taking its name from the Chumash word for 'moon,' this valley has always attracted seekers, from spiritual philosopher Krishnamurti to contemporary urban dwellers perhaps lured by the spiritual energy of Ojai's vortexes.

Downtown is defined by Ojai Ave. **Libbey Park**, with its pretty archways, has a fantastic playground, walking paths and picnic tables under the trees. Further back, catch outdoor concerts at **Libbey Bowl** amphitheatre.

WHERE TO STAY IN OJAI

Ojai Rancho Inn
On the west end of downtown, this modernized midcentury motel has pool and sauna, plus free bikes to use. **$$**

Emerald Iguana Inn
Close to downtown Ojai, this boutique inn has an attractive woodsy setting, pool and hot tub. **$$**

Ojai Valley Inn
Relaxed luxury in Spanish Colonial style, with a golf course and dreamy spa. **$$$**

Along this side of Ojai Ave and its side streets you'll find wine-tasting rooms, local boutiques like **deKor** and the indoor/outdoor **Fig**, and the gallery and theater of the **Ojai Art Center**, established in 1939.

People-watch from the corner patio of **Topa Topa Brewing Company** with Asian pub fusion food (think *okonomiyaki* tots) from **Little Sama Ojai**. Try the tea-leaf salad at the Burmese **Dutchess**, which also tempts with pastries and excellent wine list.

Across Ojai Ave, find art galleries, shops and honey tastings along the **Ojai Arcade**, which opens out to a plaza behind. The cheerfully jam-packed Sunday morning **farmers market** sets up shop in the parking lot on E Matilija St just beyond the plaza. Stroll a few more blocks west along E Matilija St to browse the maze of aisles at cherished landmark **Bart's Books**, the 'world's largest outdoor bookstore', founded in 1964.

Ojai Outdoors

HIKING, BIKING, HORSEBACK RIDING

Hiking is the leisure activity of choice in Ojai, backed as it is by the **Topatopa Mountains** and **Los Padres National Forest**.

Easily accessed from town is the **Shelf Rd Trail** in the **Valley View Preserve**, at the north end of Signal Rd in Ojai. This is a mostly flat hike with excellent views of the valley; make it an out-and-back or return through town. You'll also find the **Fox Canyon Trail** in the preserve, which you can connect with others for a more challenging loop hike.

Day-use fees are required for the easy, short hike to a waterfall (best in springtime) on the **Rose Valley Falls Trail** in the **Sespe Creek Wilderness**, about 15 miles from Ojai on Hwy 33. Another Sespe hike is the **Piedra Blanca Trail** with beautiful white sandstone boulders at the end; it's about 5 miles round-trip with a creek crossing.

Closer to town, a kid-friendly trail is the flat, not-quite-one-mile **Ojai Meadows Preserve** hike that's good for birding as it passes wetlands and meadows with views of the mountains.

Rent bikes at **The Mob Shop** on W Ojai Ave and ride along the **Ojai Valley Trail**, the Ojai section of the **Ventura River Parkway Trail**. Or take a trail-only sunset horseback ride in the Ventura River Valley Preserve to enjoy Ojai's famous 'pink moment' with **Ojai Valley Trail Riding Company**.

MEINERS OAKS FOOD SCENE

Just outside of Ojai, Meiners Oaks has great dining options for such a small community. **Ojai Deer Lodge** along Hwy 33 looks a bit divey, but this friendly tavern is Ojai's oldest restaurant, serving starters like panzanella and shishito peppers alongside its roadhouse burgers. Check the listings for live music.

In town, **The Farmer & the Cook** is run by an Ojai farmer/poet and serves real farm-to-table food at its market-cafe. The lovely **Ranch House** opened at its current location in 1956 by a couple who included family-style vegetarian meals for their weekly boarders. Their ethos purportedly inspired Alice Waters' farm-to-table philosophy, which is honored by the most recent owners who still forgo freezer or fryer. Reservations only.

GETTING AROUND

Downtown Ojai is small enough to explore on foot once you've arrived (it's a 25-minute drive from Ventura). Journeys beyond, from Meiners Oaks (3 miles) to nearby trailheads, require a car drive or bike ride.

AGNES ACKERMANN/SHUTTERSTOCK ©

Above: Pacific Ferris wheel, Santa Monica Pier (p368); Right: Rodeo Drive (p355)

THE MAIN AREAS

HOLLYWOOD
Alluring history from a bygone era. p340

GRIFFITH PARK, SILVER LAKE & LOS FELIZ
Nature, family, hipster, picturesque. p347

WEST HOLLYWOOD & BEVERLY HILLS
Shopping, architecture, design and LGBTIQ+. p353

MIRACLE MILE & MID-CITY
Museums, food, ethnically diverse. p360

LOS ANGELES

THE VIBRANTLY DIVERSE HEART OF CALIFORNIA

Perfect year-round weather meets picture-perfect skylines that kiss the cool Pacific Ocean, shining over a constantly buzzing city full of life.

Los Angeles means many things to many people. It is a city of dreams but has too much traffic. It enjoys perfect weather but there are so many mountain fires. It has the best golden-hour sunsets but the smog is terrible. All these things ring true about this enormous city in Southern California, and one thing is absolutely for sure – nothing beats the pulsating, vivacious and infamous flair of Los Angeles.

LA is home to music legends, with a long history of rock and roll on the Sunset Strip, and it's where creatives gather in Downtown. Melrose Ave is a shopping mecca, while Koreatown is a food-lover's dream. The city embodies free-spirit vibes.

Where else can you explore 75 miles of Southern California coastline that's filled with defining landmarks such as the first skatepark ever, or take a ride on the world's only solar-powered Ferris wheel over water? Where else can you hike up mountains, not only because it's trendy but because you might rub shoulders with a celebrity? And where else can you get a taste of old Hollywood just by walking down one famed street? From the mountains to the seaside, there is nothing LA can't offer. Sure, it's gritty sometimes – the homeless situation has worsened since the pandemic and iconic places have closed. But like any great city, it prevails, and has many more ups than downs.

LA is also a kaleidoscope of cultures from around 140 countries, with nearly 220 languages spoken, creating an intricate web of diversity that connects deep beneath the surface. It is a place of acceptance, and what makes LA truly shine is the diversity of its people, who uniquely come together as one. LA is the people.

Whether it's your first visit or one of many, the City of Angels always has something up its sleeve for the keen traveler, and never fails to show off its inner and outer beauty, whether that's through music, food, art or culture. Time to unravel its treasures.

MICHAEL GORDON/SHUTTERSTOCK ©

SANTA MONICA
Scenic, beach, sunsets, fresh air. p366

VENICE
Bohemian, edgy, food and outdoors. p372

DOWNTOWN
Urban, art, dining and culture. p377

BURBANK & UNIVERSAL CITY
Movie mania, family friendly, suburban. p382

Find Your Way

Los Angeles is a giant city known for its traffic with a side of road rage. It's not walking friendly with everything so spread out, so travelling by car or public transportation is highly recommended, though avoid the freeways between 5pm and 7pm.

CAR RENTAL

Renting a car is your best bet if you want to enjoy LA to the fullest. All the car-rental facilities are in the vicinity of the airport and all have shuttle services to and from. Just pay close attention to the city's erratic street signs when parking.

UBER & LYFT

No one walks around in LA – it's a thing. Locals walk through neighborhoods but that's where it ends. Make sure you download the apps for Uber or Lyft, which are typically reliable and quick to arrive anywhere in the city.

PUBLIC TRANSPORTATION

The Los Angeles metro system consists of Metro buses, DASH buses, and Metro Rail trains that go to most of the best attractions. Dockless scooters with Lime and Bird are also a great way to get around neighborhoods.

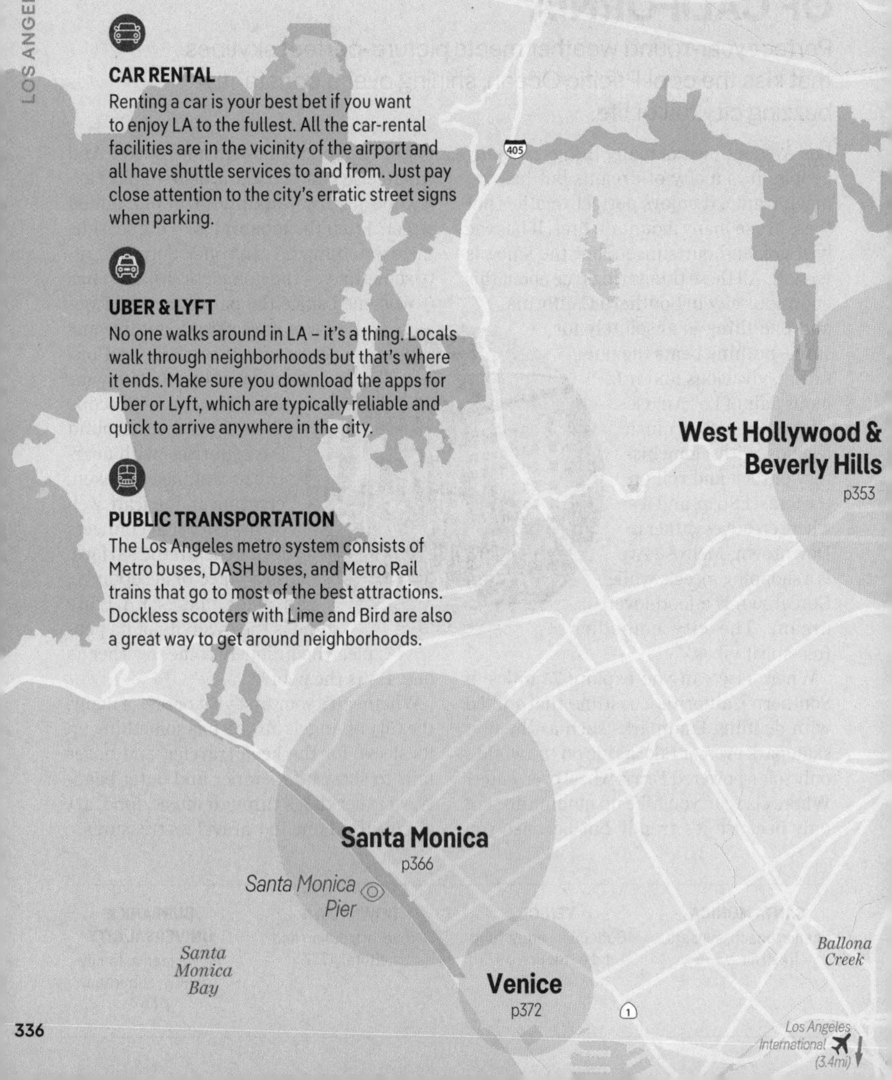

405

West Hollywood & Beverly Hills
p353

Santa Monica
p366

Santa Monica Pier

Santa Monica Bay

Venice
p372

1

Ballona Creek

Los Angeles International (3.4mi)

FROM THE AIRPORT

Los Angeles International Airport (LAX) is the city's main airport, located in Inglewood, and it's huge. It's right off the I-405; depending on traffic, it could take anywhere from 20 minutes to an hour to reach your destination.

Plan Your Days

The City of Angels can be daunting when you don't know where to start, so here are three loose recommendations on how to make the most of its great neighborhoods.

INGUS KRUKLITIS/SHUTTERSTOCK ©

Venice Beach (p375)

Day 1

Morning

- Stop for a bite at **Breakfast by Salt's Cure** (p369) on Montana Ave for some griddle hot cakes.

Afternoon

- Take a further stroll down Montana Ave to go window-shopping, then rent an e-scooter and make your way to **Third Street Promenade** (p368) for some people-watching, before going to the beach. Rent a bike and take a trip along the **Marvin Braude Bike Trail** (p366) for the ultimate California beach day.

Evening

- Bike your way to **Venice Beach** (p374) and get Instagram-worthy pictures of LA's illustrious golden-hour sunset at **Hotel Erwin** (p375) with drinks in hand. Then have dinner at **Felix** (p376).

You'll Also Want to...

With about a million things to do in this grand city, here are a few ways to truly get a dose of local life.

GO ON A NEIGHBORHOOD STROLL

Larchmont Village is a tiny historic area north of Hollywood with cafes, boutiques and a touch of the quiet life.

CATCH A LIVE GAME

See a **Dodgers**, **Lakers** or **LA Rams** game to absorb the hardcore love of LA local sports fans.

TAKE A HIKE

LA locals love hiking in various places throughout the city. Try **Runyon Canyon** in Hollywood.

AARONP/BAUER-GRIFFIN/GETTY IMAGES ©; CONOR P. FITZGERALD/SHUTTERSTOCK ©; ALEX MILLAUER/SHUTTERSTOCK ©

Day 2

Morning

- Book tickets a few days in advance and make your way to **The Broad** (p379) to see the spectacular artwork on display. The **Walt Disney Concert Hall** (p379) and **MOCA** (p379) are next door.

Afternoon

- Either take the Angels Flight funicular or a 10-minute walk to **Grand Central Market** (p380) for a selection of some of the best food from almost every country you can think of. The **Bradbury Building** (p380) is just across from the market, so pop in for a look-see.

Evening

- Visit the **Arts District** (p381) for a bit of sightseeing before heading to **Bavel** (p381) for some insanely delicious Middle Eastern fare.

Day 3

Morning

- Start your day at the **Original Farmers Market** (p362) before the hungry lunch crowds start to pour in and have some hot coffee at Du-Par's. Stop by Monsieur Marcel to scour its fine cheese, wines and imported chocolates before making your way to **The Grove shopping mall** (p362).

Afternoon

- Visit Museum Row and take in the unique sights of **LACMA** (p363), especially the famous installation of street lamps outside.

Evening

- Make your way to Koreatown for dinner at Oaxacan joint **Guelaguetza** (p365), then head straight to the **Hotel Normandie** (p364) for drinks and a bit of LA debauchery at its eponymous club.

GET IN ON LA'S BURGER OBSESSION

No stop to LA is complete without a Double-Double cheeseburger, made Animal-Style, at **In-N-Out Burger**.

BE A MALL RAT

Westfield Century City Mall, located near Beverly Hills, has eclectic shops, a Shake Shack and numerous other food vendors.

TAKE THE PERFECT PICTURE

Walk down the residential side of **Beverly Drive** around 6pm for great photos of swaying palm trees in the stellar natural light.

DINE OUT IN LAUREL CANYON

Have a laid-back Italian lunch or dinner at **Pace**, in the middle of Laurel Canyon.

HOLLYWOOD

ALLURING HISTORY FROM A BYGONE ERA

The Hollywood area might be past its heyday but its history is rich in stories of Californian glamour, and the neighborhood is filled with iconic monuments, including the Egyptian and TCL Chinese Theatres, that even the excessive souvenir shops and tour buses can't taint. The Walk of Fame is part of the bread and butter of Hollywood, and millions of visitors come each year to stroll down the somewhat dodgy but bustling city blocks to see the terrazzo sidewalks with their celebrity stars.

In 1902 Harvey Henderson Wilcox and his wife, Daeida, purchased a few hundred acres of land in Cahuenga for farming purposes, but it wasn't until real-estate mogul HJ Whitley came onto the scene that Hollywood truly started to flourish, with the building of upscale homes, markets and hotels like the Hollywood Hotel. Whitley became known as the Father of Hollywood, particularly duing the film industry's Golden Age in the 1930s.

TOP TIP

The heart of Hollywood Blvd can be a bit overwhelming with the many crowds that gather around the historic sights. A great way to see everything is by booking a walking tour, which are usually led by charismatic and knowledgeable guides. Check Viator for a list of different options.

TCL Chinese Theatre (p346)

HIGHLIGHTS
1 Hollywood Walk of Fame

SIGHTS
2 Capitol Records
3 The Egyptian
4 Hollywood Museum
5 TCL Chinese Theatre

SLEEPING
6 Hollywood Roosevelt

EATING
7 Musso & Frank

ENTERTAINMENT
8 Hollywood Bowl

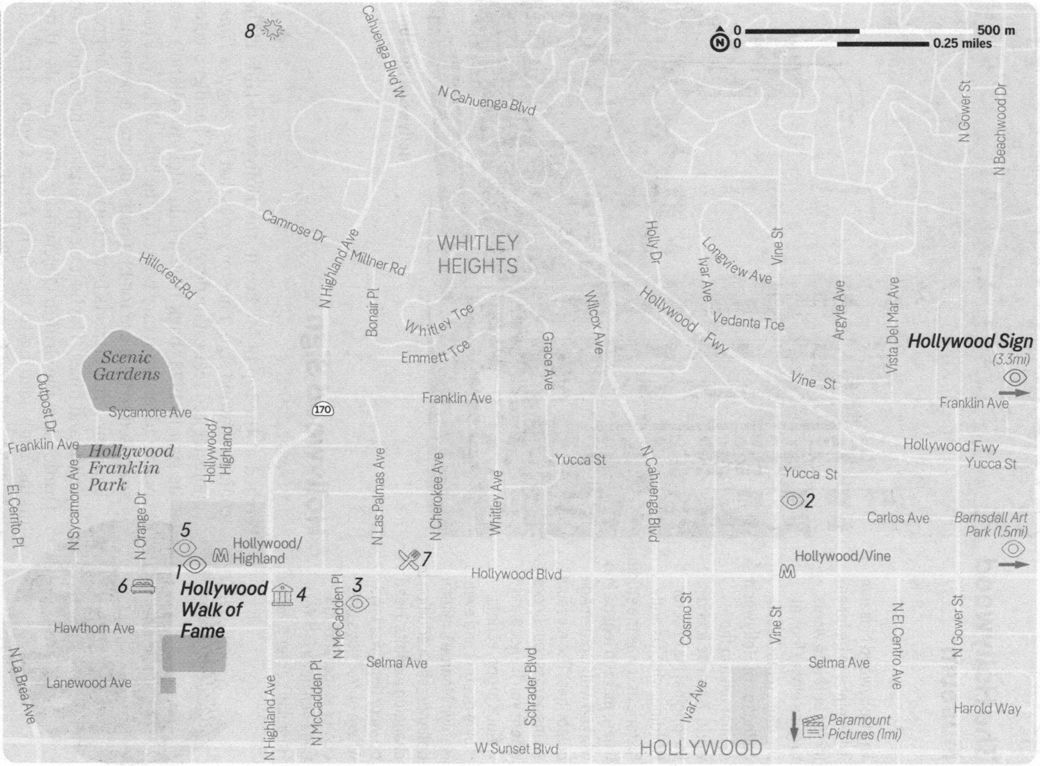

The Egyptian theatre (p346)

The Hollywood Museum

NO BUSINESS LIKE SHOW BUSINESS

The Hollywood Museum is the place to be for any movie buff who wants to get a closer look at the most remarkable collection of Hollywood memorabilia in the world. It can be found in the original Max Factor Building, which is aptly historic as it was the studio where makeup legend Max worked with Golden Age celebrities. The museum spans across four floors, where you'll encounter various props, scripts, movie posters and even Marilyn Monroe's million-dollar dress, in addition to changing exhibits. Head down to the lower level where horror films take center stage, and you can even get a feel for Hannibal Lecter's jail cell.

Hollywood Museum

Hollywood Sign

A SIGN WAS BORN

Perched at the top of Mt Lee in the Hollywood Hills is the iconic Hollywood sign. The story goes that *Los Angeles Times* publisher and real-estate developer Harry Chandler erected the sign in 1923 (back then it said 'Hollywoodland') as a way to advertise luxury homes in the hills. What was only supposed to be there for 18 months became a permanent landmark that attracts both tourists and locals for great photos and hikes. The best viewpoints can be found from Ovation and the Griffith Observatory. There are also three hiking trails leading to the sign: Brush Canyon Trail, Mt. Hollywood Trail and Cahuenga Peak Trail.

Musso & Frank

Musso & Frank

DINING LIKE THE STARS

The classic Hollywood establishment Musso & Frank has been serving the masses since 1919, making it Hollywood's oldest restaurant – it has truly stood the test of time. Dining here feels like taking a step back into the Golden Age of Hollywood, when F Scott Fitzgerald, Charles Bukowski and Marilyn Monroe graced the mahogany booths decked out with personalized coat hangers.

The servers wear waist-length red jackets, black trousers and either a tie or a bowtie to differentiate themselves from the bartenders. Start with the famous martini, which is stirred and served via a sidecar on ice, then go for a classic filet mignon or one of the daily specials like its chicken potpie.

The Hollywood Bowl

SUMMER MUSIC IN THE HILLS

This Hollywood Hills stalwart venue has been hosting live concerts since 1922. Top headliners have ranged from Billie Holiday to The Beatles, and it's the summer home of the LA Philharmonic. The amphitheater stands out for its unique silhouette, that is reminiscent of – you guessed it – a bowl, with concentric shell-like arches. This is a live-show summer haven for Angelenos, and although food and beverage prices can be a bit steep, the Hollywood Hills backdrop, the acoustics and the views make up for it all.

The Hollywood Bowl

Barnsdall Art Park

A TREASURE IN THE MIDDLE OF TOWN

Sitting pristinely in Barnsdall Art Park on Olive Hill in East Hollywood (which used to be an olive orchard) at the behest of philanthropist and oil heiress Aline Barnsdall, the Mayan-temple-inspired **Hollyhock House** is a Hollywood landmark from acclaimed architect Frank Lloyd Wright. Known to be his first Los Angeles project, this not-to-be-missed monument dating back to the 1920s also received recognition as LA's first Unesco World Heritage Site. The grounds surrounding the structure are just as eye-catching, with galleries, a theater and hilly grounds where you can picnic and catch a glorious sunset.

Frank Lloyd Wright's Hollyhock House, Barnsdall Art Park

Walk of Fame

THE PATH TO STARDOM

Nothing is more synonymous with Tinseltown than the Hollywood Walk of Fame. Created in 1958 as an ode to actors, musicians, directors and others in the entertainment industry, there are now over 2700 stars along 15 blocks running from Gower to La Brea. The area sees nearly 10 million visitors each year and although it can feel like a tourist trap with the overload of tour buses and live theatrics, it is a must-see for any film buff.

The Hollywood Roosevelt

GOLDEN ERA MEETS MODERN TIMES

There is no hotel more historically Hollywood than the Roosevelt, built in 1926 at the height of the Golden Era and still heaving with Hollywood lore. Spanish Colonial architecture meets art deco from the ground up, and it's where Marilyn Monroe lived for nearly two years (this eventually led to a suite being named after the actress) and where Shirley Temple learned to tap dance on the stairs off the lobby. You can stop in for cocktails at the Spare Room, a Prohibition-style lounge that features board games and a bowling alley, or have dinner by chef Nancy Silverton, who serves up old-world steakhouse fare with Californian flair at The Barish. Our favorite thing is to hang by the Tropicana pool that doubles as a multi-million-dollar art mural inspired by 1960s art deco. The location of Marilyn Monroe's first photo shoot, it's painted by the renowned David Hockney.

THE OVATION

Previously known as Hollywood & Highland, this mega shopping and entertainment complex includes everything from shops such as Sephora, Hot Topic and an LA Dodgers store, to restaurants like the Hard Rock Cafe, the Lucky Strike bowling alley and a night club. It's also the home of the famous Dolby Theatre (formerly the Kodak Theatre), where the red carpet gets rolled out each year for the Academy Awards. The complex is a one-stop shop that is always filled with visitors.

The Hollywood Roosevelt

ANNE CZICHOS/SHUTTERSTOCK ©

Capitol Records

RECORDING STUDIO WITH AN ILLUSTRIOUS PAST

Just a three-minute walk from the Walk of Fame, Capitol Records, the world's first circular-shaped building (looking like a giant stack of records), is just 13 floors tall and a true LA gem. The iconic tower was built in 1956, adhering to a unique, one-of-a-kind design by Welton Becket. Greats like Frank Sinatra, Nat King Cole and The Beatles recorded some of the most treasured music in history here. Don't forget to look up at the very top of the roof spire, where you'll catch a blinking light flashing 'Hollywood' in Morse code. John Lennon and Garth Brooks have their stars outside on the sidewalk.

Paramount Pictures

Paramount Pictures

THE LAST STUDIO REMNANT IN HOLLYWOOD

One of the oldest and last remaining film studios in all of Hollywood is Paramount Pictures, known for hits like *Titanic*, *Footloose*, *Indiana Jones* and *The Godfather*. It offers excellent tours year round, allowing you to get a behind-the-scenes look into the world of the industry's top producers and talent. Guided golf-cart tours, which last about two hours, take visitors through various soundstages, the prop house and a sizable New York backlot that has been featured in many movies and TV shows. Weekday-only VIP tours (4½ hours) go into a bit more depth, giving you the chance to chat with those who work on set; they include an exclusive lunch or hors d'oeuvres. Both tours are led by knowledgeable guides who offer fascinating insights into the studio's history and the movie-making process. From September to early November Paramount also runs a separate After Dark tour (2½ hours), which includes a glass of sparkling wine, snacks, scandalous Hollywood anecdotes and a trip to the adjacent Hollywood Forever Cemetery.

Capitol Records

LA's Pride Festival

THE ICONIC GAY PRIDE FESTIVAL

By far one of the largest Pride events in the country and around for nearly 50 years, the annual three-day **LA Pride** event is a fun-filled, colorful festival full of joy, divas, drag queens and lots of great music provided by various DJs and other headliners, all in support for the LGBTIQ+ community. The historic parade happens typically on a Sunday in June at the heart of Hollywood and Vine before making its way to Sunset and Ivar. Party the day away with many performances, dancers and exotic cars.

Sid Grauman's Theaters

HISTORIC THEATER HOPPING

The showman Sid Grauman is the main person responsible for Hollywood's most important theaters. In 1922 he opened his first Hollywood theater, **The Egyptian**, with nods to ancient Egypt, hieroglyphics and giant massive columns. It was here that the first movie premiere of *Robin Hood*, starring Douglas Fairbanks, was hosted. The Egyptian was restored in 1998 by American Cinematheque before being acquired in 2020 by Netflix, who are planning to restore it to its original status.

Just down the street is perhaps the most legendary cinema landmark of all time, the **TCL Chinese Theatre**, also designed by Grauman, in 1927. He went to great lengths to create his dream space, importing temple bells, pagodas and other artifacts from China. Two gigantic red columns topped by wrought-iron masks hold aloft the bronze roof. Between the columns are the two original heaven dogs guarding the theater's entrance, still standing today. With the genius idea of immortalizing celebrities with handprints and stars out on the front courtyard, the theater eventually overshadowed the Egyptian, making it the place to be in Hollywood. The theater has been designated a Los Angeles Historic-Cultural Monument and is visited by millions each year.

BEST PLACES TO DRINK IN HOLLYWOOD

Frolic Room
Anything goes at this Hollywood classic bar that sits right next to the Pantages Theatre.

Boardner's
Historic establishment that serves affordable drinks in a laid-back atmosphere.

Tramp Stamp Granny's
It refers to its piano lounge as upscale debauchery – we call it the best escape from bustling Hollywood.

Bar Lis
Escape to the French Riviera at the rooftop lounge and bar atop the Thompson Hotel.

WHERE TO EAT IN HOLLYWOOD

Providence
Michael Cimarusti's fine dining is the ultimate LA experience offering the finest of seafood with stellar service. **$$$**

Clark Street Diner
Great American greasy-spoon diner offering everything from fluffy pancakes to fried chicken. **$$**

Mashti Malone's Ice Cream
Regularly voted best ice-cream shop thanks to its unique flavors like creamy rosewater and Persian cucumber. **$**

GRIFFITH PARK, SILVER LAKE & LOS FELIZ

NATURE, FAMILY, HIPSTER, PICTURESQUE

LA's eastside neighborhoods offer hipsterism, stunning nature and laid-back, urban vibes unlike anywhere else in the sprawling city. Griffith Park, one of the US's largest municipal parks, is a refreshing escape from the hustle and bustle, with its rugged, verdant hills and trails leading to the iconic Griffith Observatory, offering some of the best views of the Hollywood sign and the LA Basin.

Sitting south is supertrendy Silver Lake (the 'Brooklyn of Los Angeles'). Its diversity of food, people, LGBTIQ+ history and constant reinvigoration keeps locals coming back for more, and you don't have to be a cool kid to fit in.

Just next door, the hilly neighborhood of Los Feliz feels calm and collected, with a sense of old-world charm – it's where many celebrities call home. With many independent shops and beautiful architectural monuments, plus its proximity to Griffith Park, it's a quaint place with good-mood energy. For a true LA day, make your way to Eagle Rock for the eclectic, down-to-earth vibe.

TOP TIP

To enjoy the hilly mountainsides of Griffith Park, rent a bike at Spokes 'N Stuff, located just southwest of the LA Zoo. The bike paths are geared to all levels and they're a great way to explore the area with the family.

Griffith Observatory (p348)

Greek Theatre

TOP: EMMA_GRIFFITHS/SHUTTERSTOCK ©; BOTTOM: SUPERJOSEPH/SHUTTERSTOCK ©

Greek Theatre

MUSIC IN THE GREAT OUTDOORS

This one-of-a-kind amphitheater sits at the very base of Griffith Park, meaning it is surrounded by nature and the rolling hills behind. The 5900-capacity Greek Theatre has been the place for performances by musical legends such as Bruce Springsteen, Carlos Santana and The Foo Fighters, among others. It is always a good idea to check the schedule of performances before making your way to the park to get the most out of the area.

LA Zoo & Botanical Gardens

A DAY IN THE WILD

Grab the family for an all-day adventure at the Los Angeles Zoo and Botanical Gardens, home to over 2000 birds, mammals and furry friends, such as the chimpanzees who live in a setting of waterfalls and beautiful rock formations that Jane Goodall herself praised as one of the world's most outstanding zoo habitats. The zoo contains more than 270 different species, of which around 60 are endangered. The giant space also oversees a botanical collection of nearly 800 different plant species and thousands of individual plants. Purchasing tickets in advance is recommended as walk-ins can't be guaranteed.

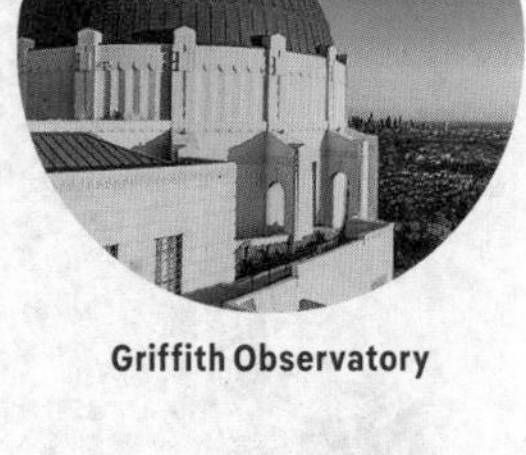

Griffith Observatory

Griffith Observatory

GET BACK TO NATURE

The dome-shaped structure of the Griffith Observatory is a historical landmark of California, and embedded in the city's history. Welsh-born Griffith J Griffith moved to LA, where he envisioned a large, green park similar to those in Europe, eventually donating land to build the eponymous Griffith Park. At the time he also offered $100,000 for an observatory to be built on the top of Mt Hollywood.

Since 1935, the observatory has been showcasing live planetarium shows, and what sets it apart is the 12-inch Zeiss telescope, which more than 600 visitors look through each day. The views from the observatory are also unmatched, with prime spots for Hollywood sign pictures. Channel your inner *La La Land* character and get ready to pose.

The Dresden

YOU'RE SO MONEY

This institution has been serving the LA crowds since 1954 and you may have seen it in the film *Swingers,* where the line 'You're so money' was made famous. The Dresden is an old-school, retro-style restaurant and bar with dimly lit rooms, arched walkways and red-wine-colored booths. Up until recently, singers Marty and Elayne had ruled the stage, though Marty has since passed away. This is nonetheless definitely the place to grab a drink before a show at the Greek – try the Blood & Sand cocktail.

The Dresden

Snow White Cottages

Snow White Cottages

STORYBOOK HOUSES

LA had a secret love for storybook/fairy-tale houses between the 1920s and 30s and prime examples are the Snow White Cottages. Built by Ben Sherwood in 1931, the eight white houses have thatched roofs, sweet window boxes and chimneys (and are even for sale!). They are said to be the inspiration for *Snow White and the Seven Dwarfs* and were built in the Tudor style with nods to French Normandy architecture. The cottages stand just a few blocks from the original site of Walt Disney's studios, where the animation legend worked from 1926 until 1940.

A Day in Atwater Village

TINY TOWN WITH BIG POWER

Thought of as one of LA's most underrated neighborhoods, this supercute millennial magnet has everything to offer the shopper in you. Atwater borders Griffith Park and Silver Lake to the west, with Glendale just to the north. Get your day started at Proof Bakery, with some of the best pastries around. After your morning fuel make your way down to the main hub for shopping on Glendale Blvd. The street is lined with unique shops like Goodies and Grain, and you should definitely make a pit stop at Tacos Villa Corona before getting drinks at the impressive Bigfoot Lodge, which is like stepping into the deep woods with its hunting-lodge decor and drinks with roasted marshmallow.

The Black Cat

GASTROPUB THAT CAUSED A MOVEMENT

When you encounter the giant Shake Shack on Sunset Blvd, make sure you look out for the Black Cat logo that leads to this historic tavern, which became a symbol for LGBTIQ+ civil rights.

The Black Cat is a Silver Lake gastropub that was one of many gay bars operating in the mid 1960s, and it was the site of the very first LGBTIQ+ civil rights demonstration in 1967 after being raided by police during NYE celebrations. In 2008 the Black Cat was recognized as a Los Angeles Historic-Cultural Monument for its significant role in the LGBTIQ+ movement and it's now an integral and inclusive neighborhod spot with a loyal following. Casual bar food is paired with great cocktails in a woody, vintage interior setting, with seating for people-watching out front. Look for the commemorative plaque right outside the building that honors the brave efforts of the tavern.

SILVER LAKE FARMERS MARKET

Get your fill of locally sourced fruits, vegetables and home-baked goods at this outdoor neighborhood farmers market that takes place at Sunset Triangle Plaza on Tuesday (from 1:30pm to 7pm) and Saturday (8am to 1:30pm). Grab a cup of artisan coffee and peruse the various stalls for treats, vintage clothing and unique gifts, all while taking in the sunshine and delicious aromas. Parking can be tricky so arrive on the early side if driving.

The Black Cat

HIGHLIGHTS
1 Griffith Observatory

SIGHTS
2 Atwater Village
3 Echo Park
4 Los Angeles Zoo and Botanical Gardens
5 Snow White Cottages

DRINKING
6 The Black Cat
7 The Dresden

ENTERTAINMENT
8 Greek Theatre

SHOPPING
9 Skylight Books

MORE IN GRIFFITH PARK, SILVER LAKE & LOS FELIZ

Local & Charismatic Echo Park

A BREAK FROM SIGHTSEEING

The low-key sibling of Silver Lake, **Echo Park** is where you can savor a taste of true LA life. It shines brightly with a list of to-dos that are the opposite of touristy. One of the city's oldest and most underrated parks, Elysian Park is the perfect escape for a hike or picnic, and has optimal views of Dodger Stadium and the downtown skyline. Make your way to Angelino Heights, one of LA's oldest neighborhoods, and take a stroll down Carroll Ave, lined with 19th-century Victorian homes that are listed on the National Register of Historic

I LIVE HERE: A LOCAL MUSICIAN'S GUIDE TO ECHO PARK

Matt Ebert, bass player in the band Joyce Manor and a lifelong LA native.

Highlight Coffee
Some of LA's best coffee, served by amazing staff in an unpretentious setting. I always go back to their curated list of pour-over coffees, but the coffee lemonade is really good, I promise.

Burgerlords
Burgerlords has perfected the vegan cheeseburger, served alongside killer fries and local beers and great natural wines. Don't miss the weekend-only breakfast burrito!

The Fable
The Fable interior (part hunting lodge, part English pub) is just right – cozy without feeling dull, and lively without being stifling. Friendly people, great drinks, good music and fair prices – a quintessential neighborhood bar.

KIT LEONG/SHUTTERSTOCK ©

Echo Park

Places. And don't leave Echo Park without catching a Dodgers game during the baseball season. Get lost in a sea of blue and gray jerseys while washing down a famous Dodger dog with an ice-cold beer or while catching a bag of peanuts from a vendor. For music lovers, The Echo and Echoplex are two venues that sit above each other and have seen legendary bands like Green Day and Nine Inch Nails grace their stages, but they're also known to showcase up-and-coming indie bands and are even known to offer free concerts.

Reading Nook at Skylight Books

COZY BOOK HAVEN

This independent bookstore is one of the city's most loved for its unique books and welcoming setting. Walk through the modest entrance and you'll encounter a tree hanging right in the middle, beneath the wood-laden, skylight ceiling. It's easy to get lost in the troves of curated books, which feature everything from literary fiction and graphic novels to titles on California history and culture. The store hosts authors as part of its exclusive events program.

WHERE TO EAT IN GRIFFITH PARK, SILVER LAKE AND LOS FELIZ

Courage Bagels
There's always a line and it's a little pricey but these are the best Montreal-style bagels on the West Coast. **$$**

Night + Market Song
Thai American chef Kris Yenbamroong serves up all the faves in an electric yet low-key setting. **$$**

Bar Moruno
Conserva boards, canned fish and upscale Spanish food give off pure Barcelona vibes. **$$$**

WEST HOLLYWOOD & BEVERLY HILLS

SHOPPING, ARCHITECTURE, DESIGN AND LGBTIQ+

The 90210 zip code is one of the most famous in the world, and is a symbol for wealthy A-list celebrities, luxe hotels and top-of-the-line shopping. In the 1920s actors Douglas Fairbanks and Mary Pickford built their home in the area, turning Beverly Hills into an immediate status symbol. Visitors come in their hundreds of thousands to take in the opulent real estate and photogenic swaying palm trees.

Riding on its coattail is the vibrant city of West Hollywood, also known as WeHo. This area has LA's finest bars, most renowned live-music shows and a dazzling Design District for any and all needs. More importantly, WeHo has been integral for the LGBTIQ+ community, making West Hollywood one of the most influential cities in the nation for its advocacy on LGBTIQ+ issues.

If you have time, also pop over to the fancy residential side of Brentwood for a taste of the good life.

TOP TIP

When you visit Beverly Hills, come with the intention of splurging on one iconic meal at longstanding Spago, chef Wolfgang Puck's flagship restaurant. No visit here is complete without the smoked salmon pizza.

Beverly Hills

SEAN PAVONE/SHUTTERSTOCK ©

WEST HOLLYWOOD & BEVERLY HILLS

SIGHTS
1 Beverly Hills Hotel
2 Greystone Mansion
3 Rodeo Drive
4 Spadena House
5 Sunset Strip
6 Virginia Robinson Gardens

EATING
7 Dan Tana's

DRINKING
8 Hamburger Mary's
9 Micky's Weho
10 Mother Lode
see 10 The Abbey
see 10 The Chapel
11 Trunks

SHOPPING
12 Melrose Avenue

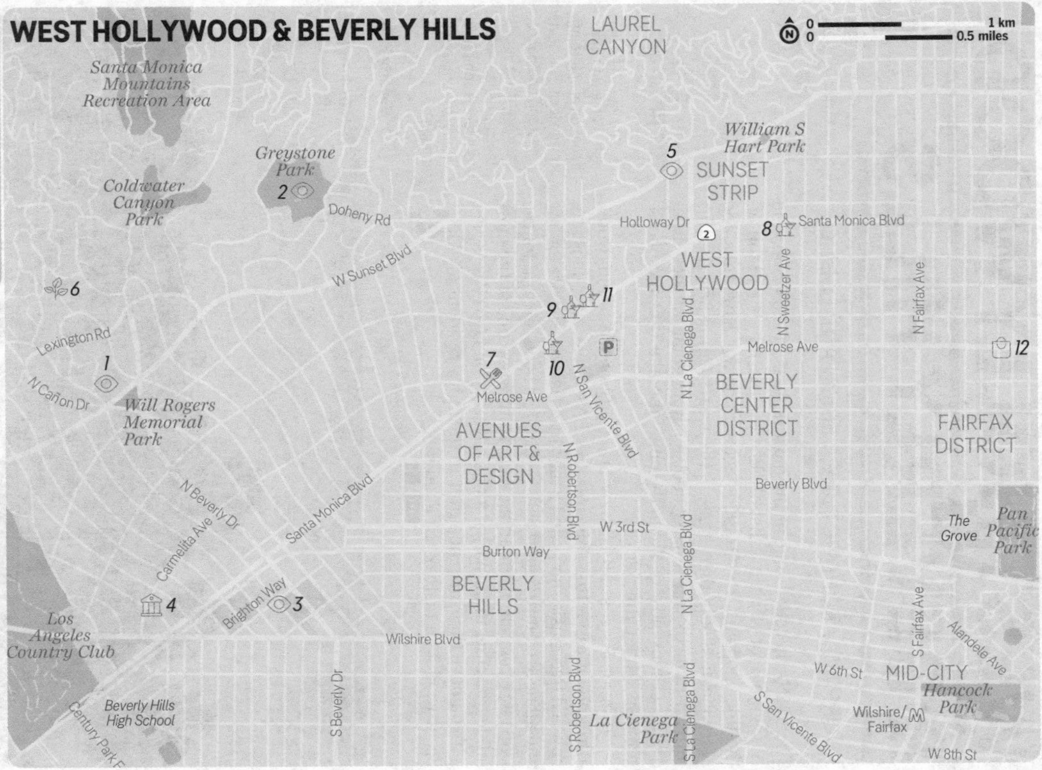

Sunset Strip (p356)

TOP: DOMINICK CORRADO/SHUTTERSTOCK ©; BOTTOM: DAVE G. HOUSER/SHUTTERSTOCK ©

Rodeo Drive

Rodeo Drive

LIFESTYLES OF THE RICH AND FAMOUS

Rodeo Drive is a small street with a big attitude. From Wilshire to Santa Monica you'll encounter palm-tree-lined roads with prestige cars, sidewalks mostly filled with tourists with money to burn and a hilly shopping corner with a cobblestone walkway. Take a leisurely stroll to enjoy window shopping and people-watching – it's an experience just to peruse the flagship stores of Chanel, Louis Vuitton and Harry Winston ('Jeweler to the Stars'), then channel your inner 'Pretty Woman' and head down to the Beverly Wilshire Hotel, where all the magic happened for Vivian Ward (played by Julia Roberts).

Virginia Robinson Gardens

THE BEGINNING OF BEVERLY HILLS

Take a trip back in to time to when Beverly Hills first came to be, at the **Virginia Robinson Gardens**, the first estate and home to be built here back in 1911. The original tenants were Virginia and Harry Robinson, retail giants of the popular Robinson department stores, who went all out with a 20th-century mansion sitting among botanical gardens, plus a Renaissance Revival pool pavilion, modeled after the famous Villa Pisani pool in Italy. The picture-perfect landscapes can be perused at the estate, which can only be seen by appointment. It is also listed on the National Register of Historic Places.

Virginia Robinson Gardens' pool

Beverly Hills Hotel

STANDING THE TEST OF TIME

This timeless hotel sits at the corner of Sunset Blvd and Beverly Dr and has been a beacon of class and glamour for over a century. Retaining an air of exclusivity for LA's elite, it is nicknamed the 'Pink Palace' for its delicate touches of pink hues offset by green, candy-striped furnishings. Add the swaying palm trees and famous Martinique banana-leaf wallpaper, and you can understand why Fred Astaire and Marilyn Monroe spent their time here. The hotel has never grown in size (even after a $100-million renovation in the 1990s) but still retains five stars. Head to the Polo Lounge or Cabana Cafe for the ultimate Beverly Hills experience, or splurge and stay in one of the 23 bungalows.

Greystone Mansion

Greystone Mansion

STUNNING MANSION WITH A HARROWING STORY

If you're going to visit any mansion in Beverly Hills, it should be the Greystone Mansion, a Tudor Revival structure built in 1927 by oil tycoon Edward Doheny. It is a popular film location, used in movies such as *Spiderman* and *There Will Be Blood*, and it's easy to see why, with the impressive grounds of perfectly mowed lawns, Italian Renaissance fountains and the 166ft walkway with enormous cyprus trees. Apart from its cinematic history, the mansion also has a dark past as the location where Edward's son, Ned Doheny, was murdered.

The Spadena House

THE FANTASY OF STORYBOOK HOUSES

If you happen to be roaming the hills on foot, make sure you have a look-see at one of the oddest-looking houses in the predominantly mansion-filled area around the corner of Walden Dr and Carmelita Ave. The Spadena House, also known as The Witch's House because of its droopy, tethered rooftops, strangely shaped wooden windows and moat that's straight out of a *Hansel and Gretel* book. The house was created by Hollywood art director Harry Oliver for studio use only, but was eventually purchased by a real estate agent who has kept its charmingly haunting vibes alive. The best time to visit is, naturally, on Halloween.

The Spadena House

TOP: NOAH SAUVE/SHUTTERSTOCK ©; BOTTOM: MICHAEL VI/SHUTTERSTOCK ©

The Sunset Strip

LEGENDARY STRIP WITH ROCK AND ROLL AT HEART

The Sunset Strip, spanning a 1.5 mile stretch in West Hollywood, has legendary status, signifying rock and roll, exclusive shopping, chic restaurants and a roaring nightlife. During the day it's business as usual, when people pop in and out of Sunset Plaza for a brow tweaking or blow-dry before having lunch at Le Petit Four or the plant-forward Mexican eatery Tocaya. When day turns to night, the strip lights up from all angles and visitors head for cocktails at the stellar Mondrian Sky Bar or art-deco Sunset Tower Hotel, before catching a live show at the Comedy Store or going all out at the Saddle Ranch for a ride on the mechanical bull.

Dan Tana's

WHERE CELEBS EAT CHICKEN PARMIGIANA

This unassuming yellow building is more than meets the eye. Serving Italian American classics since the 1960s, Dan Tana's is a place where you can rub shoulders with celebrities or watch a movie deal being made in one of the red leather booths surrounding the tables draped in red-checkered tablecloths under the magical, dim light. This place is always buzzing with life and packed to the brim, so reservations are highly recommended as the waiting line can get lengthy. Otherwise, the servers and bartenders can whip up a stiff drink while you wait for a table. Then feast on giant portions of pasta and cult faves like the Nika's salad (named after Nicky Hilton), chicken parmesan and veal piccata – these never seem to fail. The prices are high but with the old Hollywood vibe so palpable, it's worthy of a visit.

BOOK SOUP

Book Soup is a sweet bookstore that's been a Sunset Strip fave since 1975. Offering something for all kinds of readers, here among the towering, floor-to-ceiling bookshelves you will find over 60,000 titles from an array of genres, ranging from literary fiction to children's books. The customers are a mix of locals and industry folk who come in not only to pick up a book, but to attend the various events featuring A-list authors and celebrities. There's a smaller version of the store at LA's airport.

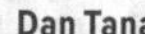

Dan Tana's

Melrose Avenue

ECLECTIC SHOPPING MECCA

The ultimate and ever-eclectic shopping mecca of West Hollywood is centered on Melrose Ave, bordering Beverly Hills and ending in Silver Lake. The stretch is long and changes vibe from luxe to funky to downright strange at points, but it's never dull. The street gained fame during the 1990s when the popular TV show *Melrose Place* aired and the infamous corner, one block north of La Cienega, now caters to high-end fashion labels. Melrose is walkable and there is plenty to keep you entertained. You'll pass the Instagram favorite pink wall of Paul Smith and the Reformation clothing store where everything is made on-site.

Once you descend on Crescent Heights, things feel a bit edgier, with sneaker shops like Adidas Original and the superfunky Posers, which focuses on '80s British culture. From Fairfax, Melrose has even more for sneakerheads with countless stores like Sportie LA and BAIT, which usually have lines around the corner for the latest drop. As you continue along, famed vintage shops like Wasteland and Crossroads Trading Co take center stage.

THE IMAGE PARTY/SHUTTERSTOCK ©

Paul Smith store on Melrose Avenue

The Abbey

AN ICON FOR THE LGBTIQ+ COMMUNITY

From its humble beginnings as a coffee shop to one of the most iconic gay nightclubs in Los Angeles today, The Abbey serves the WeHo community as much more than a nightclub thanks to owner and activist David Cooley. With around three decades in the game, the Abbey, named after its churchlike decor, is a restaurant, dance club and a community place for anyone from anywhere. Mix in the many different-flavored martinis plus a menu of upscale pub food and you'll understand why it's been called the best gay bar in the world, and who are we to argue?

MICHAEL MATTES/SHUTTERSTOCK ©

Drag Queen Bingo at Hamburger Mary's

MORE IN WEST HOLLYWOOD & BEVERLY HILLS

LGBTIQ+ Nightlife

WINE AND DINE AT THE BEST

West Hollywood is renowned for its LGBTIQ+ acceptance and with that comes some of the best places to meet, mingle, drink and dance the night away. The lengthy stretch of Santa Monica Blvd is home to most hot spots, like the iconic **Micky's Weho**, which has been on best-of-everything lists since opening its doors in 1989. With the longest-running drag shows, go-go boys and great DJ sets, it's a place to party but also a huge advocate for the community, hosting various fundraisers. **The Chapel**, the sister venue of the famed Abbey, is a packed, edgy nightclub with great DJs and weekly events that will keep you dancing. For a more low-key affair, make your way to **Mother Lode**, a dive bar that feels a touch calmer yet is still vibrant and offers great drinks. The weekends see more crowds and lots of eye candy. **Trunks**, a laid-back gay sports bar, has live TV sports, billiards and friendly crowds – it has been serving the area for over 30 years. After a night of partying, **Hamburger Mary's** is the spot to be on a Sunday afternoon, with its bottomless mimosas, brunch menu and Drag Queen Bingo.

I LIVE HERE: A LOCAL STORE OWNER'S TOP CHOICES

Tara Riceberg, second-generation Beverly Hills retailer, owner of Tesoro and self-described Curator of Happiness.

Franklin Canyon Park
An unexpected gem in the heart of Beverly Hills, with hiking trails, a picturesque lake and a pond filled with wildlife. It's been a film and TV location since the 1930s.

Fountain Room
Ironically, you'll find more locals than guests having lunch at the Fountain Room in the Beverly Hills Hotel. Order off-menu to enjoy the world-famous Polo Lounge's McCarthy Salad in casual comfort!

Edelweiss Chocolates
When the sugar cravings kick in, head over to Edelweiss. Since 1942 they've been creating chocolates by hand in their Beverly Hills factory. I'm a fan of the dark-chocolate-covered Oreo cookies!

WHERE TO DINE IN BEVERLY HILLS

Nate 'n Al's
Get a bowl of piping-hot matzo-ball soup and a Brentwood sandwich at this Beverly Hills institution. **$$**

Sugarfish
Quality sushi in a small space that is always packed with movie agents and local residents. **$$**

Wally's
This great wine bar and restaurant has outdoor seating and a huge list of wine, mescal and champagne. **$$$**

MIRACLE MILE & MID-CITY

MUSEUMS, FOOD, ETHNICALLY DIVERSE

Smack dab in the middle of LA is the multicultural, multnational Mid-City area that truly emphasizes what the city is all about – its people. It's a hodgepodge of art, natural history, fashion and is chock-full of restaurants. Mid-City encompasses the Miracle Mile (also known as 'Museum Row'), which came into effect in 1920 when AW Ross purchased 18 acres along the boulevard, hoping to rebrand the area into a shopping destination. His friends believed he was crazy, hence the name 'Miracle Mile.'

Today the area extends across Wilshire Blvd between Fairfax and Highland Ave, where a collection of famous museums like Los Angeles County Museum of Art (LACMA) and the La Brea Tar Pits stand side by side. Just north is the Fairfax district, where you'll find the Original Farmers Market and The Grove shopping mall. Things become extremely diversified as the expansive Mid-City area reaches Little Ethiopia, then Koreatown to the east, where ethnic flavors from many countries collide.

TOP TIP

Visit the Charlie Hotel West Hollywood, which was previously owned by Charlie Chaplin. The iron gates, English garden landscaping and bungalows, with their storybook architecture, will transport you back to the 1920s.

Miracle Mile

LEFT: VESPERSTOCK/SHUTTERSTOCK ©; RIGHT: STEVE CUKROV/SHUTTERSTOCK ©

SIGHTS
1 Fairfax District
2 Koreatown
3 La Brea Tar Pits
4 Los Angeles County Museum of Art (LACMA)
5 Petersen Automotive Museum

EATING
6 Gish Bac
7 Guelaguetza
8 Las 7 Regiones
9 Original Farmers Market
10 Sabores Oaxaqueños

SHOPPING
11 The Grove

0 1 km
0 0.5 miles

MELROSE/LA BREA
HANCOCK PARK
FAIRFAX DISTRICT
MID-CITY
MIRACLE MILE
WINDSOR SQUARE
WILSHIRE CENTER
The Grove
Pan Pacific Park
The Wilshire Country Club
Robert Burns Park
La Brea Tar Pit Pond
Ardmore Park
Normandie Park
Wilshire/Fairfax
Wilshire/La Brea
Wilshire/Western
Wilshire/Normandie
N Fairfax Ave
N La Brea Ave
N Highland Ave
N Rossmore Ave
Beverly Blvd
N Wilton Pl
W 3rd St
S Rossmore Ave
W 6th St
Wilshire Blvd
W 8th St
S Normandie Ave
S Fairfax Ave
W Olympic Blvd
S San Vicente Blvd
Hauser Blvd
S La Brea Ave
S Highland Ave
San Vicente Blvd
W Pico Blvd
Venice Blvd
W Washington Blvd
Crenshaw Blvd
Arlington Blvd
S Wilton Pl
S Western Ave
Irolo St

La Brea Tar Pits (p363)

The Grove

TOP: TMP - AN INSTANT OF TIME/SHUTTERSTOCK ©; BOTTOM: RITU MANOJ JETHANI/SHUTTERSTOCK ©

The Grove

OUTDOOR SHOPPING

The Grove is a great place to spend the day shopping in the great LA weather. Just beside the Original Farmers Market, this outdoor mall almost feels like Disneyland with its lively music and atmosphere. A trolley can take you on a short trip through the middle of the mall where you'll pass the dancing fountain that plays to music. Get your shopping fix at Nordstrom or Nike then take a break on the grassy knoll near the fountain.

The Original Farmers Market

FUN FOR THE ENTIRE FAMILY

A permanent fixture since 1934, the Original Farmers Market is a special place for LA locals and a must-see destination for visitors from around the world. It sits at the corner of 3rd and Fairfax – you can't miss the iconic clock tower. You'll find more restaurants than produce and butcher stalls here, but it doesn't make it any less grand. The partially covered space has various shops, famous fare from Pampas Grill and Moishe's and gourmet food boutiques like Marcel. Come here for breakfast or lunch before making your way to The Grove mall just next door.

The Original Farmers Market

Fairfax District

HISTORIC JEWISH COMMUNITY

The historic Fairfax District is bordered by Beverly Grove, La Brea and Melrose and is known as a prominent hub for LA's Jewish community, who began migrating here in the 1920s. Today, the area boasts many kosher as well as halal businesses from that time period. Landmarks like the Los Angeles Museum of the Holocaust are worth a visit, as is the 28-acre Pan Pacific Park, which is a great place for a picnic or a bit of exercise. Stop at Canter's Deli for a pastrami sandwich and drop by the weekly Melrose Trading Post, an incredibly popular flea market. Running every Sunday at Fairfax High School, it sells secondhand goods, furniture and art – book tickets in advance.

LACMA

THE LARGEST MUSEUM IN THE WEST

Standing tall and proud in the heart of Museum Row is the Los Angeles County Museum of Art (LACMA), the largest art museum in the western US. It is synonymous with Chris Burden's outdoor sculpture *Urban Light*, made of 202 cast-iron street lamps. The expansive museum buildings showcase around 149,000 objects, including a mixed collection of modernist and contemporary art pieces from around the world. There's an extensive Asian art collection, Islamic and Latin American works and the likes of Andy Warhol, Picasso, Mondrian, Klee, Kandinsky and Cézanne.

Wooly mammoth fossils, LACMA

Petersen Automotive Museum

TOP: MARK126423/SHUTTERSTOCK ©; BOTTOM: LET GO MEDIA/SHUTTERSTOCK ©

Petersen Automotive Museum

A CAR LOVER'S PARADISE

The hard-to-miss facade of the Petersen Automotive Museum is a breathtaking sight, surrounded by stainless-steel ribbons over a vibrant red exterior. Inside is one of the largest automotive collections in the world, paired with history and a bit of fun for kids, thanks to the setup inspired by the movie *Cars*. You'll find a mix of everything from Hollywood vehicles like the *Back to the Future* DeLorean and the 1992 Batmobile, as well as high-speed performers that you can even sit in. For an extra $20 you can make your way to the 4th floor for a display of rare and vintage cars that changes periodically.

La Brea Tar Pits

TIME TRAVEL TO THE ICE AGE

The La Brea Tar Pits, an Angeleno favorite, is a museum complex surrounded by bubbling tar and filled with more than 3.5 million fossils, including those found on the premises (which are on display), making this place the world's most complete record of what life was like at the end of the Ice Age, about 10,000 to 50,000 years ago. Get a feel for the mammoths and saber-toothed cats that roamed LA and check out the active dig site where you can watch paleontologists at work. The tar pits were recently recognized by the International Union of Geological Sciences as being among the First 100 IUGS Geological Heritage Sites. Purchasing advance tickets is highly recommended.

BEST PLACES TO EAT IN KOREATOWN

Jaebudo
Open until the wee hours of the morning; come here for the grilled seafood prepped Korean-style. $$

Dan Sung Sa
This local favorite is the place to be for its vast menu of sizzling meats and incredible atmosphere. $$

Soowon Galbi
Superb Korean BBQ recommended by the Michelin Guide for its prime cuts of beef grilled to perfection. $$

Guelaguetza
Oaxacan food in K Town? Yes, it's a thing and you don't want to miss these delicious bites. $$

Koreatown

MORE IN MIRACLE MILE & MID-CITY

The Center of Korean Culture in California

THE NEIGHBORHOOD THAT NEVER SLEEPS

New York might be known as the city that never sleeps, but LA's **Koreatown** could easily compete with its 'up and at 'em, 24 hours a day' mindset. Centered on about 3 sq miles and touching the outskirts of Downtown and Hollywood, this

WHERE TO STAY IN MIRACLE MILE AND MID-CITY

Hotel Normandie
In a restored 1926 art-deco building; California glamour shines throughout the property. **$$**

The Line LA
A happening hotel centrally located in Koreatown, with hip amenities and brutalist, modern vibes. **$$**

Kimpton Hotel Wilshire
Perfectly situated in Miracle Mile, this four-star property has comfy accommodations, a pool and good views. **$$$**

area was once the heart and soul of Golden Age Hollywood, when the Academy Awards took place at the Ambassador Hotel (between 1930 and 1943) and when A-listers feasted at the Brown Derby restaurant.

Nowadays Koreatown is a far cry from the Golden Age, and we think it's much better this way. Coming here feels like you have left Los Angeles and entered a bustling city in South Korea. It is home to several shopping malls, particularly KTP (Koreatown Plaza), which has an endless amount of shops and a food court selling authentic and inexpensive Korean street food. The area is made up mostly of Korean as well as Latino communities, the latter from Oaxaca in particular. You can taste some of LA's best mole at Guelaguetza, while K Town is known to have the largest concentration of nightclubs, 24-hour businesses and restaurants and karaoke bars in the country. So what are you waiting for?

Tastes of Oaxaca

OAXACAN FARE ACROSS MID-CITY

Koreatown is known for everything related to the vibrant Northeast Asian country, but it's also home to a large Oaxacan community and is therefore where you can find some of the best, most authentic Oaxacan food in Los Angeles. The story goes that Oaxacans, mainly from Sierra Juárez, migrated to LA in search of a better life and found themselves calling Koreatown and Mid-City home. The 1990s saw a boom in migration and it was also around that time that the VIP Palace, a restaurant built by Korean American businessman Hi Duk Lee, was sold to Oaxacan Fernando Lopez. Lopez preserved the exterior and facade of the building, keeping its ornate paintings and shingles, but converted the interior to the now-famed **Guelaguetza** restaurant, which serves award-winning dishes like its rich Oaxacan mole.

After Guelaguetza, more restaurants started to emerge as it became easier to source indigenous ingredients. The family-owned and operated **Las 7 Regiones** has been running for nearly 30 years and is like a second home to Oaxaquenos. Its menu is a tribute to the seven regions of Oaxaca and includes tamales wrapped in banana leaf and giant quesadillas. **Gish Bac** specializes in a weekend goat *barbacoa* that has the masses pouring in, while **Sabores Oaxaqueños** is the little sister of Guelaguetza.

WHY I LOVE MIRACLE MILE & MID-CITY

Megan Leon, writer

There are too many neighborhoods I adore in LA, but I do have a small love affair with Miracle Mile and Mid-City as it feels like the main artery of Los Angeles. Sure, it's not as beautiful or pristine as West Hollywood, and it can be rough around the edges. However, culturally speaking, this area defines LA for me. Bordering along Koreatown, touching the Jewish district, caressing Little Ethiopia, just a stone's throw from Downtown and stretching to the edge of Palms near Culver City, the latticework of cultures, history and art is a thing behold, and is something that I've always gravitated toward. And the food is a given!

WHERE TO EAT IN MIRACLE MILE AND MID-CITY

Mariscos Jalisco
This roaming food truck is a must for its delicious fried-shrimp tacos covered in homemade salsa. **$**

Roscoe's House of Chicken 'N Waffles
American soul food to the core, Roscoe's has been visited by past US presidents. **$**

n/soto
This offshoot of the high-end n/naka restaurant serves upscale Japanese *izakaya* bites with flair. **$$$**

SANTA MONICA

SCENIC, BEACH, SUNSETS, FRESH AIR

No other place captures LA beach life like Santa Monica, a true slice of the California dream. Centered between Venice and Malibu, Santa Monica is busy but somehow laid-back, with over 4 miles of coastline. With so many attractions, it can sometimes feel a touch touristy, but it never becomes annoying, and in fact it's what makes it unique and a great place for people-watching. The iconic Santa Monica Pier is the main actor but it has a strong supporting cast, including the shopping area of Third Street Promenade, charming Main Street, the art at Bergamot Station and some great restaurants. It's the place to catch the best sunsets and where you can sunbathe on the white sands that meet the giant waves of the Pacific. It is also a gateway to the beautiful beach towns of Venice, the Pacific Palisades and Malibu, which can't all be seen in one day, so plan ahead and spend a few days roaming the beaches.

TOP TIP

One of the best ways to get a feel for LA's coastline is by riding the Marvin Braude Bike Trail. The 22-mile paved path starts in Santa Monica, passing through Venice, Hermosa and Redondo Beach, finally ending in Torrance. Rent a bike at Will Rogers and take the day to breathe in the salty coastal breeze.

Third Street Promenade **(p368)**

HIGHLIGHTS
1 Santa Monica Pier

SIGHTS
2 Annenberg Community Beach House
3 Bergamot Station Arts Center
4 Getty Villa
5 Self-Realization Fellowship Lake Shrine

ACTIVITIES, COURSES & TOURS
6 Brentwood General Store

EATING
7 Breakfast by Salt's Cure
8 Father's Office
9 Locanda Portofino
10 Santa Monica Farmers Markets

SHOPPING
11 Clare V.
see 10 Third Street Promenade

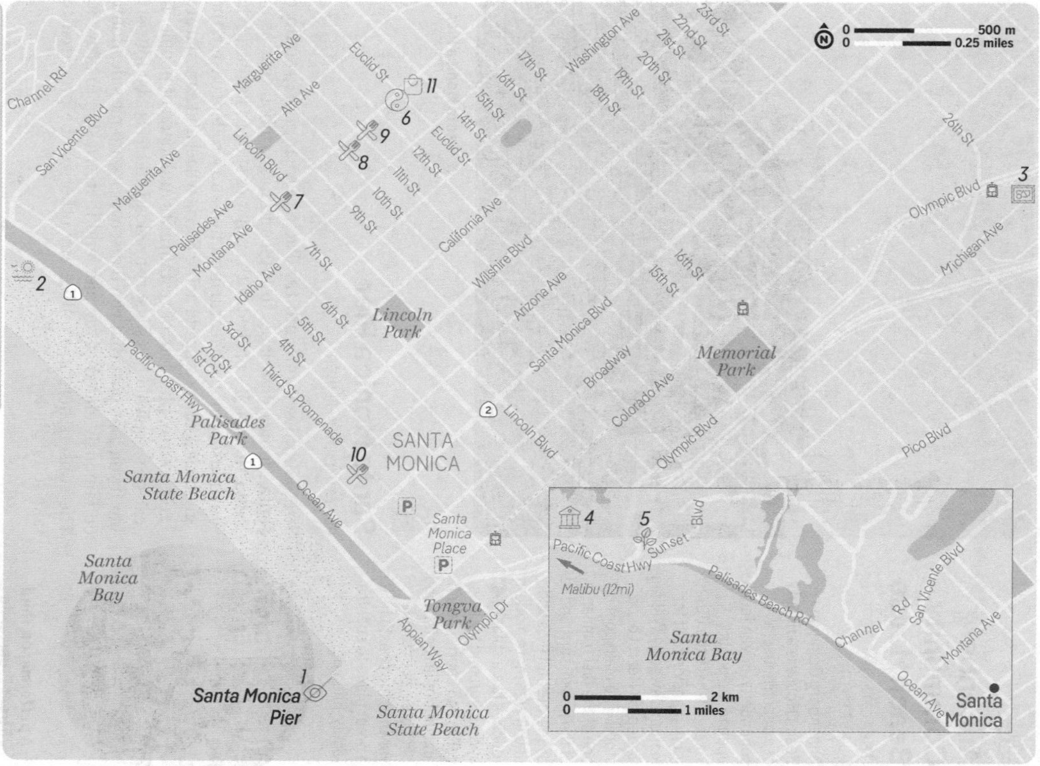

Channel Rd
San Vicente Blvd
Marguerita Ave
Alta Ave
Euclid St
Lincoln Blvd
Palisades Ave
Montana Ave
Idaho Ave
7th St
6th St
5th St
4th St
3rd St
2nd St
1st Ct
Third St Promenade
Pacific Coast Hwy
Ocean Ave
9th St
10th St
11th St
12th St
14th St
15th St
16th St
17th St
18th St
19th St
20th St
21st St
22nd St
23rd St
26th St
Washington Ave
California Ave
Wilshire Blvd
Arizona Ave
Santa Monica Blvd
Broadway
Colorado Ave
Olympic Blvd
Michigan Ave
Pico Blvd
Olympic Dr
Appian Way
Lincoln Park
Memorial Park
Palisades Park
Tongva Park
SANTA MONICA
Santa Monica Place
Santa Monica State Beach
Santa Monica Bay
Santa Monica Pier
0 500 m
0 0.25 miles

Sunset Blvd
Pacific Coast Hwy
Malibu (12mi)
Palisades Beach Rd
Channel Rd
San Vicente Blvd
Montana Ave
Ocean Ave
Santa Monica
Santa Monica Bay
0 2 km
0 1 miles

Getty Villa (p371)

Annenberg Community Beach House

A BEACH HOUSE OPEN TO EVERYONE

Annenberg Community Beach House is a beauty of a beach house, a community-driven facility open to the public, located where the 110-room mansion built for Marion Davies by William Randolph Hearst once stood. The main pool is one of the last remnants of the house, surrounded by marble and tiles and tied in with more modern touches like a splash pad and playground for kids, volleyball courts, beach and umbrella rentals and of course, spectacular views of the coastline. It's a great place to spend a family-filled day.

Santa Monica Pier

Santa Monica Pier

PLAYTIME ON THE PIER

Stretching itself out into the Pacific Ocean, the grandiose Santa Monica Pier dates to 1909 and has symbolic status in Santa Monica. It's packed with activities such as Pacific Park, an amusement park featuring a five-story roller coaster, the gigantic solar-powered Pacific Ferris wheel and a miniature golf course, plus lots of restaurants and loads of people. It can be somewhat of a sensory overload and feels a bit touristy but if you look past that you'll discover its unique side. Route 66 famously ended at the pier, and there's a sign to prove it. The sunsets here are unlike any others so be prepared to take some photos.

A performer on Third Street Promenade

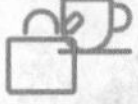

Third Street Promenade

SHOPPING AND PEOPLE-WATCHING

The shopper's paradise of the Third Street Promenade has always been a mainstay of Santa Monica. Just east of the pier, three very long blocks of car-free walking paths converge with over 80 retail shops, a mix of restaurants, kiosks selling knickknacks, and most prominently, live street performers who use the promenade as their main stage. There has been an increase in homelessness as well as tourist numbers here, but the area has always been a part of Santa Monica's charm and it still pulses with LA life. If you want to add more shopping to your agenda, the promenade ends at the luxe Santa Monica Place, a beautiful semioutdoor mall that houses Bloomingdale's, Nordstrom and other high-end stores.

Peter Fetterman Gallery at Bergamot Station

Bergamot Station

A CENTER FOR THE ARTS

The art and cultural hub Bergamot Station is a must for any visitor to Santa Monica. The site was a railroad station between 1875 and 1953, but in 1994 the sprawling 5-acre complex became one of Southern California's largest art galleries and cultural centers, and features everything from contemporary art and a hip cafe to architecture and design companies. It hosts loads of events and has rotating exhibits – check online for the latest info. Birdie G's, from acclaimed chef Jeremy Fox, is a good place to head for dinner.

Santa Monica Farmers Market

LOCAL CALIFORNIA PRODUCE HEAVEN

LA has its fair share of farmers markets in almost every other neighborhood, but none come close to the bounty and rows of colorful produce from California's rich agricultural land found at the Santa Monica Farmers Market. It's here where you'll find the best local produce, rare mushrooms, artisanal cheeses and coffees, and you'll most likely end up rubbing shoulders with some of the best chefs in the city. This is a BYO-bag place and it gets very busy, so it's best to arrive early for a memorable treat for the senses and belly. It's open every Wednesday (8:30am to 1:30pm) and Saturday (8am to 1pm).

Shitake mushrooms at the Santa Monica Farmers Market

Montana Avenue

UPSCALE SHOPPING

Cozy, chic and laid-back, charming shopper-friendly Montana Ave is just a stone's throw from downtown Santa Monica. You'll fall in love with the 10 blocks of upper-end retailers, quaint coffee shops and restaurants, which emanate completely opposite vibes to those of the madness of the Santa Monica Pier and Third Street Promenade.

Grab a morning bite at **Breakfast by Salt's Cure** before venturing down the idyllic avenue, lined with beauty boutiques and boutique shops such as **Clare V.** and **Brentwood General Store**. Dining options such as Father's Office and **Locanda Portofino** might also come with a few celebrity sightings. Get a sugar dose from the towering, delicious cakes at famed **Sweet Lady Jane**.

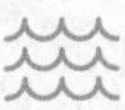

Self-Realization Fellowship Lake Shrine

TAKE A BREATHER

Hidden in the beach town of the Pacific Palisades, just steps from the Pacific Coast Hwy, is a hidden oasis for those who are seeking a bit of calm. Built in 1950, the Self-Realization Fellowship Lake Shrine was opened by Paramahansa Yogananda as a place of meditation where all religions could come together. The main attractions are the lake that's surrounded by various shrines along its pathway, along with the Windmill Chapel and a houseboat that was used by Yogananda for meditation and overnight stays. Beneath the lush greenery you'll find monuments honoring five major world religions – Buddhism, Christianity, Hinduism, Islam and Judaism – as well as an outdoor shrine where an authentic 1000-year-old Chinese stone sarcophagus holds some ashes of Mahatma Gandhi. The meditation gardens are open to the public and are free of charge (Wednesday through Sunday), but advance reservations are mandatory. Its temple is open on Sunday for services.

ORIGINAL MUSCLE BEACH

The Original Muscle Beach was actually founded in Santa Monica, not at Venice Beach as many assume. Its status boomed in the 1950s when Jack LaLanne and other famous bodybuilders and stuntmen trained here. Just south of the pier, it was completely refurbished and now serves as a common place for gymnasts and acrobats as well, and there's even a playground for children. The International Chess Park sits right beside it, where you can play a game and take a walk over the human-sized chessboard.

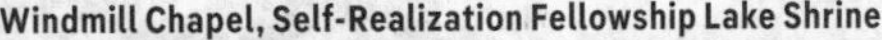

Windmill Chapel, Self-Realization Fellowship Lake Shrine

MIKELEDRAY/SHUTTERSTOCK ©

Beachfront homes in Santa Monica

MORE IN SANTA MONICA

Artworks at Getty Villa

A TOUCH OF OPULENT ROMAN LIFE

Located just north of Santa Monica in the Pacific Palisades is the remarkable Getty Villa. This impressive place was built in 1974 when billionaire J Paul Getty decided to re-create Herculaneum's Villa dei Papiri, a Roman villa that was buried in the eruption of Mt Vesuvius in 79 CE. The focus here is on the art and cultures of ancient Greece, Rome and Etruria, and there's a vast collection of classical and Renaissance-era artworks on display. Corinthian columns surround perfectly manicured gardens and an elongated pool.

Treasures of Sunny Malibu

DREAMY COASTLINE

Head north from Santa Monica and you'll fall upon the dreamy, charming and incredibly scenic seaside city of Malibu. It offers a good mix of easygoing activities, upscale residential mansions and great shopping complexes like **Malibu Country Mart** that are celebrity favorites. Nothing can beat the gorgeous views at **Point Dume** and **El Matador Beach** or the scenic hiking trail of **Escondido Falls** that has a three-tiered waterfall (when the rain is abundant). Make your way to **Malibu Village** to savor a lobster roll with warm butter from **Broadstreet Oyster** – trust us. **Malibu Pier**, the smaller sister of Santa Monica Pier, is just as fun and crowded, with cute restaurants, a few shops and great photo ops.

TONGVA PARK

Tongva Park is a truly special place worthy of a visit. Stretching over 6 acres, this appealing, meticulously designed green space sits around the corner from the Santa Monica Pier and offers a respite (if you need one) from the busy attractions in the area. The park is well lit and maintained, and features unique structures, art sculptures and various walking paths in honor of the indigenous Tongva people, who have called Los Angeles home for thousands of years. There are also palms and agave groves, cascading fountains, amphitheater seating, trim lawns and an adorable, ergonomic playground for tots.

BEST BEACHES AROUND LOS ANGELES

Zuma
Lots of parking and clean stretches of sand make this place a favorite for locals.

El Matador
This Malibu beach is one of the most beautiful in town, with rock formations and clean sands.

Surfrider Beach
This World Surfing Reserve made famous by surf legends is always packed with action.

VENICE

BOHEMIAN, EDGY, FOOD AND OUTDOORS

Founded in 1905 by Abbot Kinney, this one-of-a-kind beach town encapsulates a free-spirited, bizarre yet truly California vibe that can't be felt anywhere else in the world. For most outsiders, Venice Beach is synonymous with one place, the Boardwalk. It sits at the top of many best lists and while this is totally justifiable, it's not the place it used to be – it can get a bit weird, there are some interesting characters and it feels a touch run down. However, there are still scores of things to see, like the giant skate park and Muscle Beach, and you'll discover that Venice is a very hip and artsy area that's beaming with charisma. With the intoxicating salty sea breeze that embodies LA beach life, and from the romantic Venice Canals to the finesse of Abbot Kinney Blvd, these are the places to wander, get lost and start all over again in.

TOP TIP

Want to get a real feel for the Pacific Ocean? Head to Aloha Brothers Surf Lessons and give surfing a go right in the heart of Venice Beach. The surf school has great instructors that will guide you from the sand right into the sea.

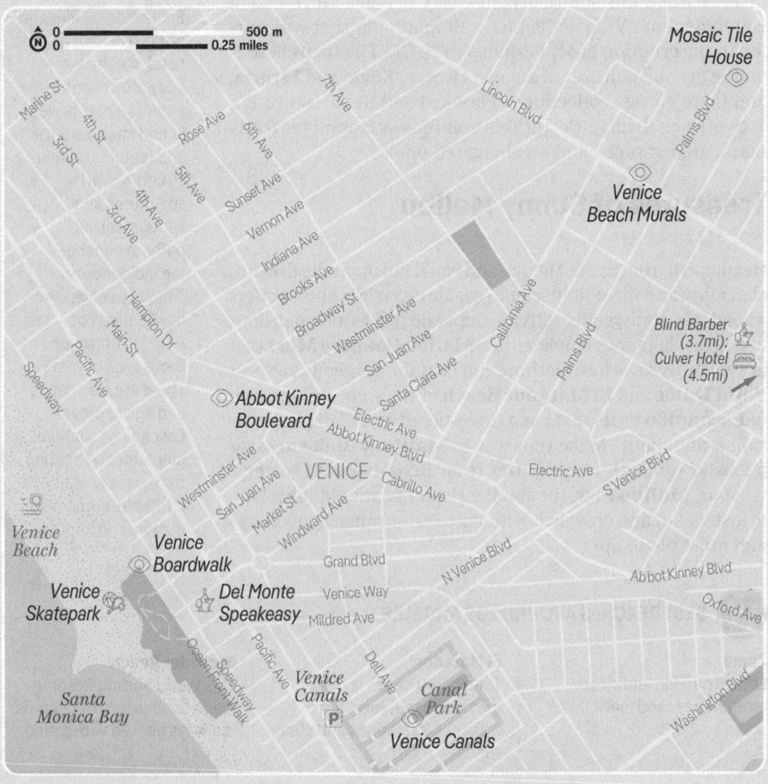

Abbot Kinney Boulevard

THE KING OF SHOPPING STREETS

A real gem in Venice Beach is Abbot Kinney Blvd, a mile-long stretch running from Washington Blvd to Santa Monica's Main St that's charmingly dotted with chic boutiques, excellent restaurants and bohemian art shops catering to any need or desire. The best way to experience the strip is by starting at the corner of Venice Blvd where the gourmet supermarket **Erewhon** is located, and making your way down the street.

Erewhon, Abbot Kinney Boulevard

Venice Canals

ITALIAN VIBES BY THE SEA

Venice Canals

If there's one thing to see in Venice, it has to be the Venice Canals that are uniquely embedded in the heart of an upper-end residential area. The picturesque canals were created in 1905 by developer and conservationist Abbot Kinney, who wanted to replicate Italy's famed waterways, dubbing the area the 'Venice of America.' What was once an expansive place of unique bridges and canals has shrunk in size, with only six canals remaining, but the beauty and charm has never faded, especially with the mix of modern and bohemian homes that line the pathways. It also serves as one of the best sunset spots in the area.

Mosaic Tile House

EYE-CATCHING COLORS IN A RESIDENTIAL AREA

The rainbow-bedazzled stucco home of couple Cheri Pann and Gonzalo Duran has been an integral part of the whimsical Venice Beach world for more than two decades, and it's still a work in progress. Located in a residential neighborhood, the Mosaic Tile House stands out with its vibrant colors of red, yellow and blue glistening from the ground up. It has been a team effort between the two artists: one creates the mosaics then the other shatters them and masterfully decorates every nook and cranny, in designs from angel wings to what seems like an underwater world of treasures. It's open on Saturdays, and it's best to make an online reservation to avoid lines.

Mural by Rip Cronk in Venice Beach

Venice Beach Murals

ART SPLASHED AGAINST THE WALLS

Venice Beach is home to an abundant collection of murals spread across the area, from the Boardwalk to Abbot Kinney Blvd. There are a few street-tour options available but if you want to venture out on your own, make sure to look out for the giant wings by Barry's Boot Camp, and the Ballerina Clown, created by Jonathan Borofsky. There is also a condensed section between Washington Blvd and Rose Ave that is walkable and worth exploring.

Skate Park

THE FIRST-EVER SKATE PARK

This oceanfront skatepark is a monumental landmark for the skating world. Venice Beach was the birthplace of skateboarding and is home to the world's most expensive skatepark (it cost $3.5 million). The 1970s saw the rise of a group of skateboarders who formed the Zephyr Skateboarding Team and soon surf shops started to pop up along Venice and Santa Monica, known then as Dogtown. Skateboarding legend Jesse Martinez fought for 20 years for the creation of a skateboarding home base; there's even a documentary called *Made in Venice* (2016) that covers this skateboarding history. Anyone can come here to skate and watch for free.

Skate Park

Del Monte Speakeasy

OLDEST SALOON IN VENICE BEACH

The Del Monte Speakeasy operated sometime between 1920 and 1930 during the Prohibition era. A place full of interesting characters, it appeared as a fruit and vegetable stand outside, with a secret bar in the basement. Now one of the oldest and coolest bars to visit in Venice Beach, it has two floors: upstairs is called the Townsend and below The Del Monte, with both retaining a mysterious, speakeasy vibe. For a true taste of Venice Beach life, come here early to sip on a hand-crafted cocktail, like a Moscow Mule, then stay for the guest DJs and eclectic crowd that fills up the space by 11pm.

Venice Beach & the Boardwalk

THE EDGY SIDE OF THE BEACH

Although this was once was *the* place to visit, Venice Beach and its Boardwalk are certainly past their prime, giving off a grittier, almost sketchy vibe since the pandemic began, with some questionable sights. With that said, it's still a very important part of LA culture, with iconic spots that still shine with local spirit. Make your way to the recently renovated Muscle Beach for optimal viewing of serious weightlifters who put on a great show. Also check out the skatepark: with the beach in the background it is the perfect spot for a golden-hour sunset you won't find anywhere else in the world. Make your way northside, where you'll find the Venice Pride Flag lifeguard tower – unveiled in 2017, in a city that has always been known as inclusive and diverse. And it wouldn't be a day at Venice Beach without browsing the souvenir shops and walking the streets filled with plumes of dubious smells.

HOTEL ERWIN

You would never know from the outside that since 1970 the Hotel Erwin, located in the heart of Venice, has been the place to be for catching one of the best sunsets in the neighborhood. Head to the High Rooftop Lounge for sundowners and small bites to take in the one-of-a-kind view of the multicolored California sunset over the Pacific Ocean. If you opt to stay at the accommodations here, it has bikes, coolers and volleyballs available to guests for the ultimate LA beach experience.

Venice Beach Boardwalk

LET GO MEDIA/SHUTTERSTOCK ©

Culver Hotel

MORE IN VENICE

Historic & Hidden Culver City

THE HEART OF SCREENLAND

Culver City is an area rich in cinematic history and has come to be known as 'the Heart of Screenland.' Sitting just between Downtown and Venice Beach, and only about 15 minutes from LAX airport, Culver City has much to offer, though it is easily passed over by visitors to LA for famous areas like Hollywood. Metro-Goldwyn-Mayer built its studios here in the 1920s, which later became **Sony Pictures Studios**, the area's largest employer (it also offers walking tours for visitors). The aviator Howard Hughes also opened his **Hughes Aircraft Company** plant here back in 1941. In modern times, Culver City has seen a major sprucing up to its downtown and it is now a vibrant area, filled with a younger crowd roaming the area for great eats or taking in shows at the **Kirk Douglas Theatre**.

Those looking for great views can head to the **Baldwin Hills Scenic Overlook**: on good days you can see across the LA Basin up to Santa Monica. History buffs can visit the **Wende Museum** and immerse themselves in artifacts and exhibits from the Cold War era. If you plan to stay in the area, look no further than the **Culver Hotel**, set in a stunning art-deco flatiron building. A 1924 historic landmark, it still retains its old Hollywood glamour. A night out in this cute neighborhood should alway include a stop at the **Blind Barber**, a hairdresser that doubles as hidden speakeasy serving great cocktails to a vibrant crowd.

BEST EATS & DRINKS IN CULVER CITY

Roberta's Pizza
Brooklyn-based pizzeria in Culver City, doling out piping-hot wood-fired pizzas. $$

Tito's
Lip-smackingly crunchy tacos loaded with beef, lettuce and cheese – one is never enough. $

Johnnie's Pastrami
This place is all about the pastrami, served to locals since 1952. $

Destroyer by Jordan Kahn
Step out of your brunch comfort zone here, where futuristic vibes collide with everyday ingredients. $$

Mandrake Bar
A hip watering hole catering to the arts crowd and anyone who loves old-school tunes.

BEST PLACES TO EAT IN VENICE

Felix
People flock here for maestro chef Evan Funke's *rigatoni all'amatriciana*. **$$$**

Gjusta
This Venice outpost is filled to the brim with diners enjoying seasonal California bites from the massive deli counter. **$$**

Cafe Gratitude
Delicious vegan dishes here are paired with an open patio and fresh sea breezes. **$$**

DOWNTOWN

URBAN, ART, DINING AND CULTURE

Downtown Los Angeles is not your typical downtown area: it's relatively small compared to others in the US, and is made up of smaller diverse neighborhoods that all converge together.

It's home to the actual birthplace of LA, El Pueblo de Los Ángeles, the oldest section of the city (dating to 1781). Mexican culture is deeply rooted here, and just as integral are the Chinese and Japanese diasporas that have long lived in the area. The first community of Chinese immigrants arrived in the 19th century, staying in the area where Union Station is located now. The second Chinatown was a bit further north, while on the other side of town, not far from the Arts District, is Tokyo Town, home to the largest population of Japanese in North America.

Downtown is a melting pot of culture and art. One corner can be full of life, the next could have the remnants of skid row, and another turn could lead you to spectacular museums and art exhibits.

TOP TIP

Downtown is an important stop for any traveler, but it's always been known for having a little bit of a dark streak, with some questionable people and sights. When in the area be aware of your surroundings. It's best not to walk around here too late at night, especially alone.

Chinatown (p380)

DOWNTOWN

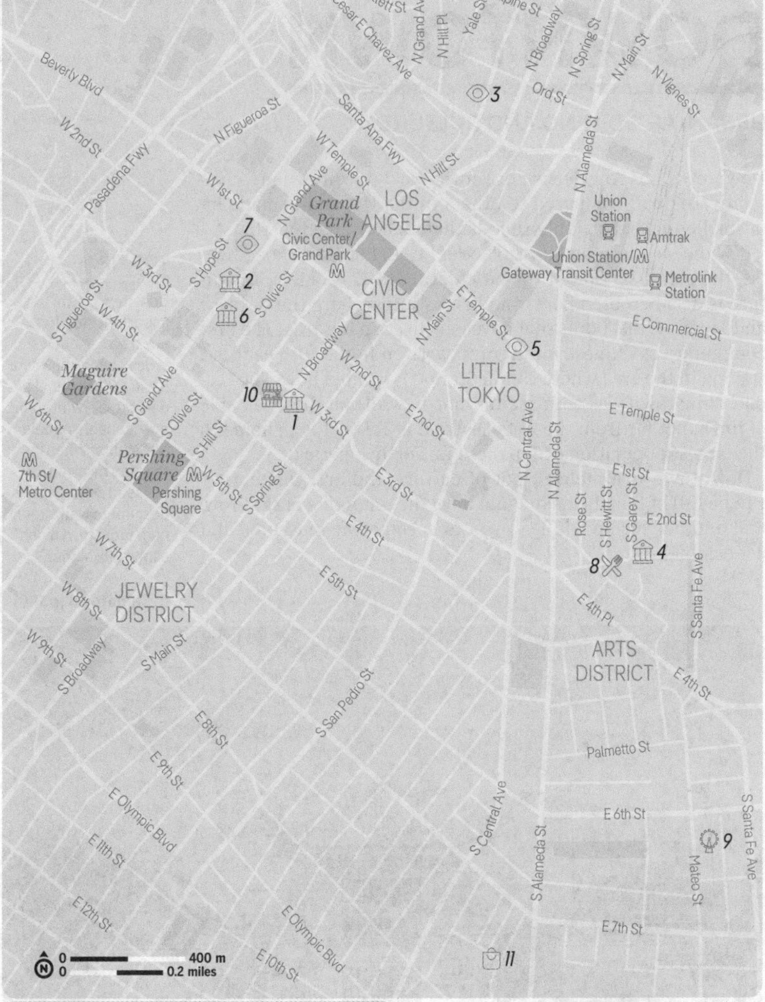

SIGHTS
1 Bradbury Building
2 Broad
3 Chinatown
4 Hauser & Wirth
5 Little Tokyo
6 MOCA
7 Walt Disney Concert Hall

EATING
8 Cha Cha Chá

ENTERTAINMENT
9 Two Bit Circus

SHOPPING
10 Grand Central Market
11 ROW DTLA

Walt Disney Concert Hall

MOCA

A BREATHTAKING COLLECTIVE

Adding to the collection of museums on Grand Ave in Bunker Hill is the **Museum of Contemporary Art (MOCA)**, where you can while away some time browsing a remarkable collection of contemporary pieces from 1940 until the present day. The only artist-founded museum in Los Angeles, it was designed by Arata Isozaki and features art by big names such as Mark Rothko, Jackson Pollock and David Hockney. After taking a look around, head to the cafe and the MOCA store.

TOP: WALTER CICCHETTI/SHUTTERSTOCK ©; BOTTOM: ROAMING PANDA PHOTOS/SHUTTERSTOCK ©

MOCA

The Broad

CONTEMPORARY ART FOR EVERYONE

The Broad

Just next door to the Walt Disney Concert Hall is the well-loved Broad, a museum housing nearly 2000 works of contemporary and post-WWII art. It was founded by philanthropists Eli and Edythe Broad, who spent nearly 50 years creating a space and art collection to make contempoary art accessible. The exterior is an innovative, honeycombed structure, while the interior features two floors of gallery space with a stunning mishmash of paintings and sculptures from celebrated artists like Jean-Michel Basquiat, Jasper Johns, Jeff Koons, Yayoi Kusama and Andy Warhol. Don't forget to stop by the gift shop. Admission is free but advanced timeslot bookings are highly recommended.

Walt Disney Concert Hall

OVER-THE-TOP ARCHITECTURE

The most eye-catching symbol of Downtown has to be the Walt Disney Concert Hall, on the corner of First St and Grand Ave. Designed by acclaimed architect, Frank Gehry, the striking building is made up of steel waves and curves that were designed specifically to enhance the acoustics. Inside the auditorium, the seating is made from Alaskan yellow cedar. A giant 6134-pipe organ, also designed by Gehry along with Manuel Rosales, is something to behold, especially when watching a live performance by the LA Philharmonic, who call this place home. The outdoor area features the Blue Ribbon garden that pays tribute to Lillian Disney and her love of Royal Delft porcelain, which Gehry used to create a mosaic-like flower fountain.

Grand Central Market

Grand Central Market

A GLOBAL CULINARY FEAST

The Grand Central Market is the place for any food lover who wants to get a feel for the many cultures of LA in one spot. Taking up the ground floor of the beaux-arts-style Homer Laughlin Building, the GCM has been a food haven since 1917, embracing the immigrant community that makes LA unique and showcasing local LA vendors and up-and-coming restaurants. From tacos de carnitas, Salvadoran *pupusas* to pad Thai, the sky is truly the limit if you're looking to immerse yourself in food culture.

Bradbury Building

OLDEST BUILDING IN DOWNTOWN

The Bradbury Building made its debut in 1893 after Lewis Bradbury, who made his fortune in the mining industry, came across young, unknown architect George Wyman, who was inspired by a more modern and science-fiction aesthetic. Wyman designed one of the most legendary buildings in downtown LA, with ornate iron railings, natural light from the glass ceiling, marble stairs and wooden moldings, with a Romanesque exterior. Much of the original architecture is still here and the building is worth a look, even though visitors are only allowed on the ground floor.

Bradbury Building

Chinatown

A MIX OF OLD AND NEW

After moving from its original location in 1938 to make way for Union Station, 'New' Chinatown has emerged as a modern-day tourist hub. You'll know you've arrived when you spot the Dragon Gate, basically the gateway to Chinatown. Far East Plaza was one of the first ethnic shopping malls in America, while down the street is Central Plaza, home to a massive statue of Bruce Lee who used to have a studio located here. Food is of most importance in the area and it's not just centered around Chinese food anymore, with some of the biggest culinary names setting up shop here. No visit to the area is complete without eating at **Pearl River Deli**, **Hop Woo** or LA institution, **Philippe The Original**, for French dip sandwiches.

MORE IN DOWNTOWN

Iconic Japanese Enclave

CULTURAL LANDMARK WITH SOUL

To the north of Downtown lies **Little Tokyo**, a robust Japanese community that's been around since the early 1900s. With the sudden boom of immigrants, naturally, local shops and restaurants began to pop up, and a few are still around to tell their story. Centered in the middle is the Japanese Village, with paper lanterns and swervy pathways, filled to the brim with shops selling all kinds of Japanese treats and knickknacks. Want to take some snacks back home? Stop by **Nijiya Market**. Searching for more history? Head to the **Japanese American National Museum** just next to The **Geffen Contemporary**, an exhibition space owned by MOCA.

Diverse, Artsy Heart of LA

IMMERSE YOURSELF IN THE CREATIVE ARTS

The Arts District is one of the coolest places in Downtown. Though it borders along the gritty side of skid row and has taken a massive blow during COVID-19 times, the feeling here is of an alternative world beaming with creativity. Since the 1970s, artists have flocked here for the low rent and working space, though with gentrification, prices have skyrocketed and the blocks on the eastern edge of Downtown now have swanky galleries and shops, hip eateries and mural-covered buildings. The **Hauser & Wirth** gallery displays contemporary art and has a great restaurant called **Manuela**, while **Two Bit Circus** is something different: dubbed a social playhouse, it has immersive entertainment, game zones and escape rooms for the entire family. While you're in the area, stop at **Cha Cha Chá** for a dose of Mexican flavors, and discover the stores of **ROW DTLA**, a destination in its own right.

I LIVE HERE: A CHEF'S BEST OF DOWNTOWN LIST

Wedchayan 'Deau' Arpapornnopparat, owner of the popular takeout window Holy Basil, with partner Tongkamal 'Joy' Yuon.

Stumptown Coffee
I go here every morning for our coffee run before our lunch service. We love their style of making coffee, from cold brew to ice latte with oat milk.

Sonoratown
After a busy lunch service we always order from Sonoratown – our personal favorites are Tripa Taco and Tripa Lorenza.

Holbox
What's not to love about this place? Our favorites are *scallop aguachile* and all the salsas.

BoomTown Brewery
Our go-to place when we want to party.

Vintage Shopping
ROW DTLA has supercool specialty boutique shops – we usually go to the General Store.

WHERE TO EAT IN DOWNTOWN

Langer's Deli
Iconic deli known for the slices of warm pastrami in its famous number 19 sandwich. **$$**

Bavel
Specializing in Middle Eastern sharing dishes in a dreamy, lush setting. Reservations are highly recommended. **$$**

Camphor
Michelin-starred Camphor is led by two Alain Ducasse–trained chefs who now bring their own skills to French cuisine. **$$$**

BURBANK & UNIVERSAL CITY

MOVIE MANIA, FAMILY FRIENDLY, SUBURBAN

Burbank might not be on everyone's must-see list given what the rest of LA has to offer, but it is nonetheless integral to the city. Dubbed the 'media capital of the world,' here you will find all the big names, such as the Walt Disney Company, Warner Bros Cartoon Network and Nickelodeon, and it's where many live studio recordings are done today. On the outskirts is Universal City, the home of the only amusement park and working studio in the world, Universal Studios Hollywood. Besides the theme park, there isn't much else to do in the area so it's best to get a little adventurous and make your way to Pasadena, which is rich in history and landmarks, and then go a bit further to San Gabriel, now hailed as the new Chinatown and offering some of the best Chinese food in the entire city.

TOP TIP

We recommend that you purchase all your theme-park and studio-tour tickets for Universal Studios Hollywood in advance to avoid long lines, and if you can, get the express pass to get more out of the day.

Wildwood Canyon Park

WILDLIFE WITH A VIEW

Wildwood Canyon Park is located in the Verdugo Mountains. Head here for a challenging hike on a clear day to get a full view of Burbank, and, if you're really lucky, downtown LA. The hike is approximately 5 miles from start to finish, and there are different paths for all levels of hikers. Make sure you bring plenty of water and pack sunscreen for hot, sunny days. If you want to make the day extra special, time your visit here for the spectacular sunset views.

Wildwood Canyon Park

Bob's Big Boy

STACK THEM BIG BOYS UP

It doesn't get any more American than Bob's Big Boy, with its famous advert featuring the cow-licked cheeky kid, who hasn't aged a bit since serving his first double-decker more than half a century ago. Slinging burgers since 1949, this is the oldest remaining location of the burger chain that serves simple eats like fried chicken and creamy milkshakes. The Burbank location also comes with a side of entertainment history, including the same booth The Beatles dined in way back in 1964. The cantilevered roof seems to float above the restaurant and recalls the work of Frank Lloyd Wright, and its 70ft-tall sign is a local landmark.

Bob's Big Boy

Warner Bros Studio Tour

AN INSIDER LOOK AT FILM AND TV

If Burbank is known for anything, it's for the famed Warner Bros Studio Tour, at one of the most important filmmaking facilities in the world. Classics including *Casablanca*, *Batman* and *Jurassic Park* and other favorites such as *Friends, Gilmore Girls, Ellen* and *La La Land* were shot on the premises, and visitors can get a real-life feel for how and where they were filmed. With various tour options available, you will be taken around the 110-acre studio by trolley, learning about its history while checking out the backlots and exhibits, including making an exclusive stop at Central Perk from *Friends*. The tours offer a fun yet authentic look behind the scenes at a major movie studio and its technical departments, including props and costumes.

Tally Rand

GOOD EATS, EASY ON THE WALLET

One of the oldest family-owned restaurants in the area, Tally Rand has been a local staple for over 60 years in Los Angeles. It does American classics well and is known for roasting its own turkeys, in addition to offering staples like buttermilk pancakes and endless varieties of sandwiches. Weekends are jam-packed with people feasting on turkey dinners, served with homemade mash, creamy gravy and cranberry sauce. The menu even states the turkey dinner was a favorite of Huell Howser, a California TV icon.

The Colony Theatre

The Colony Theatre

A THEATER WITH LOTS OF CHARM

The small but beloved Colony Theatre has grown from small-town local spot to one of the 25 most notable US theater companies, according to the Encyclopedia Britannica Almanac. Since 1975, the Colony has been a launching pad for Broadway musicals and actors with its vast variety of plays and special performances. The consistent and intriguing schedule has seen past productions such as *Guys and Dolls* and *Driving Miss Daisy*. The venue has optimal viewing wherever you sit but make sure you make your way there on the early side as the theatre can be tricky to find.

Porto's Bakery

TOP: BARRY WINIKER/GETTY IMAGES ©; BOTTOM: LEIGH GREEN/ALAMY ©

Porto's Bakery

GUAVA PASTRIES TO DIE FOR

The heart and soul of Cuban cuisine can be found at family-operated Porto's Burbank, which has been around for over five decades. It has developed a cultlike following particularly for its flaky guava and cream-cheese pastries, which have a deeper meaning than most pastries. The guava pastry called a Refugiado (refugee) is an ode to the owners' memories of Cuba and their migration to the USA. You can also get perfectly griddled Cubano sandwiches, *ropa vieja* and delicious cakes. The lines are no joke, however, and snake around the corner on most days. We recommend getting here early to avoid the hours-long queue, or calling ahead of time to preorder.

Universal Studios Hollywood

FUN FOR EVERYONE

Los Angeles is the home base of Universal Studios Hollywood – perched at the top of Universal City, this is a working studio and amusement park that gives visitors an inside look at how movies are made. Fans of *Harry Potter* can experience a replica of Hogwarts Castle, visit the shops of Hogsmeade, and even choose a wand from Ollivanders Wand Shop, before taking a ride on Harry Potter and the Forbidden Journey, which soars thrillingly above Hogwarts. Other attractions include Jurassic World: The Ride and various live shows around the large park. The studio tour, however, is by far one of the most famous experiences at the theme park. It takes you on a tram ride through the studio backlots, accompanied by a pre-recorded narration by talk-show host Jimmy Fallon. You'll drive through the famous *Jaws* and *Psycho* sets and go face to face with King Kong. It's a good idea to arrive early, before the crowds, to make the most of your time here.

SNACK TIME AT UNIVERSAL STUDIOS HOLLYWOOD

Are you a fan of *The Simpsons*? Have you ever been curious about trying the famous pink doughnut on the TV series? If so, head over to Springfield to find the doughnut shop called **Lard Lad Donuts**. If you want to sink your teeth into the brightest, sprinkle-speckled doughnut, make sure you say the secret code word 'Giant Pink,' and you'll be in for the sweetest hit of the day.

Entrance to Universal Studios Hollywood

DISNEYLAND & ORANGE COUNTY

SUN, SAND & SURF

This quintessentially beachy part of California has warm weather and sunny days year-round, and it's home to Disneyland, the state's largest tourist attraction.

You've likely heard that what makes California so great is that 'you can go to the beach and go skiing in the same day.' When people say that – and make no mistake, everyone says that and no one ever does it – they're talking about Orange County. When you're in one of the absolutely picturesque seaside cities, you're only about two hours from Southern California ski destinations. You can see the snowcapped San Gabriel Mountains especially well in Anaheim, particularly from higher-up places in and around Disneyland.

But when you're in Orange County, cold weather is likely going to be the furthest thing from your mind. This sunny, sandy stretch of paradise has 42 miles of coastline. In addition to beaches, there are nearly endless points of interest, including vibrant art museums and cultural attractions, historic areas, and nature preserves, on both land and sea, just waiting to be explored. Inland, you'll find the larger Orange County cities like Anaheim, Santa Ana and Irvine. Anaheim is home to one very, very famous mouse; nearby, Buena Park has another of California's iconic theme parks, Knott's Berry Farm. By the shore, which is where you'll want to spend the majority of your time in the OC, are all the places you've seen on television before, like Huntington Beach, Newport Beach and Laguna Beach.

DAVID MCNEW/GETTY IMAGES ©

THE MAIN AREAS

DISNEYLAND
Where childhood dreams come true. **p392**

HUNTINGTON BEACH
Surf capital of California (and the USA). **p402**

NEWPORT BEACH
A chic destination to see and be seen. **p407**

FIIPHOTO/SHUTTERSTOCK ©

Left: Disneyland (p392); Above: Huntington Beach Pier (p404)

Find Your Way

There's a lot packed into Orange County's 948 square miles, of which 16% is water. If you're only here for a short time, stick to prime beach locations for a taste of the OC lifestyle.

Huntington Beach, p402
Surf City USA is where the sport first caught on in America, way before Hawaii was a state, and surf vibes are everywhere here.

Disneyland, p392
Disneyland is a big part of Anaheim, but it's not everything. The Anaheim Packing District is a collection of rehabbed factories that house food stalls, breweries and wineries.

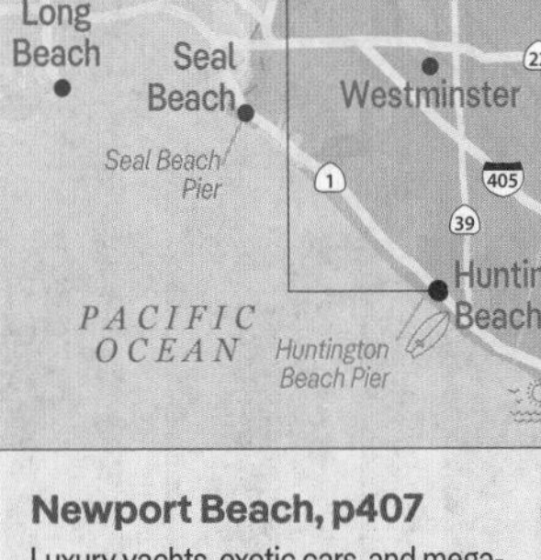

Newport Beach, p407
Luxury yachts, exotic cars, and mega-mansions balance out serene beaches, quiet waterfront restaurants and charming old-school boardwalk attractions.

CAR
The easiest and most convenient mode of transportation in Orange County is definitely to have your own vehicle. Traffic is unpredictable, you'll likely be happier being able to strategically plan around busy times of day and spend less time stuck on the freeway.

BUS
Especially if you're planning to visit the theme parks, you might want to consider skipping the parking fees and the lines to get into the garages by taking Anaheim Regional Transportation (the ART bus) to get there.

BICYCLE
One of the absolute supreme pleasures of an Orange County visit is renting a bicycle and pedaling down Pacific Coast Highway, which links all of the beach towns via a stretch of waterfront road about 40 miles long.

0 20 km
0 10 miles

SANDRA FOYT/SHUTTERSTOCK ©

Sherman Library & Gardens (p409), Newport Beach

Plan Your Time

Orange County is a place to slow down and soak in the atmosphere. Whether you're looking to bliss out on a beach or have an outdoor adventure, you're guaranteed to find beautiful places to explore.

JUANCAT/SHUTTERSTOCK ©

Crescent Bay Beach (p413)

If You Only Do One Thing

● Spend the day in **Newport Beach** (p407), where you'll get the highest concentration of quintessentially Orange County scenery and activities in one place. Within just a few miles, you can enjoy a perfectly California boardwalk and beach community on **Balboa Peninsula** (p409), complete with an old-time beach amusement park. From there, take the ferry to **Balboa Island** (p409) for one of Newport's famous frozen bananas or head to **Corona del Mar** (p409) for a stroll in its cliffside waterfront park. Change for dinner and enjoy the sunset at a posh restaurant by the harbor in **Mariner's Mile** (p409).

Seasonal Highlights

People associate Orange County with summertime, but the off-season has weather that's just as beautiful, with much smaller crowds and lower hotel prices – plus seasonal events worth exploring.

JANUARY

A three-day showcase of Vietnamese food and culture, the **Tet Festival** in Costa Mesa is the country's biggest celebration of the Vietnamese New Year.

MARCH

Head to the trails of Laguna Beach's Laguna Coast Wilderness Parks to catch some of California's famous **wildflower superbloom**.

APRIL

Jack's Surfboards Pro in Huntington Beach brings in top surfers from around the world to qualify for the World Surfing League.

MIKELEDRAY/SHUTTERSTOCK ©, LITTLENYSTOCK/SHUTTERSTOCK ©, ALLEN J. SCHABEN/LOS ANGELES TIMES VIA GETTY IMAGES ©

Three Days to Travel Around

- Next spend a day at the 'happiest place on earth', **Disneyland** (p392). For classic attractions and pure nostalgia, head to **Disneyland Park** (p394). For thrill rides, excellent food and the Marvel Cinematic Universe, choose **Disney California Adventure** (p395). A park hopper ticket gives you access to both, but if you're only planning to spend one day, stick to one and really experience all of it.

- Recover from your thrilling (and crowded) theme park day in **Laguna Beach** (p412), where the scenery is unparalleled and you can explore the seaside shops, public art and coastal landscape at your own leisurely pace.

If You Have More Time

- See Orange County by bicycle, starting in **Seal Beach** (p406) and heading south through **Huntington Beach** (p402), **Newport Beach** (p407), **Laguna Beach** (p412) and **Dana Point** (p413). The route straight through is about 40 miles, but if you veer off Pacific Coast Highway into the cities, it will be longer. Take a few days to take it slow and soak in the relaxing coastal vibes that define Orange County.

- Finally, for a marine adventure, go whale-watching or take a harbor cruise, both of which are available from every city's waterfront area.

JUNE
Newport Beach's annual **Jazz Festival** is three days of world-class concerts performed overlooking pristine nature preserves and the sweeping seascape.

JULY
Laguna Beach's world-famous **Sawdust Arts Festival** shows the creative, eclectic side of the city with a massive celebration including art lessons.

OCTOBER
For spooky fun, head to Disneyland's **Oogie Boogie Bash** Halloween party. For something scarier, try the terrifying **Knott's Scary Farm** event.

NOVEMBER
The lights go up on Sleeping Beauty Castle and the holiday festivities at **Disneyland** go into full swing, with parades, seasonal rides and fun foods.

DISNEYLAND

When Walt Disney dreamed up Disneyland, there was no other place like it – a truly immersive theme park that would delight kids and adults in equal measure. 'Here age relives fond memories of the past,' Disney said in his opening day speech on July 17, 1955, 'and here youth may savor the challenge and promise of the future.'

The park that opened in Anaheim that day, with only a handful of attractions, looked a lot different than it does today, but one thing remains the same: storytelling that feels like it blurs the line between magic and reality. It's there in everything from genre-defying rides like Star Wars: Rise of the Resistance to the 'snow' that falls over Main Street, USA every night during the holiday season, even though it has only snowed real snow three times in nearly 200 years in Orange County.

Disneyland Park (p394)

JEFFREY WHYTE/ALAMY©

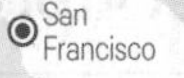

TOP TIP

Whether you're planning a day at Disneyland or an entire vacation, you're going to need to download the Disneyland app. With the app, you can keep track of ride wait times, order food, make dining reservations and lots more.

PLANNING AHEAD

Something that's different from the Disneyland of the past (and from other theme parks) is that a visit requires a fair amount of advance planning. The park requires a valid ticket, but also a park reservation for that day, made through the Disneyland app or website. Especially during busy times like school breaks and seasonal events, those reservations fill up quickly. If you're thinking about incorporating Disneyland into your travels, make sure you'll be able to get in, and secure your spot while it's still available. The same goes with dining: if you have a restaurant on your list, make a reservation when the 60-day advance window opens up for your date.

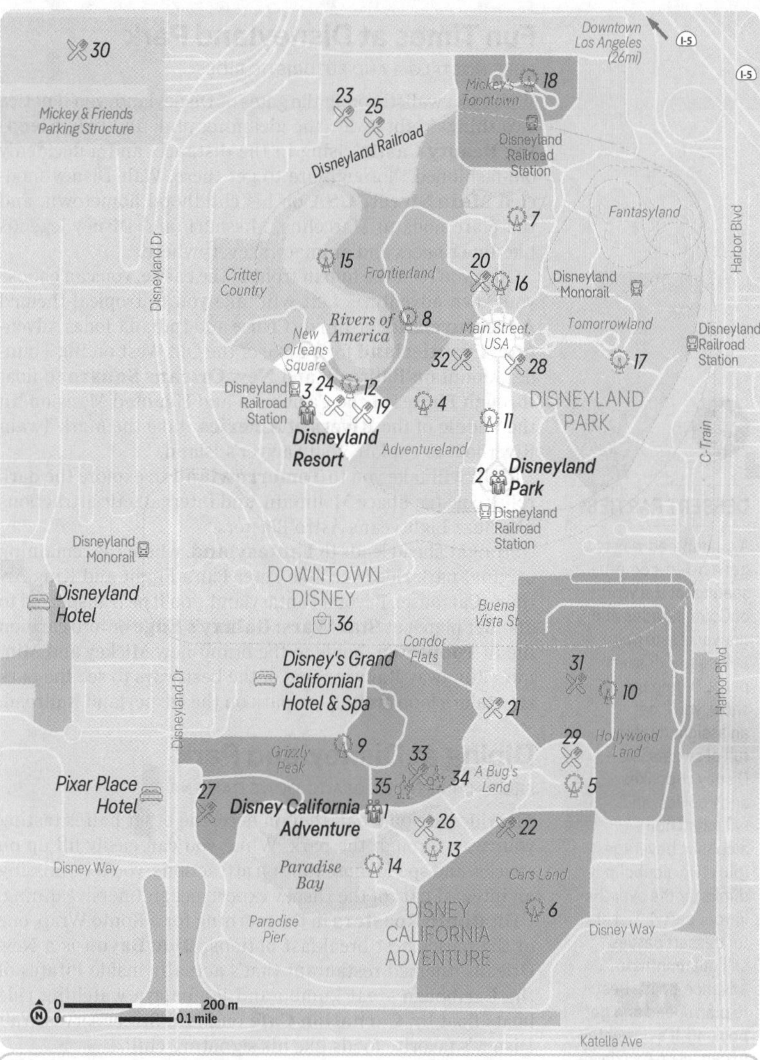

HIGHLIGHTS
1 Disney California Adventure Park
2 Disneyland Park
3 Disneyland Resort

SIGHTS
4 Adventureland
5 Avengers Campus
6 Cars Land
7 Fantasyland
8 Frontierland
9 Grizzly Peak Recreational Area
10 Hollywood Land
11 Main Street, USA
12 New Orleans Square
13 Pacific Wharf
14 Pixar Pier
15 Rivers of America
16 Sleeping Beauty Castle Walkthrough
17 Tomorrowland
18 Toontown

EATING
19 Blue Bayou Restaurant
20 Carnation Cafe
21 Carthay Circle Restaurant
22 Cozy Cone Motel
23 Docking Bay 7 Food and Cargo
24 French Market Restaurant
25 Oga's Cantina at the Disneyland Resort
26 Pacific Wharf Café
27 Paradise Garden Grill
28 Plaza Inn
29 Pym Test Kitchen
30 Ronto Roasters
31 Schmoozies
32 Walt Disney's Enchanted Tiki Room
33 Wine Country Trattoria

DRINKING
34 Mendocino Terrace
35 Sonoma Terrace

SHOPPING
36 Downtown Disney District

Fun Times at Disneyland Park

PURE NOSTALGIA AND FUTURISTIC RIDES

When you walk through the gates of Disneyland, you'll notice two things right away: the gleaming pink and blue **Sleeping Beauty Castle** rising in the distance, and a decidedly old-fashioned thoroughfare to get there. Walt Disney modeled **Main Street, USA** on his childhood hometown, and there are nods to Marceline, Missouri (and Disney legends like Imagineers and animators) everywhere.

Once you're at the hub in front of the castle, you can choose your own adventure. Left will take you to tropical-themed **Adventureland** for Jungle Cruise and Indiana Jones Adventure; **Frontierland** for a taste of the Old West on Big Thunder Mountain Railroad; and **New Orleans Square** to float through Pirates of the Caribbean and Haunted Mansion. In the middle of the **Rivers of America**, take the Mark Twain Riverboat or explore Tom Sawyer's Island.

Right will take you to **Tomorrowland** to explore the dark roller coaster, Space Mountain, and intergalactic attractions like Buzz Lightyear's Astro Blasters.

Straight ahead leads to **Fantasyland**, where the remaining original park rides are, like Peter Pan's Flight and King Arthur's Carrousel. Beyond Fantasyland, you'll be transported to another planet at **Star Wars: Galaxy's Edge** or into cartoon life in **Toontown**, home to the brand-new Mickey and Minnie's Runaway Railway. One of the best ways to see the park is to take a loop around the park on the Disneyland Railroad.

DESSERT PARTIES

A guaranteed way to get hard-to-come-by seating for the World of Color parades and fireworks is to buy tickets to a dessert party. During the show, you'll get an assigned table full of sweets like Disney cupcakes and cookies, and unlimited non-alcoholic beverages (plus two alcoholic drinks for the over-21s in your party). Tickets for dessert parties sell out months in advance, so it's best to plan ahead and get booking. It's possible to cancel up to a day before the night, if your plans change. Prices include taxes and gratuity.

Dining at Disneyland Park

FROM MAIN STREET, USA TO OGA'S CANTINA

The rides are only half the fun here, the other half is tasting your way through the park. While you can easily fill up on snacks, and spend more time on attractions, you'll be missing an integral part of the Disney experience: immersive dining.

Hit **Ronto Roasters** in the morning for a Ronto Wrap, one of the park's best breakfast options. **Blue Bayou** is a New Orleans–themed restaurant that's actually inside Pirates of the Caribbean – eat gumbo and jambalaya watching ride boats float by. **Carnation Cafe** on Main Street serves Walt Disney's favorite foods like his signature chili.

For quick service, you can't go wrong with **Plaza Inn**, which has some of the best fried chicken anywhere, plus prime parade-viewing spots. **French Market** in New Orleans Square offers jambalaya and other Cajun/Creole-inspired foods, and serves the iconic Mickey-shaped beignets people rave about.

CAN'T-MISS DISNEYLAND SHOWS

Fireworks Spectacular
Fireworks over Sleeping Beauty Castle accompanied by music and projections up and down Main Street, USA.

Fantasmic!
Nightly show on the Rivers of America featuring Sorcerer Mickey unleashing the power of imagination.

Daily Parades
Themes change with the season, but always feature Disney characters riding on floats through Main Street, USA.

Some of the most unique dining happens 'off planet' in Star Wars: Galaxy's Edge. **Oga's Cantina** isn't the bastion of 'scum and villainy' Obi-Wan described in the first movie, but it absolutely has a space cantina vibe and excellent cocktails like the Jedi Mind Trick. **Docking Bay 7** serves immersive *Star Wars*-inspired food that's some of the best, most affordable quick-service in the park.

And to round your day out with some classic Disneyland Park treats, look out for churros (with variations like s'mores and pumpkin-spice flavors); Dole Whip, a frozen pineapple treat synonymous with the **Enchanted Tiki Room**; and the collectible Disneyland popcorn buckets – a fun (and refillable) souvenir.

Big Rides at Disney California Adventure

THRILL RIDES AND MOVIE MAGIC

Across the plaza, Disney California Adventure (DCA) is a newer park with a focus on big rides and newer Disney content. DCA welcomes you in with a walk down Old Hollywood–themed Buena Vista Street, named for the street in Burbank where Walt Disney Studios sits. In **Hollywood Land**, which mimics Hollywood Blvd, there's a Monsters, Inc. ride and the Animation Academy where you can learn to draw Disney characters. That leads into **Avengers Campus**, Disney's newest land, where Marvel superheroes walk among us mere mortals, and we can feel like Spider-Man on his Web-Slingers virtual reality ride or like one of the Guardians of the Galaxy on Mission: Breakout!.

Cars Land is a truly beautiful re-creation of *Cars'* Radiator Springs, including the thrill ride Radiator Springs Racers. **Pixar Pier** is home to rides like *the Incredibles*–themed Incredicoaster, the biggest and baddest ride in either park; Toy Story Midway Mania, which puts you inside carnival games; and Mickey's Fun Wheel, a giant Ferris wheel. Don't miss Ariel's Undersea Adventure, a calm dark ride through *The Little Mermaid*'s story.

Other areas of the park represent other parts of California, like the San Francisco–inspired **Pacific Wharf** (complete with its own Ghirardelli) and the NorCal-themed **Grizzly Peak Recreation Area** that houses the unmatched Soarin' ride, which evokes the feeling of flying over some of the world's most spectacular sights.

THE OFFICE SECRET

Lamplight Lounge in Pixar Pier is a must-stop: the views of the Incredicoaster, Mickey's Fun Wheel and the lagoon are unparalleled, the food is great, and the drinks are fun (especially on the secret cocktail menu). There is also a hidden private dining room, **The Office**. How to get in is known only by die-hard fans. Do you want to see all of the original Pixar animation sketches inside for yourself? The trick is to arrive in a bigger party – the room seats 13 – and get there right when the restaurant opens for the day. Then, cross your fingers, ask a Cast Member as nicely as you can, and be prepared: you never know what Disney magic might happen.

CAN'T-MISS DCA SHOWS

World of Color
The DCA nighttime spectacular combines Disney movie clips and a water show in the lagoon.

Avengers Shows
Feats of superhero strength happen throughout the day from characters like Spider-Man and Black Widow.

Paradise Garden Concerts
Latin R&B and pop performers play the stage near the Coco and Encanto character meet-and-greets.

WHAT YOU NEED TO KNOW ABOUT GENIE+

Genie+ is similar to the former 'fast pass' but it can cost up to $29 per person. It allows you to book entry in a ride's faster Lightning Lane via the Disneyland app. You can only hold one pass at a time in a two-hour window (the app will tell you when you can book again). There are other restrictions: Genie+ can only be used once for each ride, and not all the rides are available. But if you have limited time in the parks and want to experience as much as possible, it's worth the extra investment to save yourself queuing time.

Cozy Cone Motel

DCA Dining Delights

FINE – AND FUN – DINING

Disney California Adventure (DCA) is definitely the foodie's park with many of its lands California-inspired.

There's glamorous fine dining and delectable cocktails at **Carthay Circle** and the more casual Carthay Circle Al Fresco Lounge in Hollywood Land, plus Sonoma-inspired fare at Wine Country Trattoria.

Attached to **Wine Country Trattoria** are two walk-up bars. **Sonoma Terrace** has a variety of beers and wine, plus snacks. **Mendocino Terrace** is wine-only and serves 20-plus varieties by the glass, which you can sip while you stroll the park. Unlike in Disneyland Park, alcohol is permitted throughout DCA and all restaurants offer drinks to go.

For quick service, the seasonally inspired Mexican food at **Paradise Garden Grille** is always a winner, and the **Pacific Wharf** (currently under renovation to become San Fransokyo from *Big Hero 6*) dining area has Chinese, Mexican and a San Francisco–inspired cafe with soups served in sourdough bread bowls.

The most fun by a mile is **Pym Test Kitchen** in Avengers Campus, which serves oversized/undersized food inspired by Marvel superhero Ant-Man's own shifts in size. Think tiny pas-

ATTRACTIONS THAT CHANGE WITH THE SEASON

Haunted Mansion Holiday
From September to January, Haunted Mansion gets a *The Nightmare Before Christmas* makeover.

Guardians of the Galaxy – Monsters After Dark
During Halloween this freefall ride adds 100% more scares to an already terrifying ride.

It's a Small World
This boat ride becomes a celebration of winter holidays around the globe.

ta with one giant, plant-based 'meatball' served not in a bowl but a huge spoon; or a single Pym-ini sandwich big enough to serve six, which comes in a Teeny Pym-ini version for one.

In a hurry? **Cozy Cone Motel** in Cars Land does Bacon Mac 'n' Cheese – cone-shaped bread filled with cheesy goodness; **Schmoozies** in Hollywood Land makes playful Mickey Milkshakes (pick a flavor which comes with cookie 'ears'); or you can always munch on a Mickey pretzel.

Disneyland's Festive Seasons

SEASONAL EVENTS WORTH PLANNING FOR

Disney California Adventure marks the **Lunar New Year** (usually in January or February dependent on the Chinese Lunar Calendar) with a celebration of East Asian food, culture and heritage. Food booths offer Disney takes on Chinese, Vietnamese and Korean street foods, and there are parades and musical performances.

In March and April, it's time for the **California Adventure Food & Wine Festival**. The vast and varied landscape of California's regional cuisines are the spotlight for this highly-anticipated annual festival. Not only are there food booths themed to different regions and iconic California foods (think an entire booth devoted to the artichoke, California's state vegetable), there are special dining events and chef demonstrations throughout the festival.

For those who love a spooky good time, there is no better season at Disneyland than **Halloween Time**. Halloween kicks off in September and runs through October. Both parks are fully decorated for the holiday, including an entire makeover of Cars Land with incredibly inventive Halloween decorations from auto parts: it includes a 'Haul-o-Ween' ride overlay and Cars like Lightning McQueen and Mater dressed in Halloween costumes.

Halloween also brings a highly anticipated holiday overlay of Haunted Mansion, which becomes *The Nightmare Before Christmas*-themed, and has a huge gingerbread house that changes every year. In 2022 it featured a guillotine that really dropped a blade. In DCA, the Oogie Boogie Bash is a separately ticketed Halloween party with Disney villains and trick-or-treating.

Running concurrently is **National Hispanic and Latin American Heritage Month**, which brings musical performances, special characters and incredible Mexican-inspired food to both parks.

In November **Dia de Los Muertos** celebrates those who have passed with a huge, walk-through *ofrenda* (a Dia de los

KNOW YOUR DISNEY TERMINOLOGY

At Walt Disney World, the original park is called Magic Kingdom – but at the Disneyland Resort, the original park is called Disneyland, which can get confusing. 'Disneyland' as a destination includes two theme parks: Disneyland Park, and Disney California Adventure Park, which share a plaza that makes it easy to 'park hop' back and forth between the two. The Disneyland Resort also encompasses three hotels (Disneyland Hotel, Disney's Grand Californian Hotel & Spa, and Pixar Place Hotel) and the Downtown Disney shopping and dining district. Entrance to the parks requires a ticket and reservation, but the hotels and Downtown Disney are open to the public.

RIDES TO PRIORITIZE USING GENIE+

Space Mountain
This dark coaster in Disneyland's Tomorrowland is a signature park experience and has hour-plus waits.

Toy Story: Midway Mania!
This colorful, all-ages attraction, which lets you compete for bragging rights, is a must-ride.

Big Thunder Mountain Railroad
The 'wildest ride in the wilderness' is a roller coaster with amazing views.

Muertos altar with photos of loved ones, candles and flowers) in Disneyland's Frontierland. At The Tree of Life in the Paradise Garden area of DCA, you can write a message to a departed loved one and hang it on the tree. By the end of the celebration it is filled with thousands of beautiful, moving messages.

There's nothing like Disneyland Park during the winter holidays. Sleeping Beauty Castle's halls are decked with ornate decorations and during the nightly fireworks, gingerbread-scented snow falls over Main Street. A **Christmas parade** brings Disney princesses through the streets, surrounded by dancing snowflakes and festive holiday music. The most in-demand treat at this time of year is the hand-pulled candy canes, made fresh on select days. People arrive at the park hours early to make sure they'll be able to snag one.

The California Adventure Festival sees DCA absolutely laden with festive decor during the holiday months. While all the rides with holiday overlays are in Disneyland Park, DCA has a few special things going on during this season, like Santa appearing in the Redwood Creek Challenge Trail for holiday photos.

The biggest event, though, is the **Festival of the Holidays**, which celebrates Christmas, Hanukkah, Kwanzaa, Navidad, Diwali and Three Kings Day through food, musical performances and character appearances.

THE NEW TOON IN TOWN

In January 2023 Disneyland opened Mickey and Minnie's Runaway Railway, a new ride in Toontown to commemorate the launch of the Disney100 celebration, marking 100 years of the Walt Disney Company. The trackless ride is the first-ever at Disneyland to feature Mickey and friends, and immerses you in their cartoons in surprising and delightful ways. Some Disneyland rides are so highly sought-after they have separate fees for faster access – the costs vary per day. These 'Individual Lightning Lane' passes are available for Mickey and Minnie's Runaway Railway as well as other popular rides like Radiator Springs Racers and Star Wars: Rise of the Resistance.

Staying in a Disneyland Resort

POOLS, BARS AND RETAIL THERAPY

Unlike Walt Disney World, which has more than 25 on-property hotels, Disneyland only has three, all within easy walking distance of the parks **Disneyland Hotel** is the resort's mid-tier property, but it absolutely has the most Disney magic, with touches like the headboards in the rooms that light up with Tinkerbell flying over the castle and playing 'When You Wish Upon a Star' and luxury suites with pirate, princess and Mickey themes.

The pool area with its Monorail-inspired waterslides is only for hotel guests, but the restaurants and shops in the hotel are open to the public. Goofy's Kitchen is a family-friendly buffet where classic Disney characters make the rounds and appear at each table. Tangaroa Terrace is a quick-service with Hawaiian-inspired food, including loco moco and fluffy Japanese soufflé pancakes. The real gem of the hotel, though, is Trader Sam's Enchanted Tiki Bar, a bar and restaurant (kids are welcome during the day) where volcanoes erupt, ships sink, thunder crashes inside, and you can never be sure of what will happen next.

Next on your overnighting adventures is **Disney's Grand Californian Resort & Spa**. The soaring lobby of the Grand

WALKING-DISTANCE HOTELS NEAR DISNEYLAND

J.W. Marriott
Newer luxury accommodations with fine dining and a rooftop lounge, attached to the Anaheim GardenWalk. **$$$**

Anaheim Majestic Garden Hotel
Castle-inspired architecture and room decor keep the magic going. **$$**

Candy Cane Inn
Independently-owned motel with small town charm, and recently refurbished. Very short walk to parks. **$**

Californian is an oasis from the busy parks, which is especially helpful because this luxury hotel has a direct entrance into DCA. There, you can get a hot chocolate or adult beverage from the walk-up bar, then take it to one of the cozy couches or rocking chairs by the fireplace and just sit and relax while a pianist plays Disney tunes on the grand piano.

The whole hotel is Northern California–themed – even the pool has rock waterfalls and water slides. The pool's restaurant, Craftsman Grille, is a great spot for lunch even if you can't take a dip. Storytellers Cafe offers buffet dining featuring furry Disney creatures like Chip 'n Dale. Finally, Napa Rose serves the finest food in the resort. It also has a highly in-demand princess character breakfast in the mornings.

The most budget-friendly of the Disneyland hotels, **Pixar Place Hotel**, previously Disney's Paradise Pier Hotel, is undergoing a huge makeover to create Pixar character-themed rooms and refreshed dining. The trade-off you make in paying less for this hotel is that it's the furthest walk from the parks.

Even if you don't make it inside the Disney parks, the **Downtown Disney** shopping and dining district that connects the hotels to the parks is worth a visit. There's a massive World of Disney store, as well as smaller boutiques and fun dining options, including Black Tap Craft Burgers & Shakes, which serves milkshakes topped with whole pieces of cake, and San Diego's Ballast Point Brewing Company.

The House of the Retro Future

BACK TO THE FUTURE

The **Howard Johnson by Wyndham Anaheim Hotel & Water Park** is a favorite for families visiting Disneyland, both for its proximity to the parks and its pirate-themed Castaway Cove water park. True Disneyphiles appreciate the hotel for its House of the Retro Future, a suite decorated to look like a now-closed Disney attraction.

Modeled after the Monsanto House of the Future, a walk-through attraction that was in Tomorrowland from 1957 to 1967, it showcased forward-thinking technologies that might be implemented in homes in an imagined 1986. The suite features mid-century modern decor, a record player and original art by Shag.

WHY I LOVE DISNEYLAND

Julie Tremaine, writer

Walt Disney World is bigger, but Disneyland has a charm all of its own, which I think comes from the whispers of Walt Disney's original vision still present today. On Main Street, USA and in Fantasyland especially, I can close my eyes and imagine what the park was like in 1955 when men wore suits and women wore heels to the park (not sad to skip that part), and people were experiencing this kind of truly magical immersion for the first time. My every visit is a heady mix of nostalgia, fantasy and the power of bringing joy through stories.

GETTING AROUND

Finding your way to Disneyland is pretty simple: if you're not driving, you'll likely fly into Los Angeles International Airport (LAX), Long Beach Airport (LGB) or John Wayne Orange County Airport (SNA). LAX offers many more direct, affordable flights, but is an hour or more from the resort. LGB and SNA are closer and more convenient; the Orange County airport is the closest to the parks.

If your trip only involves Disneyland and not exploring more of California, use a rideshare or hire a car service to get you to the parks; once you're at your hotel, you won't need to drive anywhere. Unlike Walt Disney World which has miles between parks, Disneyland's 'park hopping' only involves crossing a small plaza.

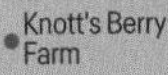

Beyond Disneyland

A delicious Orange County theme park was the first in the state, and has defined experiential entertainment for 100 years.

In 1923 Walter and Cordelia Knott opened a farmstand on their berry farm in Buena Park, introducing the boysenberry – a mix of red raspberry, blackberry and loganberry. Soon they also had a 20-seat fried-chicken restaurant that later sat 350 – and still there were hours-long waits.

To entertain hungry diners waiting up to three hours for a table, Walter began building scenes for people to peruse outside: a re-creation of George Washington's Mount Vernon, and a working volcano replica. Next, they added an Old West ghost town. Soon there were rides, even roller coasters.

Today, Knott's Berry Farm is a hugely popular theme park, but at its core, the place is still all about the berries.

TOP TIP

Knott's Berry Farm doesn't require advance park reservations. Online tickets, though, are less expensive. An express band will get you in a shorter line for nearly every ride. You can also purchase meal packages online.

Knott's Berry Farm stagecoach

KNOTT'S BERRY FARM & GHOST TOWN

CHRIS NUNEZ/SHUTTERSTOCK ©

Calico Ghost Town

Good Old Times at Knott's Berry Farm

BERRY AMUSING...

Walking into Knott's Berry Farm is to walk into a romanticized version of the Old West. The centerpiece land of the park, **Calico Ghost Town**, is based on a real silver-mining town of Calico in the Mojave Desert from California's gold-rush days. The theme-park version has real historic buildings and re-creations of others. You can take old-time photos; see a 'Burly Q revue' at the Birdcage Theater; visit the saloon or city hall; go to 'school' and generally learn about the pioneer days of California. During the summer's **Ghost Town Alive!** event, the town is full of characters like outlaws and sheriffs who give you interactive storylines to follow and solve.

Ghost Town is also home to the tallest, oldest wooden roller coaster in the West, Ghost Rider. In the Boardwalk area, Hang Time is an intense plunge coaster. In Fiesta Village, a massive refurbishment of Montezooma: The Forbidden Fortress is slated to open in summer 2023.

Beyond thrill rides, which Knott's has plenty of, there is also a really pleasant atmosphere. You can take a train ride, experience the original 1960s mine attraction, see exciting shows and performances, and learn about California's history through exhibits all over the park.

Most importantly, arrive hungry: the food is great at Knott's – and those boysenberry funnel cakes are legendary for good reason.

THE MOST DELICIOUS TIME TO VISIT

During March and April, Knott's hosts its annual **Boysenberry Festival**, when the park celebrates the fruit that made them famous. But if you think it's just a theme park filled with boysenberry pie – which, make no mistake, is excellent – then you clearly haven't experienced this culinary bonanza before.

Previous years' offerings included a fried chicken sandwich, with bacon jam and arugula (rocket), on a boysenberry-filled doughnut; boysenberry cowboy chili with mac 'n' cheese; and boysenberry blonde ale. When you need a break from eating, there are special festival concerts and entertainment – and, oh yeah, all the other rides and attractions.

GETTING AROUND

Knott's Berry Farm is only about 10 minutes away from Disneyland by car, which makes it very easy to hop over for a day trip. Because Knott's is only one park, you can see everything in a single day – so if you have the time, you should definitely make your Disney trip a 'theme parks trip' instead.

In addition to driving (there is a paid parking lot on the property) and ride-share options, Anaheim Regional Transportation (ART) is a great option for hopping over to Buena Park. The ART Bus also goes to the Anaheim Angels' stadium and the Honda Center. Manage routes and pay fares through the app, A-Way WeGo.

HUNTINGTON BEACH

San Francisco
Los Angeles
Huntington Beach

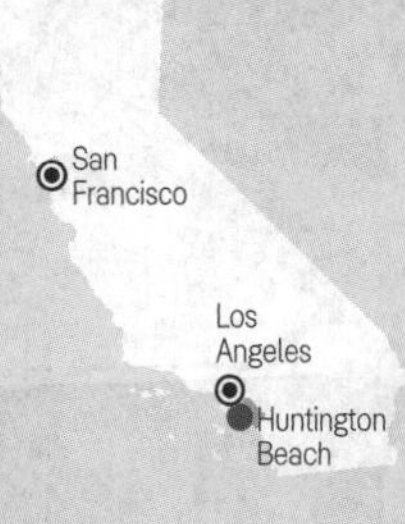

There's no place in Orange County more closely associated with surfing than Huntington Beach, also known as Surf City USA. It's where surfing first became popular in California, and it's where the sport is celebrated every day by pros and first-timers alike. Huntington Beach has 10 miles of shoreline, and a huge amount of hotels, restaurants and shops directly across Pacific Coast Highway from the sand. It's not a question of whether you'll spend time on the beach when you visit, it's a question of how you'll be able to pull yourself away when it's time to go home.

In addition to the beach itself, there are plenty of ways to enjoy the outdoors in Huntington Beach, from one of Southern California's most picturesque nature preserves to a gorgeous centerpiece park and luxury hotels that sell day passes for posh pools and cabanas without the big price tag.

TOP TIP

There are shops up and down Pacific Coast Highway renting beach chairs and boogie boards. It's also easy to find bikes and mopeds.

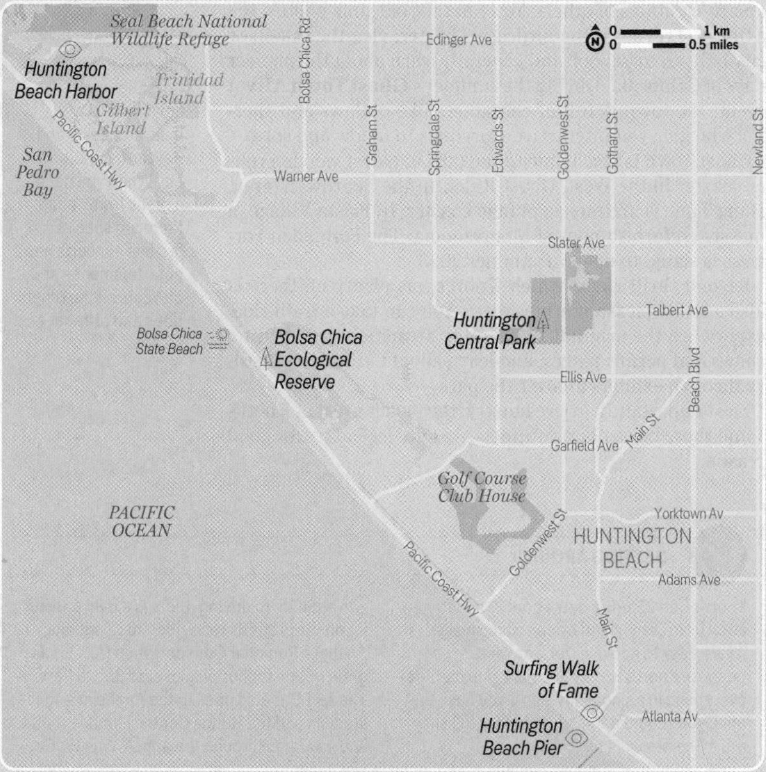
Seal Beach National Wildlife Refuge
Huntington Beach Harbor
Trinidad Island
Gilbert Island
San Pedro Bay
Pacific Coast Hwy
Bolsa Chica Rd
Edinger Ave
0 1 km
0 0.5 miles
Graham St
Springdale St
Edwards St
Goldenwest St
Gothard St
Newland St
Warner Ave
Slater Ave
Talbert Ave
Huntington Central Park
Bolsa Chica State Beach
Bolsa Chica Ecological Reserve
Ellis Ave
Beach Blvd
Main St
Garfield Ave
Golf Course Club House
Yorktown Av
PACIFIC OCEAN
HUNTINGTON BEACH
Goldenwest St
Pacific Coast Hwy
Adams Ave
Main St
Surfing Walk of Fame
Atlanta Av
Huntington Beach Pier

Competitor in the US Open of Surfing

Enjoying Surf City USA

SURF, THE OUTDOORS AND VINTAGE CARS

It's hard to overstate the importance of surfing to this town, which has ideal surfing conditions all year long and is home to several important surfing competitions and landmarks.

There's a **Surfers' Hall of Fame** outside Huntington Surf & Sport. Outside Jack's Surfboards, which has been an institution since the 1950s, you'll find the **Surfing Walk of Fame**. It also hosts an induction ceremony during the **US Open of Surfing**, the world's largest surfing competition in July. Held in September, the **International Surfing Association World Surfing Games** are an Olympic qualifying event, and **Jack's Surfboards Pro** in April is a qualifying event for the **World Surfing League**. But you don't have to be a pro to surf in Huntington: there are beginner's lessons available from surf schools all over the city.

Beyond surfing, the city hosts many other sporting events throughout the year. In October **Red Bull Straight Rhythm** is a double bill of motocross events. The **AVP Huntington Beach Open** every November is a huge professional beach-volleyball tournament.

BEACH ALL DAY, BEACH ALL NIGHT

Your beach vacation isn't complete without a beach bonfire. Three of Huntington's five beaches have fire pits available on a first-come, first-served basis: **Huntington City Beach, Huntington State Beach** and **Bolsa Chica State Beach**. Even though there are more than 500 available, they can be hard to come by in peak season, when people stake them out early in the day. However, there's a trick – rent a picnic spot, and a fire pit comes with the rental. Those can be booked through the State of California Parks Department. For $200 a day, you get a wheelchair-accessible area with two picnic tables set on a concrete pad, and a fire ring in the sand.

WHERE TO STAY AT HUNTINGTON BEACH

Paséa Hotel & Spa
Stylish beachfront hotel with a rooftop restaurant ideal for watching the sunset over the ocean. **$$**

Kimpton Shorebreak Hotel
Get the daily surf report in this stylish hotel with lobby games and courtyard firepits. **$$**

Surf City Inn
Quiet boutique hotel with harbor views and a short walk to a less busy beach. **$**

A TASTE OF HAWAII IN HUNTINGTON

There are no shortage of excellent restaurants in the area, but for a true taste of the surfing lifestyle, head to **Duke's Huntington Beach**. Founded by Duke Kahanamoku, the Hawaiian surfer and Olympic medalist who popularized the sport in America, Duke's serves Hawaiian-inspired food directly on the beach. Duke's flagship location is in Kahanamoku's hometown of Waikiki, and there are other California locations in Malibu and La Jolla, but Huntington Beach has a special connection to the legendary surfer – it's where he first introduced surfing to America in 1925. While you're there, don't miss the signature Duke's Mai Tai made with – as the menu says – 'aloha, fresh Hawaiian juices and two types of rum.'

The visual centerpiece of Huntington Beach is the **Huntington Beach Pier.** At 1850ft long, it's one of the largest piers on the West Coast. There are few pleasures more enjoyable in a beach town than taking a sunny stroll on the pier, past street musicians, people fishing, and artists selling their wares. The pier has shops and dining, and is open 5am to midnight daily. Before you arrive in Huntington Beach, you can scope out the surf on the live-streamed surf cam from the Kite Connection on the pier.

Huntington's gorgeous scenery goes way beyond the beach. The 1300-acre **Bolsa Chica Ecological Reserve** is the largest saltwater marsh in Southern California, and has five miles of walking trails with scenic overlooks. Bird lovers flock here to see the more than 300 avian species that have been spotted in the last decade.

At nearly 350 acres, **Huntington Central Park** is the largest city-owned park in Orange County. Inside the park are horseback-riding trails, a playground, disc golf, plus a dog park. In addition, the city's Central Library is in the park, as well as a nature center and three restaurants.

Huntington Beach Harbor is a residential area comprising five human-made islands with more than 500 houses. The harbor area is an ideal place to spend the afternoon kayaking or on a stand-up paddleboard in the calm waters. Private charters and electric boats are also available for hire to see the sights by water. During the holiday season, harbor homes deck themselves out for the **Huntington Harbor Cruise Of Lights**, a narrated boat tour of the festive decorations.

Every June, more than 350 cars gather for the **Huntington Beach Concours d'Elegance**, an exhibition of vintage and rare automobiles. The Concours might be the city's marquee car event, but it's far from the only one. In May over 100 vintage Volkswagen camper vans will gather for the first-ever **Kowabunga Huntington Beach Van Car Show**. In October sports cars of all stripes converge for **Cars 'N Copters On The Coast**, featuring 400 of the planet's fastest cars like Koenigseggs, Bugattis, Paganis, McLarens, Lamborghinis and Aston Martins.

GETTING AROUND

There are three airports with relatively easy access to Huntington Beach: Los Angeles International Airport (LAX), Long Beach Airport (LBG) or John Wayne Orange County Airport (SNA). LAX is an hour-plus drive, depending on traffic, which is notoriously unpredictable around Los Angeles, but offers many more flight options and is generally a more affordable option. Long Beach is closer – 30 or 35 minutes – and Orange County is around 25 to 30 minutes away.

Huntington Beach is one of the cities serviced by Orange County Transportation Authority (OCTA) buses, which run from Long Beach in the north all the way through Orange County to Dana Point near the county line. For drivers, there is ample parking, but don't forget to feed the meters (which can be paid by credit card).

Beyond Huntington Beach

The beachy destinations in Orange County have unique character and their own distinct charms, from arts to boating to festivals.

Not all beach towns are alike, even in a place like Orange County. If you're looking for cities with a lot to offer, Newport Beach and Laguna Beach are must-sees. Newport Beach has a large marina and many tony neighborhoods where you can see and be seen; Laguna Beach has a huge artistic community where you can engage with public art, galleries, theater and events.

For a quieter beach escape, explore Seal Beach to the north – it's a tiny, picturesque hamlet – or Dana Point to the south, a laid-back surfing town. But if you stay on the beach, you'll miss a lot: venture inland to connect to local communities.

TOP TIP

A unique vacation rental, the water tower in Seal Beach is a three-story round-house with panoramic views. Accessible via private elevator, it sleeps eight.

Laguna Beach

GABRIELE MALTINTI/SHUTTERSTOCK ©

INTERNATIONAL FLAVORS IN ORANGE COUNTY

Little Saigon, home to almost 40,000 Vietnamese Americans, is spread across Westminster, Garden Grove, Santa Ana and Fountain Valley. The area has over 3500 Vietnamese-owned businesses, and is widely regarded as having some of the country's best Vietnamese food. The **Asian Garden Mall** in Westminster is the is largest Vietnamese-owned dining and shopping center in the US.

Little Arabia, a neighborhood in Anaheim, is home to a concentration of residents who hail from the Middle East and Northern Africa. Here you'll see representation from Lebanese, Moroccan, Saudi Arabian and Armenian cultures, to name a few. Shop at **Altayebat Market** for Middle Eastern staples, or eat at one of many restaurants like **Sahara Falafel** or **Zait and Zaatar**.

JON BILOUS/SHUTTERSTOCK ©

Seal Beach

Kicking Back at Seal Beach

SHOPPING, SEAFOOD AND BIKE RIDES

Named after the seals that dot its shores, the city of Seal Beach is distinguished by its small, quieter beach and the quaint waterfront promenade with independent seaside shops selling seashells, chocolates and beachy fashion.

Strolling and shopping on Seal Beach's main street is an incredibly pleasant way to spend an afternoon, especially if you're looking to avoid the crowds. Stop at **Walt's Wharf** for the freshest seafood in town. When Walt and Mona Babcock started the restaurant in 1970, it served fish that Walt brought in on his own boat. Now the family owns a winery in Santa Ynez Valley and pour their own wines to accompany the local catch.

The **Hangout Restaurant and Beach Bar** serves killer breakfast burritos and burgers with an incredible water view. For something sweet, step into **Jill's Bakery** for her legendary cinnamon rolls – you'll know you're headed in the right direction by the intoxicating smell outside.

Many day-trippers bike to Seal Beach via the **San Gabriel River Bike Trail**, a 28-mile stretch of bike path next to the **San Gabriel River** that separates the city from Los Angeles County. Another major attraction in Seal Beach is the 965-acre **Seal Beach National Wildlife Preserve**, on the grounds of the Naval Weapons Station Seal Beach military base. On the last Saturday morning of the month, you can take a guided tour of the salt marsh.

GETTING AROUND

All the beach cities in Orange County are connected by Route 1, which is Pacific Coast Highway. It's an easy drive between them, but it's also an easy bike ride. If you aren't traveling with your own bike, don't worry – rental shops are up and down the coast.

If you do plan to get around by car, be ready to pay to park, either in parking lots or in metered parking spaces. All meters take credit cards, but can also be paid via an app. If you're going to be exploring for several days, you might want to download the Parkmobile app to save yourself the hassle of paying by card each time.

NEWPORT BEACH

There's no city in California quite like Newport Beach. An upscale beach community, Newport Beach has 10 distinct neighborhoods that range from quiet and residential to bustling tourist draws. The city is home to the largest recreational harbor on the West Coast, with 10 miles of waterfront that offers boating and fishing, water sports, and endless views.

Near an enormous ecological wetland preserve, it is home to more than 200 endangered species. Beyond the shore, Newport Beach has some of California's most sought-after golf courses, beloved annual cultural events and shopping that rivals Beverly Hills. You can choose to have a low-key vacation in Newport, or live like the rich and famous jet-setter set. Either way, you'll want to stay for more than a day.

TOP TIP

Every summer, Newport Beach hosts Shakespeare by the Sea performances throughout the city, which are free to attend. See shakespearebythesea.org.

Balboa Pier (p409)

NEWPORT BEACH

SIGHTS
1 Balboa Island
2 Balboa Pier
3 Civic Center Park
4 Corona Del Mar State Beach Park
5 Newport Beach Civic Center Park
6 Sherman Library & Gardens

ACTIVITIES, COURSES & TOURS
7 Mariner's Mile

SLEEPING
8 Hyatt Regency Newport Beach

EATING
9 21 Oceanfront
10 Louie's by the Bay
11 Rusty Pelican
12 Sugar 'n Spice
13 The Crab Cooker

DRINKING
14 Chihuahua Cerveza
15 Stag Bar + Kitchen

ENTERTAINMENT
16 Balboa Fun Zone

SHOPPING
17 Fashion Island

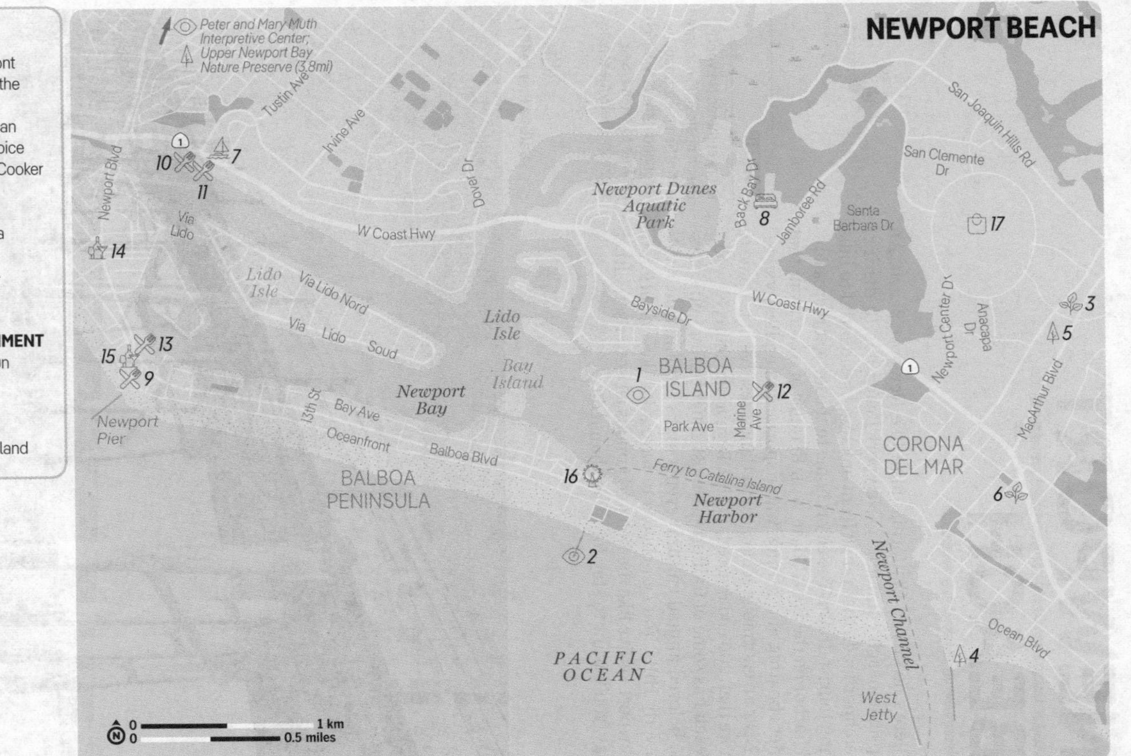

Exploring Newport Beach

MUST-SEE NEIGHBORHOODS AND ATTRACTIONS

Balboa Peninsula is where to head if you want a quintessential beach-town experience. Stroll **Balboa Pier**, rent a bike and traverse the boardwalk, or hop the ferry to **Balboa Island**. The peninsula has both casual beach bars like **Chihuahua Cerveza Taproom**, with self-serve taps, and **Stag Bar + Kitchen**, open since 1908. For fine dining with sunset views, try **21 Oceanfront** at Doryman's Oceanfront Inn. **The Crab Cooker** is a fish market and no-frills restaurant that has been serving up perfectly fresh seafood since 1951. In Balboa Village, there's **Balboa Fun Zone**, an old-time amusement park, with rides and midway games.

In addition to getting there by ferry, quaint Balboa Island is easily accessible by foot, bike or car – but parking can be hard in the cozy community. Here you can stroll shops or get a snack like Balboa Island's signature chocolate-dipped frozen banana at **Sugar n' Spice**, which inspired the Bluth family banana stand on *Arrested Development*.

Fashion Island is best known for its enormous, open-air mall full of high-end retailers like Nordstrom, Bloomingdales and Lululemon, and offers personal shopping. In the same area, **Civic Center Park** has a sculpture garden with a rotating collection of public art works, as well as dog parks and picnic areas. During the summer, **Civic Center Green** hosts free outdoor concerts.

This idyllic neighborhood is perched on the ocean cliffs and has stunning water views. Big Corona (**Corona Del Mar State Beach**) is great for swimming, while Little Corona is calmer and better for snorkeling and tide-pool observation. Even if you haven't been there before, you probably know something about Corona del Mar already: its Pirates Cove beach was featured on *Gilligan's Island*. Take the Goldenrod Footbridge to Ocean Park, then descend the staircase built into the bluff to get there.

One of Newport Beach's most beautiful destinations is the **Sherman Library & Gardens**, home to lavish botanic gardens, art exhibits and a library collection of Pacific Southwest history and artifacts.

For an adventure by sea – or just to see the superyachts docked nearby – head to **Mariner's Mile**. This is where you'll disembark for water excursions like harbor tours, gondola rides and sailing lessons. Or, rent your own Duffy boat and cruise around the harbor on your own. If you'd rather stay on land, you can't go wrong with waterfront restaurants like the **Rusty Pelican** and **Louie's by the Bay**.

TAKE A SWING IN NEWPORT

Newport is Orange County's most popular golf destination, both for pros and amateurs. Every March, the city hosts the **Hoag Classic**, an elite golf tournament on the PGA Tour Champions at **Newport Beach Country Club**.

Pelican Hill Golf Club has two courses with panoramic ocean views where you can see all the way to Catalina Island.

Tustin Ranch Golf Club regularly ranks as a crowd favorite for its landscaping, especially its lakes and waterfalls.

For beginners, the **Newport Beach Golf Course** and **Back Bay Golf Course** are both nine-hole courses. Back Bay is part of the **Hyatt Regency Newport Beach**, and greens fees for two are included in the hotel's resort fee.

WHERE TO STAY IN NEWPORT BEACH

Lido House Newport Beach
Chic luxury hotel with a popular rooftop lounge in the Lido Marina Village area. **$$$**

Resort at Pelican Hill
Immersive resort with excellent golf. It's rated best resort in the country by Forbes. **$$$**

Balboa Bay Resort
A Four Diamond waterfront hotel with a lavish spa and a marina with boat rentals. **$$$**

THE MOST SOUGHT-AFTER HOTEL RESERVATION IN TOWN

Crystal Cove is on the border between Newport Beach and Laguna Beach. While Crystal Cove State Park is technically in Laguna, the **Crystal Cove State Marine Conservation Area** is off Newport's shore, which is an area prized by scuba divers and snorkelers. Here, you can rent **Crystal Cove Beach Cottages**. These rustic cottages represent a simpler time in California's history, before there were five-star resorts up and down the shore. Rentals for up to seven people (on crystalcove.org) cost less than $300 a night, but are hard to get. The rental window opens six months before the date of your stay. Visit reservecalifornia.com exactly six months out to book.

Balboa Fun Zone (p409)

What's really the **Upper Newport Bay Nature Preserve and Ecological Reserve** is colloquially called Back Bay, which has more than 1000 acres of protected coastal wetland with a 10-mile hiking and biking trail running through it. Admission to its **Peter and Mary Muth Interpretive Center**, dedicated to local wildlife programming and education, is free.

Every June, the **Newport Beach Jazz Festival** brings in thousands of music-lovers to hear top jazz acts from around the world. The festival is on the grounds of the **Hyatt Regency Newport Beach**; both festival tickets and hotel rooms sell out well in advance of the event.

GETTING AROUND

While the airports in Los Angeles and Long Beach aren't too far away from Orange County, the most convenient airport in the area is undoubtedly John Wayne Airport (SNA), which is in Santa Ana, just a few minutes' drive from Newport. This airport is much smaller and more manageable than LAX. The downside? There are fewer direct flights into John Wayne. So for some it may be easier to fly into LAX and rent a car. Once here you can easily explore by foot, bike or public transportation.

Beyond Newport Beach

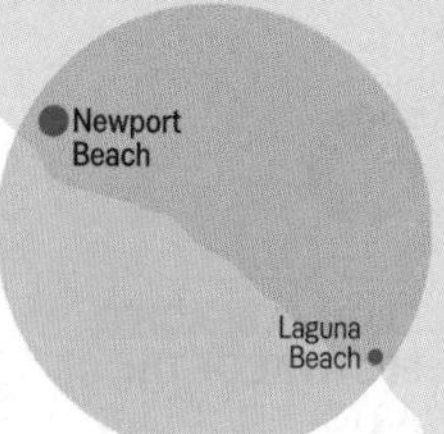

The artistic capital of Orange County, where you can explore tide pools, go hiking, and then dine out in the evening.

Laguna Beach is one of California's most beautiful coastal destinations with 7 miles of beach easily accessible from the city's main waterfront thoroughfare. Sea caves and cliffs add texture to the coastline. Water sports, like surfing and kayaking, are popular in Laguna and the mountains and canyons offer outdoor recreation away from the shore. Laguna Beach is a vibrant cultural center with an unparalleled art scene and an abundance of excellent, scenic restaurants. In short, there's a lot more to do than just hang out at the beach. Laguna Beach is also especially dog-friendly. Many restaurants, cafes, bars and shops are open to well-behaved four-legged friends, and there is an abundance of pet-friendly hotels at all price points.

TOP TIP

Many Laguna roads are 'sharrows,' shared lanes for cars and bikes, but the city offers a bike-friendly map of the best routes.

Crescent Bay Beach (p413)

LAGUNA BEACH'S FESTIVAL OF THE ARTS

Of all of California's iconic celebrations – it's got hugely popular garlic and artichoke festivals that draw tens of thousands of attendees – the **Pageant of the Masters** is one of the most unique. Laguna Beach's Festival of the Arts happens every July and August, and is an outdoor festival displaying the works of 140-plus artists, with art tours, lessons and events. But showing art isn't enough here. Laguna Beach wants you inside it. During the Pageant of the Masters, people step into life-size versions of famous works by some world renowned artists, and participate in real-life re-creations of those works. There's truly nothing like it anywhere else in the state.

JEFF GRITCHEN/MEDIANEWS GROUP/ORANGE COUNTY REGISTER VIA GETTY IMAGES ©

Sawdust Art & Craft Festival

Art Galore at Laguna Beach

ARTS, OUTDOOR ACTIVITIES AND DESTINATION DINING

Laguna Beach isn't just artsy by happenstance – the city was founded in the early 1900s as an artist colony. Today, there is art everywhere you look, literally: a phone booth isn't just a phone booth, it's a commentary on marine life preservation; and a beach overlook isn't complete without murals painted on the walkway and mosaics tiled on the railing. The city is home to **Laguna Art Museum**, which houses an all-Californian art collection and is the oldest cultural institution in the area, as well as many galleries and the **Laguna Beach Museum of Contemporary Art**. Arts and culture events take place throughout the year, including the **Sawdust Art & Craft Festival**, which has been happening annually since 1967 and offers 500 art classes during its summer event. The **Laguna**

WHERE TO STAY IN LAGUNA BEACH

Inn at Laguna Beach
Luxury beachfront hotel with a rooftop lounge with some of the area's best coastal views. **$$$**

Montage Laguna Beach
Immersive resort with three pools, a spa, several restaurants and a museum-quality fine-art collection. **$$$**

The Ranch at Laguna Beach
California's only National Geographic Lodge of the World feels rustic yet refined, in a secluded canyon. **$$$**

Beach Cultural Arts Center offers different events nearly every day, from film screenings to gallery shows to opera and theater performances.

Besides the artistic vibe of the city – which, even if you think you aren't that into art, is absolutely infectious – what makes Laguna Beach so singular is its vast and varied coastline. Beyond surfing or swimming, Laguna Beach's waterfront has tide pools that are protected environments, so they're thriving marine life habitats you can explore (as long as you look but don't touch). The best time to visit the tide pools is at low tide, usually in the morning and evening – check a tide calendar so you can get the best views.

There are many beaches in Laguna, but **Main Beach** is the one you might have seen on television before. It's famous for its scenery, its beach volleyball and surfers, and its boardwalk. **Crescent Bay Beach** is popular with surfers. Adjacent to that beach, **Crescent Bay Cove** is a green space with expansive views and tide pools. If that's the easiest to access, then **Thousand Steps Beach** is the hardest. Descend 218 steps to get to a secluded beach that has deep tide pools and a sea cave you can walk all the way through at low tide. **Diver's Cove** is ideal for snorkeling and has mild surf. **Victoria Beach** has a 'pirate tower' and a community-maintained swimming pool fed by ocean surf.

Nearby, **Santa Catalina Island** is a world away from the bustling mainland, but it's easy to reach via a one-hour high-speed ferry. OC ferries leave from Balboa Peninsula in Newport Beach and Dana Point.

Laguna Beach has no shortage of excellent dining, but all things being equal, you might as well choose a restaurant that comes with a stunning waterfront sunset. The **Cliff Restaurant** is located in Laguna Village, which is a quirky collection of shops: if you have to wait for a table at this restaurant built into the cliffside, there are worse places to do it than browsing artsy independent boutiques.

For fine dining, **Larsen** in the Hotel Laguna offers excellent seafood and better views. The **Deck on Laguna** is the city's only restaurant directly on the beach, and offers private bungalow dining. **Lost Pier Cafe** on Aliso Beach sits where a pier destroyed by El Niño once stood – in addition to coastal fare, the cafe offers bonfire kits and beach-chair rentals.

CHILLING OUT AT DANA POINT

Driving (or biking) south from Laguna Beach on Pacific Coast Highway (PCH), the next beach town you reach is Dana Point. Known for its laid-back surf culture, it's also a destination for golfers and visitors looking for quiet, pristine beaches. The benefit of a smaller community like Dana Point is that when you're on PCH, the beach is easily accessible – just find a (legal) parking space, get out of your car, and walk onto the sand.

The most child-friendly option is **Baby Beach**, where there's a roped-off section of calm water perfect for kids. **Capistrano Beach** has beach volleyball courts and a boardwalk. **Doheny State Beach** is the most popular surfing spot.

GETTING AROUND

If you're traveling in an electric vehicle, you have plenty of charging options. Newport Beach has 116 EV charging stations around town, nine of which are free to the public. Huntington Beach has 114 public charging stations, 19 of which are free to use. Laguna Beach has 27, 15 of which are free of charge. Seal Beach has 16 charging stations, and Dana Point has 10, four of which are free.

Disneyland is also EV-friendly, with 32 paid charging ports in the Mickey & Friends parking structure and 45 in the Toy Story parking lot. The cost to charge your car is in addition to the $30 fee to park.

MICHAEL J MAGEE/SHUTTERSTOCK ©

Above: La Jolla (p430); Right: San Diego (p420)

SAN DIEGO & AROUND

EXPLORE CALIFORNIA'S COOLEST CITY

The southernmost city in California has a lot to offer, including vast expanses of wilderness around it.

San Diego is a city unlike any other in California. The second largest in the state by population, San Diego has everything you could ask for in a metropolis: vibrant arts and culture, diverse and varied neighborhoods, incredible food and more entertainment than you could ever see yourself. But even with all that, the city manages to always feel relaxed. Chill coastal vibes are ingrained in every corner of this Southern California paradise.

Part of what makes San Diego so unique is that the city is directly on the border of Mexico, and there's a real cultural influence from Tijuana – its neighbor to the south – in everything from food to festivals to art galleries showcasing Chicano and Latino works.

Another thing that deeply influences the city's character: the beach. Nowhere in San Diego is more than a short drive from its 17 miles of coast. There are beaches for families and for surfers, ocean caves to explore, tide pools to observe, boats to be chartered, seaside boardwalks to stroll and stunning sunsets to appreciate. Outside San Diego proper, smaller beach communities like La Jolla and Carlsbad have cultures uniquely their own, and attractions worth driving for.

THE MAIN AREAS

SAN DIEGO
A city with something for everyone. **p420**

LA JOLLA
Enchanting coastal town full of art. **p430**

TEMECULA
San Diego's answer to Napa Valley. **p437**

Find Your Way

San Diego International Airport is in the city center and is easily accessible. Amtrak's Pacific Surfliner Train travels daily between Santa Barbara, Los Angeles and San Diego, with stops in between.

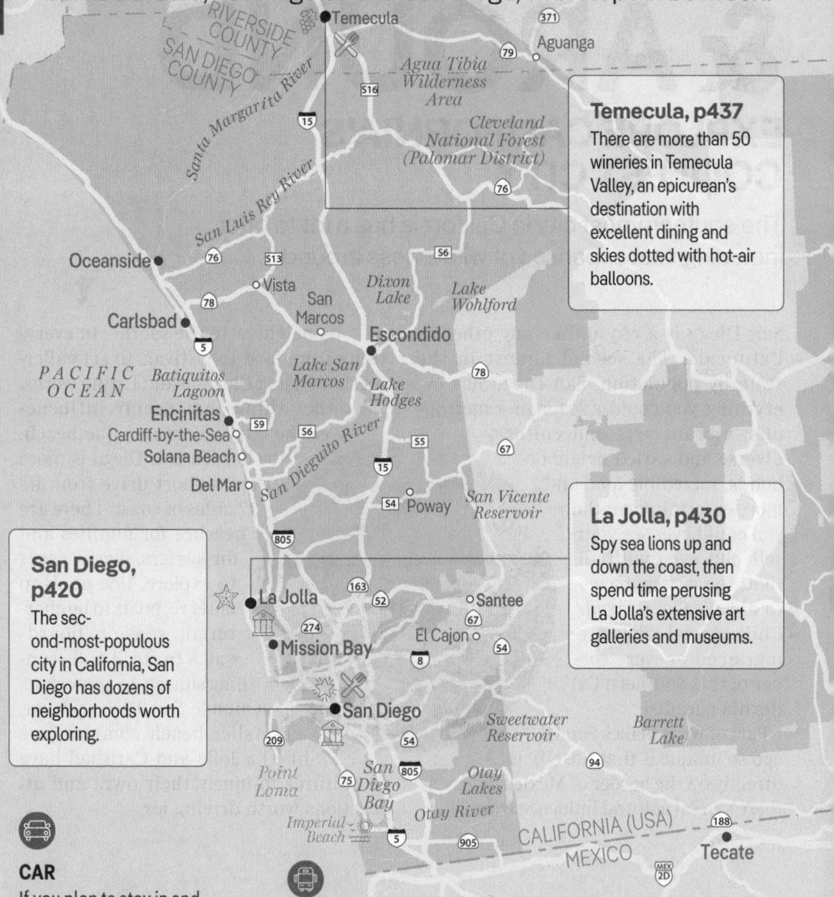

Temecula, p437
There are more than 50 wineries in Temecula Valley, an epicurean's destination with excellent dining and skies dotted with hot-air balloons.

La Jolla, p430
Spy sea lions up and down the coast, then spend time perusing La Jolla's extensive art galleries and museums.

San Diego, p420
The second-most-populous city in California, San Diego has dozens of neighborhoods worth exploring.

CAR

If you plan to stay in and around San Diego, you can get away with not having a car – but if you plan to explore some of the surrounding areas or venture up into the mountains, you're going to want to drive.

TROLLEY

San Diego has a network of trolleys that serve two purposes: they'll get you where you need to go, but they'll also give you a fair bit of history and an overview of local points of interest as you ride.

BICYCLE

The San Diego County Bicycle Coalition has extensive resources about the best and safest bicycle routes. If you're planning to get around on two wheels, you're well covered.

ESTERELV/SHUTTERSTOCK ©

Hot-air balloon, Temecula Valley (p437)

Plan Your Time

Exploring San Diego means going from the ocean all the way up into the mountains. Be prepared for a variety of climates, especially at higher elevations, where it can be cold, even in summer.

JHVEPHOTO/SHUTTERSTOCK ©

San Diego Zoo (p427)

If You Only Do One Thing

- Start with a morning on San Diego's **Imperial Beach** (p426). Take a walk on the Silver Strand watching the birds or go for a swim in the calm surf.

- In the afternoon, head to **Balboa Park** (p426) to explore one or two of the attractions there, from the **San Diego Zoo** (p427) to the 34 different **International Cottages** (p426).

- Head to **Coronado** (p425) for dinner, where you can get a waterfront table at one of the restaurants at **Hotel del Coronado** (p426) to watch the sunset. Then, find a **speakeasy** (p428) with a secret entrance – San Diego has plenty – for a nightcap.

Seasonal Highlights

When it feels like summer every day, you don't have to confine your travel to July and August. In fact, those are the busiest times to visit. Any month of the year is a good time to head to San Diego.

MARCH

See the superbloom at the **Flower Fields** at Carlsbad Ranch when 55 acres of flowers burst into living color.

APRIL

Mission Fed ArtWalk in San Diego's Little Italy is the largest art event on the West Coast and proceeds go to art education.

MAY

Hot-air balloons fill the sky during the **Temecula Valley Balloon & Wine Festival.**

LARISA GRIB/SHUTTERSTOCK ©, BRIAN G. LEWIS/SHUTTERSTOCK ©, KIT LEONG/SHUTTERSTOCK ©

Three Days to Travel Around

● Depending on whether you're flying into San Diego or driving down from the north, take a few days to go up (or down) Pacific Coast Highway. Start in the city and make your way north to **La Jolla** (p430) and **Carlsbad** (p435), or start in a smaller beach town and end up in **San Diego** (p420). Either way, you'll have a nice mix of laid-back time on the coast, and highly entertaining time in the city. Give yourself at least one night in a beachfront hotel, and one night in the city center, for a taste of everything San Diego has to offer.

If You Have More Time

● Venture out into the mountains to Temecula or Julian. Both locations offer hiking, biking and camping – but the former is a wine lover's paradise where a lot of the entertainment is at vineyards, and the latter is a tiny town with the purest expression of life's simple pleasures. Even better...visit them both and decide for yourself what you prefer. **Temecula** (p437) is especially suited to biking enthusiasts – it has 90 miles of bicycle trails. **Julian** (p442) is perfect for hikers with its proximity to the Pacific Crest Trail.

JUNE

The **San Diego County Fair** is a month-long celebration with carnival games, concerts, festivals, performances and agricultural events.

JULY

A month-long celebration of chamber music, with different performances nearly every night at **La Jolla SummerFest**.

AUGUST

Pick your own fruit in Julian for the town's **apple harvest**.

DECEMBER

Celebrate SoCal style with the San Diego Bay **Parade of Lights** with sailing vessels bedecked with thousands of Christmas lights.

SAN DIEGO

Just after Los Angeles, San Diego is California's second-most-populous city. While they're close in size, the two stand in stark contrast to each other. Traversing LA's sprawl mostly requires an automobile and could take two hours in rush hour traffic from end to end, whereas the southernmost city in California is 126 square miles smaller, and easily navigable with, or without, a car.

But don't be fooled by the size: San Diego is still a large city, packed with so many fascinating sights that you'll want to give yourself a good amount of time to explore. A stunning collection of museums in Balboa Park, the world-famous San Diego Zoo, the San Diego Padres baseball team and one of the largest Naval bases in the country are just scratching the surface of what it has to offer. Beyond the city center, there are vibrant neighborhoods worth exploring, which have unique character all their own.

TOP TIP

San Diego's huge waterfront isn't just for the navy, it's also a busy port for cruises. About 75 cruise ships dock in San Diego Bay every year, and 10 cruise lines either stop as a port of call or use the city as their start and end point.

USS Midway Museum

Gaslamp District

CATCH A GAME AT PETCO PARK

The home of the San Diego Padres is located where the Gaslamp and East Village meet. **Petco Park** encompasses the stadium, but also **Gallagher Sq**, which has an outdoor concert venue that brings in huge national touring acts. Gallagher Sq is a popular gathering spot on game days, and has a small baseball diamond in it. Petco Park offers daily guided stadium tours that take guests behind the scenes, into the press box, the Padres Hall of Fame, a luxury suite, and even down onto the field's warning track. Some hotels have sky bridges connecting to Petco Park, so you can walk straight from your room to the game.

Exploring the Heart of San Diego

DOWNTOWN, THE GASLAMP DISTRICT AND THE EMBARCADERO

The Gaslamp District downtown was named for the gas streetlights installed in the area in the late 1800s. The glowing neon signs welcoming you to this historic neighborhood tell you exactly what you need to know about it. Although the buildings are from the Victorian era, what's inside them is totally modern. There are more than 100 places to eat, drink, shop and dance in Gaslamp's 16 square blocks. This is where you'll head if you're looking for nightlife in San Diego, or to have a cocktail on a rooftop lounge. Rumors of ghost sightings swirl throughout the neighborhood, especially at the **Gaslamp Museum at the Davis-Horton House Museum**, which offers ghostly walking tours.

The waterfront area of downtown San Diego, Embarcadero, has a lot to explore, especially when it comes to maritime history. Tour the **USS Midway Museum**, a decommissioned aircraft carrier that served for 47 years, and explore the **Maritime Museum of San Diego**, a collection of historic ships that includes the 150-year-old *Star of India,* the oldest active sailing ship. The **Museum of Contemporary Art San**

WHERE TO STAY DOWNTOWN

Omni San Diego
High-rise hotel in the Gaslamp, connected to Petco Park and the San Diego Convention Center. **$$**

The Guild Hotel
Boutique hotel in a century-old building that was once a YMCA, with original architectural details. **$$$**

Pendry San Diego
Luxury hotel in the Gaslamp District with six restaurants and elegant decor. **$$$**

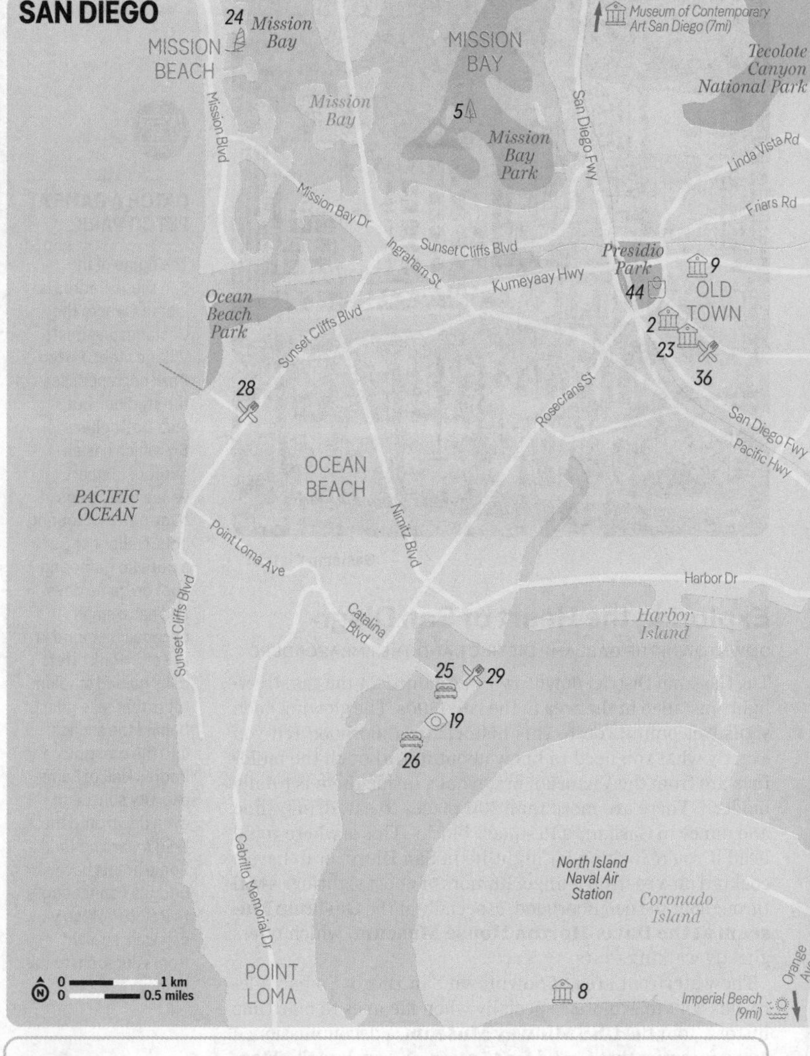

SIGHTS
1 Balboa Park
2 Casa de Estudillo
3 Centro Cultural de la Raza
4 Comic-Con Museum
5 Fiesta Island
6 Fleet Science Center
7 Gaslamp Museum at the Davis-Horton House Museum
8 Heritage Park
9 Junípero Serra Museum
10 Maritime Museum of San Diego
11 Museum of Photographic Arts
12 Museum of Us
13 New Children's Museum
see 2 Old Town San Diego State Historic Park
14 San Diego Air & Space Museum
15 San Diego Model Railroad Museum
16 San Diego Museum of Art
17 San Diego Natural History Museum
18 San Diego Zoo
19 Shelter Island
20 Spanish Village Art Center
21 Timken Museum of Art
22 USS Midway Museum
23 Whaley House Museum

ACTIVITIES, COURSES & TOURS
24 Mission Bay Aquatic Park

SLEEPING
25 Humphrey's Half-Moon Inn
26 Kona Kai Resort & Spa

EATING
27 Animae
28 Azucar
29 Bali Hai
30 Barrio Dogg
31 Ironside Fish and Oyster
32 Little Italy Food Hall
33 Neighborhood
34 Por Vida Collective
35 Station Tavern
36 Tahona

DRINKING & NIGHTLIFE
37 Hillcrest Brewing Company
38 Mothership
see 33 Noble Experiment
39 North Park Brewing
40 Prohibition
41 Thorn Street Beer
42 Trailer Park After Dark

ENTERTAINMENT
43 Landmark Hillcrest Cinemas

SHOPPING
44 Bazaar del Mundo

THE IMAGE PARTY/SHUTTERSTOCK ©

Old Town San Diego State Historic Park

OLD TOWN TROLLEY TOURS

A two-hour loop on the **Old Town Trolley** will take you from Old Town through the Gaslamp Quarter, Embarcadero, Balboa Park and Coronado, with history and information about each area as you go. If you want, you can hop on and off the trolley to explore on your own, then catch a ride back to Old Town on a later trolley. Since parking can be tricky – and sometimes expensive – in San Diego, relying on this unique form of transit is a great option...especially since the ride to get to your destination is entertainment in itself. The tour covers about 25 miles and over 100 points of interest in a full loop.

Diego occupies the city's old, historic train-station building. The **New Children's Museum** has fun, interactive science exhibits where kids can play and learn.

Discover Old Town San Diego

A TRUE STEP BACK IN TIME

The shift is abrupt: one minute you're driving through modern buildings, and the next, you've transported back in time to San Diego's Mexican and early American eras. Old Town is a true gem, with living history all around you, and cultural celebrations that get to the heart of the city's character.

Old Town San Diego State Historic Park is a stretch of 19th-century buildings where people lived and worked nearly 200 years ago. Tour an old schoolhouse, or see the spot where the first American flag was raised in San Diego, in 1846. Shops in the park represent a simpler way of life. You can make your own candles or buy penny candy. **Bazaar del Mundo**, in the center of the historic area, translates to 'marketplace of the world' and brings together merchants selling everything from jewelry to pottery.

Arguably the most iconic of Old Town's historic buildings is the **Whaley House Museum**, constructed in 1856 on land

MUST-SEE EVENTS IN OLD TOWN

Fiesta Old Town Cinco de Mayo
Three days of celebration of Mexican culture, with *lucha libre* wrestling and entertainment.

Dia de Los Muertos
One of the most important holidays in Mexican culture remembers loved ones with a procession and public altar.

Old Town Las Posadas
A holiday tradition, the Las Posadas procession is a Mexican celebration honoring biblical Christmas stories.

where hangings once took place. Today, it's rumored to be so haunted that it's been featured on many ghost-hunting television shows. **Casa de Estudillo** is an original adobe building dating back to 1825, and is furnished with antiques from the 16th to the 20th century. **Heritage Park** nearby has a collection of preserved Victorian homes. The **Junípero Serra Museum** commemorates Spanish Franciscan missionary Father Junipero Serra, when he established the state's first mission; the event is widely considered to be the first founding of California.

Beyond Downtown

NEIGHBORHOODS WORTH EXPLORING

If you truly want to experience San Diego like a local, head to North Park and South Park, just beyond Balboa Park. North Park is often called the best beer neighborhood in the country because of the number of craft-beer bars and breweries along University Ave and 30th St like **North Park Brewing** and **Thorn Street Beer**. South Park has a distinctly indie vibe, with interesting, forward-thinking galleries and vintage shopping. Grab a bite in **Station Tavern**, housed in an old trolley station.

The epicenter of San Diego's LGBTIQ+ community, Hillcrest is a place where everyone is welcome and everyone is accepted. Among home-decor boutiques and wine bars is **Hillcrest Brewing Company**, which describes itself as 'the first gay brewery in the world.' **Landmark Cinemas** screens indie and foreign films.

The city's oldest Mexican-American neighborhood, Logan Heights is a living tribute to Chicano culture, especially in Barrio Logan, an art-filled neighborhood that truly represents the city's vibrant identity. The second Saturday of every month, the **Barrio Art Crawl** is a self-guided tour through the cultural district's public art and galleries, with food and live music. In the summer **La Vuelta Car Cruise** is where owners show off their vintage and modern low-rider cars. At the gourmet coffee shop **Por Vida Collective**, try a horchata latte or one made with *mazapan,* a classic Mexican peanut candy.

Cruising the Coast

SAN DIEGO'S VARIED COASTAL COMMUNITIES

The sparkling beach on Coronado Island has been praised by Dr Beach (drbeach.org) as one of the best in the country. But if we're being honest, all of Coronado seems to shine. This coastal neighborhood is a casual departure from busy

WHY I LOVE SAN DIEGO

Julie Tremaine, writer

Of all California's large cities, San Diego truly is a marvel. It's big but not hard to navigate, full of delights but not overwhelming, full of history but also completely modern. San Diego is bursting with creative energy in everything from its emphasis on preserving and reimagining historic buildings to the public art on display virtually everywhere you turn. I find it impossible to visit this city and not leave with a longer list of things to see, do and eat than I did before I arrived.

WATERFRONT PLACES TO EXPLORE

Mission Beach
Classic beachside boardwalk with a vintage roller coaster, midway games, restaurants and beach bars.

Pacific Beach
Popular for its high-energy party atmosphere, both during the day and during nighttime bonfires.

Point Loma
Views from these cliffs are unparalleled, and there are tide pools to explore, and a lighthouse.

HOTEL DEL CORONADO'S GHOSTS

Coronado's best-known resident is the Hotel del Coronado, one of the most famous and historic hotels in California, if not the entire country. The 1888 hotel was originally built for wealthy Victorians looking to take in the ocean air, and has grown over the years to become a destination beloved for its location, its historic architecture, and, some say, its ghosts. Rooms can be very pricey at the Del, especially during high-demand times of the year. But the good news is that you don't have to be a guest to enjoy many of the hotel's attractions and restaurants.

downtown, even though it's only a few minutes away. The island is full of beach cottages and boutiques. Ferry Landing is a strollable collection of shops, restaurants and galleries.

The southernmost beach town in California is in South Bay, only a few miles from the Mexico border. **Imperial Beach** is popular for fishing, surfing, bird-watching and cycling, especially on the Silver Strand that connects Imperial to Coronado. The **Imperial Beach Outdoor Surf Museum** is a collection of surfboard benches that explain the history of surfing in the area and what it means to San Diego.

Mission Bay Aquatic Park is the place to go for water sports. This area offers everything from kayaking to water skiing, sailing and kite surfing. If you want to charter a fishing or sailing excursion, the is the place to do it. **Fiesta Island** in Mission Bay has an off-leash dog park.

Shelter Island is the closest you can get to feeling like you're in Hawaii while staying on the mainland, with hotels like the Kona Kai Resort & Spa – with a private beach – and the decidedly tropical **Humphrey's Half-Moon Inn**. **Bali Hai** is a local legend: this waterfront Polynesian restaurant has famous mai tais and decor from the South Pacific.

Museum-Hopping in Balboa Park

ART, HISTORY AND SCIENCE MUSEUMS

Balboa Park's nickname, 'the Smithsonian of the West', isn't hyperbole. San Diego's version of New York's Central Park is home to 17 museums and performance venues, Spanish Renaissance architecture, and the **San Diego Zoo**. If you try to see all of the museums in one day, you likely won't be able to – but if you just want to stroll around and appreciate their architecture from the outside, you can definitely do that in an afternoon. The 150-year-old park holds a lot but is easily walkable.

For fine-arts appreciation, try the **Museum of Photographic Arts** for its vast photography collection, the **San Diego Museum of Art** for its rotating international exhibits, or the **Timken Museum of Art** for works by European old masters. The **Centro Cultural de la Raza** is an arts center highlighting Chicano, Mexican, Indigenous and Latino culture; the **Spanish Village Art Center** is a community of more than 200 artisans showing their works.

To learn about the world, try the **Museum of Us**, dedicated to human history. The **San Diego Air & Space Museum** has the real Apollo 9 Command Module and artifacts from Amelia Earhart and Charles Lindbergh. The **Fleet Science Center** has 100 interactive science exhibits and the **San Diego Natural History Museum** has a T-rex skeleton on display.

WITH MORE TIME IN BALBOA PARK

Seventeen Gardens
The park's vast gardens include a Japanese Friendship Garden and a rose garden that blooms March-December.

The International Cottages
A gathering of 34 different countries, representing their traditions through music, arts, dance and food.

Antique Entertainment
A 1910 carousel with hand-carved animals and a miniature, rideable antique railroad train.

SARAH QUINTANS/SHUTTERSTOCK ©

Giraffes at the San Diego Zoo

Quirkier museums include the **Comic-Con Museum**, celebrating all things superhero and the city's enormous comics convention; and the **San Diego Model Railroad Museum**, the world's largest operating model railroad, which runs through a miniature California.

Wildlife Encounters at San Diego Zoo & Safari Park

TWO EQUALLY WILD EXPERIENCES

Take everything you've ever heard about the **San Diego Zoo**, and double it: that will give you some idea of how vast, and wildly impressive, this place is. Among the animals housed here are big cats (cheetahs, jaguars and leopards); elephants, giraffes and hippos; grizzly bears, polar bears and red pandas; king cobras and anacondas; and many, many more. The

ALL THE PARK'S A STAGE

Balboa Park hosts an incredible amount of live performances, from a puppet theater to the city's youth ballet company and youth symphony. The **Old Globe**, based on Shakespeare's Globe Theatre in London, has three stages and hosts productions that often head to Broadway, and it has won a Tony Award. Its annual **Shakespeare Festival** draws international attention.

One of the most unique things to do on a trip to San Diego is to attend a Sunday afternoon organ concert performed on the **Spreckels Organ**, the largest outdoor organ in the world, with more than 5000 pipes.

ANNUAL FESTIVALS

Adams Avenue Street Fair
This Normal Heights festival has 100 musical acts, 350 artist booths, carnival rides and great food.

San Diego Pride Music Festival
A massive two-day music festival that's part of Pride weekend.

Wonderfront Music & Arts Festival
This three-day festival happens up and down the Embarcadero, and brings in huge musical acts.

zoo is so large that there's a double-decker bus running a continual loop tour, and an aerial tram that flies from one side of the zoo to the other, with beautiful views of the rest of the park. The San Diego Zoo has been instrumental in saving the endangered California condor, which you can also see while you're there.

But the zoo isn't the only way to experience wildlife around here. In northern San Diego County, the San Diego Zoo has a **Safari Park** where animals roam freely in savannas. You can view them by taking guided tours through the preserve. The experiences vary depending on your interests: you can go on the **Sun Up Cheetah Safari** to see the park before it opens for the day, when cheetahs are running at top speed; or the **Roar & Snore**, where you camp in the park overnight.

ROOFTOP BARS

In a place as beautiful as San Diego, it only makes sense that there would be a lot of rooftop destinations to soak it in. The city has nearly two dozen, ranging from downtown cityscapes to beachfront oases. **Altitude Sky Lounge** in the Gaslamp is the tallest at 22 stories above the city. See and be seen at **Level Four Pool Deck** and **Lounge** or **The Rooftop by STK** – downtown rooftops that both bring in DJs and entertainment. **Kettner Exchange** in Little Italy serves an interesting wine selection and has self-serve beer taps. In Pacific Beach, **El Prez** serves gourmet tacos with ocean views.

San Diego by Night

NIGHTLIFE, GAMING AND ENTERTAINMENT

San Diego is home to the highest concentration of Native American tribes in the country (there are 18 different tribes in the county), many of which have built gaming casinos on their tribal land and use those profits to support their communities. There are 10 around San Diego.

If you love live music, opt for **Valley View Casino** in Valley Center, with seven restaurants and free nightly live entertainment. For serious gamers, **Sycuan Casino in El Cajon** has extensive table games including Sycuan-style craps and roulette. Gourmands – or just fans of cooking shows – should head to **Harrah's Resort Southern California** in Funner, home to Gordon Ramsay's **Hell's Kitchen** restaurant made famous on the TV show of the same name. If you want to spend your windfall right away, **Viejas Casino** has an attached outlet mall with 57 stores.

If you're more of a laid-back lounge person, there are many places to get creative cocktails in a lower-key atmosphere. **Prohibition** is a speakeasy hidden behind a door labeled 'Law Office, Edward Joseph O'Hare, Esq.' Inside you will find great cocktails and live music. **Noble Experiment** is a speakeasy you access by opening a fake wall of kegs in the back of a restaurant called **Neighborhood**. There, under gothic portraits and a wall of brass skulls, meticulous bartenders will craft you anything you're dreaming of.

Mothership is an outer-space-themed lounge that has been getting national attention since it opened in 2022. **Trailer Park After Dark** is all-in on the theme, decorating with artificial turf and plastic-covered sofas.

WHERE TO GO FOR LIVE ENTERTAINMENT

American Comedy Co.
Gaslamp Quarter club that brings in national headliner comedians for nightly comedy shows.

The Observatory
Once an opera house, this North Park concert hall has a varied lineup of live music.

House of Blues
A downtown music venue with Sunday gospel brunch and free live entertainment in its restaurant.

The Flavors of San Diego

A FOOD-LOVER'S CITY

San Diego is best known for Cali-Baja cuisine, a unique hybrid that combines Southern California foods with Mexican flavors and preparations. Experience it at **Barrio Dogg** in Barrio Logan, which serves internationally inspired hot dogs like the Bombero made with seven chiles and a habanero carrot slaw. In Old Town, **Tahona** serves reimagined Oaxacan cuisine and 100 varieties of mezcal.

There are many old-school and modern Italian eateries in Little Italy, where the first Italian immigrants lived when they arrived in the city, but the **Little Italy Food Hall** is a must-stop. In the expansive Piazza della Famiglia, this food destination has six food stations, a sit-down restaurant, cooking demonstrations and two bars. Nearby, **Ironside Fish and Oyster** is an upscale seafood restaurant that doesn't take itself too seriously: among the champagne and caviar are touches of mermaid decor in this refurbished 1920s factory.

Downtown, **Animae** is a fine-dining steakhouse infused with Japanese and Filipino influences from chef Tara Monsod. At **Azucar** in Ocean Beach, pastry chef Vivian Hernandez-Jackson is baking French pastries with Cuban influences.

Thien Huong, a popular Vietnamese breakfast and lunch chain, recently opened its first American restaurant in Mira Mesa, a neighborhood with a stellar collection of Filipino, Chinese, Japanese and Korean restaurants.

If you've got too many restaurants on your must-taste list and too little time to try them, solve your problem by going on a walking food tour of the city. **Wild Foodie Tours** offers an International Food Tour led by Mexican and Asian food experts with tastings of Chinese, Mexican and Filipino food at restaurants in different neighborhoods; and a Dim Sum Tour led by a Cantonese-American guide that includes a dim-sum brunch and a tour of an Asian supermarket and bakery. **Foodelicious Tours** offers a North Park 'beerucation' tour, a cocktail tour of the East Side, a Little Italy Booze and Bites tour, and a tour through Chicano foods in the Barrio Logan neighborhood.

THE MOST DECORATED RESTAURANT IN SOCAL

Addison, a fine-dining restaurant helmed by chef William Bradley, was awarded three Michelin stars in the 2022 California guide, making it one of only seven three-star restaurants in California (and the only one south of the San Francisco Bay Area).

Chef Bradley serves a nine-course tasting menu focusing on local, seasonal ingredients and the flavors of Southern California. The experience will cost you, though: dinner is $325 per person for the tasting menu. Wine pairings are recommended and come at an additional expense.

The opulent restaurant is located at the Fairmont Grand Del Mar, a truly beautiful hotel with a price tag to match.

GETTING AROUND

San Diego shares an international border with Tijuana, and it's easy for US citizens with passports to head south and explore one of the world's most visited cities. There's even a Cross Border Xpress skybridge connecting the Tijuana International Airport to San Diego.

Like any city, San Diego is challenging to park downtown and gets easier as you move away from the city center. But you might want to leave your car behind and rely on the abundant public transportation. The Red Trolley is a city-run system that is more affordable and offers more stops than the Old Town Trolley; there are 62 stations and trolleys arrive every 15 minutes. Coaster trains run up and down the coast, connecting San Diego to coastal communities to the north like La Jolla and Carlsbad. The Sprinter light rail system runs east-west from Oceanside to Escondido.

LA JOLLA

Prized for its scenery and its location, La Jolla is more than just its coastline. The city is full of creative energy, with public-art walking tours, world-renowned galleries and museums, a beloved annual music festival and a playhouse that's nationally acclaimed for its work. It might technically be considered a suburb of San Diego, but it's such an enchanting place that you may get this far, decide it's where you want to stay, and never actually make it into the city.

There is something undeniably special about La Jolla, which means 'the jewel' in Spanish. The beach town has a golden glow about it, with the warm Southern California sun reflecting off the water and the rays baking into the sand. Sea lions lounge on rocky outcroppings and splash in the waves. High above the water, La Jolla's cliffs present a different perspective on the city's 7 miles of coastline.

Sea lions at La Jolla Cove

MICHAEL J MAGEE/SHUTTERSTOCK ©

TOP TIP

Parking is tough in touristy parts of town. Once you find a spot, keep it – then walk, bike, or use public transportation. Old Town Trolley Tours has unlimited hop-on hop-off privileges.

BEST BEACHES

Directly below Scripps Park in La Jolla Village is **La Jolla Cove**, one of the most famous beaches in Southern California. The cove is great for swimming or just lounging in the sand. This is also the beach where you're almost guaranteed to see sea lions. Remember to keep your distance; some days, there are ropes in place to ensure the sea lions have enough space on the beach.

Families love **La Jolla Shores**, **Windansea** and **Torrey Pines State Beach** for their mild surf and expansive sand. Surfers love **Black's Beach** and **Tourmaline Surf Park**, which is better for beginners because of its milder surf.

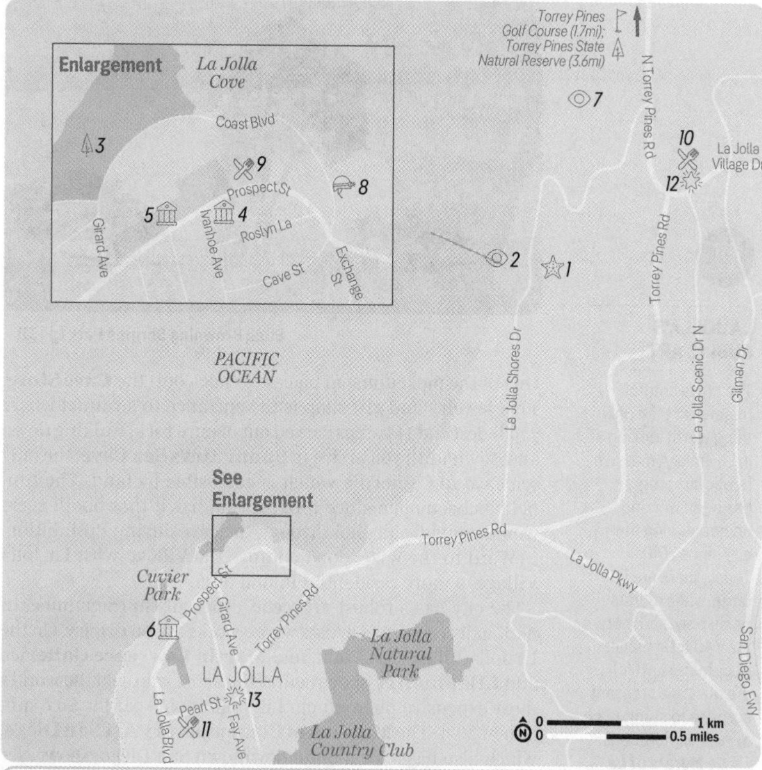

SIGHTS
1 Birch Aquarium at Scripps Institution of Oceanography
2 Ellen Browning Scripps Memorial Pier
3 Ellen Browning Scripps Park
4 LIK Fine Art La Jolla
5 Martin Lawrence Galleries
6 Museum of Contemporary Art San Diego
7 Scripps Coastal Reserve
8 Sunny Jim's Sea Cave

EATING
9 George's at the Cove
10 James' Place Prime Seafood Sushi
11 Taco Stand

ENTERTAINMENT
12 La Jolla Playhouse
13 The Comedy Store – La Jolla

SHOPPING
see 8 Cave Store

Explore La Jolla

NATURAL BEAUTY AND CREATIVE VIBES

The most strollable area of town, the Village is a picturesque collection of shops and restaurants, and includes many of La Jolla's most notable attractions – including the sea lions the city is famous for. Throughout the Village, there are many vistas from which to take in the coastline and its most vocal – and, let's face it, fragrant – inhabitants. **Ellen Browning Scripps Park** is especially picturesque. Most days, you'll see street vendors set up in and around Scripps Park, selling everything from handmade jewelry to art painted *en plein air* right there in front of you.

This is where you'll want to head if you want to walk around, see some scenery, stop for a coffee or lunch, and browse stores.

Ellen Browning Scripps Park (p431)

LA JOLLA'S PUBLIC ART

The city's natural beauty isn't the only thing worth looking at in La Jolla. A massive public-art program has been working on beautifying the city since 2010. Today, there are 15 large-scale murals on display, and more than 40 total pieces of public art, which are always a pleasant surprise to stumble on in your explorations.

The **Murals of La Jolla** website details the art and the artists, including YouTube videos, and offers a self-guided walking tour to see them for yourself. If you can't get enough of the vibrant works, take them home with you in *The Murals of La Jolla* coffee-table book, a work of art in itself that supports the project.

One of the most unusual places to check out: the **Cave Store**. This jewelry and gift shop is the entrance to a tunnel where you'll descend 144 steps carved out of pure rock, walking down and down until you arrive in **Sunny Jim's Sea Cave**, the only sea cave in California which is accessible by land. The tunnel has been open since 1902; legend has it that bootleggers would smuggle alcohol through the cave during Prohibition.

(Word to the wise: don't confuse the Village with La Jolla Village, a more residential inland area.)

The city has a robust art scene, especially in the number of nationally renowned artists whose works are on display. On the La Jolla Village Art Walk, find **Martin Lawrence Galleries** and **LIK Fine Art**, showroom of the artist who sold the world's most expensive photograph. Lik's Phantom sold for $6.5 million in 2014. The **Museum of Contemporary Art San Diego**, which also has a location in downtown San Diego, showcases works created since 1950 and has robust collections of pop art, Latin American art and works by San Diego and Tijuana artists.

La Jolla is also home to a standout local theater company, **La Jolla Playhouse**, which is nationally renowned for the quality of its works and the star power it attracts. The playhouse hosts world premieres of innovative and forward-thinking works, and brings in luminaries of the stage like Matthew Broderick to star in productions.

The **La Jolla Music Society** hosts a fine arts and music festival every summer and varied musical performances throughout the winter. The **Comedy Store**, the renowned Los Angeles comedy club, has a local outpost and brings in national acts you've definitely seen on television before.

The Torrey Pines neighborhood in northern La Jolla has some of the city's most iconic destinations: **Torrey Pines Golf Course** and **Torrey Pines State Natural Reserve**. The mu-

WHERE TO STAY IN LA JOLLA

San Diego Marriott La Jolla
Closer to UCSD and Torrey Pines, this hotel has two restaurants and an outdoor pool. **$$**

Estancia La Jolla Hotel & Spa
A Four Diamond boutique hotel with luxury amenities and 10 acres of gardens and courtyards. **$$$**

La Jolla Shores Hotel
Request a water view at this oceanfront hotel that has easy access to the beach. **$$$**

nicipal golf course, which is open to the public, is widely regarded as one of the best golf destinations in the country because of its sweeping cliffside location and the quality of its terrain. The natural reserve is a popular hiking spot prized for those same views. It's also home to a scarce species of pine tree – you guessed it, *Pinus torreyana* (Torrey pine) – which was once prevalent in California and is now preserved only in this reserve and on an island off Santa Barbara.

La Jolla has two offshore marine reserves that protect diverse marine-life habitats and are studied by oceanic research institutions: the **San Diego-Scripps Coastal Marine Conservation Area** and the **Matlahuayl State Marine Reserve**. Both make ideal locations for snorkeling and scuba diving – but if you'd rather see marine life while staying dry, you might want to head to the **Birch Aquarium**.

Part of USCD's Scripps Institution of Oceanography, the aquarium is open to the public and has more than 60 marine habitats on display, including an enormous, two-story kelp forest full of stunning marine life. Among Birch's most famous residents: a pod of little blue penguins, leopard sharks, and seahorses and seadragons. (There's also a behind-the-scenes seahorse tour for an additional fee.)

The aquarium has outdoor tide-pool tanks where people can touch the marine life inside, and offers guided explorations of natural tide pools led by an aquarium naturalist, generally in the winter and early spring. Once per month, Birch hosts **Ocean at Night**, an after-hours event that celebrates bioluminescence in all its forms (including in glowing cocktails) and has live music and entertainment.

Another part of Scripps that puts you close to the ocean: the **Ellen Browning Scripps Memorial Pier**, where oceanographic research takes place daily. You can only access the pier via student-led tours through **Scripps Community Outreach for Public Education** (SCOPE), which is the group you need to contact to schedule one.

When sunset hits, there's no better restaurant you can choose than **George's at the Cove**. This waterfront seafood restaurant has a downstairs dining room serving fine-dining cuisine, and a more casual ocean terrace rooftop with gorgeous views. Before a show, **James's Place** is an Asian-fusion restaurant serving steak and sushi in La Jolla Playhouse. The **Taco Stand** serves killer tacos with handmade tortillas and slow-roasted and braised meats; it's so popular that the quick-service restaurant has expanded with locations across Southern California and even Miami.

PAYING RESPECTS AT MT SOLEDAD

Standing atop Mt Soledad is a unique tribute to members of the US armed forces. The **Mt Soledad National Veterans Memorial** doesn't just honor the memory of soldiers who have passed away – it also honors living soldiers who were honorably discharged from their service. There are more than 5000 plaques across the memorial, each with the name and rank of a service person, a paragraph detailing their service, and any citations they have received. Family members can nominate a loved one, and thousands upon thousands of visitors to the memorial each year will be able to read their story to learn who they are and how they served.

GETTING AROUND

Because La Jolla is a suburb of San Diego, it's easily accessible through the city's public-transportation systems. The Red Trolley arrives every seven minutes in peak times and every 15 minutes on average through the day. The Old Town Trolley Tour includes La Jolla as one of 11 stops on its guided tour. The Coaster train travels north up the coast from San Diego, stopping in La Jolla also. Find schedules for all San Diego public transportation on 511sd.com.

Beyond La Jolla

Del Mar and Carlsbad are only a few miles from each other, but they have very distinct personalities.

Beachside locales like Del Mar and Carlsbad are the strongest endorsement there is for taking the long way. If you travel on the I-5 freeway, you'll miss some of the most charming parts of Southern California. Take the more leisurely Pacific Coast Highway (PCH) and you'll encounter the kind of places that stick with you long after you've left.

Del Mar is home to the annual San Diego County Fair and the Del Mar Racetrack, which has big Hollywood names associated with it. It's only 2 sq miles and with a population of just over 4000 people, but over 2 million people visit annually. Carlsbad is also boasts gorgeous beaches, plus unique attractions including the Legoland theme park.

TOP TIP

Make a detour to see two side-by-side 1920s homes in Encinitas (a renowned surfing destination) shaped like real ships.

Del Mar Racetrack

ROSAMAR/SHUTTERSTOCK ©

Seaside Walks at Del Mar

A TINY CITY WITH BIG CHARM

Don't let its petite size fool you – there's a lot to love about Del Mar, including one of the biggest annual events in the whole state. Besides the San Diego County Fair, the Del Mar Fairgrounds are also home to the **Del Mar Racetrack**. Bing Crosby was an original owner and instrumental in getting the track built. On its opening day in 1937, the crooner was at the gate greeting the first guests. The first-ever nationally broadcast horserace was at Del Mar, where Seabiscuit won by a nose. Today, the thoroughbred racing season is in late summer and late fall.

Like its name implies – *del mar* means 'of the sea' in Spanish – the coast is the main attraction in this town. There are gorgeous walking paths with both canyon and water views in the **Crest Rim Preserve**, **Del Mar Canyon Preserve**, **Scripps Bluff Preserve**, **San Dieguito Lagoon** and **Sea Cliff Park**, which has benches where you can sit on the bluff and take it all in. For something a little more active, rent a kayak or stand-up paddleboard, fish in one of the town's beach breaks, bike up and down PCH, or find a pickup volleyball game at **North Beach**.

The **Del Mar Art Walk** is a mile-long stroll that includes the city's permanent outdoor artwork and a rotating collection of pieces by visiting artists.

Blooms, Oysters & More in Carlsbad

SO MANY ATTRACTIONS, SO LITTLE TIME

There's no bad time to visit Carlsbad, but the best time is probably spring, when the Flower Fields at **Carlsbad Ranch** burst into vivid color. These 55 acres of carefully cultivated flowers bloom from March to May every year; beyond the sea of color, there's also a floral hedge maze and kids' activities at the ranch.

The city is home to a host of unique attractions, like the **Museum of Making Music**, which details the history of music and musical instruments, and hosts a concert series all year long. The **Carlsbad Barrio & Museum** celebrates the city's Mexican heritage and the families who established the area as a center of agriculture more than a century ago. The **Gemological Institute of America** houses a vast collection of stones, including the **Tower of Brilliance**, the world's largest crystal octahedron.

At **Carlsbad Aquafarm**, you can tour Southern California's only oyster farm, plus take a class in oyster shucking – or, if

SEE CALIFORNIA IN MINIATURE AT LEGOLAND

If you've ever wanted to see all of California in one day, Legoland is the place to do it – that is, if the California you want to see is all constructed out of miniature plastic bricks. This theme park has extensive, hugely impressive scale models of everything from San Francisco's Golden Gate Bridge to Napa Valley's vineyards. There are also more than 60 rides at the theme park, including those for very young kids all the way up to roller-coaster thrill rides. Two Lego hotels are on property: the **Legoland Resort Hotel** has pirate- and adventure-themed rooms, and the **Legoland Castle Hotel** is full of wizards and dragons. Both offer free hot breakfast and nightly family entertainment.

WHERE TO STAY IN DEL MAR & CARLSBAD

L'Auberge Del Mar
A luxury hotel with beach access, a spa, a fine dining restaurant and pet-friendly accommodations. **$$$**

Beach Terrace Inn
This newly renovated beachfront hotel in Carlsbad has gorgeous views and easy access to the sand. **$$**

Cape Rey Resort & Spa
This Carlsbad hotel has beach access, and a large pool for when you've had enough ocean. **$$**

FUN TIMES AT SAN DIEGO COUNTY FAIR

One of the most highly anticipated events of the year is the San Diego County Fair, which is so huge, with so much to do, that it lasts a month. More than a million people visit the Del Mar Fairgrounds in June and July for the fair, which has more than 2000 attractions and 1700 performers. There's a midway with carnival rides and games, concerts with major headliners, art and flower exhibitions, animal encounters and shows, artisan craft demonstrations, and wine, beer and spirits festivals – among many other things to do, see and eat.

ROSAMAR/SHUTTERSTOCK ©

Flower Fields at Carlsbad Ranch (p435)

you'd prefer, take a three-hour **Carlsbad Food Tour** that visits local restaurants and explains the history of the city. You can also sample the city's nine breweries on a **Scavengers Beer & Adventure Tour**.

Carlsbad also has four golf courses: **Rancho Carlsbad Golf Club** is a public course, **The Crossings** has gotten awards for its restaurant, **Park Hyatt Aviara Golf Club** has a course designed by Arnold Palmer, and **Omni La Costa Golf Course** has been played by pros like Jack Nicklaus and Tiger Woods.

GETTING AROUND

Carlsbad is about a 35 mile drive from San Diego, but it's easy to get to on the Coaster commuter train. Breeze buses transport people all through North San Diego County, including Carlsbad (and to high-congestion areas like Legoland). Find schedules for all San Diego public transportation on 511sd.com. Nearby Oceanside has a transit hub with connections to northbound local trains and to Amtrak. If you're driving, you're in luck: all public parking lots and street parking is free in the city. But pay close attention to street signs, because busier areas have three-hour parking limits where you will be ticketed if you stay longer.

TEMECULA

Most people associate Napa Valley and Sonoma County with the best wines coming out of California – but the truth is that the entire state is littered with prime grape-growing areas, even all the way down to the southernmost parts of SoCal. Temecula is only an hour away from San Diego, but it feels like an entirely different world. Pull into Temecula Valley and you'll see row after row of grapevines dotted with picturesque tasting rooms, with the Temescal and Santa Ana mountains rising up in the distance.

Beyond the more than 50 wineries, there are destination-worthy golf courses, 90 miles of cycling trails, plenty of outdoor activities, plus excellent restaurants to refuel in. Hot-air balloons are so popular here there's an annual Temecula Valley Wine & Balloon Festival every May. Time your visit to enjoy food, wine tastings, concerts (past headliners have included Brad Paisley and REO Speedwagon), and to see 50 vivid balloons in the sky.

TOP TIP

Every September, Temecula celebrates the grape with events and live entertainment at local wineries, tasting tours, farm-to-table culinary events... even grape stomping! Year round you can visit the largest country-music venue on the West Coast, the Temecula Stampede in Old Town offers line dancing, bull riding and live music.

Doffo Winery (p440)

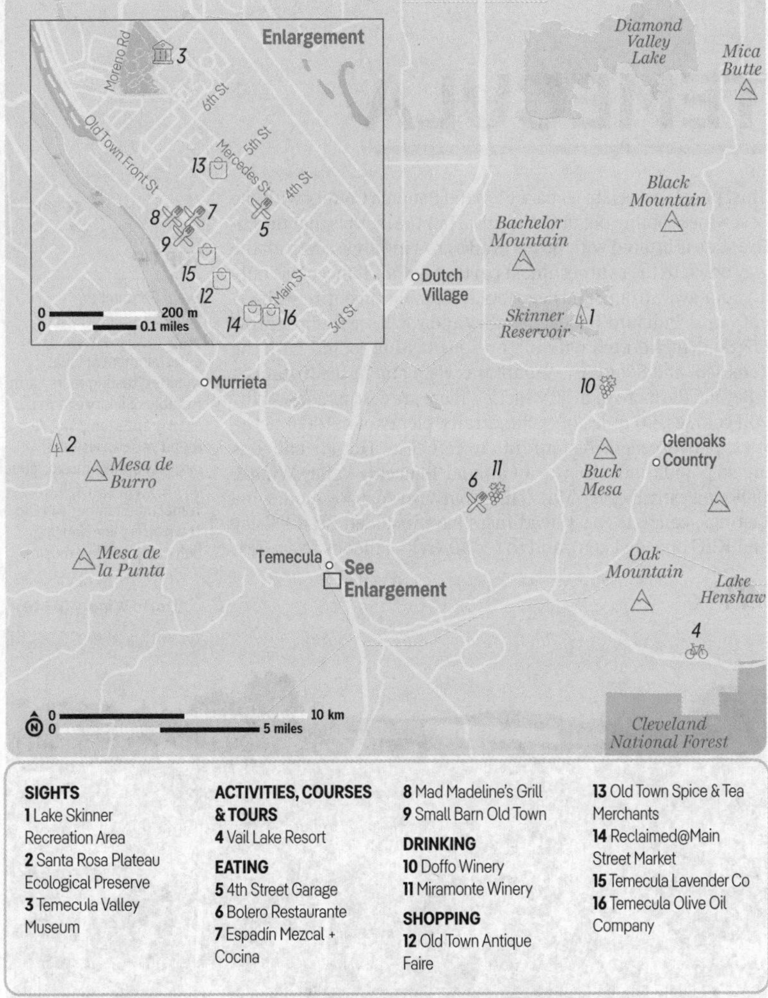

SIGHTS
1 Lake Skinner Recreation Area
2 Santa Rosa Plateau Ecological Preserve
3 Temecula Valley Museum

ACTIVITIES, COURSES & TOURS
4 Vail Lake Resort

EATING
5 4th Street Garage
6 Bolero Restaurante
7 Espadín Mezcal + Cocina
8 Mad Madeline's Grill
9 Small Barn Old Town

DRINKING
10 Doffo Winery
11 Miramonte Winery

SHOPPING
12 Old Town Antique Faire
13 Old Town Spice & Tea Merchants
14 Reclaimed@Main Street Market
15 Temecula Lavender Co
16 Temecula Olive Oil Company

Winery-Hopping in Temecula

ENJOYING WINERIES AND MUCH MORE

The heart of Temecula Valley was an important location in the Old West: after Mexico ceded California to the USA, Temecula was a stagecoach stop and home to the second-ever post office in California, after San Francisco. The **Temecula Valley Museum** explores local history from the Native Luiseno tribe to colonization through Mission San Luis Rey and Western expansion, with a miniature street scene for kids to play in and interact with.

Walking into Old Town today is very much reminiscent of the late 1800s: there are historic Old West buildings, but now they're home to antiques stores, boutiques, craft breweries

CLAUDINE VAN MASSENHOVE/SHUTTERSTOCK ©

Temecula Lavender Company

and restaurants. **Temecula Olive Oil Company** grows its own olives and presses them into robust olive oils; tastings are free in the shop. **Old Town Spice & Tea Merchants** offers 350 spices and 100 loose-leaf teas. **Temecula Lavender Company** sells products made from flowers grown on its own local lavender farm. One block on Fourth St holds several antiques shops, like **Old Town Antique Faire** and **Reclaimed@ Main Street Market**, which refurbishes vintage furniture.

Temecula Valley is a popular spot for cyclists, with more than 90 miles of biking trails and trail maps provided by **Bike Temecula Valley** bicycle coalition. **Vail Lake Resort** has an enormous bass-fishing lake, as well as horseback riding, camping, a mountain-bike park and 40 miles of hiking trails.

In the **Santa Rosa Plateau Ecological Reserve**, there are a vast number of varied terrains and ecosystems that house 200 species of native birds and 49 endangered or rare animal and plant species, including one that exists nowhere else on earth except the 9000-acre reserve. **Lake Skinner Recreation Area** in nearby Winchester has camping, horseback riding, fishing and boating on the lake.

Bolero Restaurante (with its counterpart Bolero Winery) is located in Europa Village. The restaurant serves tapas with a gourmet sensibility. Its chef Hany Ali trained and cooked throughout Europe before arriving in California. **Small Barn**,

PECHANGA RESORT CASINO

One of the largest casinos in the country is in Temecula, just minutes from Old Town. Pechanga, owned by the Pechanga Band of Indians, has 200,000 sq feet of gaming – and a lot of reasons to visit, even if gambling isn't your thing. The AAA Four Diamond property (named the best casino in the country by *USA Today*) has a large luxury hotel with an enormous pool complex and spa, a concert venue that brings in acts like The Beach Boys and comedian Kevin James, and more than a dozen restaurants including a fine-dining steakhouse and an upscale sushi bar.

WHERE TO STAY IN TEMECULA

Temecula Creek Inn
Idyllic resort with a 27-hole golf course, fine dining and complimentary shuttle service. **$$$**

Hotel Temecula
Old West vibes abound at this 1891 historic hotel in the heart of old town. **$$**

The Vine House Bed & Breakfast
Luxury inn with vineyard views and complimentary breakfast; wineries in walking distance. **$$**

SLEEP IN A WINERY

While there are many hotels in the area, if you're a wine lover on an adults getaway, you might never want to leave the vineyard. Many Temecula wineries have accommodations on property, like **Inn at Churon Winery**, where all suites have fireplaces, spa tubs and complimentary breakfast. **Ponte Vineyard Inn** is a four-diamond boutique hotel that offers discounts to wine club members. **Carter Estate Winery and Resort** is dog-friendly, and has suites in the inn and standalone bungalows for more privacy. **Europa Village** has a Spanish-inspired inn to complement its tapas restaurant and Spanish-style Bolero wines. It is also expanding with Italian and French inns, tasting rooms and restaurants.

Temecula Olive Oil Company (p438)

a farm-to-table restaurant and boutique winery, evolved from owners Dan and Cathy Gibson's small winemaking operation in their backyard. **Espadín Mezcal + Cocina** serves inspired regional Mexican food with cocktails that celebrate agave-based spirits. **4th Street Garage** offers a unique dining experience: live music, barbecue and craft brews, in a refurbished garage that houses a rotating collection of vintage cars (and encourages you to bring yours to show off). **Mad Madeline's Grill**, a vintage diner in Old Town, serves burgers and old-fashioned milkshakes.

Because the weather is dry and hot, similar to a Mediterranean climate, Temecula is especially well-suited to growing Spanish, French and Italian grape varietals. Expect to sip sangiovese and syrah – though vineyards farm more than two dozen different grapes locally. At **Doffo Winery**, Marcelo Doffo channels his Argentine and Italian heritage to make outstanding zinfandel and red blends, and also has a collection of vintage motorcycles at the winery. **Miramonte Winery**, another standout, focuses on Spanish- and Portuguese-influenced styles like tempranillo and medium-bodied red blends.

GETTING AROUND

While driving is definitely the easiest way to get to Temecula Valley, once you're there, you might want to park your car and forget about it...especially if you're planning to go wine tasting. There are plenty of options for local wine tours and car services that will leave the responsibility of the designated driver to a professional.

Borrow Our Bikes and Temecula Wine Country E-Bikes offer e-bike rentals. Sidecar Tours has something totally unique: vintage motorcycles with sidecars modified to fit two people that will transport you anywhere in the valley. There are even horse-drawn carriage wine tours courtesy of Temecula Carriage Company.

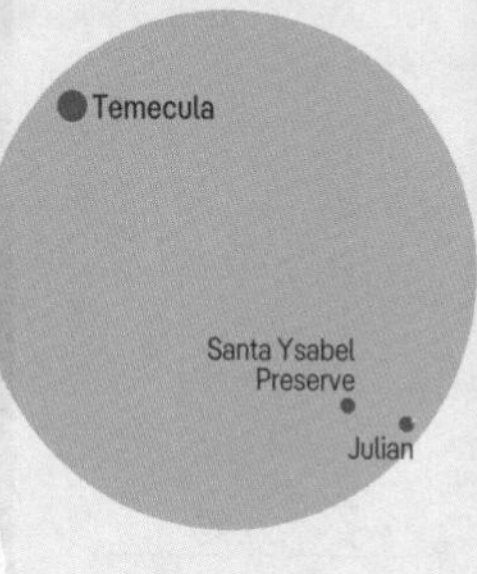

Beyond Temecula

Charming mountain town with historic gold mines, apple orchards and wildlife. Make sure you arrive hungry.

This tiny mountain town, famous for its apple pie, is an official California Historical Landmark and only an hour away from San Diego. There's one main street, lined with shops, cafes and bakeries – plus historic hotels and several small museums. Depending on your show of choice, it will either give you major *Gilmore Girls* Stars Hollow vibes or visions of *Schitt's Creek*, in the best possible way. The place is overflowing with welcoming, small-town charm.

Unlike most coastal destinations in Southern California, Julian is affordable from top-to-bottom. Most accommodations are B&Bs. Many visitors also take advantage of the surrounding landscape and camp in and around the nearby Volcan and Cuyamacas mountains.

TOP TIP

Julian is an International Dark Sky Community. Bring your binoculars or your telescope, and plan to spend some time contemplating the universe.

Julian (p442)

TRAVELINGDANI/SHUTTERSTOCK ©

Hard apple cider tasting at the Calico Ranch & Cidery

Beyond Gold-Mining History

GOLD MINING AND OUTDOOR ADVENTURES

You don't just learn about the gold-rush history in Julian, you see it for yourself. Start at the **Julian Pioneer Museum**. Staffed by volunteers, it is open for limited hours, Friday to Sunday. Inside you'll find the history of the town depicted through artifacts, exhibits and local wildlife specimens. Next, the **Old Julian Jail** (free) has been maintained by the same local man for more than 30 years.

At the **Eagle Mining Company**, you can pan for gold and tour two abandoned (but refurbished) mines. The property includes antique mining equipment and a small museum of Julian curiosities. At **Julian Mining Company**, you can pan for gold or sluice for gems, throw tomahawks and ride a mine train through a tiny mine tunnel.

The **Julian Natural History Museum** houses gold collected from Coleman Creek plus West Coast marine-life specimens. **Fort Cross Old Timey Adventures** offers farm tours with archery and old-fashioned games like slingshot shooting.

Julian is within easy distance of Anza-Borrego Desert State Park (p476), the largest in California, as well as **Cleveland National Forest**. **Laguna Mountain Recreation Area** and

STAYING AT THE JULIAN GOLD RUSH HOTEL

To truly immerse yourself in the history of Julian, there's no better accommodation than the Julian Gold Rush Hotel. This 16-room inn dates back to 1897, in the height of the town's gold rush, and is now a National Historic Landmark. Downstairs, the cozy lobby and dining room are filled with antiques like a 1914 piano. Upstairs, individually decorated rooms are named after local historical figures. Guests get a two-course breakfast in the morning and afternoon hot cider. The best part is that the hotel is directly on Main St, so it's easy to walk up and down the main drag and explore Julian from here.

WHERE TO STAY IN JULIAN

Orchard Hill Country Inn
A stay includes breakfast and afternoon hors d'oeuvres, with a paid four-course dinner on Saturdays. **$$**

Wikiup Hummingbird Inn
Quaint B&B with individually themed, luxury rooms, and a llama reserve on the property. **$$**

Julian Cabins
Individual cabins in the woods with several bedrooms, which can sleep up to 14 people. **$$$**

Cuyamaca Rancho State Park are popular camping spots. The **Pacific Crest Trail**, which runs from the Mexico border all the way up to Washington, crosses into Anza-Borrego.

One of the most popular PCT hikes in the region is to Eagle Rock, a natural rock formation in nearby Warner Springs that looks uncannily like a spread-winged eagle, and also has a waterfall close by. The nearby **Santa Ysabel Preserve** has 20 miles of trails across more than 6000 acres, and a nature center with interactive exhibits.

Did Someone Say Apple Pie?

JULIAN'S BEST BAKES

Julian's Main St smells like Christmas every day of the year. The aroma of baking apple pies wafts into the air from bakeries that fill the street. Within a two-minute walk, you'll find the **Julian Pie Company**, **Mom's Pie House** and **Apple Alley Bakery.**

Julian Pie Company bakes 16 varieties of pie – they're not all apple – with options like apple mountain berry crumb and caramel dutch apple in addition to simple fruit pies. Mom's Pie House has traditional pies and variations like apple pie sweetened only with cider rather than sugar, and apple dumplings, individually baked apples stuffed with spices. Apple Alley Bakery serves up pie and apple strudel, and offers a lunch special with soup, half a sandwich and a slice of pie for what some cups of coffee cost in Los Angeles.

Juliantla Chocolate bakes vegan apple pie. **Julian Cafe** also serves legendary pies, but more than that, it serves waffles and French toast topped with spiced apples, and a Julian apple burger stuffed with apples and blue cheese.

If you'd rather get your fruit straight from the source, there are plenty of orchards where you can pick your own fruit. **Volcan Valley Apple Farm** has 8000 apple trees across 10 acres; **Julian Farm and Orchard** has you-pick apples, berries and flowers; and **Calico Ranch & Cidery** grows apples and pears, and brews hard ciders made exclusively with fruit it grows.

GROWING A TOWN

After Fred Coleman, a 41-year-old formerly enslaved man from Kentucky, arrived in what would later be called Julian in the 1860s, he saw glinting gold in a creek, kicking off the area's gold rush that brought in an estimated $5 million. Some 30 years later, the gold was gone but the mountainous terrain and climate were uniquely suited to growing apples. Julian apples won first place at two World's Fairs: in 1893 in Chicago, and in 1915 in San Francisco. Orchards now line the mountainous terrain and are deeply ingrained in nearly every aspect of life in the town.

GETTING AROUND

Because Julian is high up in the mountains, there's no other way to reach the town than by car. But there's good news once you arrive: ample street parking is free on the quiet streets. Once you arrive, park and forget the wheels. Julian is easily walkable (manageable even for people who don't love a good walk).

You can get from one end of town to the other in 10 minutes, unless you're pulled into one of the bakeries by wafting baking smells. While Main St is an easy slope, the side streets can get hilly quickly; although almost everything you want to see in town is on the main drag.

PALM SPRINGS & THE DESERTS

HOLIDAY GETAWAY AND DESERT WILDERNESS

California's diverse desert landscapes offer hiking adventures, environmental art installations and dark skies, plus the sunny culture of Palm Springs.

The desert may evoke images of starkness and desolation, but a little immersion can quickly change one's perspective of its vast beauty. Much like the changing light can dramatically transform desert landscapes from moment to moment, living an off-grid desert minute rapidly reminds us how resilient the flora and fauna must be to survive in this boundary-pushing environment, and how much more beautiful it is for its toughness.

Hollywood may have brought Palm Springs to the country's mainstream consciousness, but this land was originally home to the Cahuilla, Serrano, Chemehuevi, Kumeyaay, Cupeño, Diegueño and Mojave tribes long before and since. The lightly worn marks of their ancient grinding mortars and rock art remain, while their trails have become modern thoroughfares. The same mesquite, piñon and cactus that provided them sustenance still flourish in the national parks and preserves today, supporting the wildlife you may glimpse with any luck, including desert tortoises and bighorn sheep.

Like the wildlife here, you'll have to adapt your rhythms to the desert environment. Self-sufficiency is key – always carry plenty of water, snacks and layers of clothing, and stay aware of changing weather. Keep an eye on the fuel gauge in your vehicle, and the level in your water bottle. You'll often find yourself unplugged whether you wish to or not, so lean into being fully present to the aliveness of the desert.

THE MAIN AREAS

PALM SPRINGS
Sunshiny holiday mecca. p450

JOSHUA TREE NATIONAL PARK
Iconic desert playground. p460

DEATH VALLEY NATIONAL PARK
Geology of extremes. p469

NICHOLAS J KLEIN/SHUTTERSTOCK ©

Left: Palm Springs (p450); Above: Zabriskie Point (p471), Death Valley National Park

ANZA-BORREGO DESERT STATE PARK
Wildflowers and dark skies. p476

MOJAVE NATIONAL PRESERVE
Desert solitude. p482

Find Your Way

California's desert region stretches from the feet of the eastern Sierra to western Nevada and south to the Mexican border. These thousands of square miles represent a spectrum of desert ecosystems, including the buoyant urban version known as Palm Springs.

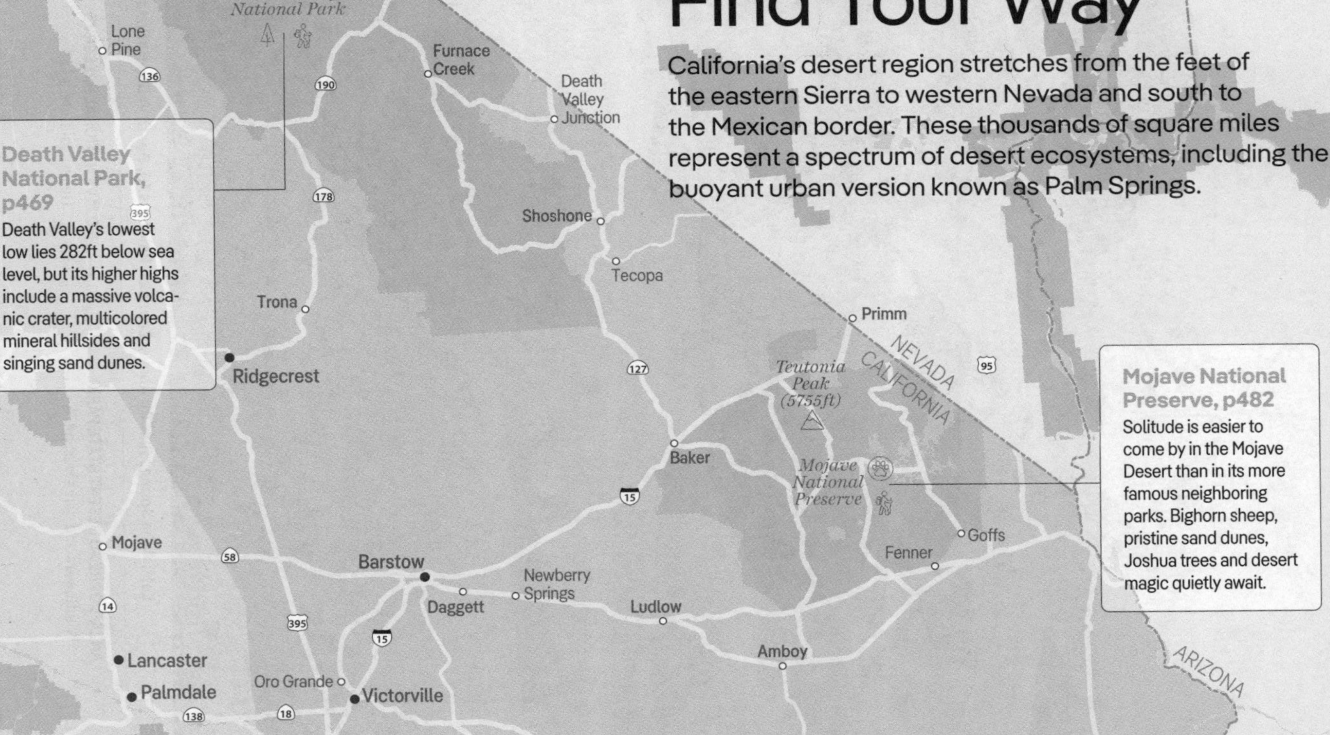

Death Valley National Park, p469
Death Valley's lowest low lies 282ft below sea level, but its higher highs include a massive volcanic crater, multicolored mineral hillsides and singing sand dunes.

Mojave National Preserve, p482
Solitude is easier to come by in the Mojave Desert than in its more famous neighboring parks. Bighorn sheep, pristine sand dunes, Joshua trees and desert magic quietly await.

Palm Springs, p450
A mecca for modernism, gay culture and spa life, Palm Springs feeds your indulgent impulses for cocktails by the pool, tempering them with hikes and healing desert air.

Joshua Tree National Park, p460
Its weird beauty extending far beyond its eponymous trees, JTree spans Mojave Desert and Sonoran Desert environments dotted with boulders, cholla and ocotillo.

Anza-Borrego Desert State Park, p476
Wildflowers and bighorn sheep are the organic draws to California's largest state park, but Ricardo Breceda's metal sculptures complement these wide-open spaces.

CAR

A car is the best way for getting around the region, allowing maximum flexibility. The desert's state and national parks encompass thousands of square miles and are not served by public transportation.

BICYCLE

In Palm Springs, many motels offer free bikes or e-bikes for their guests to use. Cycling is a fun way to get around downtown when the weather isn't excessively hot.

WALKING

To hike the desert is the best way to know it, whether it's on a paved nature trail or through a slot canyon. Prep well and allow for adjustment to plans, as the desert environment is extreme and can rapidly change.

Plan Your Time

Balance a little Hollywood-style decadence in Palm Springs with outdoor adventures in desert wilderness, discovering environmental art installations along the way.

BRENDA FITZ/SHUTTERSTOCK ©

Kelso Dunes (p483), Mojave National Preserve

If You Only Do One Thing

- For outdoor adventure, head straight to **Joshua Tree National Park** (p460) to get an up-close look at the park's iconic Joshua trees and chunky *Flintstones*-esque boulders. Take in the park's highlights on a **DIY driving tour** (p462), fitting in a short hike along the **Barker Dam Loop Trail** (p463) if you have time.

- Alternatively, take a city break in **Palm Springs** (p450) for a day of sightseeing and self-care. Go **vintage shopping** (p454) and **gallery hopping** (p454) downtown. Take time out for a spa treatment at **Sunstone Spa** (p456) or log some pool time before dinner and cocktails at **Paul Bar** (p454).

Seasonal Highlights

Summer in the desert can feel seriously hellish. High season runs mid-October through May. Spring brings wildflowers; blooms follow rains anytime of the year.

FEBRUARY

Modernism Week (p452) celebrates all things mid-century modern in Palm Springs, the most fitting city for it. Mini version in October.

MARCH

March is peak season for **wildflowers** in Anza-Borrego, though they can potentially start blooming in February.

APRIL

The desert's most famous event, **Coachella Music Festival** draws the masses over two weekends in mid- to late April.

CHARLEY GALLAY/LAUREL & WOLF/GETTY IMAGES ©; LISA PARSONS/SHUTTERSTOCK ©; TIMOTHY NORRIS/GETTY IMAGES ©

Three Days to Travel Around

- Start in **Death Valley National Park** (p469) to check off visits to **Badwater Basin** (p470), the lowest point in North America, and the spectacular colors of **Artists Palette** (p470) before spending the night in **Tecopa** (p475) for a hot-springs soak under the stars. Continue south through **Mojave National Preserve** (p482) for a beautiful, wild transect of this little-visited desert park, stopping to hike at **Kelso Dunes** (p483).

- Pick up lunch in **Joshua Tree** (p462) or **Twentynine Palms** (p467) and head into **Joshua Tree National Park** (p460) for a day or two of hiking or climbing, ending with pool time and cocktails in **Palm Springs** (p450).

If You Have More Time

- Take your time spending a couple of days each at **Death Valley National Park** (p469) and **Joshua Tree National Park** (p460), then rest and refresh for a day in **Palm Springs** (p450), perhaps fitting in a hike or horseback ride in **Indian Canyons** (p453).

- Next, head south to the Salton Sea for a look at the shoreline art installations of **Bombay Beach** (p459). Keep following Hwy 111 south to **Salvation Mountain** (p459), the cartoon-come-to-life religious monument on the edge of **Slab City** (p459).

- End with a trip to **Anza-Borrego Desert State Park** (p476), populated with metal-sculpture animals and offering an endless variety of desert hikes.

MAY

The biannual **Joshua Tree Music Festival** practices an ethos of radical inclusion in the town of Joshua Tree; also in October.

JULY

'Tis the season to avoid the searing desert floor, but Idyllwild's **Jazz in the Pines** (p459) is a cool respite.

SEPTEMBER

Go **apple picking** in Julian through October, but be prepared for crowds unless you visit midweek.

NOVEMBER

Pride is a state of mind in Palm Springs, but **Pride celebrations** in America's gayest city happen in early November.

PALM SPRINGS

San Francisco

Los Angeles

Palm Springs

One of the gayest cities in America in both senses of the word, sunny Palm Springs has long been the desert retreat of celebrities and artists. When 1930s Hollywood studios instituted the 'two-hour rule,' requiring their stars to stay geographically near enough to report to set on short notice, its reputation as decadent playground took root. More recently, it established itself as the first city in the USA to elect a 100% LGBTIQ+ city council.

Palm Springs prides itself not only on its queer culture but also on its mid-century modern identity. The 'Mid Mod' architecture and style that defined its heyday harmonized with the environment, establishing the singular desert aesthetic that endures to the present day.

Hike the trails of its Cahuilla lands, take in the vibrant art and architecture, sip tiki cocktails in the desert sunshine and experience for yourself the ebullient appeal of Palm Springs.

TOP TIP

The greater Palm Springs area sprawls out from the city proper into eight other cities, including Desert Hot Springs, Rancho Mirage, Palm Desert and Coachella. Many of the area's attractions lie outside the city of Palm Springs.

Palm Springs Art Museum (p454)

NGOC THE TRAN/SHUTTERSTOCK ©

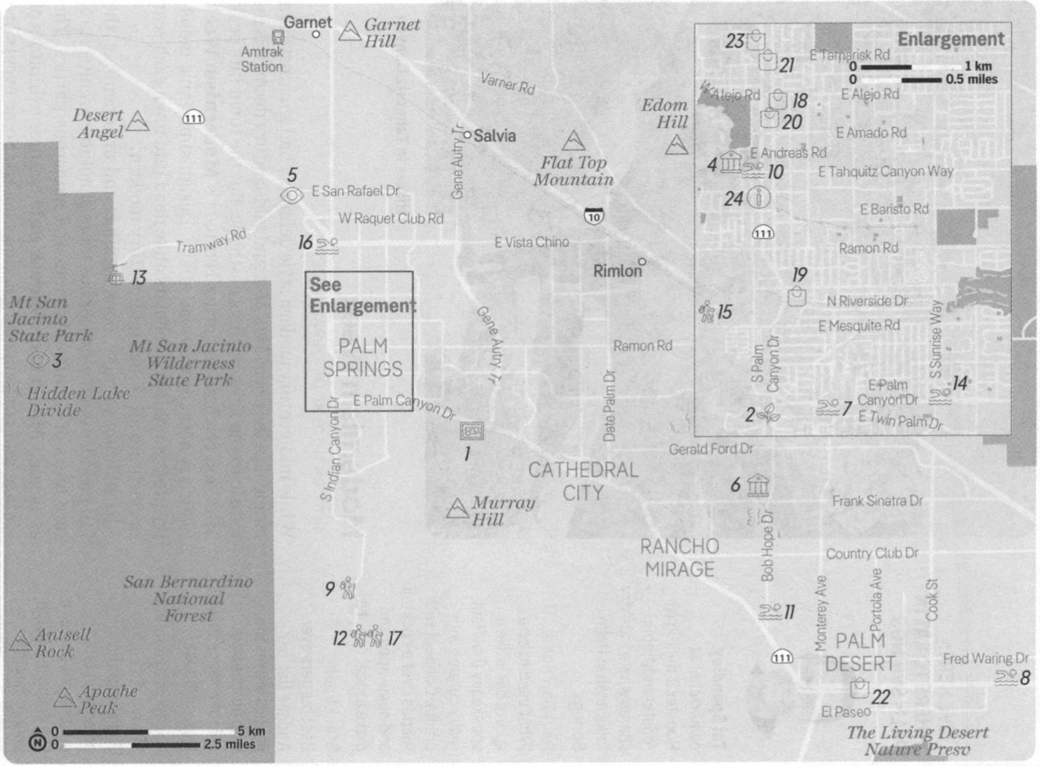

SIGHTS
1 Backstreet Art District
2 Moorten Botanical Gardens
3 Mountain Station
4 Palm Springs Art Museum
5 Palm Springs Visitor Center
6 Sunnylands

ACTIVITIES, COURSES & TOURS
7 Ace Hotel & Swim Club
see 7 Feel Good Spa
8 Hyatt Regency Indian Wells
9 Indian Canyons
10 Kimpton Rowan Palm Springs
11 Omni Rancho Las Palmas
12 Palm Canyon Trail
13 Palm Springs Aerial Tramway
see 3 Round Valley Trail
14 Saguaro Palm Springs
15 Tahquitz Canyon
16 The Pool at ARRIVE
17 Victor Trail

SHOPPING
18 Angel View Resale Store
19 Antique Galleries of Palm Springs
20 Mojave Flea Trading Post
21 Pure Atlas
22 The Fine Art of Design
23 Trina Turk

INFORMATION
24 Palm Springs Historical Society
see 3 San Jacinto State Park Ranger Station

I LIVE HERE: WHERE TO EAT IN PALM SPRINGS

Tai Spendley, owner/chef at Rooster & the Pig (@roosterandthepig), shares where industry folks nosh in Palm Springs.

Paul Bar/Food
What used to be a sports bar is like a speakeasy that Paul really curates with drama. Connect with friends over a cocktail and some apps and make a meal out of it.

Blackbook
Best burgers ever. And the flat-pan nachos are insane, with an amazing chipotle sauce they make in-house.

The Barn Kitchen at Sparrow's Lodge
Their beautiful communal table under arched trees is like dining in a Ralph Lauren magazine spread. It's a dreamy but rustic place for lunch, with fresh ingredients locally sourced as much as possible.

WKANADPON/SHUTTERSTOCK ©

Hikers in Tahquitz Canyon

Modernism Week

MID-CENTURY MODERN PALM SPRINGS

While mid-century modern style definitely had a mainstream moment in the era of *Mad Men* and mid-century decor, it is intrinsic to the Palm Springs aesthetic. But the town hits peak Mid Mod celebration during February's **Modernism Week** (which is actually a 10-day affair). Design superfans, industry professionals and scholars alike flood into town each year to celebrate all things mid-century modern.

In addition to talks, book signings and art openings, the fun includes double-decker bus tours of notable architecture, rare tours of significant homes and numerous parties. The associated **Modernism Show & Sale** features exhibitors of vintage and contemporary design and art. Some events are free, as is the nightly illumination of significant buildings along Palm Canyon Dr.

A 'mini' Modernism Week pops up in October over a long weekend for those who need a fall fix. But even if your visit doesn't coincide with the main event, there's still plenty of

YEAR-ROUND TOURS IN PALM SPRINGS

Desert Tasty Tours
Get a taste of local history and architecture with a side of Palm Springs cuisine.

Palm Springs Mod Squad
Admire from outside, and get a peek at the interiors of meticulously designed mid-century modern homes.

PS Architecture Tours
Insightful, insider tours guided by bike or car; best to book well ahead.

opportunity to explore Palm Springs modernism. The **Palm Springs Historical Society** offers various themed tours featuring modernist celebrity homes (Sinatra, Elvis, Elizabeth Taylor!), private driving tours of architectural gems and even bike tours narrated by your guide through an earpiece.

Notable buildings you can't help seeing include the cantilever-roofed **Palm Springs Visitor Center**, the Palm Springs Aerial Tramway's **Mountain Station** and the Palm Springs Art Museum (p454).

Palm Springs Hiking

TRAILS ON CITY OUTSKIRTS

Super-accessible trail adventures await just shy of downtown Palm Springs. Antsy feet can easily flee an afternoon of gallery hopping for an outdoor jaunt instead.

The Agua Caliente band of the Cahuilla tribe welcomes visitors to their gorgeous trails (entry fee required). Closest to downtown is **Tahquitz Canyon**, named after a shaman who misused his great powers to harm the Cahuilla people and was banished to a remote cave in the canyon. The mostly flat 2-mile loop leads to a seasonal waterfall and small riparian zone shaded by sycamores.

For more options, head south to **Indian Canyons**, where over 60 miles of trail traverse the backcountry. Several loop trails begin along the oasis on the **Palm Canyon Trail**, where tall palms crowd over the creek bed. An attractive 3-mile loop connects with the scenic, cactus-dotted **Victor Trail**, which opens to vistas of the valleys below.

And for something completely different, hop the **Palm Springs Aerial Tramway** at the north end of downtown for the 10-minute ride to 8516ft. Layer up, as it can be 40°F (22°C) colder than in Palm Springs. After disembarking the tram at the mountain station, walk down the paved path to the **San Jacinto State Park Ranger Station** to check in and pick up a map. The 4.5-mile **Round Valley Trail** is a wonderfully forested alpine escape from the desert heat.

Art & Landscapes

GALLERIES, GARDENS AND FESTIVALS

You may know Palm Springs as a longtime celebrity getaway, falling within the radius of Hollywood's 'two-hour rule.' It's less well known as an unofficial diplomatic retreat established in the 1960s, when Walter and Leonore Annenberg hosted foreign leaders and US presidents at **Sunnylands**, their Rancho Mirage estate. Now open to the public, its serene gardens and

SADDLE U

Smoke Tree Sta
Longtime family-run outfit offering daily horseback rides, including trail rides through the palm-lined oasis and up Murray Peak in Indian Canyons. Reservations are not necessary, but call to confirm departure times and arrive 30 minutes beforehand.

Coyote Ridge Stable
Beautiful trail riding in Morongo Valley, about 20 minutes north of Palm Springs, with another family-run stable.

Knob Hill Ranch
A bit further afield, this family-run company based in Yucca Valley takes trail rides into the west end of Joshua Tree National Park.

WHERE TO STAY IN PALM SPRINGS

Alcazar Hotel Palm Springs
Over-21-year-olds only at this stylish, truly chill Spanish-colonial boutique hotel with saltwater pool. $$

Del Marcos Hotel
Revamped from its original 1947 William F Cody design in perfectly balanced mid-century modern style. $$

Parker Palm Springs
Jonathan Adler's contemporary twist on the mid-century modern aesthetic strikes the perfect balance. $$$

ing trails are like a desert impressionist painting come to nside, there's an art gallery, cafe and home tours (when level retreats are not in session).

ore organic and intimate desert refuge is the **Moorten ical Garden**, at the southern end of Palm Canyon Dr. leads through a beautifully planted array of cacti, nts and desert flora from arid lands near and far. You o see the resident desert tortoises trucking around if not hibernating.

orth on Palm Canyon Dr to see what's on display at **rings Art Museum**, a quintessentially Palm Springs structure designed by architect E Stewart Williams. The museum's permanent collection spans Mesoamerican to modern European and contemporary California art, with rotating temporary exhibitions.

For a peek at the studios and galleries of working artists, navigate to the **Backstreet Art District**. Opening hours vary, but you may get to chat with the artists themselves. Your best bet to see the greatest breadth is to show up for **First Wednesday** art walks.

...is held every two years. Playing with and building on the landscape, international artists create arresting art installations in unexpected locations around the Coachella Valley. The often monumental art is informed by social, environmental and cultural issues and inspired by the desert. For a few months, the art becomes an element of the landscape before disappearing again with only a mirage of its existence left behind.

Shop Palm Springs

PALM SPRINGS TREASURE HUNTING

Palm Springs might be the best or worst place to hunt for mid-century modern vintage – you could unearth a mint Blenko vase amid estate castoffs, but you may pay a premium for it in the heart of the Mid Mod mecca. If you're just browsing for fun, this town has troves of vintage and retail shops to peruse.

Start on N Indian Canyon Dr at **Mojave Flea Trading Post**, a makers' market filled with artwork, clothing, homewares, jewelry, skincare and all manner of giftable baubles made in the Coachella Valley.

Moving on to N Palm Canyon Dr, stroll along the north end in the Uptown Design District to find playful retro-patterned dresses at **Trina Turk** or earthier Moroccan home decor at **Pure Atlas**. If thrifting is more your bag, pop into the nearby **Angel View Resale Store** on N Indian Canyon Dr, a local chain benefitting its eponymous nonprofit organization that serves people with disabilities.

South of downtown off S Palm Canyon Dr, **Antique Galleries of Palm Springs** occupies 12,000 sq ft of merchants selling vintage everything, spanning many eras. Find cocktail carts, Bakelite necklaces and uniquely oddball sculptures. For objects on the higher end, venture out to **The Fine Art of Design** in Palm Desert to score the Eames of your dreams.

ART GALLERIES IN PALM SPRINGS

Rubine Red Gallery
The aesthetic here leans toward modernism, representing mid-century and contemporary artists.

The Pit
Contemporary work by emerging and mid-career artists; the Palm Springs satellite of the LA gallery.

Coachella Walls
Not a gallery but a series of murals around the Coachella Valley honoring its human history.

A Palm Spring's store

Palm Springs Chill Mode

POOL, SPA, COCKTAIL, REPEAT

Let's face it – some of us are just here to relax doing nothing. If that's you, slide on your sunnies and swimsuit and park yourself by the pool. Many local hotels offer day passes to non-guests who wish to avail themselves of a lounge chair and bar service.

It's adults only at **The Pool at ARRIVE**, where the excellent food and cocktails come to you. Regular day passes can be upgraded to cabana reservations (with a food and beverage deposit), so you have a dedicated zone to chill with friends at this cool, intimate pool. Another grown-up spot is the rooftop pool at **Kimpton Rowan Palm Springs**, also with a cabana option.

FESTIVE THURSDAYS IN PALM SPRINGS

It's like a holiday every Thursday evening when N Palm Canyon Dr is closed to vehicle traffic for **VillageFest**. Several blocks of the street are lined with food stalls emanating scents of tamales and falafel, alongside local artists selling their handblown glass, paintings, textiles and metalwork. There's live music, and locals and visitors alike come out to enjoy the cool night air and festive atmosphere.

If you're not into stand-up dining, the street's restaurants and bars remain open, so you can also grab an outdoor table and people-watch to your heart's content.

WHERE TO VINTAGE-SHOP IN PALM SPRINGS

The Frippery
Your go-to source in the Uptown Design District for a de rigueur desert-chic caftan.

Iconic Atomic
Well-curated, fun selection of vintage clothing and housewares on N Palm Canyon Dr.

Gypsyland
On N Palm Canyon Dr near the visitor center, this friendly vintage spot stocks clothing and decor.

Kimpton Rowan Palm Springs (p455)

For more of a see-and-be-seen vibe, hipster stalwart **Ace Hotel & Swim Club** has a festive atmosphere, complemented by its low-key **Feel Good Spa** for a little self-care time-out. A nearby pool-party favorite is the **Saguaro Palm Springs** with its retro-tropical color-blocked backdrop. Call ahead for availability at all of these venues, especially on weekends.

Find a more family-friendly scene at the **Omni Rancho Las Palmas**, a water park in Rancho Mirage with lazy river, waterslides, ersatz beach and splashy play areas for kids. The **Hyatt Regency Indian Wells** also has a water park featuring several twisty waterslides and a lazy river.

BEST DESERT SPAS

Sunstone Spa
Make it a day of spa treatments, sauna and mineral pool at Agua Caliente Casino in Rancho Mirage.

L'Horizon Resort & Spa
Hollywood history lingers at this elegant, low-slung mid-century resort and spa with beautiful mountain views.

The Spa at Two Bunch Palms
Relaxed oasis setting with palms and mineral waters in Desert Hot Springs.

Grounded Bodyworks
Lovely downtown Palm Springs day spa if you're simply seeking a massage or primping without the whole resort experience.

GETTING AROUND

Getting around downtown Palm Springs is best on foot or by bike. Free parking is plentiful in the downtown lots; the Palm Springs Art Museum is a good choice. Many local lodgings offer free bike rentals to guests. Further out from downtown and into the great Palm Springs area, driving is the best way to get around.

Beyond Palm Springs

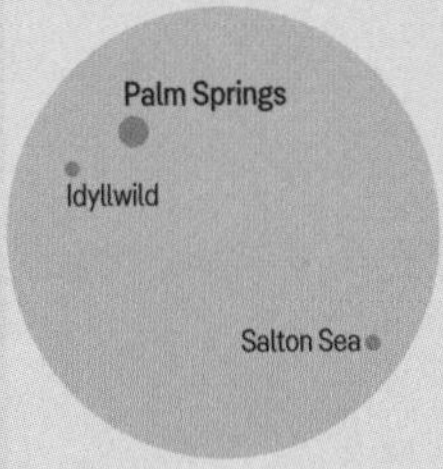

Artsy communities thrive past the edges of Palm Springs, from alpine town to receding inland sea.

From Palm Springs, heading up the hill to the forested mountains of Idyllwild is a refreshing change in perspective and temperature. Surrounded by the San Jacinto Mountains, this unpretentious little village (a dog served as mayor for most of the past decade) is a great place to hike and relax.

In the other direction – geographically and culturally – the low-lying Slabs near the Salton Sea annually rotates in a new (human) fearless leader in 'the last free place.' Transient and permanent residents populate this veritable desert island of misfit toys.

While these communities couldn't be more different, the artistic soul in each place makes them fascinating counterpoints to easy, breezy Palm Springs.

TOP TIP

Check local listings for regular art events in Idyllwild. In the Slabs, stop by the library to ask about current and upcoming live art happenings.

Bombay Beach (p459)

LEIGH GREEN/ALAMY ©

Ernie Maxwell Scenic Trail, Idyllwild

MAXIMUS, MAYOR EMERITUS

Idyllwild has been without a mayor since August 2022, when Maximus Mueller passed away after serving in the role for nine years. The beloved golden retriever succeeded Idyllwild's first Mayor Max (the nepotism at play here is an open and generally uncontroversial secret). Whether the unincorporated town will elect a new mayor remained unclear at the time of writing.

Hike & Chill Out in Idyllwild

SAN JACINTO MOUNTAINS VILLAGE

Miles of alpine hiking and mountain biking abound around Idyllwild, a sweet town in the San Jacinto Mountains. An hour's drive from Palm Springs, the temperatures get cooler as you ascend into this wild and idyllic mountain village.

Local shop **Nomad Ventures** is the place to stop for gear and intel on trail adventures. Or take a hike on the **Ernie Maxwell Scenic Trail**, about a 5-mile out-and-back through the pines and boulders with beautiful mountain views.

If roaming around town is more your speed, grab a matcha latte and house-baked cinnamon roll at local favorite **Alpaca Coffee & Tea** before your walk. Poke around in **Ephemera**

WHERE TO STAY, EAT AND DRINK IN IDYLLWILD

The Creekstone
Walking distance between town and trailheads, this rustic-chic inn rocks. **$$**

Cafe Aroma
Convivial woodsy restaurant/gallery serving New American food, cocktails and live music. **$$**

Idyllwild Brewpub
Taste a brewery flight alongside good pub food on the lovely patio in the pines. **$$**

for vintage items and **Bubba's Books** for road-trip reads and other random gems. The peaceful **Idyllwild Gardens** nursery is worth a perusal of its garden spaces and gift items.

Depending on the time of year, you could groove to live music at **Jazz in the Pines**, benefiting the Idyllwild Arts Academy, or take in a stage performance of the **Idyllwild Actors Theatre**.

If you ride the tram up from Palm Springs, you'll end up in the adjacent **San Jacinto State Park**. Low-key hard-core hikers could trek the roughly 10 miles from the Palm Springs Aerial Tramway's Mountain Station (p453) to Idyllwild with good pre-planning – it may be icy enough to require crampons and will be a daylong hike, regardless of conditions.

Salton Sea Art Communities

OUTSIDER ART FRINGING THE SALTON SEA

About 1½ hours' drive from Palm Springs, turning off Hwy 111 to **Bombay Beach** may feel like entering a ghost town, but this former holiday destination by the excessively saline, shrinking Salton Sea still retains over 200 residents. Artists have replaced migrating shorebirds, painting murals on abandoned homes and constructing art from scraps. There's even a **Bombay Beach Biennale** running art happenings from January through March. You might also catch live music at the **Ski Inn** dive bar. Cruise around town to see arted-up spaces, but if pressed for time go straight to the beach, scattered with curious sculptures and beautifully impractical structures.

About 20 miles southeast sits the area's most photographed monument, **Salvation Mountain**. This multicolored, psychedelic adobe piece of folk architecture was built by Leonard Knight, who passed away in 2014, and is now maintained by a devoted caretaker. Salvation Mountain marks the entrance of **Slab City**, an alternative community of mostly peaceful anarchy. Some residents welcome visitors to their camps, art galleries and secret gardens, and the community has a cozy library, hostel, outdoor music venue and skate park.

Follow the signs through the Slabs to tiny **East Jesus**, founded by the late Charlie Russell. Intrigued by the freewheeling lifestyle of the Slabs, he established this corner with a couple of art cars. Currently its population of six maintains this solar-powered compound, inviting artists to contribute to its ever-evolving desert installation.

I LIVE HERE: ORGANIZED ANARCHY

Mopar, Greeting Committee at East Jesus (@eastjesus), talks Slab City culture.

Slab City is a most unusual place; there's a large number of empaths out here. It's obviously an experimental community. In reality, it's anarchy...but even anarchy has cultural norms. Years ago, I was talking to a friend about the place here, and she said, 'You're living in a cult.' And she pointed out all the characteristics of the cult, and we figured out that the only thing we don't have is a charismatic leader. Every year we elect a fearless leader – someone's gotta be in charge, you know – and then at the end of the year, they're sacrificed to the fire gods. They'll step down, there'll be tears, crying, hugs, and...we never see them again.

GETTING AROUND

These destinations require a car to visit, as they are not served by public transportation. Idyllwild can be reached in about an hour from Palm Springs, heading south on Hwy 74 out of Palm Desert. Bombay Beach is less than 1½ hours to the south along Hwy 111, with Slab City another half-hour beyond.

JOSHUA TREE NATIONAL PARK

Before white settlement, natural springs at what are now the northern and southern edges of Joshua Tree National Park sustained the local indigenous Serrano, Chemehuevi and Cahuilla people. These water sources went on to enable the later-arriving cattlemen and gold prospectors to settle here in the 1870s.

The mining boom peaked in the 1920s and declined in the '30s, while activist Minerva Hoyt lobbied Congress to preserve her beloved desert environment from the human destruction she witnessed. Her efforts culminated in President Roosevelt establishing 825,000 acres as Joshua Tree National Monument in 1936.

Acting as a backdrop for old Westerns, an escape and inspiration for artists and musicians and an irresistible playground for rock climbers, Joshua Tree attained national park status in 1994. JTree's desert mystique continues to attract and entrance visitors who climb its rock faces, explore its trails and marvel at its funky geological formations and asymmetrical beauty of its namesake Joshua trees.

San Francisco

Los Angeles

Joshua Tree National Park

TOP TIP

Not only is Joshua Tree National Park irresistibly photogenic, but it's also only 2½ hours from LA, so on weekends it can seem as though all of SoCal is pouring in at once. If possible, time your trip for during the week when it's likely to be less crowded.

Climbing Intersection Rock (p462)

LEFT: SANDRA FOYT/SHUTTERSTOCK ©; RIGHT: AGAP/SHUTTERSTOCK ©

CAMPING AT JTREE

It's straight-up magical to experience sunset and sunrise in Joshua Tree National Park, to see the starry night sky above and to hear coyote howls echoing off the boulders. Several of the park's campgrounds, including **Jumbo Rocks**, are reservation-only up to six months in advance (recreation.gov). **Hidden Valley**, **Belle** and **White Tank** campgrounds are first-come, first-served and best attempted midday and midweek for a chance of snagging a spot.

Queen Mountain
Twentynine Palms Mountain
Negro Hill
Pinto Wye
Park Blvd
Bighorn Pass Rd
Sheep Pass
Ryan Mountain
Jumbo Rocks
Geology Tour Rd
Joshua Tree National Park
Malapai Hill
Lost Hors Mine Rd
Keys View Rd
Keys View
Lost Horse Mountain
The Blue Cut
Berdoo Canyon Rd
Pinto Basin Rd
Mastodon Peak Trail (16mi)
Cottonwood Spring (17mi)
Lost Palm Oasis Trail (18mi)
1
2
3
4
5
6
7
8
9
10
11
12
13
14
15
16
17
18
19
20
21
22

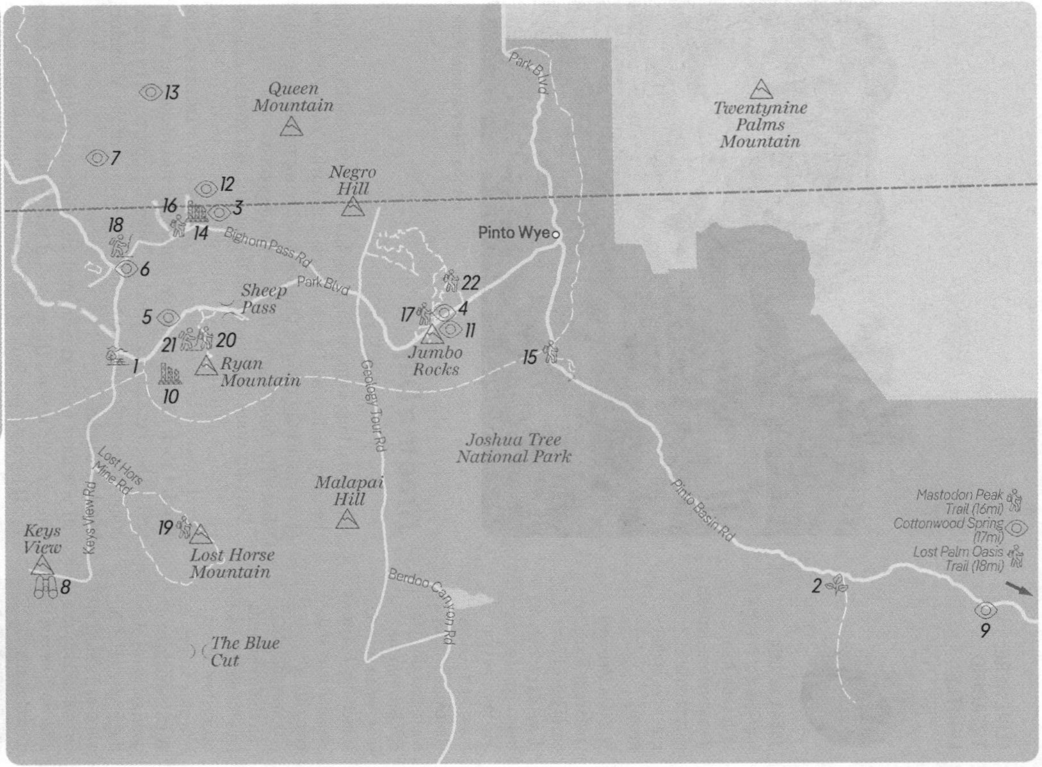

SIGHTS
1 Cap Rock
2 Cholla Cactus Garden
3 Desert Queen Well
4 Face Rock
5 Hall of Horrors
6 Intersection Rock
7 Keys Ranch
8 Keys View
9 Ocotillo Patch
10 Ryan Ranch
11 Skull Rock
12 Wall Street Mill
13 Wonderland of Rocks
14 Wonderland Ranch

ACTIVITIES, COURSES & TOURS
15 Arch Rock Trail
16 Barker Dam Loop Trail
17 Discovery Trail
18 Hidden Valley Campground
see 7 Keys Ranch Tour
19 Lost Horse Mine Trail
20 Ryan Mountain Trail
21 Saddle Rocks
22 Split Rock Loop

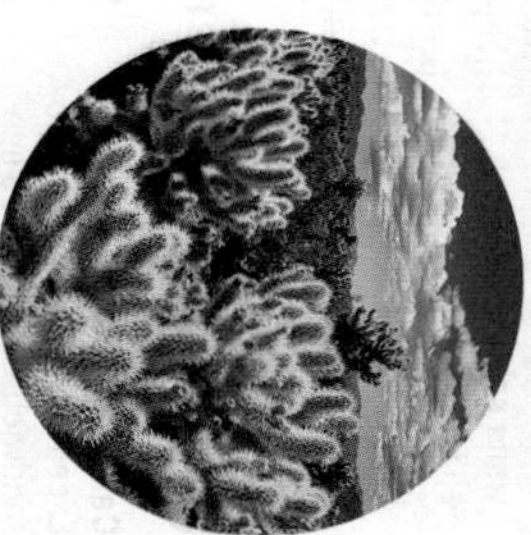

Cholla Cactus Garden (p463)

I LIVE HERE: TREADING LIGHTLY

John Lauretig, president of Friends of Joshua Tree (@joshuatreefriends), muses on best practices in the desert.

This is such a cool landscape if you've never been here – that diversity of Joshua trees, exposed rocks and the cracks in there, and people climbing them. One can't-miss thing to do? Drive up the road; when you see something that wows you, pull over and enjoy it!

One aspect that can elude visitors is how fragile the desert ecosystem is, and how slow to recover. We all need to be good stewards of these special lands, whether it's staying on trail, picking up a little trash, respecting road closures so wildlife can access water sources – it all minimizes our impact on this unique environment.

GARY C. TOGNONI/SHUTTERSTOCK ©

Joshua Tree National Park

JTree in a Day

ONE-DAY DIY HIGHLIGHTS TOUR

Make a daylong loop through Joshua Tree National Park, using the town of Joshua Tree to access the park's West Entrance. (You can easily reverse this loop, starting from Twentynine Palms; the North Entrance is often less busy.)

Driving along Park Blvd, you'll pass through swaths of Joshua trees in prickly, multi-armed welcome to their Mojave Desert zone. About 9 miles in, you'll come to **Intersection Rock** – look for climbers navigating up its cracks. Park here and walk to the back of Hidden Valley Campground to spend some time exploring the boulder landscape of the **Wonderland of Rocks**.

If you have half a day to explore, continue up this road to stretch your legs on the easy and pretty **Barker Dam Loop Trail** for a deeper look at the ecosystem and natural history. Afterward, detour south to check out **Keys View** for vistas over the San Andreas Fault, Salton Sea and to the Mexican border. Enjoy a picnic lunch at **Cap Rock**.

If you only have a couple of hours, continue on Park Blvd for another 3 miles. Stop to walk around the **Hall of Horrors** rock

WHERE TO FIND PICNIC PROVISIONS

Campbell Hill Bakery
Excellent pastries, pre-made sandwiches, pizza and a line out the door in Twentynine Palms; show up early. $

The Dez
Grab-and-go sandwiches, salads, charcuterie and coffee in Joshua Tree for your national park picnic. $

Farmers market
Both Twentynine Palms and Joshua Tree hold Saturday farmers markets from 8am to 1pm. $

formation where you may see more climbers on the backside, before continuing for another 6 miles to gawk at **Skull Rock**. Hang a right onto Pinto Basin Rd to head south to the **Cholla Cactus Garden** for the quarter-mile loop through teddy-bear cholla, then backtrack to exit through the North Entrance.

Hiking Joshua Tree

EXPLORE CLASSIC JTREE TRAILS

Joshua Tree National Park's divergent landscapes, easing from the higher-elevation Mojave Desert to the lower Colorado Desert life zones, invite deeper exploration for those with more time.

If you're hiking with kids, start at the trail designed by kids – the **Discovery Trail** offers a bit of scrambling and informative interpretive signs and is a great park intro for grown-up kids as well. At less than a mile long, it's an easy hike and close to roadside Skull Rock. For classic bouldery Joshua Tree scenery, the 2.5-mile **Split Rock Loop** is another easy one, with a short spur leading to **Face Rock**.

Hikers wanting to gain elevation can head to the lesser-trafficked northwestern corner of the park, where the 6.5-mile **Panorama Loop** takes you through Joshua trees before rising into piñon-and-juniper forest atypical to most of the park. As the name suggests, you'll find panoramic views of the Coachella and Yucca Valleys along the 1200ft climb.

A more central high is the 3-mile **Ryan Mountain Trail**, rising over 1000ft in a mile-and-a-half – breathtaking in effort but also for the expansive vistas at the top.

Finally, at the southern end of the park, the 7.4-mile **Lost Palm Oasis Trail** begins at the small oasis at Cottonwood Springs, traversing boulder-piled hills and desert washes, and ending at the gorgeous oasis named after its large grove of native California fan palms.

Rock Art & Ruins

REMNANTS OF JTREE'S HUMAN HISTORY

The mostly flat, rewardingly varied **Barker Dam Loop Trail** journeys into the park's natural history, with informative signage posted along the way. The trail skirts the dam and cattle trough used in the early 1900s, but most interestingly, a little spur leads to a shallow cave full of petroglyphs.

An easy walk takes you to the well-preserved **Wall Street Mill**, passing ore-crushing ruins, the headstone of the unfortunate loser of a shoot-out and the **Desert Queen Well**, and continues to the crumbling pink ruins of **Wonderland Ranch**.

PLAN & PREPARE

All of the 'Leave No Trace' principles (lnt.org/why/7-principles) apply when visiting Joshua Tree National Park, but it's particularly important to plan ahead and prepare for your visit. Once you enter the park, there are no services aside from vault toilets at trailheads and campgrounds, and running water only at the park entry points. Cell-phone service is nonexistent inside the park.

Bring everything you'll need: plenty of water (ie at least 2L per person for the day), salty snacks to keep your electrolytes balanced and layers so you can adjust to sudden weather changes. Have all the survival basics so you can fully enjoy the spectacular desert environment.

WHERE TO GO FOR DRINKS

Out There Bar
The friendliest little dive bar in Twentynine Palms; it's pink so you can't miss it.

GRND SQRL
Twentynine Palms gastropub with microbrews on tap, wine, good pub food and sometimes live music.

Joshua Tree Saloon
Central spot in Joshua Tree for a bite and a beer if you're not in a hurry.

I LIVE HERE: FINDING SOLITUDE

Bernadette Regan, climbing ranger at Joshua Tree National Park, talks about where to find quiet space.

I recently found a JTNP climbing brochure from 1993, encouraging climbers to leave no trace because suddenly a lot of people were coming to the park. In '93, the park averaged about a million visitors. This park was designed to give people the space for solitude, so they limited campsites and parking spots on purpose.

In 2022, we got about 3.5 million visitors. So finding solitude is a huge challenge, even though the park is the size of Rhode Island. How do you find it? Get out of your car. Don't just go to Skull Rock. If you explore a little bit further than that, you'll find quiet space.

The **Ryan Ranch** ruins, an easy half-mile walk from the road, are worth a look, the Ryan brothers having incorporated gold dust into the adobe.

For a good hike, head further south down Keys View Rd to the **Lost Horse Mine Trail**, a roughly 4.5-mile out-and-back hike to an abandoned mine and equipment. As you climb, check out the views down on Pleasant Valley and the basalt-iced Malapai Hill popping up on the plain.

History buffs will want to book a tour of the national historic site of **Keys Ranch**, accessible only by ranger-led walk from October to May. Exploring the small homestead brings to life the challenges of living in this environment.

At the park's southern end, it's only about a quarter-mile walk beyond the coolness of **Cottonwood Spring** to some trailside *metates* (grinding stones) left by the Cahuilla. It's easy to imagine people gathering here and preparing food together near this life-sustaining water source.

Rock Climbing in Joshua Tree

GUIDED CLIMBING IN THE PARK

Standing at the base of the tank of monzogranite, your hands begin to sweat through the chalk you've just dipped into for grippiness. Seeing some likely features to grab, you've never been so conscious of your fingers as you hold onto the cool rock before placing a foot on an obvious bump. Making your first move, you push yourself up with your foot to reach the higher little depression that you saw from the start. Your other foot leaves the desert floor and you're on the rock, which now seems a lot bigger than it did from the ground.

Fortunately, you are roped up and on belay with an experienced climbing partner certified to teach rock climbing in Joshua Tree National Park. They've begun by introducing you to the basics while you're still on the ground, literally showing you the ropes.

The town of Joshua Tree has over 400 certified climbing guides and over 30 companies who offer climbing lessons. All certified guides have medical training and teaching experience, with permission to teach in the park. The best way to find the right guide is to call around and chat with someone personally to see if you vibe with them. If so, climb on.

With over 10,000 climbs in the park, more experienced climbers can start with some bouldering and beta at **Hidden Valley Campground**, and numerous centrally accessed climbs at Hall of Horrors or **Saddle Rocks**.

JOSHUA TREE CLIMBING GUIDES

California Climbing School
Family-run company promoting safety, environmental stewardship and diversity in the outdoors.

Cliffhanger Guides
A small, owner-operated outfit offering customized guiding with an emphasis on safety and fun.

Stone Adventures
Another local family-run company offering guided climbs for all levels.

Barker Dam (p462)

Joshua Tree Drive-Through

SEEING JTREE VIA ROAD TRIP

Even if your time is limited on an interstate road trip, you can still soak up some classic Joshua Tree vibes on your journey. Reverse this trip's orientation as necessary.

Starting from the park's West Entrance, experience a moving meditation as you drive through the undulating Joshua tree forest along Park Blvd. Pause at **Intersection Rock** to watch rock climbers honing their technique, moving along to walk out to the Hall of Horrors and Skull Rock, both natural roadside attractions.

After the turn south on Pinto Basin Rd, stretch your legs for half an hour on the short **Arch Rock Trail**. Have a snack here or at the Cholla Cactus Garden about 8 miles south, taking care not to hug the cute but spiky teddy-bear cholla. Continue south about 3 miles to the **Ocotillo Patch**, whose graceful succulents may be popping out in red blooms after a rain and whose green stalks signal the transition into the park's Colorado Desert zone.

Drive onward to **Cottonwood Spring**, stopping for a short walk into this palm- and cottonwood-shaded oasis. If you have time, take at least part of the **Mastodon Peak Trail** for a last look at JTree's geological beauty and a peek at *metates* from its human history. The Cottonwood exit spills you onto I-10 to Palm Springs or Phoenix.

JOSHUA TREE DESTINY

The Joshua tree, the elegantly Seussian namesake of the park, is showing some effects of climate change. While this plant species – known as *hunuvat chiy'a* or *humwichawa* in the Cahuilla language – continues to reproduce sexually in a symbiotic relationship with the yucca moth, research has shown it to reproduce asexually in parts of its cooler northern range. This cloning response embodies the species' resilience in the face of climate change but also signals environmental stress. In the springtime, look out for its clusters of cream-colored blossoms signifying renewed hope for the future survival of this desert icon, and tread carefully in its home.

GETTING AROUND

Driving is the best way to experience Joshua Tree National Park, as there is no public transportation and you'll be inspired to pull over for unexpectedly stunning sights. Crossing north to south, expect the journey to take about 1¼ hours nonstop, but keep in mind that you'll definitely stop.

If you have a bike or e-bike with you, the park roads make for a gorgeous cycling tour. Always stay on established park roads.

Beyond Joshua Tree National Park

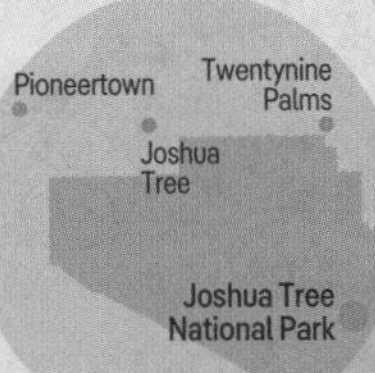

Find enduring outdoor art installations, new infusions of energy to gateway towns and a real town originally established as a film set.

Over the last few years, new energy has revitalized the park's gateway towns of Joshua Tree and Twentynine Palms along Twentynine Palms Hwy (Hwy 62), making it worthwhile to spend some time poking around the local shops and surprisingly diverse eateries. Even more captivating are the outdoor sculpture gardens and art installations – both permanent and pop-up – dotting the desert. Moving through these human-made landscapes, often created with discarded objects, presents a thought-provoking contrast to the natural artscapes of the park.

Branching off from Twentynine Palms Hwy is another living art piece: Pioneertown, a film set constructed as a backdrop for old Westerns that was and still is an actual tiny town.

TOP TIP

Bring plenty of water and sun protection to the art sites. You may not be hiking, but you'll get a lot of sun exposure, as there is little or no shade.

Pioneertown Motel (p468), Pioneertown

NOAH SAUVE/SHUTTERSTOCK ©

***Untitled, (Aku'aba)*, 2000, Noah Purifoy Outdoor Desert Art Museum**

Desert Art Installations

OUTDOOR ART INSTALLATIONS AND SCULPTURE GARDENS

When you come to the high desert, you can't help but feel a sense of the freedom afforded by these wide-open, exposed spaces.

For Noah Purifoy, who lived and made art in Joshua Tree the last 15 years of his life, art was a means of creating social change. His first major work of assemblage art came from wreckage salvaged from the 1965 Watts Riots in LA. His architectural and playful sculptures were constructed from discarded materials, including lunch trays, vacuum-cleaner parts, bicycle tires and toilets. In the town of Joshua Tree, about 10 minutes north of the West Entrance to the park, the **Noah Purifoy Outdoor Desert Art Museum** preserves these works he left behind, as pieces of it slowly and inevitably succumb to the desert conditions. There's so much to look at with each turn through this space; allow yourself time to wander. While in the neighborhood, make a detour to the **Transmission** sculpture by Daniel Popper.

About 10 minutes' drive northeast of the park's North Entrance and Twentynine Palms, the **Glass Outhouse Art**

INTEGRATRON SOUND BATH

Aerospace engineer George Van Tassel built the wood-domed **Integratron** in the 1950s, incorporating structural elements based on writings of Nikola Tesla and, he claimed, communications from extraterrestrials.

The Integratron was a machine for rejuvenating cell tissues, as it was designed to channel a frequency specified by the aliens. Regardless of their provenance, the dome's acoustics provide a perfect setting for sound baths using crystal singing bowls said to be tuned to each of your chakras. One-hour public sessions can be booked a month or two in advance to soak up the high-desert vibes for yourself.

WHERE TO SHOP

Habitat
Great selection of handmade art and homewares at this locally owned Twentynine Palms boutique.

Coyote Corner
This Old West storefront in Joshua Tree sells fun souvenirs and more practical camping gear.

The Station
Locally designed goodies, retro-tinged souvenirs and vintage finds in an old Joshua Tree gas station.

YUCCA VALLEY FUN

Lest you believe you're in some dusty, forgotten backwater, remember that you have a plan B if a last-minute attempt to crash Pappy & Harriet's failed anticlimactically. On weekends, there's a good chance to hear good live music at **Giant Rock Meeting Room** in Yucca Valley. This surprisingly cool little corner of Twentynine Palms Hwy is also home to **La Copine**, one of the most acclaimed area restaurants, as well as **Frontier Cafe** (which keeps earlier hours). Find local handmade wares at **Mojave Flea** and home goods at the playful **Wine & Rock**.

Gallery lives up to its name, offering a functional glass outhouse outfitted with reflective glass walls for privacy from the outside and panoramic views from inside. Besides the marquee piece is a tiny chapel open 24 hours, a gallery (to which friendly owner Laurel Siedl accepts any artist who wishes to show there) and a cheeky sculpture garden filled with a kookily delightful concatenation of desert assemblage.

Ask around at the galleries of Joshua Tree's **East Village** for current installations on your visit.

A Slice of the Wild West

NEW OLD WEST TOWN

Built in the 1940s as a movie set for filming Westerns, **Pioneertown** has weathered its booms and busts. It was originally conceived as a permanent set that could also house and support film production staff, but its economy collapsed in the 1950s as the Western genre faded in popularity. The town's population has ebbed and flowed over the decades, and is now fittingly enjoying a contemporary revival as a social-media backdrop.

A short 25-minute drive from the national park's West Entrance, Pioneertown still has residents and horses. And aside from its popularity for Instagram photo shoots, its block-long row of Old West facades houses actual shops selling cool locally made wares, including artisanal skincare, pottery and artwork. On Saturday afternoons you might witness **Wild West shoot-outs** (donations appreciated).

Afternoons are best to find businesses open, and weekends are typically way more crowded. If staying overnight, book a room at the **Pioneertown Motel** well in advance in case a popular act is playing that night.

Consider hiking around the **Pioneertown Mountains Preserve** as a respite from any tourist density you may encounter in town. A few trails lead through terrain that varies from riparian zones to piñon-and-juniper scrub. Head back into town for some Mexican food and a beer at the **Red Dog Saloon** or soak in the storied atmosphere at music venue **Pappy & Harriet's**. Check out the little shops at the Yucca Valley turnoff on your way in or out.

GETTING AROUND

You'll need a car to explore the sights outside the national park. Pioneertown Rd veers off Twentynine Palms Hwy in Yucca Valley, winding 5 miles into the mountains.

The area's outdoor art installations are all over the map, and spending half a day driving around finding them is part of the adventure.

DEATH VALLEY NATIONAL PARK

San Francisco
Death Valley National Park
Los Angeles

An ancestral and contemporary home to the Timbisha Shoshone people, the land now known as Death Valley National Park represents the largest US national park in the lower 48 states. The park is probably best known for boasting the lowest point in North America at 282ft below sea level. Its highest point is Telescope Peak (11,049ft), making it a land of extremes, but not just in elevation.

Despite the ominous name, Death Valley's vast desertscapes are alive with geological wonders. Between the hexagonal quilt of salt flats at Badwater Basin, the startling greens and pinks of Artists Palette, the wind-shaped sand dunes and the smooth marble-walled slot canyons, it may radically morph the image that the word 'desert' summons to your mind.

Borax mining put it on the proverbial map, but its uniquely austere wildness kept it there and garnered its protected status as a national park.

TOP TIP

'Don't die' – this blunt message is on park signage everywhere, because the desert is not messing around. Have on hand at least a gallon of water per person per day, fill up your gas tank before setting out, and understand that your cell service will be mostly nonexistent. Plan wisely to play safely.

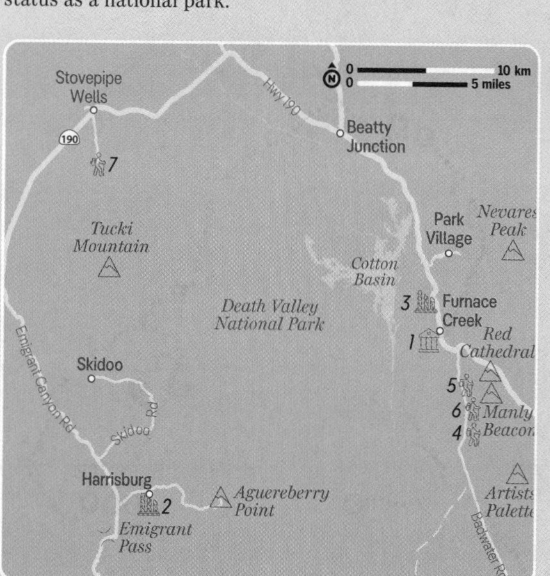

SIGHTS
1 Borax Museum
2 Eureka Mine
3 Harmony Borax Works

ACTIVITIES, COURSES & TOURS
4 Desolation Canyon
5 Golden Canyon
6 Gower Gulch
7 Mosaic Canyon Trail

DRIVE-THROUGH HIGHLIGHTS

If you're only driving through Death Valley between other destinations, you can still survey some of the park's greatest hits as you travel across the changing desert landscape. Reverse the route to suit your trajectory.

From the west along Hwy 190, stop at **1 Father Crowley Vista Point** for a view into Rainbow Canyon and possibly a sighting of military jets in training. After returning eastbound on Hwy 190, turn right onto Panamint Valley Rd and drive 15 miles before hanging a left onto Wildrose Canyon Rd. Drive to the end of the road for a little wander into the 1870s-era **2 beehive-shaped charcoal kilns** before heading back to the junction with Emigrant Canyon Rd to continue north until it joins Hwy 190.

Stop for a bite or a cold drink and top up your gas tank in **3 Stovepipe Wells** if you like; 2 miles east, blaze your own trail through the fascinating, ever-shifting **4 Mesquite Flats Sand Dunes**. Then press on past Furnace Creek, taking the turnoff down Badwater Rd to drive 17 miles to North America's lowest point, **5 Badwater Basin**. Walk the half-mile out to the alien-looking **6 salt flats** for the full experience of strange awe, then backtrack up the road for the short detour onto Artists Dr to take in the colorfully otherworldly mineral hillsides of **7 Artists Palette**. Artists Dr runs one-way, south to north, so it's best to drive it after visiting Badwater Basin.

Return to Hwy 190, now veering southeast, stopping at **8 Zabriskie Point** for classic views of the badlands below in all their gorgeousness. Try leaving enough time to drive the 14-mile road up to **9 Dante's View** for a dramatic look down on Badwater Basin and Death Valley before leaving the park.

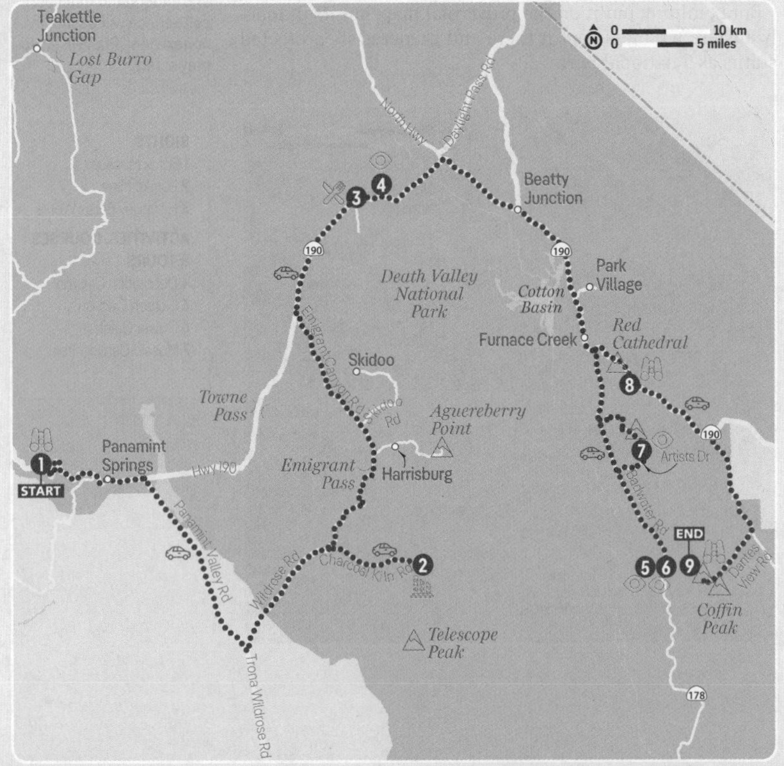

ROMAN KHOMLYAK/SHUTTERSTOCK ©

Hiking trail through Mosaic Canyon

Death Valley Trails

BEST HIKES IN DEATH VALLEY

True, it's the lowest (in North America, at 282ft below sea level), the hottest (in the world, when it hit 128°F/53°C in summer 2022) and the driest (of the US national parks) – but Death Valley is an amazing place to hike. Because of its brain-melting extremes, it's best to hike before 10am and after 4pm during the hottest seasons. Be prepared for dips in temperature after dark and stay aware of flash-flood warnings.

Flash floods are the reason that sinously winding slot canyons like **Mosaic Canyon** even exist, and hikers have them to thank for this canyon's beautifully exposed layers of juxtaposed Noonday dolomite and Mosaic Canyon breccia (mudflow carbonates studded with inclusions of rock fragments).

A quite differently spectacular gallery of wondrous geology is **Golden Canyon**, off the northern end of Badwater Rd. Take the **Golden Canyon–Gower Gulch loop** that starts in a narrow slot and climbs along a towering golden wall before dropping you into the badlands visible from Zabriskie Point.

I LIVE HERE: FAVORITE HIKES

Christine Sceppe, sales manager at the Oasis at Death Valley (@oasisatdeathvalley), shares her favorite hikes in the park.

Golden Canyon–Gower Gulch loop
The geology here is so interesting, with many different deposits of mineral in beautiful layers of sedimentary rock.

Ubehebe Crater
Standing on the edge of this huge, open crater makes you feel so small. It only takes five minutes to get to the bottom of the crater but 45 minutes to get back up.

Dante's Ridge
The trail goes on top of the peaks out to Mt Perry, over 4 miles each way, and the whole time you have the most amazing view of the entire valley.

WHERE TO STAY IN DEATH VALLEY

Furnace Creek Campground
Desert campground centrally located in the park; reservations highly recommended October to April. **$**

Panamint Springs Resort
Comfortable, rustic rooms and cabins, plus a restaurant and bar on the park's west side. **$**

Oasis at Death Valley
Built in 1927, this remodeled historic hotel is sited at a natural spring in a garden setting. **$$**

THE FIRST PEOPLE OF DEATH VALLEY

Timbisha Shoshone people lived in the Panamint Range for centuries, visiting the valley every winter to gather acorns, hunt waterfowl, catch pupfish in marshes and cultivate small areas of corn, squash and beans. After the federal government created Death Valley National Monument in 1933, the tribe was forced to move several times and was eventually restricted to a 40-acre village site. Years of protests and lobbying by tribal activists resulted in President Clinton signing the Timbisha Shoshone Homeland Act in 2000, transferring 7500 acres of land back to the tribe and creating the first Native American reservation inside a US national park. Today, a few dozen Timbisha live in the **Indian Village** near Furnace Creek.

Desolation Canyon is another stunner, with splashes of pink, green and purple from iron oxides and chlorite, and the payoff of a beautiful view at the end. This out-and-back involves some minor scrambling in a couple of spots.

Human History in Death Valley

NATIVE AMERICANS, BORAX AND GOLD MINERS

Death Valley may not have wound up as a national park were it not for mining, as counterintuitive as that sounds.

The gold rush in 1849 initiated the intermittent influx of prospectors and miners to Death Valley. Though miners often didn't succeed in the harsh conditions, Pete Aguereberry managed to work at his **Eureka Mine** for almost 40 years after discovering gold there in 1905. You can see the closed mine and camp, where his cabin compound still stands.

Further south down Wildrose Canyon Rd, explore the **beehive-shaped charcoal kilns** lined up neatly by the road. Built by the Modock Mines, the kilns were used to make charcoal for fueling ore-refining operations.

But it was the discovery of borax (used for detergents among other purposes) that paved the way for tourism at Death Valley. Borax mining and processing began in Death Valley in the 1880s and was laboriously transported out via wagons pulled by 20-mule teams. When the lucrative mineral was discovered in a more easily accessed location, the Pacific Coast Borax Company built what is now the Inn at Death Valley, heavily promoting it as a holiday destination, to create an alternative revenue stream. The company later lobbied to establish Death Valley as a national park.

Nowadays, you can walk the interpretive trail at the **Harmony Borax Works** site near Furnace Creek. Then stroll around the rusty mining equipment, mule-drawn wagons and other sculptural skeletons in the back of the **Borax Museum** at the Ranch in Furnace Creek.

GETTING AROUND

As a car is necessary for traveling around the park, make sure you check current road closures ahead of your trip at nps.gov/deva. Heavy monsoon rains of 2022 washed out sections of several park roads, making some entrances and sections of the park inaccessible. At the time of writing, the Olancha entrance from Hwy 395 had reopened for access from the west. On the east side, entrances from Beatty and Death Valley Junction were open.

Beyond Death Valley National Park

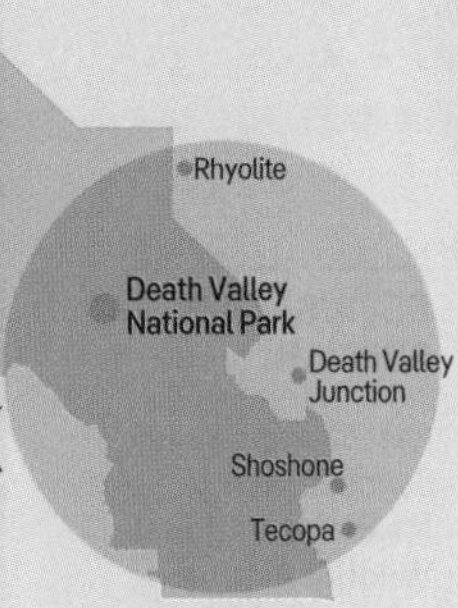

These are lands of wide-open spaces, where the Sierra Nevada looms west of the park and tiny desert communities dot the east.

Hwy 395 runs north to south, near the west side of Death Valley. Along Hwy 395 lies the Eastern Sierra town of Lone Pine, a lovely gateway town on the park's west side. Stop here for a little mountain hiking, a big dinner and a fuel fill-up.

The park's eastern gateways are a different world altogether, where the desert stretches into Nevada, scattered with ghost towns, hot springs, oases and hidden rivers. Taking Hwy 127 south out of Death Valley Junction makes for a scenic road trip, meandering through small communities in greener desert zones to Mojave National Preserve. Fascinating cave dwellings, reed-fringed hot springs and outdoor art are worth the stops on your drive.

TOP TIP

The distances between services can be big on both rural highways. Before entering or upon leaving the park, top up your gas tank when the opportunity arises.

Amargosa Opera House (p474)

LOGAN BUSH/SHUTTERSTOCK ©

Dublin Gulch cave house, Shoshone

DEVIL'S HOLE PUPFISH

East of Death Valley Junction, **Ash Meadows National Wildlife Refuge** provides habitat for 26 species endemic to the region. Its most famous inhabitant is the endangered Devil's Hole pupfish, the rarest fish on the planet. Occupying 93°F (34°C) geothermal water in **Devil's Hole**, whose depth remains unknown, this little fish is a miracle that swam back from the brink of total extinction. If you visit Devil's Hole, a tiny outpost of Death Valley National Park enclosed within Ash Meadows, you can peer into this mysterious pool from the viewing platform high above; however, you'll need binoculars to see the pupfish.

Ghost-Town Arts

GHOST TOWNS AND DESERT CREATIONS

The spectral white-and-turquoise adobe **Amargosa Opera House** anchors **Death Valley Junction** with weather-beaten gravitas. Its story is compelling enough to have inspired a 2000 documentary about Marta Becket, the former ballerina who began performing one-woman shows here in 1968. Learn more on a tour, offered daily, or stay in the idiosyncratic adjacent hotel, decorated with her hand-painted murals. Not much else exists here except for the road into the park (a 20-minute drive along Hwy 190) and the sky above.

Further north on Hwy 95, Beatty, NV, serves as the hub for the park's northeastern Daylight Pass entrance. Head west

WHERE TO STAY

Amargosa Hotel
Stay overnight at Marta Becket's spiritual home in dead-quiet Death Valley Junction. $

Stagecoach Hotel & Casino
Swimming pool, slot machines and comfortable remodeled rooms for basing yourself in Beatty. $

Atomic Inn
Friendly, clean, quirky motel in Beatty, with all the basics. $

on Daylight Pass Rd (Hwy 374) for 6 miles through the hills and down to the ghost town of **Rhyolite**, once a prospering gold-rush town along the Las Vegas and Tonopah Railroad. Partial walls of the town's bank and shops lead up the road to the grand **Rhyolite Railroad Depot**, overlooking valley views. Interpretive signage helps to conjure the bustling town in its prime.

Just outside Rhyolite, you may glimpse unexpected shapes in your peripheral vision. Whatever you look at first, you'll eventually stumble on the eerie figures of Albert Szukalski's *The Last Supper*, the flagship sculpture of the outdoor **Goldwell Museum**. Walk around to view several artists' open-air work, day or night. From the main road, it's another 5 miles to the park entrance.

JAPANESE AMERICAN GHOST TOWN

From Lone Pine, you can take a side trip to the starkly beautiful **Manzanar National Historic Site** (p623) – this sensitively curated memorial of US government injustice is a must-visit in the Eastern Sierra.

Delights of Shoshone & Tecopa

RUINS, HOT SPRINGS AND THRIVING PUPFISH

Twenty-seven miles south of Death Valley Junction, **Shoshone** (with a population of only 22) may seem like just an oasis pit stop, but after your gas fill-up and a bite at the century-old **Crowbar Cafe & Saloon**, walk it off at this outpost's fascinating sights.

As ghost towns go, **Dublin Gulch** deviates from the norm with its cave dwellings carved out of the limestone by miners in the early 1900s. Insulating in the cold winters and cool in the blazing summers, these caves were ingeniously livable.

More exceptional is Shoshone's extinction story gone right. The **Shoshone pupfish** was believed extinct by 1970, but in 1986 a small population was identified in a local ditch. Since then, conservation efforts have resulted in the species bouncing back, and it's now numbering at over 1000. From a little loop trail, you can see the current descendants happily zipping around the pond habitats created expressly for them.

South of Tecopa, drive out to **China Date Ranch** not for the date shakes – though you should enjoy one – but to hike a refreshingly riparian section of the **Amargosa River Trail**. You can tackle a 2-mile loop from the ranch parking lot, and add the spur to a slot canyon for a 3-miler.

HOT-SPRINGS DETOUR

Treat your hike-weary muscles to mineral spring water at **Delight's Hot Springs Resort**, which has an outdoor pool, clean showers and private pool cabanas where you can soak au naturel. You can also opt for a day pass. In your state of post-hot-springs bliss, float down the driveway to the teeny **Tecopa Brewing Company** to see what's on tap to pair with a pulled-pork sandwich.

GETTING AROUND

As in Death Valley National Park, it's necessary to have a car to get around this area. Try to avoid driving in the area at night – the two-lane highways and rural roads are quite dark, especially if there's little to no moonlight.

ANZA-BORREGO DESERT STATE PARK

San Francisco

Los Angeles

Anza-Borrego Desert State Park

It's a superbloom superstar, an outdoor menagerie of metal-sculpture animals and an International Dark Sky Park. At over 1000 sq miles, Anza-Borrego is California's largest state park, with hundreds of miles of established roads and endless possibilities for backcountry camping under a shockingly starry night sky. The land was traditionally occupied by the Santa Rosa Band of the Cahuilla tribe and the Kumeyaay people, and still bears the marks of their lives in the petroglyphs and *morteros* (mortars) visible today.

Anza-Borrego's high season runs from mid-February through March, when the wildflowers suddenly paint the desert in splashes of yellow, pink and magenta. The park's diminutive hub of Borrego Springs can quickly overflow with photo-hungry visitors when blooming peaks, but its all-season allure lies in its folded badlands, hidden oases, slot canyons and desert plains graced by joyous outdoor art.

TOP TIP

In the mercurial way of the desert, Anza-Borrego's much anticipated wildflower season is fleeting and unpredictable. Conditions have to come together with the right alchemy for desert wildflowers to blossom, but you can hear a weekly update on the Wildflower Hotline at 760-767-4684.

Anza-Borrego Desert State Park

JNJPHOTOS/SHUTTERSTOCK ©

WHY I LOVE ANZA-BORREGO

Wendy Yanagihara, writer

In the spring of 2017 I'd heard the Anza-Borrego superbloom buzz, so on a Monday I threw my camping gear into the car and squeezed into the last site at Culp Valley before dusk. In the morning I sat on a boulder watching the sun rise over the Salton Sea and fell in love with the park before I even saw a single desert sunflower of the gazillion that would blind me later that day. The pure delight of seeing the desert floor awash with color still sticks with me.

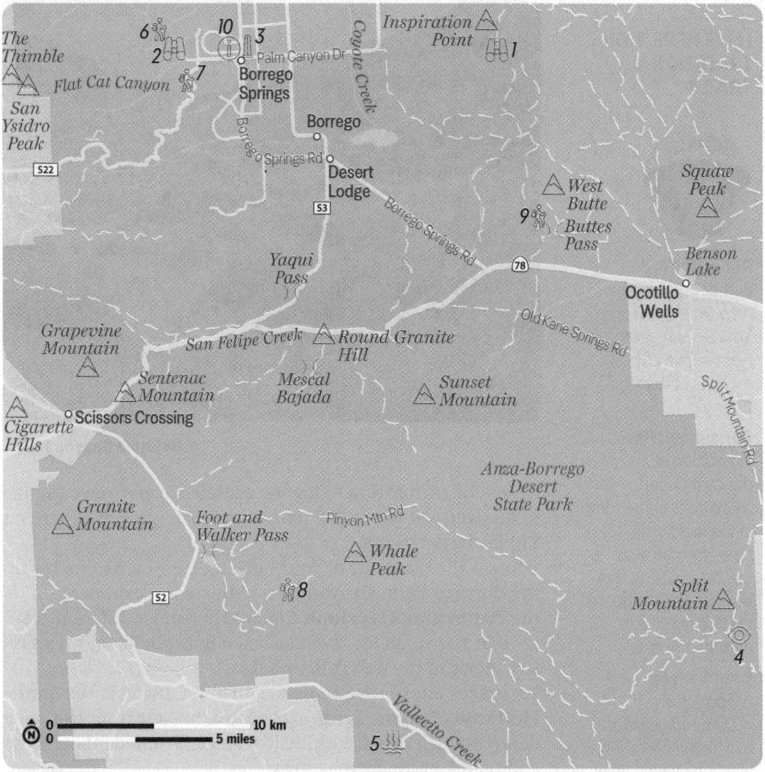

SIGHTS
1 Fonts Point
2 Panorama Overlook
3 Sky Art
4 Wind Caves

ACTIVITIES, COURSES & TOURS
5 Agua Caliente Regional Park
6 Borrego Palm Canyon Nature Trail
7 Hellhole Canyon Trail
8 Pictograph Trail
9 Slot Canyon

INFORMATION
10 Anza-Borrego Desert Natural History Association

Hiking Anza-Borrego

NATURE TRAILS AND ROUTE-FINDING ADVENTURES

Many visitors to Anza-Borrego Desert State Park wind up hiking the **Borrego Palm Canyon Nature Trail,** but it's popular for good reason. The trail is an easy one and fun for kids to explore, and it ends at the **Borrego Palm Canyon Oasis**, named after its native California fan palms. The oasis itself is

WHERE TO EAT AND DRINK IN BORREGO SPRINGS

Red Ocotillo
A lovely little garden hideaway for breakfast, lunch, dinner and happy hour. **$$**

Kesling's Kitchen
Wood-fired pizza is usually on the ever-changing menu of quality eats; also has grab-and-go items. **$$**

Carmelita's Mexican Grill & Cantina
Good Mexican classics and margaritas at this local favorite in the mall. **$**

I LIVE HERE: NON-TRADITIONAL TRAILS

Robin Halford, author of *Hiking in Anza-Borrego Desert*, Vols 1–3, suggest hikes within 25 minutes of Borrego Springs.

Cannonball Run
In addition to the cannonball formations embedded in the mudstone here, you can also see the uplifting that occurred eons ago, that's almost like natural rock art.

Cool Canyon
A wonderful meandering canyon at a higher elevation, with different vegetation and cooler temperatures than on the desert floor.

Bill Kenyon Trail
This out-and-back isn't difficult, with wonderful cacti and other desert flora along the trail. You end up with a really nice view across Hwy 78 to a bajada, where you have several alluvial fans coming together.

UNDERAWESTERNSKY/SHUTTERSTOCK ©

Hellhole Canyon Trail

closed for restoration following a 2020 fire, but you can hike to an overlook to see the palms recovering nicely. There's a $10 fee to park here.

To get the most out of your parking fee, you can follow up the Borrego Palm Canyon hike with some elevation gain on the **Panorama Overlook** that starts from a different trail-head at the same lot. Even as you climb, you'll enjoy expansive views of the desert floor below.

A longer alternative to Borrego Palm Canyon is the 5-mile **Hellhole Canyon Trail** nearby, taking you from the open desert to lush oases with little waterfalls, maidenhair ferns and palms untouched by fire.

Because flash floods can swiftly erase trails and signage, many hikes in Anza-Borrego follow washes, drainages and ridges in place of established trails. If you're heading into the desert, it's a great idea to pick up a topographic map and hiking guidebook so you have detailed directions in hand, as cell-phone coverage is unreliable.

The Sky Art of Borrego Springs

BORREGO SPRINGS' ENVIRONMENTAL SCULPTURES

A dragon rears up from the desert floor, its serpentine back swelling and falling behind it, seemingly passing under the road. Nearby, saber-toothed tigers stalk a herd of horses on alert, and a family of mammoths stretch out their trunks as they lope. They're all real, albeit in sculpture form, in the

WHERE TO STAY IN BORREGO SPRINGS

Hacienda del Sol
Updated rooms and casitas with mid-century design flair, walkable to everything in town. **$$**

Borrego Valley Inn
Romantic, quiet and close to town, this pink adobe refuge has gorgeous views of the mountains. **$$**

La Casa del Zorro
Resort-style hotel beyond downtown Borrego Springs, with pool, bar and restaurant in a landscaped setting. **$$**

open plains of Borrego Springs. Artist Ricardo Breceda has created and installed over 130 sculptures – animals mythical, prehistoric and contemporary – that dot the landscape, all of which comprise the **Sky Art** of Galleta Meadows. The fantastical sculptures were commissioned by late landowner and philanthropist Dennis Avery, with the land they occupy intended for conservation and open to the public.

Part of the fun is stumbling upon them in the wild as you drive along the main arteries of Palm Canyon Dr and Borrego Springs Rd. You'll glimpse them from a distance and close in, noticing that even though motionless, they look on the verge of springing dynamically to life. But if you want to make a tour of the sculptures, you can pick up a critter-locator map at the **Anza-Borrego Desert Natural History Association** store in town.

The sculptures are a big draw for Borrego Springs, and thousands of visitors come to see them each year. Try to keep your impact low by driving where there are preexisting tracks, and not touching these beloved metal masterpieces.

STARGAZING IN BORREGO SPRINGS

Approved in 2009 as the only certified Dark Sky Community in California, Borrego Springs is a stellar place for stargazing. The park's visitor center in Borrego Springs offers guided stargazing on dark new-moon nights, and you may catch a star party behind the **Borrego Springs Library**, where astronomers set up telescopes to tour the night sky. Check out the website of the **Borrego Dark Sky Coalition** (abdnha.org/borregodarksky) for upcoming events.

Anza-Borrego South to North

PETROGLYPHS, DIVERSE LANDSCAPES AND HOT SPRINGS

Pack a lunch and start early for your drive south through the park's Pinyon Mountains and beautiful higher-elevation piñon and juniper country. From the junction of Hwy 78 and County Rd S2, drive 6 miles to the Blair Valley turnoff, a dirt road at Mile 22.9. A map posted there shows the way to the **Pictograph Trail** (high-clearance vehicle recommended to the trailhead). The pretty hike to the **petroglyphs** is lined with small boulders, cholla and brittlebush, opening up to valley views at **Smugglers Overlook**.

If a hot-spring dip appeals to you, continue south about 15 miles to **Agua Caliente Regional Park**, a San Diego County regional park within Anza-Borrego. Here, hot springs feed three indoor and outdoor developed pools, with $3 granting you access to showers and day use of the pools. Note: the indoor pool is adults only; weekends are often packed.

Return toward Borrego Springs the way you came, this time staying on Hwy 78 to the junction with the inconspicuous Buttes Pass Rd. It's 1½ miles to the **Slot Canyon** trailhead, where there's a day-use fee. This is another easy hike through a cool slot canyon, ending at **wind caves**, so called because the wind eroded the sandstone into these smooth formations.

End your day with sunset at **Fonts Point**, with the dramatic panorama of Borrego Valley to the west and Borrego Badlands to the south shown in their best light.

GETTING AROUND

If you plan on backcountry hiking or camping, it's ideal to drive a high-clearance 4WD vehicle in Anza-Borrego. But even 4WD vehicles can wind up spinning their wheels in loose sand, so have gear on hand in case you need to dig out your rig. Bring a shovel and some carpet remnants or old floor mats for traction.

Beyond Anza-Borrego Desert State Park

Discover a quaint mining town, forest lake and wolf conservation center west of Anza-Borrego.

Wild wolf encounters, lake fishing and mining-town ambience await in Julian, only an hour southwest of Borrego Springs but a world away at 4226ft. In contrast to Anza-Borrego's austere badlands and sun-baked valley floor, the mountains offer respite from the heat.

A popular midway point on the two-hour drive between San Diego and Anza-Borrego, Julian makes a nice stop to stretch your legs and take in some cool mountain air. The old town's few blocks can get jammed with pedestrians and run out of street parking on the weekends. This is especially true during the fall, peaking for the Julian Apple Festival in October.

TOP TIP

Julian is best on weekdays when there's fewer visitors, as the main attraction is the very tiny old-town district.

Lake Cuyamaca

UNWIND/SHUTTERSTOCK ©

ALLISON CHERRY/SHUTTERSTOCK ©

Apple pie in Julian

Julian Mountain Retreat

APPLE PIES AND MOUNTAIN HIGHS

Leaving Anza-Borrego from the west on Hwy 78, the road curves upward into oak and pine meadowlands, spilling into the little mountain town of Julian. Driving in, you'll see the Victorian-style storefronts that date back to the early 1900s, when gold mining brought an influx of settlers. Nowadays Julian is most famous for its **apple pie**, abundant at bakeries along the main drag.

Stroll the few blocks of old-town **Main St** to shop for goat's-milk soap, sample a slice of pie and take the self-guided historical walking tour. From September through mid-October you can pick several varieties of your own apples at a local **u-pick orchard**. Year-round, book a beautiful guided trail ride on horseback with **Integrity Stables**.

One of the area's unique encounters is at the **California Wolf Conservation Center** south of Julian, where you'll learn about wild wolf conservation efforts while observing a few ambassador wolves that reside at the center. Advance reservations are required.

Find more leisurely outdoor pursuits 9 miles south of Julian at the woodsy **Lake Cuyamaca**. Go fishing or walk the flat 3-mile perimeter trail before having a pint over views of the lake at **The Pub**. It's an outpost of **Nickel Beer Company**, whose little taproom on the east end of Julian occupies the former jailhouse.

JULIAN'S BLACK HISTORY

According to the US census of 1880, 33 of the 55 Black residents of San Diego County lived in Julian; several landmarks around town honor some of its notable Black citizens.

Coleman Creek was named after AE 'Fred' Coleman, the local cattleman who first discovered gold in Julian, leading to the only gold rush in San Diego County and Julian's mining boom.

In town, former slave Albert Robinson and his wife Margaret Tull Robinson ran a successful restaurant, which they tore down to build the Robinson Hotel in 1897. Now the charming **Julian Gold Rush Hotel**, it's the oldest continuously operating hotel in Southern California and is on the National Register of Historic Places.

GETTING AROUND

You'll need your own wheels to get to Julian, which is located some 30 miles southwest of Borrego Springs at the junction of Hwy 78 and Hwy 79.

MOJAVE NATIONAL PRESERVE

Occupying a swath of wilderness between two interstate highways (I-15 and I-40), Mojave National Preserve is a less visited desert park guaranteeing space for solitude. Spanning Mojave, Sonoran and Great Basic Desert zones, its landscape varies from sand dunes to piñon-and-juniper woodland. With a higher density of Joshua trees than in Joshua Tree National Park, the preserve offers all of the wild Mojave Desert beauty without the selfie-snapping human component.

Very few visitor amenities exist here, especially after recent monsoon damage to some of the preserve's roads. At the time of writing, only one of the two visitor centers was open and only from Friday to Monday. But for the self-sufficient traveler, Mojave National Preserve is truly a refuge and a rich setting for sitting with the elemental delights of the desert.

TOP TIP

Ahead of entering Mojave National Preserve, print a basic map showing passable roads, which is updated regularly by the National Park Service website (nps.gov/moja/road-conditions.htm). The monsoons of 2022 destroyed sections of road in the preserve, where GPS coverage is unreliable and an old-fashioned map may save your day.

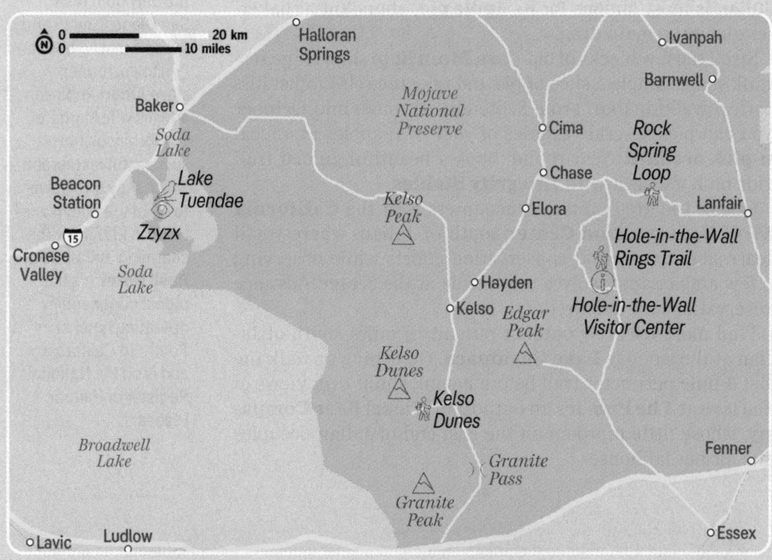

CLAY PARTNERS/SHUTTERSTOCK ©

Kelso Dunes

Mojave Transect

SOLITUDE AND STUNNING SAND DUNES

Heading east on I-15 from Baker, the Cima Rd turnoff leads south into the wilderness of Mojave National Preserve. Cruise south through the desert scrub and Joshua trees (many of which got charred by the August 2020 Dome Fire).

Turning east on Cedar Canyon Rd, drive 11 miles to the **Rock Spring Loop** trailhead for the easy 1.5-mile loop hike, passing a rock house built in 1929 and spring-fed pools in the boulders, with mountain views all around.

From here, choose your own adventure: if you want to hear the singing sands of **Kelso Dunes**, backtrack to Kelso Cima Rd and continue south to the turnoff for the dunes. Budget about 2½ hours to hike to the top, a soft-sand challenge best tackled before 10am and the heat of the day, or toward sundown to soak up the dramatic light.

Alternatively, circle around the long way (due to road damage) for a classic Mojave hike. Keep heading east on Cedar Canyon Rd to turn right on Lanfair Rd, southward to I-40. You'll loop westward on I-40 before turning north back into the preserve on Essex Rd. Connect with Black Canyon Rd to

DESERT TORTOISES

The desert tortoise is a threatened species found in the Mojave Desert Preserve as well as California's larger desert region. Though the species has been around for millions of years, its populations have declined over the past several decades. Stressors include rising temperatures from climate change, disease, human encroachment on their desert habitats and even ravens, which prey on baby tortoises.

Consider it a blessing if you luck out seeing a desert tortoise in the wild. In fact, always check under your parked car before driving away, and watch out for tortoises trundling across roads.

WHERE TO CAMP IN MOJAVE NATIONAL PRESERVE

Hole-in-the-Wall
First-come, first-served campground currently only accessible from the south on Essex Rd. $

Mid Hills
Higher-elevation first-come, first-served campground best for tent camping; accessible on Cedar Canyon Rd. $

Kelso Dunes
Backcountry camp here for sunrise solitude in the early hours, when you're likely to have the dunes to yourself. $

Bighorn sheep

SCRAPPY ROAD RACERS

Spotting a bighorn sheep can come down to luck and timing, but you're likely to see a roadrunner cross your path in your desert travels. The greater roadrunner's scientific name of *Geococcyx californianus* means 'Californian earth cuckoo' (which could apply to many state residents), and its common name seems 100% accurate when you see them zipping across roadways. Roadrunners not only bravely mate for life but also prey on scary delicacies like scorpions and rattlesnakes.

Hole-in-the-Wall Visitor Center (open 10am to 4pm Friday through Monday).

From here, hike the 1.3-mile **Hole-in-the-Wall Rings Trail**. Formed by a volcanic eruption whose gases left air bubbles in the cooling rock, the namesake holey walls on this fun hike include steep sections featuring bolted rings for handholds.

Mojave Wildlife-Watching

WILD DENIZENS OF THE MOJAVE

From Baker, the Zzyzx Rd turnoff is just a few miles west on I-15, after which it's 5 miles south to **Zzyzx**. Established as a health spa by quack doctor Curtis Springer in 1944, he named Zzyzx so as to be 'the last word' in health. Springer was evicted 30 years later by the Bureau of Land Management as he had no legitimate claim to the land, with the structures then left to the mercy of the desert's unforgiving elements.

From the parking area, walk the quarter mile to **Lake Tuendae** – time your arrival here in the morning or evening and you have a good chance of spotting **bighorn sheep**. The lake is also a great locale for **birding** – spot hundreds of species here, including the western tanager and various flycatchers. The half-mile loop trail around the lake is flat and an easy stroll.

The Lake Tuendae (north) side of the road is open to the public from dawn to dusk. On the road's south side, the old resort buildings now function as the California State University's Desert Studies Center, a working field station (private property).

Link this experience with a drive through the preserve, whether you're entering via the south or north.

GETTING AROUND

You'll need your own vehicle to access Mojave National Preserve, as there's zero public transport. Though several main roads may still be closed due to monsoon damage, much of the preserve remains accessible if you have the time to explore.

Beyond Mojave National Preserve

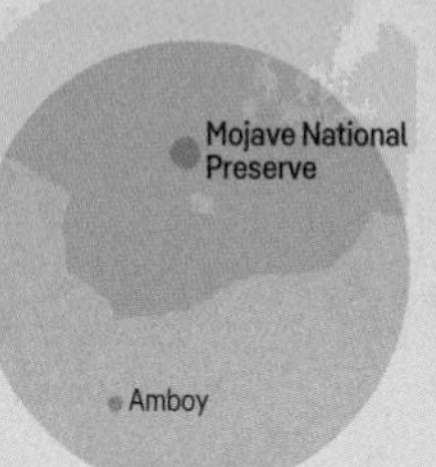

Embrace slow travel by taking yourself on a time-warp road trip along a stretch of the historic Mother Road.

Wide-open desert flies by as you travel the interstates above and below Mojave National Preserve. But if you're not quite ready for highway travel and a straight shot back to urban hubs, take the long way to explore a smidge of old Route 66.

Unfortunately, flash flooding on Route 66 has washed out several 1930s-era bridges and sections of roadway connecting Amboy with Ludlow to the west and Goffs to the east. It's unclear when this section of Route 66 will be repaired, so an east–west through-drive is likely impossible anytime soon. Still, the romance of the Mother Road endures even in the short stretches, with unexpected roadside sights popping up through the shimmering heat waves.

TOP TIP

Look for 'Route 66' painted on the road, for a photo opp proving that you're driving the historic highway.

Amboy Crater (p487)

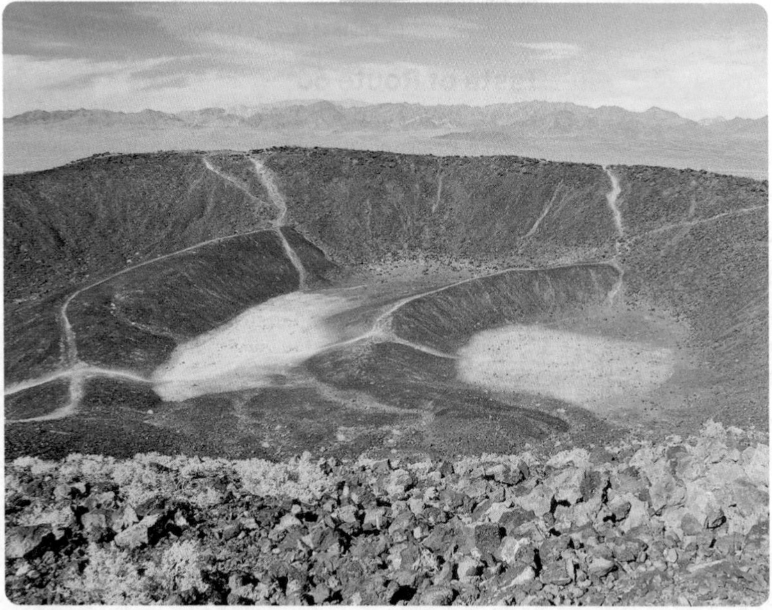

OLOS/SHUTTERSTOCK ©

Route 66 through the Mojave National Preserve

Taste of Route 66

MOJAVE TO JOSHUA TREE

Connect Mojave National Preserve with a drive to Joshua Tree National Park (p460). Leaving Mojave National Preserve along Kelbaker Rd, cross I-40 to continue south for about 11 miles until the road intersects with **Route 66** (National Trails Hwy). The path eastward is blocked, so your only choice is to take a right.

Route 66 stretches ahead of you for miles, passing the odd graffitied road sign. Look for the pair of **Chinese stone lions** guarding the otherwise empty desert on the south side of the highway, adding unexpected mys-

ROAD-TRIP LINK

Make a grand desert road trip by stitching any or all of these drives together to sightsee while getting from points A to B: **drive-though highlights** (p470), **Mojave transect** (p483) and/or **Joshua Tree drive-through** (p465).

Roy's Motel & Cafe

tery to the archetypical Americana feel of this drive. In about 6 miles you'll approach the town of **Amboy**, marked by its towering atomic-age sign for **Roy's Motel & Cafe**. Though Roy's no longer offers lodging, you can fill up your gas tank here and grab a cold drink to sip. Stretch your legs, checking out the active post office (serving the zero residents of Amboy) and the exterior of the Amboy School.

Cut across the train tracks to check out **Amboy Crater**, a cinder cone in one of the youngest volcanic fields in the USA (it last erupted around 10,000 years ago).

Return to Route 66, backtracking eastward about a mile to the turnoff on Amboy Rd, which travels south through the high desert to Twentynine Palms (p467), gateway to Joshua Tree National Park.

CIRCLE THE CRATER

Eerily quiet but for your footsteps crunching along the lava-chunk-lined trail, **Amboy Crater's** remoteness, extreme heat and volcanic landscape feels like entering another world entirely. NASA thought so, too, and test-drove the Mars Rover in these lava fields. The trail leads into the breach in the crater where lava spilled out, providing entry into the crater itself, where you can hike up to the rim (only 80ft up) and trek along its perimeter. Allow about two hours to complete the mostly flat, 3-mile hike to and around the crater. Bring at least a liter of water, try to finish your hike before 10am and avoid hiking during the summer in this particularly harsh environment.

GETTING AROUND

You'll definitely need your own vehicle to get anywhere around the area. As is advisable around these parts, fill up your gas tank when you can. Roy's Motel & Cafe in Amboy is the only fuel stop along this lovely, lonely desert drive.

TIAGO IGNOWSKI/SHUTTERSTOCK ©

Above: McArthur-Burney Falls (p497); Right: Castle Crags State Park (p496)

NORTHERN MOUNTAINS

CALIFORNIA'S UNSUNG MOUNTAIN PARADISE

Vast forests, lofty peaks and high deserts delight, with the surreal, pyramid-shaped Mt Shasta winking at you around every turn.

'Hidden California' gets bandied around casually, but the northeastern corner of the state does seem forgotten. Prepare yourself for something completely different from the sunny West Coast clichés: vast expanses of wilderness – some 24,000 protected acres – divided by rivers and dotted with cobalt lakes, horse ranches and Alpine peaks. Further east is a stretch of shrubby high desert cut with amber gorges, caves and dramatic light that's a photographer's dream. The topography resembles the older mountains of the Rockies more than the relatively young Sierras. The towns are tiny but friendly, with few comforts; come to get lost in vast remoteness. Even the two principal attractions, Mt Shasta and Lassen Volcanic National Park, remain relatively uncrowded even at the peak of summer.

You'll want a car out here to explore the interstates and country roads: places where you can drive for hours without seeing another soul – or a gas station (fill up when you can). Wonders like McArthur-Burney Falls and Lava Beds National Monument are far from everything but worth the trip. Or base yourself at Mt Shasta or Lassen Volcanic National Park where there are enough hiking trails to fill several months, plus lakes, biking and fishing. Spiritual seekers will be drawn to Shasta's mountain magic and counterculture vibes. Load up on crystals and try to find a vortex.

THE MAIN AREAS

MT SHASTA REGION
Mountain vortexes to lava tubes.
p494

MT LASSEN REGION
Fantastic volcanic landscapes.
p502

REDDING & SHASTA LAKE
Houseboating and camping.
p511

Find Your Way

I-5 divides the better-known mountain areas to the east from the lesser-visited forests, small towns and lakes to the west. Hwy 89 in the principal route to get around Mt Lassen.

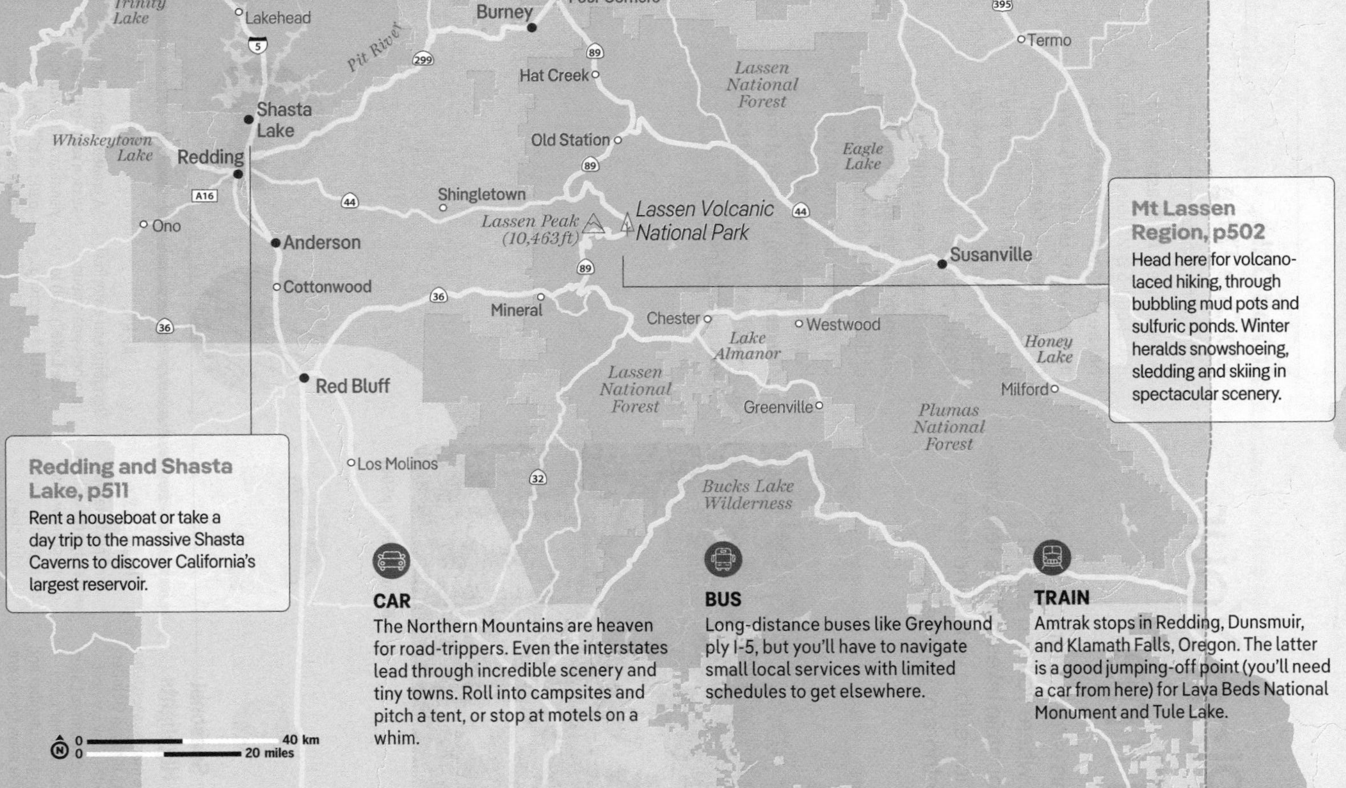

Redding and Shasta Lake, p511

Rent a houseboat or take a day trip to the massive Shasta Caverns to discover California's largest reservoir.

Mt Lassen Region, p502

Head here for volcano-laced hiking, through bubbling mud pots and sulfuric ponds. Winter heralds snowshoeing, sledding and skiing in spectacular scenery.

CAR

The Northern Mountains are heaven for road-trippers. Even the interstates lead through incredible scenery and tiny towns. Roll into campsites and pitch a tent, or stop at motels on a whim.

BUS

Long-distance buses like Greyhound ply I-5, but you'll have to navigate small local services with limited schedules to get elsewhere.

TRAIN

Amtrak stops in Redding, Dunsmuir, and Klamath Falls, Oregon. The latter is a good jumping-off point (you'll need a car from here) for Lava Beds National Monument and Tule Lake.

Plan Your Time

This is road-tripping Shangri-la, where you can stop at mountain lakes, pitch a tent, hike to incredible vistas and see a plethora of wildlife.

NORA YUSUF/SHUTTERSTOCK ©

Bumpass Hell (p506)

If You Only Do One Thing

● Magnificent **Mt Shasta** (p494) is just off I-5 (you'll see it for miles before you reach it) so there's no excuse not to pull into Mt Shasta City, then drive as far as you can up the mountain – in summer you can get up to 7800ft, and in winter 6950ft. Wherever you end up, take as long a hike as time allows and enjoy the incredible energy of this forested, dormant volcano. On your way out, you might be inspired to shop for a **crystal souvenir** (p495), then eat at one of the town's excellent and healthy **restaurants** (p494).

Seasonal Highlights

The main season runs May through October with many services closed in winter. Lakes are warmish July through September and winter snow sports are best from December through March.

FEBRUARY

The best times for **winter sports** with the deepest snow base, plus a good chance of blue skies.

APRIL

Songbird and waterfowl numbers peak around **Tule Lake** (p501) for epic bird-watching.

MAY

A great month for off-season **road-tripping**; visitation at the national parks is still low. Most services are now open.

BRENT DOSCHER/AURORA PHOTOS/GETTY IMAGES ©; NG STUDIO PHOTOGRAPHY/SHUTTERSTOCK ©; FORREST MORRISEY/SHUTTERSTOCK ©

Three Days to Travel Around

● From the Bay Area, head first to **Lassen Volcanic National Park** (p503) and spend a day driving the park and hiking to the bubbling and bright 'mini Yellowstone' **Bumpass Hell** (p506).

● The next day take back-road Hwy 89 for incredible views of Mt Shasta, and detour to the impressive **McArthur-Burney Falls** (p497). Spend the night in tiny, charming **McCloud** (p498), where you can start or end the day with a forest stroll.

● On day three, spend the day exploring Mt Shasta, either **hiking on the mountain** (p496) or relaxing and swimming in **Castle Lake** (p498).

If You Have More Time

● Follow the three-day itinerary, taking more time in the national park and on Mt Shasta, then take Hwy 97 east from Weed to **Tule Lake** (p501) for a day or more of canoeing and oohing and aahing over bald eagles, waterfowl and osprey.

● From here it's only 12 miles to the fantastic **Lava Beds National Monument** (p500) where you could spend a few days exploring caves, above-ground lavascapes and Native American historical sites scrawled with petroglyphs. Then loop back via Yreka and down Hwy 3 through mountains and charming small towns to **Weaverville** (p517) and **Redding** (p511).

JUNE

Scenic hiking with lingering mountain snow, gushing waterfalls and blooming **wildflowers** in the lowlands.

JULY

Summer is in full swing and the **High Sierra Music Festival** (p510) rocks the town of Quincy.

AUGUST

It's hot outside, perfect for high-country **camping** at Almanor or Siskiyou lakes – if there are no forest fires.

OCTOBER

Leaves begin to turn with **foliage** best mid-month on Mt Shasta and Lassen Peak; expect warm days and cold nights.

MT SHASTA REGION

'Lonely as God, and white as a winter moon,' wrote poet Joaquin Miller about this lovely mountain. The sight of it is so awe-inspiring that the new-age claims about its power as an energy vortex sound plausible even after a first glimpse.

There are many ways to explore Mt Shasta and the surrounding Shasta-Trinity National Forest: take scenic drives or get out and hike, mountain bike, raft, ski or snowshoe. Around the mountain sit four excellent little towns: Dunsmuir, Mt Shasta City, McCloud and Weed. Each has a distinct personality, but all hold a wild-mountain sensibility and first-rate amenities. Find the snaggle-toothed peaks of Castle Crags just 6 miles west of Dunsmuir.

A long drive northeast of Mt Shasta and a world away is the eerily beautiful Lava Beds National Monument, a blistered badland of petrified fire. The contrasting wetlands of Klamath Basin National Wildlife Refuges lie just west.

TOP TIP

There are great views of Mt Shasta from I-5, but leaving the interstate and driving east will afford even better angles. Be sure to account for the time you'll need to pull over again and again to take in all the majesty and snap photos.

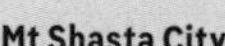

Mt Shasta City

JMOORI7/GETTY IMAGES ©

BEST RESTAURANTS IN MT SHASTA CITY

Bistro 107
Get excellent burgers and hearty hot sandwiches at this homey little joint. $$$

Lily's
Asian- and Mediterranean-touched salads, fresh sandwiches and all kinds of veggie and gluten-free options. $$

Crave
Street tacos, sandwiches, barbeque, vegetarian...it's all good. Setting is basic but comfy and friendly. $$

Poncho & Lefkowitz
Surrounded by a picnic tables, this classy, wood-sided food cart turns out juicy Polish sausages, tamales and burritos. $

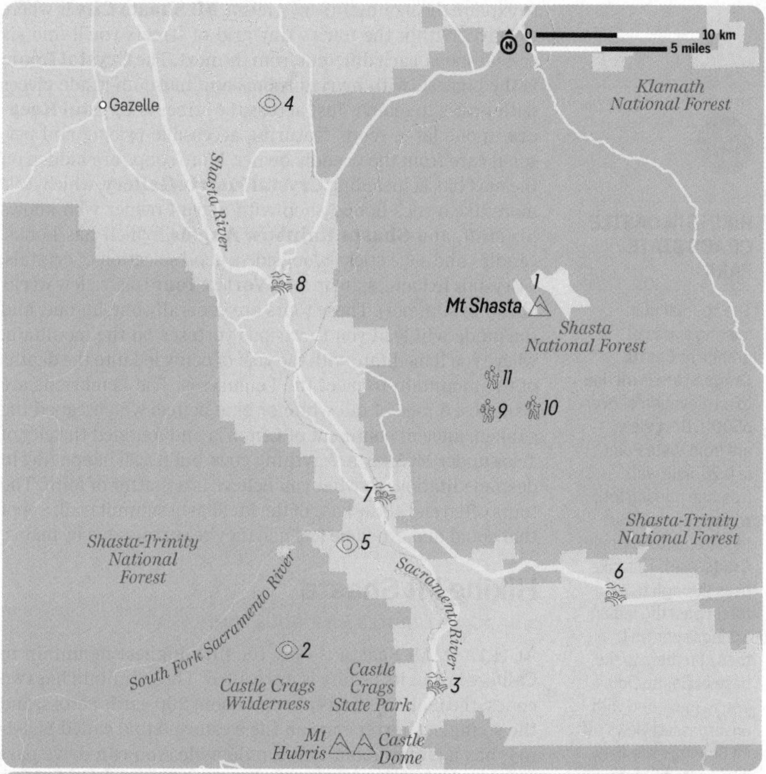

HIGHLIGHTS
1 Mt Shasta

SIGHTS
2 Castle Lake
3 Dunsmuir
4 Lake Shastina
5 Lake Siskiyou
6 McCloud
7 Mt Shasta City
8 Weed

ACTIVITIES, COURSES & TOURS
9 Bunny Flat
10 Lower Panther Meadow
11 Sierra Club Horse Camp

Crystal Shops & Vortex Tours

A MYSTICAL ENERGY CENTER

Mt Shasta is considered a power center, where mythical ley lines cross, producing a high concentration of electromagnetic energy on par with Stonehenge, Machu Picchu and the pyramids of Giza. Whatever you believe, there's no denying that the mountain exudes intense beauty and majesty. If you want

WHERE TO DRINK IN MT SHASTA

Handsome John's Speakeasy
It's so local that people may look at you in surprise when you walk in.

Pipeline Craft Taps & Kitchen
Gastropub right in town with an excellent craft brew selection.

Cooper's Bar & Grill
Good, strong drinks and a decent pub food menu.

to explore the mountain's mysticism, **Mt Shasta City** is where to start. Within the town's tiny grid of streets you'll find six crystal shops, each different from the next. The **Crystal Room** is the biggest, with myriad rooms and museum-grade pieces with prices to match. Just across the street is **Crystal Keepers** in one large room, featuring accessible pricing and personal care from the friendly owner. More shops are hidden on the next block, including **Crystal Matrix Gallery**, which feels more like a rock-hound shop with a gruff owner who knows his stuff, and **Shasta Rainbow Angels**, which has books, candles and sage sticks alongside a good selection of crystals.

Crystals in hand, sign up for a **Vortex Tour** (plan a few weeks ahead in summer). These tours are generally one-on-one, and the guide will lead you to various vortexes on the mountain, where you'll meditate with the goal of being led into the depths of the mountain to meet the Lemurians. The Lemurians are a supposed race of tall white or blue beings who escaped the sunken, ancient continent of Lemuria and founded the city of Telos under Mt Shasta. Anything goes, but it's all happening in deep meditation, so what you believe is a matter of faith. The tours often end at the base of the Mt Shasta summit trail, a spot that could make anyone feel like they're surrounded by magic.

HIKING IN CASTLE CRAGS STATE PARK

The spectacular, soaring spires of granite at **Castle Crags State Park** rise to an elevation of over 6500ft. Best views are from Vista Point (a 0.25-mile walk from the parking lot), where you can start the strenuous 2.7-mile **Crags Trail**. This hike rises through the forest past the Indian Springs spur trail, then clambers to the base of Castle Dome. You're rewarded with unsurpassed views of Mt Shasta, especially if you scramble the last 100 yards or so up into the rocky saddle gap. The park also has a number of more gentle trails; 8 miles of the Pacific Crest Trail passes through the park.

Hiking Mt Shasta

WOODLAND STROLLS, AMBITIOUS SUMMIT

At 14,179ft, Mt Shasta is only the fifth-highest mountain in California, but its beauty is unrivalled. The mountain has two cones: the main cone has a crater about 200 yards across, and the younger, shorter cone on the western flank, called Shastina, has a crater about half a mile wide. You can drive part way up the mountain via the Everitt Memorial Hwy (Hwy A10) and enjoy exquisite views at any time of year.

The moderate 3.5-mile out-and-back hike to the beautiful stone 1922 **Sierra Club Horse Camp** hut leaves from **Bunny Flat** (6940ft) and is open year-round, though you'll want snowshoes in winter. It's popular for a reason: the forested trail isn't too steep, and the views of the mountain are spectacular. Bunny Flat is also the starting place of the challenging **Avalanche Gulch**, the easiest route to the summit, best done between May and September. Although it's only about 10 miles round-trip, the vertical climb is more than 7000ft, so acclimatizing to the elevation is critical – many hikers overnight at Helen Lake (10,443ft). This route requires crampons, an ice axe and a helmet, all of which can be rented locally. Rockslides, while rare, are also a hazard. If you want to make the climb without gear, the only option is the **Clear Creek**

WHERE TO STAY IN MT SHASTA CITY

LOGE
Dorms, gear lockers, shared bathrooms and covered campsites geared toward social, active folks. **$$**

Mt Shasta Ranch Bed & Breakfast
Two-story 1923 house with rooms and cottages just outside of town. **$$**

Strawberry Valley Inn
Cozy, well-run motel in town with B&B-like touches and, fittingly, good breakfasts. **$$**

Crags Trail, Castle Crags State Park

Route (10 miles round-trip), which leaves from the east side of the mountain. In late summer this route is usually manageable in hiking boots, though it should also be done as an overnight hike. Novices or those wanting to climb the more technical Cascade Gulch or West Face Gully routes should contact the Mt Shasta Ranger Station for a list of available guides.

The section of highway beyond Bunny Flat is only open when it's snow-free (mid-June to October). This road leads to **Lower Panther Meadow**, where short trails connect the campground to a Wintu sacred spring in the upper meadows near the Old Ski Bowl (7800ft) parking area. Several other gorgeous trails leave from here, including a 7-mile downhill jaunt to Bunny Flat. Shortly after Panther Meadows is the highlight of the drive, **Everitt Vista Point** (7900ft), where a short interpretive walk leads to a stone-walled outcrop affording exceptional views of Lassen Peak to the south, the Mt Eddy and Marble Mountains to the west and the whole of Strawberry Valley below.

There's a charge to climb beyond 10,000ft: a three-day summit pass costs $25; an annual pass is $30. Contact the ranger station for details. You must obtain a free wilderness permit any time you go into the wilderness, whether you're on the mountain or in the surrounding areas.

MCARTHUR-BURNEY FALLS MEMORIAL STATE PARK

Worth the 41-mile detour from McCloud, these 129ft falls are fed by a spring that flows year-round at the same temperature, a nippy 42°F (6°C). It might not be California's highest waterfall, but it may be the most beautiful (Teddy Roosevelt considered it the eighth wonder of the world). Clear water surges over the top and also from springs in the waterfall's face. Hiking trails include a portion of the Pacific Crest Trail, but it's the 1.3-mile **Burney Falls Trail** that you shouldn't miss. It's an easy loop for families and allows close-up views of water rushing right out of the rock.

Shasta Mountain Inn Retreat & Spa
Victorian B&B with incredible views, gardens and spa; walking distance to town. **$$$**

Inn at Mt Shasta
Very central and hip, this newly updated motel is well managed. **$$**

Mt Shasta Resort
Divinely situated on the shores on Mt Siskiyou, with traditional rooms and chalets. **$$**

TOP SHASTA WINTER ACTIVITIES

There's no end of winter fun around Mt Shasta. For pristine snowscapes, try snowshoeing on trails leaving from Castle Crags State Park or the Bunny Flat Trailhead on Mt Shasta. For more excitement, ski, snowboard or sled at family-friendly **Mt Shasta Ski Park**. You can also cross-country ski on the scenic, groomed trails of **Mt Shasta Nordic Center**, take a thrilling snowmobile tour with **Fun Factory Rentals**, or ice-skate at **Siskiyou Ice Rink**, right in the heart of Mt Shasta City. Locals love to go ice fishing for trout at Castle Lake. You can rent most gear in Mt Shasta City at **Fifth Season Sports**.

Small-Town Bliss

OIUTDOOR FUN, GREAT FOOD

The small towns surrounding Mt Shasta and Mt Shasta City are not only excellent bases for outdoor fun, but they also hold some of the region's best dining. Little **Dunsmuir**, a railroad stop with an adorable historic downtown, has cafes, restaurants, galleries and a spirited artistic community. The Mediterranean-inspired fare at **Café Maddalena** is the best restaurant in the region. **Weed** has suffered some serious fire damage over the years, but you can still get an 'I love Weed' T-shirt, stop for a craft brew at the excellent **Mt Shasta Brewing Company Alehouse & Bistro** or drive 19 miles northeast of town to **Mt Shasta Lavender Farm** (blooms are best in June and July) to view the mountain above a sea of purple. The most interesting town is arguably **McCloud**, a scenic hamlet with excellent hiking, fishing and a snow park at its doorstep. Also here is the **McCloud Dance Country Ballroom**, where you can take popular square or ballroom dancing classes. The 1916 refurbished jewel, the **McCloud Hotel**, has both fine dining and more casual fare.

Mountain Lake Majesty

RELAX BY THE WATER

There are a number of pristine mountain lakes near Mt Shasta, some of which are only accessible by dirt roads or hiking trails. The closest, largest and busiest lake to Mt Shasta City is lovely **Lake Siskiyou**. There's a huge campground here where you can join the family revelry, splashing around, sunbathing (in summer) and making new friends. Another 7 miles up in the mountains, southwest of Lake Siskiyou, lies quieter and more remote **Castle Lake**, an unspoiled gem surrounded by granite formations and pine forest. Try your luck hiking in a quarter mile to nab a free, primitive campsite in the conifers. Then swim, fish and chill; in winter folks ice-skate on the lake. **Lake Shastina**, near Weed, is great for paddling a kayak or canoe when its calm, or windsurfing when the regular winds here pick up. It has a jaw-dropping view of Mt Shasta.

GETTING AROUND

This region is best explored by car in order to get to all the remote roads, trailheads and campsites. However, the Amtrak Coast Starlight Train stops in Dunsmuir, and Greyhound buses stop in Weed. You could catch local bus services to get around from either of these towns, but schedules are erratic.

Beyond Mt Shasta Region

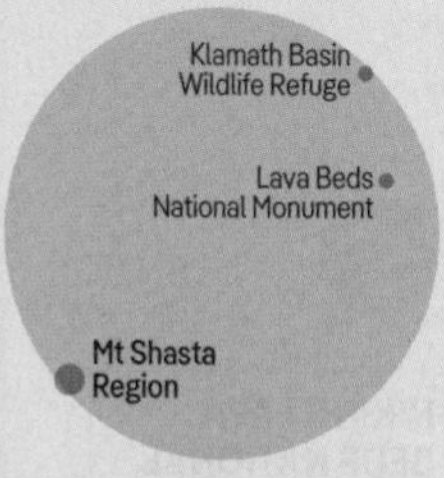

Klamath Basin Wildlife Refuge
Lava Beds National Monument
Mt Shasta Region

From caving to bird-watching, this remote corner of the state is worth the long drive.

One of California's most remote areas holds two special places that would be overrun by tourists were they closer to, well, anything. Lava Beds National Monument is a remarkable 47,000-acre landscape of lava flows, craters, cinder cones, spatter cones, amazing lava tubes and petroglyphs. More than 800 caves have been found in the monument and they average a comfortable 55°F (13°C) no matter the season. Only a 15-minute drive away is the Klamath Basin Wild Refuge, where you can drive, canoe or hike to gaze on a spectacular array of birdlife. This network of lakes extends over the Oregon border and is a key nesting and resting area on the Pacific Flyway.

TOP TIP

When caving it's essential you bring a high-powered flashlight or headlamp, good shoes and long sleeves. Do not go alone.

Lava Beds National Monument (p500)

HIKING LAVA BEDS NATIONAL MONUMENT

Schonchin Butte Lookout
This tall black cone (5253ft) rewards with magnificent vistas after a steep 0.75-mile trail.

Petroglyph Point
The Modoc carved these patterned petroglyphs at the far northeastern end of the monument (0.25-mile hike) thousands of years ago. There's a short trail at the top of the hill that offers amazing views over the plains and Lower Klamath Lake.

Stronghold Trail
Two self-guided trails (0.5 mile to 1.5 miles) wend through the labyrinthine landscape of Captain Jack's stronghold.

DAVIDHOFFMANN PHOTOGRAPHY/SHUTTERSTOCK ©

Geese, Klamath Basin Wildlife Refuge

Caving at Lava Beds National Monument

LAVA TUBES AND PETROGLYPHS

A wild landscape of charred volcanic rock and rolling hills, this remote national monument is reason enough to visit the region. Off Hwy 139, immediately south of Tule Lake National Wildlife Refuge, Lava Beds is roughly 90 miles northeast of Mt Shasta City. Spending a day or two exploring the two dozen or so caves open to the public here will be unlike any other caving experience you've ever had, simply because of the sheer variety.

Every cave is unique, and the short, one-way Cave Loop drive provides access to many of them. **Mushpot Cave**, the one nearest to the visitor's center, has lighting and information signs and is an easy, beautiful introductory hike for all levels. More challenging options include the naturally lit **Sunshine Cave**; the long and winding but easily accessible **Labyrinth**; the rugged, lava-formation-filled **Hercules**

WHERE TO STAY NEAR LAVA BEDS NATIONAL MONUMENT

Indian Well Campground
Forty-three first-come, first-served campsites are available here, half a mile from the monument. **$**

Winema Lodge
Ten basic yet homey motel rooms between Klamath Basin Wildlife Refuge and Lava Beds National Monument. **$**

Wild Goose Lodge
In Merrill, Oregon, 9 miles out of Tule Lake, this is a good-value motel with country charm. **$**

Leg; the gold-ceilinged **Golden Dome**; and the azure-hued **Blue Grotto**. Good brochures with details of each cave are available from the visitor's center; staff will also inform you which are currently open. **Symbol Bridge Cave**, reached via an easy 0.8-mile hike, is rarely visited, and is filled with outrageous petroglyphs, likely from early traveling Native Americans on vision quests.

Rangers at the visitor's center loan mediocre flashlights (and sell helmets and kneepads in the summer) for cave exploration and lead summer interpretive programs, including campfire talks and guided cave walks.

Bird-watching in Klamath Basin Wildlife Refuge

BALD EAGLES, RAPTORS AND WATERFOWL

The Klamath Basin Wildlife Refuge straddles the Oregon–California border, providing habitats for a stunning array of birds migrating along the Pacific Flyway. Some stop over only briefly; others stay longer to mate, make nests and raise their young. Spying them is an intensely magical experience regardless of the time of year you visit.

After perusing the small but excellent **museum**, grab a map at the visitors center and head off on a self-guided driving tour that will take you to some of the best viewing points. For even better views from the water, try out the self-guided canoe trails in the **Tule Lake** and **Klamath Marsh** refuges, which are usually open from July 1 to September 30; canoes are available for free at the visitor center. Canoe trails in the **Upper Klamath** refuge are open year-round with rentals available at Rocky Point Resort.

What you see will depend on the season. The spring migration peaks during March, when over a million birds may fill the skies. In April and May songbirds, waterfowl and shorebirds arrive, some to nest while others stay to build up their energy before continuing north. In summer, ducks, Canada geese and other water birds nest here. The fall migration peaks in early November. In and around February, the area hosts the largest wintering concentration of bald eagles in the lower 48 states, with 1000 in residence (but you should only expect to see a few at a time). Eagles prey on migrating geese, and yes, seeing one catch a goose can be quite dramatic.

Tule Lake (in California) and Upper Klamath and Klamath Marsh across the border in Oregon are all about 85 miles northeast of Mt Shasta City.

CAPTAIN JACK'S STRONGHOLD

Captain Jack, a Modoc Native also known as Chief Kintpuash, used a naturally formed fort in Lava Beds National Monument as a stronghold after returning with his band to their ancestral homeland at Lost River in 1873. For about half a year, just 51 Modoc warriors were able to hold off the US Army, which sometimes numbered as many as three hundred soldiers. Eventually, the Army cut off access to the nearest water supply, the group was defeated and Captain Jack surrendered. He was executed in 1873 and the surviving Modoc were relocated to a reservation in Oklahoma.

GETTING AROUND

You'll need your own wheels to get around the region.

MT LASSEN REGION

Mt Lassen Region
San Francisco
Los Angeles

The dramatic crags, volcanic formations and Alpine lakes of Lassen Volcanic National Park are surprisingly quiet when you consider that they are only a few hours from the Bay Area. Snowed in through most of the winter, the park blossoms in late spring. While it's only 50 miles from Redding, and thus close enough for a day trip, to do it justice you'll want to spend a few days exploring the area along its scenic, winding roads. The park is surrounded by the vast Lassen National Forest, which is so big that it's hard to comprehend: it covers 1.2 million acres of wilderness in an area called the Crossroads, where the granite Sierra, volcanic Cascades, Modoc Plateau and Central Valley all meet. At the mountain's base lies the summer playground of wooded Lake Almanor, where you'll find lodging, a few restaurants and amenities. Sadly, you'll also see plenty of scorched areas from the 2021 Dixie Fire.

TOP TIP

From Lassen Volcanic National Park you can take one of two very picturesque routes: Hwy 36, which heads east past Chester, Lake Almanor and historic Susanville; or Hwy 89, which leads southeast to the cozy mountain town of Quincy.

Lake Almanor (p506)

WALTER SOMERS/500PX/GETTY IMAGES ©

WHY I LOVE THE MT LASSEN AREA

Celeste Brash, writer

Some of the earliest photos of me are as a cowboy-hat-toting toddler at my aunt's house in Susanville. Whenever I come back to these mountains and lakes, it feels like coming home. I love the freshness of the clear rivers, the pine smell in the mountains and the untarnished kindness in the small towns. Mt Lassen's geothermal features never cease to amaze and entertain. I was sad to see so much scorched land on this trip, but the regrowth and resilience of nature and the communities make one believe in miracles. Visiting the region is one way to help Lassen get back on its feet.

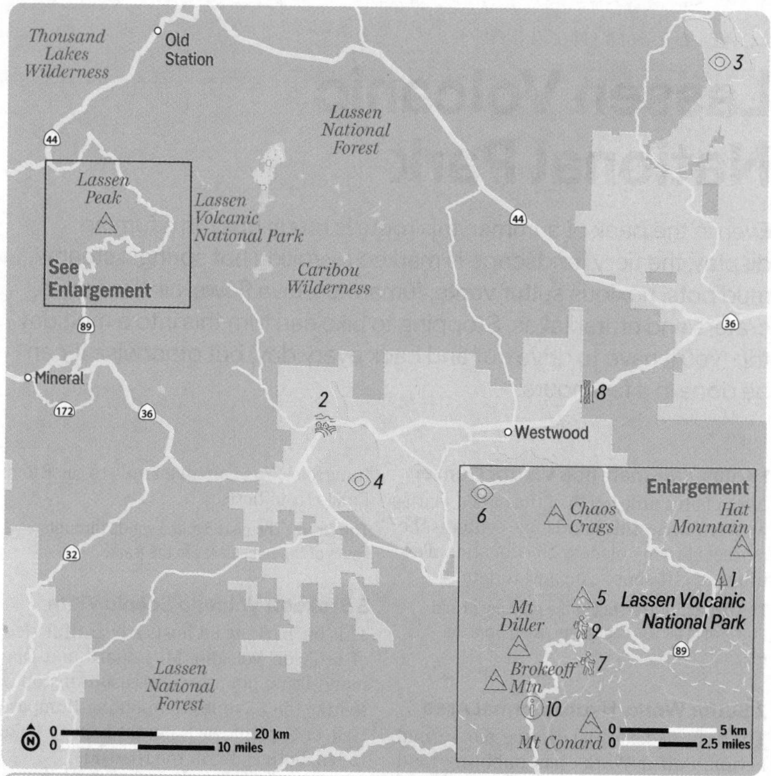

HIGHLIGHTS
1 Lassen Volcanic National Park

SIGHTS
2 Chester
3 Eagle Lake
4 Lake Almanor
5 Lassen Peak
6 Manzanita Lake

ACTIVITIES, COURSES & TOURS
7 Bumpass Hell
8 Coppervale Ski Hill
9 Lassen Peak Trail

INFORMATION
10 Kohm Yah-mah-nee Visitor Center

Hiking Lassen Volcanic National Park

LAVA-FORMED FIERY LANDSCAPES

The smoldering terrain within this 106,000-acre national park stands in stunning contrast to the green (though partially charred by fire) conifer forest that surrounds it. That's in summer; in winter, tons of snow ensures you won't get too far inside its borders without the appropriate gear and some

WHERE TO STAY IN THE MT LASSEN REGION

Drakesbad Guest Ranch
Enjoy a hot-springs-fed swimming pool and horseback riding in the park. Check for post–Dixie Fire updates. **$$$**

The Walker Mansion
Quaint B&B with restaurant serving high tea and a country mercantile on-site. **$**

Village at Child's Meadows
This recently remodeled yet old-fashioned mountain resort sits 9 miles from the park's southwest entrance. **$$**

ROAD OR HIKING TRIP

Lassen Volcanic National Park

Even in the peak of summer, this route is rarely busy. In a fuming display, the fiery landscape is marked by roiling hot springs, steamy mud pots, noxious sulfur vents, fumaroles, lava flows, cinder cones, craters and crater lakes. Stopping to hike can turn this into a multiday trip (you'll have to drive out and back every day) but otherwise it can be done in a few hours.

1 Kohm Yah-mah-nee Visitor Center

About half a mile north of the park's southwest entrance, this handsome center is the perfect starting place with educational exhibits, a gift shop, cafe and toilets.

The Drive: Turn left out of the parking lot and drive 1 mile till you see steam rising from the rocks.

2 Sulfur Works Hydrothermal Area

The best roadside place to see geothermal action, Sulfur Works has bubbling mud pots, hissing steam vents, fountains and fumaroles. You can hike 1 mile to the Ridge Lakes from here.

The Drive: The next 5 miles winds through some of the best vistas in the park.

3 Brokeoff Volcano Scenic Vista

This big parking lot hosts a beautiful view of Brokeoff Volcano, Mt Conard and Diamond Peak, but a better reason to stop is to hike the 1.5 miles to bubbling Bumpass Hell, or to picnic by Emerald Lake or Lake Helen, both right off the roadside.

MICHEAL LEE/SHUTTERSTOCK ©

Hat Creek Meadow

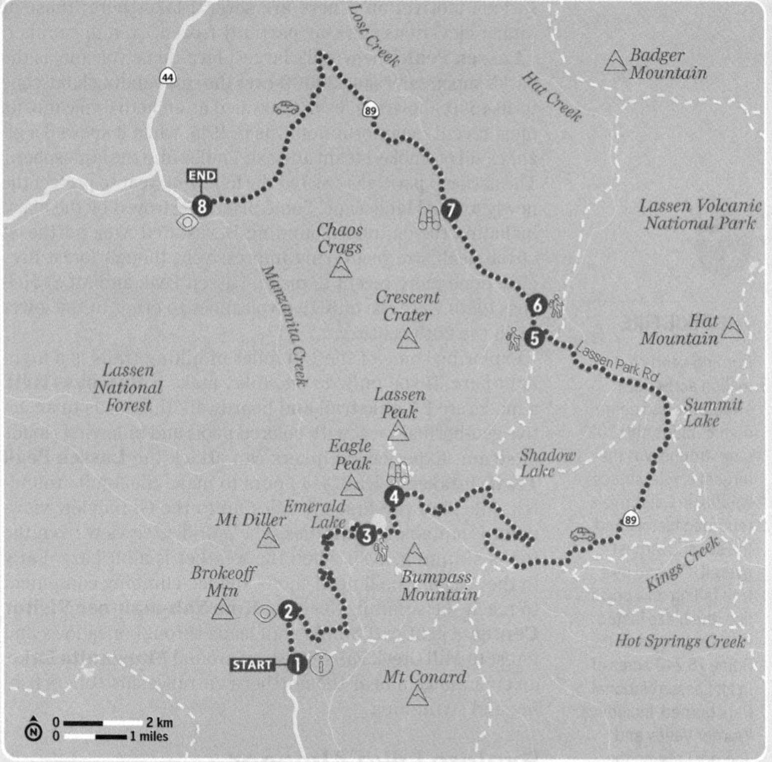

The Drive: In just over a mile turn into the parking lot; Lassen Peak looms on your left.

4 Lassen Peak Scenic Vista

Even if you're not going to take the 5-mile trail to the peak, the sight of the rocky slopes up close is awe inspiring.

The Drive: There are several places to stop over the next 11 miles, including Kings Creek Meadow and Summit Lakes; both were partially burned in the Dixie Fire.

5 Hat Creek Meadow

This spot is one of the best for fall foliage and there's a dreamy 1.25-mile walk to Hat Creek Meadow and a gorgeous waterfall.

The Drive: It's a quick half mile to your next stop on the right.

6 Devastated Area

The 0.25-mile interpretive loop through the former eruption area is fascinating.

The Drive: The scenery becomes lusher over the next 7.5 miles. Make a quick stop at Emigrant Pass, once plied by covered wagons.

7 Chaos Crags

This giant field of rock rubble is the result of a massive slide in the 1660s. It's worth pulling over and gazing out at the weird and wild terrain.

The Drive: It's about a mile through light forest to your final stop.

8 Manzanita Lake

The northwest park entrance is home to Loomis Museum (open May to October) and a 1.8-mile loop around Manzanita Lake, where there are kayak rentals in summer. Just across the road is the smaller Reflection Lake, which has great views of Lassen Peak.

serious motivation. There are several lakes here; those at higher elevations can stay partially frozen, even in summer.

Lassen Peak, the world's largest lava-dome volcano, is the park's superstar, rising 2000ft over the surrounding landscape to 10,463ft above sea level. Classified as an active volcano, its most recent major eruption was in 1915, when it spewed a giant cloud of smoke, steam and ash 7 miles into the atmosphere. The national park was created the following year to protect the newly formed landscape. Some places destroyed by the blast, including the ominous-sounding Devastated Area northeast of the peak, are recovering impressively, though forest fires have done more recent damage. Lassen Peak and Mt St Helens (1980) were the only two volcanoes to erupt in the lower 48 in the 20th century.

Exploring some of the 150 miles of hiking trails is a highlight here. If you only do one hike, make it **Bumpass Hell**, a moderate 1.5-mile trail and boardwalk that leads to an active geothermal area, with colored pools and billowing clouds of steam. Experienced hikers can attack the **Lassen Peak Trail**; it takes at least 4½ hours to make the 5-mile round-trip hike, but the first 1.3 miles up to the Grandview viewpoint is suitable for families. The 360-degree view from the top is stunning, even when the weather is a bit hazy. Early in the season, you'll need snow- and ice-climbing equipment to reach the summit. Near the **Kom Yah-mah-nee Visitor Center**, a gentler 2.3-mile trail leads through meadows and forest to Mill Creek Falls. The trail around **Manzanita Lake**, an emerald gem near the northern entrance, also offers fishing and swimming.

THE DIXIE FIRE

Burning nearly a million acres, 1329 structures and entire communities, this 2021 catastrophe was the largest single-source wildfire in California's recorded history and the second largest overall. Caused by a tree falling on a power line, the blaze lasted for over three months. Some 73,240 acres of In Mt Lassen National Park burned, including Warner Valley and Juniper Lake on the eastern side, and the Summit Lakes area in the north. The park is slowly reopening hiking trails and affected areas, but the vistas over a never-ending sea of burned trees are a stark reminder. It's best to check in at the visitor center for updates on what's open.

Explore Lake Almanor

RUGGED SHORES AND MOTORBOATING

Calm, turquoise Lake Almanor lies 40 miles southwest of Lassen Volcanic National Park and is a top spot in which to base yourself. The lake's 52 miles of coastline is surrounded by lush meadows and tall evergreens, and has a quiet spot for everyone. Pitch a tent or book a lake house in the ritzy northeastern section, where there are even a few gated communities. On the rugged southern end are miles and miles of nothing but pine trees. Wherever you find yourself, plunge in, rent a boat, go stand-up paddleboarding and take in the views of Lassen Peak. Motorboats ply the waters in summer and with properties continually being developed all around the shores, it seems the word is getting out about this once-secret spot.

WHERE TO CAMP IN THE MT LASSEN REGION

PG&E Recreational Area Campgrounds
Many sites are tent-centric and more tranquil than the others surrounding Lake Almanor. $

Lassen Volcanic National Park Campgrounds
The park has seven developed campgrounds that are open between May and October. $

Bucks Lake Campgrounds
There are several camping areas around the lake, some of which quite rustic. Great for tranquility. $

Cool Off at Eagle Lake

SUMMER GETAWAY

Those who have the time to get all the way out to Eagle Lake, California's second-largest natural lake, are rewarded with a stunningly blue jewel on the high desert plateau. From late spring until fall, this lovely spot, about 15 miles northwest of Susanville, is a fantastic, off-the-beaten-path place to cool off, swim, fish, boat and camp. On the south shore, you'll find a 5-mile, paved **recreational trail** that weaves through pine trees and is great for walking, biking or casting a fishing line. Keep your eyes peeled for bald eagles. There are several busy campgrounds here, administered by Lassen National Forest and the Bureau of Land Management. **Eagle Lake Marina**, close by, has shower and laundry facilities, and can help you get out onto the lake with a fishing license.

Winter Fun

SLED, SKI OR SNOWSHOE

Winter is magical around Mt Lassen and there's no shortage of activities to keep the blood pumping. A great place to start is the **Kohm Yah-mah-nee Visitor Center**, which has several sledding hills to choose from. People out here can get pretty wild, so start on the smaller slopes before joining the scrum. For a more peaceful experience, try **snowshoeing**. Joining a ranger-led walk in the park is a good idea if you're new to the sport – these are usually available from January through March, and snowshoe rental is included. Alternatively, there are several great snowshoe trails from the visitor center that you can do on your own, featuring wintry white mountain views; rentals are available in Redding or at **Bodfish Bicycles** in Chester.

About 20 miles east of Chester is the family-friendly **Coppervale Ski Hill**, run by Lassen College. Ski or snowboard the eight well-groomed trails, try out the half-pipe, or skip the hills altogether and go cross-country skiing.

THE STATE OF JEFFERSON

Welcome to the state of Jefferson. The name comes from Thomas Jefferson, who once envisioned a separate republic on the West Coast. You'll notice billboards and bumper stickers ('Jefferson: A State of Mind') endorsing the proposed 51st state, and as you travel the two-lane blacktop in Northern California and southern Oregon, they start to make more sense. For one, these folks are mostly conservatives surrounded by a sea of Democrats.

The State of Jefferson was originally proposed in 1941 by a band of well-armed locals, who were irate about terrible road conditions. Today, Jefferson encompasses over 3 million people across some 30 counties. You can tune into regional news by listening to Jefferson Public Radio (ijpr.org).

WHERE TO EAT IN THE MT LASSEN REGION

Red Onion Grill
The finest Italian fare on Lake Almanor; casual setting in Westwood. **$$**

Cravings
City-worthy coffee and cooking with small-town smiles and service; located in Chester. **$$**

Lassen Ale Works
From fish-and-chips to steaks in a renovated 1862 saloon; located in Susanville. **$$**

Beyond Mt Lassen Region

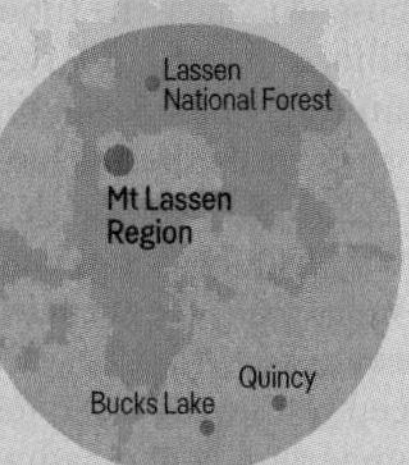

This is backcountry at its finest: little known, little trodden, and filled with glorious mountain scenery, kind folks and outdoor activities.

The gold rush–era region of Plumas County was named for the Feather River that flows through it (*plumas* means 'feathers' in Spanish). Located at the far north of the Sierra Nevada, it holds over 100 lakes. This is an all-season outdoor paradise, with hiking, rafting, skiing, fishing and more, serviced by the friendly and pretty mountain town of Quincy.

The county seat is Susanville, which has good services and some mountain-biking options (the spectacular 25.4-mile Bizz Johnson Trail ends here) but little else. Several small towns in the county were destroyed by the 2021 Dixie Fire and you'll still see plenty of scarred forest along with buds of regrowth.

TOP TIP

Consider donating to the Dixie Fire Fund in partnership with Plumas Bank to help these communities with recovery (nevadafund.org/donate/dixie-fire-fund).

Rock Lake, Bucks Lake Wilderness

CAMINOR/SHUTTERSTOCK ©

DAVIDRH/SHUTTERSTOCK ©

Plumas County Courthouse (p510), Quincy

Chill Out at Bucks Lake

SWIM, PADDLE & FISH

This clear mountain lake is cherished by locals in the know. Surrounded by pine forests, the lightly developed banks are like a deep breath of fresh air. Set up camp or check in to a woodland cabin, then just chill out. Take a leisurely swim in summer, drop a line for some trout or rent a canoe or paddleboard to cruise around. Need more exercise? The region is lined with beautiful hiking trails, including the Pacific Crest Trail, which passes through the adjoining 21,000-acre **Bucks Lake Wilderness** in the northwestern part of Plumas National Forest. In winter, the last 3 miles of Bucks Lake Rd are closed by snow, making it ideal for cross-country skiers. It's about 90 miles southwest of Lassen Volcanic National Park, via the white-knuckle Bucks Lake Rd (Hwy 119).

STARGAZING SPECTACULAR

Astronomy buffs and recreational stargazers make a point of visiting Lassen Volcanic National Park at night, though the lack of light pollution extends throughout the region, including Buck's Lake. The area's natural darkness offers a prime opportunity for viewing the Milky Way and other celestial wonders; the annual **Lassen Dark Sky Festival** takes place in the park one weekend in August. During the festival you can partake in solar scope viewing, learn about constellations, and hear talks or chat with experts from the Astronomical Society of the Pacific, NASA and more. Clear skies are common in all seasons.

Quincy Delights

HISTORY LESSONS WITH SNACKS

Aside from being an excellent base for hiking, fishing, river floating and more in the Plumas National Forest and Feather River area, idyllic Quincy is a lovely little artist and student town to explore in its own right.

WHERE TO STAY IN QUINCY

Greenhorn Guest Ranch
Think of this place as the cowboy version of the getaway resort in *Dirty Dancing*. **$$$**

Ranchito Motel
Friendly, good-value motel in the eastern half of town, with a Mexican ranch feel. **$**

Quincy Courtyard Suites
Beautifully renovated suites in the 1908 Clinch building, overlooking Quincy's main drag. **$$**

QUINCY'S MUSIC FESTIVAL

If you're lucky enough to be in Quincy at the end of June or early July, check out the **High Sierra Music Festival**, a four-day family-fun extravaganza (camping included) that brings a five-stage smorgasbord of art and music from a spectrum of cultural corners (indie rock, classic blues, folk and jazz). Past acts include Thievery Corporation, Lauryn Hill, Primus, Ben Harper and Neko Case. Sure, a curmudgeonly local might call it the Hippie Fest, but it's pretty tame in comparison to some of Northern California's true fringe festivals. If you plan to attend, reserve a room or campsite a couple of months in advance.

Just about everything you need is on, or close to, two one-way streets: Main St, with traffic heading east; and Lawrence St, with traffic heading west. Jackson St runs parallel to Main St one block south, and is another main artery, making up Quincy's low-key commercial district.

Start with a leisurely visit to **Plumas County Museum**, a multistory old-timey place. Peruse hundreds of historical photos and relics from the county's pioneer and native Maidu days, its early mining and timber industries, and the construction of the Western Pacific Railroad. The 1921 **Plumas County Courthouse** next door is worth popping into to see enormous interior marble posts and staircases, and a 1-ton bronze-and-glass chandelier in the lobby. Then wander through town, checking out the handful of art galleries before stopping into **Quincy Provisions** for excellent baked goods and coffee, or healthy eats and good beer at the local favorite, **Pangea Café and Pub**.

Quincy is 71 miles southeast of Lassen Volcanic National Park.

Hiking in Lassen National Forest

WILDERNESS EXPERIENCE

This forest has 460 miles of trails, ranging from a brutal 120-mile section of the famous Pacific Crest Trail to ambitious day hikes (the 12-mile **Spencer Meadows National Recreation Trail**) and just-want-to-stretch-the-legs-a-little shorter jaunts (the 3.5-mile **Heart Lake National Recreation Trail**). Near the intersection of Hwys 44 and 89 is the most spectacular feature of the forest, the pitch-black 600-yard **Subway Cave** lava tube. Other points of interest include the 1.5-mile volcanic **Spattercone Crest Trail**, **Willow** and **Crater Lakes**, **Antelope Peak** (7684ft), and the 900ft-high, 14-mile-long **Hat Creek Rim** escarpment.

For those seeking to get far off the beaten track, the **Caribou Wilderness** and the **Thousand Lakes Wilderness** are high-altitude gems, while **Ishi Wilderness** (named after Ishi, the last surviving member of the Yahi people) is at a much lower elevation.

GETTING AROUND

Truckee (p589) close to Lake Tahoe and I-80, is a little over 60 miles south of Quincy on Hwy 89.

REDDING & SHASTA LAKE

Redding & Shasta Lake
San Francisco
Los Angeles

North of Red Bluff, the dusty central corridor along I-5 starts to give way to panoramic mountain ranges on either side. Redding, with its hot and congested downtown that blends to open space along the scenic Sacramento River, is the last major outpost before the small towns of the far north, and the surrounding lakes make for easy day trips or overnight campouts. If you get off the highway – like, way off – this can be an exceptionally rewarding area of the state to explore. A surge of good eating and drinking spots in Redding makes it an excellent pit stop for a meal if you're taking a long road trip on the interstate. And if you stay the night, Redding has a handful of excellent craft breweries, wineries and the Cascade Theater, a 1935 art deco gem that hosts some up-and-coming top-tier bands.

TOP TIP

Packer's Bay is the best area for leg-stretcher hikes with easy access off I-5, but the prettiest trail (outside of summer months when it's intensely hot) is the 7.5-mile loop known as the Clikapudi Trail. To get there, follow Bear Mountain Rd several miles until it dead-ends.

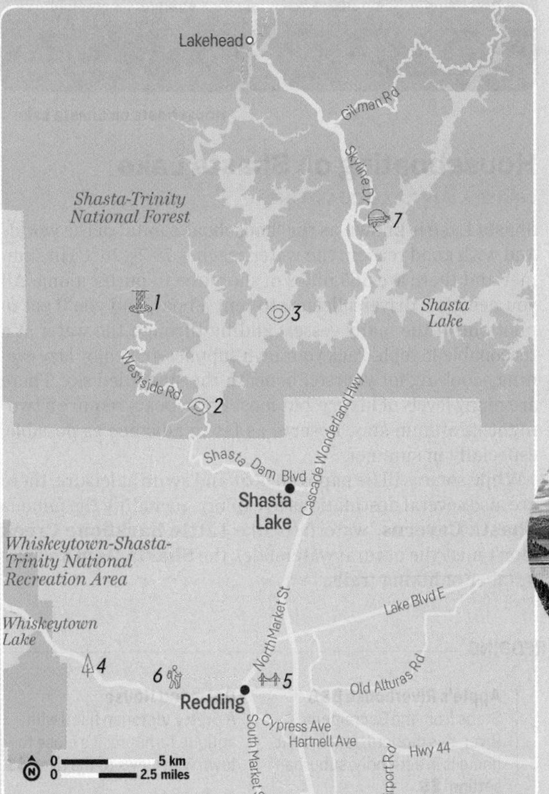

SIGHTS
1 Little Backbone Creek
2 Shasta Dam
3 Shasta Lake
4 Shasta State Historic Park
5 Sundial Bridge

ACTIVITIES, COURSES & TOURS
6 Sacramento River Trail
7 Shasta Caverns

Shasta Lake

BRYAN RAMSEY/SHUTTERSTOCK ©

BEST PLACES TO EAT IN REDDING

Moonstone Bistro
Organic, local, free-range, line-caught – the Moonstone checks all the boxes. Plus it's insanely delicious – don't skip dessert. $$$

Jack's Grill
Regulars line up to get the best steaks around at this dark cavern of a restaurant. No reservations. $$$

The Park
A rotating collection of food trucks with an assortment of lawn games and live music on warm weekends. Regular carts include crepes and pizzas. $$

Wilda's Grill
Hot dogs with crazy toppings, healthy falafel and Buddha rice bowls. $

RONNIE GREGORY/SHUTTERSTOCK ©

Houseboats on Shasta Lake

Houseboating on Shasta Lake

CRUISE A FORESTED COASTLINE

Shasta Lake is known as the 'houseboat capital of the world,' and with good reason: the water reaches 78°F (26°C) in summer and there are 365 miles of shoreline to putter along. All you need is a driver's license to rent a boat, and you'll get to pilot one of the many vessels gliding through the water at a reasonable 15 mph. Pack your own supplies and enjoy lazy evenings cooking for yourself beneath the star-filled sky. There are many levels of luxury, but most houseboats require a two-night minimum stay. Reserve as far in advance as possible, especially in summer.

While some will be happy to float and swim at leisure, there are also several destinations to explore, including the famous **Shasta Caverns**, waterfalls like **Little Backbone Creek** (don't miss the natural waterslide), the **Shasta Dam** and any number of hiking trails.

WHERE TO STAY IN REDDING

Americana Modern Hotel
Very central and newly upgraded with a minimalist style. **$$**

Apple's Riverhouse B&B
Steps from the Sacramento River, this modern, ranch-style home is in a friendly, suburban setting. **$$**

Desmond House
A pretty Victorian filled with antique furniture; it's close to town with views of the river. **$$**

And while you're out on the water, be sure to keep an eye peeled for wildlife: this massive lake hosts the largest reservoir populations of ospreys and bald eagles in California. Ospreys are best seen from March to October and peak in May and June, which is their nesting season. Look for bald eagles (white head, brown body) year-round, which nest primarily in tall coniferous trees. If you're lucky you might see one swoop down to catch a fish or even a waterfowl. Other birds to look out for are double-crested cormorants, western grebes and mallard ducks. On land, look for acorn woodpeckers, quail and wild turkeys.

Get Deep at Shasta Caverns

UNDERGROUND GEOLOGICAL WONDERLAND

Located high in the limestone megaliths at the north end of Shasta Lake are the impressive Shasta Caverns. Tours through the many chambers dripping with massive formations operate daily and include a boat ride across Shasta Lake. Guides are fantastic and will help you spot bald eagles en route to the caves as well as answer all sorts of geeky geology questions within the caverns. Once inside, it's a one-hour meander along lighted trails and some 600 steps, passing a wondrous array of formations, including waterfall-like curtains of limestone, impressively large stalactites and stalagmites, Jurassic fossils and coral-like helicites. Bring a sweater as the temperature inside is 58°F (14°C) year-round. On Friday and Saturday evenings in summer, the company also runs sunset buffet dinner cruises on the lake. Call and check what's on, particularly in winter, since the website schedule can be misleading.

Explore Shasta State Historic Park

GHOSTS OF THE PAST

This state park, 6 miles west of Redding on Hwy 299, preserves the ruins of an 1850s gold rush mining town called Shasta – not to be confused with Mt Shasta City. When the gold rush was at its heady height, everything and everyone passed through this Shasta. But when the railroad bypassed it to set up in Poverty Flats (present-day Redding), poor Shasta lost its raison d'être. The 1861 courthouse is now a museum, housing an amazing gun collection, gallows out back and spooky holograms in the basement; it's a thrill ride. Afterward, pick up walking-tour pamphlets from the information desk and follow trails to the beautiful Catholic cemetery, brewery ruins and other historic sites.

THE DAM AT SHASTA LAKE

On scale with the enormous natural features of the area, the colossal 15-million-ton **Shasta Dam** is second in size only to Grand Coolie Dam in Washington state and second in height only to Hoover Dam in Nevada.

Built between 1937 and 1949, its 487ft spillway is nearly three times as high as Niagara Falls. Woody Guthrie wrote 'This Land Is Your Land' here while he was entertaining dam workers. The Shasta Dam visitors center offers a 21-minute video shown on request, and self-guided walking tours across the vertiginous top of the dam are available from 6am to 10pm daily. It's located at the south end of the lake on Shasta Dam Blvd.

SHASTA LAKE HOUSEBOAT RENTALS

Shasta Marina at Packers Bay
One of the biggest outfits, but maintains great service. **$$$**

Holiday Harbor
Has a camping and RV park and rents stand-up paddleboards near the busy marina. **$$$**

Bridge Bay Resort
Also has a lakeside lodge and rents small fishing and leisure crafts. **$$$**

CALIFORNIA'S LAST GREAT PLACE

Etna (population 680), toward the north end of Scott Valley on Hwy 3, is known by its residents as 'California's Last Great Place,' and they might be right. Folks are uncommonly friendly, birdsong is more prevalent than road noise, and if you're in town in summer, you'll see lots of weather-beaten individuals with backpacks: those are hard-core hikers taking a break from the nearby 2650-mile Pacific Crest Trail.

If you're taking the scenic route instead of I-5, stop at the excellent **Etna Brewing Company**, the ultra-homey **Paystreak Brewing** or **Denny Bar Co**, a flashy distillery that offers craft spirits, cocktails, tastings and great food.

Sundial Bridge, Redding

Discover Local Nature via the Sundial Bridge

AN ARCHITECTURAL WONDER

Resembling a beached cruise ship, the shimmering-white Sundial Bridge, designed by renowned Spanish architect Santiago Calatrava, spans the bucolic shores of Sacramento River and is one of Redding's marquee attractions. The bridge and partially working sundial attracts visitors from around the world, who come to marvel at this unique feat of engineering and artistry. Stroll across the bridge for a surprisingly glamorous selfie against its unique silhouette.

The bridge also connects with 80 miles of trails in the **Redding Trails** network, which loops through parks, along rivers and up hills for strolling, hiking and mountain biking. The star is the paved **Sacramento River Trail**, which meanders for 17 miles along the river all the way to Shasta Dam. You can easily turn this into a shorter loop by crossing the river and turning around after 5.5 miles.

At the other end of the bridge, a glass-deck pedestrian overpass connects to the **Turtle Bay Exploration Park**, an artistic, cultural and scientific center for all ages. Don't miss the arboretum gardens, a butterfly house (open seasonally) and a 22,000-gallon, walk-through river aquarium full of regional aquatic life.

GETTING AROUND

Taking the mountainous Hwy 3 – which runs from Weaverville to Yreka, via Trinity Lake and the small, picturesque communities of Etna and Fort Jones – is a fun alternative to I-5. It adds around one hour to the drive – check road conditions in winter.

Beyond Redding & Shasta Lake

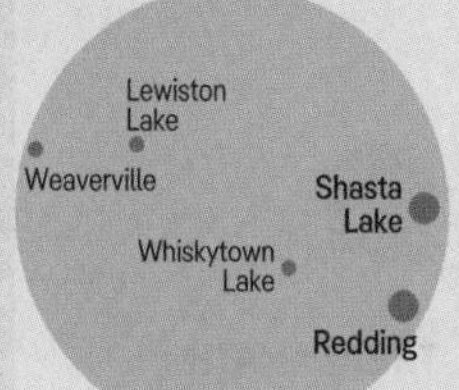

The sun-baked lowlands of Redding blend into mountains, lakes and wild rivers dotted with eclectic towns.

Here are some of the most rugged towns and wilderness areas in California – just difficult enough to reach to discourage big crowds. The Trinity Scenic Byway (Hwy 299) winds spectacularly along the Trinity River and beneath towering cliffs as it makes its way from the plains of Redding to the coastal redwood forests around Arcata. It cuts through some of the northern mountains' most pristine wilderness and passes through the vibrant gold rush town of Weaverville. Heavenly Hwy 3 heads north from Weaverville through the Trinity Alps – a stunning granite range dotted with Alpine lakes – past the shores of Lewiston and Trinity Lakes, over the Scott Mountains and finally into mountain-rimmed Scott Valley.

TOP TIP

Take off-the-beaten-path Hwy 299 to the coastal redwoods, then head up or down Hwy 1 for a whole other adventure.

Redwood forest

THE KLAMATH KNOT

A conglomeration of coastal mountains – **Klamath** and **Siskiyou Mountains** – gives this region the nickname 'the Klamath Knot.' Coastal temperate rainforest gives way to moist inland forest, creating a diversity of habitats for many species, some found nowhere else in the world. Around 3500 native plants live here. Local fauna includes northern spotted owls, bald eagles, tailed frogs, several species of Pacific salmon, wolverines and mountain lions. One theory for the extraordinary biodiversity of this area is that it escaped extensive glaciation during recent ice ages. This may have given species refuge and longer stretches of favorable conditions during which to adapt.

ZACK FRANK/SHUTTERSTOCK ©

Joss House Historic State Park, Weaverville

Whiskeytown Lake by Land & Water

A HISTORIC TWIST

Sparkling Whiskeytown Lake takes its name from an old mining camp. In the 1960s, a 263ft dam was built, the few remaining buildings of the original Whiskeytown were relocated and the camp was submerged beneath the rising waters.

Just 15 minutes from Redding, the lake's serene 36-mile forested shoreline is the perfect place to camp while enjoying non-motorized water sports. On the western side, the Tower House Historic District contains the **El Dorado** mine ruins and the pioneer **Camden House**, open for summer tours. On the southern shore of the lake, **Brandy Creek** is ideal for swimming; on the northern edge of the lake, **Oak Bottom Marina** rents out boats. The 1.2-mile hike to roaring **Whiskeytown Falls** follows a former logging road and is a good choice if you're only making a quick stop. Camp at tightly packed **Oak Bottom Campground** near the shore for longer stays.

The main trails and campsites are mostly open, but the area is still recovering from the 2018 Carr Fire that burned

WHERE TO STAY IN WEAVERVILLE

Indian Creek Lodge
Comfy fishing lodge 8 miles out of town along the banks of the Trinity River. **$$**

Weaverville Hotel & Emporium
Upscale historic-landmark hotel in the heart of downtown, refurbished in grand style. **$$$**

The Weaverville Whitmore Inn
Classic Victorian B&B with a wraparound deck on the edge of downtown. **$$**

virtually all of the recreation area. However, it's a surprisingly beautiful time to visit, with lush regrowth contrasting with the sienna-colored charred trees. The visitors center has knowledgeable staff who can answer your questions and let you know which areas are open.

Weaverville's Chinese Heritage

DISCOVER A GOLD RUSH COMMUNITY

Roughly an hour's drive west of Redding, Weaverville is the place to learn about Northern California's original Chinese immigrant community. The walls of the 1874 **Joss House Historic State Park** basically talk – they're papered with 150-year-old donation ledgers from the once-thriving community, first gold prospectors and later workers who built so much of Northern California's infrastructure. The blue-and-gold **Taoist temple** is the oldest in California that's still in use and contains an ornate altar, more than 3000 years old, which was brought here from China. Next door to the Joss House you'll find gold-mining and cultural exhibits, plus vintage machinery, memorabilia, an old miner's cabin and a blacksmith shop. The adjoining schoolhouse was the first to teach Chinese students in California.

Fly-Fishing on Lewiston Lake

REEL IN TROPHY TROUT

This narrow 9-mile lake connects Trinity Lake with Trinity River and offers sublime fly-fishing. If you didn't bring a rod or if you're new to the sport, hook up with a guiding service like **Trinity River Adventures**, who will ferry you through the slow-moving, marsh-lined channels in the search for several species of trout, many weighing 4lb or more. Aside from the plentiful fish, this is a serene alternative to the other lakes in the area because of its 10mph boat speed limit. Early in the evening you may see ospreys and bald eagles diving for their dinner. Even if you're not fishing, head to the **Trinity River Fish Hatchery**, where juvenile salmon and steelhead are held before being released into the river. The only marina on the lake, **Pine Cove**, has free information about the lake and its wildlife, boat and canoe rentals, and guided off-road tours.

The adorable town of **Lewiston**, 40 minutes west of Redding, is little more than a collection of rickety historic buildings beside the Trinity River; the lake is about 1.5 miles north of town. It's worth stopping here to peruse antiques at the photogenic **Country Peddler**, or stop to eat, drink or stay the night at the quirky **Old Lewiston Inn**.

WINE TASTING AT TRINITY LAKE

Placid Trinity Lake, California's third-largest reservoir, sits beneath dramatic snowcapped peaks, 6 miles north of Lewiston Lake. Trinity Center, its main town, is another 30 miles away. In the off-season it's serenely quiet, but in the summer, multitudes come here for swimming, fishing and other water sports. Even if you're just driving through, it's worth detouring to the little-known, utterly picturesque **Alpen Cellars**. Specializing in riesling, Gewürztraminer, chardonnay and pinot noir, the vineyard is open for tours, tastings and picnicking on its idyllic riverside grounds. **Pinewood Cove Resort**, spread over 22 acres on the lake shore, offers quality camping, cabins and marina facilities.

WHERE TO EAT IN WEAVERVILLE

Cafe on Main
Creative, internationally inspired cuisine makes for the best dining this side of I-5. **$$**

Trinideli
Decadent sandwiches are served at the back of the most hopping bar in town. **$**

Mamma Lama
Delightful coffeehouse that also serves breakfast, light meals and microbrews. **$**

SACRAMENTO & THE CENTRAL VALLEY

GRITTY, BODACIOUS AND SOULFUL

Drive the region that put the 'western' in country-and-western music. Make discoveries that inspire, entertain, inform and delight amid the wide-open spaces.

The Central Valley is a vast expanse of green between the Sierra Nevada and Pacific Ocean, divided into the Sacramento Valley in the north and the San Joaquin Valley in the south. For millennia, the rivers cutting through them flooded seasonally, creating extremely fertile soil. Today, those waterways are tamed by mighty public works projects that support massive agricultural endeavors and life itself in thirsty Southern California. Half the produce in the USA is grown in these valleys – including almost every almond, olive and tomato.

Most travelers just pass through, zipping along the freeways to more popular parts of the state. But those who pause are rewarded with compelling historical spots, thriving craft beer and wine scenes, scenic byways and quirky small towns. It's a vast region for driving – getting lost in seemingly endless flat expanses can be both inspirational and thrilling. (The crop duster scene in *North by Northwest* was shot northwest of Bakersfield.)

Sacramento mixes history and culture with great food and drink. Every non-glitzy aspect of California is celebrated at the annual California State Fair. Wine is foundational to the valley's produce and you can enjoy fine vintages in the vast vineyards around Lodi.

Bust the flatland cliché by hitting the world-class white water on the Kern River. And as you drive the valley's byway, Hwy 99, know that you'll find the best Mexican food ever at nearly every exit.

PHOTOSOUNDS/SHUTTERSTOCK ©

THE MAIN AREAS

SACRAMENTO
Historic, lively capital.
p524

SACRAMENTO VALLEY
Farmlands and Chico nightlife.
p534

SAN JOAQUIN VALLEY
Gritty heart of the state.
p536

RICH LONARDO/SHUTTERSTOCK ©

Left: Olive trees, Bakersfield (p540); Above: Tower Bridge (p527), Sacramento

Find Your Way

The Central Valley covers an enormous swath of California: from Red Bluff to Bakersfield is over 400 miles. The wide-open spaces here are awe-inspiring and are easily reached from the rest of the state.

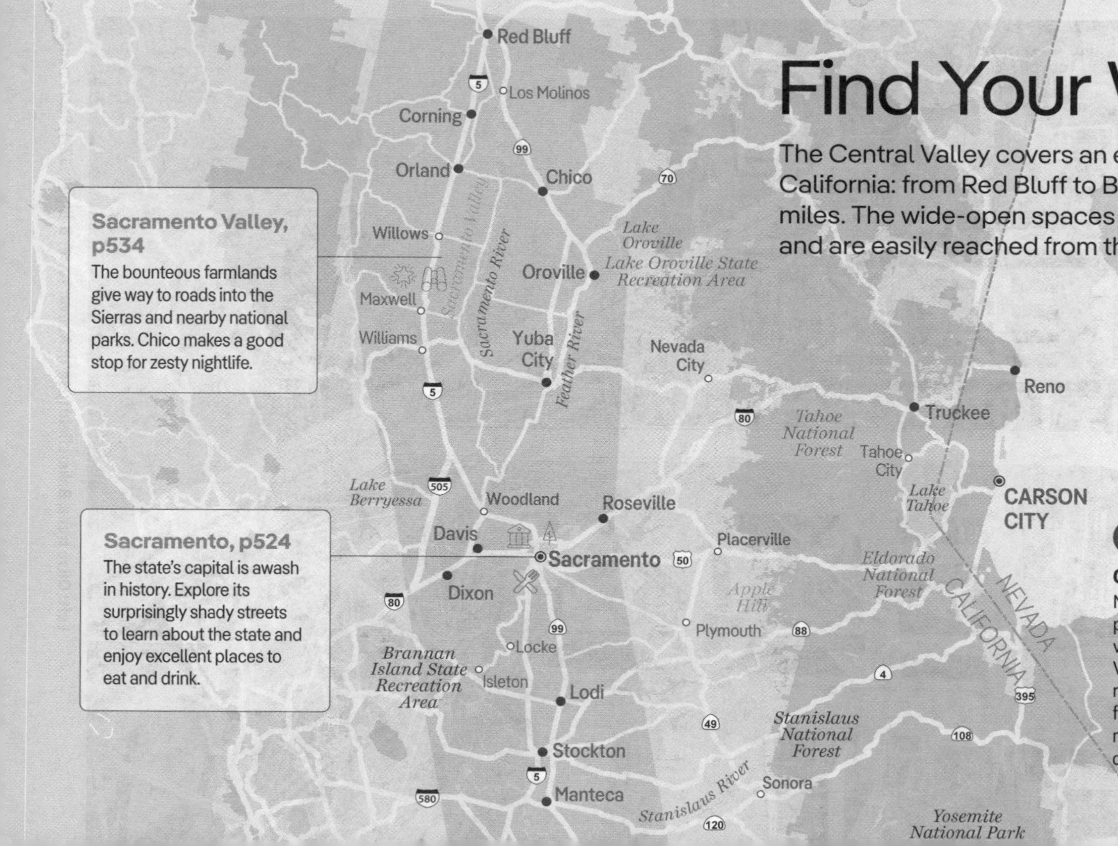

Sacramento Valley, p534
The bounteous farmlands give way to roads into the Sierras and nearby national parks. Chico makes a good stop for zesty nightlife.

Sacramento, p524
The state's capital is awash in history. Explore its surprisingly shady streets to learn about the state and enjoy excellent places to eat and drink.

CAR
Motorcycle, convertible, rugged pickup or electric cruiser – pick your vehicle of choice for the Central Valley's wide-open roads, many running arrow-straight across table-flat lands where the distant horizon never seems to get closer. The valley demands your own wheels.

Red Bluff
Los Molinos
Corning
Orland
Chico
Willows
Sacramento Valley
Sacramento River
Oroville
Lake Oroville
Lake Oroville State Recreation Area
Maxwell
Williams
Yuba City
Feather River
Nevada City
Reno
Truckee
Tahoe National Forest
Tahoe City
Lake Tahoe
CARSON CITY
Lake Berryessa
Woodland
Roseville
Davis
Sacramento
Placerville
Dixon
Eldorado National Forest
Apple Hill
Plymouth
NEVADA
CALIFORNIA
Locke
Brannan Island State Recreation Area
Isleton
Lodi
Stanislaus National Forest
Stockton
Manteca
Sonora
Stanislaus River
Yosemite National Park

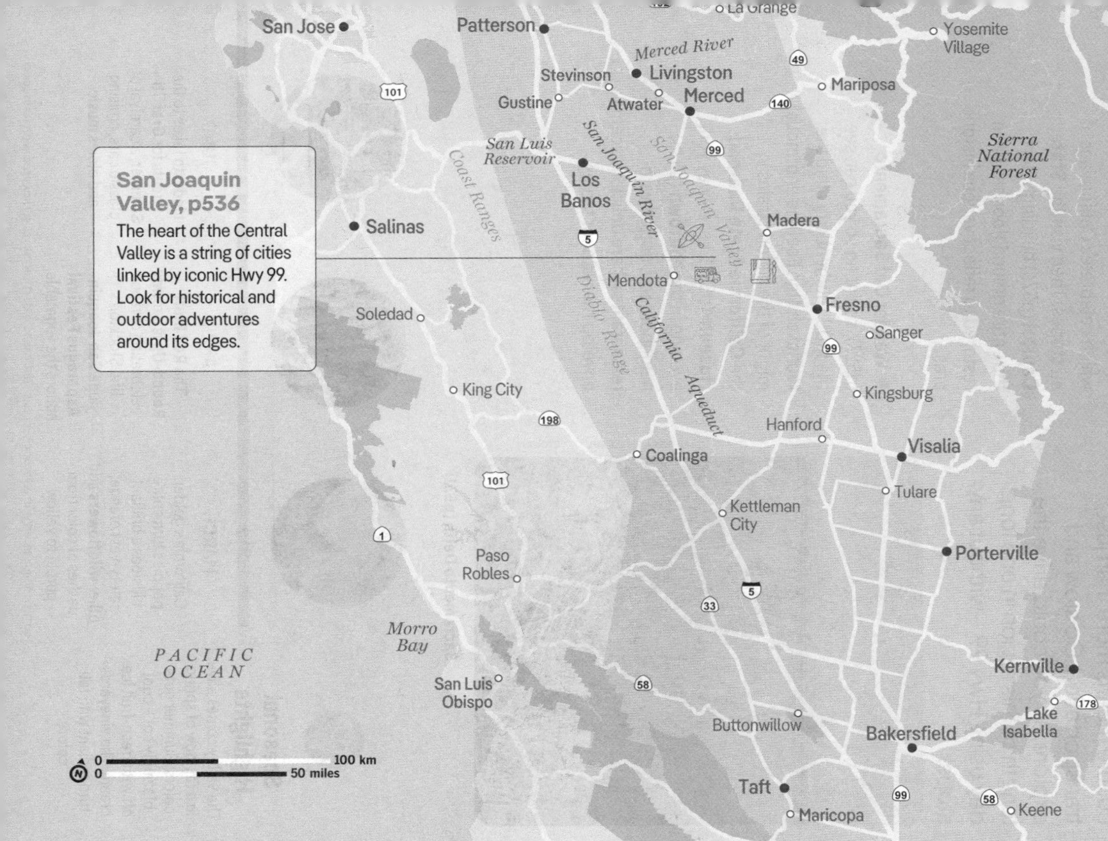

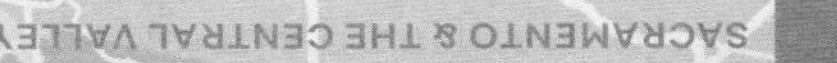

San Joaquin Valley, p536

The heart of the Central Valley is a string of cities linked by iconic Hwy 99. Look for historical and outdoor adventures around its edges.

TRAIN

The Central Valley has surprisingly good train service. All the main cities of the San Joaquin Valley such as Fresno and Bakersfield are linked to Sacramento and the Bay Area by fast and frequent Amtrak trains.

BUS

Buses provide bare-bones service across the valley. Amtrak buses provide important links out of the region to Lake Tahoe, the Gold Country, Yosemite and LA. Local buses in the larger cities like Sacramento will get you around and to some nearby attractions.

San Jose
Patterson
La Grange
Yosemite Village
Merced River
Stevinson
Livingston
Gustine
Atwater
Merced
Mariposa
Sierra National Forest
San Luis Reservoir
Los Banos
San Joaquin River
San Joaquin Valley
Coast Ranges
Salinas
Madera
Mendota
Diablo Range
California Aqueduct
Fresno
Sanger
Soledad
King City
Kingsburg
Hanford
Visalia
Coalinga
Tulare
Kettleman City
Porterville
Paso Robles
Morro Bay
PACIFIC OCEAN
San Luis Obispo
Buttonwillow
Bakersfield
Kernville
Lake Isabella
Taft
Maricopa
Keene
0 100 km
0 50 miles

Plan Your Time

Hit the valley roads, where car culture means more than just transportation. Go slow and explore, as you could drive the length of this region in one long day using Hwy 99 – without any stops!

MARISSA SISCO/SHUTTERSTOCK ©

Sacramento Delta (p531)

If You Only Have One Day

- Head to Sacramento via the **Sacramento Delta** (p531) with its sinuous drives through a lost California. In the state capital, drop by the **California Museum** (p526), which celebrates Californians of all stripes. Then visit the **State Capitol** (p526) building where the entire ground floor has been restored to reflect various historic eras.

- Wander **Old Sacramento** (p527), squinting so you can see the 1800s authenticity amid the tourist clutter. Feel the enormous might of the historic trains in the **California State Railroad Museum** (p527). Laze away your evening in the **Midtown** (p528) neighborhood, dotted with restaurants where delicious scents envelop the outdoor tables.

Seasonal Highlights

The valley comes alive in a rainbow of spring colors. Summer gets blazingly hot – cool off with fresh-fruit ice cream. The vineyards turn radiant with fall colors.

MARCH

California's golden poppies turn entire hillsides a brilliant safety-vest orange; other **wildflowers** add dashes of color from purple to yellow.

APRIL

The **Red Bluff Round-Up** is a rowdy celebration of ranch life. Stockton's huge **San Joaquin Asparagus Festival** honors the vegetable.

JUNE

Modesto takes to the streets for **Graffiti Summer**, a carnival of classic cars, cruising and oldies music.

MATTHEW SCHUKNECHT/SHUTTERSTOCK ©; CARRIE ANNE CASTILLO/GETTY IMAGES ©; BLANCA RIVAS/SHUTTERSTOCK ©

Three Days to Travel Around

- Spend your first day as directed in **Sacramento** (p524). Then hit the open road on historic Hwy 99, the spine of the Central Valley. Head south for a root beer at a historic stand in **Modesto** (p538). Stop by **Castle Air Museum** (p538) in Merced to see decades of famous military aircraft.

- Satisfy lunch cravings at one of the excellent Mexican restaurants that line Hwy 99. In Fresno, get down for the weirdness at **Forestiere Underground Gardens** (p538). At night in Bakersfield, have a filling **Basque dinner** (p540), then feel the passion of the Bakersfield sound at **Buck Owens' Crystal Palace** (p540).

If You Have More Time

- Head north up the Sacramento Valley to the beer heaven that is **Chico** (p535). Watch for migrating birds in the vast marshes and open plains. To the south, make time for experiences beyond Central Valley clichés. Seek out **Colonel Allensworth State Historic Park** (p539) for a different side of California. Continue south to the outdoor spectacle at **Antelope Valley California Poppy Reserve** (p541).

- East of Bakersfield, seek out the **white-water adventure** (p540) of your dreams in Kernville. Finally, drop down to **César E Chávez National Monument** (p539) and learn about the man and the movement that radically changed the Central Valley and its people.

JULY

One of the state's biggest parties, Sacramento's **California State Fair** showcases agriculture, thrill rides, improbable junk food and more.

AUGUST

Farmers markets across the valley burst with waves of bounty as peak seasons for many fruits and vegetables converge.

SEPTEMBER

Old Sacramento comes alive in early September for **Gold Rush Days**, with horse races, historic costumes, music and gold panning.

NOVEMBER

The very end of the growing season sees the **Pomegranate Festival** in Madera, with cooking contest and a focus on dried fruits and nuts.

SACRAMENTO

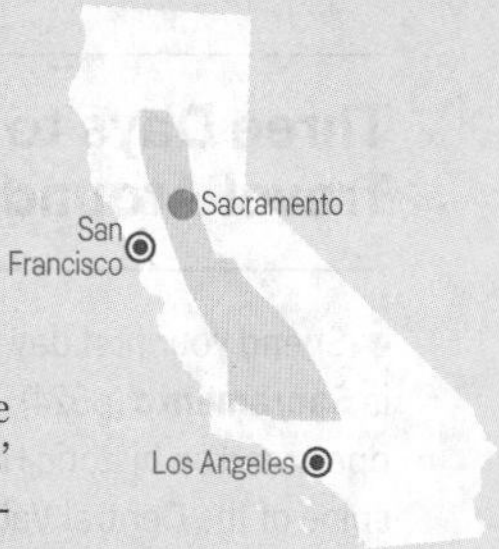

Sacramento
San Francisco
Los Angeles

Sacramento is a city of contrasts. It's a former cow town where state legislators' SUVs go bumper-to-bumper with farmers' muddy, half-ton pickups at rush hour. It has sprawling suburbs, but also new lofts and upscale boutiques squeezed between aging mid-century storefronts. Its sights range from rows of gold-rush-era historical buildings to cutting-edge art museums.

The people of 'Sac' are a resourceful lot that have fostered small but energetic food, art and nightlife scenes. Numerous breweries keep this city well stocked with award-winning beers, and the ubiquitous farmers markets and farm-to-fork fare are another point of pride.

In addition to offering plenty of reasons to stop off as part of any itinerary that passes through, the city is hard to miss as it's the crossroads of Interstates 5 and 80. And it's roughly halfway between San Francisco and Lake Tahoe, so some of the state's most popular destinations are not far away.

TOP TIP

Sacramento is very diffuse; sights and nightlife are spread throughout the city and the central core (the Grid), where numbered streets run north–south and lettered streets run east–west. Old Sacramento is at the west end of the Grid. Distances from here to appealing Midtown to the east are long.

California State Capitol Museum (p526)

SIGHTS
1 California Museum
2 California State Capitol Museum
3 California State Capitol Park
4 California State Railroad Museum
5 Crocker Art Museum
6 Old Sacramento
7 Sacramento History Museum
8 State Indian Museum
9 Sutter's Fort State Historic Park
10 Tower Bridge

EATING
11 K Street Mall
12 Midtown
13 Tower District

ENTERTAINMENT
14 Golden 1 Center

SHOPPING
15 20th St

Sutter's Fort State Historic Park (p527)

SACRAMENTO'S EARLY HISTORY

Sacramento embodies much of California's history. Indigenous peoples fished the rivers and thrived before colonists arrived. By the 1800s, the native communities were largely wiped out and control changed from Spanish to Mexican to American hands. In 1847, John Sutter came seeking fortune and built a fortified outpost.

Beginning in 1848, gold rushers stampeded to the fast-growing town around the trading post now christened 'Sacramento.' It became the state capital in 1850. In the following decades, a quarter of a million Chinese people arrived in California, many working as indentured servants. They built much of the Central Pacific Railroad, which began construction in Sacramento in 1863, and connected to the Union Pacific in Promontory, UT, in 1869.

Locomotive at the California State Railroad Museum

Revel in the California Museum

CELEBRATE GOLDEN STATE ACHIEVEMENTS

This eclectic, modern museum has rotating exhibits that focus on the contributions of the state's diverse residents. A recent one celebrated the immense contributions and accomplishments of Chinese immigrants; others have focused on the state's Native American culture. It's also home to the **California Hall of Fame**: the only place to simultaneously encounter César Chávez, Serena Williams and Steve Jobs.

California's Historic State Capitol

MONUMENTAL BUILDING AND GROUNDS

The gleaming dome of the **California State Capitol Museum** is Sacramento's most recognizable structure. The renovated ground floor functions as a working museum and important offices have been restored to their period glory. Outside, **California State Capitol Park** is an alluring and eclectic mix of elaborate gardens and memorials. Take time to read the labels on the myriad trees as they show the state's vast range of species, from date palms to coast redwoods.

WHERE TO EAT IN SACRAMENTO

Localis
A relaxed Midtown temple to Central Valley produce and California cuisine. Book ahead, especially for patio tables. **$$**

Chando's Cantina
North of Downtown, Chando's serves Tijuana-style street food like superb tacos until late on weekends. **$**

Ginger Elizabeth Patisserie
Exquisite French-inspired baked goods in Midtown; excellent breakfast and lunch items. **$**

Explore Old Sacramento

HISTORIC CENTER WITH FASCINATING MUSEUMS

The historic river port next to downtown, **Old Sacramento** is the city's top visitor draw. The kitschy gold-rush-era atmosphere makes it good for a stroll, especially on summer evenings. California's largest concentration of buildings on the National Register of Historic Places is found here. However, like with an aging Hollywood star, the massive reconstructions give Old Sacramento an odd artificiality.

Of the 100 buildings, 35 are mostly original to the gold rush era (get a guide from the visitor center). If you ignore the tatty gift shops, fudgeries and tourist-trap eateries, you can get an engaging sense of the past. Join the **Underground Tour** run by the on-site **Sacramento History Museum**, which explores the tunnels under the streets that date from the time before everything was raised 18ft due to floods.

The top sight is the **California State Railroad Museum**, which recreates the completion of the Transcontinental Railroad and has a huge collection of restored and notable locomotives and cars. On many days (weather permitting) you can go for a train ride along the river, which gives the riverfront a lively air, all in the shadow of the iconic **Tower Bridge** (featured in 2017's Oscar-winning *Lady Bird*).

Housed in the ornate Victorian mansion (with sprawling contemporary additions) of a railroad baron, the **Crocker Art Museum** has excellent collections. Works by California painters and European masters hang beside an enthusiastically curated collection of contemporary art.

NOTABLE GOVERNORS

Sacramento has been home to California's governors since 1850. The state has elected many colorful characters, none more notorious than its first governor, Peter Burnett. An avowed racist, he played a significant role in the genocide of California's indigenous people. In contrast, the 30th governor, Earl Warren (1943–53) went on to serve as the chief justice of the USA, presiding over decisions that liberalized civil rights.

More recently, former actor Ronald Reagan (1967–75) used the office as a springboard to the presidency. The 38th governor, Arnold Schwarzenegger (2003–11) was notable for his intemperate statements and huge budget deficits.

An 1850s Fort Full of Ambience

DIG INTO JOHN SUTTER'S HISTORIC FORT

Originally built by John Sutter, the mostly reconstructed site of **Sutter's Fort State Historic Park** was once the only trace of white settlement for hundreds of miles. Stroll within its walls, where displays including furniture, medical equipment and a blacksmith shop recreate life in the 1850s.

Sutter was an entrepreneur, who was also a con artist and itinerant debtor – qualities that survive to this day in Silicon Valley. He enslaved the local Native American population to create his fortune, which was lost after gold-seekers swamped his lands.

TO THE GOLDFIELDS!

As others got rich, John Sutter met financial ruin at the gold discovery site in **Marshall** (p551). Sacramento anchored the gold rush and entrepreneurs like Leland Stanford became powerful and wealthy (see his mansion in Downtown Sacramento).

Kin Thai Stree Eatery
Busy Midtown cafe with a vibe like an Asian street market. **$**

Aioli Bodega Espanola
Spanish tapas in a garden near the capital, plus a long wine list. **$$**

Casa Tulum Restaurant
Just east of Midtown, serving excellent Mexican fare that goes beyond the clichés; good chipotle salsa. **$**

I LIVE HERE: BEST EATS IN SACRAMENTO

Sacramento is a California melting pot and that's reflected in its restaurants. Sacramento food blogger **Gennifer Rose** (@genniferrose_blog) says the city is filled with great eats, including the following favorites:

'**Cafeteria 15L** is a Sacramento staple near the Capitol that serves New American comfort food in a modern setting. On the menu you'll find American classics with an unexpected twist.

The ultra-trendy **Beast + Bounty** restaurant is in the up-and-coming R District, southeast of Midtown. It serves fresh fare (seafood, pizza, salads and pasta) inside a bright, airy venue.

Take a trip to Vietnam with a meal at Midtown's **Saigon Alley Kitchen**. You'll find both traditional Vietnamese cuisine and new takes on classics. The ambience and food are stylish.'

Ponder California's Indigenous History

APPRECIATE THE STATE'S NATIVE CULTURES

It's with some irony that the small **State Indian Museum** sits in the shadow of Sutter's Fort. The excellent exhibits and handicrafts on display – including the intricately woven and feathered baskets of the Pomo – are traces of cultures nearly stamped out by the immigration fervor Sutter ignited. Enthusiastic docents provide context on the exhibits. A $200-million replacement in West Sacramento is in the works.

Cheer on the Sacramento Kings

ROOT FOR THE UNDERDOG

The local professional basketball team has a passionate following in Central California despite having the worst record in the NBA over the last two decades. Games are played in the glitzy **Golden 1 Center**.

Savor Farmers Markets

REAP THE REWARDS OF RICH AGRICULTURE

Sacramento lies at the center of some of the continent's most fertile farmlands, so you're never far from a mind-blowing year-round farmers market in the city (check out marketlocations.com). Most will have food trucks, excellent morning coffee vendors and street performers. One of the very best is on Saturday mornings in Midtown on **20th St**.

Wine & Dine Downtown

SACRAMENTO'S BEST EATING AND NIGHTLIFE DISTRICTS

Lively **Midtown** begins east of 17th St and is an appealing mix of older buildings, huge shade trees and a zesty assortment of shops, restaurants and bars. A cruise up J St and nearby parallel streets passes a number of creative-but-affordable restaurants where tables spill onto the sidewalks in the summer.

South of Midtown, at the corner of Broadway and 16th St, the **Tower District** is dominated by the Tower Theatre, a beautiful 1938 art deco movie palace. From the theater, head east on Broadway to a stretch of the city's most eclectic and affordable eateries.

The **K Street Mall**, known by locals as 'The Kay,' is the once-moribund central business district. It's been transformed into a weekend hot spot for nightlife. The pedestrian mall draws partiers to the ever-changing lineup of trendy restaurants and clubs.

WHERE TO DRINK BEER IN SACRAMENTO

Fieldwork Brewing Company
Bustling brewpub in Midtown. Over 20 rotating taps of excellent draft beer; hoppy IPAs are the specialty.

Ruhstaller BSMT
This cozy basement bar on The Kay serves up red ales and Kolsch alongside experimental brews.

Bike Dog Broadway Taproom
Bright and cheery taproom in the Tower District, with a big lineup of house brews.

CASSIOHABIB/SHUTTERSTOCK ©

Golden 1 Center

Parks, Trails & Verdant Paths

BREATHE DEEPLY AMID URBAN NATURE

Snuggled into a curve of the American River, **River Bend Park** is a real treat for those looking for some green space in Sacramento. Trails crisscross peaceful riparian landscapes defined by twisted oak trees, grassy meadows and rocky river shorelines.

The **American River Parkway** includes a nice walking, running and cycling path called the **Jedediah Smith Memorial Trail** that's accessible from Old Sacramento.

Sacramento is also a fantastic city to cruise around by bike, especially given how its highlights are widely scattered. There are plenty of bike lanes, and **Lime** has rideshare e-bikes and e-scooters available in the center using its app.

PRIZE PIGS, FUNNEL CAKES & THRILL RIDES

If you're anywhere near Sacramento during the last two weeks in July, don't miss the enormous **California State Fair** at the Cal Expo grounds. Since its inception in 1854, the fair has hosted horse racing, blue-ribbon livestock and agricultural exhibits showcasing California's bounty.

Nowadays many come for the deep-fried Snickers bars and corn-dog eating contests. Other crowd-pleasers include tastings of high-end wines, a huge array of carnival rides, and concerts with nostalgic acts whose names often feature in 'dead or alive' trivia contests.

Many days at this family-friendly event feature various themes. Midweek is the best time to come; weekend crowds can be overwhelming. Hotels across the region fill up during the fair weeks.

GETTING AROUND

Sacramento International Airport has plenty of flights and is the nearest major option for those traveling to Yosemite National Park.

Sacramento is also a hub for Amtrak service. Trains and buses from the station next to Old Sacramento serve Lake Tahoe, the Central Valley south to Bakersfield and the Bay Area. It's a stop for the distance *Coast Starlight* (Seattle to LA) and the *California Zephyr*, which links the Bay Area to Chicago via the spectacular run through the Sierras and Truckee on the original route of the Transcontinental Railroad.

Sacramento Regional Transit buses cover the center and SacRT also runs a trolley between Old Sacramento and Downtown, as well as Sacramento's light-rail system, which is of limited usefulness as it's designed for commuting from outlying communities.

Beyond Sacramento

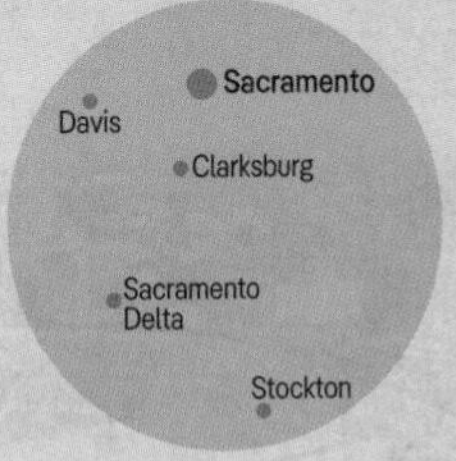

The Sacramento Delta's little levee-protected towns and reed-covered islands seem stuck in the 1930s and make for ideal backroads exploring.

Sacramento's waterfront on its namesake river is just the start of the sprawling web of waterways that form the Sacramento Delta and eventually flow into the San Francisco Bay. The wetlands cover a huge swath of the state and extend south all the way to Stockton and the edge of the San Joaquin Valley. It's easy to get happily lost here and forget you're surrounded by two of the state's largest metropolitan areas: Sacramento and San Francisco. On weekends, locals gun powerboats on the wandering rivers and cruise winding levee roads beneath twisted oak canopies.

Just north, Davis is one of California's most delightful college towns. It's surrounded by lush vineyards and orchards.

TOP TIP

The Sacramento Delta makes a wonderful day trip from the Bay Area. From the East Bay to the levees is only about an hour's drive.

Sacramento National Wildlife Refuge (p532)

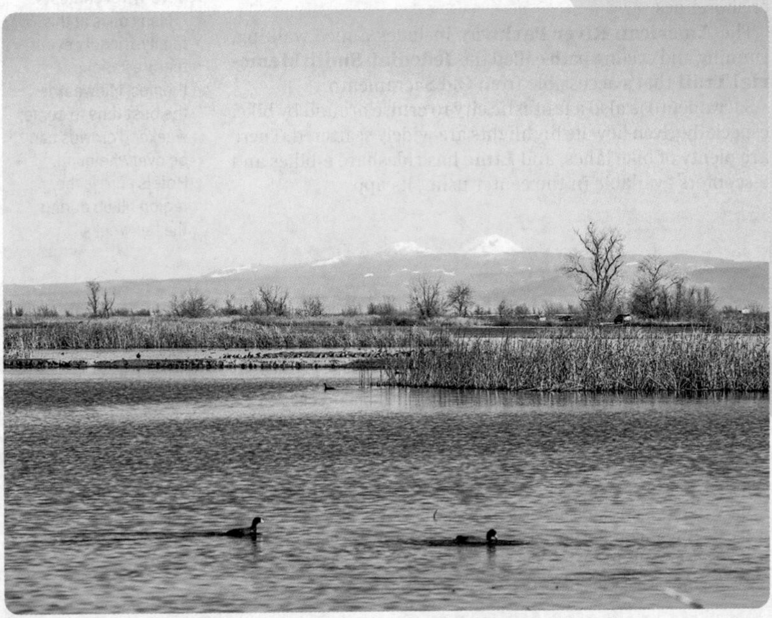

The Surprising Sacramento Delta

HARDSCRABBLE HISTORY AND RICH LOCAL LIFE

If you have the time to smell the grassy breezes of the Sacramento Delta on the slow route between San Francisco and Sacramento, don't miss traveling the region's roads that wind around islands linked by iron bridges. Everything is within one hour's drive of Sacramento. Winding Hwy 160 follows the curvaceous Delta levees. Hwy 12 is another good option, as are other two-laners crisscrossing this watery wonderland, such as the evocatively named Grand Island Rd. You will lazily make your way past orderly vineyards, vast orchards, sandy swimming banks, bird-thronged parks and little towns with long histories.

Locke is the most fascinating of the Delta towns. Tucked below a levee, its main street feels like a ghost town. The colorful **Dai Loy Museum** recalls the town's Chinese heritage that dates back 100 years; dusty *pai gow* tables and an antique safe are among the highlights. Nearby, the **Locke Boarding House Museum State Park** preserves the lodging of the hard-working Southern Pacific track workers. Anchoring Main St is **Al's Place**, a saloon that's been pouring since 1915. Below are creaking floorboards; above, the ceiling is covered in crusty dollar bills and more than one pair of erstwhile undies. The bar food is excellent.

Isleton – so-called 'Crawdad Town USA' – has a long, historic main street with shops, restaurants, bars and buildings that reflect the region's Chinese heritage. **Delta Queen** is a vintage B&B that makes for a vintage escape. The town's **Cajun Festival**, at the end of June, draws folks from across the state, but you can get very lively crawdads year-round at **Bob's Bait Shop**.

Rio Vista is a humble burg with a nice little waterfront on the Sacramento River. Nearby are good and unpretentious cafes and bars.

Across the Delta you'll see signs for the **Delta Loop**, a drive that passes boater bars and marinas where you can rent something to take on the water. At the end is the **Brannan Island State Recreation Area**, which has boat-in, drive-in and walk-in campsites.

You'll notice signs across the region protesting plans to divert even more fresh water away from the region. Since the 1930s, 75% of the water from the major rivers flowing into the Delta has been diverted to the Central Valley for agriculture and to Southern California.

LOCKE'S RICH CHINESE HERITAGE

Locke was founded by Chinese laborers who also built the levees that ended perpetual flooding in the Sacramento Delta. This allowed agriculture to flourish and created waterways that helped inland ports grow.

After a malicious fire wiped out the settlement in 1912, a group of community leaders approached land baron George Locke for a leasehold; at the time, California didn't allow people of Chinese descent to own property. Locke became the only freestanding town built and managed by Chinese people in the USA.

These days the weather-beaten buildings are protected on the National Register of Historic Places. Somewhat miraculously, these tightly packed old wood structures have avoided the fires that are the bane of California's historic old towns.

WHERE TO DRINK BEYOND SACRAMENTO

Mei Wah Beer Room
Fantastic restored drinking den in Isleton with an opulent Chinese-accented interior, good beer selection and patio.

Davis Beer Shoppe
Mellow Davis beer hall with 650 varieties of craft beer, bottled and on tap.

Hemly Cider
Pear-growing family with six generations of experience in the Delta makes cloudy pear cider from their own orchards.

HAVENS FOR BIRDS & BATS

The Sacramento Delta serves as a rest stop for countless migrating species that arrive in such great numbers they are a spectacle even without binoculars.

October to February
Four million waterbirds winter in the warm tules (marshes) on their way along the Great Pacific Flyway. **Sacramento National Wildlife Refuge** offers tours.

October to January
Endangered chinook and steelhead fight their way upstream to spawn. Spot them along Sacramento's **American River Parkway**.

March to June
Cabbage white, painted lady and western tiger swallowtail butterflies come to party. Sacramento National Wildlife Refuge has details.

June to August
Hundreds of thousands of Mexican free-tailed bats shelter under the Yolo Causeway in **Davis**.

ALESSANDRARC/SHUTTERSTOCK ©

Locke Boarding House Museum State Park (p531)

A Tour of Local Wineries

TASTING UNIQUE DELTA VINTAGES

The wines of the **Clarksburg** region along the Sacramento River, a 30-minute drive from Sacramento, have a great reputation, benefiting from the blazing sun and cool delta breezes. The **Old Sugar Mill** is the hub of a thriving community of local winemakers. Peruse the tasting rooms and enjoy a bottle on the outdoor patio overlooking vineyards. The region's best-known winery, **Bogle**, is a few miles southwest of Clarksburg via the winding County Rds 141 and 144. It's set among vineyards on a 6th-generation family farm, and is very proud of its sustainable practices.

University Life & Fascinating Museums

LEARN YOUR WAY AROUND UC DAVIS

Much of Davis' energy comes from the free-spirited students who flock to the **University of California, Davis** (UC Davis), which boasts one of the nation's leading viticulture departments. Bikes outnumber cars two to one, and students

WHERE TO EAT BEYOND SACRAMENTO

Rogelio's
Isleton classic serving a mash-up of Mexican and Chinese dishes, with Italian and American standards, too. **$$**

Lucy's Cafe
No-nonsense Italian-accented fare near the Rio Vista waterfront. **$**

Mustard Seed
Creative takes on California cuisine using local bounty in downtown Davis. **$$**

make up half the population. The town, a 20-minute drive west of Sacramento, makes a good pit stop when traveling in or out of the Bay Area.

Strolling the shady downtown, you'll pass family-operated businesses (the city council has forbidden any store over 50,000 sq ft – sorry, Wal-Mart) and public art projects.

The university is all about agriculture, and new types of produce that end up in your supermarket are developed here. The 100-acre **UC Davis Arboretum** is a must-see for its well-marked botanical collections. Afterward, follow the peaceful 3.5-mile loop along one of the state's oldest reservoirs, dug in the 1860s.

The campus has two notable cultural centers. The **Jan Shrem and Maria Manetti Shrem Museum of Art** features features contemporary artists working across a wide range of mediums in a dreamy modern space. The **John Natsoulas Center for the Arts** is marked by a giant mosaic cat on the way into town; the ceramic calico cat guards one of the state's most vibrant small contemporary art galleries.

College students love to eat and drink cheaply, and downtown has many lively spots for a quick dose of Asian noodles or a slice of pizza. The **Davis Farmers Market** is renowned for being one of the best in the country, and features over 150 food vendors, plus picnic supplies and buskers. For nightlife, downtown bars lure students with drink specials, open-mic nights, karaoke and trivia.

Shipbuilding Meets Downtown Living

SLEEPER-HIT WATERFRONT STOCKTON

Stockton, a 30-minute drive southwest of Sacramento, is the surprise port city at the east end of the Delta. Huge terminals load ships with bulk products like grain for shipment to Asia. It was once the main supply hub for gold rushers and during WWII it became a major center of American shipbuilding.

The waterfront redevelopment is one of the valley's successful efforts at revitalization and makes for a good stroll along with the adjoining downtown. Slightly north, you'll find **Miracle Mile**, a second hub of bars and restaurants.

Of all the Central Valley food celebrations, perhaps none pay such creative respect to the main ingredient as Stockton's **San Joaquin Asparagus Festival**, which brings together more than 500 vendors to serve the prized green stalks – more than 10 tons of them! – every way imaginable. It sprouts at the San Joaquin County Fairgrounds over three days in April.

WINE TASTING IN LODI

Lodi's underrated wineries – easily accessed from I-5 or Hwy 99 – make for a fun, budget-friendly afternoon of tasting. The vineyards include some of the world's oldest zinfandel vines. Some favorites:

Jessie's Grove anchors Lodi's wine producers. The winery grounds are a perfect wine-drinking setting.

Harney Lane is a sweet family outfit with a fab tempranillo. The tree-covered patio is sublime.

Bokisch offers a high-quality take on Spanish varietals in a peaceful country setting. Enjoy live music and social evenings.

Acquiesce delivers a bright selection of white wines that buck Lodi wine tradition. The picpoul blanc and the roussanne are wonderful.

d'Art features a bold-yet-smooth cabernet sauvignon that's as inviting as the tasting room, which doubles as a local art gallery.

GETTING AROUND

Exploring the Delta will require your own vehicle.

Davis is on the Amtrak regional network; Yolobus local bus service has routes to Sacramento.

Stockton has Amtrak regional service to the Bay Area, Sacramento and the San Joaquin Valley. Altamont Commuter Express trains serve San Jose.

SACRAMENTO VALLEY

The Sacramento River, California's largest, rushes out of the northern mountains from Shasta Lake before hitting the Sacramento Valley basin above Red Bluff. It snakes south across grassy plains and orchards before skirting the state capital, fanning across the delta and draining into San Francisco Bay.

The valley is most beautiful in the bloom of spring, when delicate flowers bejewel the orchards and hillsides. If you're driving through the region to one of California's marquee attractions, swing though Chico for a fun vibe, good eats and famous drinks.

Since so much is grown in the Sacramento Valley, enjoying the fresh, seasonal food in the region is easy. Look for fruit-and-nut stands along the highways, many selling what you can see growing in the surrounding farmlands. Every city has farmers markets, many open year-round. The vendors are experts – some will patiently take you through their vast range of produce.

TOP TIP

The backbone of the Sacramento Valley is I-5, which connects with other major highways like I-80. However, this stretch of the state's north–south spine is no more interesting than the San Joaquin Valley portion. Instead, get close to valley towns and farmlands on Hwys 45, 70 and 99.

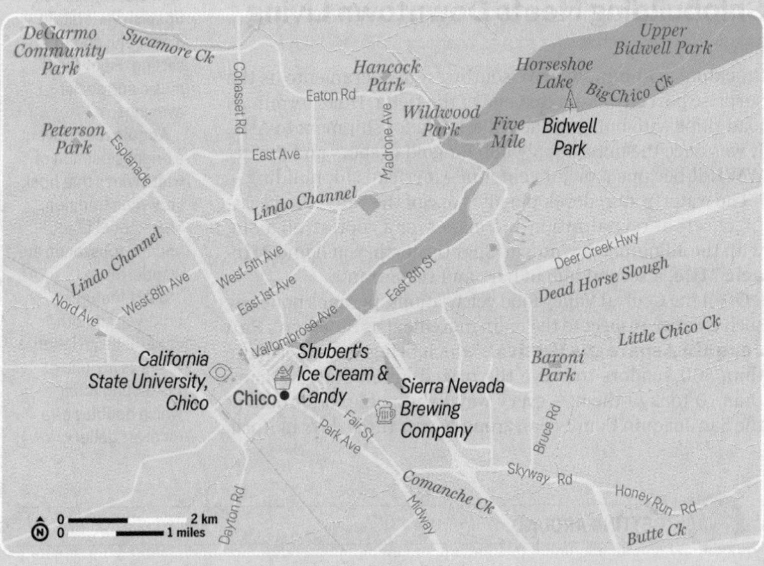

Sierra Nevada Brewing Company's pale ale

Party Town & Iconic Brewery

GOOD TIMES IN CHICO

With its huge student population, Chico has the wild energy of a college kegger during the school year, and a lethargic hangover during summer. The oak-shaded downtown and lively **California State University, Chico** make it one of Sacramento Valley's most attractive hubs. Folks mingle late in the restaurants and bars here, which open onto patios when it's warm.

Though the city – like the rest of the valley – wilts in the summer heat, the swimming holes in impressive **Bidwell Park** offer an escape, as does floating down the gentle Sacramento River. The park stretches 10 miles northwest of downtown with lush groves and miles of trails.

For many, Chico's top attraction has pilgrimage status: this is the home of the legendary **Sierra Nevada Brewing Company**. Founded in 1979, the brewery was one of the pioneers of the craft beer revolution. Today, Sierra Nevada continues to try out new styles of beer at the various taprooms at its huge brewery complex near Hwy 99. Take a self-guided tour or go for one of the deep-immersion (not literally) sessions with a brewmaster. Soak up the suds in the excellent restaurant.

All ages will delight in **Shubert's Ice Cream & Candy**, a beloved old-time shop where five generations of Shuberts have produced delicious homemade ice cream, chocolates and confections.

TOP SACRAMENTO VALLEY CITIES

Amid the grapes, nuts, lemons, tomatoes and plethora of tree fruits, the Sacramento Valley has a few cities worth your time.

Red Bluff – one of California's hottest towns – makes a fine pit stop on the way to the famous parks to the northeast. Shop for Western wear downtown, then get a dose of history at **William B Ide Adobe State Historic Park**, which preserves an original 1850 one-room adobe house.

Quiet **Oroville** has restored 19-century wooden homes that recall its past as a gold-rush town. The restored 1863 **Chinese Temple & Museum Complex** offers a fascinating glimpse into Oroville's Chinese legacy. Hwy 70 heads northeast to the magnificent **Feather River Canyon**.

GETTING AROUND

The Sacramento Valley is where you need your own vehicle. Quiet two-lane roads far from the busy highways are great for cycling, but otherwise you'll need the freedom of driving to explore the region. Amtrak and Greyhound buses provide service that's barely serviceable.

SAN JOAQUIN VALLEY

San Francisco
San Joaquin Valley
Los Angeles

The southern half of California's Central Valley, named after the San Joaquin River, sprawls from Stockton to the Tehachapi Mountains, southeast of Bakersfield. Everything stretches to the horizon in straight lines – train tracks, two-lane blacktop and long irrigation channels.

The tiny towns scattering the region meld their Main St Americana appeal with the cultural influence of the Latinx labor force.

This is a place of seismic, often contentious, development. Arrivals priced out of coastal cities have resulted in patches of urban sprawl. What were once ranches and vineyards are now nostalgically named developments, and water rights is the issue on everyone's minds.

The valley's cities are not compelling, but each has attractions to lure you off Hwy 99, the spine of the San Joaquin. Distances here are long: it's over 220 miles from Modesto south to Bakersfield. Look to the edges for the scenic Kern River area and the Antelope Valley wildflowers.

TOP TIP

To really see the region, skip I-5 and travel on Hwy 99 – a freeway with nearly as long a history as the famous Route 66 to the south. Crank up the twangy country and western or the booming *norteño* (accordion-driven Mexican folk music). Exit often for bushels of farm-fresh produce.

Colonel Allensworth State Historic Park (p539)

ZACK FRANK/SHUTTERSTOCK ©

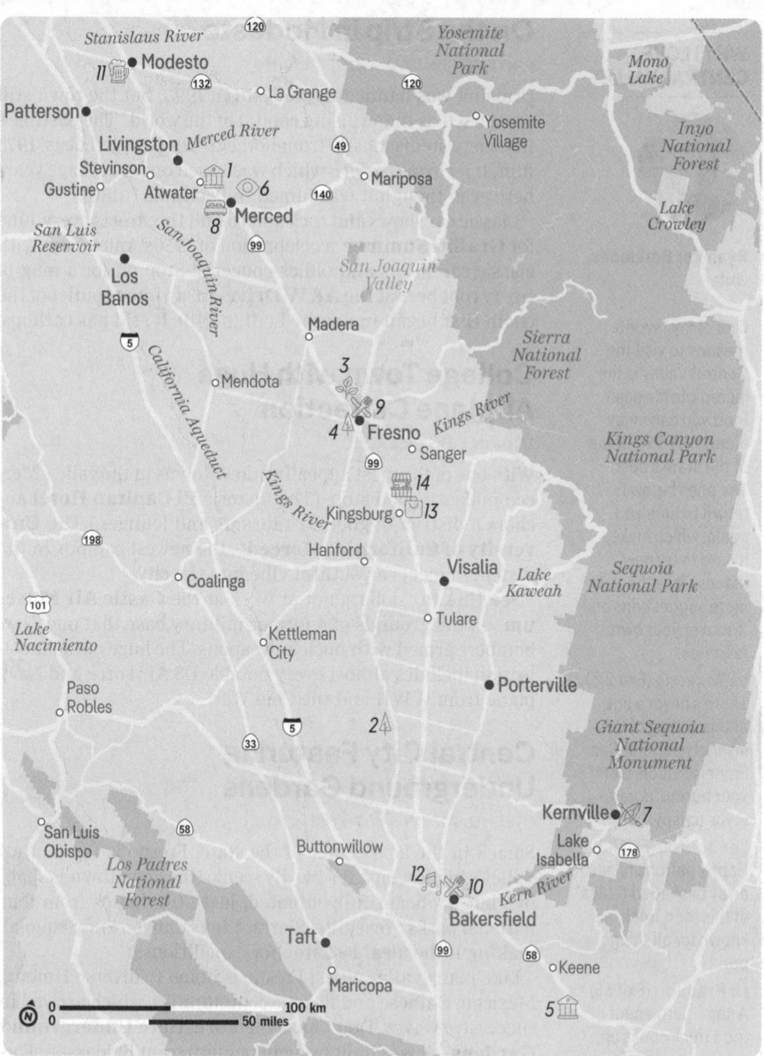

SIGHTS
1 Castle Air Museum
2 Colonel Allensworth State Historic Park
3 Forestiere Underground Gardens
4 Roeding Park
5 Tehachapi Railroad Depot
6 University of California, Merced

ACTIVITIES, COURSES & TOURS
7 Kernville

SLEEPING
8 El Capitan Hotel

EATING
9 Tower District
10 Wool Growers

DRINKING
11 A&W Drive-In

ENTERTAINMENT
12 Buck Owens' Crystal Palace

SHOPPING
13 Draper St
14 Sun-Maid Market

WHY I LOVE CENTRAL VALLEY

Ryan Ver Berkmoes, writer

One of my favorite reasons to visit the Central Valley is the incredible Mexican food you can enjoy along Hwy 99 – some of the state's best! The ones below I return to time and again, which makes it hard to try new places. Take them as mere suggestions and discover your own favorites.

La Taqueria (Exit 213) There's never a line at this sibling of the insanely popular San Francisco icon. Get your burrito '*dorado* style' (crispy).

Los Toritos (Exit 115) Happy patrons fill an array of shaded tables at this food truck known for all things pork.

La Pasadita (Exit 65) A semi-permanent food truck cooks up sublime *vampiros* – a sort of cheesy tostada, only better.

On the Strip in Modesto

VINTAGE CENTRAL VALLEY LIVING

Cruising was banned in Modesto in 1993, but the town still touts itself as the 'cruising capital of the world.' The pastime's notoriety stems mostly from homegrown George Lucas' 1973 film *American Graffiti,* which was based on his teenage years here even though it was filmed in Petaluma (p180).

Classic car shows and rock and roll fill the streets every June for **Graffiti Summer**, a celebration of 1950s Americana with classic car shows and oldies concerts. Stop off for a mug of frosty root beer at the **A&W Drive-In**, a vintage outlet of the chain that began in nearby Lodi in 1919. It still has carhops.

College Town with Huge Airplane Collection

TOURING TIDY MERCED

With one of the most appealing downtowns in the valley, Merced makes a good stop. (The historic **El Capitan Hotel** anchors a district of good restaurants and lounges.) The **University of California, Merced** – the newest campus in the system – injects a youthful vibe into the city.

See USA tax dollars not at work at the **Castle Air Museum**, on the grounds of a former military base that once saw bombers armed with nuclear weapons. The huge outdoor collection includes almost every notable US Air Force and Navy plane from WWII and the Cold War.

Central City Featuring Underground Gardens

FRESNO BUZZING WITH HISTORY

Smack in the arid center of the state, Fresno is the Central Valley's biggest city. It's hardly scenic (the downtown is shabby), but it's beautifully situated, just 90 minutes from four national parks (Yosemite, Sierra, Kings Canyon and Sequoia), making it the ideal last stop for expeditions.

Like many valley cities, Fresno is home to diverse Hmong, Mexican, Chinese and Basque communities, which arrived in successive waves. Don't miss the **Forestiere Underground Gardens** – it was built by Sicilian immigrant Baldassare Forestiere, who dug out some 70 acres beneath the hardpan soil to plant citrus trees, starting in 1906. With a unique skylight

WHERE TO DRINK IN THE SAN JOAQUIN VALLEY

17th Street Public House
Stylish bar right in the heart of Merced's revitalized downtown.

Cedar View Winery
Great patio for sampling wines and Sierra views in the countryside east of Fresno.

Kern River Brewing Company
Hub for rafting guides and outdoor types, with a rotation of award-winning seasonal beers.

system, Forestiere created a beautiful subterranean space for commercial crops and his own living quarters.

Hidden away in **Roeding Park** is a moving memorial to the many local Japanese Americans who died serving the USA in WWII. Their sacrifice is bittersweet given that their families were being held in concentration camps across the Western USA at the time. Thousands came from the Central Valley where, more often than not, their farms and homes were seized by their neighbors in their absence.

One of the most interesting parts of town is the **Tower District**, north of downtown – an oasis of gay-friendly bars, bookstores, music clubs and interesting restaurants.

Delicious Treats & Nordic Kitsch

SAMPLING SWEDISH KINGSBURG

Around 1873, a rail stop called 'Kings River Switch' was established and two Swedes arrived. Their countrymen soon followed and by 1921, 94% of Kingsburg's residents – as it had become known – were of Swedish heritage. Today, the Swedish past mixes with more recent Mexican immigrants who drive the agricultural economy.

Draper St, the main drag, is decked out with swaths of faux half-timbered schtick, all in the shadow of the landmark coffee-pot water tower. Gift shops and little bakeries selling buttery pastries and good coffee abound. Note: everything is closed on Sunday.

Don't miss all things raisin at the **Sun-Maid Market**. Pose next to the giant Sun Maid statue, then wander in for free samples and a selection of snacks.

Earliest African American Town

THE ABANDONED TOWN OF ALLENSWORTH

Some 10 miles west of Hwy 99 at Earlimart, **Colonel Allensworth State Historic Park** is an anomaly in the valley: a town built by and for African Americans. Named after its founder, a formerly enslaved person who later became a chaplain in the US Army, Allensworth comprised several dozen houses by 1910. Unfortunately, the same water woes that bedevil the valley today caused the town to go into terminal decline. It was abandoned by the 1930s. Today, it's a state park and buildings are being restored. The land here is table-top flat and, except for passing trains, the only sound is the wind whipping across the plain.

HONORING CÉSAR CHÁVEZ

The **César E Chávez National Monument** is at Nuestra Señora Reina de la Paz, the national headquarters of the United Farmworkers of America and the home of civil rights leader César Chávez from 1971 until his death in 1993. On view are exhibits on Chávez' work, his office and grave. It's in **Keene**, 27 miles southeast of Bakersfield.

Chávez was 11 when his family lost their farm and became migrant farm workers in California. At 14, he left school to labor in the fields. Eventually, he became a champion of nonviolent social change, leading controversial strikes while negotiating for better working conditions in the fields. His 1960s activism led to enormous improvements in the lives of California's farmworkers.

WHERE TO EAT IN THE SAN JOAQUIN VALLEY

8th St Taco Trucks
Browse this ever-changing assortment of superb food trucks near H St in Modesto. **$**

Branding Iron
A roadhouse favorite of ranchers in Merced, who order huge platters of steak. **$$**

Banzai Japanese Bar & Kitchen
High-concept Japanese fare in Fresno; the spicy garlic edamame is addictive. **$$**

Pilgrimage to the Bakersfield Sound

BOOMING BAKERSFIELD RISING FROM THE EARTH

Nearing Bakersfield, the landscape has evidence of California's other gold rush: rusting rigs burrow into Southern California's vast oil fields. Black gold was discovered here in the late 1800s, and Kern County, the southernmost along Hwy 99, still pumps more than some OPEC countries.

This is the setting of Upton Sinclair's *Oil!*, which was adapted into the 2007 Academy Award–winning film, *There Will Be Blood*. In the 1930s the oil attracted a stream of 'Okies' – farmers who migrated out of the Great Plains – to work the derricks. The children of these tough-as-nails roughnecks put the 'western' in country and western by creating the 'Bakersfield Sound' in the mid-1950s, with heroes Buck Owens and Merle Haggard waving a defiant middle finger at the silky Nashville establishment.

The obvious music choice as you explore the region is Owens' classic 'Streets of Bakersfield,' which combines the gritty local sound with lashings of Mexican *norteño*. Immerse yourself in the vibe at **Buck Owens' Crystal Palace**, the north-side music club that's part museum, honky-tonk and steakhouse. (Owens died in 2006.)

Downtown Bakersfield has been spruced up, which is evident in the upbeat mix of restored buildings and new restaurants, theaters and clubs. Just east, Bakersfield is blessed with Basque culinary traditions brought by shepherds in the 1800s. Restaurants such as **Wool Growers** serve family-style feasts of myriad courses that are meaty, garlicky and good.

GOOD SCENTS ON THE BLOSSOM TRAIL

When the Central Valley fruit and nut trees are in bloom, the winding roads around Fresno and Visalia make for a lovely afternoon drive. The 62-mile **Fresno County Blossom Trail** (goblossomtrail.com) is stunning between February and March, with the orchards awash in the pastel petals of apricot, almond, peach, nectarine, apple and citrus. Return in summer to taste the results.

Route maps are available online, though DIY is possible if you don't mind occasional detours on the backroads between Sanger, Reedley, Orange Cove, Selma, Fowler and Kingsburg. Don't miss lunch at **School House Restaurant** in Sanger. Dating from 1921, it serves elevated classic American cuisine in a vintage setting with pulley-powered fans and the like.

White Water & Family Floats

RIDING THE KERN RIVER

A half-century ago, Kern River originated on the slopes of Mt Whitney and journeyed close to 170 miles before finally settling into the Central Valley. Now, after its wild descent from the high country – 60ft per mile – the Kern is dammed in several places and almost entirely tapped for agricultural use.

Kernville, a cute little town straddling the river, is a hub for water sports. The pristine upper reaches, north of Kernville, boast class IV and V rapids during spring runoff and offer some of the most awe-inspiring white-water trips in the USA. Below Lake Isabella, the Kern is tamer and steadier. Rafting outfitters run trips from May to August, depending on conditions. There's something for nearly every age and skill level.

WHERE TO FIND FARMERS MARKETS IN THE SAN JOAQUIN VALLEY

Original Merced Certified Farmers' Market
One of the valley's premier markets, held every Saturday morning.

Vineyard Farmers Market
The freshest seasonal food from surrounding farms beneath wood arches covered in vines in Fresno.

Downtown Market
A hive of activity on Saturday mornings in Bakersfield; excellent coffee vendors.

Kern River

Old-School Train Station & Cafes

CHUGGING THROUGH TEHACHAPI

Midway between the San Joaquin Valley and the Mojave Desert, the tidy town of Tehachapi is a fine stop for its historic main drag, which has several good, retro cafes. However, the real star is the **Tehachapi Railroad Depot** – a reconstructed train station with a museum dedicated to the very busy train tracks outside, which link much of California with the rest of the USA (don't miss the little used-book section within).

The depot is built to a standard design of the Southern Pacific Railroad that dates back to the 1870s. Stations such as this were once a ubiquitous feature of town centers across the state.

THE SURPRISING ANTELOPE VALLEY

Seemingly a scruffier version of the Mojave Desert, the Antelope Valley is a dry annex to the Central Valley. Somewhat isolated and over the hill from Bakersfield, it has surprises for those willing to look.

The **Antelope Valley California Poppy Reserve** explodes in color every spring and is popular with fans of the brilliantly orange state flower. The reserve is also filled with a wide range of native wildlife and is good for hiking.

Set against the granite outcrops of the Piute Butte, the **Antelope Valley Indian Museum** displays thousands of indigenous artifacts.

Back toward Bakersfield, **Fort Tejon State Historic Park** is the site of one of the myriad atrocities committed against California tribes in the 1800s.

GETTING AROUND

Amtrak's San Joaquin service follows Hwy 99 and links the main valley cities with Sacramento and the Bay Area. There's connecting bus service onward to the LA Basin from the Bakersfield train station. Other buses connect to Yosemite and Sequoia National Parks.

Although you'll see plenty of construction – such as the huge new concrete trestles over Hwy 99 north of Fresno, California's much-hyped high-speed rail line linking the Bay Area with LA via the San Joaquin Valley is years away from completion.

The main cities have local buses for getting around town.

Above: Firehouse No 1 Museum (p556), Nevada City; Right: Hiking trails beyond Auburn (551)

GOLD COUNTRY

DELIGHTFUL TOWNS, BEAUTIFUL PARKS AND HISTORY

Discover the place that put the gold in the Golden State.

Hollywood draws the dreamers and Silicon Valley lures fortune-hunters, but this isn't the first time droves of aspiring young folk have streamed into the Golden State. After a sparkle in the American River caught James Marshall's eye in 1848, more than 300,000 prospectors from around the world started digging for gold in the Sierra foothills. Soon California entered statehood with the official motto 'Eureka,' solidifying its place as the land of opportunity.

The miner forty-niners are gone, but a ride along Hwy 49 through sleepy towns, past clapboard saloons and along oak-lined byways is a return to the unprecedented ride that was modern California's founding: ubiquitous historical markers tell tales about the gold rush, and share details about its devastating impact on the indigenous peoples here and the exploitation of non-white labor.

One thing never in dispute is the quality of California's food, which can be hearty, healthy and even creative thanks to plenty of fresh farm ingredients on offer. And as you'd expect for a place that's both hot (in summer) and popular with tourists, top-notch ice cream is a major feature. At night, many of the towns have vintage hotels that have been restored to a level of comfort likely greater than they offered in the 19th century. And get your anticipation ready as the wine-tasting scene is booming.

Make your own discoveries in beguiling towns such as Nevada City, Auburn, Placerville, Sutter Creek, Columbia and Sonora. Head off into nature for a hike or a float and don't miss the eerily poignant gold discovery site itself.

THE MAIN AREAS

AUBURN
Engaging Gold Country gateway. **p548**

NEVADA CITY
Cute, engrossing and historic. **p555**

SONORA
Characterful hub of the south. **p559**

Find Your Way

The Gold Country's core from Nevada City to Sonora can be driven in only a couple hours on the region's spine, Hwy 49, which means most of your time will be happily spent outside your car!

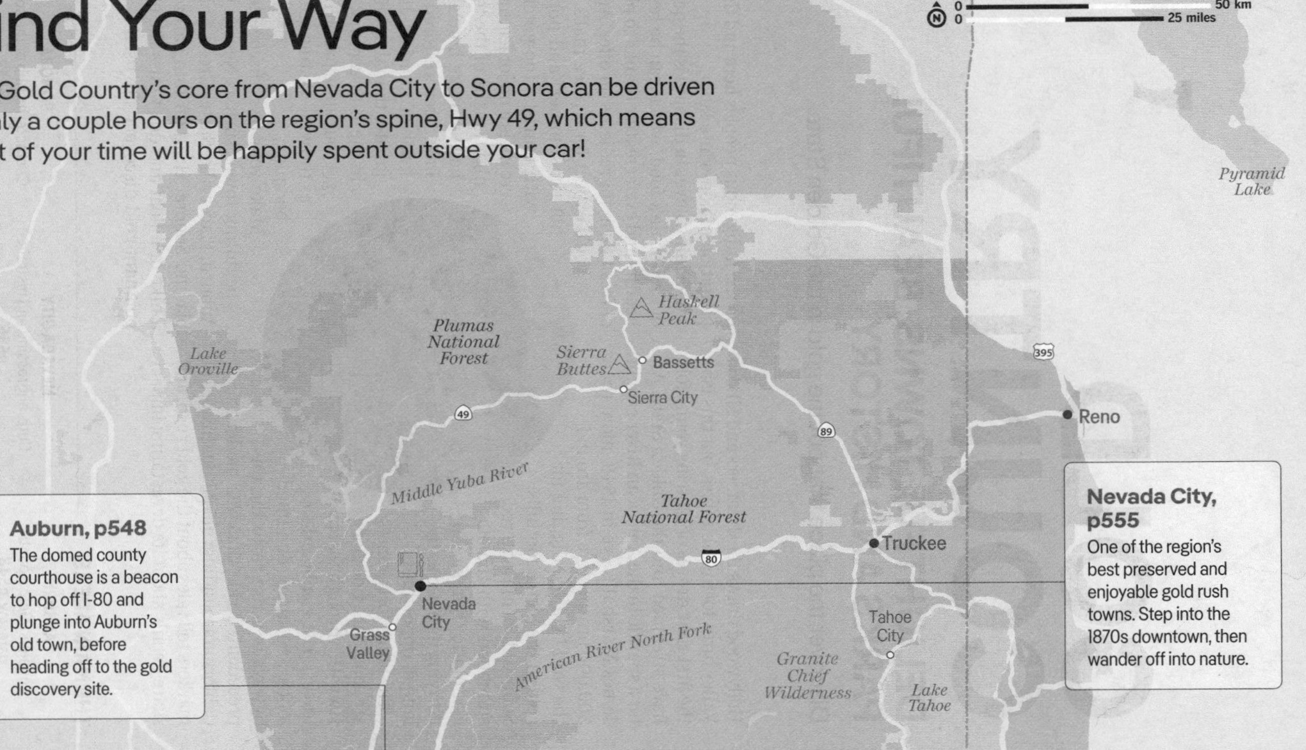

CAR

The Gold Country is best enjoyed with your own wheels. There's really no other option for navigating Hwy 49 and exploring all the sights. Distances are short, so your fuel needs will be minimal (or do it all with only one charge).

TRAIN

There's limited train service to Auburn. Amtrak also runs connecting buses here and to Placerville as part of its I-80 and Hwy 50 routes to Lake Tahoe. Otherwise, public transport is of minimal use.

BICYCLE

Experienced cyclists can navigate Hwy 49, although the lack of bike lanes, narrow shoulders and hilly curves will be a challenge. For quieter rides, travel outside summer and use back roads, although these are better for exploring just one area.

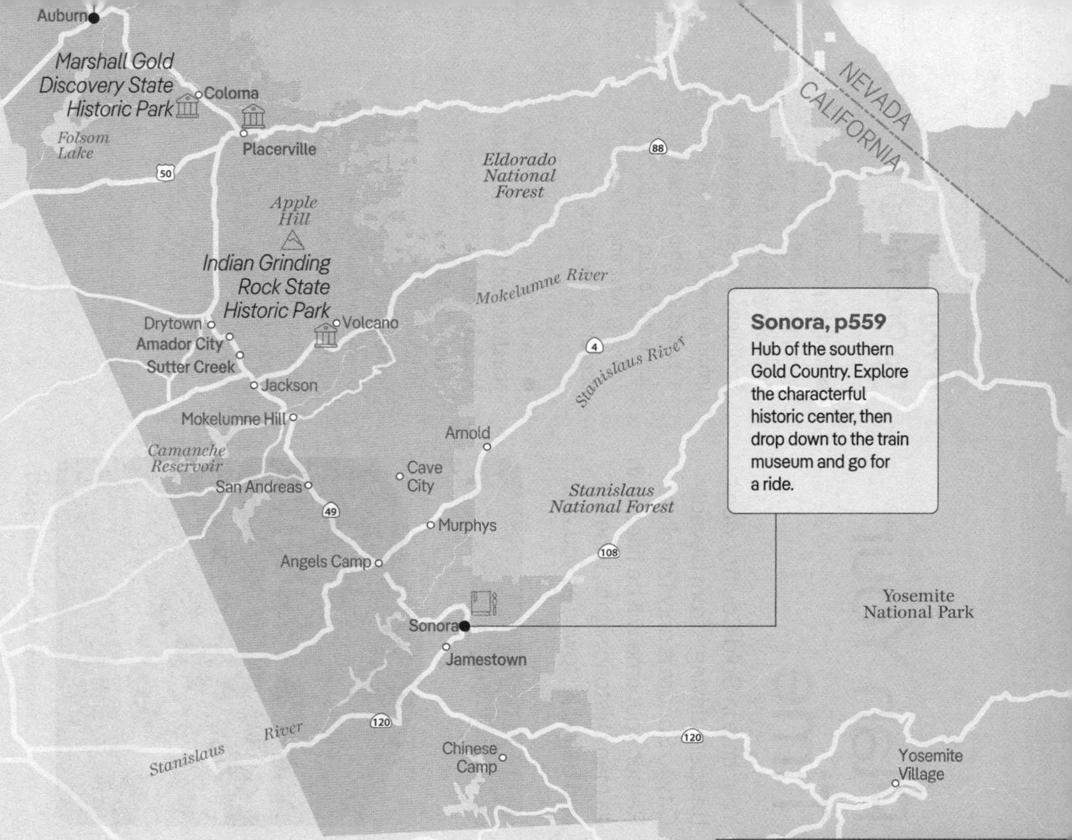

Sonora, p559
Hub of the southern Gold Country. Explore the characterful historic center, then drop down to the train museum and go for a ride.

Plan Your Time

Your time in Gold Country won't be spent driving – from Nevada City to Sonora is only 125 miles. Rather, your time will be filled with as many historic sights, wineries and beguiling towns as you wish.

HANK SHIFFMAN/SHUTTERSTOCK ©

Yuba River at Downieville (p558)

If You Only Do One Thing

- With only one day, drive the section of Hwy 49 between the compelling towns of **Auburn** (p548) on I-80 and **Placerville** (p551) on Hwy 50. This will give you a taste of the region's beautiful scenery of rolling foothills, coursing rivers and forests of conifers and live oaks.

- It will also allow a visit to the **Marshall Gold Discovery State Historic Park** (p551), the origin of Gold Country's name. This multifaceted park can easily occupy half a day – more if you go on a hike or two. Meanwhile, the two bookend towns are vintage delights with great eating and drinking.

Seasonal Highlights

Winter is cold, but that makes many sights more evocative. Hills turn brilliant green in spring, while the bountiful summer is hot. Fall sees the wine harvest.

JANUARY

Gold Country towns hold special events and festivals around the January 24 **anniversary of gold's discovery**.

MAY

Angels Camp hops for joy at the **Calaveras County Fair & Jumping Frog Jubilee**, famed for its namesake contest.

JUNE

Look for **farm tours and u-pick offers** as you drive Hwy 49 through the prime summer growing season.

DEVIN POWERS/SHUTTERSTOCK ©; MIKLUHA_MAKLAI/SHUTTERSTOCK ©; MIN C. CHIU/SHUTTERSTOCK ©

Three Days to Travel Around

- Three days is the sweet spot for a visit to Gold Country. You can fully enjoy essential Auburn sights, the state historic park and Placerville. And you can also venture along the must-see portions of Hwy 49 north and south. The north includes the preserved treasure that is **Nevada City** (p555), where you can stroll the wonderful town center and hike into the countryside.

- The south section of Hwy 49 gives you a rapid-fire succession of charmers, including **Sutter Creek** (p553), **Angels Camp** (p563), **Columbia** (p562), **Sonora** (p559) and **Jamestown** (p562). Cozy **Murphys** (p563) is the briefest of detours. Fill your days with wine-tasting and frolic.

If You Have More Time

- Take the many fascinating detours off Hwy 49. Tiny **Volcano** (p554) and the meaningful **Indian Grinding Rock State Historic Park** (p554) are on one of the best back roads into the Sierras. Venture north to remote **Downieville** (p558) and **Sierra City** (p558) for alpine action. Stop off at engrossing **Malakoff Diggins State Historic Park** (p558).

- Go **white-water rafting** (p552) on the American River. Wander sinuous country roads to taste wine in **Amador County** (p553) and **pick apples** (p552) east of Placerville. Spend a night in the historic small towns of Nevada City, Sutter Creek, Murphys and Columbia and soak up the timeless vibe.

JULY

Amador County stages its huge **county fair** in Plymouth. Like other Gold County counties, it celebrates food, wine, flowers and more.

AUGUST

The Sierra foothills are hot and you'll find **music festivals** across Gold County, most with a country-and-western or rock theme.

OCTOBER

Amador County vineyards host the three-day **Big Crush Harvest Festival**, featuring special wines, food and music.

DECEMBER

Postcard-perfect **Nevada City** becomes a Christmas card of joyous events each Sunday before December 25.

AUBURN

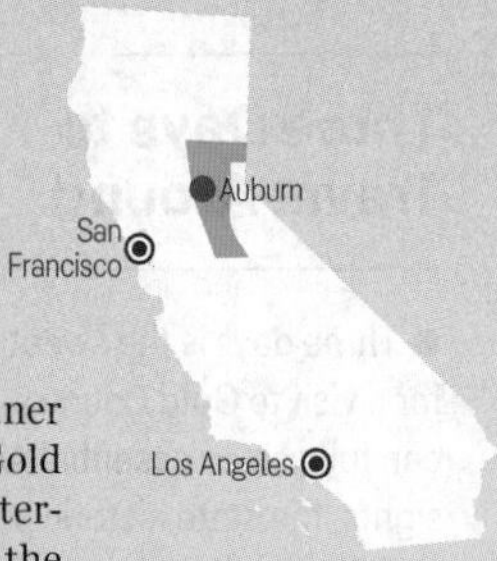

Look for the big man: a 45-ton effigy of French gold panner Claude Chana marks your arrival in Placer County's Gold Country. Its hallmarks are all here – ice-cream shops, interesting historic districts and antiques. A major stop on the Central Pacific's transcontinental route, the Union Pacific's busy main line still looms over old Auburn.

At the town's center, and an icon for those whizzing by on I-80, the domed 1898 Placer County Courthouse neatly straddles Auburn's two main areas: the restored and somewhat kitschy Old Town to the southwest and the charming and commercial Historic Downtown to the northeast. As the county seat, Auburn was able to prosper even as other early gold rush towns vanished. Today, it's a popular stop for those driving I-80 between the Bay Area and the Sierras.

Los Angeles

TOP TIP

The Historic Downtown is great for browsing amid cafes and popular local restaurants. Stop into the Chamber of Commerce for oodles of area info and pick from busy breakfast spots. Auburn Alehouse anchors Old Town and brews its own fine beer, which goes well with its good, casual eats.

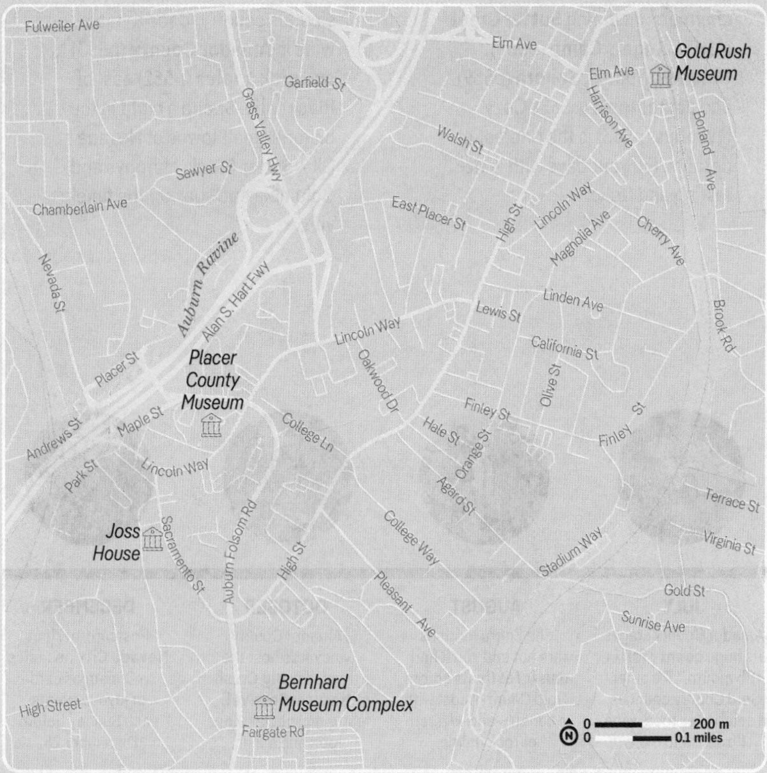

MARK MILLER PHOTOS/AGEFOTOSTOCK/ALAMY ©

Placer County Museum

Touring Gold Country History

RICH HISTORY AND MUSEUMS

Stroll the Old Town for buildings dating from the 1850s. On the south side, the **Bernhard Museum Complex**, built in 1851 as the Traveler's Rest Hotel and later serving as the home of the Bernhard family, exhibits depictions of typical 19th-century farm life. Volunteers in period garb show you around.

Built by the Yue family in the 1920s, the clapboard **Joss House** stands on 'Chinese Hill,' one of many Chinese communities established during the gold rush. After a 'mysterious' fire ripped through the settlement, the family converted their home into a public space for worship, seasonal boarders and a school.

The 1st floor of the historic courthouse is home to the **Placer County Museum**. It has Native American artifacts and an 1877 stage coach. Don't miss the museum's gold collection, which features huge chunks of unrefined gold.

Up in the Historic Downtown in the old Auburn train station, the **Gold Rush Museum** includes a reconstructed mine and gold panning, both great for kids.

Venture a short distance south along Hwy 49 for a deeper taste of Gold Country, including the site where gold was discovered.

OUTDOOR ACTION

The fact that Auburn is sometimes called the 'Endurance Sport Capital of the World' will give you a sense of how good the area is for cycling, trail running and other heart-pounding activities.

Much of the action is centered on Auburn State Recreation Area. A park of deep gorges, it's cut by the rushing waters of the North and Middle Forks of the American River, which converge beneath a bridge on Hwy 49, 4 miles south of town. In early spring, this is immensely popular for white-water rafting, with class II to class V runs. In late summer, calmer waters allow for sunning and swimming, especially around the confluence. Numerous trails are shared by hikers, mountain bikers and horses.

GETTING AROUND

Auburn is the public transit gateway to Gold Country. Amtrak runs one train daily on the Capital Corridor route to Sacramento and on to the Bay Area. The *California Zephyr* stops on its daily run between the Bay Area and Chicago via Truckee, Reno and Denver. Amtrak Thruway buses provide additional service to Sacramento and Reno.

Local buses link Auburn to Neva da City and Grass Valley on weekdays.

Beyond Auburn

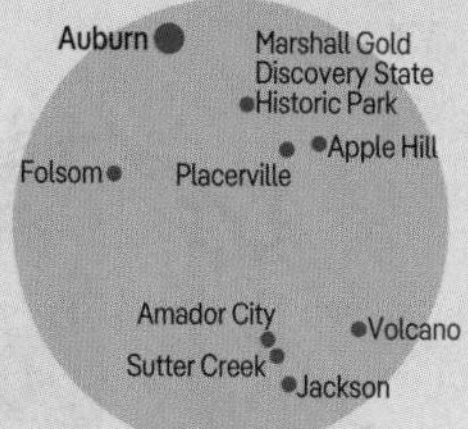

The spine of Gold Country, Hwy 49, winds through the hills, linking towns redolent with an 1850s appeal.

In the heart of the pine- and oak-covered Sierra foothills, this is where gold was first discovered – Spanish-speaking settlers named it El Dorado County after the mythical city of riches.

Today, visitors discover evocative rolling hillsides dotted with historic towns, sun-soaked terraces and the fertile soil of one of California's burgeoning wine-growing regions. This central part of Gold Country comprises some of its most compelling sights – and that's after you've spent a few engrossing hours at the very place where a glint of gold caught James Marshall's eye in 1848. Surprises abound, including an amazing Indian site that's thousands of years old.

TOP TIP

This is the most visited portion of Gold Country. Travel here midweek if possible to avoid weekend crowds and prices.

Marshall Gold Discovery State Historic Park

LARA RED/SHUTTERSTOCK ©

Where the Gold Rush Began

CONTEMPLATE THE PAST

The **Marshall Gold Discovery State Historic Park** comprises a fascinating collection of buildings in a bucolic riverside setting at the site of James Marshall's discovery. Compared to the stampede of gun-toting, hill-blasting, hell-raising settlers that populate tall tales along Hwy 49, the park is a place of relative tranquility. It's a half-hour drive southeast of Auburn.

Recent investments have given the site much-improved signage. The museum provides background on the discovery, and also tells the stories of some of the forgotten early settlers here, such as a group of African-American former enslaved peoples.

There's a fascinating replica of **Sutter's Mill**, which (figuratively) put the wheels in motion that led to finding gold. Follow a short path along the south fork of the American River to the place where James Marshall made his fateful discovery and started the revolutionary birth of the 'Golden State,' with its horrific consequences for the state's indigenous peoples.

Check out the displays on panning and hydraulic mining, along with the 1860 **Wah Hop Chinese Store**. The village of Coloma is barely there, although you can get refreshments in summer. Fittingly, you can try your hand at gold panning.

ALL THAT GLITTERS IS TRAGIC

John Sutter, who had a fort in Sacramento (p527), partnered with James Marshall to build a sawmill on the swift stretch of the American River at Coloma in 1847. It was Marshall who discovered gold here on January 24, 1848, and though the men tried to keep their findings secret, prospectors from around the world stampeded into town.

In one of the ironies of the gold rush, the men who made this discovery died nearly penniless. Many of the new immigrants who arrived seeking fortune were indentured, taxed and bamboozled out of anything they found. Meanwhile, the world of the local Native American Nisenan people was collapsing due to disease and displacement.

Monumental Hikes

WALKING GOLD COUNTRY HILLS

The **James Marshall Monument** marks the spot where the man was buried in 1885, a penniless ward of the state. You can drive a short road here, but it's much better to meander on foot up to the monument, which overlooks the discovery site.

A 3-mile **hike** follows a steep route up from Coloma. Take High St from the town center, then Marshall Park Way, winding through oak woodland to the monument, via James Marshall's barebones cabin and an 1865 Catholic church and pioneer cemetery. You then join the **Monroe Ridge Trail**, which leads along the ridge, looping back down into Coloma.

For a hike that honors the legacy of the many Chinese miners and laborers, hit the 2.5-mile **Gam Saan Trail** that links the discovery site with **Hennigsen Lotus Park**, a small riverfront park built on the site of Chinese mining camps.

Compelling Placerville

THE OLD WEST COMES ALIVE

Pronounced PLASS-er-ville, local wags cherish its wild reputation as 'Hangtown' – a name earned when a handful of men swung from the gallows in the mid-1800s. It's a compelling and

WHERE TO EAT AND DRINK BEYOND AUBURN

Farm to Fork Cafe
The name sums up the foodie philosophy at this new-agey cafe in Coloma. $

Pies of the World
Tiny spot on Placerville's Main St, serving delicious and savory pies. A top lunch stop. $

Heyday Café
Local ingredients and creative cuisine keep visitors happy in the heart of old Placerville. $$

RAFTING THE AMERICAN RIVER

Coloma-Lotus Valley surrounds Sutter's Mill. It's a great launching pad for rafting adventures. The South Fork of the American River gets the most traffic, since it features exciting rapids but is still manageable. Adrenaline junkies who have never rafted before should try the Middle Fork.

Half-day rafting trips usually begin at Chili Bar and end close to the Marshall Gold Discovery State Historic Park (p551). Full-day trips put in at the Coloma Bridge and take out at Salmon Falls, near Folsom Lake. The half-day options start in class III rapids and are action-packed (full-day trips start out slowly, then build up to class IV as a climax). The season usually runs from May to mid-October, depending on water levels.

atmospheric little place to explore while traveling on Hwys 49 and 50. It's a lovely hour-long drive southeast of Auburn.

Busy **Main St** may look like a movie set, but it's lined with stores catering to local needs, which saves Placerville from sugary artificiality. Most of the buildings date from the 1850s, including the spindly **Bell Tower**, a relic that once rallied volunteer firefighters. About 1 mile north of town, **Hangtown's Gold Bug Park & Mine** stands on the site of four mining claims that yielded gold from 1849 to 1888. You can descend into the mine on a self-guided audio tour.

Save your sweet tooth for **Annabelle's**, a fantastic chocolate shop (with wine tasting!) in El Dorado, 5 miles southwest of Placerville.

Bounties of Farms & Vineyards

RIPE EXPLORATION IN APPLE HILL

Bountiful Apple Hill, a 20-sq-mile area east of Placerville and north of Hwy 50, has more than 50 orchards, farms and wineries. Growers sell directly to the public, usually from August to December, and some let you pick your own; bakeries offer all manner of apple treats. Plan on 90 minutes' driving to get here from Auburn.

Get a Charge Out of Folsom

FOLLOW IN THE FOOTSTEPS OF JOHNNY CASH

The town that became Folsom began – like so many others – during the early days of the gold rush. Its position on the American River proved fortuitous as early dams spurred developments like the state's first commercial electrical generation, an accomplishment preserved at the Power House Museum and State Park. The 19th-century downtown is a walkable delight. Just upstream, **Folsom State Prison** is the place Johnny Cash immortalized in 'Folsom Prison Blues.' It's an easy 30-minute drive southwest from Auburn.

Vintage Shops & Back Road Walks

GOLD-DUSTED AMADOR CITY

Blissfully located off Hwy 49, Amador City was once home to the Keystone Mine – one of the most prolific gold producers in California – but after the mine closed in 1942, the town lay deserted. In the 1950s, a family bought the dilapidated buildings and converted them into antique shops – a harbinger of things to come for the region. The narrow back roads east of here are ideal for idyllic countryside walks. Getting here from Auburn is a one-hour drive south.

WHERE TO EAT AND DRINK BEYOND AUBURN

Taste
Offers a list of top regional wines paired with creative California cuisine in Plymouth. $$

Sina's Backroads Café
Popular Sutter Creek retro cafe noted for filling and tasty breakfasts, and locally roasted coffee. $

Sutter Creek Provisions
Huge array of local wines and brews, serving a changing, mostly vegetarian menu. Get your picnic here. $$

VENEMAMA/GETTY IMAGES ©

Bell Tower, Placerville

Perfectly Preserved Sutter Creek

ICONIC GOLD RUSH TOWN

Perch on the balcony of one of the gracefully restored buildings on this particularly scenic Main St and view Sutter Creek, a gem of a Gold Country town with raised arcade sidewalks and high-balconied buildings with false fronts.

Get a town walking-tour map from the excellent visitors center and begin exploring the 1860s buildings, many bearing traces of the homelands of the Cornish, Yugoslavian and Italian immigrants who built them. **Miners Bend Park** at the town's south end offers history in the open air. There are many good food and lodging options, and a dozen wine tasting rooms let you try wines from the region. Follow Hwy 49 for almost 90 minutes to get here from Auburn.

An Undiscovered Mine

GET OFF THE BEATEN PATH

Jackson has historic buildings and a small downtown, but it feels more functional than alluring. The main attraction is the **Kennedy Gold Mine**. The ominous steel headframe is 125ft high and the shafts date from 1860. Guided tours take you around the site.

GOLD COUNTRY WINE TASTING

Carpeting the beautiful rolling hills of Gold Country, you'll find scores of vineyards amid the gnarled oaks. Most of the old towns along Hwy 49 have several bars and shops where you can taste (and buy) the local vintages.

Amador County has a thriving circuit of family wineries that have not a whiff of pretension about them (unlike Napa, there are no rapacious charges for tastings here). The county itself lays claim to the US's oldest zinfandel vines – vintages are bold, richly colored, earthy and constantly surprising. Many wineries line Shenandoah Rd, while Sutter Creek is good for tasting rooms. El Dorado County, Placerville and the Sonora region (p563) are also prime spots for wine tasting.

Volcano Union Inn
Vintage hotel with the best restaurant in the Volcano area. Creative, seasonal food. $$

Mel & Faye's Diner
Retro Jackson diner with a modern verve. Great versions of all the classics from breakfast to dinner. $

Liar's Bench
Timeless boozer under a neon martini sign in Placerville; a top stop when you're weary of wine.

Sutter Creek's Main St (p553)

The somewhat undiscovered settlement of **Mokelumne Hill** is 7 miles south of Jackson. Settled by French trappers in the early 1840s, it's a good place to see historic buildings without a glut of antique stores and gift shops. Driving here from Auburn takes about 90 minutes, but plan on many stops along the way.

Sleepy Hamlet with Time-Traveling Shop

LONELY VOLCANO

One of the fading plaques in Volcano, 12 miles upstream from the town of Sutter Creek, tellingly calls it a place of 'quiet history.' Even though the little L-shaped village on the bank of Sutter Creek yielded tons of gold and a Civil War battle, today it slumbers away in remote solitude. It exudes an end-of-the-road vibe, even if the road eventually joins Hwy 88 in the Sierras. Wending your way here from Auburn can take almost two hours.

Little Sutter Creek is lined here with large sandstone rocks that were blasted from surrounding hills by hydraulic mining before being scraped clean of their gold.

In continuous use since 1852, the fantastically atmospheric **Country Store** has creaky floorboards and a long wooden counter. You can get a simple burger and a beer you select from the cooler.

NATIVE HERITAGE

Indian Grinding Rock State Historic Park is a sacred area for the local Miwok. The awe-inspiring centerpiece is a limestone outcrop covered with 360 faint petroglyphs – some over 2000 years old – and more than 1100 ancient mortar holes called *chaw'se,* used for grinding acorns and seeds into meal.

There's a small museum, a traditional wooden roundhouse and a village site. Miwok continue to hold ceremonies here featuring crafts, dances and games. Look for the display of elaborate feathered dance capes.

Trails weave through the park with signs describing the plants and animals and their significance to the Miwok. The park is in a lonely patch of forest on the road to the equally lonely town of Volcano.

GETTING AROUND

Amtrak runs Thruway buses that stop in Placerville on their route between Sacramento and Lake Tahoe via Hwy 50. Otherwise, the only way to easily travel through the region is with your own wheels.

NEVADA CITY

Nevada City has a an abundance of charm, but it doesn't like to brag. The main attraction is the town itself: its restored buildings, all brick and wrought-iron, wear their past proudly, aided by exhaustive histories. The strollable streets are lively in summer, while in December the blanketing snow and twinkling lights are something from a storybook. Signs in windows for readings and meetings reveal the residents' strong progressive streak.

The town is justifiably proud of its rich cultural life. The Miners Foundry (1856) was once an industrial building used to manufacture Pelton water wheels. It's now an eclectic arts center, hosting music, theater, dance and other gigs. The stolid brick Nevada Theatre dates from 1865 and has welcomed the likes of Jack London, Emma Nevada and Mark Twain to its stage. Today it's used for offbeat films and theater. The beloved Onyx Theatre is another haven for unusual film series.

TOP TIP

From Nevada City, a pine-needle-carpeted trail leads to Deer Creek, where the photogenic Angkula Seo Suspension Bridge honors the Nisenan people, the area's original inhabitants. The bridge links to trails back to downtown for a pleasant 3.5-mile loop. Or detour to the Chinese Tribute Bridge further along the creek.

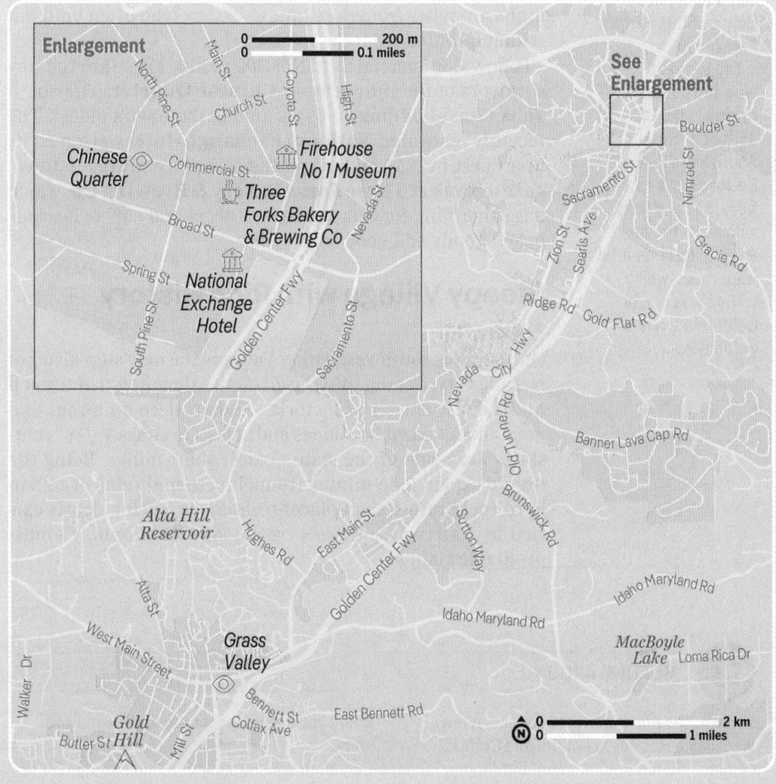

SOUTH YUBA RIVER STATE PARK

Cool off with a dip at **South Yuba River State Park**, which has popular swimming holes and hiking trails. It's beautiful here throughout the year, especially from April to June when the rivers are rushing and the wildflowers are out. The park consists of several units along various stretches of the river. Hiking trails lace the wilderness, and with some effort you can reach Malakoff Diggins State Historic Park (p558).

The **longest wooden covered bridge** in the USA, all 251ft of it, crosses the South Yuba River at Bridgeport. It dates from 1862 and links with many trails. Revel in this beautiful wilderness, which in 1848 was one of California's richest goldfields.

SENATOREK/GETTY IMAGES ©

Yuba River

Gold Country's Star Town

WALKING NEVADA CITY

Start at the **Firehouse No 1 Museum**, which holds a small and carefully curated exhibit in a stately 1861 building. From stunning Nisenan baskets to preserved Victorian bridal wear, its collections tell the story of the local people. The prize exhibits are relics from the Chinese settlers who often built but seldom profited from the mines.

Follow Commercial St to Nos 309 to 316. These are the tiny survivors of the 19th-century **Chinese Quarter**. The South Yuba Canal Building (1855) is among the town's oldest. The recently renovated **National Exchange Hotel** welcomed its first guest in 1854 and is still the best place to stay in town. Take a break at **Three Forks Bakery & Brewing Co**, which has something for everyone: great beers and coffee, luscious baked goods and good sandwiches.

Sleepy Village with Rich History

GRASS VALLEY

Only 4 miles southwest, Grass Valley is the ugly step-sister of Nevada City. But dig into the attractive downtown and you'll find a dense cluster of Victorian and art deco buildings and great independent boutiques and cafes. On Grass Valley's outskirts are some of the state's oldest shaft mines. Being the first to exploit lode-mining (tunneling to find veins of gold in hard rock) rather than placer techniques (sifting debris carried by waterways), these were among Gold Country's most profitable claims.

GETTING AROUND

Local buses provide limited service. A few weekday buses serve Auburn and Colfax, where you can connect to Amtrak buses and trains.

Beyond Nevada City

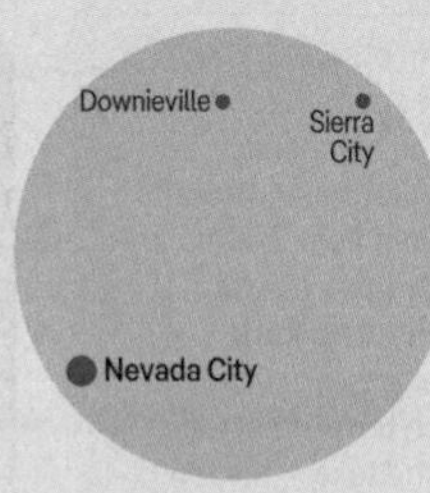

Civilization disappears as you ascend Hwy 49 into the Sierras. The drama of the gold rush is replaced by pure wilderness awe.

The forty-niners hit it big in Nevada County – the richest score in the region known as the Mother Lode. Beyond the resulting wealth you can see written on the facades of Nevada City, you'll find lovely, remote wilderness areas, a clutch of historic parks and fascinating remnants of the long-gone miners, including a ghost town.

The northernmost segment of Hwy 49 follows the North Yuba River through some stunning, isolated parts of the Sierra Nevada, known for great wilderness adventure. An entire lifetime outdoors could hardly cover the trail network that hikers, mountain bikers and skiers blaze every season. In summer, snow remains at the highest elevations and many places have roaring fireplaces year-round.

TOP TIP

Take Hwy 20 east into the Sierras instead of I-80. It's a gorgeous drive and there are many pull-outs to enjoy the view.

Stocking Flat Bridge on the Deer Creek Tribute Trail in Nevada County

DIGGING INTO THE PAST

An otherworldly testament to the mechanical determination of the gold hunt, **Malakoff Diggins State Historic Park** is a place to get lost on fern-lined trails and take in the raw beauty of a landscape recovering from brutal hydraulic mining. There is a mesmerizing ghost town here.

California's largest hydraulic mine left behind massive gold and crimson cliffs and small mountains of tailings. The forestland has recovered since the legal battles between mine owners and downstream farmers shut down the mine in 1884.

Tours of the town provide the chance to see some impressive gold nuggets. The 1-mile **Diggins Loop Trail** is the quickest way to get a glimpse of the scarred moonscape.

BILL FREEMAN/ALAMY ©

Mountain biking in Downieville

Mountain Biking, Monster Hiking

DOWNHILL POWER IN DOWNIEVILLE

Downieville, the biggest town in remote Sierra County (though that's not saying much), is located at the confluence of the North Yuba and Downie rivers. With a reputation that quietly rivals Moab (Utah), this is one of the premier places for **mountain-biking** in the USA, and a staging area for true wilderness adventures. By car, it's a winding one-hour drive from Nevada City.

The **Downieville Downhill**, a world-class mountain biking trail, shoots riders over the Sierra Buttes and a molar-rattling 5000ft down into town. There are plenty of other scenic biking trails to explore, including **Chimney Rock**, **Empire Creek** and **Rattlesnake Creek**.

As with most gold rush towns, it wasn't always fun and games: the first justice of the peace was the local barkeep, and a placard tells the story of the racist mob that hanged a Chicana woman named Josefa on the town bridge in 1851, the only recorded lynching of a woman in California.

Rugged Mountains, Fantastic Fishing

OUTFITTING IN SIERRA CITY

Sierra City is the primary supply station for people headed to the **Sierra Buttes**, a rugged, rocky shock of mountains that are probably the closest thing to the Alps you'll find in California without hoisting a backpack. It's also the last supply point for people headed into the fishing paradise of the **Lakes Basin**. There's just one main drag in town, and all commerce happens here. The hotels often have the best restaurants – when they're open, that is. Wintertime is quiet. Plan on upwards of 90 minutes to drive here from Nevada City.

GETTING AROUND

The only way to get here is with your own vehicle.

SONORA

Settled in 1848 by miners from Sonora, Mexico, this portion of the goldfields was once a cosmopolitan center of commerce and culture, with parks, elaborate saloons and the Southern Mines' largest concentration of gamblers and gold. Racial unrest drove the Mexican settlers out and their European immigrant usurpers got rich on the Big Bonanza Mine, where Sonora High School now stands. That single mine yielded 12 tons of gold in two years (including a 28lb nugget).

Today, people en route to Yosemite National Park or starting the Hwy 49 Gold Country tour from the south use Sonora as a staging post. The historic center is so well preserved that it's a frequent backdrop in films. Washington St is the vintage main drag. Don't miss the 1885 Opera House, which was built on the bones of a flour mill. Local civic boosters built the grand courthouse with its landmark clock tower in 1898.

TOP TIP

Ditch the car in Sonora, which is often clogged with stop-and-go traffic. It's an unpleasant place to be stuck while slow-moving SUVs jockey for one of the few places to parallel park along Washington St/ Hwy 49. One block east, there's a hassle-free lot on Stewart St.

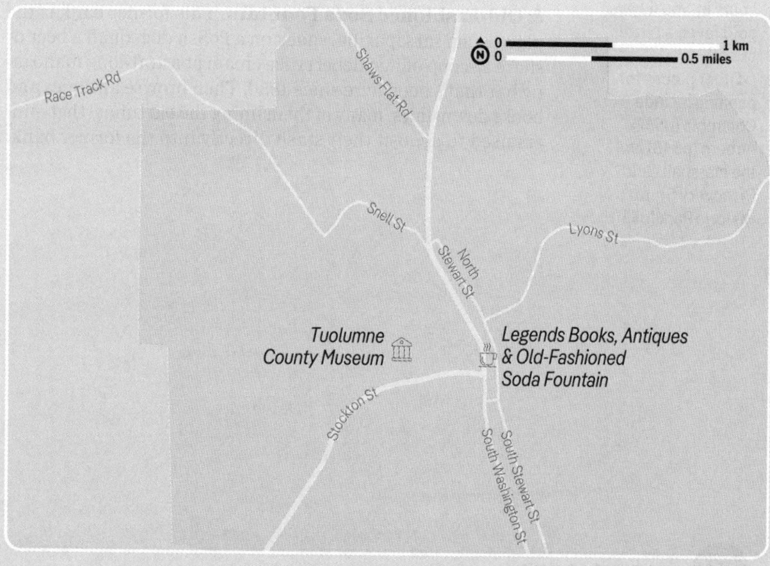

GOLD PANNING

Over 170 years after the gold rush, people still try their luck in the rivers and streams of the Sierras. For some it's a hobby, while for others it becomes an obsession. And there's definitely still gold to be found, although for the weekend prospector, this can take years of bent-back effort.

You can try your luck near Sonora: Miner John and his crew at **California Gold Panning Lessons** provide all needed equipment at Woods Creek and beyond. Be warned, real prospecting involves lots of digging. A couple of hours in, you'll have gold fever, a blister or both.

Other places for panning include Columbia (p562), Auburn (p548) and the Marshall Gold Discovery State Historic Park (p551).

Untold Stories

HISTORIC NUGGETS

In the former 1857 Tuolumne County Jail, you'll find the great little **Tuolumne County Museum**, with a fortune's worth of gold displayed in the form of nuggets and gold-bearing quartz. Each of the former jail cells spotlights a different theme, one of which is the little-told story of African Americans during the gold rush. You can learn about former enslaved man William Suggs, who set up a leather harness business, built a mansion in the town and successfully campaigned to overturn segregation in local schools.

Running the Rapids

READY, SET, PADDLE!

Sonora is a popular white-water rafting base. The **Upper Tuolumne River** is known for class IV and V rapids, while the **Stanislaus River** is more accessible with class III rapids. Family-run **All-Outdoors California Whitewater Rafting** runs tours of all the local rivers, including, ahem, fully immersive ones lasting several days.

Sodas Above, Books Below

BROWSE VINTAGE FINDS

Sonora has cafes and restaurants to rival those across Gold Country, but none compare to **Legends Books, Antiques & Old-Fashioned Soda Fountain**. This former bank is the place to sip sarsaparilla, snack on a Polish dog, quaff a beer or share a scoop of huckleberry ice cream at a 26ft-long mahogany bar that's been here since 1850. Then browse antiques and books downstairs, many of them lining the old tunnel that miners used to deposit their stash directly into the former bank.

GETTING AROUND

There's limited local bus service. However, on certain days in summer, a free shuttle links the sights in Columbia, Sonora and Jamestown.

Yosemite National Park lies 60 scenic miles south on Hwy 120.

Beyond Sonora

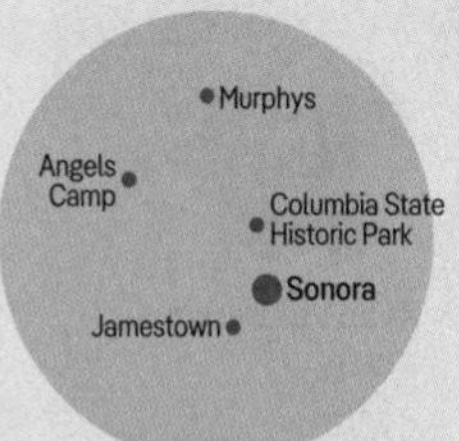

Wine, water and steam are just a few of the highlights in this region, which boasts some of Gold Country's most authentic sights.

The southern region of Gold Country is hot as blazes in the summer, so cruising through its historic gold rush hubs will demand more than one stop for ice cream. The tall tales of yesteryear come alive through one of the region's most famous former residents: author Mark Twain, who got his start writing about a jumping frog contest in Calaveras County.

Cute little Murphys is a popular wine-tasting destination, and tasting rooms line Main St. Columbia preserves – and recreates – an authentic gold rush town in a non-commercial setting. Tiny Jamestown, in the shadow of Sonora, is home to one of the region's most popular sights, Railtown, which is a dream destination for train fans.

TOP TIP

The historic towns in the region feature several old hotels that have been restored: the perfect antidote to the national chains.

Jamestown

TRAVELVIEW/SHUTTERSTOCK ©

WHY I LOVE RAILTOWN

Ryan Ver Berkmoes, writer

Railtown 1897 State Historic Park is the photogenic sister to Sacramento's rail museum (p527). I first went there as a kid, and the thrill has never waned. Once known as the Sierra Railroad, the narrow-gauge track transported ore, lumber and miners. On some weekends and holidays, you can go for a 6-mile ride through the area's beautiful rolling hills, something I heartily recommend. The emerald-green grasses of spring are complemented by golden fields dotted with poppies at other times.

Volunteers show you the roundhouse and restored station, or you can wander on your own. Don't miss steam engine number 3, which has appeared in countless films and TV shows, including *Back to the Future III*, *Unforgiven* and *High Noon*.

GARY CRABBE/ENLIGHTENED IMAGES/ALAMY ©

Ironstone Vineyards

Scrappy Jamestown

LEAVE THE NOISE BEHIND

Diminutive **Jamestown** is just 3 miles south of Sonora. Founded around the time of Tuolumne County's first gold strike in 1848, it has more authenticity than traffic- and tourist-thronged Sonora. Busy Hwy 49 bypasses Jamestown to the west. The usual antique stores fill dusty storefronts in the small center. But it does have two excellent hotels preserved since the 1800s: the **National Hotel** and the **Jamestown Hotel**. And Railtown is a short walk east.

Millions in Gold

PRESERVED GOLD COUNTRY TOWN

More than any other place in Gold Country, **Columbia State Historic Park** blurs the lines between present and past with its carefully preserved gold rush town. In 1850 Columbia was

WHERE TO EAT BEYOND SONORA

Joma's Artisan Ice Cream
Makes small batches of creamy treats, many with seasonal fruit. In Murphys. **$**

Grounds
This casually elegant Muphys cafe serves superb breakfasts, good lunches and weekend dinners. **$$**

Service Station
This good American cafe in Jamestown has a big patio, good selection of beer and local wine. **$**

founded as the 'Gem of the Southern Mines,' and as much as $150 million in gold was found here. The center of Columbia (which comprises the preserved state park) looks much as it did in its heyday. It's only 10 minutes by car north from Sonora.

The blacksmith's shop, theater, hotels and saloon are all carefully framed windows into California's past. The yesteryear illusion of Main St is shaken by only a smidgen of commercialization. Diversions include gold panning, stagecoach rides and breezy picnic spots. The restored **City Hotel** is a good place to stay and means you can wander the streets after the throngs are gone.

Prospect for Adventure

ABOVE OR BELOW GROUND

Murphys is one of the more scenic communities along the southern stretch of Gold Country, befitting its nickname as 'Queen of the Sierra.' Its location 8 miles east of Hwy 49 (30 minutes from Sonora) gives it an appealing end-of-the-road quality. Wine bars and upscale pubs good for a pint abound – many, predictably, with Murphy's in the name and shamrocks on the wall. In a solid 1856 brick storefront, **Pop the Bubbly** has a name that says all you need to know. Good local wines include those from **Ironstone Vineyards** and **Newsome-Harlow**.

For kids and adults who like a sense of adventure with their cave tour, **Mercer Caverns** obliges. You'll walk a quarter of a mile on 440 twisting steps through the spectacular caverns. Think of it as a self-propelled thrill ride.

Hop Through Angels Camp

GO ON, KISS THE FROG

On the southern stretch of Hwy 49, one figure looms over all others: literary giant Mark Twain, who got his first big break with the short story *The Celebrated Jumping Frog of Calaveras County* (1865). It was written and set in Angels Camp, and they make the most of it. There are gentlemanly Twain impersonators and statues, and bronze frogs on Main St honoring jumping contest champions of the past many decades. Today, the town is an attractive mix of buildings, but does suffer from traffic on Hwys 4 and 49. It's barely 30 minutes drive northwest from Sonora.

GOLD COUNTRY'S BIGGEST TREES

In the forests above the foothills of Gold Country, few big trees survived the widespread logging that occurred during the gold rush. One place you can still see old-growth magnificence, however, is at **Calaveras Big Trees State Park**.

Home to giant sequoia trees that reach as high as 250ft with trunks that are over 25ft in diameter, these leftovers from the Mesozoic era are thought to weigh upwards of 2000 tons. The giants are distributed in two large groves, one easily seen on the **North Grove Trail**, a 1.5-mile self-guided loop, near the park entrance. On the more remote **South Grove Trail**, it's a 5-mile round-trip hike to Agassiz Tree, the park's largest specimen.

GETTING AROUND

There's limited local bus service in southern Gold Country. On certain days in summer, a free shuttle links the sights in Columbia, Sonora and Jamestown. There are also summer buses from Jamestown and Sonora to Yosemite, 60 scenic miles south.

LAKE TAHOE

BEACHES, SKIING, MOUNTAINS AND CASINOS

Shimmering in myriad shades of blue and green, the USA's largest alpine lake beckons with beaches, water sports and hikes in summer, and world-class skiing in winter.

Straddling the California–Nevada state line, Lake Tahoe sits at 6245ft and is one of the highest-elevation lakes in the country. Driving around the 72-mile shoreline is a spellbinding adventure, with curves, viewpoints and trails galore.

The lake was formed a mere 25 million years ago when the surrounding mountains were created through uplift and the region where the lake now lies sank between two fault lines. Mt Pluto in the north ejected lava that created a natural dam, allowing water to remain and continue to rise – today it's the second-deepest lake in the USA. Glaciers went on to carve the valleys and inlets where you'll find bodies of water like lovely Emerald Bay and Fallen Leaf Lake.

The first people in the region, the Washoe, arrived over 10,000 years ago, trapping, hunting and fishing the rich terrain. The modern-day word Tahoe was derived from a mispronunciation of their phrase *Da ow a ga,* which means 'edge of the lake.'

It wasn't until the 1860s – during the mining of silver in the Comstock Lode in nearby Nevada City – that Tahoe became a center of trade, using the nearby Central Pacific Railroad, and the forest was widely cut to help build mine shafts.

Today, the brilliant-blue lake, its reforested shores and its encircling horned peaks counts among California's premier year-round nature destinations.

BX PHOTOGRAPHY/GETTY IMAGES ©

THE MAIN AREAS

SOUTH LAKE TAHOE & STATELINE
Buzzing casino central. **p570**

TAHOE CITY
Hub for idyllic western shore. **p579**

NORTHERN SHORE
Laid-back lakeside charm. **p584**

TRUCKEE
Historic foodie town replete with skiing options. **p589**

NKNEIDLPHOTO/SHUTTERSTOCK ©

Left: Truckee (p589); Above: Lake Tahoe

Find Your Way

Lake Tahoe is a majestic mountain jewel surrounded by ski runs, hiking trails, forests and unique settlements. Each part of the 72-mile shoreline offers a chance to experience the Sierra dream your way.

Truckee, p589

In recent years, this former ski bum's Old West hangout has burgeoned into a gourmet hot spot amid myriad ski resorts and the adventure activities of nearby Donner Lake.

Tahoe City, p579

The lake's western shore radiates out from small Tahoe City, an unspoiled series of state parks, calm coves and pristine ski runs.

Northern Shore, p584

Home to cool cats and the upper crust alike; development is more understated and amenities rich, with beautiful beaches to boot.

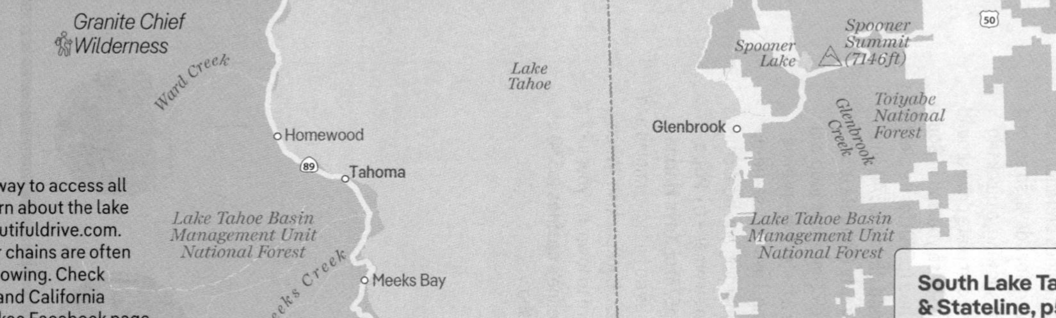

CAR

Driving is the easiest way to access all that Tahoe offers. Learn about the lake loop drive at mostbeautifuldrive.com. In winter, snow tires or chains are often required if it's been snowing. Check Caltrans (dot.ca.gov) and California Highway Patrol – Truckee Facebook page (facebook.com/chp.truckee) for current requirements.

BUS

Once you're at Tahoe, save the hassle of parking with free local buses and shuttles. Tahoe Transportation District serves the south shore, and bike-rack-equipped Tahoe Area Rapid Transit serves the north and some of the west. During ski season, most resorts run free shuttles to the mountains.

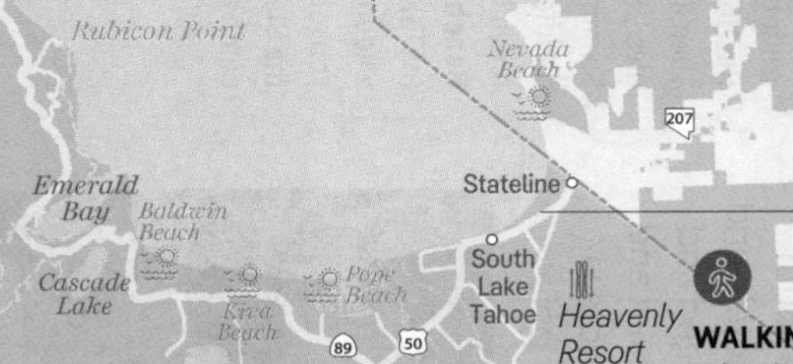

South Lake Tahoe & Stateline, p570

Dive deep into casino life and the busy epicenter of Tahoe's most developed shore, where marinas, ski resorts and slot machines vie for your attention.

WALKING

Tahoe is a hiker's paradise. With proper preparation anyone can find a trail to meet their needs, from ADA-accessible to backcountry technical. Check locally to learn the state of the trails, double-check you've brought everything you need to be safe and always hike within your abilities.

Plan Your Time

Lakeside life changes as you circulate. Generally, the south shore is bustling with motels and casinos, the west is rugged and old-timey, the north is quiet and upscale, and the east shore is undeveloped. Pick your poison.

ASIF ISLAM/SHUTTERSTOCK ©

Activities at Lake Tahoe

Pressed for Time

- The sun shines on Tahoe three out of every four days, so as long as it's not snowing, a quick trip calls for a complete drive around its shores. Base yourself in **South Lake Tahoe** (p570) for its plentiful **wining and dining** (p574) and the **Heavenly Gondola** (p572). Then, the 72-mile lake loop will give you a taste of everything. Swimming, kayaking, stand-up paddleboarding and boat cruises prevail in summer – try **Pope Beach** (p573) or **Keys Marina** (p573) – as do hiking, camping and wilderness backpacking. When you return to town, try your luck at the Stateline's **casinos** (p574) or catch a show.

Seasonal Highlights

Summer is beach time, with warm days and mild nights. Winter is snowy and mountain passes can close in storms. Fall and spring have moderate temperatures.

MARCH

WinterWonderGrass is a great little festival of bluegrass and acoustic roots music, where the stage is encircled by the snow. **Snowfest** lights up North Lake Tahoe.

APRIL

Snow thaw begins (great waterfalls!) but not many trails or resorts are open for summer. Heavenly Village hosts a huge **Easter Egg Hunt**.

JUNE

Beach season kicks off and wildflowers bloom, while **hiking** and mountain-biking trails are clear for use.

COREY RICH/AURORA OPEN RF/CAVAN IMAGES/ALAMY ©; GEORGE ROSE/GETTY IMAGES ©; PHOTOGRAPHYBY_JENNY/SHUTTERSTOCK ©

Three Days to Travel Around

- If staying longer, you'll actually have time to hike the **Rubicon Trail** (p576) to **Emerald Bay** (p576). Then, sun yourself before kayaking to **Fannette Island** (p576). Grab lunch in **Tahoe City** (p579), lakeside at **Tahoe National Brewing Company** (p581) or at one of the many cafes. Head up to **Truckee** (p589) and the **Donner Lake** (p591) area for mountain biking or water sports, before a night out in Truckee bar-hopping and fine dining.

- If it's winter, you'll replace hiking with snowshoeing and mountain biking with skiing at resorts like the enormous **Palisades Tahoe** (p593), with its thronging Olympic Valley and its chiller Alpine Meadows.

If You Have More Time

- With even more time, slow your roll and stay longer at each spot you visit around the lake. Swim like royalty at **Kings Beach** (p586) before hiking the **Mt Rose Wilderness** (p586) or the **East Shore Trail** (p586). Or go horseback riding or paddleboating at **Zephyr Cove** (p578). If you're a gambler, hunker down at **Stateside's casinos** (p574).

- During winter, take the **Heavenly Gondola** (p572) and ski the famed resort, or ski and board further afield at **Kirkwood** (p576), **Northstar** (p591) and **Boreal** (p589). Cross-country ski at **Royal Gorge** (p591) or take the tykes tubing at **Hansen's Resort** (p573) or **Soda Springs** (p589).

JULY

Valhalla Art, Music & Theatre Festival is a summerlong cultural bonanza of music and theater held at a 1930s Nordic style hall.

AUGUST

Lake Tahoe Shakespeare Festival (p588) starts in July and continues into August, with outdoor performances staged lakeside.

SEPTEMBER

Cooler temperatures, colorful foliage and fewer tourists after Labor Day make it a favorite for **low-key hikers**.

DECEMBER

Snow sports boom at resorts around the lake, but storms can bring hazardous roads requiring vigilance and planning.

SOUTH LAKE TAHOE & STATELINE

South Lake Tahoe & Stateline
San Francisco
Los Angeles

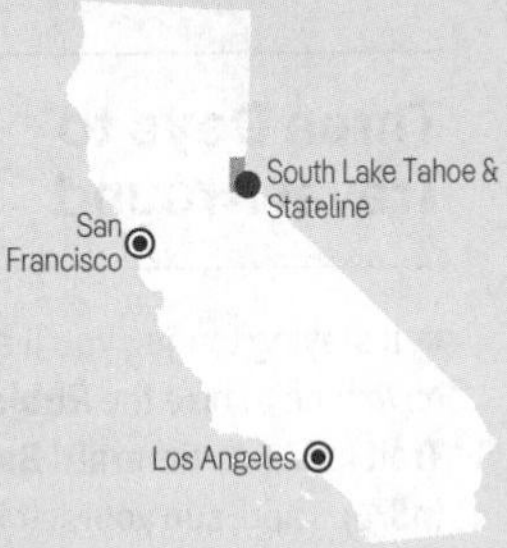

South Lake Tahoe is a chockablock commercial strip bordering the lake, framed by picture-perfect alpine mountains. It sits at the foot of the world-class Heavenly mountain resort, and buzzes from the gambling tables in the large casinos just across the border in Stateline, Nevada. Lake Tahoe's south shore draws visitors with a cornucopia of activities, lodging and eating options, especially for summer beach access and powdery winter snow.

South Lake Tahoe's main east–west thoroughfare is a 5-mile stretch of Hwy 50 called Lake Tahoe Blvd. Most hotels and businesses hover around the state line and Heavenly Village. The siren song of blackjack and slot machines calls the masses to the casinos containing hotels, restaurants, live entertainment and bars.

During busy times, this hub of activity gets highly congested. Although arguably it's overdeveloped, density is lower away from the casinos, with the thick blanket of trees hiding much of the excess.

TOP TIP

Hotels, resorts and vacation apartments abound, and casinos offer basic cheap lodging. Stay as close to the lake as possible to allow for car-free outings. Try to avoid accommodations on busy Hwys 50 and 89. In winter, Stateline lodging is convenient for the Heavenly Gondola up to the resort.

Hot-air balloon over Lake Tahoe

LEFT: DREWTHEHOBBIT/SHUTTERSTOCK ©; RIGHT: PIERRE WILLIOT/SHUTTERSTOCK ©

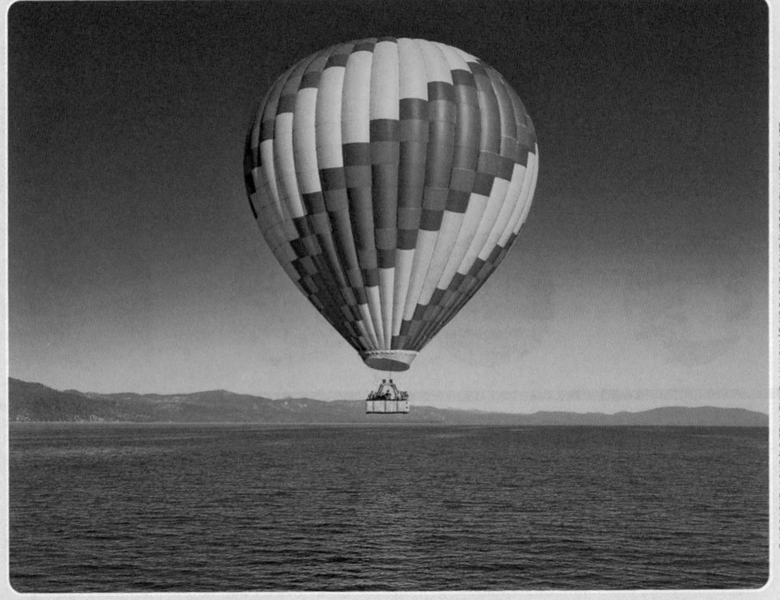

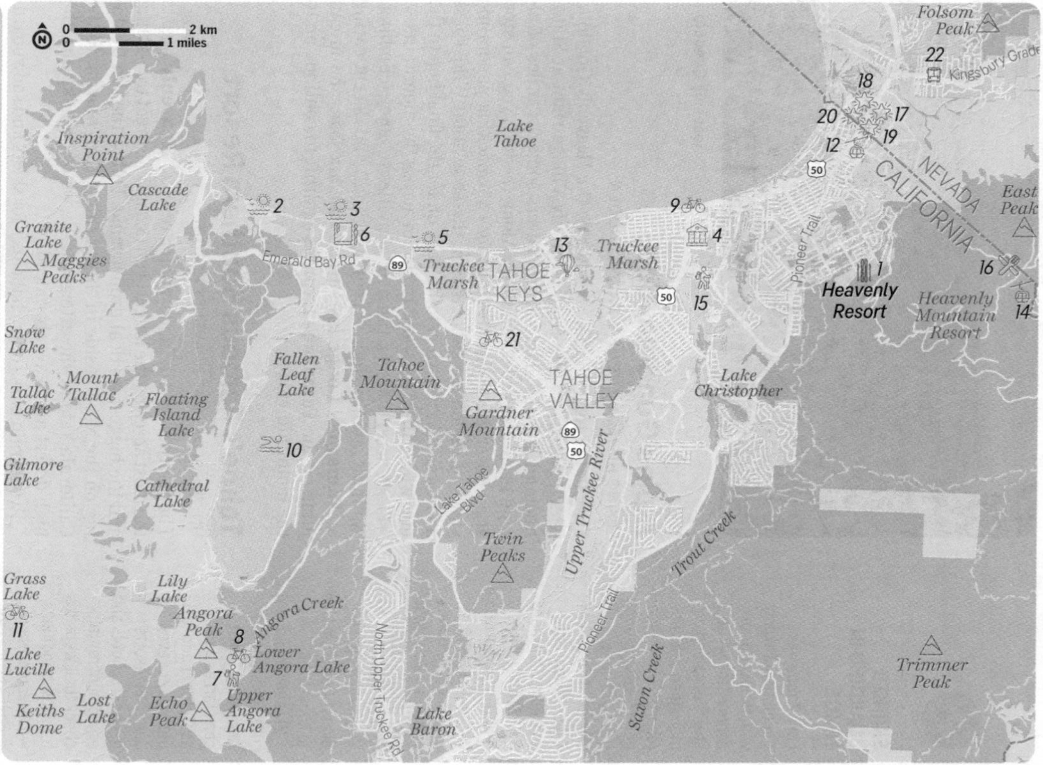

HIGHLIGHTS
1 Heavenly Resort

SIGHTS
2 Baldwin Beach
3 Kiva Beach
4 Lake Tahoe Historical Society Museum
5 Pope Beach
6 Tallac Historic Site

ACTIVITIES, COURSES & TOURS
7 Angora Lakes
8 Angora Lakes Trail
9 El Dorado Beach
10 Fallen Leaf Lake
11 Grass Lake
12 Heavenly Gondola
13 Lake Tahoe Balloons
14 Tamarack Express
15 USFS Taylor Creek Visitor Center

EATING
16 Tamarack Lodge

ENTERTAINMENT
17 Bally's Lake Tahoe
18 Hard Rock Hotel Lake Tahoe
19 Harrah's
20 Harvey's

TRANSPORT
21 Anderson's Bike Rental
22 Wanna Ride

Angora Lakes (p573)

PIERRE WILLIOT/SHUTTERSTOCK ©

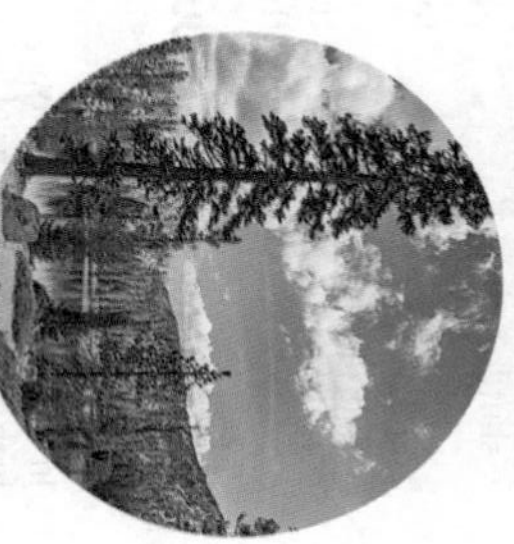

SKIING & BOARDING IN TAHOE

Lake Tahoe has phenomenal skiing, with thousands of acres of the white stuff beckoning at more than a dozen resorts. Winter-sports complexes include the giant, jet-set slopes of South Lake Tahoe's Heavenly, as well as Palisades (p593) and Northstar (p591) in the north. No less enticing are the insider playgrounds like Sugar Bowl (p589) and Homewood (p583). Tahoe simply has a hill for everybody, from kids to kamikazes.

Ski season generally runs November to April, although it can start as early as October and last until May or even June. All resorts have ski schools and equipment rental; check their websites for snow conditions, weather reports and free ski-season shuttle buses.

Look for info and discounts at skilaketahoe.com.

GG5795/SHUTTERSTOCK ©

Heavenly Gondola

Alpine Gondola Ride

FLYING HIGH ON THE HEAVENLY GONDOLA

Soar to the top of Tahoe as you ride the Heavenly Gondola, which sweeps you up from Heavenly Village right at Stateline and Hwy 50. The journey covers some 2.4 miles of alpine beauty in just 12 minutes. Along the way, you can stop at an observation deck (9123ft) for gobsmacking panoramic views of the entire Tahoe Basin, the Desolation Wilderness and Carson Valley, then jump back on for the final hop to the top, where lifts, runs and trails fan across the mountains.

From here, there's a range of activities to enjoy (climbing, ziplining, tubing and, of course, skiing!) and decent eating at **Tamarack Lodge** restaurant, cafe and bar; or you can jump on the **Tamarack Express** chairlift to continue up to the mountain ridge.

Tahoe's Famous Southern Resort

HIT THE SLOPES AT HEAVENLY RESORT

The 'mother' of all Tahoe winter resorts, **Heavenly** boasts the most acreage, the longest run (5.5 miles), great tree-skiing and the biggest vertical drop around. Follow the sun by skiing on the Nevada side in the morning, then moving to the California side in the afternoon. Views of the lake and the high desert are heavenly indeed.

Two terrain parks offer challenges for skiers and snowboarders of all skill levels. Stats: 28 lifts, 3500 vertical feet, 97 runs. Even if you're not skiing, you can get a solid taste of this winter wonderland by riding the Heavenly Gondola.

In summer, the gondola is also the way to access miles of trails such as the **Skyline Hiking Trail**, which has top-of-the-world views across two states.

WHERE TO EAT IN SOUTH LAKE TAHOE

Himmel Haus
In the forest near Heavenly, with a huge deck, steins of German beer and schnitzels. **$$**

Cafe Fiore
Upscale Italian without pretension, this tiny romantic eatery has an award-winning 300-vintage wine list. **$$$**

Sprouts
Energetic, mostly organic cafe that gets kudos for its juices, smoothies, rice bowls, burrito wraps and salads. **$**

Hit the Beaches

GENTLE GOLDEN LAKESIDE SANDS

In South Lake Tahoe, the grandest strands beckon – **Pope Beach**, **Kiva Beach** and **Baldwin Beach** – each with picnic tables and barbecue grills. Find them all along Emerald Bay Rd (Hwy 89). Just south, **Fallen Leaf Lake**, where scenes from the Hollywood flicks *The Bodyguard* and *City of Angels* were filmed, is also a favorite for summer swims.

Get your *brrrrr* ready. The clear waters of Lake Tahoe are brisk, if not frozen, for much of the year. Peak temperatures in late summer might reach 70°F (21°C) near shore.

Lake Boating, Water Sports & Balloons

TAKE TO THE LAKE'S BLUE WATER

Outside winter, Lake Tahoe's famous blue water awaits your exploration. You can rent powerboats, pontoon boats, sailboats and Jet Skis, as well as human-powered kayaks, canoes, paddleboats, stand-up paddleboards (SUPs) and more. Marinas with rentals dot the south shore, and Keys Marina even hosts **Lake Tahoe Balloons** if you want to reach 10,000ft for breathtaking views of the lake and the Sierra Nevada.

Guided kayak trips venture into the lake's nooks and crannies. Otherwise, you can go for a sightseeing cruise on boats big and small, fast and slow.

Hiking Galore

TRAILS FOR EVERY LEVEL

At Tahoe you are always near a great hike. Several easy ones begin near the **USFS Taylor Creek Visitor Center** off Hwy 89. The mile-long, mostly flat **Rainbow Trail** loops around a creek-side meadow. The gentle, rolling 1-mile **Moraine Trail** follows the shoreline of **Fallen Leaf Lake**. Up at cooler elevations, the mile-long round trip to **Angora Lakes** is another family-friendly trek.

For longer and more strenuous day hikes to alpine lakes and meadows, several major trailheads provide easy access to the evocatively named Desolation Wilderness (p578). The end point of the Heavenly Gondola is the starting point to many more high-alpine trails.

Cycling & Mountain-Biking Playground

ROLLING FLAT, SHREDDING STEEP

All those slopes, hills and trails make a playground for all types of cyclists. The **South Lake Tahoe Bike Path** is a level,

WINTER FUN OFF THE SKIS

Major ski resorts such as Heavenly offer sledding and tubing hills. The region's Sno-Parks, found in state parks and some ski resorts, provide all sorts of snowy fun. For private groomed sledding and tubing hills, swing by **Hansen's Resort** in South Lake Tahoe or **Adventure Mountain**, south of town.

Away from the slopes, Tahoe's cross-country ski resorts are usually open December to March, sometimes into April. Most rent equipment and offer lessons; some run tours into the frozen wilderness.

On crisp quiet nights, what could be more magical than a full-moon snowshoe tour? These rambles, found at state parks and ski resorts, are very popular. Or, enjoy ice skating right in the heart of **Heavenly Village**.

WHERE TO DRINK IN SOUTH LAKE TAHOE

Idle Hour
Sample flights of wines at this super-casual lakeside bar with a big deck.

South Lake Brewing Company
Up to 16 beers on tap daily in a large pub with a good outdoor seating, too.

The Hangar – Taproom & Bottle Shop
Top microbrews on tap and beautiful setting in a grove of trees with fire pits.

leisurely ride suitable for anyone. It heads west from **El Dorado Beach**. The **Lake Tahoe Bicycle Coalition** (tahoebike.org) has an info-packed website with good maps, and you can get bikes at **Anderson's Bike Rental**.

For expert mountain bikers, the fabled 6-mile **Mr Toad's Wild Ride**, with its steep downhill sections and banked turns reminiscent of its namesake Disneyland theme-park ride, is thrilling. It's south of town near **Grass Lake** and Luther Pass.

Among myriad other options, the **Angora Lakes Trail** is steep but technically easy and rewards you with sweeping views of Mt Tallac and Fallen Leaf Lake. The **Tahoe Area Mountain Biking Association** (tamba.org) provides plenty of local info, or check with **Wanna Ride** (wannaridetahoe.com).

Casino Sparkle

TRY YOUR LUCK

Just over the border in Nevada, four large casino and hotel complexes loom over the lake. All have vast gambling floors with little natural light that are open 24/7. Big-name performers appear at well-spaced intervals, while lesser lights offer regular live entertainment in various bars, lounges and clubs.

Harvey's is the oldest casino and has rooms in a tower right on the lake. Under the same ownership, **Harrah's** is the most opulent and liveliest casino. Its 18th-floor bar and restaurant have sweeping views that anyone can enjoy from the public space by the elevators. **Bally's Lake Tahoe** is straightforward, while **Hard Rock Hotel Lake Tahoe** is bedecked with an overlay of rock-and-roll motifs and memorabilia. All offer discount rooms during much of the year.

Dive into Tahoe's History

WASHOE CULTURE TO FLAPPER LIFE

Sheltered by a pine grove and bordering a wide, sandy beach, **Tallac Historic Site** sits on the archaeologically excavated grounds of the former Tallac Resort, a swish vacation retreat for San Francisco's high society around the turn of the 20th century. It has been transformed into a community arts hub. Explore the grounds and check out the many grand old estates and buildings.

Near the center of South Lake Tahoe, the small but interesting **Lake Tahoe Historical Society Museum** displays artifacts from Tahoe's past, including Washoe tribal baskets and vintage black-and-white films.

I LIVE HERE: WHERE TO EAT & DRINK IN SOUTH LAKE TAHOE

Sidellis Lake Tahoe (@sidellislaketahoe) brewmaster **Chris Sidell** shares a few favorite meals.

Primos Italian Bistro offers a lovely night out indulging – but not over-splurging. Don't miss the carbonara pasta (yes, homemade) with South Lake Brewing Company's Pillow Line Pale Ale.

MacDuff's Pub is a must, with faves like shepherd's pie and fish-and-chips paired with Clockwork White Ale. It warms you up inside and out, plus it's walking distance from Sidellis, my brewpub!

Lake Tahoe Pizza Company is a win for its salad bar alone, but the pizzas are scrumptious too, especially Barnyard Massacre or Southwestern Chicken. Bonus: the crusts are handmade. Wash them down with OB Amber beer.

GETTING AROUND

Reno-Tahoe International Airport is the closest major airport. It's 55 miles northeast and is linked to the south shore by shuttle buses. Amtrak has Thruway bus service from the Sacramento train station.

South Lake Tahoe has two transportation hubs: one is just south of the 'Y' intersection of Hwys 50 and 89; the other is centrally located at Stateline. Tahoe Transportation District local buses serve the south shore and are free. During winter ski season, most resorts run free shuttles to the mountains.

Beyond South Lake Tahoe & Stateline

Rubicon Trail
Desolation Wilderness
Emerald Bay State Park
South Lake Tahoe & Stateline
Sierra-at-Tahoe
Kirkwood
NEVADA
CALIFORNIA

Unspoilt Tahoe nature at its finest unfurls around the western shore and deep into the southern mountains.

It doesn't take long to leave the relatively urban charms of South Lake Tahoe and Stateside, NV, behind. The lake's densely forested western shore around Emerald Bay is idyllic. Hwy 89 sinuously wends past gorgeous state parks with swimming beaches, hiking trails, pine-shaded campgrounds and historic mansions. Several trailheads access the rugged splendor of the Desolation Wilderness.

To the south lie countless square miles of rugged mountain terrain. Some portions are scarred from the 2021 Caldor Fire, but plenty of dense forest and even the odd ski resort remain. Mountain peaks are frosted by snow throughout the year.

Heading north on Hwy 50 into Nevada, the lake's shoreline opens up, which makes for sunny beaches.

TOP TIP

In winter, snow tires or chains may be required for your vehicle. Check the CalTrans (dot.ca.gov) website for more information.

Fannette Island in Emerald Bay (p576)

WHY I LOVE WESTERN LAKE TAHOE

Alexis Averbuck, writer

DL Bliss State Park – along Hwy 89, 2 miles north of Emerald Bay – always lives up to its name for me. It has the western shore's nicest beaches, **Lester Beach** and **Calawee Cove**, and I love the trail to the **Balancing Rock**, a giant chunk of granite perched on a stone pedestal. In spring and fall, it's quiet and isolated.

Near Calawee Cove is the northern end of the Rubicon Trail, a huge highlight. Insider tip: parking at the cove usually fills up by 10am, in which case it's a 2-mile walk from the park entrance to the beach. Park staff can tell you where else to access the trails.

Teal Waters, Pristine Island

EXPLORING EMERALD BAY STATE PARK

Sheer granite cliffs and a jagged shoreline hem in glacier-arved Emerald Bay, a teardrop cove just west of South Lake Tahoe. Its most captivating aspect is the water, which changes from clover-leaf green to light jade depending on the angle of the sun. **Fannette Island**, Tahoe's only island, is set perfectly in the park's center. An uninhabited granite speck, it holds the vandalized remains of a tiny 1920s teahouse, and is known by some as Bambi's Island.

You'll spy panoramic pullouts all along Hwy 89, including at **Inspiration Point**. Just south, the road shoulder evaporates on both sides of a steep drop-off, revealing a postcard-perfect view of Emerald Bay to the north and **Cascade Lake** to the south.

A park highlight, **Vikingsholm Castle** is a rare example of ancient Scandinavian-style architecture. Completed in 1929, it has trippy design elements aplenty, including sod-covered roofs that sprout wildflowers in late spring. The mansion is reached by a steep 1-mile trail, which also leads to a visitor center.

The park's campgrounds are excellent places to commune with nature. **Eagle Point** has amenities like hot showers, while **USFS Bayview** is close to Inspiration Point and is purposely primitive.

Hiking to Coves & Historic Lighthouse

WALKING THE MAGNIFICENT RUBICON TRAIL

A brilliantly scenic trail on Lake Tahoe's western shore, Rubicon Trail ribbons along the lakeshore for 4.5 mostly gentle miles from Vikingsholm Castle (add a mile for the downhill walk to the castle from Hwy 89) in Emerald Bay State Park. It leads past small coves perfect for taking a cooling dip, and treats you to great views along the way north to DL Bliss State Park.

Add an extra mile to loop around and visit the restored **historic lighthouse**, a square wood-enclosed beacon (that looks a lot like an outhouse) constructed by the Coast Guard in 1916. Poised above 6800ft, it's the USA's highest-elevation lighthouse.

FOR MOUNTAIN LOVERS

Lake Tahoe and the Sierras remain perennial natural magic in California, but mountainous beauties abound. Whether it's **Yosemite** (p600), **Sequoia & Kings Canyon National Parks** (p611), **Mt Shasta** (p494) or **Mt Lassen** (p502), you can explore boundlessly.

Low-Key, High-Country Ski Resort

SKIING COOL KIRKWOOD

Off-the-beaten-path Kirkwood, set in a high-elevation valley, gets great snow and holds it longer than almost any

WHERE TO STAY NEAR SOUTH LAKE TAHOE

DL Bliss State Park Campground
Gorgeous campground on the western shore with 150 sites, some near the beach. **$**

Wylder Hotel Hope Valley
Delightful option in the Hope Valley, with snug pine cottages, yurts and camping, plus a wealth of activities. **$$**

Camp Richardson Resort & Marina
A complex of cabins, campsites and motel rooms, plus its own beach and marina. **$$**

GALINA BARSKAYA/SHUTTERSTOCK ©

Sowboarding with Lake Tahoe views

other Tahoe resort. It has stellar tree-skiing, gullies, chutes and terrain parks, and is the only Tahoe resort with backcountry runs accessible by snowcats. Novice out-of-bounds skiers should sign up in advance for backcountry safety-skills clinics.

It's 35 miles southwest of South Lake Tahoe via Hwy 89; check kirkwood.com for a list of ski-season shuttles. Stats: 15 lifts, 2000 vertical feet, 86 runs.

Snowboarding Thrills

RIPPING AT SIERRA-AT-TAHOE

About 18 miles southwest of South Lake Tahoe, discover snowboarding central at Sierra-at-Tahoe where six raging terrain parks meet a 17ft-high superpipe. A great beginners' run meanders gently for 2.5 miles from the summit, but there are also gnarly steeps and chutes for speed demons.

Kids get four 'adventure zones,' while adults-only **Huckleberry Gates** tempts with steep-and-deep backcountry terrain for experts. Stats: 14 lifts, 2200 vertical feet, 47 runs. The resort has made a remarkable comeback since the Caldor Fire.

ON & BELOW EMERALD BAY

Fannette Island is accessible by boat, except during Canada goose nesting season (typically February to mid-June). Rent kayaks at Vikingsholm from **Kayak Tahoe**, or rent boats in South Lake Tahoe (or catch narrated bay cruises or speedboat tours) and Meeks Bay (p583).

Much of Lake Tahoe seems bottomless (it reaches a depth of 1644ft), but divers prepared for a chilly plunge can explore the bottom on the **Emerald Bay Maritime Heritage Underwater Trail** (parks.ca.gov), discovering sunken barges and recreational boats, complete with underwater interpretive markers.

Elsewhere in the bay, divers can find a submerged rockslide and other artifacts at a historic dumping ground, all part of the unique **Underwater State Parks of Emerald Bay** and DL Bliss State Park (p576).

WHERE TO EAT NEAR SOUTH LAKE TAHOE

Getaway Cafe
Far to the south of Hwy 50, this remote cafe is famed for its huge portions of classic American fare. **$$**

Beacon Bar & Grill
Waterfront joint with a popular summertime deck right on the lake off Hwy 89 at Camp Richardson. **$$$**

Sunset Bar & Grill
Lives up to its name with stunning dusk views across the lake at Zephyr Cove Resort. **$$**

HIGHLIGHTS OF ZEPHYR COVE

Zephyr Cove is the gem of Hwy 50 as you head north from Stateline.

Kayaking
Survey the azure expanse of the lake aboard a kayak launched from the cove.

Beach
Frolic on the sandy swimming beaches and play beach volleyball.

MS Dixie II paddle wheeler
Ply Lake Tahoe's 'big blue' year-round with a variety of sightseeing, drinking, dining and dancing cruises, including a narrated two-hour daytime trip to Emerald Bay (p576).

Zephyr Cove Stables
Reserve ahead for forest and meadow horseback rides.

Zephyr Cove Resort & Marina
This historic family resort has vintage cabins scattered in the trees.

HOTRAVEL_RU/SHUTTERSTOCK ©

Eagle Falls trail

Hiking & Backpacking the Desolation Wilderness

LIVE YOUR BACKCOUNTRY DREAM

Sculpted by powerful glaciers eons ago, the (relatively) compact Desolation Wilderness (fs.usda.gov/detail/eldorado/specialplaces) spreads south and west of Lake Tahoe and is the most popular spot in the Sierra Nevada. It's a 100-sq-mile wonderland of polished granite peaks, deep-blue alpine lakes, glacier-carved valleys and resplendent pine forests that thin quickly at the higher elevations. In summer, wildflowers nudge out from between the rocks.

All this splendor makes for exquisite backcountry exploration. Six major trailheads provide access from the Lake Tahoe side. **Tallac** and **Eagle Falls** get the most traffic, but solitude comes quickly once you've scampered past the day hikers.

Permits are required year-round for both day and overnight explorations. Quotas are in effect from late May through the end of September. Over half of the permits for the season may be reserved online, usually starting in late March or April; the other permits are available on a first-arrival basis on the day of entry only. Get maps, information and permits at the USFS Taylor Creek Visitor Center.

GETTING AROUND

Heavy snowfall sometimes closes Hwy 89 north of the Tallac Historic Site (p574). The section of Hwy 89 between South Lake Tahoe and Emerald Bay is also known as Emerald Bay Rd.

Avoid the South Lake Tahoe traffic when trying to reach places elsewhere by driving the Pioneer Trail, which branches east off the Hwy 89/50 junction (south of the 'Y' junction) and reconnects with Hwy 50 at Stateline.

TAHOE CITY

The western shore's commercial hub, Tahoe City straddles the junction of Hwys 89 and 28, making it almost inevitable that you'll find yourself breezing through at least once during your round-the-lake sojourn.

Tahoe City takes full advantage of its lakeside location. Views south over the water are spectacular, and many restaurants and pubs have large decks that are good for savoring the vistas. You can take in downtown's top sights on a 1-mile walking loop from the North Lake Tahoe Visitor Center. Follow Mackinaw Rd to Commons Beach, then stroll the coastal path to the pier. After checking out the clarity of the lake, walk to N Lake Blvd. Cross Fanny Bridge and explore the Gatekeeper's Museum and adjacent park.

The area is within easy reach of half a dozen winter resorts like Alpine Meadows and Olympic Valley at Palisades Tahoe.

TOP TIP

Tahoe City is the best place north of South Lake Tahoe to buy supplies and rent gear. The main drag, N Lake Blvd, is packed with outdoor outfitters, touristy shops, restaurants, bakeries and cafes – an excellent pit stop. The unpretentious nightlife scene includes several restaurants with live music.

Cycling in Tahoe City (p581)

TAHOE CITY

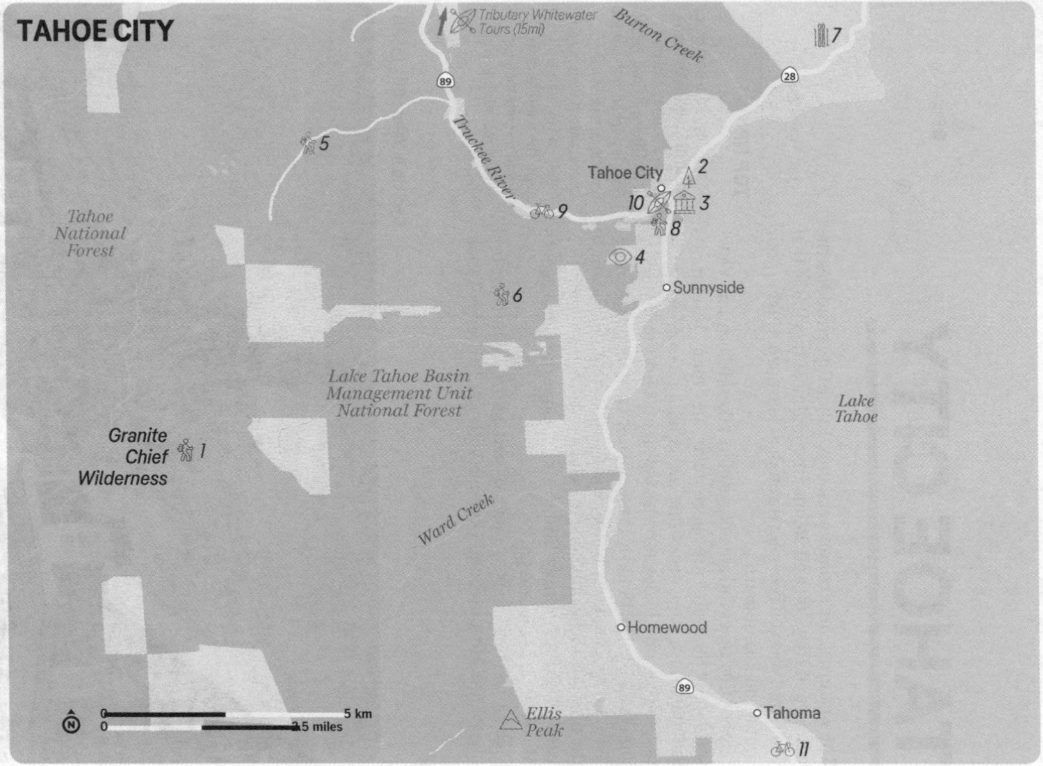
Tributary Whitewater Tours (15mi)
Burton Creek
89
28
7
Truckee River
5
Tahoe City
2
10
3
9
8
4
Sunnyside
6
Tahoe National Forest
Lake Tahoe Basin Management Unit National Forest
Lake Tahoe
Granite Chief Wilderness
1
Ward Creek
Homewood
89
Tahoma
Ellis Peak
11
0 5 km
0 2.5 miles

HIGHLIGHTS
1 Granite Chief Wilderness

SIGHTS
2 Commons Beach
3 Gatekeeper's Museum & Marion Steinbach Indian Basket Museum
4 Tahoe Treetop Adventure Parks

ACTIVITIES, COURSES & TOURS
5 Five Lakes Trail
6 Paige Meadows
7 Tahoe Cross-Country
8 Tahoe Rim Trail
9 Truckee River Bike Trail
10 Truckee River Raft Rentals
11 West Shore Bike Path

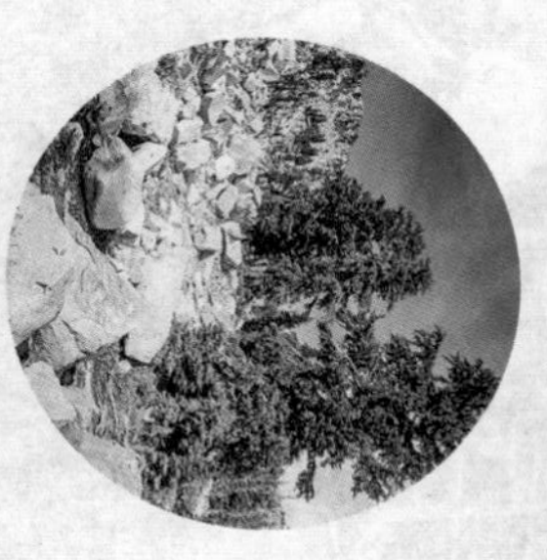

Granite Chief Wilderness

DANIEL DRSW/SHUTTERSTOCK ©

Hiking, Cycling & Rafting Around Tahoe City

SUMMER FUN IN NORTHWEST TAHOE

Explore the fabulous trails of the **Granite Chief Wilderness** north and west of Tahoe City. Recommended day hikes include the moderately strenuous **Five Lakes Trail** (5 miles round trip) and the easy trek to **Paige Meadows**, leading on to the **Tahoe Rim Trail**. Paige Meadows is also good terrain for novice mountain bikers.

The paved 4.5-mile **Truckee River Bike Trail** runs from Tahoe City toward Palisades, while the multiuse **West Shore Bike Path** heads 9 miles south to Ed Z'berg Sugar Pine Point State Park (p583), including highway-shoulder and residential-street sections. Both are fairly easy rides; rent bicycles from any of several shops along N Lake Blvd.

Commons Beach is a small, attractive park with sandy and grassy areas, picnic tables, barbecue grills, a climbing rock and a playground, as well as free summer concerts. There's mellow rafting on the Truckee River – inquire with **Truckee River Raft Rentals** or **Tributary Whitewater Tours**. Or you can hit the zip lines and swinging bridges at **Tahoe Treetop Adventure Parks**.

Tahoe History & Basket Artistry

CELEBRATE ARTS AND ARTIFACTS

In a reconstructed log cabin close to town, **Gatekeeper's Museum & Marion Steinbach Indian Basket Museum** has a small but fascinating collection of Tahoe memorabilia, including relics from the early steamboat era and tourism explosion around the lake. However, the don't-miss exhibit is the exquisite array of Native American baskets collected from more than 85 indigenous California tribes.

Cross-Country Skiing for Everyone

GLIDING ON FOREST TRAILS

Run by a nonprofit group, **Tahoe Cross-Country** (tahoexc.org) has over 40 miles of groomed tracks (21 trails) that wind through lovely forest and are suitable for all skill levels. Group lessons come with good-value equipment-rental packages. Half-day trail-pass discounts are also available. Ask about skate clinics and beginners' cross-country lessons.

BEST EATS & SLEEPS IN TAHOE CITY

Mediterranean Cafe Tahoe
Mix it up with fast, casual Med fare that can easily be made vegan. $

Tahoe National Brewing Company
Good beer, creative pub eats and outdoor patio with fires within view of the lake. $$$

New Moon Natural Foods
Tiny but well-stocked natural-foods store with a gem of a deli that concocts scrumptious food to go. $

Mother Nature's Inn
Eight quiet motel-style rooms with a tidy country look within walking distance of Commons Beach. $

GETTING AROUND

Tahoe City is right at the junction of Hwys 28 and 89. Tahoe Truckee Area Regional Transit (TART) runs free buses between Tahoe City, Incline Village and Truckee.

Beyond Tahoe City

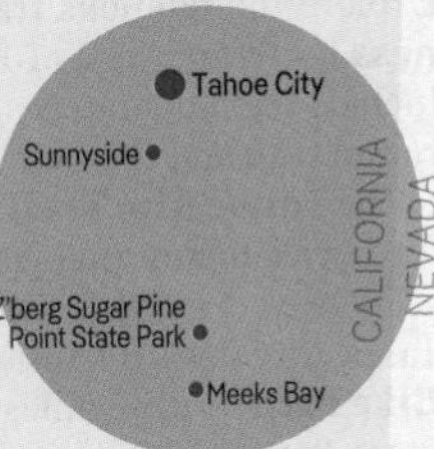

Tahoe's western edge invites leisurely exploration of the forested shores and long days boating its sparkling waters.

The 18 miles of Hwy 89 that link Tahoe City and Emerald Bay on the western shore are some of the lake's most iconic. Myriad shades of green (the trees) mix with vistas of blue (the lake). In winter, an overlay of white makes it all too evocative.

Peaks rise to the west, blanketed by thick stands of conifer. The lakeshore is dotted with beaches, piers, campgrounds, resorts and state parks. There are year-round activities, from swimming to skiing. Film buffs will want to keep their eyes peeled for the famous Fleur du Lac Estate in Homewood. It's here that Michael Corleone threw his son's first communion celebration in the vaunted *Godfather II* (1974).

TOP TIP

Although 18 miles may not seem far, allow plenty of time for slow-moving cars and countless appealing stops. Campgrounds abound.

Meeks Bay

CHERI GAGNE/GETTY IMAGES ©

Warmer Waters, Steeper Trails

EXPLORING MEEKS BAY AND BEYOND

With a wide sweep of shoreline, shallow Meeks Bay, 11 miles south of Tahoe City and best reached with your own wheels, has warm water by Tahoe standards and is fringed by a beautiful, sandy beach. West of Hwy 89 is a trailhead for the **Meeks Bay Trail** leading into the Desolation Wilderness (p578). A mostly level, shaded path parallels **Meeks Creek** before heading steeply uphill through the forest to **Lake Genevieve** (9 miles round trip), **Crag Lake** (10 miles round trip) and other backcountry ponds, all surrounded by scenic Sierra peaks.

Play in One of Tahoe's Best State Parks

CORNUCOPIA OF LAKESIDE ACTIVITIES

Ed Z'berg Sugar Pine Point State Park occupies a promontory blanketed by a fragrant mix of pine, juniper, aspen and fir. It has a swimming beach, hiking trails, kayaking in summer and, in winter, over 2 miles of groomed cross-country trails. A paved bike path travels north for 9 miles to Tahoe City.

Historic sights include the modest 1872 **cabin** of an early Tahoe settler, and the considerably grander 1903 Queen Anne–style **Hellman-Ehrman Mansion**.

The park is named after Edwin L Z'berg (1926–75), a conservationist assemblyman who fought for Tahoe's preservation.

Lakeside Breakfast & Biking

CYCLING AND PADDLING AT SUNNYSIDE

Lakeshore hamlet Sunnyside, 2 miles south of Tahoe City, is a hub for cycling. Rent a bike and glide along the path that follows the shoreline north and south. Or, rent a stand-up paddling set and hit the busy local beaches.

For sustenance, everyone heads to the **Fire Sign Cafe**, where superb breakfasts and lunches are served in summer on the outdoor patio.

TAHOE'S LAID-BACK WINTER RESORT

The trees lining Hwy 89 open up when you reach **Homewood**. Six miles south of Tahoe City, this quiet and very alpine-looking hamlet is popular with summertime boaters who dock at its marina and, in winter, skiers and snowboarders.

The Homewood winter resort proves that bigger isn't always better. Locals and in-the-know visitors cherish the awesome lake views, laid-back ambience, smaller crowds, tree-lined slopes and open bowls (including the excellent but expert 'Quail Face'). Families love the wide, gentle slopes. It's also the best place to ski during stormy weather. Stats: eight lifts, 1650 vertical feet, 67 runs.

Homewood also boasts one of the lake's most elegant accommodations in the form of the **West Shore Inn**, a luxurious six-room lakeside inn.

GETTING AROUND

Hiking and cycling trails allow non-drivers to explore portions of the western shore.

However, you'll really need your own vehicle to do it justice.

NORTHERN SHORE

San Francisco
Northern Shore
Los Angeles

Northeast of Tahoe City, Hwy 28 cruises through a string of cute, low-key towns, many fronting superb sandy beaches, with reasonably priced roadside motels and hotels, plus lodges and holiday apartments of myriad stripes, all crowded together along the lakeshore.

Oozing old-fashioned charm, the north shore is a blissful escape from the teeming crowds of South Lake Tahoe, Tahoe City and Truckee, but still puts you within easy reach of winter ski resorts and snow parks, and summertime swimming, kayaking, hiking trails and more.

The state line between California and Nevada neatly bisects the northern shore. Most famously, it passes right through the lobby of now-closed but once-notorious Cal-Neva Resort, which has a colorful history involving ghosts, mobsters and various Ratpackers, including Frank Sinatra who once owned the joint. Nearby flashing neon marks several old-school casinos that are as humble as the numerous cafes lining the highway.

TOP TIP

The northern shore combines all of the attributes that make Tahoe a compelling destination, from the lake to popular Northstar ski resort in the mountains immediately to the north. Given the enormous range of campgrounds, cabins, holiday condos, motels and resorts large and small, there's accommodations for everyone.

Snow covering Kings Beach State Recreation Area (p586)

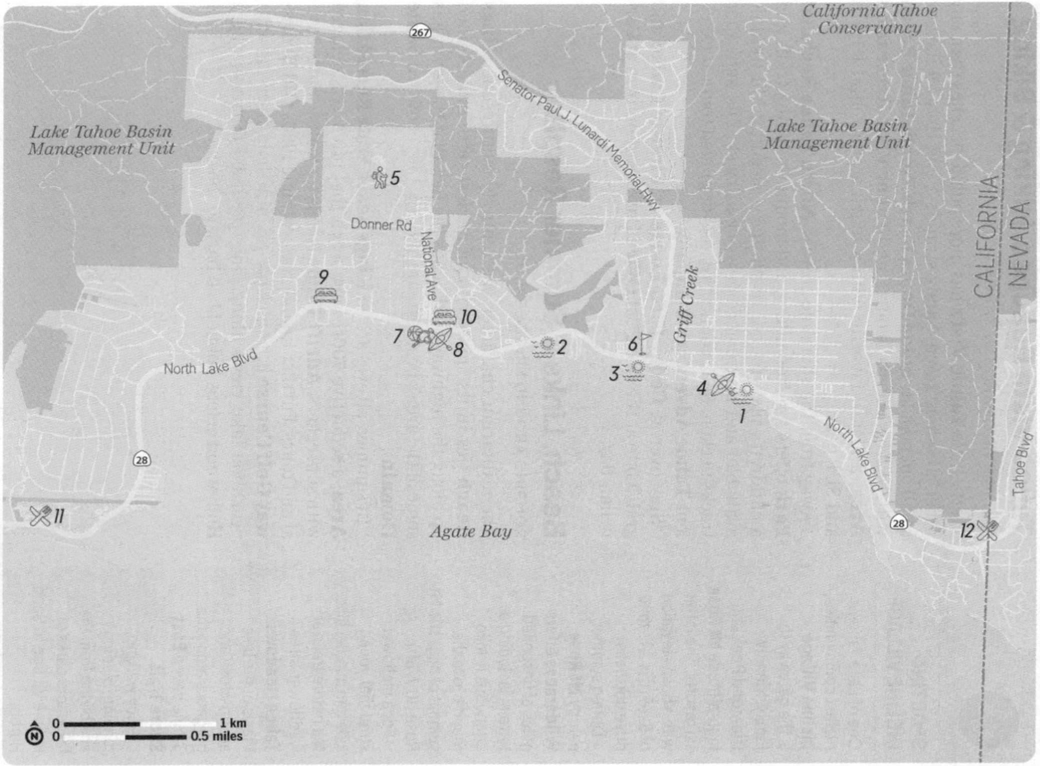

SIGHTS
1 Kings Beach State Recreation Area
2 Moon Dunes Beach
3 North Tahoe Beach

ACTIVITIES, COURSES & TOURS
4 Adrift Tahoe
5 North Tahoe Regional Park
6 Old Brockway Golf Course
7 Tahoe Adventure Company
8 Tahoe Vista Recreation Area

SLEEPING
9 Cedar Glen Lodge
10 Firelite Lodge

EATING
11 Old Post Office Café
12 Soule Domain

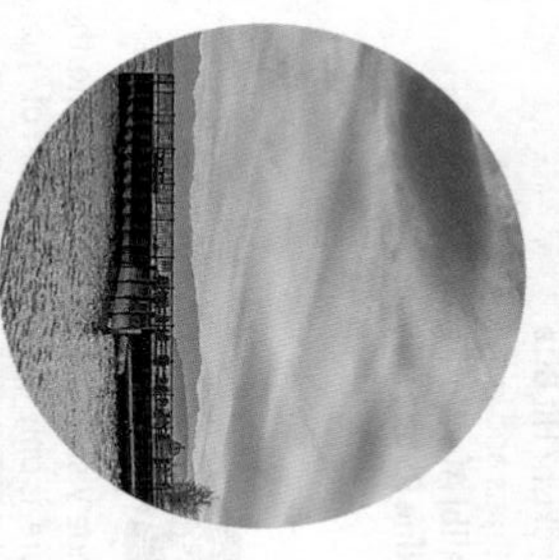

Tahoe Vista Recreation Area (p586)

SPORTING INCLINE VILLAGE

One of Lake Tahoe's ritziest communities, **Incline Village** is the gateway to family-friendly **Diamond Peak** and high-altitude **Mt Rose** ski resorts. The latter, with a base elevation of 8269ft, is a 12-mile drive northeast.

During summer, nearby **Mt Rose Wilderness** offers miles of unspoiled terrain, including a strenuous 11-mile round trip to the summit of majestic Mt Rose (10,776ft).

For a mellower stroll that young kids can handle, hike the nature trails at wildflower-strewn **Tahoe Meadows**. Views of the lake are up-close and gorgeous along the 3-mile paved **East Shore Trail**.

Enjoy walking, running, blading and biking from the lakeshore parks of Incline Village to Sand Harbor.

Peckish? Hit **Bite** for tapas and wine or **Alibi Ale Works Incline Public House**.

Tahoe Vista Beaches, Hiking & Biking

THE MYRIAD CHARMS OF TAHOE VISTA

Pretty little **Tahoe Vista** has more public beaches than any other lakeshore town. Sandy strands along Hwy 28 include small but popular **Moon Dunes Beach**, **North Tahoe Beach** with beach-volleyball courts, and **Tahoe Vista Recreation Area**, a locals' favorite with a marina and rental kayaks and SUP gear.

Away from the shoreline crowds, **North Tahoe Regional Park** offers forested hiking and mountain-biking trails and a children's playground. In winter, a sledding hill (rentals available) and ungroomed cross-country ski and snowshoe tracks beckon. Seek council, rentals or guided tours at excellent **Tahoe Adventure Company**.

Stay over at **Cedar Glen Lodge** or **Firelite Lodge** and grab a bite at the **Old Post Office Cafe**, west of town at Carnelian Bay.

Beach, Links & Summer Respite

ROMPING AROUND KINGS BEACH

The utilitarian character of fetchingly picturesque **Kings Beach** lies in its smattering of modest retro motels lined up along the highway (and belies the fact that the town has some of the area's best restaurants – try the renowned **Soule Domain**).

In summer, all eyes are on **Kings Beach State Recreation Area**, a seductive 700ft-long beach that often gets deluged with sunseekers. **Adrift Tahoe** is tops for water-sports rental and tours. Further inland, the nostalgic 1920s **Old Brockway Golf Course** is a quick par-36, nine-hole diversion with peekaboo lake views along pine-tree-lined fairways where Hollywood celebs hobnobbed back in the day.

GETTING AROUND

Tahoe Vista, near the heart of the northern shore, is only 12 miles southeast of Truckee via Hwy 267. Free Tahoe Truckee Area Regional Transit (TART) buses run between Tahoe City and Incline Village, making stops in Tahoe Vista, Kings Beach and Crystal Bay. There are connections to Truckee.

Beyond Northern Shore

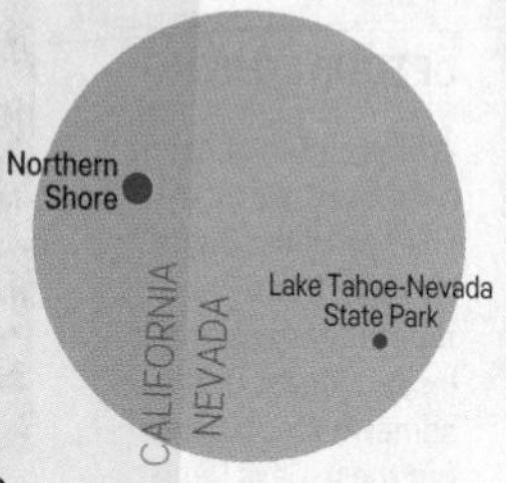

Prettily preserved, Tahoe's eastern shore remains the lake's least developed zone and is a wonderland to explore.

Lake Tahoe's eastern shore lies entirely within Nevada. Much of it is relatively undeveloped thanks to George Whittell Jr, an eccentric San Franciscan playboy who once owned a lot of this land, including 27 miles of shoreline. Upon his death in 1969, it was sold off to a private investor, who later wheeled and dealed most of it to the US Forest Service and Nevada State Parks. And lucky for us, because today the eastern shore offers some of Tahoe's best and least-crowded scenery and outdoor diversions.

The eastern shore is linked by Hwys 28 and 50, which run for 22 beautiful miles between Incline Village in the north and Zephyr Cove in the south.

TOP TIP

Pack a picnic from the good delis on the northern or southern shores and look for your ideal waterfront lunch spot.

Spooner Lake (p588)

LAURA MAEVA/SHUTTERSTOCK ©

DETOUR TO RENO

With a clutch of big casinos in the dusty shadow of the Sierra Nevada, **Reno** has a reputation for being a lesser Vegas. That's somewhat accurate, but these days Reno is much more. In the last 10 years, Reno has become host to server farms supporting familiar Silicon Valley names, and the formerly gritty **Midtown District** offers funky bars, top-notch restaurants and vibrant arts spaces.

Sights around town include the **National Automobile Museum**, the **Nevada Museum of Art** and the **Nevada Historical Society Museum**.

Only an hour from Lake Tahoe on I-80 or Hwy 50, it's a fun urban adventure.

TERESA MUNSON/SHUTTERSTOCK ©

Sand Harbor

Bounty of Activities

PLAY YOUR WAY THROUGH LAKE TAHOE-NEVADA STATE PARK

Stretching from the lake to the peaks of the Carson Range, the **Lake Tahoe-Nevada State Park** has beaches, lakes and miles of trails.

Just 3 miles south of Incline Village stretches crowd-pleasing **Sand Harbor**, where two sand spits form a shallow bay with brilliant, warm turquoise water and white, boulder-strewn beaches backed by dunes. There's also a visitor center with exhibits about the lake, a seasonal restaurant and snacks year-round.

The views west across Lake Tahoe feature distant snow-capped peaks and sublime sunsets. It gets busy here, especially during July and August when the **Lake Tahoe Shakespeare Festival** is underway. It mixes works by the Bard and contemporary pieces, performed outdoors by the lake.

At the park's southern end, just north of the Hwy 50 and Hwy 28 junction, **Spooner Lake** is popular for catch-and-release fishing, picnicking, nature walks, backcountry camping and cross-country skiing. Spooner Lake is also the start of the famous 14-mile **Flume Trail**, a holy grail for experienced mountain bikers. It's a mix of spectacular views and sometimes technical, generally leg-shaking biking that's not for the faint of heart.

GETTING AROUND

East Shore Express shuttle buses link Sand Harbor with Incline Village; otherwise you'll need your own vehicle to explore the eastern shore. If you're riding the Flume Trail, you can arrange for a pick-up from the end through bike rental shops in Incline Village and South Lake Tahoe.

TRUCKEE

San Francisco
Truckee
Los Angeles

Cradled by mountains and the Tahoe National Forest, Truckee is a thriving town steeped in Old West history. It was put on the map by the railroad, grew rich on logging and ice harvesting, and even had its brush with Hollywood during the 1924 filming of Charlie Chaplin's *The Gold Rush*. Today tourism fills much of the city's coffers, thanks to a well-preserved historic downtown and its proximity to Lake Tahoe, I-80 and nearly a dozen winter resorts.

The aura of the Old West still lingers over Truckee's teensy one-horse downtown, where railroad workers and lumberjacks once milled about in raucous saloons, bawdy brothels and shady gambling halls. With a recent influx of families and entrepreneurs from the Bay Area, most of the late-19th-century buildings now contain creative restaurants and upscale boutiques. Donner Memorial State Park and pristine Donner Lake are just 3 miles west. The surrounding peaks are laced with hiking and rock-climbing routes.

Truckee River

TOP TIP

Truckee's downtown is south of I-80. The Union Pacific Railroad main line cuts through the middle on a route that dates from the late 1860s, when the Central Pacific Railroad was building the first transcontinental railway line. West of the center and north of I-80 is a long schmear of strip malls.

BEST SKI RESORTS

Besides top choices like Palisades Tahoe (p592), Royal Gorge (p591) and Northstar California (p591), try the following.

Sugar Bowl
Cofounded by Walt Disney in 1939 and known for its gullies and chutes plus stellar alpine views.

Boreal
Usually the first to open each season, with 41 runs and night skiing.

Soda Springs
Tops with tots, who enjoy the ski school, snow-tubing, sledding and pint-sized snowmobiles.

Donner Ski Ranch
Tiny, family-owned winter resort where generations of Californians have learned to ski.

HIGHLIGHTS
1 Northstar California Resort

SIGHTS
2 Old Jail
3 Pioneer Monument
4 West End Beach

ACTIVITIES, COURSES & TOURS
5 Donner Lake
6 Donner Memorial State Park
7 Royal Gorge

SLEEPING
8 Gravity Haus Truckee-Tahoe

EATING
9 Full Belly Deli
10 Moody's Bistro & Lounge
11 Pianeta
12 Red Truck
13 Squeeze In
14 Stella
15 Trokay

DRINKING
16 Donner Creek Brewing
17 Truckee Brewing Company

Old West & Foodie Boomtown

ABSORBING HISTORIC TRUCKEE

Truckee's old downtown dates from the 19th century and is an attractive and evocative place to explore. It's compact and easily walked, and you'll find the excellent visitor center in the old train depot. Continuously in use until the 1960s, the **Old Jail** is in a tiny 1875 redbrick building filled with relics. George 'Machine Gun' Kelly was reportedly once held here for shoplifting.

Good cafes, restaurants and breweries abound. Among the best choices are **Squeeze In** for incredible omelets; **Full Belly Deli** for stacked sandwiches; **Pianeta** for cocktails and Italian fare; and **Moody's Bistro & Lounge** for creative cuisine.

Locals love **Red Truck** cafe (at the local airport!) for its Asian-inflected casual eats; or go ahead and put on the ritz at **Stella** or **Trokay**. Get craft beer at **Truckee Brewing Company** or myriad other haunts, and if you can't make it back to your place, stay over at **Gravity Haus Truckee-Tahoe**.

Keep Moving Around Donner Memorial State Park

EDGES OF DONNER LAKE THEN AND NOW

At the eastern end of Donner Lake, Donner Memorial State Park occupies one of the sites where the doomed Donner Party got trapped in 1846–7. Though its history is gruesome, the park is gorgeous and has a sandy beach, hiking trails and wintertime cross-country skiing and snowshoeing. The visitor center has historical exhibits and a film reenacting the Donner Party's plight.

There are also displays about the Chinese workers who turned from gold mining to building California's railways. Outside, the **Pioneer Monument** honors the families who came to California, and a short trail leads to a memorial at one of the cabin sites.

High-Mountain Water Sports

LIVING IT UP ON DONNER LAKE

Warmer than Lake Tahoe, tree-lined Donner Lake is great for water sports. **West End Beach** is popular with families for its swimming area and kayak, paddleboat, SUP and inner-tube rentals. The surrounding ring of granite peaks soars high above the tree line, creating a dramatic tableau. Stop in at nearby **Donner Creek Brewing** for beer, cider, paninis and sandwiches.

HIT THE SLOPES

Skiing Royal Gorge

Nordic-skiing aficionados won't want to pass up a spin around **Royal Gorge**, the largest cross-country resort in North America, with its 85 miles of groomed track crisscrossing 6000 acres of terrain. It has great skating lanes and diagonal stride tracks and also welcomes telemark skiers and snowshoers.

Skiing Popular Northstar

An easy 7 miles south of I-80, hugely popular **Northstar California Resort** has great intermediate terrain as well as long black runs. Northstar's relatively sheltered location makes it a top choice when it's snowing, and the eight terrain parks and pipes are top-ranked. Advanced and expert skiers can look for tree-skiing challenges on the back of the mountain.

GETTING AROUND

Greyhound buses stop at Truckee's train depot, as do Amtrak Thruway buses and the daily *California Zephyr* train west to Sacramento and Emeryville/San Francisco and east to Reno, Denver and Chicago.

Tahoe Truckee Area Regional Transit (TART) links downtown with Donner Lake and Palisades Tahoe. With connections, you can reach Tahoe City and the northern shore. During ski season, shuttles run to many area ski resorts.

Beyond Truckee

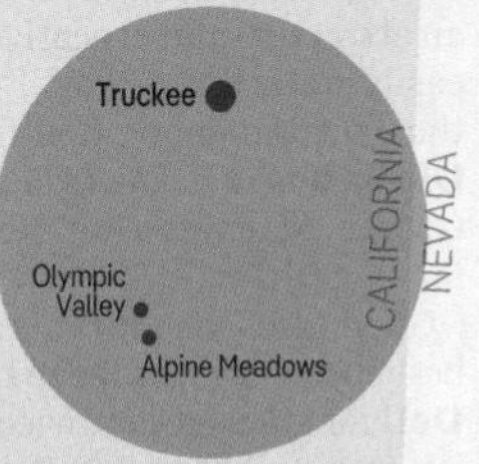

Placed on the map by the 1960 Winter Olympic Games, Palisades Tahoe remains one of California's favorite ski areas.

Palisades Tahoe is the largest ski resort around Lake Tahoe. Among the world's top ski areas, the stunning setting amid granite peaks makes it a superb destination in any season, and this deluxe family-friendly resort stays almost as busy in summer as in winter.

Formerly known as Squaw Valley, the resort – which hosted the 1960 Winter Olympics – changed its name in 2021 to end racist and sexist associations.

Palisades Tahoe consists of two main ski areas: Alpine Meadows, which is the less glossy resort to the south; and Olympic Valley, which is the mega-size, world-class, see-and-be-seen resort. A spectacular new 2.4-mile-long gondola linking the two ski areas opened in 2022.

TOP TIP

Check the palisadestahoe.com for deals on lift tickets. There are discounts on certain days of the week such as Thursday.

Palisades Tahoe

EQROY/SHUTTERSTOCK ©

Ski Like an Olympian

HITTING THE VILLAGE AND SLOPES AT OLYMPIC VALLEY

The base of Olympic Valley, 12 miles south of Truckee, is known as '**The Village**.' It's a lavish alpine-style resort with restaurants, bars and lots of shopping. Lifts and gondolas climb to the many ski areas, including Alpine Meadows, over the ridge.

The aptly named **High Camp** (8200ft) is at the top of a steep cable-car run. Here you'll find restaurants, an ice-skating rink in winter and **Olympic Museum**, a fun retro exploration of the 1960 Olympics, featuring a film and much memorabilia.

Hard-core skiers thrill to white-knuckle cornices, chutes and bowls, while beginners practice their turns in a separate area on the upper mountain. Stats: 30 lifts, 2850 vertical feet, more than 175 runs. Other activities in winter include disco tubing at night, cross-country skiing and more.

There's a great après-ski scene. A tiny dive in The Village, the **Slot**, is beloved for its steady-flowing shots. Nearby and more mannered, **Le Chamois & Loft Bar** offers pizza and beer with fab mountain views. For daytime sustenance, **Wildflour Baking Co** makes everything from scratch.

Laid-Back Runs on the Back of the Ridge

MELLOWING OUT AT ALPINE MEADOWS

The Alpine Meadows base camp of Palisades Tahoe, 14 miles south of Truckee, is a no-nonsense resort with challenging terrain and without the fancy attitude or crowds of its companion Olympic Valley (linked by a new gondola). It gets more snow than Olympic Valley and is the most backcountry-friendly resort around. Boarders jib down the mountain in a terrain park designed by noted winter-resort architect Eric Rosenwald. Stats: 13 lifts, 1802 vertical feet, more than 100 runs. It's also easily accessible from Tahoe City (p579).

SUMMER AT PALISADES

Much summertime action centers on High Camp, reached by a cable car, which offers swimming, geocaching, roller-skating and lots of spectacular hiking.

Activities down below include a ropes course with zip lines operated by **Olympic Valley Treetop**. There's a 50ft-high alpine tower, six short zip lines and 16 tree platforms linking various challenges.

Many trails radiate from High Camp, or try the moderate **Shirley Lake Trail** (round trip 5 miles), which follows a sprightly creek to waterfalls, granite boulders and abundant wildflowers. Longer and more advanced trails loop into the Granite Chief Wilderness (p581) to the west. Options include a section of the 2659-mile **Pacific Crest** route. The area is notable for its dramatic cirques (amphitheater-like valleys).

GETTING AROUND

Tahoe Tuckee Area Regional Transit (TART) buses link Olympic Valley with Truckee and Tahoe City. Connections serve much of the northern shore and some of the western shore.

Above: Vernal Fall (p603), Yosemite National Park; Right: Sequoia National Park (p611)

YOSEMITE & THE SIERRA NEVADA

FORMIDABLE AND EXQUISITE ADVENTURER'S WONDERLAND

Like a backbone rising up over central California, the Sierra Nevada encompasses colossal canyons and some of the highest peaks in the country.

In the Sierra Nevada, everything feels a little less tame, a lot more wondrous, and far, far bigger than in other parts of California. The natural environs are ferociously beautiful and brimming with superlatives: the world's biggest trees, the world's oldest trees, the highest waterfall in North America, the lowest point in North America and the highest mountaintop in the contiguous USA.

Formed by tectonic plate crushing against plate and then sculpted by glaciers, this land and its innumerable lakes, meadows, forests and mountains has served as inspiration – and a playground – for people through the ages and from all over the world. To present-day Californians, though, it's something more: lifeblood. The melted Sierra snowpack hydrates more than 75% of the state's residents and large swaths of farmland across the Central Valley, which produces a quarter of the nation's food. In recent years, climate change has become a dire threat to that water supply, and to the ecosystems, inhabitants and recreational opportunities across the region.

Visitors will notice that sizable stretches of the Sierra's landscape have already been transformed by catastrophic wildfire, drought, floods and severe storms, not to mention the surge of people de-stressing in wild places but not always respecting them.

In so many ways, the Sierra Nevada is more important than ever. And at least for now, its inconceivable beauty still abounds.

BENNY MARTY/SHUTTERSTOCK ©

THE MAIN AREAS

YOSEMITE NATIONAL PARK
Epic Sierra Nevada scenery. p600

SEQUOIA & KINGS CANYON NATIONAL PARKS
A vast canyon and very, very big trees. p611

EASTERN SIERRA
Crazy mountains and surreal desert landscapes. p619

Find Your Way

The Sierra Nevada stretches 400 miles long and approximately 70 miles wide (covering 25% of California). We've selected the region's three national parks along with its lesser-explored eastern expanse as hubs for you to discover its natural landscapes, history and culture.

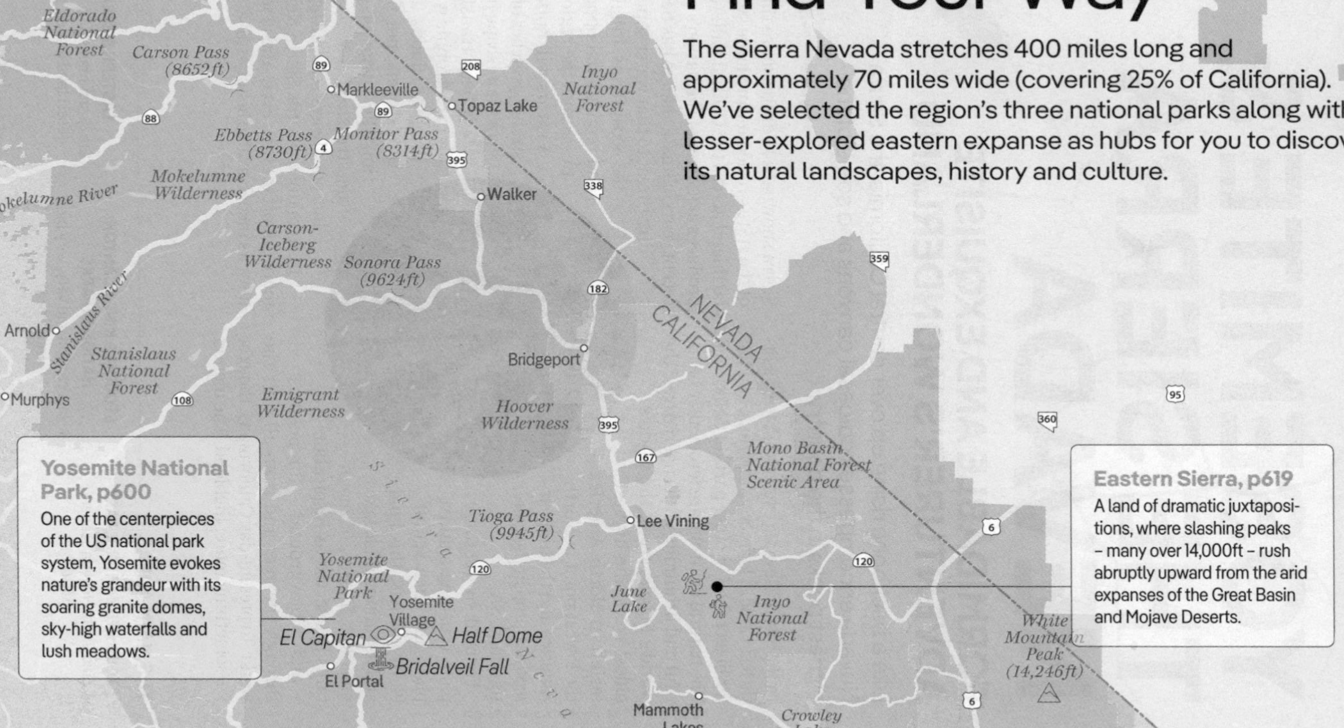

Yosemite National Park, p600

One of the centerpieces of the US national park system, Yosemite evokes nature's grandeur with its soaring granite domes, sky-high waterfalls and lush meadows.

Eastern Sierra, p619

A land of dramatic juxtapositions, where slashing peaks – many over 14,000ft – rush abruptly upward from the arid expanses of the Great Basin and Mojave Deserts.

CAR

Driving is by far the most popular way to get to and around the Sierra Nevada. In Yosemite National Park this means traffic, smog and sometimes frustrating battles for parking spaces during peak summer months.

BUS

Yosemite Area Regional Transport System (YARTS) buses connect Yosemite to Merced, and to gateway towns and the Eastern Sierra in summer. Sequoia Shuttle runs from Visalia and Three Rivers to Sequoia National Park during summer. Eastern Sierra Transit Authority buses stop at all Hwy 395 towns.

WALKING

The best way to experience the Sierra Nevada is on your own two feet. Try to ditch all other forms of transportation and hit the trails for at least a day or two.

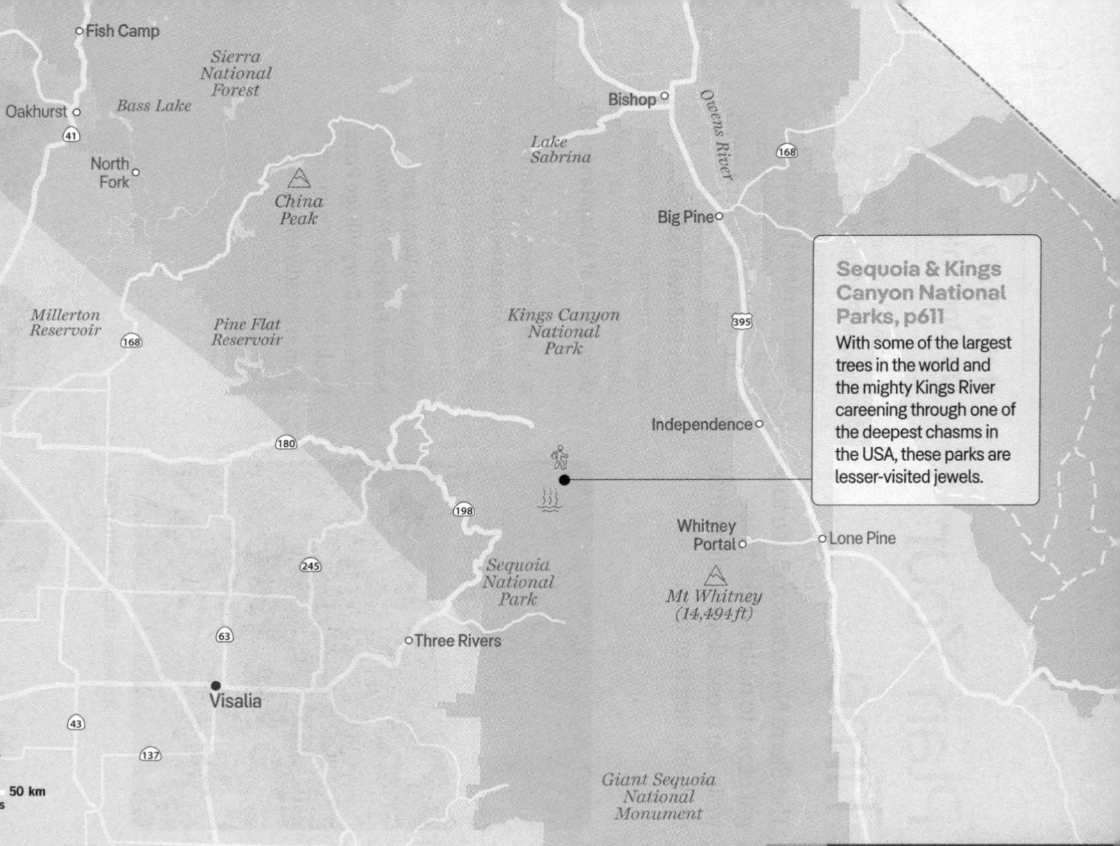

Sequoia & Kings Canyon National Parks, p611

With some of the largest trees in the world and the mighty Kings River careening through one of the deepest chasms in the USA, these parks are lesser-visited jewels.

Mariposa
Fish Camp
Sierra National Forest
Oakhurst
Bass Lake
North Fork
China Peak
Bishop
Owens River
Lake Sabrina
Big Pine
Millerton Reservoir
Pine Flat Reservoir
Kings Canyon National Park
Independence
Whitney Portal
Lone Pine
Mt Whitney (14,494ft)
Sequoia National Park
Three Rivers
Visalia
Giant Sequoia National Monument
140
41
168
395
180
198
245
63
43
137
0 50 km
0 25 miles

Plan Your Time

The Sierra Nevada is a place to get close to nature. Hike those trails, ski those slopes, climb that rock and hug that tree.

IMON DANNHAUER/SHUTTERSTOCK ©

A hiker on Glacier Point (p602)

If You Only Do One Thing

- Spend the day in **Yosemite National Park** (p600). To avoid parking or reservation problems, consider a **tour of the valley floor** (p602). If DIY is more your style, stop at **Tunnel View** (p602) on your way in, take the hike up to misty **Bridalveil Fall** (p602) and look for seemingly microscopic climbers working their way up the sheer granite of **El Capitan** (p602).

- In the afternoon, head to the historic **Ahwahnee Hotel** (p604) for a well-deserved cocktail or coffee and lunch, before setting out on a hike to **Vernal and Nevada Falls** (p603). Reward yourself at **Curry Village Pizza Deck** (p601) and get some restful sleep in a nearby tent cabin.

Seasonal Highlights

There's no bad time to visit. Spring is lovely for wildflowers and waterfalls, summer is great for high-altitude drives and low-altitude hikes, while fall colors and winter snow dustings are magic.

JANUARY

Snow sports reign supreme. At the Ahwahnee, top chefs from around the country lead **cooking demonstrations** and offer kitchen tours.

FEBRUARY

For two weeks at the end of the month, the thin, seasonal cascade of **Horsetail Fall** (p605) becomes Yosemite's most photographed attraction.

APRIL

By the end of the month, the dogwoods start to bloom and the **waterfalls** begin awakening. Also, anglers rejoice for the start of **fishing season**.

MATTHEW CONNOLLY/SHUTTERSTOCK ©; WIRESTOCK CREATORS/SHUTTERSTOCK ©; STEVEN CASTRO/SHUTTERSTOCK ©

Three Days to Travel Around

- After a day in Yosemite, give yourself at least two more, especially in summer. If you're ambitious, hike Four Mile Trail to **Glacier Point** (p602), or maybe just drive there. On your last day in the park, drive to the Tioga Pass, gaze at Half Dome's glorious reflection in **Mirror Lake** (p603) and sleep under the stars in **Tuolumne Meadows** (p604).

- Exit the park through the Tioga Pass gate for some adventuring in the Eastern Sierra. Visit **Bodie State Historic Park** (p627), the spookiest ghost town ever, then mosey around the also-haunting tufas of **Mono Lake** (p626). Don't go home without hitting one of the many **hot springs** (p625).

If You Have More Time

- Keep right on trucking down **Hwy 395** (p620), taking your sweet time hiking around lakes and visiting all the **crazy stuff** (p624) caused by volcanic activity, especially the **Devils Postpile** (p624). Hit up some of the area's best museums near Bishop – definitely visit the **Manzanar National Historic Site** (p623) – and take a gander at the blob-like red boulders at the **Alabama Hills** (p620).

- Swing back around to the other side of the Sierra and check out the **world's biggest trees** (p605) at Sequoia National Park. Then wind your way through to neighboring Kings Canyon for spelunking in **Boyden Cavern** (p614) and some gorgeous **hikes** (p613).

MAY

Cascades gush and Bishop celebrates **Mule Days** (p621), a unique rodeo-like event where 'packers' (backcountry cowboys) show their skills.

SEPTEMBER

Crowds recede, waterfalls trickle. **Yosemite Facelift** cleans up trash, while **Dark Sky Festival** (p616) graces Sequoia and Kings Canyon.

OCTOBER

Fall colors light up the Sierra Nevada and **leaf-peeping photographers** joyride looking for the best shot.

DECEMBER

The parks are frosted and mostly solitary, but the Ahwahnee holds its **Bracebridge Dinner** (p605; part feast, part Renaissance fair).

YOSEMITE NATIONAL PARK

The crown jewel of California's national parks is defined by its plunging waterfalls, soaring trees, wildflower-dotted valleys and majestic domes. Carved by ancient glaciers, these stunning granite features have been gazed upon by devoted humans for some 8000 years.

The original caretakers, the Ahwahneechee people, were violently displaced in the mid-1800s by white settlers. After roads and inns began springing up, conservationists petitioned Congress to protect the area. In 1864 President Abraham Lincoln signed the Yosemite Grant, which ceded the land to California as a state park. This decision, paired with the efforts of conservationist John Muir, led to a congressional act in 1890 creating Yosemite National Park.

Today, the show-stopping park is also a Unesco World Heritage Site and is visited by millions of people each year. Look up above the crowds, though, and you'll feel awed by the park's unrivaled natural splendors.

TOP TIP

Before driving to Yosemite, find out if you'll need a reservation for your visit and secure it through recreation.gov. If reservations are sold out, you can enter by booking lodgings within the park, taking a guided tour, obtaining a wilderness permit or Half Dome permit, or riding a YARTS bus.

Bridalveil Fall (p602)

ALEXANDER DEMYANENKO/SHUTTERSTOCK ©

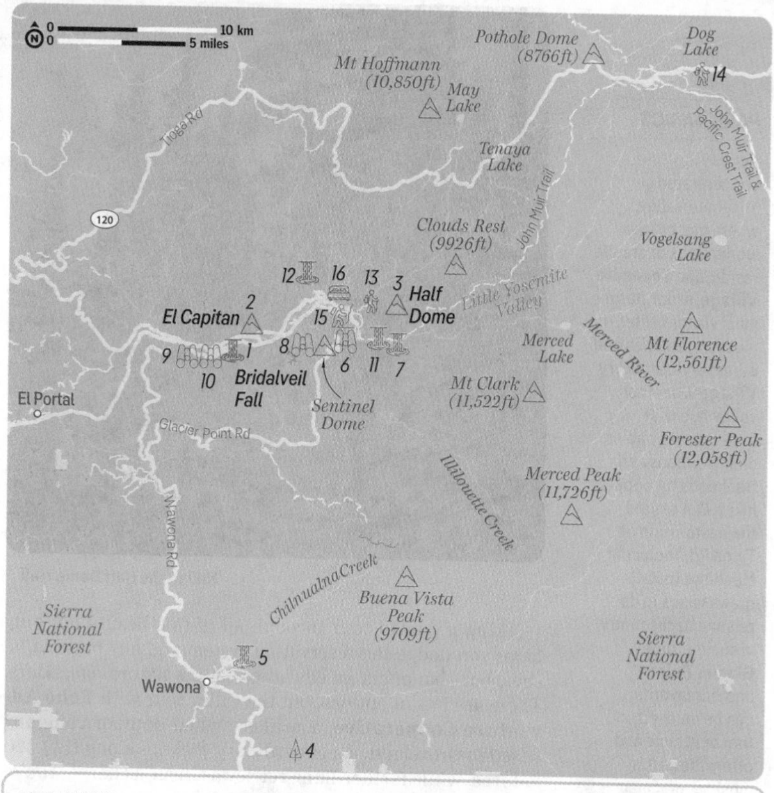

HIGHLIGHTS
1 Bridalveil Fall
2 El Capitan
3 Half Dome

SIGHTS
4 Mariposa Grove
5 Chilnualna Falls
6 Glacier Point
7 Nevada Fall
8 Sentinel Dome
9 Tunnel View
10 Valley View
11 Vernal Fall
12 Yosemite Falls

ACTIVITIES, COURSES & TOURS
13 Mirror Lake
14 Tuolumne Meadows
15 Yosemite Mountaineering School

SLEEPING
16 Ahwahnee Hotel

Iconic Yosemite

A TOUR OF THE VALLEY FLOOR

Spectacular, meadow-carpeted Yosemite Valley stretches for 7 miles, bisected by the rippling Merced River and hemmed in by some of the most majestic chunks of granite anywhere on earth. Ribbons of water, including some of the highest waterfalls in the USA, plummet and crash in thunderous displays.

BEST RESTAURANTS IN YOSEMITE NATIONAL PARK

Ahwahnee Dining Room
Mind the dinner dress code at this lavish establishment, where dishes are exquisite and beautifully presented. **$$$**

Mountain Room Restaurant
Plates of NY strip steak, roasted acorn squash and mountain trout, with killer views of Yosemite Falls. **$$$**

Curry Village Pizza Deck
Enjoy pizza at this revamped and buzzing eatery that becomes a chatty après-hike hangout in the afternoon. **$$**

R.M. NUNES/SHUTTERSTOCK ©

Hiking the Half Dome trail

PARK BASICS

Activity is concentrated in Yosemite Valley, where most of the iconic slabs of granite reside, and **Yosemite Village**, which has the main visitor center, a museum, eateries and other services. **Curry Village** is another valley hub with motel rooms, cabins, dining options and trailheads for popular hikes. Out toward the eastern end of Tioga Rd, Tuolumne Meadows (p604) draws hikers to its pristine backcountry in summertime. **Glacier Point**, another favorite, can be reached on foot or vehicle and offers the park's most spectacular views. **Wawona**, the park's southern focal point, has good infrastructure and enormous trees. In the northwestern corner, **Hetch Hetchy** offers waterfall hikes and an up-close look at San Francisco's water supply.

Taking a guided tour through all of this beauty not only helps you dodge the reservation system and any parking issues, but also offers an education on the natural splendors. There are lots of options, but the valley tour with **Echo Adventure Cooperative**, a worker-owned outdoor company based in Groveland, is extraordinary. Pickups along Hwy 120 are free, while farther-flung retrievals incur a charge. You're then whisked into the park in a passenger van, all the while getting to know your guide, who is likely a climber and definitely a long-time local. At the first stop, **Tunnel View**, you'll drink in vistas of the entire valley: **El Capitan** towering on the left, **Bridalveil Fall** plunging on the right, and glorious **Half Dome** front and center. For a closer look at heavenly Bridalveil Fall, you'll take a raised boardwalk to new viewing platforms directly in the spray zone of this 620-footer. Pack rain gear if it's spring (seriously) and aim your camera at the fall's misty rainbows.

After a quick stop at **Yosemite Valley Chapel**, the oldest structure in the park, you'll cruise around the corner and boom: there's Half Dome. The park's spiritual centerpiece is 87 million years old and has a 93% vertical grade – the sheerest cliff in North America. You will not suffer for lack of pho-

WHERE TO STAY INSIDE YOSEMITE NATIONAL PARK

Ahwahnee Hotel
Sumptuous historic property on the valley floor, with killer views, a famous dining room and a heated pool. **$$$**

Curry Village
A collection of motel rooms, wood cabins and canvas tent cabins in the heart of Yosemite. **$**

Yosemite Valley Lodge
Low-slung complex of rustic lodgings, eateries, a lively bar and a pool a short walk from the base of Yosemite Falls. **$$**

to opportunities, but definitely save some battery for **Mirror Lake**, the picture-perfect spot for capturing Half Dome's reflection. Heading back through Curry Village, the stunning granite **Royal Arches** will appear on your left as you continue on to **Yosemite Falls**, a hypnotizing cascade in the heart of the valley. A quick trail leads to the bottom, but adventurers prefer clambering up the grueling one to the top. Spring runoff turns these falls into thunderous cataracts, but they're reduced to a trickle by late summer. Mere minutes away is El Capitan, one of the world's largest granite monoliths. The road offers several good spots from which to watch climbers reckoning with El Cap's series of cracks and ledges, including the famous 'Nose.'

Your parting gift is **Valley View**, a bottom-up valley vista and a lovely spot to dip your toes in the Merced River. Here you'll have a last glance at Bridalveil Fall, **Cathedral Rocks** and El Capitan, and in the distance there's also the tip-top of Half Dome, bidding you farewell. Other recommended operators include **Yosemite 360 Tours** (out of Tenaya Lodge), **Yosemite Valley Floor Tour** (led by park rangers and naturalists out of Yosemite Valley Lodge) and **YExplore Yosemite Adventures** (custom experiences out of Sonora).

Hiking & Backpacking in Yosemite

SUPERLATIVE CALIFORNIA TRAILS

Over 800 miles of trails cater to hikers of all abilities. Take an easy half-mile stroll on the valley floor; venture out all day on a quest for viewpoints, waterfalls and lakes; or go camping in the remote outer reaches of the backcountry.

Some of the park's most popular hikes start right in Yosemite Valley, including the most famous of all: the top of Half Dome (17 miles round trip). It follows a section of the John Muir Trail, is strenuous and requires ascending fixed cables that rangers install seasonally. Depending on snow conditions, this may occur as early as late May or as late as July, and the cables usually come down in mid-October. To whittle down the cables' notorious human logjams, the park requires hikers to obtain permits, but the route is nerve-racking nonetheless. The less ambitious or physically fit can follow the same trail as far as **Vernal Fall** (2.6 miles round trip), the top of **Nevada Fall** (6.5 miles round trip) or idyllic **Little Yosemite Valley** (8 miles round trip). The **Four Mile Trail** (9.2 miles round trip) to Glacier Point is a strenuous but satisfying climb to a glorious viewpoint.

MAIN PARK ENTRANCES

Arch Rock Entrance
Hwy 140 runs through the Merced River Canyon before entering Yosemite Valley on the western side of the park.

Big Oak Flat Entrance
Hwy 120 W runs east from Groveland through Stanislaus National Forest before entering the park on its west side.

South Entrance
The southern entrance to the park along Hwy 41 is just north of the town of Fish Camp and minutes to Mariposa Grove.

Tioga Pass Entrance
Hwy 120 E traverses the park as Tioga Rd, connecting Yosemite Valley with the Eastern Sierra.

CLIMATE CHANGE

For a more in-depth discussion on how **climate change** is impacting the people of California and altering the state's landscapes, see p660.

Wawona Hotel
Stay in a Victorian building filled with period furnishings at this National Historic landmark from 1879. **$$**

Camp 4
A walk-in campground at 4000ft near Yosemite Falls' base; popular with climbers and notable in the sport's history. **$**

High Sierra Camps
Five backcountry camps along a 49-mile loop offering beds, sheets and some meals. Reservations by lottery. **$**

I LIVE HERE: WHERE TO SEE WILDFLOWERS

Mirella Gutierrez, a National Park Service contract specialist living and working in Yosemite, recommends where to find blooming trees and wildflowers.

Yosemite Valley
I love driving through the valley to see the Pacific dogwoods, which typically bloom in late April and early May. They can also be found along the walk to Mirror Lake.

Hetch Hetchy
When I want a half-day hike with some elevation change, I hike Wapama Falls. The best time to go is mid- to late May, when purple, yellow, red and pink wildflowers bloom.

Clouds Rest
There are many high-elevation hikes along Tioga Rd, but Clouds Rest has always been a favorite. Wildflowers can be seen all along the trail in July and August.

Along Glacier Point Rd, Sentinel Dome (2.2 miles round trip) is an easy hike to the crown of a commanding granite dome. And one of the most scenic hikes in the park, the **Panorama Trail** (8.5 miles one way), descends to the valley (joining the John Muir and Mist Trails) with nonstop views, including of Half Dome and Illilouette Fall. If you've got kids in tow, easy destinations include **Mirror Lake** (2 miles round trip, or 4.5 miles via the Tenaya Canyon Loop) in the valley, and the **McGurk Meadow** trail (1.6 miles round trip) on Glacier Point Rd, which has a historic log cabin to romp around in. The Wawona area features giant sequoias (the world's largest trees) and one of the park's prettiest – and often overlooked – hikes, to **Chilnualna Falls** (8.6 miles round trip). Best done between April and June, it follows a cascading creek to the top of the dramatic falls.

The highest concentration of hikes lies in the high country of **Tuolumne Meadows**, which is only accessible in summer. One rewarding and popular combo hike is **Dog Lake and Lembert Dome** (5 miles round trip), but the meadow's best hike has to be **Cathedral Lakes**, a 7.6-mile jaunt through stunning forests and meadows to a pair of lakes that shimmer beneath the jagged Cathedral Peak (10,911ft). Backpacks, tents and other equipment can be rented from the **Yosemite Mountaineering School**. The school also offers two-day Learn to Backpack trips for novices ($400 per person), and all-inclusive three-, four- and five-day guided backpacking trips ($450 to $750 per person), which are great for inexperienced and solo travelers.

An Ahwahnee Experience

THE SIERRA'S STYLISH SIDE

Maybe you hiked all the way to the top of Yosemite Falls. Maybe you just bumped around the village and bought a T-shirt. Either way, a much-deserved break awaits at the crème de la crème of Yosemite lodgings and the very picture of rustic elegance: the Ahwahnee Hotel. Dating back to 1927, this majestic hotel was built from granite, concrete and steel to attract wealthy guests. But these days all park visitors have the right to wander beneath the soaring ceilings, relax in atmospheric lounges before mammoth stone fireplaces and peer through massive windows at Glacier Point, Half Dome and Yosemite Falls.

If the lobby looks familiar, perhaps it's because it inspired the lobby of the Overlook Hotel, the ill-fated inn from Stanley Kubrick's film *The Shining*. Those less inclined to stay

BEST PLACES FOR CULTURE IN YOSEMITE NATIONAL PARK

Yosemite History Center
Some of the park's oldest buildings were brought to this center. Peer inside, read the history and ride stagecoaches.

Ansel Adams Gallery
Ansel Adams, photographic prints are shown, and walks and classes are on offer in this Yosemite Village gallery.

Indian Village
Behind the Yosemite Museum, an interpretive trail winds through reconstructed 1870s Ahwahnee village.

Ahwahnee Hotel dining room

FRANCISCO BLANCO/SHUTTERSTOCK ©

the night may enjoy a meal in the baronial dining room or a casual drink in the piano bar, admiring the leaded-glass, sculpted tiles, Native American trappings, German Gothic chandeliers and Turkish rugs. At Christmas the hotel hosts the **Bracebridge Dinner**, a combination of banquet and Renaissance fair. Book early, and for high season and holidays book rooms a year ahead. A word to the wise: the hotel is a dead zone for cell-phone reception.

Strolling the Mariposa Grove

500 OF THE WORLD'S BIGGEST TREES

The Mariposa Grove looms large in the southern region of Yosemite National Park. Its 500 mature giant sequoias stand more than 200ft high and date back over 2000 years, having survived countless fires. As recently as 2022, the grove was threatened by wildfire. Yet again these resilient trees persevered, but that is not to say that the trees are invincible.

A visit begins with either a 2-mile shuttle-bus ride from the welcome plaza or a 2-mile hike along the **Washburn Trail**, which follows a 19th-century stagecoach route. On the right as you enter the lower grove, the **Fallen Monarch** tree and its exposed roots illustrate the sequoias' shallow but diffuse

YOSEMITE FIREFALL

For two weeks in late February, if the sky is clear and the water flow sufficient, visitors can behold a fiery spectacle at **Horsetail Fall**. As the ribbon of water drops off the edge of El Capitan and catches the sunset, it blazes like a stream of molten lava. Photographers flock to the El Capitan Picnic Area for the best angle, and the park service limits visitation and parking to reduce the congestion.

Many compare it to witnessing the former Glacier Point Firefall, which started in 1872 and lasted through to the 1970s. That event involved sending actual burning hot embers over the top of Glacier Point and into the valley 3000ft below.

BEST PICNIC SPOTS IN YOSEMITE NATIONAL PARK

Olmsted Point
Settle into this lunar landscape with stunning views down Tenaya Canyon to the back side of Half Dome.

Tenaya Lake
Sit along the shoreline after an easy stroll around one of the park's largest and prettiest natural lakes.

Inspiration Point
Hike the steep 1.3-mile trail to this gorgeous spot and venture out on a spur trail to feast.

GREG EPPERSON/SHUTTERSTOCK ©

Rock climbing in Yosemite

YOSEMITE'S DREAMIEST WATERFALLS

Yosemite Falls
The tallest waterfall in North America, dropping 2425ft in three tiers; it's a brutal hike to the top.

Bridalveil Fall
In the valley, gusts blow this 620-footer side to side – the Ahwahneechee called it Pohono (Spirit of the Puffing Wind).

Vernal & Nevada Falls
These two Merced River beauties fall 317ft and 594ft respectively.

Chilnualna Falls
These falls plummet into a deep chasm; an appealing Wawona day hike.

Wapama Falls
By the Hetch Hetchy reservoir, this 1000-footer is reached on a 5-mile hike from O'Shaughnessy Dam.

life-support system, while many wind-toppled, weakened and scarred trees nearby offer evidence of a changing climate.

Keeping walking, and a half-mile up you'll encounter the 800-year-old **Grizzly Giant**, a monster of a tree whose branches are thicker than the trunks of local pines. The walk-through **California Tunnel Tree** is close by, and the favored spot for photos. Incredibly, this tree continues to survive, even though its heart was chopped out in 1895. In the upper grove, the more famous **Fallen Wawona Tunnel Tree**, however, fell over in a heap in 1969 due to a large hole gouged decades earlier. It's about a mile round trip from the Fallen Wawona Tunnel Tree to the wide-open overlook at **Wawona Point** (6810ft), which takes in the entire area.

Going Wild

OUTDOOR ADVENTURE IN YOSEMITE

There are a great many ways to adventure within this outdoor wonderland. For example, with its sheer spires, polished domes and soaring monoliths, Yosemite is legendary for its **rock climbing**. Most climbers, including famous ones, stay at Camp 4 near El Capitan, especially in spring and fall. In summer, another base camp springs up at Tuolumne Mead-

BEST SLABS OF GRANITE IN YOSEMITE NATIONAL PARK

El Capitan
Summiting the sheer granite and splintering cracks of this monolith is a vertigo-conquering achievement.

Half Dome
A pinnacle so popular that hikers need a permit to scale it; a must-reach-it obsession for millions.

Sentinel Rock
Yosemite's easiest granite-dome scramble rewards with 360-degree views of high peaks and falls.

ows Campground. Climbers looking for partners post notices on bulletin boards at either campground.

Although mountain biking isn't permitted, **cycling** (or e-biking) along the 12 miles of paved trails is a popular and environmentally friendly way of exploring the valley. It's also the fastest way to get around when traffic is at a standstill.

In early summer, **floating** along the Merced River is a leisurely way to soak up valley views. Raft rentals for a 3-mile trip are available in Curry Village and include a shuttle ride back to the rental kiosk. Down in Wawona, the South Fork of the Merced offers some of the best stream **fishing** in the park, and on a hot summer day, of course, nothing beats **swimming** in the cool river. Whatever you do, don't jump in near a waterfall, or even pretend you're going to. People have died that way.

The white coat of winter opens up a different set of options, as the valley becomes a quiet, frosty world of snow-draped evergreens, ice-coated lakes and gleaming white mountains for **winter sports**. Cross-country skiers can explore 350 miles of skiable trails and roads, while the family-friendly **Badger Pass Ski Area** has been beckoning skiers and snowboarders since 1935. You'll also find opportunities around the park for snowshoeing, ice-skating, snow camping, sledding and tubing.

Artistic Inspiration

ART IN YOSEMITE

From its very beginnings, Yosemite has inspired a body of art nearly as impressive as the landscape itself. The artists who came to Yosemite with the first generation of tourists revealed its extraordinary beauty, even as miners, ranchers and lumbermen were tearing it apart. From the illustrations of Thomas Ayres to the photographs of Carleton Watkins, art played a key role in establishing Yosemite as a national park. Yosemite's best-known photographer was Ansel Adams. An early proponent of the idea that photography could adhere to the same aesthetic principles used by fine artists, he also became an advocate for the preservation of the wilderness. Today you can visit the **Ansel Adams Gallery** in Yosemite Village to view prints of his work.

THE PLIGHT OF YOSEMITE'S TREES

Rising temperatures coupled with drought have led to the demise of millions of Yosemite's trees, which in a weakened state become vulnerable to invading bark beetles. A dry, dead tree is also highly flammable. Throw in woody debris left over from a century of fire suppression and Yosemite starts to look like a tinderbox, with fires burning hotter and faster than ever before. In response, park officials are performing prescribed, or deliberate, fires when possible, and allowing fires to burn naturally if they don't threaten lives or infrastructure. They'd like to thin the forests to prevent catastrophic fires, but some environmentalists take issue with the practice, and in 2022 stalled the efforts with lawsuits.

GETTING AROUND

Yosemite is accessible year-round from the west (via Hwys 120 W and 140) and south (Hwy 41), and in summer also from the east (via Hwy 120 E). Roads are plowed in winter, but snow chains may be required at any time. Rock slides have periodically shut down sections of road for weeks or months at a time, and Glacier Point Rd was experiencing delays for an improvement project at the time of research.

Gas up year-round at Wawona or Crane Flat inside the park (you'll pay dearly), at El Portal on Hwy 140 just outside its western boundary, or at Lee Vining at the junction of Hwys 120 and 395 outside the park in the east.

Beyond Yosemite National Park

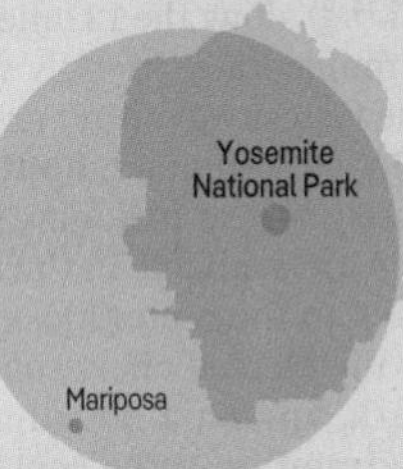

The gateway towns to Yosemite National Park are worth more than a passing glance out the car window.

About halfway between Merced and Yosemite Valley, Mariposa is the largest and most interesting of the national park's gateway hubs. Established as a mining and railroad town during the gold rush, it has loads of Old West character and a couple of good museums dedicated to the area's heritage, plus a rollicking nightlife.

To the north along Hwy 120 W perches Groveland, a little town with restored gold-rush-era buildings and loads of old-timey charm. Down south along Hwy 41, travelers can ride a historic steam train in Fish Camp, and just south of there, quotidian Oakhurst offers some unexpected, one-of-a-kind lodgings.

TOP TIP

The roads from the gateway towns into Yosemite – especially scenic Hwy 41 through the Merced River Canyon – become traffic-clogged in high season. Plan accordingly.

Mariposa

LENSTRAVEL/SHUTTERSTOCK ©

EBBETTS PASS DRIVING TOUR

For outdoor fanatics looking for an alternative to Yosemite National Park, or perhaps just a scenic way to get between the park and Lake Tahoe, there's the drive along Ebbetts Pass Scenic Byway (scenic4.org).

On this 61-mile section of Hwys 4 and 89, head east from **1 Arnold**, gaze up at the giant sequoias of **2 Calaveras Big Trees State Park** (p563) and stop at the family-friendly **3 Bear Valley Ski Resort**. Snow adventures dominate in winter, while mountain-biking trails and glamping tents rule in the summer; nearby, the Bear Valley Adventure Company is a one-stop shop for outdoor pursuits. Continuing east, the stunningly beautiful **4 Lake Alpine** is skirted by granite, has great beaches and boasts excellent water sports, fishing and hiking. A handful of campgrounds line the lakefront; also here is the rustic Lake Alpine Lodge.

The next stretch is the most dramatic, when the narrow highway continues past picturesque Mosquito Lake and the Pacific Grade Summit (8060ft) before slaloming through historic Hermit Valley and finally winding up and over the 8730ft summit of **5 Ebbetts Pass**. On the final stretch near Markleeville, you'll notice quite a bit of damage from the 2021 Tamarack Fire. Consider detouring northwest to relatively little-known Hope Valley Wildlife Area, a gorgeous reserve of meadows, streams and forests ringed by high Sierra peaks. Nearby the adventure base camp **6 Wylder Hotel** offers glamping, dreamy cabins and delicious food.

Note that Ebbetts Pass closes after the first major snowfall and doesn't reopen until June, but Hwy 4 is usually plowed from the west, often as far as Bear Valley.

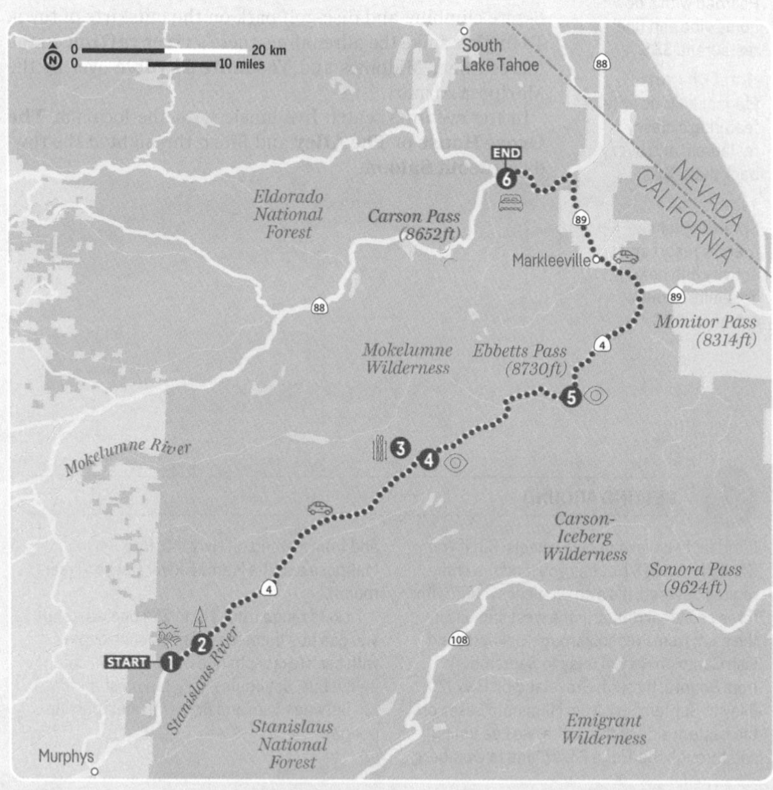

BEST STAYS OUTSIDE YOSEMITE NATIONAL PARK

Rush Creek Lodge
Luxe, country-chic resort and mountain-adventure destination with hot tubs and a fabulous Yosemite-inspired spa. $$$

Yosemite Bug Rustic Mountain Resort
A long-standing budget-friendly oasis with eclectic accommodations, a beloved restaurant and a spa. $

Narrow Gauge Inn
A 26-room inn near the Sugar Pine Railroad with a down-home vibe and fine restaurant. $$$

Hotel Charlotte
Elegant historic hotel featuring a classy restaurant and buzzy back patio. $$

Tenaya Lodge
Sprawling family-friendly resort and activity hub near Yosemite's south entrance. $$$

Gateway Gold

A CULTURE TOUR OF MARIPOSA

This no-stoplight former gold-rush town about an hour's drive from Yosemite packs quite the cultural punch. Dive into Mariposa with a wander around the historic downtown, which recently underwent a $6.3 million renovation and features the oldest courthouse in continuous use (since 1854) west of the Mississippi. Grab a late-morning libation at **1850 Brewing Company**, where the beers are brewed on-site and the cocktail of choice, Tipsy Cow Tipper, comes with peanut-butter-flavored whiskey.

Museum time! The **Mariposa Museum & History Center** brings the town's past to life with old menus, train tickets, photos and the like, and a new Miwuk exhibit features expertly woven baskets, jewelry, arrowheads and more. Over at the county fairgrounds, rock hounds will dig the **California State Mining & Mineral Museum**, where the 13lb 'Fricot Nugget' (the largest crystalized gold specimen from the California gold-rush era) is proudly displayed. The newest cultural offering in town, **Yosemite Climbing Museum**, contains memorabilia stretching back to when the sport's pioneers were making their own gear. Climbing enthusiasts should also check out the **Yosemite Boulder Farm**, a new 6-acre climbing and disc-golf park on the outskirts of town. To further spike the adrenaline, there's **river rafting** on the Merced near Midpines and **Yosemite Skydive** over by the Mariposa Airport.

In the evenings, catch live music with the locals at **The Grove House** or **The Alley** and finish the night at the rowdy **Hideout Saloon**.

GETTING AROUND

It's ideal to have your own wheels. But if you don't, the YARTS bus has you (and the entire region) covered. It's a convenient system with three seasonal routes in the west and one in the east: from Fresno, through Oakhurst and Fish Camp on Hwy 41 (May to September); from Sonora, through Groveland on Hwy 120 (May to September); from Mammoth Lakes on the eastern side of the Sierra, via Lee Vining and through the Tioga Pass (June to October); and from Merced on Hwy 140, through Mariposa and the Merced River Canyon (year-round).

Tickets range from $10 to $22 one way, and you can buy them in advance online or pay with cash (exact change only) or credit card on the bus. Schedules vary, but most routes run between 5am and 8pm with multiple runs per day.

SEQUOIA & KINGS CANYON NATIONAL PARKS

Far from the hubbub of Yosemite Valley, some 200 miles to the southwest, these side-by-side parks comprise a quieter stretch of the Sierra. Here it's easy to find solitude within wildflower-strewn meadows or by an alpine lake, to unwind before a gushing waterfall or to pull off a deserted highway and gaze into a dramatic gorge. People mainly visit, however, for the parks' forests, which feature some of the planet's largest giant sequoias. If you've ever wanted to see these magnificent trees, now is the time.

Over the last few years, climate change has threatened these groves like never before. In 2020 and 2021, two incredibly intense fires scorched thousands of sequoias living within the parks, killing 20% of species. Burn areas and other impacted park features remained off-limits to visitors at the time of research, but the undeniable beauty of the parks endures.

TOP TIP

Although administered as a single unit by the National Park Service (NPS), Sequoia and Kings Canyon National Parks are actually two national parks. Sequoia has more famous sequoias (including General Sherman, the world's largest tree), while Kings Canyon is better known for its canyons, valleys, waterfalls and mountain peaks.

Sequoia National Park

SEQUOIA & KINGS CANYON NATIONAL PARKS

SIGHTS
1 Boyden Cavern
2 General Grant Grove
see 3 General Sherman Tree
3 Giant Forest
4 Giant Forest Museum
5 Mineral King
6 Mist Falls Trail
7 Moro Rock

ACTIVITIES, COURSES & TOURS
8 Eagle Lake
9 High Sierra Trail
10 Rae Lakes Loop

SLEEPING
11 Silver City Mountain Resort

Superlative Sequoias

VISITING THE WORLD'S BIGGEST TREES

Build your big-tree anticipation with a primer on their intriguing ecology and history at the Giant Forest Museum off the Generals Hwy within Sequoia. Hands-on exhibits teach about the life stages of the trees, which can live for more than 3000 years, and the fire cycle that releases their seeds and allows

BEST PLACES TO SLEEP IN SEQUOIA AND KINGS CANYON NATIONAL PARKS

Pear Lake Ski Hut
A rustic backcountry hut (6 miles of cross-country skiing or snowshoeing required) that sleeps 10, with a wood stove. **$**

Silver City Mountain Resort
These cozy, rustic cabins in remote Mineral King offer a unique and memorable mountain experience. **$$**

Wuksachi Lodge
The parks' most upscale option, with stone fireplaces, forest views and generic motel-style rooms. **$$$**

them to sprout on bare soil. The museum is housed in a historic 1920s building designed by Gilbert Stanley Underwood, famed architect of the Ahwahnee Hotel (p604).

Now you're ready for the big time. Jump on the shuttle (recommended) or drive five minutes up the highway to **Giant Forest**, a 3-sq-mile grove that protects around half of the world's most gargantuan tree specimens. Among them is the world's biggest by volume, the General Sherman tree, rocketing 275ft into the sky. Pay your respects then consider doing the **Congress Trail**, a paved 2-mile pathway that begins near the General Sherman tree and takes in the **Washington Tree** (named in honor of George Washington) and the see-through **Telescope Tree**.

For even more big tree action later in the trip, there's the **General Grant Grove** over in Kings Canyon. Take the paved half-mile **General Grant Tree Trail**, an interpretive walk that visits a number of mature sequoias, including the 27-story **General Grant Tree**. This giant holds triple honors as the world's second-largest living tree (by trunk volume), a memorial to US soldiers killed in war and the nation's official Christmas tree since 1926.

Hit the Trails

ALL THE ICONIC HIKES

More than 850 miles of maintained trails await your footsteps in both national parks. From sun-bleached granite peaks soaring above alpine lakes to wildflower-dotted meadows and roaring waterfalls, this is a hiker's paradise.

Which day hikes appeal most will largely depend on your preferences and stamina. Are you the sort who appreciates a quick ascent to the tippy-top of a granite dome to enjoy panoramic views over 150 miles of mountain range? Do **Moro Rock**, just south of the Giant Forest. If you'd prefer a more secluded jaunt to a glacially carved tarn, Mineral King's **Eagle Lake** has you covered. For anyone craving a satisfying 9-mile walk along a riverside and up a natural granite staircase to the park's largest waterfall, Cedar Grove's **Mist Falls Trail** is perfect.

For those more interested in overnight hikes, you too have come to the right place. **Mineral King**, **Lodgepole** and **Cedar Grove** offer the best backcountry trail access, while the **Jennie Lakes Wilderness** in the Sequoia National Forest boasts pristine meadows and lakes at lower elevations. The most popular multiday trek in Kings Canyon is **Rae Lakes Loop**, which skirts a chain of jewel-like lakes over 41 glorious miles. And the **High Sierra Trail**, a 49-mile stunner along

PARK BASICS

Sequoia and Kings Canyon are both accessible by car only from the west, via Hwy 99 from Fresno or Visalia. It's 46 miles east on Hwy 198 from Visalia into Sequoia National Park – you pass through the gateway town of Three Rivers before entering the park. From Fresno, it's 57 miles east on Hwy 180 to Kings Canyon. The two roads are connected by the Generals Hwy, inside Sequoia. There is no access to either park from the east.

There are five main regions of the parks to explore: Foothills, Mineral King and the Giant Forest (and Lodgepole area) within Sequoia, and Grant Grove and Cedar Grove within Kings Canyon.

John Muir Lodge
A stone-and-timber retreat in Grant Grove Village offering homespun rooms, a cozy fireplace and tent cabins. **$**

Cedar Grove Lodge
The only indoor sleeping option in the canyon, this riverside lodge offers 21 simple motel-style rooms. **$$**

Sequoia High Sierra Camp
A mile's hike into the Sequoia National Forest, this off-the-grid resort and its bungalows are glamping nirvana. **$**

I LIVE HERE: BEST HIKES IN SEQUOIA

Krista Simonic, passionate Sierra Nevada native and owner of Sequoia Guides, shares her favorite hikes in Sequoia and Kings Canyon.

Crescent Meadow & Tharp's Log
This 1.8-mile loop is my favorite place to look for wildlife and wildflowers. There are dozens of amazing sequoias, and one you can climb inside!

General Sherman Tree & Congress Trail
Begin in the morning to avoid crowds and venture into the heart of the Giant Forest. You'll see burnt but still thriving trees that command inspiration.

Tokopah Falls
This 3.2-mile out-and-back trail follows the Marble Fork of the Kaweah River into Tokopah Valley, with towering rock cliffs above and a misty waterfall reward.

a dramatic ridge, offers epic views and river crossings, concluding at Mt Whitney.

Park-approved, bear-proof food canisters are mandatory for wilderness trips.

Spelunking at Boyden Cavern

GETTING DOWN UNDERGROUND

Among hundreds of caves that have been discovered in and around Sequoia and Kings Canyon National Parks, privately owned **Boyden Cavern** (accessed via the Kings Canyon Scenic Byway) is the only one currently open to the public. Carved out by an underground river some 100,000 years ago, the marble cavern was known to Native American tribes in the early 1800s and a survey crew found it later in the century. Putnam Boyden, a Hume Lake logger, liked the idea of opening it for sightseers. He bought the cave, moved in and offered tours for 5¢.

Its current owners charge $16 to $20, depending on the day, but the experience is largely the same. Visitors hike a short but incredibly steep trail to the entrance before ducking into the cave, where the temperature quickly drops to 55°F (13°C). Stalactites hang like daggers from the ceiling and milky-white marble takes the shape of things like ethereal curtains, a dripping stack of pancakes and even 'cave bacon,' as the guides call it.

Enjoy poking around the ancient wonder and keep your eyes peeled for the shrews, spiders, scorpions and (of course) bats, but try not to touch the sensitive formations. Guided tours ranging from 45 minutes to an hour run daily during summer. Book tickets in advance online at boydencavern.com.

Adventuring in Mineral King

SECLUSION IN THE SIERRA

A scenic subalpine valley at 7500ft, Mineral King is Sequoia's backpacking mecca and a good place to find solitude. Gorgeous and gigantic, its glacially sculpted valley is ringed by massive mountains, including the jagged 12,343ft Sawtooth Peak. The area is reached via Mineral King Rd – a winding, steep and narrow 28-mile road not suitable for recreational vehicles (RVs) or speed demons; it's usually open from late May through October. Plan on spending at least one night, and ideally several.

Scattered along the last 6 miles of road are two first-come, first-served park campgrounds, a ranger station and the private **Silver City Mountain Resort**. This rustic, old-fashioned

BEST PLACES TO EAT IN SEQUOIA AND KINGS CANYON NATIONAL PARKS

Peaks Restaurant
Wuksachi Lodge serves up an excellent breakfast buffet, soup-and-salad lunch fare and gourmet dinners. **$$$**

Silver City Mountain Resort Restaurant
The only restaurant in Mineral King serves lip-smacking burgers and homemade pie. **$**

Grant Grove Restaurant
Grab an outdoor table at this solid lodge restaurant serving traditional and seasonal American dishes. **$$**

KINGS CANYON SCENIC BYWAY DRIVING TOUR

John Muir once called Kings Canyon a rival of Yosemite, and this jaw-dropping scenic drive may well be why. It enters one of North America's deepest canyons, traversing the forested Giant Sequoia National Monument and shadowing the Kings River all the way to Road's End.

Begin at the **1 Grant Grove turnoff** and drive about 3 miles up Hwy 180, then pull over to drink in the mountain panorama at **2 McGee Vista Point**. Continue winding downhill through the Sequoia National Forest past the turnoff to Converse Basin Grove, a solemn reminder of the 19th-century logging of giant sequoias. Head deeper into the canyon, as the road serpentines past chiseled rock walls laced with waterfalls. Stop for superb scenery at **3 Junction View**, about 10.5 miles from Grant Grove, and **4 Yucca Point**, another 3.5 miles further.

Continue around ear-popping curves for 5 miles and you'll reach the entrance to **5 Boyden Cavern**, a privately owned marble wonder filled with curious rock formations and bats. Take the highly entertaining 45-minute tour, then keep on driving. The road bottoms out and runs parallel to the Kings River, its roar ricocheting off granite cliffs soaring high above. Soon you'll reach **6 Grizzly Falls**, often a torrent in late spring.

The scenic byway reenters the national park just over 2.5 miles further along, passing the Lewis Creek bridge and a riverside beach. At Cedar Grove Village, you can stop at the visitor center and market before continuing to the Roaring River Falls and pretty Zumwalt Meadow trailheads. More hiking and swimming holes (like Muir Rock) await at **7 Road's End**, where the only way to keep going across the Sierra Nevada is on foot.

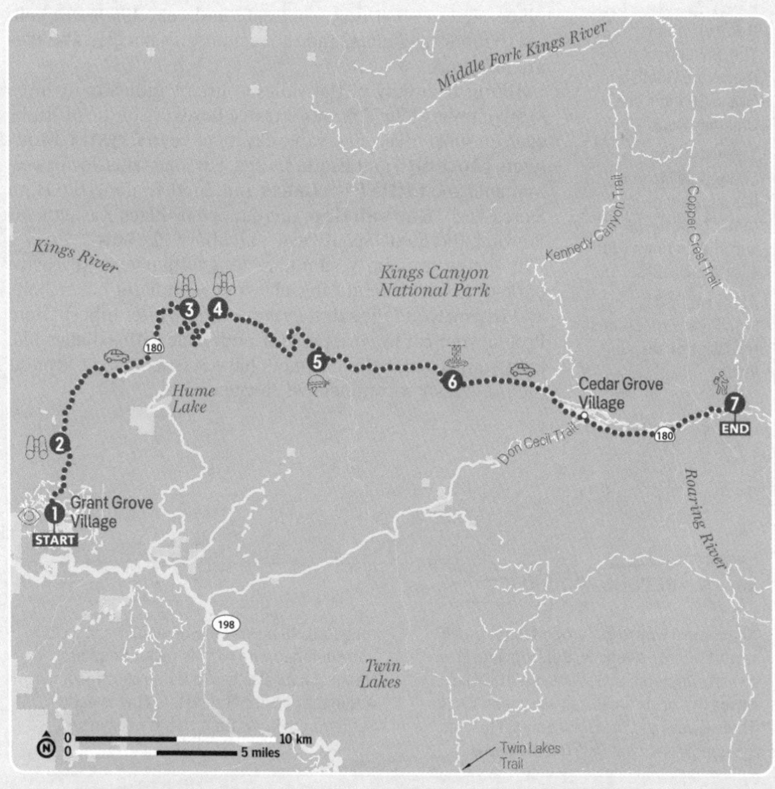

BEST OUTDOOR ACTIVITIES IN SEQUOIA & KINGS CANYON NATIONAL PARKS

Stargazing
The annual Dark Sky Festival includes star parties, ranger programs, solar viewing and NASA astronaut talks.

Horseback riding
Summer rides from Grant Grove Stables and Cedar Grove Pack Station in Kings Canyon and Horse Corral Pack Station in Sequoia.

Rock climbing
The most popular routes are Obelisk, Grand Sentinel and Chimney Rock.

Snowshoeing
Lodgepole Market has snowshoes for rent. Check the parks' website for ranger-led snowshoe walks.

River rafting
King River Expeditions runs trips on the Kings River.

SEBASTIEN BUREL/SHUTTERSTOCK ©

Mosquito Lakes

place offers everything from cute and cozy 1950s-era cabins to modern chalets, and the restaurant's burgers and pies are delicious.

Hiking from any of the valley's three trailheads involves steep climbs along strenuous trails. Be aware of the altitude, even on short hikes. Enjoyable day hikes go to **Crystal**, **Monarch**, **Mosquito** and **Eagle Lakes**. For long trips, locals recommend the **Little Five Lakes** and, further along the High Sierra Trail, **Kaweah Gap**, surrounded by Black Kaweah, Mt Stewart and Eagle Scout Peak – all above 12,000ft.

In spring and early summer, hungry marmots terrorize parked cars at Mineral King, chewing on radiator hoses, belts and wiring to get the salt they crave after winter hibernation. Protect your car by wrapping the underside with a diaper-like tarp – apparently the marmots have learned to get around the previously recommended chicken wire.

GETTING AROUND

The easiest way to get around these parks is with your own vehicle. But from late May to early September, Sequoia Shuttle runs buses five or six times daily between Visalia, Three Rivers and the Giant Forest Museum in Sequoia National Park (reservations required). All buses are wheelchair-accessible and equipped with bicycle racks. Sequoia National Park also has four free shuttle routes within the park (operating late May to early September); Kings Canyon has no shuttles.

Beyond Sequoia & Kings Canyon National Parks

Though lesser known and little explored, the gateway towns to Sequoia and Kings Canyon punch above their weight.

When park lodgings fill up in summertime and visitors are relegated to the gateway towns of Visalia and Three Rivers, some are surprised at how much they enjoy these two (very different) bases.

The agricultural prosperity and well-maintained downtown of Visalia, in the foothills of the Sierra Nevada, make it a convenient stop en route to the parks, and its old-town charm offers a reason to stay and stroll among the original Victorian homes, restaurants and shops.

A half-hour's drive closer to the park, and named for the convergence of three Kaweah River forks, Three Rivers is a friendly small town populated by retirees and artsy newcomers. The main drag, Sierra Dr (Hwy 198), is sparsely lined with cozy lodgings, eateries and shops.

TOP TIP

The helpful folks at the Visalia Convention & Visitors Bureau will hook you up with maps and brochures for touring the region.

Kaweah River

BEST PLACES TO SLEEP & EAT IN VISALIA & THREE RIVERS

Lamp Liter Inn
A family-owned Visalia spot with clean country cottages, a pool and a Sequoia Shuttle stop out front. $$

Buckeye Tree Lodge
A cute collection of recently upgraded hotel rooms and cabins, some with patio and balcony views of the river. $$

Three Rivers Hideaway
A friendly and convenient campground right outside the Ash Mountain Entrance to Sequoia. Cabins also available. $

Quesadilla Gorilla
A fast-growing Central Valley chain that specializes in from-scratch quesadillas with fresh ingredients. $

RUBEN QUINTANA/GETTY IMAGES ©

Kaweah Oak Preserve

Kickin' It in Visalia

OAK TREES AND BOOZE

The main draw in the area is the **Kaweah Oak Preserve**, about 7 miles east of Visalia (which is a 45-minute drive from the park). The preserve features 344 acres of majestic oak trees, which once stretched from the Sierras to (long-gone) Tulare Lake in the valley. A gorgeous setting for easy hikes, it's a glimpse of the valley ecosystem before orchards and vineyards took over, and more than 300 plant and animal species inhabit the preserve, including bobcats, great horned owls and woodpeckers.

For travelers interested in some hands-on experience, the preserve offers stewardship opportunities, with no long-term commitment necessary. You can work in the native plant nursery or help with trail maintenance. Email education@sequoiariverlands.org for more info. For those who'd rather hike and then drink beer, Visalia delivers with three excellent breweries. **Brewbakers Brewing Company** is often jam-packed with hikers thirsty for craft booze, while **Barrelhouse Brewing Co.** has a spacious taproom and hosts live music on weekends. **Sequoia Brewing Company** is a sports-themed brewpub with beers named for local landmarks (eg General Sherman IPA and the General Grant ESB). Up the road, **Three Rivers Brewing** is run by an award-winning craft-beer maker, and has a tasty rotation of reds, IPAs, sours and stouts on tap.

GETTING AROUND

Hwy 198 runs north from Visalia through Three Rivers to Sequoia National Park's Ash Mountain Entrance. The road to remote Mineral King veers off Hwy 198 at the northern end of Three Rivers, just south of the park's Ash Mountain Entrance.

Sequoia Shuttle buses run five to six times daily between Visalia and the Giant Forest Museum ($20 round trip, 2½ hours, including park entry fees) via Three Rivers; reservations required.

EASTERN SIERRA

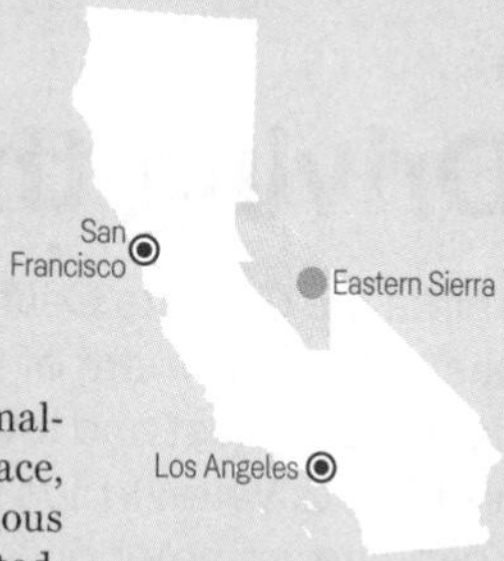

The lesser-explored side of the Sierra is a compelling amalgam of high desert, rural towns and blissfully empty space, backed by some of the tallest mountains in the contiguous USA. Many are over 14,000ft and frequently snow dusted, shooting skyward from the arid Great Basin and Mojave Deserts. It's a dramatic juxtaposition, and a landscape far less accessible than its western counterpart. But those who make the journey are rewarded with said beauty, plus pine forests, lush meadows, ice-blue lakes, simmering hot springs and glacier-gouged canyons.

The Eastern Sierra Scenic Byway (Hwy 395 officially) runs the entire length of the range. Turnoffs dead-ending at the foot of the mountains deliver you to pristine wilderness and countless trails, including the famous Pacific Crest Trail, John Muir Trail and the main Mt Whitney Trail. Add to that two major ski areas, the hauntingly gorgeous Mono Lake and California's best-preserved ghost town, and it's no wonder that the Eastern Sierra is suddenly on everybody's to-do list.

TOP TIP

Recent years have seen an influx of itinerants and van dwellers cruising Hwy 395, hiking, climbing or skiing by day, and boondocking on Bureau of Land Management property by night. If you aim to join the ranks of these dispersed campers, be sure to respect the land and other visitors, and pack out your trash.

Mono Lake (p626)

ROAD TRIP

Driving the 395

This is the ultimate California road trip, a south–north route tracing the eastern escarpment of the mighty Sierra Nevada. The road passes near the highest and lowest points in the continental USA (Mt Whitney and Death Valley), plus three national parks and the back entrance to Yosemite (summer only).

1 Lone Pine

Start in diminutive Lone Pine at the **Museum of Western Film History**, investigating the paraphernalia from hundreds of movies. Then head to the nearby orange, round-earthen mounds of the transcendental **Alabama Hills**, where many of the Old West Hollywood movies were shot. Even if you don't plan to climb the jagged 14,505ft peak of Mt Whitney, the drive to the **Whitney Portal** is gorgeous in its own right.

The Drive: Wind back down the mountain and through the sage-speckled desert, then head north on Hwy 395.

2 Manzanar National Historic Site

Just up the road near the tiny town of Independence is the Manzanar National Historic Site, a museum that tells the story of one of the darkest chapters in US history (p623). On this barren, windswept land, a former WWII-era concentration camp incarcerated thousands of Japanese Americans between 1942 and 1945. Also in Independence is the **Eastern California Museum**, with exhibits on the area's Native American history.

The Drive: Hop back on the 395 and keep on truckin' north.

DENNIS SILVAS/SHUTTERSTOCK ©

Road to Lone Pine and Mt Whitney

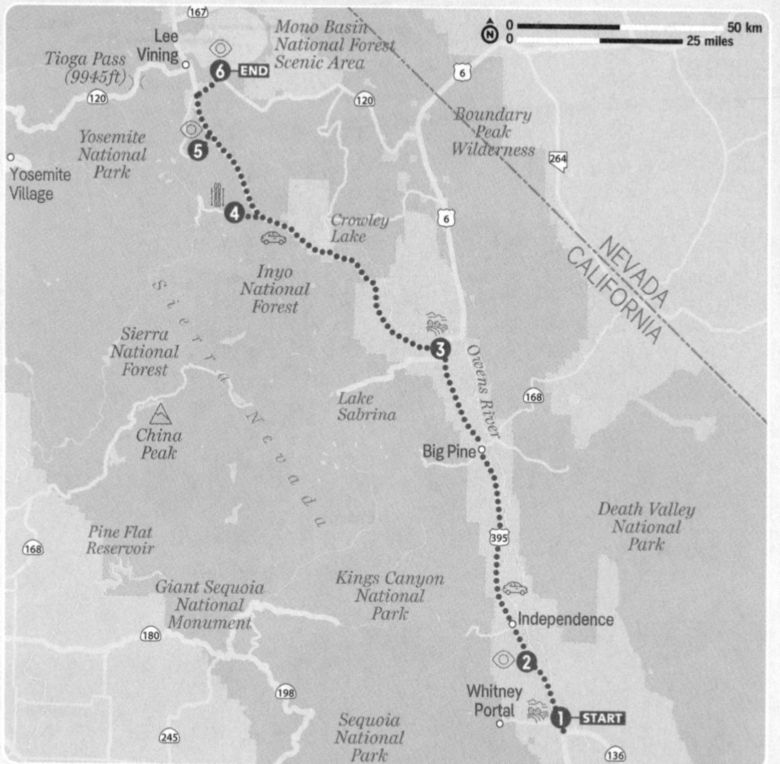

3 Bishop

You could spend a few days bumpin' around Bishop, the second-largest town in the Eastern Sierra, where hiking, cycling, fishing and climbing are all on offer. Set aside some time for the **Laws Railroad Museum & Historic Site**, where you sift through relics of the Old West and explore antique railcars. Consider timing your visit to correspond with **Mule Days** in May (a festival celebrating the mule).

The Drive: Return to Hwy 395, then veer off to the west through Inyo National Forest on Rte 203, which becomes Mammoth's Main St.

4 Mammoth Lakes

In the year-round resort town of Mammoth Lakes, the mountain's ski season can run into June, with backcountry hikes galore and a massive mountain-biking park. Don't miss Reds Meadow (p624), just west of Mammoth Mountain, and the surreal 10,000-year-old Devils Postpile National Monument (p624).

The Drive: Hop back on Hwy 395 and head for the scenic June Lake Loop.

5 June Lake Loop

The June Lake Loop drive traces the lake and meanders through a horseshoe canyon under the shadow of Carson Peak. Especially scenic in fall, the road is backed by the Ansel Adams Wilderness Area (p624) and its world-class high-country trails. Rainbows abound in springtime, and in summer the lake beach becomes quite the party scene.

The Drive: Head east on Rte 120 to Mono Lake's South Tufa area.

6 Mono Lake

North America's second-oldest lake is a quiet and mysterious 70-sq-mile expanse of deep blue water. The glassy surface reflects jagged Sierra peaks, young volcanic cones and the unearthly tufa towers that make the lake so distinctive.

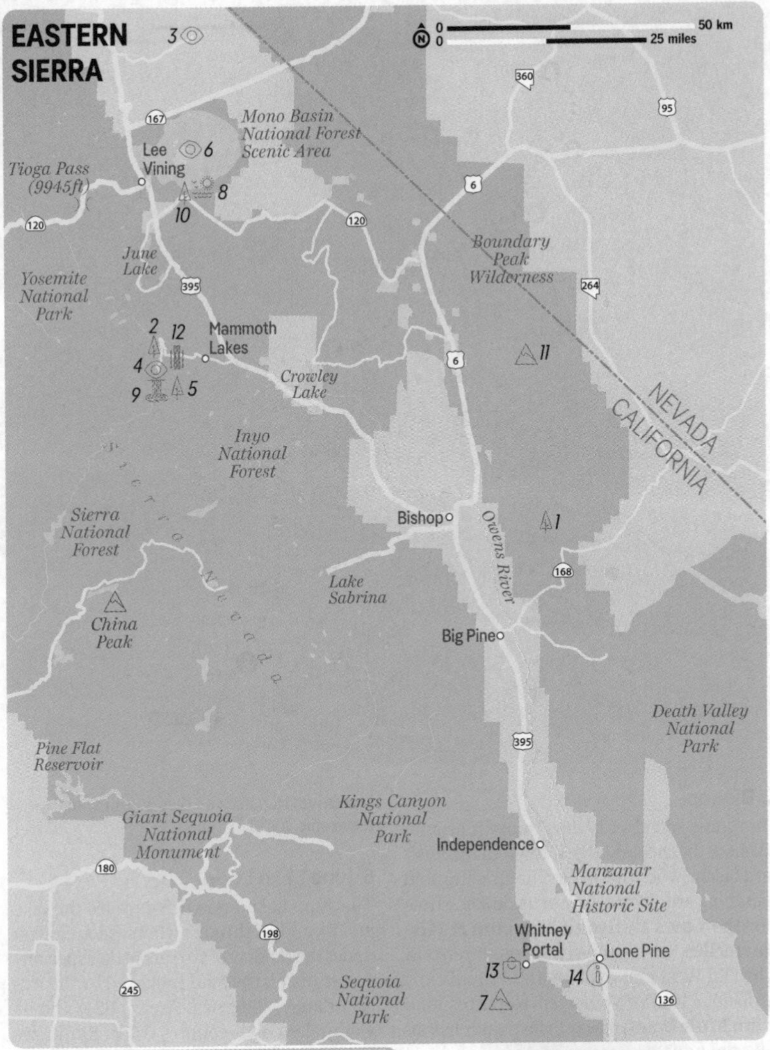
EASTERN SIERRA
0 50 km
0 25 miles
3
Mono Basin National Forest Scenic Area
Lee Vining
6
Tioga Pass (9945ft)
8
10
June Lake
Yosemite National Park
Boundary Peak Wilderness
2
12
Mammoth Lakes
4
9
5
Crowley Lake
11
NEVADA
CALIFORNIA
Inyo National Forest
Sierra National Forest
Sierra Nevada
Bishop
Owens River
1
Lake Sabrina
China Peak
Big Pine
Death Valley National Park
Pine Flat Reservoir
Kings Canyon National Park
Giant Sequoia National Monument
Independence
Manzanar National Historic Site
Whitney Portal
Lone Pine
13
14
7
Sequoia National Park
360
95
167
6
120
120
395
264
6
168
395
180
198
245
136

SIGHTS
1 Ancient Bristlecone Pine Forest
2 Ansel Adams Wilderness Area
3 Bodie State Historic Park
4 Devils Postpile National Monument
5 John Muir Wilderness Area
6 Mono Lake
7 Mt Whitney
8 Navy Beach
9 Rainbow Falls
10 South Tufa
11 White Mountain Peak

ACTIVITIES, COURSES & TOURS
12 Mammoth Mountain

SHOPPNG
13 Whitney Portal Store

INFORMATION
14 Eastern Sierra Interagency Visitor Center

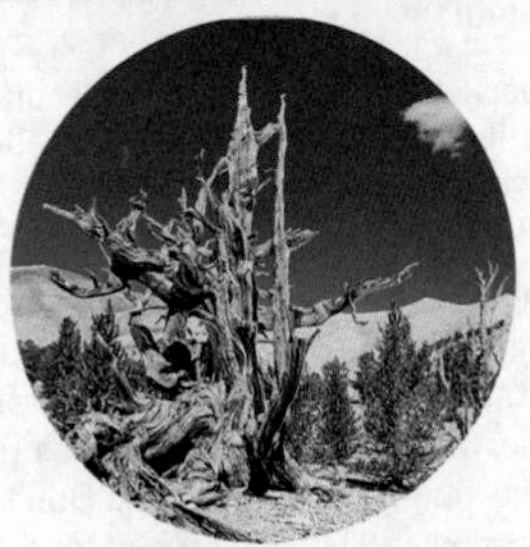

Ancient Bristlecone Pine Forest

OLICLIMB/SHUTTERSTOCK ©

Hiking Mt Whitney

ONE MAJESTIC MONOLITH

The mystique of Mt Whitney (14,505ft) captures the imagination, and conquering it becomes an obsession for many. The main **Mt Whitney Trail** (the easiest and busiest one) leaves from Whitney Portal, about 13 miles west of Lone Pine via Whitney Portal Rd (closed in winter), and climbs about 6000ft over 11 miles. It's a super-strenuous, really, *really* long walk that'll wear out even experienced mountaineers, but it doesn't require technical skills if attempted in summer or early fall. Earlier or later in the season, you'll likely need an ice axe and crampons, and to stay overnight.

Many people in good physical condition make it to the top, although only superbly conditioned, previously acclimatized hikers should attempt this as a day hike. Breathing becomes difficult at these elevations, and altitude sickness is a common problem. Rangers recommend spending a night camping at the trailhead and another at one of the two camps along the route: **Outpost Camp** at 3.5 miles or **Trail Camp** at 6 miles up the trail.

Permits are sometimes hard to come by, but if you're lucky enough to snag one, pick it up along with pack-out kits (hikers must pack out their poop) at the **Eastern Sierra Interagency Visitor Center** in Lone Pine (p620), and get the latest info on weather and trail conditions. Near the trailhead, the **Whitney Portal Store** sells groceries and snacks. It also has public showers and a cafe that serves enormous, delicious pancakes. The message board on its website is a good starting point for Whitney research.

Walk in the World's Oldest Forest

RESPECT YOUR ELDERS

For encounters with some of the earth's oldest living things, plan at least a half-day trip to the **Ancient Bristlecone Pine Forest**. These otherworldly-looking trees are found above 10,000ft on the parched slopes of the White Mountains where almost nothing grows, and that allows the bristlecones to thrive.

To reach the groves, take Hwy 168 east 12 miles from Big Pine to White Mountain Rd, then turn left (north) and climb the curvy road 10 miles. Park at the solar-powered **Schulman Grove Visitor Center** (open mid-May to October) and if Ranger Skip Vasquez is working, pick her brain. She knows absolutely everything about bristlecones, and gives talks twice a day.

If you're lucky, she'll accompany you on the 1-mile Discovery Trail through the **Schulman Grove**, a fantastic introduction to these gnarled and wind-battled stalwarts. Otherwise,

UNDERSTANDING MANZANAR

A shameful chapter in the nation's history is memorialized at the **Manzanar National Historic Site**, where between 1942 and 1945, 11,070 people of Japanese ancestry were incarcerated by the US government. Little remains of the dusty war relocation center, but a stark wooden guard tower alerts drivers to veer off Hwy 395 and enter the camp's only remaining building, the former high-school auditorium. Inside, a superb interpretive center tells the heartbreaking stories of the former residents who languished here yet managed to create a thriving community. There's also a 22-minute documentary and a self-guided 3.2-mile driving tour, where visitors can explore a recreated mess hall and barracks, a reconstructed women's latrine and the haunting camp cemetery. A visit is one of California's historical highlights and should not be missed.

BEST PLACES TO STAY IN THE EASTERN SIERRA

Bodie Hotel
Experience an 1800s boardinghouse transported to Bridgeport from Bodie in all its rickety (but restored!) glory. **$$**

Double Eagle Resort & Spa
Fancy for June Lake, these two-bedroom log cabins and balcony hotel rooms exude rustic elegance. Great spa. **$$$**

Whitney Portal Hostel & Hotel
Perfect launchpad for Mt Whitney trips, with affordable dorms and modern motel rooms with views. **$**

BEST CRAZY LANDFORMS IN THE EASTERN SIERRA

Hot Creek Geological Site
Steaming, bubbling cauldrons, with water shimmering in tropical shades of blue and green. Near the airport.

Earthquake Fault
Near Mammoth Lakes, this sinuous fissure half a mile long gouges a crevice 20ft deep into the earth.

Black Point Fissures
These narrow crags opened when a lava mass cooled and contracted 13,000 years ago on Mono Lake's north shore.

Panum Crater
The youngest (640 years old), smallest and most accessible of the craters between Mono Lake and Mammoth Mountain.

interpretative panels tell the story of how Dr Edmund Schulman's curiosity about old trees led him to this grove in 1953, where he found the world's first known 4000-year-old tree. Four years later he found **Methuselah**, the world's oldest (known) living tree, at around 4700 years. Its location is secret, but there are plenty more wizened survivors to admire and photograph. Just be sure to stay on the trail to avoid damaging the fragile root systems.

A second grove, the **Patriarch Grove**, is set within a dramatic open bowl and reached via a 12-mile graded dirt road. Four miles further on you'll find a locked gate, which is the departure point for hikes to **White Mountain Peak** – at 14,246ft, it's the third-highest mountain in California.

Playing Outside in Mammoth Lakes

WHEEEEEEEEEE!

Mammoth Lakes is a famous mountain-resort town endowed with larger-than-life scenery – active outdoorsy folks worship at the base of its imposing 11,053ft Mammoth Mountain. Long-lasting powder clings to these slopes, and when the snow finally fades, the area is an outdoor wonderland of mountain-biking trails and endless alpine hiking.

Mammoth Lakes rubs up against the **Ansel Adams Wilderness Area** and **John Muir Wilderness Area**. Both are laced with fabulous trails leading to shimmering lakes, rugged peaks and hidden canyons. Major trailheads leave from the **Mammoth Lakes Basin**, **Reds Meadow** and **Agnew Meadows**; the last is accessible from June through September, and for the most part only by shuttle.

From various spots along the Reds Meadow area, long-distance backpackers with wilderness permits and bear canisters can easily jump onto the **John Muir Trail** (to Yosemite to the north and Mt Whitney to the south) and the **Pacific Crest Trail** (fancy walking to Mexico or Canada?).

From the last Saturday in April, the dozens of lakes that give the town its name lure fly- and trout-fishers from near and far. California fishing licenses, gear and advice are available at sporting-goods stores throughout town.

RESPONSIBLE TRAVEL

For more tips on how to travel lightly in California and help conserve the state's precious natural resources, see p640.

Get Down with the Devil

THE STRANGE THINGS VOLCANOES DO

The rawness and relative newness of the volcanic formations in the Eastern Sierra are a reminder of the region's active and ongoing evolution. And the most

BEST PLACES TO EAT IN THE EASTERN SIERRA

Silver Lake Resort Cafe
Hearty breakfasts are the bomb in this old-timey cafe within an eponymous 1916 cabin compound on June Lake. **$$**

Erick Schat's Bakery
Deservedly hyped tourist mecca in Bishop packed with fresh bread, dipping oil, jams and other goodies. **$**

Whoa Nellie Deli
Mobil-gas-station restaurant famous for Mono Lake views, live bands and amazing food. **$$**

Mammoth Lakes Basin

astounding landmark formed in the current era of volcanic activity is the **Devils Postpile National Monument**, located west of Mammoth Lakes.

To reach it, visitors must park near Mammoth Mountain Inn and hop on the shuttle bus in front of the Adventure Center, which transports you to one of the most beautiful and varied landscapes in the region. Exit the shuttle at the Devils Postpile Ranger Station and take the easy half-mile trail around the feature, which is perched atop a hill. As you walk, consider that about 80,000 to 100,000 years ago, a violent volcanic vent filled the river canyon in which you stand with lava 400ft deep. The lava cooled so quickly that it formed one of the world's most impressive examples of columnar basalt, reaching up to 60ft high. These multisided columns are virtually symmetrical, and their honeycomb formation can be viewed up close by taking a short trail up the hill.

From the monument, continue on a 2.5-mile hike through fire-scarred forest to awe-inspiring **Rainbow Falls**, where the San Joaquin River gushes over a 101ft basalt cliff. Your chances of seeing a rainbow forming in the billowing mist are highest at midday. The falls can also be reached via an easy 1.5-mile walk from the Reds Meadow area, which has a cafe, store, campground, pack station and shuttle stop.

BEST HOT SPRINGS IN THE EASTERN SIERRA

Keough's Hot Springs
Historic complex featuring a tepid outdoor pool and a hotter soaking pool. Locals bathe nearby in complimentary 'hot ditches.'

Buckeye Hot Spring
Secluded piping-hot spring with several pools beside Buckeye Creek – handy for a cooling dip. Clothing optional.

Travertine Hot Spring
Natural pools amid impressive rock formations just outside of Bridgeport. Can become kind of a scene after dark.

The Inn at Benton Hot Springs
A historic resort outside of already-remote Benton, with antique-filled rooms and campsites featuring private soaking tubs.

Convict Lake Resort Restaurant
Impress your date by going to this classy establishment for fresh rainbow trout. **$$$**

Lakefront Restaurant
Incredibly romantic French-California restaurant in the delightful Tamarack Lodge on the twin lakes. **$$$**

Ohanas 395
Slow-cooked kalua-pig tacos and poke bowls are delish at this Hawaiian soul food truck on June Lake. **$**

ZACK FRANK/SHUTTERSTOCK ©

Bodie State Historic Park

WATER FIGHT

In the 1930s Los Angeles expanded and bought up water rights in the Mono Basin, diverting streams feeding Mono Lake. The lake water dropped, doubling its salinity and threatening its ecological balance. In 1976, environmentalist David Gaines found that, if left untouched, Mono Lake would dry up within 20 years. To avert disaster he formed the Mono Lake Committee. Years of legal action followed, and eventually the committee succeeded. In 1994 the city was forced to reduce its diversions to allow the lake to rise by 20ft. Unfortunately, that hasn't happened. Recent drought means the lake is receding, which creates dust and other environmental issues. To learn more, visit the **Mono Lake Committee Information Center & Bookstore** in Lee Vining.

Diving into Mono Lake

AND OTHER WAYS TO ENJOY IT

After drinking in the glassy blue-green expanse of Mono Lake while driving along Hwy 395, you'll likely want an immersion. Next up, the **Mono Basin Scenic Area Visitor Center** is a short drive north of Lee Vining, where you'll find exhibits on the lake's history, wildlife and geology, and an interpretative trail overlooking the lake.

Rangers give patio talks on weekends, and they also lead excellent walking tours about 20 minutes away at the **South Tufa** area on the lake's rim. This is where you'll find the largest number of tufa: limestone towers resembling tall, thin sand castles, rising from the lake. They form when minerals are released from subterranean springs, and a mile-long loop trail meanders through these bizarre formations, with interpretative signage for hikers. Looking out over the lake, you may notice that the brackish water teems with buzzing alkali flies and brine shrimp, both considered delicacies by

BEST DAY HIKING NEAR LAKES

Little Lakes Valley
A chain of alpine lakes sparkling in pine-dotted bowls between snow-tipped summits, starting at 10,000ft.

Convict Lake
Gorgeous lake with a gentle 2-mile trail and a crazy history (an 1871 shoot-out with escaped prisoners).

Lundy Canyon
Out past Lundy Lake, this 6-mile out-and-back threads a secluded canyon with beavers and waterfalls.

dozens of migratory bird species that return year after year. So do about 60% of the state's population of California gulls, which nest on the lake's volcanic islands in spring and summer.

If you want more activities, rent water toys or take a guided tour that gets you out on the water. In summer and early fall, visitors put in at **Navy Beach**, a short drive or hike from South Tufa, with kayaks, canoes and paddleboards. Gliding among the tufa is a quintessential California experience, and swimming is also quite memorable thanks to the salty, buoyant water. Just be sure you don't have any open cuts, and avoid menacing the tufa.

Time Traveling in Bodie

AN AUTHENTIC GHOST TOWN

At **Bodie State Historic Park**, a gold-rush ghost town is preserved in a state of 'arrested decay.' Weathered buildings sit frozen in time on a dusty, windswept plain where gold was first discovered in 1859. Within 20 years the place grew from a rough mining camp to an even rougher boomtown with a population of 10,000 and a reputation for lawlessness. Fights and murders were commonplace, the violence no doubt fueled by liquor dispensed in the town's 65 saloons, some of which did double duty as brothels, gambling halls or opium dens. The hills disgorged some $34 million worth of gold and silver in the 1870s and '80s, but when production plummeted, so did the population, and eventually the town was abandoned to the elements.

To get here, head east through the sage-dappled hills for 13 miles (the last 3 miles are unpaved) on Hwy 270, about 7 miles south of Bridgeport. Give yourself two hours to wander the abandoned town, peering through the windows of weather-beaten buildings. You'll see stocked stores, furnished homes, workshops filled with tools and a schoolhouse with homework assignments still scrawled on the chalkboard. The jail is still here, as are the fire station, a bank vault and many other buildings. The former **Miners' Union Hall** houses a museum and visitor center, and daily ranger talks take place at the museum and a church. There's also a tour of the **stamp mill**, where quartz rock containing gold and silver was crushed with iron rods. To complete the experience, spend the night at the **Bodie Hotel**, a former boardinghouse and brothel that was transported to nearby Bridgeport in the 1800s.

THE CURSE OF CERRO GORDO

In 2018, social-media influencer Brent Underwood bought Cerro Gordo, an abandoned silver mining town 20 miles east of Lone Pine. He and a partner paid $1.4 million for the 360-acre property and 22 structures, including the American Hotel and its intact saloon. Intent on preserving the history, Underwood moved to the town and began revamping it to attract visitors.

Then everything started to go wrong: the pandemic hit, the famous hotel burned down, and a '1000-year flood' took out the road. Underwood has pressed on, rebuilding the hotel, installing a movie theater and exploring abandoned mine shafts. The place seems to be a cursed and haunted work in progress, but it's open for daytime visits for anybody willing to attempt the drive.

GETTING AROUND

The Eastern Sierra is easiest to explore under your own steam. Keep in mind that some mountain roads close in winter, as do most of the passes that take you over the Sierras from east to west, including Tioga Rd (Hwy 120) to Yosemite.

Eastern Sierra Transit Authority runs buses all along Hwy 395 between Lone Pine and Reno, NV ($59, six hours), with stops in Mammoth Lakes, Lee Vining and Bridgeport (fares between stops vary). The buses run once a day in either direction between Monday and Friday.

VanNess Ave California
59
& Market
Streets

TOOLKIT

The chapters in this section cover the most important topics you'll need to know about in California. They're full of nuts-and-bolts information and valuable insights to help you understand and navigate California and get the most out of your trip.

Arriving p630

Getting Around p631

Money p632

Accommodations p633

Family Travel p634

Health & Safe Travel p635

Outdoor Safety p636

Food, Drink & Nightlife p638

Responsible Travel p640

LGBTIQ+ Travelers p642

Accessible Travel p643

Driving Highway 1 p644

Nuts & Bolts p645

San Francisco (p55)

Arriving

California has a dozen airports with flights from out of state. Many also have international services. You can also reach California by train from neighboring states and beyond. Most people, however, arrive in the state in their own vehicles via interstate freeways that offer scenic previews of what lies ahead.

Easy Visas

Under the US Visa Waiver Program (VWP), visas are not required for citizens of 39 countries for stays up to 90 days with an approved passport valid for six months beyond your stay.

Complex Visas

Regulations for non-VWP visas change regularly. For up-to-date information about requirements, check the visa section on the **US Department of State** (travel.state.gov) website.

Cell Phones

Foreign phones usually work in California. Buy prepaid SIM cards locally. Coverage can be spotty in remote areas such as the far northern coast, in the mountains and Sierra Nevada.

Wi-Fi

Wi-fi is nearly ubiquitous in the state that is home to Silicon Valley, as it is in much of the world. Free networks abound in civic centers, restaurants, hotels and more.

Public Transport from Airport to City Center

	Los Angeles	San Francisco	San Diego
TRAIN	$2	$10	N/A
BUS	$10	$3	$3
TAXI	$30-55	$50-70	$20-40
RIDESHARE	$35-50	$35-60	$15-35

THE SCENIC WAY TO CALIFORNIA

There are four Amtrak routes to California from the rest of the USA. Each offers superb scenery.

From Seattle and Portland, the *Coast Starlight* serves Sacramento, the Bay Area and Santa Barbara, en route to Los Angeles. The ride along the coast is stunning.

From Chicago and Denver to the Bay Area, the *California Zephyr* traces the route of the first Transcontinental Railroad as it enters the state at Truckee high in the Sierras.

Also from Chicago, the *Southwest Limited* reaches LA via the beautifully stark desert, as does the *Sunset Limited* from New Orleans, Houston and Tucson.

Getting Around

While the car is king in this state, there are many options to get around the region by train, ferry, bus and trail.

TRAVEL COSTS

Rental
From $35/day

Gas
Approx $4/ gallon

EV charging
$0.25/kWh

Train ticket from LA to San Diego
From $35

Hiring a Car

There's no advantage between airport and city location rates for rental cars. Both vary widely depending on season and demand. Don't rent a car if all you'll do is park it at the hotel – for example, ride BART into San Francisco, then get a one-day rental for Napa.

Road Conditions

After years of neglect due to fractured state finances, California's voters approved an extra gas tax that is funding repair and construction of roads statewide. You may get caught in work-related delays. But the result is that road conditions in the state are rapidly improving.

TIP

Download the **Caltrans QuickMap** (quickmap.dot.ca.gov/QM/app.htm) app, which shows road conditions statewide.

ROAD HABITS

Californians spend a lot of time in their cars – 25 hours a week is common in LA. Certain rules and habits are enshrined in the state's road culture that may not be immediately apparent to visitors.

On scenic and mountainous roads, pull over so that residents can whizz past.

Motorcycles are allowed to ride between cars on freeways. It's called lane-splitting.

Car-pool lanes are tightly regulated. If you have the correct number of passengers, use them and fly past coagulated traffic.

DRIVING ESSENTIALS

Drive on the right.

Speed limit is usually 65mph on freeways, 55mph on two-lane highways and 35mph in cities.

.08

Blood alcohol limit is 0.08%.

Bus, Train & Ferry

California has more public transit options than many think. The LA region is well covered with a dense network, as is the Bay Area. When taking a ferry to Sausalito or Catalina Island, the ride is part of the adventure. Amtrak's regional trains are fast and reasonably frequent.

Public Transit Tickets

In LA, it's the TAP app; in the Bay Area it's the Clipper Card app. Both let you ride the various forms of transit in their respective regions with a tap of your phone. Refill their stored value online or just use your phone's payment options.

Plane

Californians use planes the way people in other places use trains. The environmental cost aside, service between the state's 12 major airports and numerous smaller ones is frequent and cheap, especially for tickets bought in advance. One downside is that, barring a clear day and a window seat, you miss the scenery.

Money

CURRENCY: **US DOLLAR ($)**

Credit & Debit Cards

Visa and Mastercard are accepted everywhere; American Express and Discover are spottier. The USA has finally fully adopted chip-and-pin systems for cards, although some small businesses have not. Debit cards may require extra security checks at gas stations, rental car counters etc.

Digital Payments

After a surprising lag compared with Europe and Asia, the home to Apple and Google has finally caught up with digital payments. Residents commonly pay for everything with a tap of their phone and can go weeks without ever using cash. (Save $1 bills for the tip jars in coffee bars etc.)

Taxes & Refunds

California state sales tax (7.25%) is added to the retail price of most goods and services (groceries are an exception). Local sales taxes may add on up to 3%. Tourist lodging taxes vary statewide, but average 10.5% to 14% in major cities. No tax refunds are available to international visitors.

HOW MUCH FOR...

Beach parking
Free–$10

Bridge toll
$9

Driving Hwy 1
Free

ATM fee
$3

HOW TO... Save Some Dollars

Buy an **America the Beautiful Pass** (store.usgs.gov/pass), which costs $80 and grants unlimited entry to all US National Parks – 28 of which are in California – plus national wildlife refuges and more. It's good for one year from the purchase date and is an incredible value considering that it can pay for itself after visiting just three parks. (For example, the vehicle entrance fee at Yosemite alone is $35.)

Scan this QR code to buy an America the Beautiful Pass

WHAT TO TIP

Tipping is *not* optional: it's part of workers' wages.

Bartenders 15% to 20% per round; minimum $1 per drink.

Concierges Nothing for simple information, up to $20 for securing last-minute restaurant reservations etc.

Hotel bellhops $2 or $3 per bag; minimum $5 per cart.

Housekeeping staff $2 to $4 daily.

Parking valets At least $2 when your car keys are handed back.

Restaurant servers 15% to 25%.

Taxi/rideshare drivers 10% to 15% of the fare, rounded up to the next dollar.

LOCAL TIP

There's no good pass for California's nearly 300 state parks. Some are free, but many charge $10 or more to enter. Do like many residents: park outside and walk in.

Accommodations

A Bed for Every Taste

With its many beautiful destinations and innovative spirit, California has hundreds of cool, unique accommodations. Find solitude at a desert campsite or feed all your desires with decadent city luxury. Aside from the usual motels and hotels, there are offbeat options like retro motels, vacation rentals right on the beach, campsites perched in dramatic locations and myriad forms of glamping.

Retro Motels

The humble motel has been revitalized over the last few years, with many tired models receiving makeovers that have given them a second act. Designed with an eye to the mid-century aesthetics and consciously addressing contemporary needs, these roadside spots are hot little properties that can be stylish but affordable options. Look for brilliantly restored neon signs.

Estate Wineries

Immerse yourself in a wine-country retreat with views of vineyard rows. Go big at a high-end chateau, complete with spa treatments and South of France ambience, or choose from a wide range of more low-key winery digs. California's wine regions aren't limited to Napa and Sonoma Counties, and accommodation styles can be as individual as their winegrowers and makers.

HOW MUCH FOR A NIGHT IN...

a hotel
$100–300 and up

a hostel
from $30

a campsite
from $25

Don't Camp, Glamp

California may not have invented glamping, but it has perfect backdrops and set pieces for the concept. Iconic national parks and private entities alike have placed canvas safari tents and yurts in gorgeous settings like Yosemite, Kings Canyon and Big Sur. Much of the state maintains a temperate climate for most of the year, making glamping a realistic option almost everywhere.

See the Forest from the Trees

Commune with the redwoods in a tree house. Widely viewed on Instagram, human-size nests and birdhouse-clad pods are some of the more feral-feeling luxury aeries you can settle into for the night. Some meet the definition of shelter better than others, so check details, weather reports and your comfort zone before committing. Confirm basic details such as sanitation and water availability.

VACATION RENTAL LIMITS

Vacation rentals are a charged topic in California. In a state with a catastrophic shortage of affordable housing, any housing stock removed from availability for the masses provokes strong reactions. Once-affordable rural areas have become weekend retreats for the urban affluent, forcing residents who work in the shops and cafes to scramble for housing they can afford. In wealthy areas, residents have grown weary of beach houses turned into party pads for tech bros. In response, cities and towns statewide have imposed limits on vacation rentals.

Family Travel

California is a tailor-made destination for family travel. The kids will be begging to go to theme parks, and teens to celebrity hot spots. Then take 'em into the great outdoors – from sunny beaches shaded by palm trees to misty redwood forests and four-seasons mountain playgrounds. Even getting around is fun, from stops at roadside diversions to the adventure of a train or ferry.

Prams, Strollers & Babies

Urban areas are great for strollers,but if you plan on enjoying the great outdoors, child carriers are definitely a better option. Some attractions offer rental strollers. Basics are available in supermarkets and drugstores 24/7, while organics and specialty items can be found at higher-end supermarkets, big-box stores and boutiques. Bathrooms with changing facilities are common, as are family bathrooms.

Dining Out

Casual eateries typically have high chairs and children's menus available. Cleverer eateries won't just cut down on portions for small-size diners but will offer special kid-tested items so that everybody at the table feels special. Roadside restaurants on tourist routes often have extra inducements for families to stop, such as playgrounds, amusing displays or a chance to pet a winsome barnyard animal.

Car Travel

Any child under the age of six or weighing less than 60lb must be buckled up in the car's back seat in a child or infant safety seat – reserve one ahead when renting a car. Bring in-car distractions for inevitable traffic delays.

Don't Get Caught Short

Some rides may have minimum-height requirements and/or age requirements. Let younger kids know about possible limitations in advance, to avoid disappointment – or tears standing in front of the cut-out clown with the 'riders must be this tall' requirement.

KID-FRIENDLY PICKS

Disneyland (p392) Kids of all ages, even teens, and the young-at-heart adore the 'Magic Kingdom.'

Knott's Berry Farm (p401) SoCal's original theme park offers thrills-a-minute, especially on spooky Halloween nights.

Monterey Bay Aquarium (p260) Meet aquatic denizens of the deep at a national marine sanctuary.

Santa Cruz Beach Boardwalk (p252) An old-timey amusement park on a great beach.

Yosemite National Park (p600) Epic Sierra Nevada scenery, with gushing waterfalls, alpine lakes and glacier-carved peaks.

KEEPING COSTS DOWN

California is not cheap. Cost-conscious families can need help to avoid sticker shock.

In hotels and motels, look for 'kids stay free' and/or 'free breakfast' promotions. Motels are cheaper on average; most have two queen- or king-size beds, and many have fridges and microwaves.

If you're visiting theme parks, carry a cooler in the car and have a picnic in the parking lot (ensure you have park re-entry permission before you do) to avoid expensive and often junk-foodie options inside.

From endless beaches, mountains and urban parks for frolicking, some of the most family-friendly activities in California are free.

FROM LEFT: WIRESTOCK CREATORS/SHUTTERSTOCK ©, RICHARD STEPHEN/SHUTTERSTOCK ©

Health & Safe Travel

INSURANCE

Travel insurance to cover theft, loss and medical problems is essential, especially for international visitors. Domestic visitors should confirm they have proper coverage. Some policies do not cover 'risky' activities such as scuba diving, motorcycling and skiing, so read the fine print. Given upheavals like COVID-19, trip-cancellation insurance is a worthwhile expense.

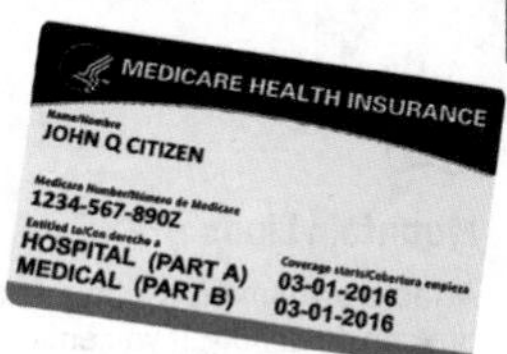

Earthquakes

Earthquakes happen all the time, but most are undetectable. If you're caught in a serious temblor:

- If possible, stay in an open outdoor space.
- If indoors, get under a desk or table or stand in a doorway.
- Protect your head and stay clear of windows, mirrors or anything that might fall.
- Don't head for elevators or go running into the street.

Wildfires

The wildfire season gets ever-longer (at least June through November). Fires limit access to roads and parks, and can cause vacationers and residents to flee for their lives. Of late, fires have affected the Santa Cruz Mountains, Napa and Sonoma Wine Country, Big Sur, Yosemite National Park, Sequoia and Kings Canyon National Parks, Lake Tahoe and all the national forests.

MARIJUANA

Cannabis is legal in California for medicinal and 21-plus recreational use. Shops sell myriad forms of marijuana. Driving under the influence is illegal.

WILDFIRE DANGER RATINGS

Low (Green) Control of fires is generally easy.

Moderate (Blue) Fires can start from accidental causes.

High (Yellow) Fires can start easily from most causes.

Very High (Orange) Fires start easily and spread rapidly.

Extreme (Red) Fires start quickly, burn intensely and are hard to control.

Smoking

Smoking is prohibited inside all public buildings, including airports, shopping malls and transport stations. No smoking is allowed inside restaurants, although it may be tolerated at outdoor tables (ask first). At hotels you must specifically request a smoking room, but some properties are entirely nonsmoking. In some areas you can't smoke outside near a business.

THOUSANDS WITHOUT HOMES

Despite billions spent annually to combat California's homelessness crisis, the number of people living on the streets keeps growing inexorably. You'll see unhoused people – the current descriptor of choice – in large cities and small towns, living in tents, under tarps, in battered RVs etc. Solving the causes, which include housing costs, mental health and substance-abuse problems, is an elusive goal.

Outdoor Safety

California's great outdoors is mostly safe, but there are a few warnings to heed and precautions to take to ensure you avoid danger.

Mountain Lions

Attacks on humans by mountain lions are rare, but can be deadly. If you encounter a mountain lion on a hiking trail, stay calm, pick up small children, face the animal and retreat slowly. Make yourself appear larger by raising your arms or grabbing a stick. If the lion becomes menacing, shout or throw rocks at it. If attacked, fight back aggressively.

Snakes & Spiders

Snakes and spiders are common throughout California, not just in wilderness areas. There are many more species than just the rattlers seen in Westerns. Always look inside your shoes before putting them on when camping. Snake bites are rare, but occur most often when a snake is stepped on or provoked (eg poked with a stick). Antivenom is available at most hospitals.

BEARS

The California grizzly bear (as seen on the state flag) was extinct by 1924, less than 75 years after gold was discovered. Black bears remain common and are often attracted to campgrounds, where they may find food or trash stashed in tents and cars. Always use bear-proof containers.

If you encounter a black bear, don't run. Stay together, keep small children next to you and keep back at least 100m. If the bear starts moving toward you, back away slowly; have bear spray at the ready.

Sharks

Despite the hype of TV channels seeking ratings, sharks are not a real concern in the ocean off the California coast. Since records began being kept in 1851, only 24 people have been killed by sharks in the state. Still, the image of a beady-eyed great white cruising along looking for a meal inspires fear at a base level.

Jellyfish

Unlike sharks, the many species of jellyfish in the Pacific Ocean are worthy of your concern. The California shoreline is home to many species through the year and several come equipped with poisonous stingers, which – while not deadly – can cause extreme pain. Always look into the water to check if you see jellyfish. If stung, plain old urine is an effective pain reliever.

Packing for Mountain Hiking

Instead of cotton, wear synthetic or woolen clothing that retains warmth even when wet. Carry waterproof layers and high-energy snacks.

Don't Feed the Animals

Never feed or approach wild animals, not even harmless-looking critters – it causes them to lose their innate fear of humans, which in turn makes them dangerously aggressive. Many birds and mammals carry serious diseases that can be transmitted through bites.

FROM LEFT: VOBLENKO EVGENIIA/SHUTTERSTOCK ©, ANDREA IZZOTTI/SHUTTERSTOCK ©

Hypothermia

Temperatures in the mountains and desert can quickly drop below freezing. Rain or high winds can lower your body temperature fast. Symptoms of hypothermia include exhaustion, numbness, shivering, stumbling and muscle cramps.

For mild hypothermia, get dry and change into warm clothing. Drink hot liquids (no caffeine or alcohol) and eat. For severe hypothermia, seek immediate medical attention.

Heat Exhaustion & Heatstroke

On hot days, drink plenty of water. A daily minimum of 3L per person is recommended when you're active outdoors. Dehydration can cause heat exhaustion, often characterized by heavy sweating, fatigue, lethargy, nausea, etc. Continuous exposure to high temperatures can lead to possibly fatal heatstroke. Immediate hospitalization is essential. Meanwhile get out of the sun, douse with cool water and fan continuously.

Avalanches

As you marvel at all the snowy peaks in the Sierra Nevada, take a moment to realize that deadly avalanches can occur at any time and even on terrain that seems relatively flat. It's vital that people venturing off groomed slopes check avalanche conditions first. Whether you're backcountry ski-touring or simply hiking or snowshoeing, you'll want to rent a homing beacon.

SUNSCREEN

Sun lotion with an SPF of 30 blocks 97% of dangerous solar rays; SPF 50 blocks 98% and SPF 100 blocks 99%.

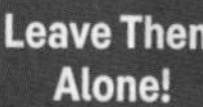

Leave Them Alone!

Disturbing or harassing specially protected species – including many marine mammals such as whales, dolphins and seals – is a crime, subject to enormous fines. Watch for signs indicating natural areas that have been declared off-limits to allow birds to nest in spring.

BEACH LIFEGUARD FLAGS

Green flag
Water is safe.

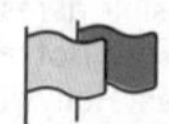

Yellow/blue flag
Potential dangers.

Orange flag
No lifeguard on duty.

Red flag
Beach is closed to the public.

Sneaker Waves

One of the biggest causes of death along the California coast are sneaker waves. These are dramatically larger waves that suddenly appear and wash people off the rocks or sand before they can flee to safety. If you're not swimming, keep a good distance from the water and never turn your back toward it.

LIFEGUARDS OR NOT

Despite what you could surmise from *Baywatch*, most California beaches do not have lifeguards. Rather, your safety is entirely left up to you. Should you get in trouble in the water and begin waving your hand overhead for help – the universal signal – it's unlikely salvation will come from an official source.

Where lifeguards roam, they're primarily found on Southern California beaches. Elsewhere in the state, you may see them on a few state and local beaches.

Food, Drink & Nightlife

When to Eat

Breakfast Usually between 7:30am and 11am. Residents most often grab this meal on the go.

Brunch Enjoyed from 11am until 3pm on weekends. Often boozy.

Lunch Generally served between 11:30am and 2:30pm. Lunch out tends to be for social or business purposes. Booze is rarely consumed.

Dinner Between 5pm and 9pm, and later in coastal cities.

MENU DECODER

Californian casual Few restaurants require more than a dressy shirt, slacks and shoes that aren't flip-flops. At most places, T-shirts, shorts and sandals are fine.

Corkage You can bring your own wine to most restaurants; a 'corkage' fee of $15 to $30 usually applies.

Entree Always confusing to non-Americans – the word for the main course.

Heirloom Trendy term for types of produce meant to evoke varieties grown in the past.

Split-plate If you ask the kitchen to divide a plate between two (or more) people, there may be a small split-plate surcharge.

Allergies and dietary restrictions Travelers with food allergies or dietary restrictions are in luck – vegetarian and vegan fare is all the rage in California and many restaurants are used to catering to specific dietary needs.

Where to Eat

Whether you're into fine dining or searching for the ultimate surf-shack taco, California will spoil you. Make reservations online at least a month ahead for top tables.

Cafes and diners Coffee shops are what many would call a diner. Hours vary, but expect breakfasts and comfort food.

Farmers markets Vendors selling superb local produce and prepared foods.

Food trucks Get fresh, imaginative food to go, often in a parking lot.

Destination dining Top restaurant in a high-end hotel or wine-country resort.

Tips & Tricks of Californian Dining

Californians love to swipe right with restaurants, especially places deemed new and unmissable. It's essential to reserve a table as far in advance as possible at restaurants with buzz or perennial popularity. Hot tables in a trend-loving place like West Hollywood will be booked up weeks in advance.

Destination restaurants like the Napa Valley's French Laundry (p164) have become tick boxes for some diners whose main interest is bagging another famous meal. An entire market has been created for secondary sales of table reservations – people pay hundreds of dollars for a booking. Trust us, there's always a fine alternative restaurant.

How to tip (p632) is already a minefield for non-Americans not used to the practice. Now some restaurants in the Bay Area and LA have introduced mandatory tip fees. But they often leave the door open to additional tipping (!), meaning the 'service fees' are the equivalent of the hated mandatory resort fee.

HOW MUCH FOR A...

Coffee
$2–5

Glass of local wine
From $6

Craft beer
$5–8

Burrito
$9–12

Bowl of cioppino
$25

Dungeness crab sandwich
From $15

California sushi roll
$9

Cup of artisanal ice cream
$5

HOW TO...

How to Eat & Drink Like a Californian

Start your morning with a pricey coffee. Some have it black, but most adulterate their brew with something like oat milk and various flavorings. Breakfast might be a Greek-style yogurt or something simple from an artisanal bakery; fare like omelets and hash browns is saved for a special occasion or weekend brunch.

Lunch can easily be from a food truck near work; Mexican food trucks or 'taco trucks' are the most popular, and are often superb and relatively cheap. Lunch might also be something light like salad that's consumed at one's desk. And while many won't admit to this, the long lines outside In-N-Out Burger (p662) prove that all California meals aren't created healthy.

After-work drinks at a brewery while sitting outside on a patio are popular 12 months a year. Sure, sometimes temperatures might even get down into the 50s, but that's what overhead heaters are for.

Dinner at home might feature whatever is fresh at the local farmers market (many are open year-round). Favorite dining-out choices are Vietnamese, Japanese, regional Chinese, Italian (pasta is favored over pizza), the catch-all Mediterranean (which is a lot like Californian!), regional Mexican (of course), other Central American cuisines and regional American. A trendy cocktail and/or a local wine is a favorite accompaniment. Restaurants are uniformly casual and, since COVID-19, many feature year-round outside dining.

Bars tend to close early, so even in cities like San Francisco or LA, the streets get quiet by midnight.

Food Trucks

California has about 1000 food trucks (p46) operating across the state. Some are found in clusters; others operate alone. Some are in the same spot every day, but others move around.

HOW TO TASTE WINE

Clutch your wallet The days of free tastings are long gone at the vaunted vineyards of Napa and Sonoma Counties (and elsewhere), where a 45-minute tasting costs $30 or more.

Swirl Before tasting a just-opened bottle of wine, swirl your glass to oxygenate the wine and release the flavors.

Sniff Dip your nose (without getting it wet) into the glass for a good whiff. This sniff prompts your senses and your salivary glands to fully appreciate the wine.

Swish Take a swig, and roll it over the front of your gums and sides of your tongue to get the full effect of complex flavors and textures on all your taste buds. After you swallow, breathe out through your nose to appreciate the finish.

If you're driving or cycling, don't swallow Sips are hard to keep track of at tastings, so perfect your graceful arc into the spittoon.

Take it easy There's no need for speed, even if the winery seems to be hurrying you along. Plan to visit three wineries a day maximum.

No need to buy No one expects you to buy – but it's customary to buy a bottle before winery picnics, and tasting fees are sometimes refunded with purchases.

Join the club? Many wineries push their own 'wine clubs' with promises of free future tastings and discounts. Before plunking down the dough, ask yourself: 'Will I ever come here again?'

Responsible Travel

Climate Change & Travel

It's impossible to ignore the impact we have when traveling, and the importance of making changes where we can. Lonely Planet urges all travelers to engage with their travel carbon footprint. There are many carbon calculators online that allow travelers to estimate the carbon emissions generated by their journey; try resurgence.org/resources/carbon-calculator.html. Many airlines and booking sites off er travelers the option of off setting the impact of greenhouse gas emissions by contributing to climate-friendly initiatives around the world. We continue to offset the carbon footprint of all Lonely Planet staff travel, while recognising this is a mitigation more than a solution.

California's near-permanent drought means that everybody can help save water, including visitors. The state has a list of easy things anyone can do to save water, many of which may be new to some (drought.ca.gov/water-saving-tips).

A thicket of regulations governs California's fishing industry. Learn about the best sustainable practices and try your luck fishing with **Sea Forager Expeditions** (p74) along San Francisco's waterfront.

Rent an Electric Car

Car rental companies have embraced hybrid and electric vehicles. You usually have a choice at California locations. If rates seem high, shop around as discounts do pop up. The state has thousands of charging stations (afdc.energy.gov/fuels/electricity_locations.html).

Scan this QR code to find charging stations

Container Cash

Look for 'CA CASH REFUND' or 'CA CRV' on beverage containers sold in California, including plastic water bottles and beer cans (although not wine bottles). The minimum refund is 5¢ for containers under 24oz and 10¢ for containers 24oz or greater.

You can collect the money at any of more than 2000 recycling points in the state. Find them online at calrecycle.ca.gov/BevContainer/RecyclingCenters.

Scan this QR code to find bottle and can recycling points

SAVE ON PLASTICS

Rinse out resealable beverage containers and fill them with tap water. One plastic bottle will last the duration of your trip. If you're given a plastic straw (banned in many parts of California), rinse and reuse it.

WHERE AND HOW TO CYCLE

Bikes, e-bikes and e-scooters are easily rented at all of California's main tourist areas. **CalBike** (calbike.org/go_for_a_ride/map_routes) has dozens of links to online and downloadable maps of bike routes, lanes and paths statewide.

Sustainable Wineries

California has dozens of wineries committed to sustainable practices – important, given the amount ofwater, pesticides and herbicides that some others use.

In the Napa Valley, look for Matthiasson Winery (p159), Pride Mountain Vineyards (p170), Preston (p199), Porter Creek (p196) and Pax Wines (p189).

The Sacramento Delta's best-known winery, Bogle (p532), is very proud of its sustainable practices.

South in Paso Robles is Vina Robles (p281), with six certified sustainable wine estates. Further south in Los Olivos is Foxen Winery (p323).

Many public water fountains in California now have spigots, so water bottles can be refilled easily.

Help the beaches: adopt any trash you see as your own and toss it – this works elsewhere too!

RESOURCES

greenbusinessca.org Search for green businesses by categories.

happycow.net Vegetarian and vegan restaurants in California and beyond.

saveourshores.org Sponsors frequent events to improve the beaches at the Monterey Bay National Marine Sanctuary.

Driving between San Francisco and LA emits about 150kg of carbon dioxide for an average-size car; flying emits 140kg per passenger. A bus emits 80kg per passenger; a train only 40kg. Calculate your trip and options at native.eco/for-individuals/calculators/#Travel.

LGBTIQ+ Travelers

Inclusivity tends to be the norm in California, and its embrace of all things LGBTIQ+ is cause for both admiration and ridicule in other parts of the USA. But it's a large and diverse state in terms of demographics and culture, and though largely progressive, attitudes vary from region to region. To generalize, the agricultural parts of the state are less tolerant.

Notable Months

There aren't any bad months for LGBTIQ+ travel in California, but there are months that are famous for their special events. First, of course, is June, when pride events such as fabulous parades take over cities like LA (p346) and San Francisco (p93) and smaller communities. Long Beach gets a head start, holding its events in May, while San Diego's (p420) are in July. Palm Springs lets its great weather shine for its pride month in November. Head to the hills in March for Mammoth Gay Ski Week.

LGBTIQ+ HISTORY

For insight into LA's fascinating queer history, download the free **Pride Explorer** (thelavendereffect.org/pride-explorer) app, which offers self-guided walking tours of LA. In San Francisco, visit the GLBT History Museum (p92), America's first gay-history museum, which showcases more than 50 years of San Francisco LGBTIQ+ ephemera.

GET MARRIED IN CALIFORNIA

Though it's legal across the USA, many LGBTIQ+ couples prefer to marry in a state known for its queer welcome. In California, you needn't be a citizen or take a blood test. Just fill out a form at a county clerk's office, pay a fee and get a license. Then get hitched!

Queer Havens

Many places in California are queer-friendly, but the following are at another level: San Francisco's Castro District (p91), the center of everything; West Hollywood (p353) and its extraordinary nightlife; Guerneville (p195) for summer escapes amid the redwoods; Santa Cruz (p250), where lesbians could be open in the 1970s; and Palm Springs (p450), with languid days spent by the (mid-century) pool.

Employment

The California Fair Employment and Housing Act makes it illegal for an employer to fire, demote, fail to hire, harass or otherwise discriminate against anyone due to their sexual orientation, gender identity and/or gender expression.

LGBTIQ+ RESOURCES

Advocate (advocate.com/travel) News, LGBTIQ+ travel features and destination guides.

Damron (damron.com) Long-running, advertiser-driven gay travel guides and app.

LGBT National Help Center (lgbthotline.org) Counseling, information and referrals for people of all ages; special resources for youths.

Out Traveler (outtraveler.com) Free online magazine articles with travel tips, destination guides and resortreviews.

Accessible Travel

More populated areas of California are reasonably well equipped for travelers with disabilities, although older properties may have limitations.

Park Passes

US residents with a permanent disability quality for a free lifetime pass, which waives entry fees to all national parks. California State Parks' disabled discount pass ($3.50) gives 50% off parking and camping fees.

Buses

Public transit buses are all accessible by law. Ramps that deploy automatically when the bus is lowered to the curb are the norm. The driver may have to assist with securing wheelchairs once inside the bus.

Trains

In the Bay Area, BART is fully accessible; Caltrain has four minor stations that are not accessible. In Southern California, Metro trains and stations are all accessible. Amtrak requires advance notice for accessibility service.

AIRPORT

California's airports comply with accessibility laws. Assistance is available through your airline.

Scan this QR code for details on beaches with wheelchairs

Beach Accessibility

California lags behind the EU in providing accessibility for all on its beaches, which are mostly left in a natural state and don't include ramps into the water. However, the California Coastal Commission does provide a useful resource of over 100 beaches with available wheelchairs designed for use on the sand. These devices can be reserved and are free to use; some are motorized. See the CCC website for full details (coastal.ca.gov/access/beach-wheelchairs.html).

RESOURCES

Search for the name of your destination plus 'accessibility' – for example, 'Disneyland accessibility' brings up comprehensive information.

Access Northern California (accessnca.org) Extensive links to accessible-travel resources, including outdoor recreation opportunities, lodgings, tours and transportation.

California State Parks (access.parks.ca.gov/home.asp) Searchable online map and database of accessible features at state parks.

Yosemite National Park Accessibility (nps.gov/yose/planyourvisit/accessibility.htm) Detailed information for Yosemite, including services for deaf visitors.

The US Department of Justice (ada.gov) enforces the Americans with Disabilities Act (ADA). It makes this statement on its comprehensive website: 'Disability rights are civil rights.' The Act covers many areas of public life including employment, transportation, accommodations and telecommunications.

ACCOMMODATIONS

Hotels built since 1993 must meet modern accessibility requirements. Major chains usually have rooms adapted for accessibility needs, but you should book in advance and double-check they have what you require. Holiday rentals and vintage properties may not be accessible.

Driving Highway 1

Resplendent Hwy 1, the Pacific Coast Highway, unfurls for 656 miles along some of the world's most beautiful shoreline. Take in dramatic sea cliffs, sun-soaked surfing towns, untrod beaches and the Golden Gate Bridge en route to buzzing Santa Monica and the bling of the beaches in the Orange County and San Diego beyond.

THE ROUTE

Hwy 1 starts out a mere redwood-lined lane and snakes along the craggy coast in far northern California. As you approach San Francisco, it loops across the Marin Headlands (p117) and the Golden Gate Bridge (p62). It's less curvy as it wends down and through Santa Cruz (p250) and is occasionally even a highway en route to Santa Barbara (p300), Los Angeles (Santa Monica; p366) and San Diego (p420).

Wildlife Spotting

Elk roam the Lost Coast (p216) and Point Reyes (p121), which is also home to myriad seabirds. Marine life is rich throughout, with highlights in Point Reyes, Rodeo Beach (p117), Monterey Bay (p260), Morro Bay (p290) and Crystal Cove (p410). Elephant seals dwell in Point Reyes, Año Nuevo (p148) and Piedras Blancas (p278). Glancing offshore anywhere along the coast can reveal whales migrating.

Pull Over

There are plenty of reasons to pull off Hwy 1. Turnouts abound, which will allow you to let locals continue on their way as you happily dawdle.

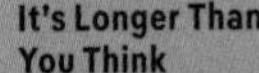

It's Longer Than You Think

Short as some of the distances may seem, beyond slow-driving tourists (you?) certain areas can bottleneck. This is especially true of the area just north of and through San Francisco, the corridor south of Santa Cruz (rough in rush hours) and certainly the Los Angeles fringes. Time your journey accordingly.

STOP FOR THE NIGHT

If you're driving the whole highway, you'll need to break for the night along the way. Beyond obvious large cities, other top spots to sleep include Eureka (p225), Fort Bragg (p215), Mendocino (p208), Santa Cruz (p250), Monterey (p258), Carmel (p264), Big Sur (p267), Cambria (p276) and Laguna Beach (p412). State parks have campgrounds – some where you reserve in advance.

Nuts & Bolts

OPENING HOURS

Businesses, restaurants and shops in tourist areas may close earlier and on additional days during the winter off-season (November to March). Standard hours:

Banks 9:30am–5pm weekdays

Bars 4pm–2am

Restaurants 11am–3pm and 5:30pm–10pm daily, some open later Friday and Saturday

Shops 10am–7pm Monday to Saturday, 11am–6pm Sunday (many open later)

Toilets

Free public restrooms are easy to find inside shopping malls, public buildings, libraries, gas stations and some transportation hubs, as well as at parks and beaches.

GOOD TO KNOW

Time Zone
Pacific Standard Time (GMT/UTC -8 hours)

Country Code
1

Emergency number
911

Population
40 million

Weights & Measures

Imperial (except 1 US gallon equals 0.83 imperial gallons).

Water

Tap water in California is good quality and is safe to drink. (San Francisco's comes from snow melt and is excellent.)

Electricity 120V/60Hz

Type A
120V/60Hz

PUBLIC HOLIDAYS

On the following holidays, banks, schools and government offices (including post offices) are closed, and transportation, museums and other services may operate on a Sunday schedule. Holidays falling on a weekend are usually observed the following Monday.

New Year's Day January 1

Martin Luther King Jr Day Third Monday in January

Presidents' Day Third Monday in February

Cesar Chavez Day March 31

Memorial Day Last Monday in May

Independence Day July 4

Labor Day First Monday in September

Indigenous Peoples' Day Second Monday in October

Veterans Day November 11

Thanksgiving Day Fourth Thursday in November

Christmas Day December 25

CALIFORNIA

STORYBOOK

Our writers delve deep into different aspects of Californian life

A History of California in 15 Places

Native Americans called this land home for some 15,000 years before European arrivals gave it a new name: California.

Ryan Ver Berkmoes

p648

Meet the Californians

Expect a friendly, smile-filled welcome paired with a sense of self-reliance and independence.

Alexis Averbuck

p652

The Myth of California

Movies, music, and literature all contribute to the Golden State's larger-than-life reputation.

Anita Isalska

p654

Where Diversity Reigns Supreme

California, home to America's most diverse population, outstrips even New York as the nation's biggest melting pot.

Megan Leon

p658

Climate Crisis

California is on the leading edge of the global climate crisis. Fortunately, green initiatives are fighting back – hard.

Anita Isalska

p660

In-N-Out Burger

Simple, down-to-earth In-N-Out Burger is as quintessentially Californian as the Hollywood sign or Santa Monica Pier.

Megan Leon

p664

Street performers in Uptown (p128), Oakland

A HISTORY OF CALIFORNIA IN 15 PLACES

On a Pacific island ruled by Amazon queen Califia, women warriors wear golden armor and ride dragons... Recognize the story? Today the heroine of Garci Rodríguez de Montalvo's 1500 Spanish novel is better known as the namesake of California, and the basis of Hollywood superhero Wonder Woman. Who can resist a place like this? By Ryan Ver Berkmoes.

FIVE HUNDRED NATIVE American nations called this land home for some 15,000 years before 16th-century European arrivals gave it a new name: California. Spanish conquistadors and priests came here for gold and God, but soon relinquished their flea-plagued missions and ill-equipped presidios (forts) to Mexico. Their main legacy? The near-extermination of indigenous peoples.

The unruly territory was handed off to the USA in the Treaty of Guadalupe Hidalgo mere months before gold was discovered in 1848. A virtual flood of prospectors and settlers washed over California in a short time – the first of many such influxes. Generations of California dreamers have made the trek to these Pacific shores for gold, glory and self-determination, making homes and history on America's most fabled frontier.

The Golden State has surged ahead and is poised to become the world's fourth-largest economy, much of that fueled by successive booms in the last 100 years: Hollywood, aerospace, computers and the internet. But like a kid that's grown too fast, California still hasn't figured out how to handle such rapid growth, including housing shortages, traffic gridlock and breathtaking costs of living. Today, California flaunts its international status and is taking leading roles in such global issues as environmental standards, online privacy, marriage equality and immigrant rights.

1. Indian Grinding Rock State Historic Park

19,000 YEARS OF CIVILIZATION

Human settlement began in Native California as early as 19,000 years ago. Native Californians passed knowledge of hunting grounds and turf boundaries from generation to generation in at least 100 distinct languages.

Indian Grinding Rock State Historic Park is a sacred area for the local Miwok, one of the 500 indigenous groups that have been identified so far. The centerpiece is a limestone outcrop covered with faint, ancient petroglyphs and mortar holes used for grinding acorns and seeds.

By 1870, California's indigenous population had been decimated by 90%, due to introduced European diseases, conscripted labor, violence, marginalization and hunger in their own fertile lands.

For more on the park, see page 554.

2. Mission San Luis Obispo de Tolosa

MISSIONS AND GENOCIDE

For the glory of God and its tax coffers, in 1769 Spain decided to establish missions across California that would be run by local converts. Franciscan friar Junípero Serra established Mission San Diego de Alcalá in 1769. Another 20 missions followed, eventually reaching Sonoma.

Mission San Luis Obispo de Tolosa in San Luis Obispo was the fifth California mission. It was founded by Serra in 1772 and, like the others, was never a big success. Native Californians balked at life as slaves; they died in droves.

In 1821, Mexico (which included California) won its independence from Spain and the mission system soon collapsed.

For more on San Luis Obispo, see page 285.

3. Monterey Custom House

WHERE AMERICAN CALIFORNIA BEGAN

In 1822, a newly independent Mexico ended the Spanish trade monopoly and stipulated that any traders bringing goods to Alta (Upper) California must first unload their cargoes in Monterey at the Custom House. It didn't last.

In 1846, Mexico and the USA went to war. Meanwhile, legions of Americans were already arriving in California, lured by its obvious bounties. When Mexico ordered them out in 1846, they declared independence here and raised the US flag. Mexico could not compete and hostilities ended with the Treaty of Guadalupe Hidalgo, in which Mexico ceded much of its northern territory (including Alta California) to the USA.

For more on Monterey, see page 258.

4. Marshall Gold Discovery State Historic Park

GOLD! GOLD! GOLD!

Given the drama spawned at Marshall Gold Discovery State Historic Park, you'd never know it from this tranquil riverside park today. John Sutter and James Marshall built a sawmill here in 1847, and a few months later Marshall saw something glittering in the American River. When San Francisco tabloid publisher Sam Brannan heard gold flakes were found in the Sierra Nevada foothills, he published the rumor as fact, figuring it might sell some newspapers. It did. Word spread, gold fever swept the world and thousands of people poured into California in 1849. Native Californians who'd survived the mission era were soon overwhelmed by the gold rush.

For more on park, see page 551.

5. Truckee Train Station

TRANSCONTINENTAL RAILROAD STOP

'The Big Four' – Collis P Huntington, Leland Stanford, Mark Hopkins and Charles Crocker – got rich not from mining but by selling shovels (and lending money) to miners during the gold rush. From their Sacramento base, these oligarchs of the day built enormous business empires.

To reach East Coast markets, the Big Four rounded up Chinese miners left unemployed due to mechanization and racism to build the first transcontinental railroad. Over 12,000 toiled in brutal conditions blasting tracks and tunnels through the Sierra Nevada. Today, the same line – completed in 1869 – remains a vital link and passes right by the old Truckee Train Station.

For more on Truckee, see page 589.

6. Angel Island Immigration Station

WEST COAST ELLIS ISLAND

Denied gold rush mining claims, many Chinese prospectors opened service-based businesses that became the basis for the Chinatowns that were once found in nearly every California city and town. However, discriminatory Californian laws restricting housing, employment and citizenship for anyone born in China were codified with the 1882 US Chinese Exclusion Act, which remained US law until 1943.

One legacy of the law can be found on Angel Island in the San Francisco Bay. The Immigration Station operated from 1910 to 1940. It was a detention center for Chinese immigrants and many were cruelly held for long periods before ultimately being sent back to China. Many left only mournful graffiti behind.

For more on Angel Island, see page 71.

7. San Francisco's Dolores Park

REFUGE FROM EARTHQUAKE FLAMES

California's 'robber barons' (Leland Stanford et al) built Nob Hill mansions in San

Francisco with their fortunes. The City by the Bay dominated the West Coast and attracted notables such as William Randolph Hearst, who took over his first newspaper here in 1887.

But San Francisco's grand ambitions came crashing down on April 18, 1906, when earthquake and fire reduced the city to rubble. With flames destroying what the shaking didn't, thousands escaped the inferno in Dolores Park. Cross 20th St to the fire hydrant (still painted golden) that saved the neighborhood, and take in the view of city's skyline today.

For more on Dolores Park, see page 98.

8. Hollywood Sign

THERE'S NO BUSINESS LIKE SHOW BUSINESS

The 1906 earthquake hobbled San Francisco, opening the door for Los Angeles. SoCal boosters like *Los Angeles Times* publisher and real estate developer, Harry Chandler, were busy building an empire out of what had been Spanish and Mexican land-grant ranches and desert.

In 1923, Chandler had a 'Hollywoodland' sign erected in the hills to advertise a luxury home development (the first of many!). Conceived as temporary, the sign arrived with the meteoric rise of the film studios. Soon 'land' decayed away and, as they say, a star was born as the sign became the literal symbol for the entertainment industry, known generically as Hollywood.

For more on Hollywood, see page 340.

9. Manzanar National Historic Park

CALIFORNIA'S CONCENTRATION CAMP

In the 1930s, Japanese Americans had thriving farms and businesses across California. Many others were jealous of this success, and people like William Randolph Hearst sought political power by fueling ethnic hatred and division.

After the attack on Pearl Harbor by Japan on December 7, 1941 sparked the US entry into WWII, Hearst and company saw their chance: they would stop opposing the policies of the normally progressive President Franklin Roosevelt. In return, he'd allow nearly 120,000 Japanese Americans to be rounded up and sent to concentration camps scattered in desolate corners of the west, including what's now Manzanar National Historic Site (pictured right) in the Eastern Sierra.

For more on Manzanar, see page 623.

10. Rosie the Riveter WWI Home Front National Historic Park

ALL HANDS ON DECK

No place better symbolizes the win-at-any-cost WWII war effort than the old Kaiser shipyards on the San Francisco Bay in Richmond. From 1942 until 1946, a whopping 747 ships were built here – an extraordinary accomplishment, made more so because much of the vast workforce had been marginalized before the war: women and African Americans.

The societal changes caused by this upheaval of the social order are still felt today, as detailed at the Rosie the Riveter WWII Home Front National Historic Park. Meanwhile, names like Douglas and Lockheed created the Southern California aerospace industry, which fueled California's first postwar boom.

For more on park, see page 137.

11. Disneyland

NOTHING MICKEY MOUSE ABOUT IT

It was the dawn of the California dream in 1955 when California's middle class exploded along with the population. Increased wages allowed the whole family to take a holiday and drive the Chevy on a new freeway to Disneyland, Walt's new idealized fantasyland.

Families flocked here from their new tract houses spreading like crabgrass in suburbs across the LA Basin, the San Fernando Valley, across San Jose up north and all around the San Francisco Bay and beyond. Today, Disneyland is yet another California first and, at its core, remarkably unchanged from Walt's original vision for Main Street, USA, Sleeping Beauty Castle, Frontierland, Adventureland and Tomorrowland.

For more on Disneyland, see page 392.

12. Golden Gate Park

TURN ON, TUNE IN, DROP OUT

The Summer of Love really started on January 14, 1967 in San Francisco's Golden Gate Park, when Human Be-In blew minds, gave Timothy Leary a stage and celebrated all things psychedelic. Free speech was

the mantra and Haight-Ashbury became the place to be.

Passions soon turned to racial injustice and the Vietnam War. Starting with UC Berkeley, college campuses across the USA were roiled by unrestrained, at times violent, protests. Yet the social upheavals also jump-started the careers of California's 'law and order' politicians Ronald Reagan (who was elected governor in 1966) and Richard Nixon (elected president in 1968).

For more on the park, see page 103.

13. César E Chávez National Monument

MARCHING FOR HUMANITY AND DIGNITY

César Chávez and Dolores Huerta formed United Farm Workers (UFW) in 1962 to champion the rights of immigrant laborers, bringing the issues of fair wages and pesticide health risks to the nation's attention. Committed to non-violence and intent on defending the laborers' interests, they led marches that highlighted the abuses of the laborers and risked the violent wrath of San Joaquin Valley sheriff deputies.

The UFW masterminded the successful late-1960s table-grape boycott, which spawned a wave of issue-oriented boycotts. The César E Chávez National Monument, located within the undulating Tehachapi Mountains, was Chávez' home and the UFW headquarters from 1971 until his death in 1993.

For more on the monument, see page 539.

14. GLBT History Museum

THE ROAD TO MARRIAGE EQUALITY

San Francisco Supervisor Harvey Milk became the first openly gay man elected to public office in California in 1977. He lived in the Castro, now home to the GLBT History Museum. Milk sponsored a gay-rights bill before his murder by a political opponent in SF's iconic City Hall.

In 2004, then-mayor Gavin Newsom ordered marriage licenses to be issued for same-sex couples, a first in the USA. However, in 2008 California voters narrowly passed a proposition defining legal marriage as between man and woman. California courts ruled it unconstitutional, and in a surprise decision, the US Supreme Court upheld marriage equality in 2013. The museum covers this saga and much more.

For more on the GLBT History Museum, see page 92.

15. Apple Park

FAKE IT TILL YOU MAKE IT

At the 1977 West Coast Computer Faire, 21-year-old Steve Jobs and Steve Wozniak introduced the Apple II, a personal computer with unfathomable memory (4KB of RAM!) and microprocessor speed (1MHz!). But the question remained: what would ordinary people do with all that computing power?

The rest, of course, is history. What's now known as Silicon Valley has spawned countless millionaires and products that have changed lives worldwide. Boom-and-bust cycles are the norm, which is worth remembering as you navigate the antiseptic minimalism of the visitor center at Apple Park, the hubristic bunker of the multi-billion-dollar corporate headquarters in Cupertino.

For more on Apple Park, see page 142.

MEET THE CALIFORNIANS

Expect a friendly, smile-filled welcome paired with a sense of self-reliance and independence. It's the expression of a live-and-let-live ethos. Alexis Averbuck introduces her people.

COMPARED WITH THE rest of the USA, many Californians see our state as a laid-back, free-thinking multicultural society that gives everyone a chance to live however we like.

Indeed, many powerful movements that have changed the world began here. Chicano pride, Black Power, the Farm Workers movement and LGBTIQ+ pride all built political bases here. In 2017, then-governor Jerry Brown signed a law making California a 'sanctuary state,' thereby preventing local law enforcement from aiding federal authorities in detaining undocumented immigrants.

That's for good reason. Throughout California's history, immigration has been a core aspect of the state's very existence. It had a thriving indigenous population for over 10,000 years, but Native Californians were decimated when California was colonized by Spain, Mexico and even Russia, then became a US state. Today, around 11 million Californians are immigrants. One of every four arrivals in the USA settles in California.

The idea of California lives in world lore, and some stereotypes are not strictly wrong. For example, nearly 70% of Californians do live in coastal areas. And, yes, the Cali self-help and new-agey movements were successfully pioneered and marketed here since well before their 1970s heyday. Similarly, SoCal's movie and music industries are wildly influential – though nowadays, Silicon Valley and the state's powerful tech industry jockey for the title of top influencer.

But life here is not charmed. The rising cost of housing has reached a crisis level, leading to a huge spike in homelessness. Six of the 10 most expensive US housing markets are in California, and buying or even renting a home these days is out of reach for many Californians. The home-ownership rate has dropped to 55%, down from a 60.7% peak in 2006. The high cost of living is also prompting more middle- and low-income Californians (especially millennials) to migrate to other states with more affordable pastures.

Also, it's true that Californians drive a lot. We spend at least $1 out of every $5 earned on car-related expenses. But at least Californians are zooming ahead of the national energy-use curve in the use of smog-checked cars and are buying more hybrid and fuel-efficient cars. In 2022, Governor Gavin Newsom signed into law sweeping measures to hasten the use of clean energy and protect us from polluters. Generally, we always back initiatives that promote a clean environment – keeping California a progressive oasis in our rough-and-tumble national politics.

WHO & HOW MANY?

With almost 40 million residents, California is the most populous state in the USA. It is also poised to become the fourth-largest economy in the world. Cue jokes about seceding from the nation.

Clockwise from top left: Surfers at Newport Beach (p407); vintner in Napa Valley (p161); parade audience in San Diego (p420); festivalgoer in Oakland (p125)

TYPICAL CALIFORNIAN?

I grew up in Oakland, a child of two people with wildly different backgrounds. My mother's family has been here for seven generations. One of my ancestors on her side was among the first female Spanish-land-grant holders in the Los Angeles area. She in turn married a German immigrant.

My father's family arrived from Eastern Europe via NYC to East LA (Boyle Heights, to be specific) in the 1940s. They were Jewish communists who were persecuted during Joseph McCarthy's Red Scare – proof that California's institutions are not always tolerant. My parents were both teachers, and during my youth we spent many years living overseas, speaking other languages, but always returned to Oakland.

California is a land of immigration, innovation and change, and my family history is as multifaceted as many people here. It shows is that the only thing typical in California is that there is no such thing as a typical Californian.

Sunset at Venice Beach (p375), Los Angeles
DIEGOMARIOTTINI/SHUTTERSTOCK ©

THE MYTH OF CALIFORNIA

The Golden State's reputation precedes it. Movies, music and literature all contribute to California's larger-than-life mythology. By Anita Isalska

THIS IS A PROMISED land, the stories say. In California, you can reinvent yourself and soar to success among beautiful people and under blue skies. But dramatic falls are as much a part of the California myth as meteoric rises. For well over a century, legends of boom and bust have been core to the Californian story.

The cheerful beats and exuberant lyrics of bands like the Beach Boys, part of the 1960s California Sound, introduced the world to the romance, carefree lifestyle and surf culture of the West Coast. Meanwhile, Hollywood has long presented a glittering image of California's wealth, sunshine and sexual freedom. So it's no wonder the world tends to see California through rose-tinted glasses.

But dreaming of California isn't a modern phenomenon: the state has a mythology of aspiration, grit and heady success that has built up over centuries. These stories often come with a shadow: some of the most compelling and enduring art about California is tinged with themes of sorrow, nostalgia and bitter failure – because when the highs are this high, there's a heck of a long way to fall.

The Origins of the California Dream

Understanding the origins of the California myth can provide context that enriches your travels and will clue you in for local bar talk, where you'll hear locals extol California's unsurpassed charms in one breath, and bemoan its ruination in the next.

The concept of the California dream as we know it was born during the short-lived gold rush of 1848–55. When a glimmer of gold was sighted in a river in the western Sierra Nevada, rumors spread as fast as horses and ships could carry them. They inspired fortune-seekers not only to flock from further east, but also to embark on weeks-long journeys from overseas, with the hope of getting rich quick and securing a new start in this land at the edge of the Earth.

More than 300,000 people arrived, turning San Francisco into a gold-rush boomtown practically overnight and accelerating the demise of the area's Native

American communities. For those who toiled out east in frontier communities, California represented an alternative to Puritan ideals – a Shangri-la of warm weather and and abundant resources. And though few struck it rich, the gold rush sealed California's reputation: the myth was born.

The state's rapid growth into an agricultural and industrial powerhouse continued to amplify California's formidable reputation. While city workers unionized, farm laborers continued to languish in harsh conditions with low pay. This meant that when the Dust Bowl and the Great Depression of the 1930s sparked a rush to California, multitudes of 'Okies' and 'Arkies' (migrants, often from Oklahoma and Arkansas) arrived to an unwelcoming place where they had no choice but to work in miserable conditions as farm laborers.

John Steinbeck paints the scene in *The Grapes of Wrath* (1939), in which the Joad family flee Oklahoma's hardships and drought, learning along the way that California might not be the land of milk and honey they're hoping for. When they arrive, workers are abundant, pay is light and conditions are wretched. Real-life Californians who achieved their dreams during this grueling period often did so by profiting from the forced labor of Native Americans, and from the poorly paid labor of Okies and Arkies.

Happiness, Prosperity & Tragedy

Ambitions of wealth and fame aside, California maintains a reputation of happiness and prosperity. It has the fourth-highest average per capita income among the 50 states and, at the time of writing, a GDP poised to overtake Germany's and make the state the world's fourth-largest economy. California also generally ranks in the top five for 'happiness studies' across the USA, as well as in health and fitness rankings.

When the living is this good, there's a whole lot to lose. No wonder California is the perfect setting for tragedies with almost Shakespearean story arcs. Cautionary tales abound in many odes to California in literature, music and movies, many of them suffused with disillusionment, alienation and even outright horror.

One common narrative is a hero (or, usually, an antihero) who strives to access or hold onto California's glittering wealth and incredible pleasures. He or she fails to do so, and is either brought down by a tragic flaw (like vanity or pride), or is simply chewed up and spat out – perhaps by the Hollywood machine, or by callous characters determined to climb their own ladders to success.

Movies from the golden age of Hollywood are awash with characters mourning their failure or bitterly nostalgic for bygone success. The 1950 film noir *Sunset Boulevard* immerses us in its Hollywood setting (even borrowing the names of real producers and directors to heighten the verisimilitude) as it reveals the slow descent into madness of deluded silent-film star Norma Desmond, who craves a comeback on the silver screen. Then there's cruel, petulant Jane Hudson sporting childlike dresses and curls in *What Ever Happened to Baby Jane?* (1962). Unable to cope with life after child stardom, Jane finds satisfaction only in sadism directed at the sister whose beauty and career she so envies.

More recently, it's the Silicon Valley dream that gets skewered on the big and small screens. In *The Social Network* (2010), the character inspired by Facebook CEO Mark Zuckerberg winds up rich, successful and alone. Across decades of film, the enduring theme is that California's giddying wealth and opportunity becomes a self-imposed cage, whether you're a Hollywood grande dame sequestered in her decaying mansion or a tech billionaire alone in his huge office.

The image of being in California's thrall is common. As The Eagles sang in *Hotel California* (1977), 'you can check out any time you like, but you can never leave.' The enigmatic lyrics of this classic song are ripe for numerous interpretations: California is a place of siren calls to pleasure and unbridled freedom, but it's also rife with grotesque images and a terror that can't be outrun.

A Storied State of Reinvention

The Red Hot Chili Peppers capture a similar mood in *Californication* (2000), which lays bare the artifice and illusion of the

California dream. In the song, California is 'the edge of the world and all of Western civilization,' a place of lost innocence, soulless capitalism and so much plastic surgery.

'Californication' as a concept long predates the Chilis – or the unrelated TV series of the same name, a darkly funny narrative of frailty, addiction and redemption. The term was first coined in 1966 to refer to runaway overdevelopment of land, but it's since come to mean the aggressive exporting of California. This could be physical, like the current exodus of Californians to other states. San Francisco and Los Angeles lead the USA in numbers of outbound moves, and it's an unwelcome trend, as Californians have a reputation for bringing gentrification and rising prices with them. Californication can also be spiritual: California has an outsized presence in global culture and, through Hollywood, is blamed for the imposition of American culture throughout the world.

With this image of an unstoppable and deadening cultural force in mind, it's apt that sci-fi horror *Invasion of the Body Snatchers* (1956) is set in California. In the movie, emotionless alien clones replace the residents of a fictional California town, Santa Mira, one by one. In a state that prizes individuality and ambition above all else, could there be a greater horror than existing as an impassive, unfeeling being, doomed to live out the days in utter conformity?

AS SO MANY BALLADS, BOOKS AND MOVIES CONVEY, CALIFORNIA IS BEST UNDERSTOOD AS A COLLISION OF EXTREMES: THE DREAM AND THE DOWNFALL, ALL ROLLED INTO ONE.

Ask Californians whether their storied state has lost its luster, and you'll be greeted with eye rolls: they've heard it all before. The 'death of the California dream' narrative is a recurring cliché, part of the natural cycle of optimism and disillusionment that naturally accompanies a place held to such mythic standards. In fact, as *LA Times* writer Michael Hiltzik found, people were talking about the 'California nightmare' as far back as the 1850s, when transplants from other states bemoaned California's levels of crime and corruption, and its failure to meet gilded expectations.

As so many ballads, books and movies convey, California is best understood as a collision of extremes: the dream and the downfall, all rolled into one. Accepting this duality unlocks a deeper understanding of California's people and places. You'll encounter extravagant wealth alongside the direst poverty. You'll hear barstool yarns about reinvention and fortune-building in the same breath as stories of burnout and lost opportunity. Under the rays of the sun, listening to the rasping ocean, you yourself might be tempted to risk it all for a taste of your own California dream. Because even if it all goes up in flames, what a glorious ride it will be.

Rodeo Drive (p355), Los Angeles

WHERE DIVERSITY REIGNS SUPREME

California, home to America's most diverse population, outstrips even New York as the nation's biggest melting pot. By Megan Leon

CALIFORNIA, THE THIRD-LARGEST state in the USA, is a rich tapestry of cultural difference. Statistics show that 27% of Californians were foreign-born – considerably more than the national state average. Significantly, the Caucasian population of California is decreasing in absolute terms, making it more of a minority than ever, with the increase in immigration.

California ranks first in the land for racial and ethnic diversity, and third for socio-economic diversity. It is the state's willingness to embrace diversity that has made it into such a welcome haven for those looking to start a new life. People from over 140 countries call California home and the number of languages that are spoken within the many ethnic enclaves of its cities surpasses a staggering 200.

Historically, California was inhabited by Native American tribes such as the Chumash and Miwok and had numerous

Traditional Aztec clothing

languages being spoken from mountain to sea. The Portuguese explorer Juan Rodriguez Cabrillo was the first European to set foot in California back in 1542, but the Spanish would not fully explore the state for around another 200 years. They consolidated their acquisition by building 21 missions as well as five presidios (forts) in San Diego, Monterey, San Francisco, Santa Barbara and Sonoma. Dotting the coast, the missions were established in part to convert Native Californians to Catholicism.

After Mexico gained independence from Spain in 1821, California became a part of the fledgling Mexican empire. Olvera St in what is now Downtown LA served as an important community hub and is still densely inhabited by the Hispanic community.

CALIFORNIA IS NOT ONLY KNOWN FOR ITS SCENIC DRIVES AND CINEMATIC HISTORY, IT IS A MULTINATIONAL DESTINATION THAT COMES TOGETHER HARMONIOUSLY.

The Asian community is equally prominent: California has one of the largest Asian American populations of any US state. San Francisco, for example, is home to the second-highest proportion of Asian American residents, after Hawaii. Back in 1870, nearly 100,000 Chinese Americans already resided in the Golden State. Today, thriving communities are found in San Francisco's famous Chinatown and around the Bay Area, and in Japan Town (one of the only three left in the USA) and the rebuilt Chinatown in LA, which still has people flocking over for authentic food and feel.

Chinatown in Los Angeles is uniquely bordered by Tokyo Town. Japanese Immigrants have historically settled in this downtown area, with 70,000 people living there by 1910. Nearby is the historic area of El Pueblo de Los Ángeles, now almost a 'living museum' of Mexican-Californian culture. Colorful stalls and restaurants line the streets, proclaiming this Latinx culture and merging into the Chinese and Japanese areas. Not far off is the iconic Korea Town, where Koreans make up around 9% of the population. The city of LA has attracted Korean immigrants since 1880, and now houses one of the most significant of all Korean American populations.

It doesn't end there. California, home to the biggest Thai population outside Thailand, is home to the only Thai Town in the USA in North Hollywood. You can be assured of finding excellent pad thai, jungle curries and other classics in some of the best Thai restaurants in America. An adventurous spirit can also lead you to a plenitude of vibrant eclectic enclaves from Ethiopia, Cambodia, Armenia, the Philippines and Vietnam. California has more than scenic drives and cinematic history – it is a multinational destination that comes together harmoniously creating a unique footprint in the whole of the USA.

The feeling here is that everyone is welcome, and a walk down any street can be filled with the sweet sounds of languages from far-off places. Spanish, Vietnamese, Korean, Farsi, Russian and Tagalog are just some of the sounds you can catch when traveling through the city. This is one of the biggest perks of visiting this American escape – you'll be feeling like you are exploring the world.

Chinese lanterns, San Francisco (p55)

CLIMATE CRISIS

California is on the leading edge of the global climate crisis. Fortunately, green initiatives are fighting back – hard. By Anita Isalska

ALTHOUGH THE WHOLE world is facing up to the reality of the climate crisis, California is especially vulnerable to its effects. The challenges – wildfires, endless drought and rising sea water levels – are near-apocalyptic.

According to the California Environmental Protection Agency's Office of Environmental Health Hazard Assessment (OEHHA), annual air and ocean temperatures have been rising since records began in 1895. This is indubitably due to human activity. Average temperatures have risen by 3°F, and are projected to rise by another 2°F degrees by 2040. Most noticeable in Southern California, the trend is accelerating: more than half of the 20 warmest years in California occurred after 2000.

Warmer seas mean rising sea levels, and this is a huge problem in a state where more than 26 million people live near the sea. Authorities are fast-tracking the expensive work of 'coastal armoring,' and California has already spent billions of dollars improving seawalls and fortifying wetlands. Not only has the sea risen by 6in since 1950, but the rise has also accelerated to a pace of 1in per decade. Combined with El Niño weather events, which can bring intense rainfall, more Californians than ever are at risk of experiencing floods.

The impact of the climate crisis on Californians intersects with racial and economic inequalities. A study by UC Irvine showed that Black and low-income households in the Los Angeles Basin are at greatest risk of impact by flooding – a risk up to 79% higher than for white residents.

Freak Weather Events

Rising tides and rising temperatures are even more dangerous when freak weather events occur. The *Indicators of Climate Change in California* report (2022) warned that weather extremes are getting more intense and less predictable – a particular concern given California's seasonal wildfires.

The 2020 wildfire season broke records when more than 6565 sq miles burned. Rural communities experience the greatest danger from wildfires, but in recent years urban dwellers have been unable to ignore the extreme smoke pollution. On September

Hwy 1 and Big Sur (p268)

2020's infamous 'orange sky day,' Bay Area residents woke to a sun that never rose, so thick was the smoke.

But Californians are fighting back: 2022 experienced a comparatively subdued fire season, with 'only' 565 sq miles burned, and fewer structures damaged. This was a testament to a slew of wildfire response measures. CAL FIRE has put in place an expanding network of high-tech cameras in fire-prone areas, helping firefighters respond to even the smallest wisp of smoke. Meanwhile, scientists are harnessing AI to model wildfire spreading, enabling firefighters to deploy their resources more precisely.

Lessons from California's First Nations

Climate change isn't the only accelerant of California's worsening wildfires: forest management may also be key. In 2022, the Wildfire and Forest Resilience Task Force announced a plan to expand the use of 'beneficial fire,' a concept passed down through generations of Native American people.

A UC Berkeley study showed that the Klamath Mountains forests have doubled in size since the native Karuk and Yurok tribes were stewarding the land. These original custodians carried out controlled burns to prevent overgrowth, cultivating diverse landscapes of plains, hills and forests. When European settlers arrived, they logged then replanted trees close together, creating overgrown forests that can carry fires over a wide area.

Burnt sequoias in Sequoia National Park (p611)

The Impact of Tourism

The fragile beauty that draws around 260 million visitors to California in a single year is at the mercy of visitor's behavior.

At popular destinations like Big Sur, where overtourism has caused soil erosion from excessive tourist footfall, many blame social media for popularizing the area's photogenic locations. In 2019, signs appeared at Bixby Bridge reading 'Overtourism is killing Big Sur.'

Then came the pandemic, forcing all tourist activity to suddenly hit the brakes. At the height of COVID-19, California shut down its tourist sites for more than a year. When California reopened with a bang (a $95-million bang, according to their promotional budget), Californians were nervous about a return to the overtouristed status quo.

Sustainable Futures

Fortunately, California has an extensive set of programs to encourage sustainable travel. The National Park Service is increasingly shifting to renewable or alternative energy sources, with some parks heading quickly toward carbon-neutral status. One example is the Golden Gate National Recreation Area (itself a victim of overtourism, as the USA's third-most-visited park in 2021). Winter sports giant Vail Resorts has committed to achieving carbon-neutral status by 2030, while the SIP (Sustainability in Practice) certified program highlights increasing numbers of wineries using sustainable practices.

California may be at the sharp edge of climate change, but it's also mounting some robust measures to meet these challenges. The state has been reducing its greenhouse gas emissions since 2004, and will ban the sale of new fossil-fuel-powered cars from 2035.

There are also efforts to harness California's abundant sunshine for solar power. Rooftop solar alone won't meet the population's energy needs but devoting land to this use is hotly debated. Wildlife conservationists want solar sites in the cities, far from protected land, meanwhile urban dwellers want the sites far from view.

Many more hurdles lie ahead, but the urgency of the climate crisis, mixed with cutting-edge technology and research, are equipping the population for a heck of a fight.

IN-N-OUT BURGER

Simple, down-to-earth In-N-Out Burger is as quintessentially Californian as the Hollywood sign or Santa Monica Pier. By Megan Leon

THE LATE, GREAT Anthony Bourdain said of In-N-Out's burgers: 'This is like a ballistic missile...a perfectly designed protein delivery system.' But what makes In-N-Out so special? How can a humble burger joint cause never-ending disputes between diehard lovers and haters? The answer owes something to nostalgia, but much more to the chain's original owners, who vowed to use always the freshest, highest-quality ingredients available.

The story of this beloved joint started back in 1948 when a WWII veteran by the name of Harry Snyder and his new wife, Esther, decided to open up shop in the suburban neighborhood of Baldwin Park.

Around that time there was a major boom in fast-food joints popping up around the country, from the golden arches of McDonald's to another West Coast favorite – Carl's Jr. Yet In-N-Out stood apart and for many reasons. While other chains relied on frozen items like beef patties, Harry and Esther insisted on using only fresh ingredients.

Each day Harry and Esther would shop for fresh produce, visiting the butcher for

Clockwise from top left: In-N-Out Burger sign; Double-Double cheeseburger; drive-through, Anaheim; take-out packaging

TOP LEFT: SUNDRY PHOTOGRAPHY/SHUTTERSTOCK © TOP RIGHT: SHENGYING LIN/SHUTTERSTOCK © BOTTOM LEFT: WILD AS LIGHT/SHUTTERSTOCK © BOTTOM RIGHT: THE IMAGE PARTY/SHUTTERSTOCK ©

ground beef and assembling everything by hand. Every single burger was made to order, all the potatoes were cut on the spot before being fried to order. Then, as now, there were absolutely no freezers nor microwaves in any In-N-Out location.

In addition to serving the freshest burgers in town, Harry wanted to give his guests a way to order without ever having to leave their cars. After many nights working away in his garage, he introduced a two-way speaker box that would let guests order from outside, marking the official birth of the Drive-Thru concept. While this fast-food breakthrough quickly gained traction, it took nearly two years for Fred and Esther to open a second location.

A refusal to turn to the franchise model long distinguished In-N-Out from its competitors. For as long as they could, Harry and Esther kept the Southern Californian business in the family. Keeping In-N-Out a family concern was equally important to the Snyders' son Rich, who became the company's president after his father passed away from cancer in 1976.

Rich made it clear that he would continue his father's legacy and never change what he grew up with. This made sense, as it was a formula of proven popularity. In-N-Out has always kept its menu small, focusing on classic hamburgers and cheeseburgers. Later introductions included Double-Doubles (burgers with two patties and two slices of cheese) and the not-so-secret 'Animal-Style' menu.

The first Animal-Style burger was cooked at In-N-Out in 1961. Now a trademarked term that people immediately correlate with In-N-Out, it's one of the chain's most popular burgers. Animal-Style burgers feature the same components as regular burgers, except that the beef patties are grilled in mustard and then elevated by extra secret spread, extra pickles and grilled onions.

Eventually, the Animal-Style was brought to bear on In-N-Out's fries, with grilled onions, cheese and the same secret sauce adorning their freshly cut and cooked fries. Ironically, it's been the very freshness of In-N-Out's fries that has provoked much of the debate surrounding the chain.

The fries at In-N-Out have always been cut on-site, making use of a device that slices the potatoes immediately before they're fried. The end product is a not-so-crisp tray of potatoes that tends to be slightly mushy. To some, they just don't compare to the fries made from frozen potatoes in other fast-food joints. Those in the know tend to order their In-N-Out fries well done. Once super-crisp, the fries can stand up to the ravages of heavy toppings and long drives!

In-N-Out expanded beyond its Southern Californian homeland in 1992, when the first restaurant opened in Las Vegas. It was a big move for a small business that makes a point of only opening new locations within 300 miles of its patty-making facilities. However, the success of the Las Vegas experiment soon led to openings in other western states, including Arizona, Utah, Texas and Oregon.

While In-N-Out has never reached America's East Coast, the increasingly iconic burger brand has opened new outlets around the world. Attracting hungry crowds as far away as Asia, the chain can now boast more than 330 locations, with more to surely come.

For those who do get the chance to hit up a location, there are a few unique things to look out for. You'll find palm trees outside most stores, but see if you can find two crossed trees, planted to form an 'X'. These are homages to Harry Snyder's favorite film, *It's a Mad, Mad, Mad, Mad World.* Released in 1963, the comedy features a group of motorists stranded in the California desert, hunting for treasure buried under crossed palms.

More curios can be found by those in the know on In-N-Out's cups and French-fry boats. Look underneath and discover Bible verses – legacies of born-again evangelical Christian Harry Snyder.

This simple burger joint has become symbolic of California, and in particularly of Los Angeles. Landing at LAX airport and heading straight to In-N-Out is a ritual, a rite of passage, an essential Californian experience. Some may argue it's not the state's greatest burger, and it's true that visitors will enjoy myriad other choices featuring every kind of ingredient under the sun. But In-N-Out Burger provides more than just food. It represents a feeling of home, promises familiar joys and is the kind of place that always delivers on expectations.

INDEX

A

Academy of Sciences 103
accessible travel 643
accommodations 633
activities 48–51, *see also individual activies*
air travel 631
Alameda 131
Alamo Square 84
Alcatraz 71
Amador City 552
amusement parks 23
  Balboa Fun Zone 409
  Disneyland 392-9, **393**
  Knott's Berry Farm 401
  Legoland 435
  Mission Bay Aquatic Park 426
  Paramount Pictures 345
  Santa Cruz Beach Boardwalk 252
  Santa Monica Pier 368
  Universal Studios Hollywood 385
  Warner Bros Studio Tour 383
Angel Island 117
Angel Island Immigration Station 71
Angels Camp 563
Annenberg Community Beach House 368
Antelope Valley 541
Anza-Borrego Desert State Park 476-9, **477**
  accommodations 478
  beyond Anza-Borrego Desert State Park 480-1
  food 477
  travel within 479
Apple 142, 651
Apple Park 651
aquariums
  Aquarium of the Bay 73
  Birch Aquarium 433
  Monterey Bay Aquarium 260
Arcata 231
Atherton 142
Atwater 349
Auburn 548-9, **548**
  beyond Auburn 550-4
  travel within 549

Bakersfield Sound 540
Balboa Park 426-7
Ballard 325
ballooning 167
Battery Bluff 63
Bay Area 108-49
  itineraries 112-13
  travel within 110-11, **110-11**
beaches 16
  Avila Beach 291-2
  Baker Beach 64
  Capitola 254
  Corona Del Mar State Beach 409
  Crescent Bay Beach 413
  Dana Point 413
  Dillon Beach 124
  El Capitán State Beach 310
  Gazos Creek State Beach 149
  Glass Beach 215
  Gray Whale Cove State Beach 149
  Half Moon Bay State Beach 146
  Huntington Beach 402-4
  Imperial Beach 426
  Jalama Beach 319
  Kings Beach 586
  La Jolla Cove 430
  Leadbetter Beach 304
  Limantour Beach 122
  Main Beach 413
  Mattole Beach 219
  Mission Beach 425
  Montara Beach 149
  Moss Beach 149
  Muir Beach 119
  Ocean Beach 106
  Original Muscle Beach 370
  Pacific Beach 425
  Pacifica State Beach 148
  Pescadero State Beach 149
  Pfeiffer Beach 269
  Pismo Beach 292
  Point Reyes Beach 122
  Refugio State Beach 310
  Rodeo Beach 117-18
  San Buenaventura State Beach 329
  Santa Cruz 252-3
  Seal Beach 406
  South Lake Tahoe 573
  Stinson Beach 119
  Surfrider Beach 371
  Tahoe Vista 586
  Thousand Steps Beach 413
  Venice Beach 375
  Zephyr Cove 578
beer *see* breweries
Berkeley 132–135, **133**
  beyond Berkeley 136-8
  food 134
  shopping 134
  travel within 135
Beverly Hills Hotel 355
bicycling *see* cycling
Big Sur 267–271
  itineraries 32
  travel within 271
Bigfoot 256
bird-watching 484, 501, 532
Bishop 621
Bob's Big Boy 383
Bodie State Historic Park 627
books 43
breweries 45
  Barrelhouse Brewing Co 618
  Brewbakers Brewing Company 618
  Littorai 189
  Mt Shasta Brewing Company Alehouse & Bistro 498
  North Park Brewing 425
  Santa Cruz 253
  Sequoia Brewing Company 618
  Sierra Nevada Brewing Company 535
  Thorn Street Beer 425
  Valley Brewers 315
bridges
  Bay Bridge 82
  Bixby Bridge 268
  Golden Gate Bridge 62
  Tower Bridge 527
  Sundial Bridge 514
Bucks Lake 509
Buellton 317-18
bus travel 631

Caffe Trieste 72
Calistoga 171-2
Calle 24 99-100
Cambria 276-9, **276**
camping 14, 633
cannabis 229, 635
canoeing, *see* kayaking & canoeing
Cape Mendocino 218
Capitol Records 345
Capitola 254
car travel 631, *see also* road trips & scenic drives
Carlsbad 435-6
Carmel Valley 264
Carpinteria 311
casinos 428, 439, 574
Castle Lake 498
caving 500-1
cell phones 630
Central Coast 245-93
  itineraries 248-9
  travel within 246-7, **246-7**
Central Valley, the 518-41
  itineraries 522-3
  travel within 520-1, **520-1**
Cerro Gordo 627
César E Chávez National Monument 651
Chabot Space & Science Center 129
Charlie Brown 185
children, travel with 49, 634
Chinatown (Los Angeles) 380
Chinatown (San Francisco) 70

Map Pages **000**

City Lights Books 69, 72, 73
Clear Lake 240-3
climate 40-1
climate change 640
climate crisis 660-1
climbing 275
clothes 42
Coit Tower 69
Comstock 264
Cottage Row 84
credit cards 632
Crescent City 239
culture 652-3, 654-7, 658-9
Culver City 376
cycling 49, 51, 641
17-Mile Drive 265
Auburn 549
Cambria 278
Devil's Slide Coastal Trail 148
Edna Valley 287, **287**
Napa Valley 162
Richmond-San Rafael Bridge 138
River Bend Park 529
Santa Barbara 306-7
Santa Cruz 253
South Lake Tahoe 573-4
Tahoe City 581
Tahoe Vista 586
Ventura River Parkway Trail 328
Yosemite National Park 607
cycling tours 287, **287**

D

Dan Tana's 357
Dana Point 413
Death Valley National Park 469-72, **469**
accommodations 471
beyond Death Valley National Park 473-5
history 472
travel within 472
Del Mar 435
Deserts, the 444-87
itineraries 448-9
travel within 446-7, **446-7**
disabilities, travelers with 643
Disneyland 386-413, 392-9, 650, **393**
accommodations 398-9
beyond Disneyland 400-1
entertainment 394
festivals & events 390-1
food 394-5, 396
itineraries 390-1
planning 392
seasonal travel 396-7
travel seasons 390-1
travel within 388-9, 399, **388-9**
distilleries 149, 182, 281
diversity 658-9
diving 51
Downieville 558
Dublin Gulch 475
Dunsmuir 498

E

Eagle Lake 507
earthquakes 635
Eastern Sierra 619-27, **622**
accommodations 622-623
food 624-625
travel within 627
Echo Park 351-2
Edna Valley 287
electricity 645
etiquette 43
Etna 514
Eureka 225-9
accommodations 227
beyond Eureka 230-1
drinking 228
food 228
travel within 229
walking tours 226, **226**

F

Fairfax District 362
family travel 49, 634
Fern Canyon 234-5
Ferndale 218, 222
Ferry Building 82
ferry travel 631
festivals & events 41
Adams Avenue Street Fair 427
Bay to Breakers 82
Bombay Beach Biennale 459
Cajun Festival 531
California Avocado Festival 45, 299
California State Fair 41, 529
Capitola Art & Wine Festival 45, 250
Carnaval 100
Cherry Blossom Festival 85
Coachella Valley Music & Arts Festival 41, 448
Desert X 454
Field of Light 281
Fillmore Jazz Fest 85
Flor y Canto Literary Festival 100
Frameline Film Festival 92
Graffiti Summer 41, 522
Gravenstein Apple Fair 45, 189
Half Moon Bay Art & Pumpkin Festival 146
High Sierra Music Festival 41, 510
Huntington Beach Concours d'Elegance 404
Kelseyville Pear Festival 45, 243
LA Pride 346
Laguna Beach's Festival of the Arts 412
Lake Tahoe Shakespeare Festival 588
Modernism Week 452-3
Monterey Jazz Festival 41
Noir City film festival 129
Outside Lands 41, 107
Portola Music Festival 101
Salute to American Graffiti 41, 182
San Diego County Fair 436
San Diego Pride Music Festival 427
San Joaquin Asparagus Festival 45, 533
Sawdust Art & Craft Festival 412
SF Pride 41, 93-4
Shakespeare Festival 427
Sonoma Harvest Fair 45, 155
US Open of Surfing 403
VillageFest 455
Wine & Food Affair 45, 155
WinterWonderGrass 41, 568
Wonderfront Music & Arts Festival 427
film 23, 43, 654-7
film studios
Sony Pictures Studios 376
Paramount Pictures 345
Universal Studios Hollywood 385
Warner Bros Studio 383
fishing 509, 517, 607
fog 41
Folsom 552
food 12-13, 44-7, 638-9, 662-3, *see also* festivals, oysters, *individual locations*
food trucks 46
forests, *see also* national parks & reserves, parks & gardens, state parks & reserves
Ancient Bristlecone Pine Forest 623-4
Forest of Nisene Marks 257
Giant Forest 613
Lassen National Forest 510
Los Osos Elfin Forest 291
Fort Bragg 215
Fort Mason 66
Freestone 192
Fresno 538-539

G

galleries, see museums & galleries
glamping 633
Glen Ellen 178
Gold Country 543-63
itineraries 546-7
travel within 544-5, **544-5**
Golden Gate Bridge 62
Golden Gate Park 650-1
golf 409, 432, 586
Google 142
Grass Valley 556
Grateful Dead House 90
Grauman, Sid 346
Greystone Mansion 356
Griffith Observatory 348
Grove of the Titans 235-6

H

Half Moon Bay 145-6, **145**
beyond Half Moon Bay 147-9
drinking 146
food 146
travel within 146
Healdsburg 197-199, **198**
beyond Healdsburg 200-1
health 635
Hearst Castle 279
Heavenly 572
highlights 10-27
hiking 49, 51
Avenue of the Giants 222-4
Bill Kenyon Trail 478
Bob Jones Trail 291
Bolinas Ridge Trail 124
Borrego Palm Canyon Nature Trail 477-8
Cambria 277-8
Cannonball Run 478
Castle Crags State Park 496
Coastal Trail 106, 235
Convict Lake 626
Cool Canyon 478
Death Valley 471-2
Desolation Wilderness 578

hiking *continued*
Devil's Slide Coastal Trail 148
Downieville 558
Eureka 228-9
Franklin Canyon Park 359
Fresno County Blossom Trail 540
Golden Gate Bridge 115
Grove of the Titans 235-6
Half Moon Bay 146
Heavenly 572
High Sierra Trail 613-14
Idyllwild 458-9
Joshua Tree National Park 463
Kings Canyon National Park 613-614
Lassen National Forest 510
Lassen Volcanic National Park 503, 504-5, 506, **505**
Lava Beds National Monument 500
Little Lakes Valley 626
Lundy Canyon 626
Mammoth Lakes 624
Mariposa Grove 605-6
McArthur-Burney Falls Memorial State Park 497
Mendocino 212-13
Mendocino Headlands Trail 210-11
Montaña de Oro State Park 292-3
Mt Livermore 117
Mt Shasta 496-8
Mt Whitney 623
Muir Woods National Monument 118-19
Palisades 593
Palm Springs 453
Palo Alto 140
Pinnacles National Park 275
Redding Trails 514
Redwood National & State Park 234
Redwood Skywalk 228-9
River Bend Park 529
Royal Gorge 591
Rubicon Trail 576
safety 636
Santa Cruz 253
Sausalito 115
Sequoia National Park 613-14
South Yuba River State Park 556
Tahoe City 581
Tahoe Vista 586
Yosemite National Park 603-4
history 24-5, 648-51
Hollywood 650, *see also* Los Angeles
Hollywood Bowl 343
Hollywood Roosevelt 344
Hollywood sign 342
Homewood 583
horseback riding
Half Moon Bay State Beach 146
Huntington Central Park 404
Kings Canyon National Park 616
Palm Springs 453
Sequoia National Park 616
Sonoma 176
Zephyr Cove 578
hot air balloons 573
hotels 633
hot springs 14
Calistoga 171-2
Delight's Hot Springs Resort 475
Eastern Sierra 625
Harbin Hot Springs 243
Paso Robles 282
Roman Spa Hot Springs 172
houseboating 512
Huntington Beach 402-4, **402**
accommodations 403
beyond Huntington Beach 405-6
itineraries 39
travel within 404
Hwy 1 644
Hwy 101 272-5, **273**

I

Idyllwild 458-9
Incline Village 586
In-N-Out Burger 662-3
Isleton 531
itineraries 32-9, 58-9, 112-13, *see also individual locations*

J

Jackson 553-4
Jamestown 562
Jefferson 507
Joshua Tree National Park 460-5, **461**
accommodations 460
beyond Joshua Tree National Park 466-8
drinking 463
food 462
planning 463
travel within 465
Julian 442-3

kayaking & canoeing 48
Berkeley 138
Emerald Bay 577
Half Moon Bay State Beach 146
Mendocino 211, 212-13
Monterey Bay 260-1
Moss Landing 257
Oakland 127
Point Reyes 124
Russian River Valley 195
San Diego 426
San Francisco 82
Santa Barbara 305
South Lake Tahoe 573
Truckee 591
Zephyr Cove 578
Kelso Dunes 483
Kennedy Gold Mine 553
Kernville 540
Kings Canyon National Park 611-16, **612**
accommodations 612-13
beyond Kings Canyon National Park 617-18
food 614
planning 613
travel within 616
Kingsburg 539
Kirkwood 576
kiteboarding 48
Klamath 239
Knott's Berry Farm 401
Koreatown 364-5

La Brea Tar Pits 363
Laguna Beach 412-13
La Jolla 430-3, **431**
accommodations 432
beyond La Jolla 434-6
itineraries 39
travel within 433
Lake Almanor 506
Lake Shastina 498
Lake Sonoma 201
Lake Tahoe 564-93
itineraries 35, 568-9
travel within 566-7, **566-7**
language 42
Lassen Volcanic National Park 503, 504-5, 506
Legoland 435
Lewiston 517
LGBTIQ+ travelers 642
GLBT History Museum 92, 651
Guerneville 195
Los Angeles 346, 358, 359
Palm Springs 449
San Diego 427
San Francisco 41, 92, 93-4
literature 654-7
Little Arabia 406
Little Saigon 406
Little Tokyo 381
Locke 531
Lone Pine 620
Los Alamos 324
Los Angeles 335-85
accommodations 344, 355, 364
Beverly Hills 353-9, **354**
Burbank 382-5, **382**
Downtown 377-81, **378**
drinking 346, 349, 350, 352, 374, 375, 376, 381
entertainment 343, 348, 379, 384
festivals & events 346
food 342, 346, 352, 357, 359, 364, 365, 376, 380, 381, 383, 384, 385
Griffith Park 347-52, **351**
Hollywood 340-6, **341**
itineraries 38, 338-9
LGBTQ+ travelers 346, 358, 359
Los Feliz 347-52, **351**
Mid-City 360-5, **361**
Miracle Mile 360-5, **361**
nightlife 358, 359
Santa Monica 366-71, **367**
shopping 344, 350, 355, 357, 358, 362, 368, 369, 373, 381
Silver Lake 347-52, **351**
travel within 336-7, **336-7**
Universal City 382-5, **382**
Venice 372–376, **372**
West Hollywood & Beverly Hills 353-9, **354**
Los Gatos 142
Los Olivos 320-1, **320**
beyond Los Olivos 322-5
drinking 321
travel within 321
Los Osos 291
Lost Coast, the 216-20, **217**
beyond the Lost Coast 221-4
drinking 217
food 217
hiking 217, 220
travel within 220

Map Pages **000**

M

Malibu 371
Mammoth Lakes 621, 624
marijuana 229, 635
Marin County 108-49
  food 118
  itineraries 112-13
  travel within 110-11, **110-11**
Marin Headlands 117-18
marine reserves
  Fitzgerald Marine Reserve 149
  Matlahuayl State Marine Reserve 433
  San Diego-Scripps Coastal Marine Conservation Area 433
Mariposa 610
Mariposa Grove 605-6
markets 12
  Barlow Market 189
  Castro Farmers Market 94
  Davis Farmers Market 533
  Downtown Market 540
  Eureka 228
  Ferndale 222
  Grand Central Market 380
  Mission Community Market 99
  Oakland 127
  Occidental 191
  Original Farmers Market 362
  Original Merced Certified Farmers' Market 540
  Sacramento 528
  Santa Monica Farmers Market 369
  Sebastopol 188
  Silver Lake Farmers Market 350
  Vineyard Farmers Market 540
McCloud 498
measures 645
Meeks Bay 583
Meiners Oaks 333
Melrose Avenue 358
Mendocino 208-12, **208**
  accommodations 210
  beyond Mendocino 213-15
  drinking 210-11
  food 210-11
  shopping 209
  travel within 212
Merced 538
Meta 142
military sites 106
  Battery Bluff 63
  Fort Baker 115
  Fort Mason 66
  Sonoma Barracks 175
Mill Valley 119
Mineral King 614, 616
missions
  Mission San Francisco Solano 175
  Mission San Luis Obispo de Tolosa 649
  Mission San Miguel Arcángel 284
  Mission Santa Bárbara 305
  San Buenaventura Mission 328
Modesto 538
Mojave National Preserve 482-4, **482**
  accommodations 483
  beyond Mojave National Preserve 485-7
  travel within 484
money 632
Mono Lake 626
Monterey 258-62, **259**
  activities 262
  beyond Monterey 263-6
  food 260
  history 262
  travel within 262
Monte Rio 195
Morro Bay 290
mountain biking 49, 51, *see also* cycling
  Downieville 558
  Downieville Downhill 558
  Idyllwild 458-9
  Mr Toad's Wild Ride 574
  Redding Trails 514
  Santa Barbara 307
  South Lake Tahoe 574
mountains
  Klamath 516
  Mt Diablo 131
  Mt Lassen 502-7
  Mt Livermore 117
  Mt Shasta 496-8
  Mt Soledad 433
  Mt Tamalpais 119-20
  Mt Whitney 623
  Siskiyou Mountains 516
Mt Lassen region 502-7, **503**
  accommodations 503, 506
  beyond Mt Massen region 508-10
  food 507
Mt Shasta City 496, **495**
Mt Shasta region 494-8, **495**
  accommodatons 496-7
  beyond Mt Shasta region 499-501
  drinking 495
  food 494
  travel within 498
Murphys 563
museums & galleries
  Academy of Sciences 103
  Antelope Valley Indian Museum 541
  Asian Art Museum 78
  Balboa Park 426-7
  BAMPFA (Berkeley Art Museum and Pacific Film Archive) 135
  Barnsdall Art Park 343
  Beat Museum 72
  Bergamot Station 369
  Bernhard Museum Complex 549
  Bigfoot Discovery Center 256
  Bodie State Historic Park 627
  Broad 379
  California Museum 526
  California State Capitol Museum 526
  California State Mining & Mineral Museum 610
  California State Railroad Museum 527
  Cambria Historical Museum 277
  Cantor Arts Center 140
  Castle Air Museum 538
  César E Chávez National Monument 539
  Charles M Schulz Museum 185
  Chinese Historical Society of America 68
  Chinese Temple & Museum Complex 535
  Clarion Alley 99
  Colonel Allensworth State Historic Park 539
  Columbia State Historic Park 562
  Comic-Con Museum 427
  Computer History Museum 142
  Contemporary Jewish Museum (CJM) 78
  Crocker Art Museum 527
  Dai Loy Museum 531
  de Young Museum 103
  di Rosa Center for Contemporary Art 163
  Elverhøj Museum of History and Art 313
  Exploratorium 80
  Firehouse No 1 Museum 556
  Fort Tejon State Historic Park 541
  Gaslamp Museum at the Davis-Horton House Museum 421
  Gatekeeper's Museum & Marion Steinbach Indian Basket Museum 581
  Geffen Contemporary 381
  Glass Outhouse Art Gallery 467-8
  GLBT History Museum 92, 651
  Goldwell Museum 475-6
  Hans Christian Andersen Museum 313
  Hauser & Wirth 381
  Hollywood Museum 343
  Imperial Beach Outdoor Surf Museum 426
  Institute for Contemporary Arts San Francisco (ICASF) 101
  Intel Museum 142
  Jack London State Historic Park 179
  Jan Shrem and Maria Manetti Shrem Museum of Art 533
  Japan Center 84
  Japanese American National Museum 381
  John Muir National Historic Site 138
  Julian Pioneer Museum 442
  Kelley House Museum 209
  La Brea Tar Pits 363
  La Haye Art Center 175
  Laguna Art Museum 412
  Laws Railroad Museum & Historic Site 621
  Letterform Archive 101
  Los Angeles County Museum of Art (LACMA) 363
  Manzanar National Historic Site 620
  Mariposa Museum & History Center 610
  Maritime Museum of San Diego 421
  Marshall Gold Discovery State Historic Park 551, 649
  Martin Lawrence Galleries 432
  Mendocino Art Center 211-12
  Minnesota Street Project 101
  Morris Graves Museum of Art 227
  Museum of Contemporary Art (MOCA) 379
  Museum of Contemporary Art San Diego 421, 424, 432
  Museum of Sonoma County 185
  Museum of the African Diaspora (MoAD) 78

museums & galleries *continued*
Museum of Ventura County 328
Museum of Western Film History 620
National Maritime History Museum 73
National Steinbeck Center 274
Noah Purifoy Outdoor Desert Art Museum 467
Oakland Museum of California 127
Old Town San Diego State Historic Park 424-5
Olympic Museum 593
Palm Springs Art Museum 454
Petaluma Historical Library & Museum 181
Petersen Automotive Museum 363
Phoebe A Hearst Museum of Anthropology 134
Railtown 1897 State Historic Park 562
Rosie the Riveter WWI Home Front National Historic Park 137, 650
Rubine Red Gallery 454
San Diego Air & Space Museum 426
Santa Barbara Maritime Museum 305
Santa Barbara Museum of Art 306
Santa Barbara Museum of Natural History 305
Sebastopol Center for the Arts 187-8
SF Camerawork 66
SFMOMA (San Francisco Museum of Modern Art) 79
Sky Art 479
State Indian Museum 528
Sutter's Fort State Historic Park 527
Tallac Historic Site 574
Tech Interactive 144
Temecula Valley Museum 438
Tuolumne County Museum 560
Venice Beach Murals 374
Wende Museum 376
Wildling Museum of Art & Nature 315
William B Ide Adobe State Historic Park 535
Yosemite Climbing Museum 610
music 43, 88, 654-7
Capitol Records 345

N

Napa 156-160, **157**
accommodations 160
beyond Napa 161-4
drinking 159
festivals & events 160
food 158
travel within 160
wineries 158
Napa & Sonoma Wine Country 151-201
itineraries 154-5
travel within 152-3, **152-3**
national parks & reserves 51, *see also* forests, parks & gardens, state parks & reserves
Channel Islands National Park 331-2
Crissy Field 63
Death Valley National Park 469-72, **469**
Joshua Tree National Park 460-5, **461**
Kings Canyon National Park 611-16, **612**
Lassen National Forest 510
Mojave National Preserve 482-4, **482**
Muir Woods National Monument 118
Pinnacles National Park 275
Redwood National & State Parks 232-6, **233**
Rosie the Riveter WWII Home Front National Historic Park 137, 650
Sequoia National Park 611-16, **612**
Yosemite National Park 600-7, **601**
navigation
Central Coast 246-7, **246-7**
Central Valley, the 520-1, **520–521**
Deserts, the 446-7, **446-7**
Disneyland 388-9, **388-9**
Gold Country 544-5, **544-5**
Lake Tahoe 566-7, **566-7**
Los Angeles 336-7, **336-7**
Marin County & Bay Area 110-11, **110-11**
Napa & Sonoma Wine Country 152-3, **152-3**
North Coast & Redwoods 204-5, **204–205**
Northern Mountains 490-1, **490-1**
Orange County 388-9, **388-9**
Palm Springs 446-7, **446-7**
Sacramento 520-1, **520-1**
San Diego 416-17, **416-17**
San Francisco 56-7, **56-7**
Santa Barbara County 296-7, **296-7**
Sierra Nevada 596-7, **596-7**
Yosemite National Park 596-7, **596-7**
Nevada City 555-6, **555**
beyond Nevada City 557-8
food 556
travel within 556
Newport Beach 407-10, **408**
accommodations 409, 410
beyond Newport Beach 411-13
food 409
travel within 410
nightlife 638-9, *see also individual locations*
North Coast 202-43
festivals & events 206-7
itineraries 206-7
seasonal travel 206-7
travel within 204-5, **204-5**
Northern Mountains 489-517
itineraries 492-3
travel within 490-1, **490-1**
Northern Shore 584-6, **586**
beyond Northern Shore 587-8
travel within 586
Northwood 195

Oakland 125-9, **126**
beyond Oakland 130-1
drinking 127, 128
food 127
travel within 129
Occidental 191
Ojai 332-3
Olympic Valley 593
opening hours 645
Orange County 386-413
itineraries 390-1
travel within 388-9, **388-9**
Oroville 535
oysters 124, 435

Pacifica 148
painted ladies 84
Palisades Tahoe 592-3
Palm Springs 444-87, **451**
accommodations 453-4
beyond Palm Springs 457-9
festivals & events 448-9
food 452
itineraries 38, 448-9
LGBTIQ+ travelers 449
shopping 454, 455
tours 452
travel seasons 448-9
travel within 446-7, 456, **446-7**
Palo Alto 139-40, **139**
beyond Palo Alto 141-2
Paramount Pictures 345
parks & gardens, *see also* forests, national parks & reserves, state parks & reserves
Agua Caliente Regional Park 479
Alamo Square 84
Balboa Park 426-7
Barnsdall Art Park 343
Bidwell Park 535
Bolsa Chica Ecological Reserve 404
Dolores Park 98, 649-50
Ellen Browning Scripps Park 431
Forest of Nisene Marks 257
Franklin Canyon Park 359
Golden Gate Park 103, 650-1
Hood Mountain Regional Park 178
Huntington Central Park 404
Japanese Tea Garden 103
Kaweah Oak Preserve 618
Los Angeles Zoo and Botanical Gardens 348
Los Osos Elfin Forest 291
Lotusland 310
Mendocino Coast Botanical Gardens 215
Moorten Botanical Garden 454
Presidio 64-5
River Bend Park 529
Romano Gabriel Wooden Sculpture Garden 227
San Francisco Botanical Garden 103

Map Pages **000**

Santa Barbara Botanic Garden 305
Sherman Library & Gardens 409
Sonoma Botanical Garden 178
Sonoma Valley Regional Park 178
Sugarloaf Ridge State Park 178
Tilden Regional Park 135
Tongva Park 371
Tunnel Tops 63
UC Botanical Garden 135
Ventura Botanical Garden 329
Virginia Robinson Gardens 355
Wildwood Canyon Park 383
Paso Robles 280-2, **280**
beyond Paso Robles 283-4
food 281
history 282
travel within 282
people 652-3
Pescadero 149
Petaluma 180-2, **181**
Petco Park 421
Petrolia 218
Pioneertown 468
Pismo Beach 292
Placerville 551-2
Point Reyes 121-2, **121**
beyond Point Reyes 123-4
travel within 122
Point Reyes National Seashore 124
public holidays 645

Quincy 509-10

rafting 14, 49
American River 552
Auburn 549
Kern River 540
Kings Canyon National Park 616
Sequoia National Park 616
Stanislaus River 560
Tahoe City 581
Upper Tuolumne River 560
Rainbow Honor Walk 92
Red Bluff 535
Redding 511-14, **512**
accommodations 512
beyond Redding 515-17
food 512–515
Redwood National & State Parks 232-6, **233**
accommodations 234
beyond Redwood National & State Parks 237-9
food 234
travel within 236
redwoods
Armstrong Redwoods State Natural Reserve 196
Big Basin Redwood State Park 256
Henry Cowell Redwoods State Park 257
Humboldt Redwoods State Park 219
Redwood National & State Parks 232-6, **233**
Redwood Skywalk 228-9
redwoods region 202-43
festivals & events 206-7
itineraries 206-7
seasonal travel 206-7
travel within 204-5, **204-5**
Reno 588
responsible travel 640-1
Rhyolite 474-5
Rio Vista 531
road trips & scenic drives 18-19
17-Mile Drive 265
Big Sur 268-9, **269**
Death Valley 470, **470**
Ebbetts Pass 609, **609**
Far North Coast 238-9, **239**
Hwy 1 214, 644
Hwy 395 620-1, **621**
Joshua Tree National Park 465
Kings Canyon Scenic Byway 615, **615**
Lost Coast 218-19, **219**
Mono Lake 626
Redwood National & State Parks 235
Route 66 486-7
San Marcos Pass 317
Santa Rita Hills 318, **318**
Sonoma County 192
rock climbing 49
Joshua Tree National Park 464
Kings Canyon National Park 616
Route 66 486-7
Sequoia National Park 616
Yosemite National Park 606
Rodeo Drive 355
Route 66 486–487
Russian River Valley 193-6, **194**
accommodations 194
drinking 196
food 195
itineraries 37
travel within 196

Sacramento 518-41, **525**
beyond Sacramento 530-3
drinking 528
festivals & events 522-3
food 526-7, 528
history 526
itineraries 522-3
travel seasons 522-3
travel within 520-1, 529, **520–521**
Sacramento Delta 531
Sacramento Valley 534-5, **534**
safe travel 635
safety 635
driving 40
outdoor 636-7
Salinas 274-5
San Diego 415-43, **422-3**
accommodations 421
drinking 425, 428
entertainment 421, 427, 428
festivals & events 418-19, 427
food 429
itineraries 418-19
LGBTIQ+ travelers 427
nightlife 428
seasonal travel 418-19
travel within 416-17, 429, **416-17**
San Diego Zoo 427-8
San Francisco 55-107
accommodations 64, 75, 82, 85, 93
activities 58-9
Avenues, the 102-7, **104-5**
Castro, the 91-4, **91**
Chinatown 67-75, **68**
Civic Center 76-82, **77**
Dogpatch 95-101, **96-7**
Downtown 76-82, **77**
drinking 74–75, 89, 94, 106
festivals & events 81, 85, 90, 92, 93-4, 101, 107
Fillmore 83-5, **83**
Fisherman's Wharf 67-75, **68**
food 64, 66, 70, 72-3, 75, 79, 81, 82, 85, 89, 90, 93, 99, 101, 106, 107
Golden Gate Bridge 60-6, **61**
Golden Gate Park 102-7, **104-5**
Haight, the 86-90, **87**
Hayes Valley 86-90, **87**
itineraries 32, 58-9
Japantown 83-5, **83**
LGBTIQ+ travelers 41, 92, 93-4
Marina, the 60-6, **61**
Mission, the 95-101, **96-7**
North Beach 67-75, **68**
Pacific Heights 83-5, **83**
Presidio 60-6, **61**
shopping 94
SoMa 76-82, **77**
travel seasons 58-9
travel within 56-7, **56-7**
San Francisco Opera 88
San Francisco Symphony 88
San Joaquin Valley 536-41, **537**
San Jose 143-4, **143**
San Luis Obispo 285-8, **285**
beyond San Luis Obispo 289-93
cycling tour 287, **287**
itineraries 33
travel within 288
walking tour 286, **286**
San Mateo 142
San Miguel 284
San Rafael 120
San Simeon 278
Santa Barbara 300-8, **302-3**
accommodations 304
beyond Santa Barbara 309-11
drinking 307
entertainment 306
food 301, 305, 308
itineraries 33
shopping 308
travel within 308
Santa Barbara County 294-333
itineraries 298-9
travel within 296-7, **296-7**
Santa Clara 142
Santa Cruz 250-4, **251**
beyond Santa Cruz 255-7
drinking 252
food 252
itineraries 32
travel within 254
Santa Monica Pier 368
Santa Rosa 183-5, **184**
Santa Ynez Valley 325
Saratoga 142
Sausalito 114-15, **114**
beyond Sausalito 116-20
itineraries 36
travel within 115
scuba diving 49, 577

Seal Beach 406
Sebastopol 186-9, **187**
beyond Sebastopol 190-2
festivals & events 189
food 189
shopping 188
travel within 189
Self-Realization Fellowship Lake Shrine 370
Sequoia National Park 611-16, **612**
accommodations 612-13
beyond Sequoia National Park 617-18
food 614
itineraries 34
planning 613
travel within 616
Shasta Caverns 513-14
Shasta Dam 513
Shasta Lake 511-14, **512**
accommodations 512
beyond Shasta Lake 515-17
Shelter Cove 219
Sierra City 558
Sierra Nevada, the 595-627
itineraries 598, 598-9
travel within 596-7, **596-7**
Silicon Valley 141, 142
skateboarding 100
skate parks 374
skiing 48
Alpine Meadows 593
Badger Pass Ski Area 607
Boreal 589
Diamond Peak 586
Donner Ski Ranch 589
Heavenly 572
Homewood 583
Kirkwood 576
Lake Tahoe 572
Mt Lassen 507
Mt Rose 586
Mt Shasta 498
Northstar California Resort 591
Olympic Valley 593
Palisades Tahoe 593
Soda Springs 589
South Lake Tahoe 573
Sugar Bowl 589
Tahoe Cross-Country 581
Yosemite National Park 607
Skylight Books 352
Slab City 459
sledding 507, 573
smoking 635
snorkelling 49, 51, 260-1
snowboarding 48
Homewood 583
Lake Tahoe 572
Mt Lassen 507
Mt Shasta 498
Sierra-at-Tahoe 577
snowshoeing
Kings Canyon National Park 616
Mt Lassen 507
Mt Shasta 498
Royal Gorge 591
Sequoia National Park 616
Yosemite National Park 607
Snow White Cottages 349
Solvang 312-15, **313**
beyond Solvang 316-19
food 314
travel within 315
Sonoma 173-6, **174**
accommodations 175
activities 176
beyond Sonoma town 177-9
drinking 175
food 174
shopping 175-6
travel within 176
Sonoma Wine Country 151-201
itineraries 154-5
travel within 152-3, **152-3**
Sonora 559-60, **559**
beyond Sonora 561-3
food 560
shopping 560
travel within 560
South Lake Tahoe 570-4, **573**
beyond South Lake Tahoe 757-8
drinking 573, 574
food 572–573, 574
travel within 574
Spadena House 356
spas 332, 456
spelunking 614
Stanford University 140
stargazing 509, 616
Stateline 570-4, **573**
beyond Stateline 575-8
state parks & reserves, *see also* forests, national parks & reserves, parks & gardens
Andrew Molera State Park 268-9
Antelope Valley California Poppy Reserve 541
Anza-Borrego Desert State Park 476-9, **477**
Armstrong Redwoods State Natural Reserve 196
Big Basin Redwood State Park 256
Bodie State Historic Park 627
Calaveras Big Trees State Park 563
California State Capitol Park 526
Castle Crags State Park 496
Castle Rock State Park 256
China Camp State Park 120
Colonel Allensworth State Historic Park 539
Columbia State Historic Park 562
DL Bliss State Park 576
Donner Memorial State Park 591
Ed Z'berg Sugar Pine Point State Park 583
Emerald Bay State Park 576
Fort Tejon State Historic Park 541
Garrapata State Park 268
Gaviota State Park 310
Hearst San Simeon State Park 279
Henry Cowell Redwoods State Park 257
Humboldt Lagoons State Park 238-9
Humboldt Redwoods State Park 219
Indian Grinding Rock State Historic Park 554, 648
Julia Pfeiffer Burns State Park 269
Lake Tahoe-Nevada State Park 588
Los Osos Oaks State Reserve 291
Malakoff Diggins State Historic Park 558
Marshall Gold Discovery State Historic Park 551, 649
McArthur-Burney Falls Memorial State Park 497
Montaña de Oro State Park 292
Olompali State Historic Park 120
Point Lobos State Natural Reserve 266
Railtown 1897 State Historic Park 562
Redwood National & State Parks 232-6
Samuel P Taylor State Park 120
San Juan Bautista State Historic Park 274
Shasta State Historic Park 513
Sinkyone Wilderness State Park 220
South Yuba River State Park 556
Sue-meg State Park 238
Sutter's Fort State Historic Park 527
Underwater State Parks of Emerald Bay 577
William B Ide Adobe State Historic Park 535
St Helena 165-8, **166**
activities 167
beyond St Helena 169-72
shopping 167
travel within 168
Sunnyside 583
Sunset Strip 356
surfing 16, 48, 51
Huntington Beach 403-4
La Jolla 430
San Francisco 106
Santa Barbara 304
Santa Cruz 252
Surfrider Beach 371
Sutter Creek 553
swimming 48, *see also* beaches

T

tacos 128
Tahoe City 579-81, **580**
accommodations 581
beyond Tahoe City 582-3
food 581
travel within 581
Tahoe Vista 586
taxes 632
Temecula 437-40, **438**
accommodations 439
beyond Temecula 441-3
food 438–439
travel within 440
theaters
Castro Theatre 92, 93
Colony Theatre 384
Egyptian, the 346
Geary Theater 81
Grand Lake Theatre 129
Great American Music Hall 81
Greek Theatre 348
La Jolla Playhouse 432
Magic Theatre 66

Map Pages **000**

Santa Barbara 306
Strand Theater 81
TCL Chinese Theatre 346
Walt Disney Concert Hall 379
theme parks, *see* amusement parks
tipping 632
Tomales 124
tours, *see also* cycling tours, roads trips & scenic drives, walking tours
Channel Islands 331
winery 324
Yosemite National Park 601-3
train travel 631
travel to/from California 630
travel within California 631
treehouses 633
Trinidad 238
Trinity Lake 517
Truckee 589-91, **590**
beyond Truckee 592-3
food 590-91
itineraries 35
travel within 591
tubing 573, 593, 607

Universal Studios Hollywood 385
University of California, Berkeley 134-5
University of California, Davis 532-3
USS Hornet 131

Venice Beach 375
Venice Canals 373
Ventana Wilderness 270-1
Ventura 326-9, **327**
beyond Ventura 330-3
drinking 328
food 328, 329
shopping 329
travel within 329
Victorian mansions 226
Visalia 618
visas 630
Volcano 554
volcanoes
Amboy Crater 487
Devils Postpile National Monument 624-5
Lassen Volcanic National Park 503, 506
Nine Sisters 288
volunteering 250

walking 49, 51
walking tours
Eureka 226, **226**
San Luis Obispo 286, **286**
Walk of Fame 342
Walt Disney Concert Hall 379
Warner Bros Studio Tour 383
water 645
Wave Organ 65-6
weather 40-1
Weaverville 517
Weed 498
weights 645
whale-watching 49
Mendocino 211
Monterey Bay 253-4, 260-1
Point Reyes 122
Santa Barbara 306
Whiskeytown Lake 516-17
wi-fi 630
wildfires 635
wildlife 27
wildlife reserves
Ash Meadows National Wildlife Refuge 474
California Wolf Conservation Center 481
Elkhorn Slough 257
Humboldt Bay National Wildlife Refuge 231
Klamath Basin Wildlife Refuge 501
Monarch Trail 253
Monterey Bay National Marine Reserve 253
Pismo State Beach Monarch Butterfly Grove 292
Sacramento National Wildlife Refuge 532
Tule Elk Reserve 122
Winchester Mystery House 144
windsurfing 48
wineries 22, 45
accommodations 633
Acquiesce 533
Adelaida Vineyards 281
Alexander Valley 201
Alpen Cellars 517
Amador County 553
Amizetta Vineyards 170
Ampelos 319
Apple Hill 552
Bartholomew Estate Winery 176
Bed & Barrel at Stonehouse Cellars 243
Blue Fox Cellars 264
Boatique Winery 243
Boekenoogen Winery 264
Bogle 532
Bokisch 533
Brassfield Estate Winery 243
Carhartt Family Wines 321
Chacewater Winery & Olive Mill 243
Chalone Vineyard 273
Chappellet Winery 170
Clear Lake 241-3
Cuvaison Winery 162
d'Art 533
Dawn's Dream Winery 265
Demetria 323
Doffo Winery 440
Donum Estate 163
Dry Creek Valley 199
Eberle Winery 281
Equinox Sparkling Wine 253
Fiddlehead Cellars 319
Flying Goat Cellars 319
Foxen Canyon Wine Trail 323-4
Foxen Winery 323
Francis Ford Coppola Winery 201
Freeman vineyards 189
Frog's Leap 170
Furthermore Wines 191
Ghost Block Estates 170
Gundlach-Bundschu 176
Hanzell Vineyards 176
Harney Lane 533
Healdsburg 199
Hendry 159
Herman Story Wines 281
Hess Pearsson Estates 162
Idlewild 198
Indigené Cellars 281
Iron Horse Vineyards 191
Jessie's Grove 533
Joseph Phelps 168
Joullian Vineyards 264
Kaz Winery 242
Kunde winery 179
Lasseter Family Winery 178
Laujor Estate Winery 242-3
Lodi 533
Lompoc 319
Martinelli winery 191
Matthiasson Winery 159
Mayo Family Winery & Reserve Room 179
McKenzie-Mueller Winery 162
Miramonte Winery 440
Napa 158, 159
Napa Valley 162-3
Napa Valley Gondola 158
Napa Valley Wine Train 158
Nichelini Family Winery 170
Olof Cellars 242
Palmaz 159
Paso Robles 281
Pride Mountain Vineyards 170
Quixote Winery 163
River Road Wine Trail 273
Riverbench 324
Robledo 162
Russian River Valley 196
Santa Barbara 301
Sebastopol 188-9
Shannon Mercantile 243
Sinegal Estate 168
Soda Rock Winery 201
Sonoma Valley 179
St Helena 168, 170
Talisman Wines 178
tasting tips 639
Temecula 438-9, 440
tours 324
Tres Sabores 168
Vina Robles 281
VJB Cellars 179
Wild Diamond Vineyards 242
Women's Building 98
Woodside 142

Yosemite Firefall 605
Yosemite National Park 595-627, **601**
accommodations 602-3, 604-5
beyond Yosemite National Park 608-10
festivals & events 598-9
food 601
itineraries 34, 598-9
planning 602
travel seasons 598-9
travel within 596-7, 607, **596-7**
Yosemite Valley 601-3
Yountville 164

Zephyr Cove 578
zip lining 593
zoos
Los Angeles Zoo and Botanical Gardens 348
San Diego Zoo 427-8
Sequoia Park Zoo 228-9
Turtle Bay Exploration Park 514

"Nothing is more synonymous with Tinseltown than the Hollywood Walk of Fame (p342)."

MEGAN LEON

"Pause at Intersection Rock (p465; Joshua Tree National Park) to watch climbers honing their technique."

WENDY YANAGIHARA

LEFT: ZIKG/SHUTTERSTOCK ©, RIGHT: LUNAMARINA/SHUTTERSTOCK ©

THIS BOOK

Design Development
Marc Backwell

Content Development
Mark Jones, Sandie Kestell, Anne Mason, Joana Taborda

Cartography Development
Katerina Pavkova

Production Development
Sandie Kestell, Fergal Condon

Series Development Leadership
Darren O'Connell, Piers Pickard, Chris Zeiher

Destination Editor
Daniel Bolger

Production Editor
Kathryn Rowan

Book Designer
Clara Monitto

Cartographer
Rachel Imeson

Assisting Editors
Nigel Chin, Peter Cruttenden, Charlotte Orr, Christopher Pitts, Brana Vladisavljevic, Tasmin Waby

Cover Researcher
Norma Brewer

Thanks Clare Healy, Karen Henderson, Alison Killilea, Amy Lysen, Bohumil Ptáček

Paper in this book is certified against the Forest Stewardship Council™ standards. FSC™ promotes environmentally responsible, socially beneficial and economically viable management of the world's forests.

Published by Lonely Planet Global Limited
CRN 554153
10th edition – August 2023
ISBN 978 1 83869 181 3

10 9 8 7 6 5 4 3 2 1
Printed in Malaysia